**Soho and
Trafalgar Square**

**Bloomsbury and
Fitzrovia**

**Covent Garden
and the Strand**

**Holborn and the
Inns of Court**

**Smithfield and
Spitalfields**

The City

Bloomsbury
and Fitzrovia

Smithfield
and
Spitalfields

Holborn and the
Inns of Court

Covent
Garden
and the
Strand

ho and
afalgar
quare

The City

RIVER THAMES

South Bank

Southwark and
Bankside

Vhitehall and
Westminster

**Whitehall and
Westminster**

**Piccadilly, Mayfair
and St James's**

South Bank

**Southwark and
Bankside**

EYEWITNESS TRAVEL

LONDON

EYEWITNESS TRAVEL

LONDON

Main Contributor **Michael Leapman**

LONDON, NEW YORK,
MELBOURNE, MUNICH AND DELHI
www.dk.com

Project Editor Jane Shaw
Art Editor Sally Ann Hibbard
Editor Tom Fraser
Designers Pippa Hurst, Robyn Tomlinson
Design Assistant Clare Sullivan

Contributors
Michael Leapman, Christopher Pick, Lindsay Hunt

Photographers
Max Alexander, Philip Enticknap,
John Heseltine, Stephen Oliver

Illustrators
Brian Delf, Trevor Hill, Robbie Polley

This book was produced with the assistance
of Websters International Publishers.

Printed and bound in China

First published in the UK in 1993
by Dorling Kindersley Limited,
80 Strand, London WC2R 0RL, UK

16 17 18 19 10 9 8 7 6 5 4 3 2 1

Reprinted with revisions 1994, 1995, 1996, 1997, 1999, 2000 (twice),
2001, 2002, 2003, 2004, 2005, 2006, 2007, 2008, 2009, 2010, 2011,
2012, 2013, 2014, 2015, 2016

Copyright 1993, 2016 © Dorling Kindersley Limited, London

A Penguin Random House Company

ISBN 978-0-24120-954-7

MIX
Paper from
responsible sources
FSC™ C018179
www.fsc.org

Front cover main image: The iconic Tower Bridge

◀ St Paul's Cathedral, as seen from One New Change

Contents

Portrait of Sir Walter Raleigh (1585)

Introducing London

Bedford Square doorway (1775)

London
Area by Area

The Broadwalk at Hampton Court (c.1720)

Bandstand in St James's Park

Beefeater at the Tower of London

Houses of Parliament

Survival Guide

St Paul's Church, Covent Garden

Travellers' Needs

HOW TO USE THIS GUIDE

This Eyewitness Travel Guide helps you get the most from your stay in London with the minimum of practical difficulty. The opening section, *Introducing London*, locates the city geographically, sets modern London in its historical context and describes the events of the London year. *London at a Glance* is an overview of the city's highlights. *London Area by Area* takes you round the city's areas of interest. It describes all the main sights

with maps, photographs and detailed illustrations. In addition, six planned walking routes take you to parts of London you might otherwise miss.

Well-researched tips on where to stay, eat, shop, and on entertainment are in *Travellers' Needs*. *Children's London* lists highlights for young visitors, and *Survival Guide* tells you how to do anything from posting a letter to using the Underground.

London Area by Area

The city has been divided into 16 sightseeing areas, each with its own section in the guide. Each section begins with a short introduction summing up the character and history of this part

of the city. The key sights of interest to visitors are numbered and clearly located on an *Area Map*; these sights are also numbered on the pages that follow to help navigation around

the section. Each section has a large-scale *Street-by-Street Map* that focuses on an especially interesting part of the area, usually one in which a cluster of attractions can be found.

Colour-coded tabs help you find the section you want.

A locator map shows you where you are in relation to surrounding areas. The extent of the *Area Map* is highlighted.

Numbered circles pinpoint all the listed sights on the area map. St Margaret's Church, for example, is ❻

Recommended restaurants in the area are listed and plotted on the map.

1 Area Map
For easy reference, the sights in each area are numbered and located on an *Area Map*. To help the visitor, the map also shows Underground and mainline train stations.

Stars indicate the sights that no visitor should miss.

A locator map shows you where you are in relation to surrounding areas. The area of the *Street-by-Street Map* is shown in red.

A suggested route for a walk takes in the most attractive and interesting streets in the area.

2 Street-by-Street Map
This gives a bird's-eye view of the heart of each sightseeing area. The numbering of the sights ties in with the *Area Map* and the fuller descriptions on the pages that follow.

London at a Glance

Each map in this section concentrates on a specific theme: *Remarkable Londoners, Museums and Galleries, Churches, Parks and Gardens* and *Ceremonies*. Top sights are shown on the map; other sights are described on the following two pages.

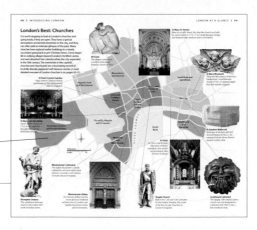

Each sightseeing area is colour-coded.

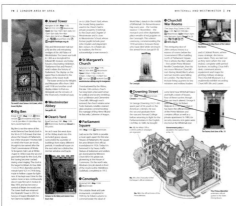

Practical Information lists all the information you need to visit every sight, including a map reference to the *Street Finder* at the back of the book.

Numbers refer to each sight's position on the *Area Map* and its place in the chapter.

3 Detailed information on each sight

All the important sights in each area are described in depth in this section. They are listed in order, following the numbering on the *Area Map*. Practical information on opening hours, telephone numbers, websites, admission charges and facilities available is given for each sight. The key to the symbols used can be found on the back flap.

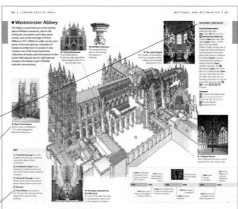

The Visitors' Checklist provides the practical information you need to plan your visit.

Stars indicate the most interesting architectural details of the building, and the most important works of art or exhibits on view inside.

Major features of the sight are listed and described in a key.

4 London's major sights

These are given two or more full pages in the sightseeing area in which they are found. Historic buildings are dissected to reveal their interiors; museums and galleries have colour-coded floorplans to help you find important exhibits.

INTRODUCING LONDON

GREAT DAYS IN LONDON

For things to see and do, visitors to London are spoiled for choice. Whether you're here for several days, or after a small taste of this great city, you'll want to make the most of your time. Over the following pages, you'll find itineraries for some of the best attractions London has to offer, arranged first by theme and then by length of stay. Price guides on pages 10–11 include travel on public transport and food plus admission charges for two adults; family prices are for two adults and two children.

Café at the National Portrait Gallery with a view of Trafalgar Square

History and Culture

Two adults
allow at least £200 (less with a picnic lunch)

- **Art at the National Gallery**
- **Houses of Parliament**
- **Buckingham Palace**

Morning
Begin the day in **Trafalgar Square** (see p106) at 10am, when the **National Gallery** (see pp108–11) opens. Allow yourself an hour and a half here. The gallery is free, but visitors are encouraged to make a donation. Afterwards, go for a coffee at the Portrait Restaurant on the top floor of the neigh-bouring **National Portrait Gallery** (see p106), which has a great view over Trafalgar Square and Nelson's Column. Set off down Whitehall to Parliament Square, a 15-minute walk that may be extended by the passing distractions of Horse Guard's Parade, **Banqueting House** (see p84) and **Downing Street** (see p79). See the **Houses of Parliament** (see pp76–7) before visiting the next highlight, the magnificent **Westminster Abbey** (see pp80–83). If the sun is shining, **St James's Park** (see p96), one of London's most pleasant green spaces, is ideal for a picnic lunch. If not, try Inn the Park (book ahead; 020 7451 9999) by the park's lake.

Afternoon
On the far side of St James's Park is **Buckingham Palace** (see pp98–9). During the summer months you can visit the State Rooms, while all year the Queen's Gallery has changing exhibitions. For tea, head up past St James's Palace onto Piccadilly, where there are several cafés and patisseries, such as Richoux at No. 172. Opposite, the **Royal Academy** (see p94) hosts some of the city's biggest art exhibitions, including the annual summer exhibition. For the best evening entertainment, get tickets for a West End play or show. These should be booked in advance (see p339), although last-minute tickets are sometimes on sale at the theatre box offices.

Shopping in Style

Two adults
allow at least £55 (plus shopping money)

- **Historic shops of St James's**
- **Old Bond Street for style**
- **Browsing trendy Covent Garden and the Piazza**

Morning
Start in Piccadilly and **St James's Street** (see pp92–3), home of suppliers to royalty and historic fashion names: John Lobb the bootmaker is at No. 9 and Lock the hatter at 6. Turn right into Jermyn Street for high-class men's tailors such as Turnbull & Asser and New & Lingwood, outfitters to Eton College. Floris the perfumer at 89 was founded in 1730 and the cheese shop Paxton & Whitfield at 93 has been here since 1740. Walk through Piccadilly Arcade to **Fortnum & Mason** (see p317), where you can treat yourself to an indulgent sundae at the Parlour before stocking up on

Burlington Arcade, a historic shopping mall off Piccadilly

Greenwich, a UNESCO World Heritage site

English classics such as fine teas and preserves. Walk through **Burlington Arcade** *(see p94)* for window-shopping of the highest calibre, before heading up **Old** and **New Bond** streets *(see p319)*, the smartest shopping addresses in town. Try South Molton Street for fashion and Oxford Street for **Selfridges** department store *(see p317)*. The café at the **Wallace Collection** *(see p230)*, just behind, is a sophisticated lunch setting.

Afternoon
Head to **Covent Garden** *(see pp116–17)* and browse the Piazza's craft stalls. Mainstream shops line the square and nearby Floral Street is renowned for fashion. The streets that radiate from **Seven Dials** *(see p120)* are home to one-off boutiques, street style and intriguing emporiums.

A Day on the River

Two adults
allow at least £180

- Take the boat to Greenwich
- Explore the *Cutty Sark*
- View the Thames from Tower Bridge

Morning
Take the half-hour boat trip from the Embankment or London Eye piers to **Greenwich** *(see pp242–7)*, and enjoy excellent views of St Paul's, the Tower and the City along the way. There are fine views too from Greenwich's Royal Observatory. Explore the

immaculately restored *Cutty Sark*, located next to the river, and pick up street food for lunch from **Greenwich Market** *(see p336)*.

Afternoon
On the return boat trip, stop at Tower Millennium pier for **Tower Bridge** *(see p157)*, where a glass-floored walkway gives a unique river view. Next, walk along the South Bank where you might catch a free live show at the Scoop amphitheatre by **City Hall** *(see p187)*. The old warehouses of Butler's Wharf, east of the bridge, house good restaurants.

A Family Fun Day

Family of four
allow at least £270

- Take the kids to the Tower
- Lunch at St Katharine Docks
- Ride the London Eye
- Explore Chinatown

Morning
Head to the **Tower of London** *(see pp158–61)*, London's top visitor attraction and an established family favourite. Book tickets to avoid the queue. The fascinating castle and Crown Jewels will take at least a couple of hours to explore. For lunch, head across the road to **St Katharine Docks** *(see p162)* where, alongside the various yachts and pleasure cruisers, there are several good places to eat.

Predators at the London Aquarium

Afternoon
A walk along the south bank of the Thames is full of things to see – like the replica *Golden Hinde II* *(see p179)* – and free entertainment. In summer, the area around the **Royal Festival Hall** *(see p192)* has fountains, sand pits and lots of events suitable for children. Next stop, the **London Eye** is a thrilling trip above the city *(see p193;* online bookings can be made in advance at www.londoneye.com).

Vertigo sufferers need not feel left out – there is plenty of entertainment at and below ground level to choose from, especially in **County Hall** *(see p192)*. This leisure complex is home to the Sea Life London Aquarium (great for younger kids) and the London Dungeon (for teenagers). Afterwards, head to **Chinatown** *(see p112)*, situated in and around Gerrard Street, which has many superb restaurants, colourful shops and a vibrant streetlife. Go for an early Chinese supper of *dim sum* (small dishes).

Admiring the view from the London Eye, South Bank

2 Days in London

- Enjoy a panoramic spin on the London Eye
- Admire Wren's masterpiece, St Paul's Cathedral
- Take a Beefeater tour of the Tower of London

Day 1

Morning Inspect monuments to England's kings and queens on a self-guided tour of **Westminster Abbey** *(see pp80–83)*. Don't miss the intricate Lady Chapel and peaceful cloisters. Next, wander through **Parliament Square** *(see p78)* into idyllic **St James's Park** *(see p96)*, with its pelicans and black swans, reaching **Buckingham Palace** *(see pp98–9)* in time for the 11:30am Changing the Guard ceremony. In autumn or winter head to **Horse Guards Parade** *(see p84)* instead. Then walk through stately **Trafalgar Square** *(see p106)* into the West End. Buy theatre tickets for the evening at discounted prices from the official cut-price booth on **Leicester Square** *(see p107)*.

Afternoon Head to **Chinatown** *(see p112)* for *dim sum*, then spend an hour or two admiring works by Van Eyck, Van Gogh and Constable at the **National Gallery** *(see pp108–11)*. If there's time before the show, head to Covent Garden's **Piazza and Central Market** *(see p118)* to watch the street performers.

Day 2

Morning The **Tower of London** *(see pp158–61)* is a must-see. Two hours is enough time to join an entertaining Beefeater tour and inspect murderous-looking Tudor weaponry in the White Tower. Then head to the **Monument** *(see p156)*, Sir Christopher Wren's splendid 17th-century column built to commemorate the Great Fire of London. Climb its spiral staircase for a spectacular view that takes in landmarks old and new. Next, walk to Wren's glorious masterpiece, **St Paul's Cathedral** *(see pp152–5)*. Highlights include the Whispering Gallery, the spectacular dome and the crypt.

Naval gunship HMS *Belfast* moored in front of Tower Bridge

Afternoon Cross the Millennium Bridge to Bankside, taking in views of **Tower Bridge** *(see p157)*. Grab lunch from one of the artisan food stalls or cafés at **Borough Market** *(see p180)*, then stroll to **Shakespeare's Globe** *(see p181)* and its fascinating museum (tours of the auditorium are available on days when there's no performance). Next door is **Tate Modern** *(see pp182–5)*, housing paintings and art installations on a magnificent scale. End the day with a ride on the **London Eye** *(see p193)*, timing it, if you're lucky, as the sun sets over the city.

3 Days in London

- Uncover England's history at Westminster Abbey and the Houses of Parliament
- View contemporary art at Tate Modern
- Meet the old masters at the National Gallery

Day 1

Morning Visit the **Tower of London** *(see pp158–61)*: explore the armoury, infiltrate the torture chambers and admire the Crown Jewels. Afterwards, have a drink by the colourful quayside at **St Katharine Docks** *(see p162)*, then cross **Tower Bridge** *(see p157)* to Shad Thames: its scrubbed-up dockside warehouses are now pricey apartments. Walk along the river to one of London's oldest markets, **Borough** *(see p335)*, where you're spoiled for choice for lunchtime treats (not Sunday).

Afternoon A 5-minute walk away is one of London's newest

but most recognizable sights, the **Shard** *(see p186)*. Speed up 72 floors to the very top, where the trains and boats far below look like toys. Walk along the riverside and stop off to look around **HMS** *Belfast* *(see p187)*, now a floating naval museum, before detouring into **Southwark** *(see pp178–9)* for one of London's most macabre attractions: the **Old Operating Theatre** *(see p180)*. Located in St Thomas's Church, the surgery dates from before the use of anaesthetics.

Day 2

Morning Get to **Westminster Abbey** *(see pp80–83)* early to explore its royal memorials. Nearby rise the Neo-Gothic **Houses of Parliament** *(see pp76–7)* and **Big Ben** *(see p78)*. Cross the river and head for the **Southbank Centre** *(see pp190–91)*, which includes the **Hayward Gallery** *(see p192)* and the **Royal Festival Hall** *(see p192)*. Nearby is the **London Eye** *(see p193)* and the aquarium at **County Hall** *(see p192)*.

A performance in progress at Shakespeare's Globe in Southwark

Afternoon Wander the galleries of **Tate Modern** *(see pp182–5)*. Then walk over the Millennium Bridge for views back of **Shakespeare's Globe** *(see p181)* and **Tower Bridge** *(see p157)*, reaching **St Paul's Cathedral** *(see pp152–5)* in time for evensong.

Day 3
Morning Start the day in literary **Bloomsbury** *(see pp126–7)*, and give yourself a couple of hours at the magnificent **British Museum** *(see pp128–31)* – either join a highlights tour or select a few galleries to visit, such as the Greek or Egyptian collections.

Afternoon Head to **Leicester Square** *(see p107)* for cheap theatre tickets, then walk to **Trafalgar Square** *(see p106)* and spend a few hours at the **National Gallery** *(see pp108–11)* and the adjacent **National Portrait Gallery** *(see pp106–7)* for world-famous art. Stroll in **St James's Park** *(see p97)* for a peek at **Buckingham Palace** *(see pp98–9)* before the theatre.

5 Days in London

- Visit Buckingham Palace, the Queen's official home
- Discover ancient treasures at the British Museum
- Explore South Kensington's world-class museums

Day 1
Morning Begin at **Tower Bridge** *(see p157)*, from where you can see one of Britain's great battleships, **HMS Belfast** *(see p187)*. Next, spend two hours at the **Tower of London** *(see pp158–61)* and have lunch at **St Katharine Docks** *(see p162)*.

Afternoon Allow time to see two of Sir Christopher Wren's masterworks, **St Paul's Cathedral** *(see pp152–5)* and the **Monument** *(see p156)*, before heading to **Southwark** *(see pp178–9)* and the **Shard** *(see p186)*, then viewing contemporary art at **Tate Modern** *(see pp182–5)*. End the day with a play *(Apr–Oct)* at **Shakespeare's Globe** *(see p181)*.

Day 2
Morning Start the day with some culture at the **National Gallery** *(see pp108–11)*, and the **National Portrait Gallery** *(see pp106–7)*, with its fascinating collection of paintings and photographs. Then soak up the ambience of Soho with a wander through **Berwick Street Market** *(see p112)* and **Soho Square** *(see p112)*. Head to **Chinatown** for a spot of lunch *(see p112)*.

Afternoon Walk to **Covent Garden** *(see pp116–17)* and take a backstage tour of the **Royal Opera House** *(see p119)*, then explore London's social history at the **London Transport Museum** *(see p118)*. Afterwards, peruse the hip shops of **Neal Street** *(see p119)*.

Day 3
Morning Start the day at the **British Museum** *(see pp128–31)*, a treasure trove charting two million years of human civilization. Don't miss the Ancient Egyptian mummies and the Rosetta Stone.

Afternoon Head to **Trafalgar Square** *(see p106)*, then stroll along **The Mall** *(see p97)* to **Buckingham Palace** *(see pp98–9)* to visit the State Rooms *(Jul–Sep)*. End the day by relaxing in **St James's Park** *(see p96)*.

Day 4
Morning Start with a spin on the **London Eye** *(see p193)*, then head to **Westminster Abbey** *(see pp80–83)*. This incredible building has witnessed

Assembled crowds watch a daredevil street performer in Covent Garden's Piazza

Al fresco eating and drinking at picturesque Gabriel's Wharf

coronations and royal weddings. If it's summer, book a tour of the **Houses of Parliament** *(see pp76–7)*, or at other times queue to see the Lords and Commons in action. As you leave, look up at **Big Ben** *(see p78)*.

Afternoon Make your way to the **Imperial War Museum** *(see pp194–5)*, with its poignant exhibition on the Holocaust. For something lighter, walk through the vibrant **Southbank Centre** *(see pp190–91)* to the boutiques and cafés of **Gabriel's Wharf** *(see p195)*.

Day 5
Morning South Kensington's three world-class museums are worth the best part of a day, even if you are selective. Arrive early (they all open at 10am) as they can be very popular. Start with either the **Science Museum** *(see pp210–11)*, with its hands-on experiments and aircraft simulators, or the **Natural History Museum** *(see pp206–7)* for animatronic dinosaurs and touch-screen creepy-crawlies.

Afternoon The tearooms of the **Victoria and Albert Museum** *(see pp214–17)* are the most beautifully decorated in London, so have a reviving lunch there before discovering one of the world's finest collections of decorative art, with extraordinary pieces from across the globe. Finish the day by walking up to **Kensington Gardens** *(see p212)* to take a look at the Albert Memorial, the Palace and the Peter Pan statue.

Putting London on the Map

London, the capital of the United Kingdom, is a city of over eight million people covering 1,606 sq km (620 sq miles) of southeast England. It is built on the River Thames and is at the centre of the UK's road and rail networks. From London visitors can easily reach the UK's other main tourist attractions.

Western Europe

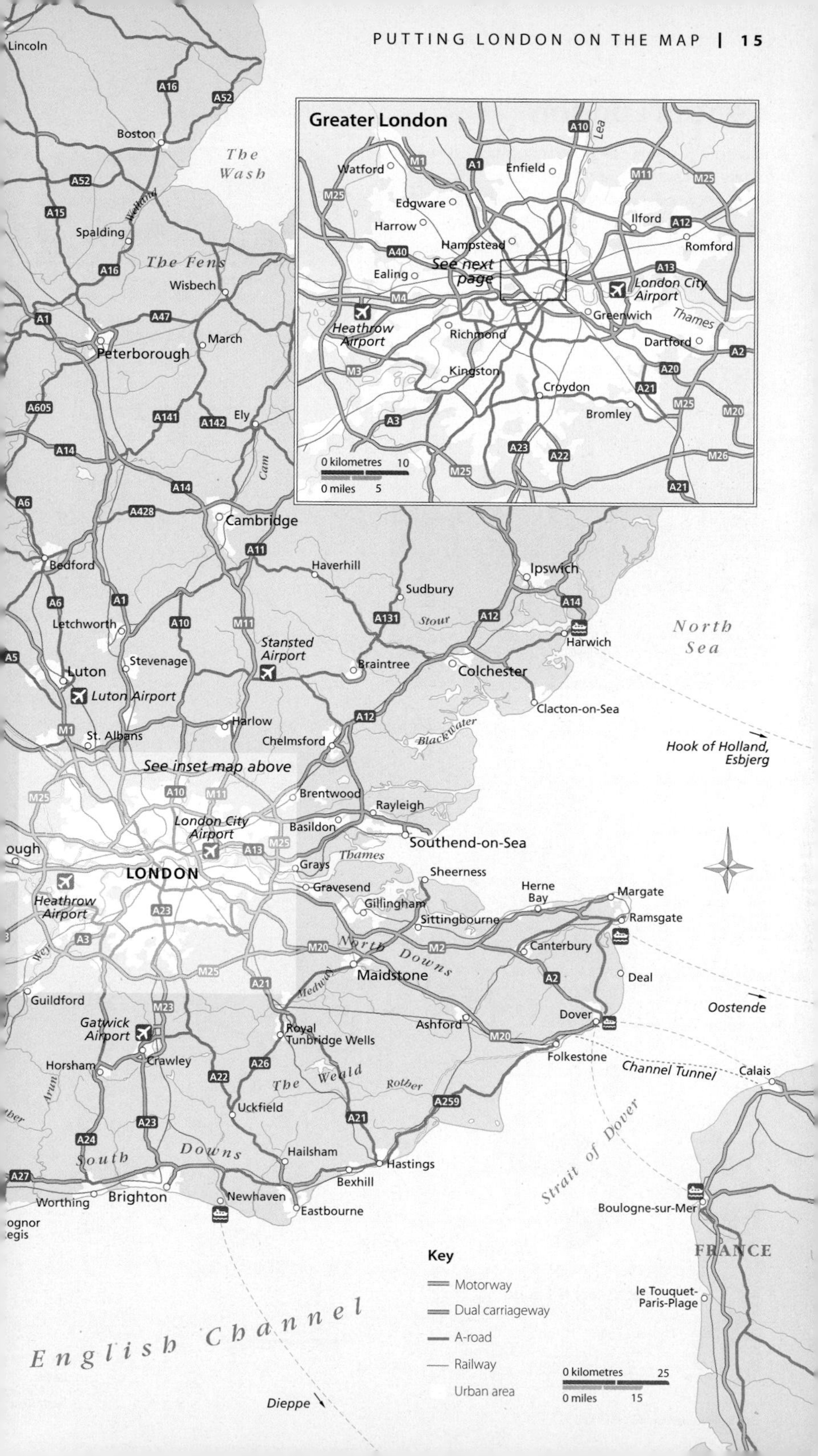

Greater London

Watford
A1
A10 *Lee*
Enfield
M1
Edgware
M25
Ilford
M11
M25
Harrow
Hampstead
Romford
A40
Ealing
A12
London City
Airport
A13
M4
Heathrow
Airport
Greenwich
Thames
Richmond
Dartford
A2
See next page
Kingston
A20
Croydon
A21
M25
M20
Bromley
A3
A23
A22
M26
M25
A21

0 kilometres 10
0 miles 5

Lincoln
A16
A52
Boston
A52
A15
Spalding
A16
Wisbech
The Fens
The Wash
March
A47
Peterborough
A1
A605
A141
A142
Ely
A428
Cam
Bedford
A14
Cambridge
A6
A1
A11
Letchworth
A10
Haverhill
A5
Luton
Stevenage
M11
Sudbury
Ipswich
Luton Airport
Stansted
Airport
A131
Stour
A12
A14
Harwich
M1
St. Albans
Harlow
Braintree
Colchester
*North
Sea*
See inset map above
Chelmsford
A12
Clacton-on-Sea
A10
M11
Blackwater
ough
Brentwood
Rayleigh
M25
London City
Airport
Basildon
Southend-on-Sea
*Hook of Holland,
Esbjerg*
A13
Grays
Thames
Sheerness
LONDON
Gravesend
Margate
Heathrow
Airport
A23
Gillingham
Herne
Bay
Ramsgate
Sittingbourne
A3
M20
North Downs
M2
Canterbury
M25
A21
Maidstone
A2
Deal
Oostende
Guildford
Medway
Ashford
M23
Dover
Gatwick
Airport
Royal
Tunbridge Wells
M20
Folkestone
Channel Tunnel
Calais
Horsham
A22
A26
Crawley
The Weald
Rother
A24
A259
A23
Uckfield
A21
South Downs
Hailsham
Hastings
Worthing
Brighton
Bexhill
Boulogne-sur-Mer
ognor
egis
Newhaven
Eastbourne
FRANCE
Strait of Dover
*le Touquet-
Paris-Plage*

Key

Motorway
Dual carriageway
A-road
Railway
Urban area

0 kilometres 25
0 miles 15

English Channel

Dieppe

Central London

Most of the sights described in this book lie within 14 areas of central London, plus two outlying districts of Hampstead and Greenwich. Each area has its own chapter. If time is short, you may decide to restrict yourself to the five areas that contain most of London's famous sights: Whitehall and Westminster, The City, Bloomsbury and Fitzrovia, Soho and Trafalgar Square, and South Kensington.

Tower of London
For much of its 900-year history the Tower was an object of fear. Its bloody past and the Crown Jewels make it a major attraction (see pp158–61).

National Gallery
This gallery has over 2,300 paintings, and the collection is particularly strong on Dutch, early Renaissance Italian and 17th-century Spanish painting (see pp108–11).

Natural History Museum
Life on Earth and the Earth itself are vividly explored at the museum, through a combination of interactive techniques and traditional displays (see pp206–7).

0 kilometres   1

0 miles   0.5

For keys to symbols see back flap

Buckingham Palace
The office and home of the monarchy, the palace is also used for state occasions. The State Rooms open to the public in the summer *(see pp98–9)*.

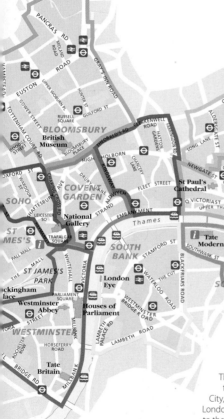

Museum of London
This museum, on the edge of the Barbican complex in the City, provides a lively account of London life from prehistoric times to the present day *(see pp170–71)*.

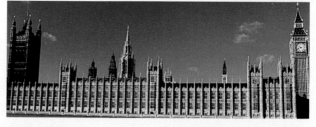

Houses of Parliament
The Palace of Westminster has been the seat of the two Houses of Parliament, called the Lords and the Commons, since 1512 *(see pp76–7)*.

THE HISTORY OF LONDON

In 55 BC, Julius Caesar's Roman army invaded England, landing in Kent and marching northwest until it reached the broad River Thames at what is now Southwark. There were a few tribesmen living on the opposite bank but no major settlement. However, by the time of the second Roman invasion 88 years later, a small port and mercantile community had been established here. The Romans bridged the river and built their administrative headquarters on the north bank, calling it Londinium – a version of its old Celtic name.

London as Capital

London was soon the largest city in England and, by the time of the Norman Conquest in 1066, it was the obvious choice for national capital.

Settlement slowly spread beyond the original walled city, which was virtually wiped out by the Great Fire of 1666. The post-fire rebuilding formed the basis of the area we know today as the City of London but, by the 18th century, London had enveloped the settlements around it. These included the royal City of Westminster, which had long been London's religious and political centre. The explosive growth of commerce and industry during the 18th and 19th centuries made London the biggest and wealthiest city in the world, creating a prosperous middle class who built the fine houses that still grace parts of the capital. The prospect of riches also lured millions of the dispossessed from the country-side and from abroad. They crowded into insanitary dwellings, many just east of the City, where docks provided employment.

By the end of the 19th century, 4.5 million people lived in inner London and another 4 million in its immediate vicinity. Bombing during World War II devastated many of the central areas and led to substantial rebuilding in the second half of the 20th century, when the docks and other Victorian industries disappeared.

The following pages illustrate London's history by giving snapshots of significant periods in its evolution.

A map of 1580 depicting the City of London and, near the lower left corner, the City of Westminster

◀ A 15th-century manuscript showing the Tower of London with London Bridge in the background

Roman London

When the Romans invaded Britain in the 1st century AD, they already controlled vast areas of the Mediterranean, but fierce opposition from local tribes (such as Queen Boudicca's Iceni) made Britain difficult to control. The Romans persevered, however, and had consolidated their power by the end of the century. Londinium, with its port, developed into a capital city; by the 3rd century, there were some 50,000 people living here. But, as the Roman Empire crumbled in the 5th century, the garrison pulled out, leaving the city to the Saxons.

Extent of the City
AD 125   Today

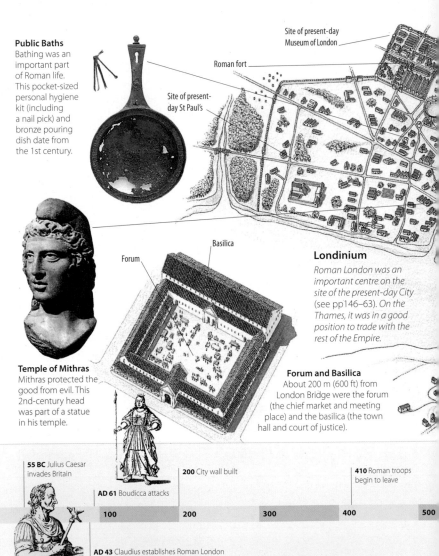

Site of present-day Museum of London

Roman fort

Public Baths
Bathing was an important part of Roman life. This pocket-sized personal hygiene kit (including a nail pick) and bronze pouring dish date from the 1st century.

Site of present-day St Paul's

Basilica

Forum

Londinium
Roman London was an important centre on the site of the present-day City (see pp146–63). On the Thames, it was in a good position to trade with the rest of the Empire.

Temple of Mithras
Mithras protected the good from evil. This 2nd-century head was part of a statue in his temple.

Forum and Basilica
About 200 m (600 ft) from London Bridge were the forum (the chief market and meeting place) and the basilica (the town hall and court of justice).

55 BC Julius Caesar invades Britain

200 City wall built

410 Roman troops begin to leave

AD 61 Boudicca attacks

100   200   300   400   500

AD 43 Claudius establishes Roman London and builds the first bridge

London Wall
The tombstone of a Roman legionnaire was built into the city wall. The writing tablets in his left hand suggest he did clerical work.

Amphitheatre
Entertainment was brutal. Gladiators, dressed like this figurine, fighting to the death, was a popular spectacle.

Where to See Roman London

Most traces of the Roman occupation are in the City (see pp146–63) and Southwark (see pp176–87). The Museum of London (see pp170–71) and the British Museum (see pp128–31) have extensive collections of Roman finds. There's a Roman pavement in the crypt of All Hallows by the Tower (see p157), and the foundations of the Temple of Mithras are on view near the site on Queen Victoria St. In the 1980s an amphitheatre was found below the Guildhall (see p163).

This section of the Roman wall, built in the 3rd century to defend the city, can be seen from the Museum of London.

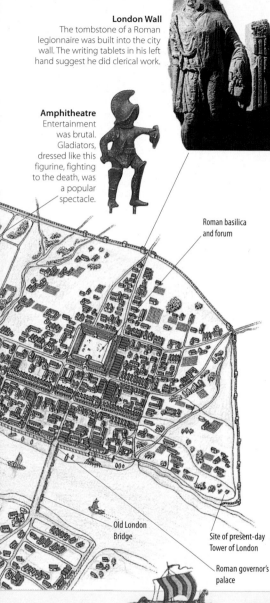

Roman basilica and forum

Old London Bridge

Site of present-day Tower of London

Roman governor's palace

This well-preserved Roman mosaic, a 2nd-century pavement, was found in 1869 in the City. It is now in the Museum of London.

604 King Ethelbert builds first St Paul's

834 First Viking raids

1014 Norse invader Olaf pulls down London Bridge to take the city

| 600 | 700 | 800 | | 1000 |

871 Alfred the Great becomes king of Wessex

Medieval London

The historic division between London's centres of commerce (the City) and government (Westminster) started in the mid-11th century when Edward the Confessor established his court and sited his abbey *(see pp80–83)* at Westminster. Meanwhile, in the City, tradesmen set up their own institutions and guilds, and London appointed its first mayor. Disease was rife and the population never rose much above its Roman peak of 50,000. The Black Death (1348) reduced the population by half.

Extent of the City
☐ 1200   ▦ Today

London Bridge

The first stone bridge was built in 1209 and lasted 600 years. It was the only bridge across the Thames in London until Westminster Bridge (1750).

Houses and shops projected over both sides of the bridge. Shopkeepers made their own merchandise on the premises and lived above their shops. Apprentices did the selling.

The Chapel of St Thomas, erected the year the bridge was completed, was one of its first buildings.

St Thomas à Becket
As Archbishop of Canterbury he was murdered in 1170, at the prompting of Henry II, with whom he was quarrelling. Thomas was made a saint and pilgrims visited his Canterbury shrine.

Iron railings

Dick Whittington
The 15th-century trader was thrice mayor of London.

The piers were made from wooden stakes rammed into the riverbed and filled with rubble.

Stag Hunting
Such sports were the chief recreation of wealthy landowners.

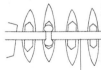

The arches ranged from 4.5 m (15 ft) to 10 m (35 ft) in width.

1042 Edward the Confessor becomes king

1086 Domesday Book, England's first survey, published

1191 Henry Fitzalwin becomes London's first mayor

1050   **1100**   **1150**   **1200**   **1250**

1066 William I crowned in Abbey

1065 Westminster Abbey completed

1176 Work starts on the first stone London Bridge

1215 King John's Magna Carta gives City more powers

1240 First parliament sits at Westminster

Chivalry
In later eras, medieval knights were idealized for their courage and honour. Edward Burne-Jones (1833–98) painted George, patron saint of England, rescuing a maiden from the dragon.

Geoffrey Chaucer
The poet and customs controller *(see p43)* is best remembered for his *Canterbury Tales*, which creates a rich picture of 14th-century England.

Where to See Medieval London

Only a few buildings survived the Great Fire of 1666 *(see pp26–7)*: the Tower *(see pp158–61)*, Westminster Hall *(see p76)*, and Westminster Abbey *(see pp80–83)*, and a handful of churches *(see p50)*. The Museum of London *(see pp170–71)* contains artifacts, while Tate Britain *(see pp86–9)* and the National Gallery *(see pp108–11)* display paintings. Manuscripts, including the Domesday Book, are found at the British Library *(see p133)*.

The Tower of London was started in 1078 and became one of the few centres of royal power in the largely self-governing City.

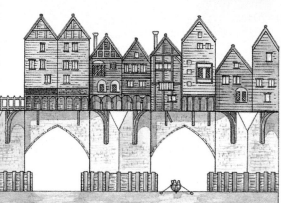

Plan of the Bridge
The bridge had 19 arches to span the river, making it for many years the longest stone bridge in England.

A 14th-century rose window is all that remains of Winchester Palace near the Clink on Bankside *(see p179)*.

Many 13th-century pilgrims went to Canterbury.

1348 Black Death kills thousands

1394 Westminster Hall remodelled by Henry Yevele

The Great Seal of Richard I, who spent most of his 10-year reign fighting abroad.

1350	1400	1450

1381 Peasants' Revolt defeated

1397 Richard Whittington becomes mayor

1476 William Caxton sets up first printing press at Westminster

Elizabethan London

In the 16th century the monarchy was stronger than ever before. The Tudors established peace throughout England, allowing art and commerce to flourish. This renaissance reached its zenith under Elizabeth I, when explorers opened up the New World, and English theatre, the nation's most lasting contribution to world culture, was born.

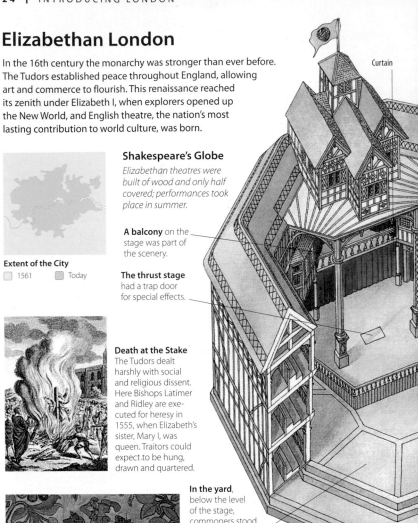

Curtain

Shakespeare's Globe

Elizabethan theatres were built of wood and only half covered; performances took place in summer.

Extent of the City

🟦 1561   🟦 Today

A balcony on the stage was part of the scenery.

The thrust stage had a trap door for special effects.

Death at the Stake

The Tudors dealt harshly with social and religious dissent. Here Bishops Latimer and Ridley are executed for heresy in 1555, when Elizabeth's sister, Mary I, was queen. Traitors could expect to be hung, drawn and quartered.

In the yard, below the level of the stage, commoners stood to watch the play.

Hunting and Hawking

Popular 16th-century pastimes are shown on this cushion cover.

Rat catchers, and other pest controllers, could not prevent epidemics of plague.

1535 Sir Thomas More executed for treason

1536 Henry VIII's second wife, Anne Boleyn, executed

1530

1534 Henry VIII breaks with the Roman Catholic church

1540

1547 Henry dies, succeeded by his son Edward VI

1550

1553 Edward dies, succeeded by his sister Mary I

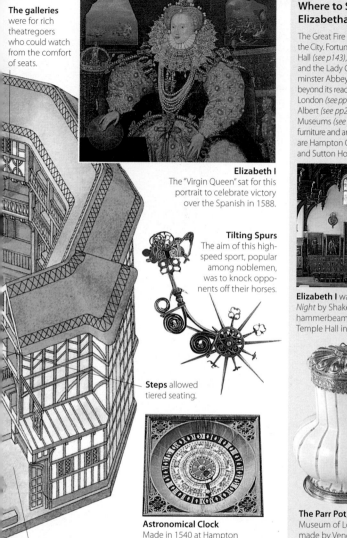

The galleries were for rich theatregoers who could watch from the comfort of seats.

Elizabeth I
The "Virgin Queen" sat for this portrait to celebrate victory over the Spanish in 1588.

Tilting Spurs
The aim of this high-speed sport, popular among noblemen, was to knock opponents off their horses.

Steps allowed tiered seating.

Audience entrance

Astronomical Clock
Made in 1540 at Hampton Court, this device shows the sun moving round the earth.

Where to See Elizabethan London

The Great Fire of 1666 wiped out the City. Fortunately, Middle Temple Hall *(see p143)*, Staple Inn *(see p145)* and the Lady Chapel inside Westminster Abbey *(see pp80–83)* were beyond its reach. The Museum of London *(see pp170–71)*, Victoria and Albert *(see pp214–17)*, and Geffrye Museums *(see p252)* have fine furniture and artifacts. Further afield are Hampton Court *(see pp260–63)* and Sutton House *(see p252)*.

Elizabeth I watched *Twelfth Night* by Shakespeare under the hammerbeam roof of Middle Temple Hall in 1603.

The Parr Pot, now in the Museum of London, was made by Venetian craftsmen in London in 1547.

1563 Plague sweeps Europe

1558 Mary I's death makes Elizabeth queen

1570 Francis Drake makes first voyage to the West Indies

1584 Walter Raleigh's first attempt to colonize America

Gloves made from imported silk and velvet

1588 Drake defeats Spanish Armada

1591 First play by Shakespeare produced

1603 Elizabeth dies, James I accedes

| 1560 | 1570 | 1580 | 1590 |

Restoration London

Civil War broke out in 1642 when the mercantile class demanded that some of the monarch's power be passed to Parliament. The subsequent Commonwealth was dominated by Puritans under Oliver Cromwell. The Puritans outlawed simple pleasures, such as dancing and theatre, so it was small wonder that the restoration of the monarchy under Charles II in 1660 was greeted with rejoicing and the release of pent-up creative energies. The period was, however, also marked with two major tragedies: the Plague (1665) and the Great Fire (1666).

Extent of the City
☐ 1680   ☐ Today

St Paul's was destroyed in the fire that raged as far west as Fetter Lane *(map 14 E1)*.

London Bridge itself survived, but many of the buildings on it were burned down.

Oliver Cromwell
He led the Parliamentarian army and was Lord Protector of the Realm from 1653 until his death in 1658. At the Restoration, his body was dug up and hung from the gallows at Tyburn, near Hyde Park *(see p213)*.

Charles I's Death
The king was beheaded for tyranny on a freezing day (30 January 1649) outside Banqueting House *(see p84)*.

Charles I
His belief in the Divine Right of Kings angered Parliament and contributed to the Civil War.

1605 Guy Fawkes leads failed attempt to blow up the King and Parliament

1620

1623 Shakespeare's First Folio published

1625 James I dies, succeeded by his son Charles I

1630

Feathered helmet worn by Royalist cavaliers.

1640

1642 Civil War starts when Parliament defies the king

1649 Charles I executed, Commonwealth established

1650

Newton's Telescope
Physicist and astronomer Sir Isaac Newton (1642–1727) formulated the law of gravity.

Samuel Pepys
His exuberant diaries tell us much about courtly life of the time.

The Tower of London
was just out of the fire's reach.

Where to See Restoration London

Wren's churches and his St Paul's Cathedral *(see p51 and pp152–5)* are, with Inigo Jones's Banqueting House *(see p84)*, London's most famous 17th-century buildings. Other fine examples are Lincoln's Inn *(see p140)* and Cloth Fair *(see p168)*. The Museum of London *(see pp170–71)* has a period interior. The British Museum *(see pp128–31)* and the V&A *(see pp214–17)* have large pottery, silver and textile collections.

Ham House *(see p258)* was built in 1610 but much enlarged later in the century. It has the finest interior of its time in England.

The Great Fire of 1666
An unidentified Dutch artist painted this view of the fire, which burned for five days, destroying 13,000 houses.

The Plague
During 1665, carts collected the dead and took them to communal graves outside the city.

Peter Paul Rubens painted the ceiling in 1636 for Inigo Jones's Banqueting House *(see p84)*. This is one of its panels.

1664–5 Plague kills 100,000

1666 Great Fire

1685 Charles II dies, Catholic James II becomes king

1692 First insurance market opens at Lloyd's

1660

1670

1680

1690

1660 Monarchy restored under Charles II

A barber's bowl made by London potters in 1681.

1688 James ousted in favour of Protestant William of Orange

1694 First Bank of England set up by William Paterson

Georgian London

The foundation of the Bank of England in 1694 spurred the growth of London and, by the time George I came to the throne in 1714, it had become an important financial and commercial centre. Aristocrats with West End estates began laying out elegant squares and terraces to house newly rich merchants. Architects such as the Adam brothers, John Soane and John Nash developed stylish medium-scale housing. They drew inspiration from the great European capitals, as did English painters, sculptors, composers and craftsmen.

Extent of the City
☐ 1810 ☐ Today

Portman Square was on the town's outskirts when it was started in 1764.

Manchester Square was laid out in 1776–8.

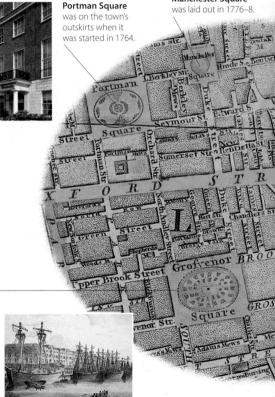

Great Cumberland Place
Built in 1790, it was named after a royal duke and military commander.

Grosvenor Square
Few of the original houses remain on one of the oldest and largest Mayfair squares (1720).

Docks
Purpose-built docks handled the growth in world trade.

1714 George I becomes king

1727 George II becomes king

1760 George III becomes king

1768 Royal Academy of Art established

1720 | **1740** | **1760** | **1770**

1717 Hanover Square built, start of West End development

1729 John Wesley (1703–91) founds the Methodist Church

1759 Kew Gardens established

John Nash
Nash shaped 18th-century London with variations on Classical themes, such as this archway in Cumberland Terrace, near Regent's Park.

Georgian London
The layout of much of London's West End has remained very similar to how it was in 1828, when this map was published.

Where to See Georgian London

The portico of the Theatre Royal Haymarket *(see pp340–41)* gives a taste of the style of fashionable London in the 1820s. In Pall Mall *(see p96)* Charles Barry's Reform and Travellers' Clubs are equally evocative. Most West End squares have some Georgian buildings, while Fournier Street *(see p174)* has good small-scale domestic architecture. The Victoria and Albert Museum *(V&A, see pp214–17)* has silver, as do the London Silver Vaults *(see p145)*, where it is for sale. Hogarth's pictures, at Tate Britain *(see pp86–9)* and Sir John Soane's Museum *(see pp140–41)*, illustrate social conditions.

This English long-case clock (1725), made of oak and pine with Chinese designs, is in the V&A.

Berkeley Square
Built in the 1730s and 1740s in the grounds of the former Berkeley House, several characteristic original houses remain on its west side.

Ironwork
Crafts flourished. This ornate railing is in Manchester Square.

Captain Cook
This Yorkshire-born explorer discovered Australia during a voyage round the world in 1768–71.

Signatories of the American Declaration of Independence

1802 Stock Exchange formally established

1820 George III dies, Prince Regent becomes George IV

1830 George IV dies, brother William IV is king

| 1790 | 1800 | 1810 | 1820 | 1830 |

1776 Britain loses American colonies with Declaration of Independence

1811 George III goes mad, his son George is made Regent

1829 London's first horse bus

Victorian London

Much of London today is Victorian. Until the early 19th century, the capital had been confined to the original Roman city, plus Westminster and Mayfair to the west, ringed by fields and villages such as Brompton, Islington and Battersea. From the 1820s, these green spaces filled rapidly with terraces of houses for the growing numbers attracted to London by industrialization. Rapid expansion brought its challenges. The first cholera epidemic broke out in 1832, and in 1858 came the Great Stink, when the smell from the Thames became so bad that parliament had to go into recess. Joseph Bazalgette's sewerage system (1875), involving pumping stations on both sides of the Thames, eased the problem.

Extent of the City
☐ 1900 ■ Today

Pantomime
The traditional family Christmas entertainment – still popular today *(see p340)* – started in the 19th century.

Nearly 14,000 exhibitors came from all over the world, bringing more than 100,000 exhibits.

The building was 560 m (1,850 ft) long and 33 m (110 ft) high.

Soldiers marched and jumped on the floor to test its strength before the exhibition opened.

Massive elm trees growing in Hyde Park were left standing and the exhibition was erected around them.

The Crystal Fountain was 8 m (27 ft) high.

Carpets and stained glass were hung from the galleries.

1836 First London rail terminus opens at London Bridge

1837 Victoria becomes queen

1851 Great Exhibition

A Wedgwood plate in typically florid Victorian style

1861 Prince Albert dies

| 1840 | 1850 | 1860 |

1840 Rowland Hill introduces the Penny Post

Season ticket for Great Exhibition

1863 Metropolitan Railway, world's first underground system, is opened

Railways
By 1900 fast trains, such as this *Scotch Express*, were crossing the country.

Where to See Victorian London

Grandiose buildings best reflect the spirit of the age, notably the rail termini, the Kensington Museums *(see pp202–17)* and the Royal Albert Hall *(see p209)*. Leighton House *(see p222)* has a well-preserved interior. Pottery and fabrics are in the Victoria and Albert Museum, and the London Transport Museum *(see p118)* has buses, trams and trains.

Crystal Palace
Between May and October 1851, 6 million people visited Joseph Paxton's superb feat of engineering. In 1852, it was dismantled and reassembled in south London, where it remained until destroyed by fire in 1936.

Formal Dress Under Victoria, elaborate men's attire was replaced by more restrained evening wear.

The Public Record Office in Chancery Lane is an example of Victorian Gothic architecture.

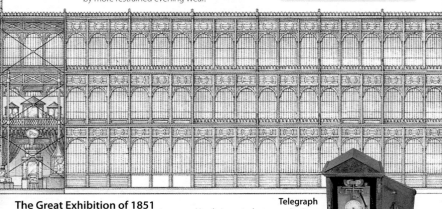

The Great Exhibition of 1851
The exhibition, held in the Crystal Palace in Hyde Park, celebrated industry, technology and the expanding British Empire.

Telegraph
Newly invented communications technology, like this telegraph from 1840, made business expansion easier.

1870 First Peabody Buildings, to house the poor, built in Blackfriars Road

1890 First electric Underground line, from Bank to Stockwell, opens

1891 First LCC public housing built, in Shoreditch

1901 Queen Victoria dies; Edward VII accedes

70   1880   1890   1900

A special box for carrying top hats

1889 London County Council (LCC) established

1899 First motor buses introduced

Commemorative fan for the Boer War, which ended in 1903

London and Two World Wars

During World War I, Zeppelin airships bombed the city, and the sight of injured soldiers returning from the front to be treated at Charing Cross Hospital became familiar. The society that emerged from the war embraced the innovations of the early 20th century – the motor car, telephone and commuter transport. Then came the Depression of the 1930s, the effects of which had barely worn off when World War II began. The city was once again bombarded, though on a vastly bigger scale, most notably during the Blitz of 1940–41.

Extent of the City
☐ 1938   ☐ Today

Commuting
London's new outer suburbs were made popular by the underground railway. In the north was "Metroland", named after the Metropolitan line, which penetrated Hertfordshire.

Communications
The radio provided home entertainment and information. This is a 1933 model.

High Fashion
The sleek flowing new styles contrasted with the fussy elaboration of the Victorians and Edwardians. This tea gown is from the 1920s.

Formal evening wear, including hats for both sexes, was still compulsory when going to smart West End night spots.

A London Street Scene
Maurice Greiflenhagen's painting (1926) captures the bustle of London after dark.

Medals like this one from 1914 were struck during the campaign for women's votes.

1910 George V succeeds Edward VII

1910

1920

Cavalry was still used in the Middle Eastern battles of World War I (1914–18).

1921 North Circular Road links northern suburbs

1922 First BBC national radio broadcast

Victory march
American flags were flown in peace parades on the streets of London to celebrate the end of World War I.

World War II and the Blitz

World War II saw large-scale civilian bombing for the first time, bringing the horror of war to Londoners' doorsteps. Thousands were killed in their homes. Many people took refuge in Underground stations and children were evacuated to the safety of the countryside.

George VI
Oswald Birley painted this portrait of the king who became a model for wartime resistance and unity.

As in World War I, women were recruited for factory work formerly done by men who were away fighting.

Seven new theatres were built in central London between 1924 and 1931.

Early motor buses had open tops, like the old horse-drawn buses.

Bombing raids in 1940 and 1941 (the Blitz) caused devastation all over the city.

Throughout the period newspaper circulations increased massively. In 1930, *The Daily Herald* sold 2 million copies a day.

1929 US stock market crash brings world Depression

1939 World War II begins

25

1930

1927 First talking pictures

1936 Edward VIII abdicates to marry US divorcée Wallis Simpson. George VI accedes

1940 Winston Churchill becomes prime minister

Postwar London

Much of London was flattened by World War II bombs.
Afterwards, the chance for imaginative rebuilding was missed –
some badly designed postwar developments have since been
razed. But, by the 1960s, London was such a dynamic world
leader in fashion and popular music that *Time* magazine dubbed
it "swinging London". Skyscrapers sprang up, but some stayed
empty as the 1980s boom gave way to 1990s recession.

Extent of the City
- [ ] 1959
- [ ] Today

The Beatles
The Liverpool pop group, pictured in 1965,
had rocketed to stardom two years earlier with
songs of appealing freshness and directness.
The group symbolized carefree 1960s London.

Festival of Britain
After wartime,
the city's morale
was lifted by the
Festival, marking
the 1851 Great
Exhibition's
centenary
(see pp30–31).

Margaret Thatcher
Britain's first female
prime minister (1979–90)
promoted the market-
led policies that fuelled
the 1980s boom.

The Royal Festival Hall (1951)
was the Festival's centrepiece and
is still a landmark *(see p192)*.

Telecom Tower (1964), at
189 m (620 ft) high, dominates
the Fitzrovia skyline.

The Lloyd's Building (1986) is
Richard Rogers' Post-Modernist
emblem *(see pp162–3)*.

1948 Olympic Games
held in London

1952 George VI
dies; his daughter
Elizabeth II accedes

*Minis became a symbol of
the 1960s; small and
manoeuvrable, they typified
the go-as-you-please mood
of the decade.*

1945	1950	1955	1960	1965

1951 Festival
of Britain

1945
End of World War II

1954
Food rationing,
introduced
during World
War II, abolished

1963
National Theatre
founded at the Old Vic

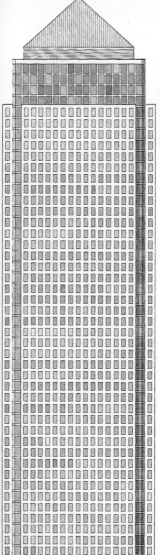

One Canada Square (1991) in Canary Wharf *(see p253)* was designed by César Pelli.

Docklands Light Railway
In the 1980s, new, driverless trains started to transport people to the developing Docklands.

Post-Modern Architecture

Since the 1980s, architects have reacted against the stark shapes of the Modernists. Architect Richard Rogers emphasizes structural features; others, like Terry Farrell, adopt a more playful approach using pastiches of Classical features.

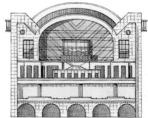

Charing Cross (1991) has Terry Farrell's glasshouse on top of the Victorian station *(see p123)*.

Youth Culture

With their new mobility and spending power, young people began to influence the development of British popular culture in the years after World War II. Music, fashion and design were increasingly geared to their rapidly changing tastes.

Punks were a phenomenon of the 1970s and 1980s. Their clothes, music and hair were designed to shock.

The Royal Wedding
The marriage between Prince Charles and Lady Diana Spencer turned the new Princess of Wales into a global style icon.

1977 Queen's Silver Jubilee; work starts on the Underground's Jubilee line

1981 Prince Charles and Lady Diana Spencer marry at St Paul's Cathedral

1984 Thames Barrier completed

1986 Greater London Council abolished

1992 Canary Wharf development opens

1970	1975	1980	1985	1990	1995

1971 New London Bridge built

1982 Sovereignty disputes over South Atlantic islands lead to the Falklands War between Britain and Argentina

1985 Ethiopian famine prompts Live Aid relief campaign

Vivienne Westwood's clothes won prizes in the 1980s and 1990s.

Modern London

In 1997 Tony Blair entered Downing Street as prime minister after New Labour secured a landslide victory. The following years saw the city busy with grand building projects and new cultural attractions to mark the year 2000, including the Tate Modern; the London Eye; the Millennium Dome (now the O2 arena) and the Millennium Bridge. Soon after, Great Britain joined in the international effort against terrorism and London became the stage for mass protests against the invasion of Iraq. July 2005 saw the city blighted by a horrific terrorist attack on its transport system. In 2012, London was celebrating again as it hosted a hugely successful Olympic Games.

2004 One of London's most distinctive buildings, 30 St Mary Axe, also known as "the Gherkin", opens

1997 Tony Blair enters Downing Street

2000 Ken Livingstone becomes London's first directly elected mayor

2003 Over a million people march in London against the second Iraq war

2005 London's public transport system suffers a major terrorist attack

1995	2000	2005	
	Livingstone		Johnson
1995	2000	2005	

2000 A series of new projects opens for the millennium, including the Tate Modern, London Eye and Millennium Bridge

1997 Princess Diana's funeral procession brings London to a halt

2003 The congestion charge is introduced in central areas of the city prone to heavy traffic

2008 Boris Johnson becomes London mayor

2002 Celebrations held around the city for the Queen's Golden Jubilee

2010 "Boris Bikes" available to ride around the city in a new cycle hire scheme

Celebrations for the Queen's Diamond Jubilee

2011 Prince William marries Catherine Middleton

2012 The Queen celebrates her Diamond Jubilee and London hosts the Olympic Games

2013 A new royal heir, George Alexander Louis, is born to Prince William and Catherine

2015 Princess Charlotte is born

2010	2015	2020

Khan

2010	2015	2020

2016 Sadiq Khan becomes London mayor

2013 The tallest building in the city, the Shard, opens

2015 The Conservative party wins the general election

The Shard

2011 Thousands of people riot across the city, resulting in looting, arson and violence

2010 The Conservatives and the Liberal Democrats form a coalition government

Kings and Queens in London

London has been the royal capital of England since 1066, when William the Conqueror began a tradition of holding coronations in Westminster Abbey. Since then, successive kings and queens have left their mark on London and many of the places described in this book have royal associations: Henry VIII hunted at Richmond, Charles I was executed on Whitehall and the young Queen Victoria rode on Queensway. Royalty is also celebrated in many of London's traditional ceremonies – for more details on these, turn to pages 56–9.

1413–22 Henry V

1509–47 Henry VIII

1399–1413 Henry IV

1485–1509 Henry VII

1553–8 Mary I

1483–5 Richard III

1066–87 William the Conqueror

1087–1100 William II

1100–35 Henry I

1135–54 Stephen

1327–77 Edward III

1050	1100	1150	1200	1250	1300	1350	1400	1450	1500	1
Norman		Plantagenet					Lancaster	York	Tudor	
1050	1100	1150	1200	1250	1300	1350	1400	1450	1500	1

1154–89 Henry II

1189–99 Richard I

1199–1216 John

1216–72 Henry III

1307–27 Edward II

1272–1307 Edward I

1461–70 and 1471–83 Edward IV

1547–53 Edward VI

1422–61 and 1470–1 Henry VI

1377–99 Richard II

Matthew Paris's 13th-century chronicle showing kings Richard I, Henry II, John and Henry III.

1483 Edward V

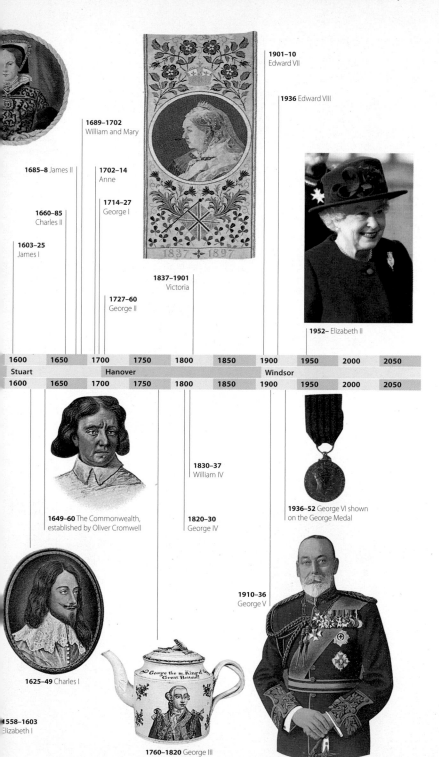

1901–10 Edward VII

1936 Edward VIII

1689–1702 William and Mary

1685–8 James II

1702–14 Anne

1714–27 George I

1660–85 Charles II

1603–25 James I

1837–1901 Victoria

1727–60 George II

1952– Elizabeth II

| 1600 | 1650 | 1700 | 1750 | 1800 | 1850 | 1900 | 1950 | 2000 | 2050 |

Stuart   Hanover   Windsor

| 1600 | 1650 | 1700 | 1750 | 1800 | 1850 | 1900 | 1950 | 2000 | 2050 |

1830–37 William IV

1649–60 The Commonwealth, established by Oliver Cromwell

1820–30 George IV

1936–52 George VI shown on the George Medal

1625–49 Charles I

1910–36 George V

1558–1603 Elizabeth I

1760–1820 George III

LONDON AT A GLANCE

There are nearly 300 places of interest described in the *Area by Area* section of this book. These range from the magnificent National Gallery *(see pp108–11)* to the gruesome Old Operating Theatre *(see p180)*, and from ancient Charterhouse *(see p168)* to modern Canary Wharf *(see p253)*. To help you make the most of your stay, the following 18 pages are a time-saving guide to the best London has to offer. Museums and galleries, churches, and parks and gardens each have a section, along with guides to remarkable Londoners and ceremonies in London. Each sight mentioned is cross-referenced to its own full entry. Below are the top ten tourist attractions to start you off.

London's Top Ten Tourist Attractions

St Paul's
See pp152–5.

London Eye
See p193.

National Gallery
See pp108–11.

Changing the Guard
Buckingham Palace, see pp98–9.

Hampton Court
See pp260–63.

Westminster Abbey
See pp80–83.

British Museum
See pp128–31.

Houses of Parliament
See pp76–7.

Tower of London
See pp158–61.

Victoria and Albert Museum
See pp214–17.

◄ The spectacular Great Court at the British Museum

Remarkable Londoners

London has always been a gathering place for the most prominent and influential people of the time. Some of these figures came to London from other parts of Britain or from countries further afield; others have been Londoners born and bred. All of them have left their mark on London, by designing great and lasting buildings, establishing institutions and traditions, or by writing about or painting the city they knew. Most of them have also had an influence that spread out from London to the rest of the world.

Venus Venticordia by Dante Gabriel Rossetti

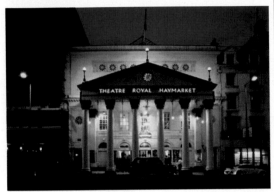

John Nash's Theatre Royal Haymarket (1821)

Architects and Engineers

A number of people who built London still have works standing. Inigo Jones (1573–1652), London-born, was the father of English Renaissance architecture. He lived and worked at Great Scotland Yard, Whitehall, then the residence of the royal architect – he was later succeeded by Sir Christopher Wren (1632–1723).

Wren's successors as the prime architects of London were his protégé Nicholas Hawksmoor (1661–1736)

and James Gibbs (1682–1754). Succeeding generations each produced architects who were to stamp their genius on the city: the brothers Robert (1728–92) and James Adam (1730–94), then John Nash (1752–1835), Sir Charles Barry (1795–1860), Decimus Burton (1800–81), Alfred Waterhouse (1830–1905), Norman Shaw (1831–1912), and Sir George Gilbert Scott (1811–78). Sir Joseph Bazalgette (1819–91) built London's sewer system and the Thames Embankment. More recently, Sir Norman Foster (1935–) has

left his mark with such iconic buildings as 30 St Mary Axe, known as "the Gherkin".

Artists

Painters in London, as elsewhere, often lived in enclaves, for mutual support and because they shared common priorities. During the 18th century, artists clustered around the court at St James's to be near their patrons. Thus both William Hogarth (1697–1764) and Sir Joshua Reynolds (1723–92) lived and worked in Leicester Square, while Thomas Gainsborough (1727–88) lived in Pall Mall. (Hogarth's Chiswick house was his place in the country.)

Later, Cheyne Walk in Chelsea, with its river views, became popular with artists, including the masters J M W Turner (1775–1851), James McNeill Whistler (1834–1903), Dante Gabriel Rossetti (1828–82), Philip Wilson Steer (1860–1942) and the sculptor Sir Jacob Epstein (1880–1959). Augustus John (1879–1961) and John

Historic London Homes

Four writers' homes that have been recreated are those of the romantic poet **John Keats** (1795–1821), the historian **Thomas Carlyle** (1795–1881), the lexicographer **Dr Samuel Johnson** (1709–84), and the prolific and popular novelist **Charles Dickens** (1812–70). The house that the architect **Sir John Soane** (1753–1837) designed for himself remains largely as it was when he died, as does the house where the psychiatrist **Sigmund Freud** (1856–1939) settled after fleeing Austria before World War II.

Apsley House, on Hyde Park Corner, was the residence of the **Duke of Wellington** (1769–1852), hero of the Battle of Waterloo. The life and music of Baroque composer **George Frideric Handel** (1685–1759) are recalled at his former home in Mayfair. Finally, the rooms of Sir Arthur Conan Doyle's fictional detective **Sherlock Holmes** have been created in Baker Street.

Carlyle's House

Plaques
All over London, the former homes of well-known figures are marked by plaques. Look out for these, especially in Chelsea, Kensington and Mayfair, and see how many names you recognize.

No. 3 Sussex Square, Kensington

No. 27b Canonbury Square, Islington

No. 56 Oakley Street, Chelsea

Singer Sargent (1856–1925) had studios in Tite Street.

Throughout the 20th century, independent galleries located in Cork Street, Mayfair, launched the careers of many London-based artists, including Irish-born Francis Bacon (1909–1992). Bacon is, however, most associated with the Soho of the 1950s and 60s, where his set, including painter Lucian Freud (1922–2011), gathered. In the late 1980s, a group of artists known as the Young British Artists, including Damien Hirst and Tracey Emin, emerged from Goldsmiths College of Art. They were associated with Hoxton and the East End, where the art scene has thrived in recent decades. Artist duo Gilbert & George also live and work in the area, incorporating photographs of the East End into their work.

off Sloane Street, near the Cadogan Hotel, where the flamboyant Oscar Wilde (1854–1900) was arrested in 1895 for homosexuality. Playwright George Bernard Shaw (1856–1950) lived at No. 29 Fitzroy Square in Bloomsbury. Later the same house was home to Virginia Woolf (1882–1941) and became a meeting place for the Bloomsbury Group, which included Vanessa Bell, John Maynard Keynes, E M Forster, Roger Fry and Duncan Grant.

Current authors with works set in modern London include Monica Ali, who wrote *Brick Lane*, Ian McEwan and Zadie Smith, who often focuses on her native northwest London. Sarah Waters has explored the city through novels set in different historic periods, as has Peter Ackroyd, also the writer of the magisterial *London: The Biography* and *Thames: Sacred River*.

Novelist Zadie Smith

poverty-stricken childhood in the slums of London.

In the 20th century, a school of fine actors blossomed at the Old Vic, including Sir John Gielgud (1904–2001), Sir Ralph Richardson (1902–83), Dame Peggy Ashcroft (1907–91) and Laurence (later Lord) Olivier (1907–89), who was appointed the first director of the National Theatre. In recent years, numerous London-born actors who have achieved a global level of fame on the big screen have chosen to return to the London stage, including Benedict Cumberbatch, Chiwetel Ejiofor, Jude Law, Tom Hiddleston and Carey Mulligan.

Laurence Olivier

Writers

Geoffrey Chaucer (c.1345–1400), author of *The Canterbury Tales,* was born in Upper Thames Street, the son of an innkeeper. William Shakespeare (1564–1616) and Christopher Marlowe (1564–93) were both associated with the theatres in Southwark, and may have lived nearby.

Poets John Donne (1572–1631) and John Milton (1608–74) were both born in Bread Street in the City. Donne, after a profligate youth, became Dean of St Paul's. The diarist Samuel Pepys (1633–1703) was born off Fleet Street.

The young novelist Jane Austen (1775–1817) lived briefly

Actors

Nell Gwynne (1650–87) won more fame as King Charles II's mistress than as an actress. However, she did appear on stage at Drury Lane Theatre; she also sold oranges there. The Shakespearean actor Edmund Kean (1789–1833) and the great tragic actress Sarah Siddons (1755–1831) were more distinguished players at Drury Lane. So were Henry Irving (1838–1905) and Ellen Terry (1847–1928), whose stage partnership lasted 24 years. Charlie Chaplin (1889–1977), born in Kennington, had a

Where to Find Historic London Homes

London's Best: Museums and Galleries

London's museums are filled with an astonishing diversity of treasures from all over the world. This map highlights 15 of the city's most important galleries and museums, whose exhibits cater to most interests. Some of these collections started from the legacies of 18th- and 19th-century explorers, traders and collectors. Others specialize in one aspect of art, history, science or technology. A more detailed overview of London's museums and galleries is on pages 46–7.

British Museum
This Anglo-Saxon helmet is part of a massive collection of antiquities.

Wallace Collection
Frans Hals's *Laughing Cavalier* is a star attraction in this museum of art, furniture, armour and *objets d'art*.

Royal Academy of Arts
Major international art exhibitions are held here, and the renowned Summer Exhibition, when works are on sale, takes place every year.

Regent's Park and Marylebone

Kensington and Holland Park

South Kensington and Knightsbridge

Piccadilly Mayfair a St James

Natural History Museum
All of life is here, with vivid displays on everything from dinosaurs (like this Triceratops skull) to butterflies.

Chelsea

Science Museum
Newcomen's steam engine of 1712 is just one of many exhibits that appeal to both novice and expert.

Victoria and Albert Museum
A museum dedicated to decorative arts with literally millions of objects in its collection. This Indian vase is from the 18th century.

National Portrait Gallery
Important British figures
are the subjects of paintings
and photographs. This
is Vivien Leigh, by
Angus McBean (1954).

National Gallery
The world-famous
paintings in the
national collection
are mainly European
and date from the
15th to the 19th
centuries.

British
Museum

Museum of London
London's history is told
through fascinating
objects such as this
15th-century reliquary.

National Portrait
Gallery

Tower of London
The Crown Jewels
and a vast collection
of arms and armour
are found here. This
armour was worn by
a 14th-century
Italian knight.

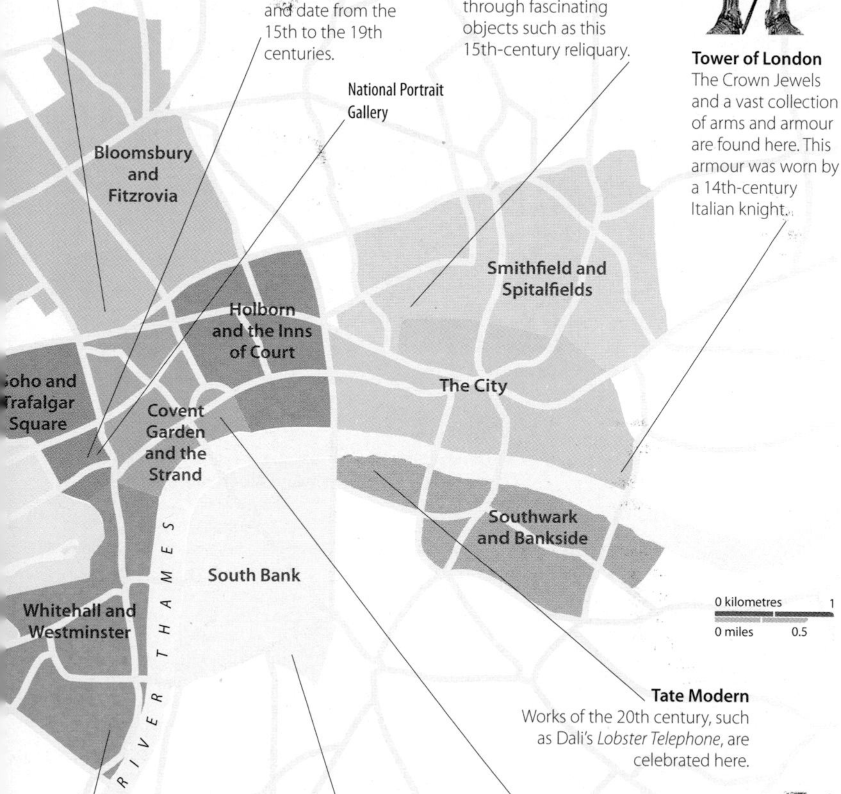

**Bloomsbury
and
Fitzrovia**

**Smithfield and
Spitalfields**

**Holborn
and the Inns
of Court**

**Soho and
Trafalgar
Square**

The City

**Covent
Garden
and the
Strand**

**Southwark
and Bankside**

South Bank

RIVER THAMES

0 kilometres 1

0 miles 0.5

**Whitehall and
Westminster**

Tate Modern
Works of the 20th century, such
as Dali's *Lobster Telephone*, are
celebrated here.

Tate Britain
Formerly the Tate Gallery,
this museum showcases
an outstanding collection
of British art from the 16th
century to the present.

Imperial War Museum
Displays, film and special
effects are used to recreate
20th-century battles. This
is one of the earliest tanks.

Courtauld Gallery
Well-known works, such as
Manet's *A Bar at the Folies-Bergère*,
line its galleries.

Exploring Museums and Galleries

London boasts an astonishingly rich and diverse collection of museums. The city's position for centuries at the hub of world-wide trade has been partly responsible for this extraordinarily rich cultural heritage. Britain's rule of a far-flung empire has also played its part. The world-renowned collections are impressive, but find time for the city's range of smaller museums, which are often more peaceful than their grander counterparts. Brimming with character, they cover every imaginable theme, from buses and toys to electricity and water power.

Geffrye Museum: Art Nouveau Room

Antiquities and Archaeology

Some of the most celebrated artifacts of ancient Asia, Egypt, Greece and Rome are housed in the **British Museum's** fine collection. Other antiquities, including books, manuscripts, paintings, busts and gems, are displayed in **Sir John Soane's Museum**, which is one of the most idiosyncratic to be found in London.

The **Museum of London** contains much of archaeological interest from all periods of the city's history.

Eclectic collection at Sir John Soane's Museum

Furniture and Interiors

The Museum of London recreates typical domestic and commercial interiors from the Roman period right up to the present day. The **Victoria and Albert Museum** (or V&A) contains complete rooms rescued from now vanished buildings, plus a magnificent collection of furniture ranging from the 16th century to work by

Design Museum display of chairs

contemporary designers. On a more modest scale, the **Geffrye Museum** consists of fully furnished period rooms dating from 1600 to the 1990s. Former homes of individuals, such as the **Freud Museum**, give insights into the furniture of specific periods, while **18 Stafford Terrace** offers visitors a perfectly preserved example of a late Victorian interior.

Costume and Jewellery

The **V&A's** vast collections include English and European clothes of the last 400 years, and some stunning jewellery from China, India and Japan. The priceless Crown Jewels, at the **Tower of London**, should not be missed; they include the world's largest cut diamond, the First Star of Africa, set in the Sceptre with the Cross. **Kensington Palace's** Ceremonial Dress Collection includes pieces worn by many notable royals. The **British Museum** displays ancient Aztec, Mayan and African costume.

Crafts and Design

Once again, the **Victoria and Albert Museum** (V&A) is the essential first port of call; its collections in these fields remain unrivalled. The **William Morris Gallery** shows every aspect of the 19th-century designer's work within the Arts and Crafts movement. The **Design Museum** focuses on modern design including products and fashion. The **Fashion and Textile Museum** mounts temporary exhibitions about many aspects of fashion.

Military Artifacts

The **National Army Museum** uses vivid models and displays to narrate the history of the British Army. Near Whitehall, the **Guards Museum** and **Household Cavalry Museum** focus on the Foot Guards and mounted royal regiments respectively. The **Tower of London** holds part of the national collection of arms and armour; an impressive display can be found at the **Wallace Collection**. The **Imperial War Museum** has recreations of World War I trenches and the Blitz. The **National Maritime Museum** has the definitive display on Lord Nelson and his naval battles and the **Florence Nightingale Museum** illustrates the hardships of 19th-century warfare.

Imperial War Museum

Toys and Childhood

Teddy bears, tin soldiers and doll's houses are some of the toys that can be seen in **Pollock's Toy Museum**. The collection includes Eric, "the oldest known teddy bear". The **V&A Museum of Childhood** and the **Museum of London** are a little more formal, but still fun, and illustrate aspects of the social history of childhood, with both offering some interesting children's activities.

Science and Natural History

Computers, electricity, space exploration, industrial processes and transport can all be explored at the **Science Museum**. Transport enthusiasts are also catered for at the **London Transport Museum**. Other specialized

museums include the **Faraday Museum**, covering the development of electricity, and the **London Museum of Water & Steam**, focusing on water power. Greenwich's **Royal Observatory** charts both the history of astronomy and the creation of GMT, by which the world still sets its clocks. The **Natural History Museum** mixes displays on animal life with ecological exhibits. Both the **Grant Museum of Zoology** and the **Horniman Museum** have superb Victorian collections of taxidermy specimens and skeletons.

Visual Arts

The particular strengths of the **National Gallery** are early Renaissance Italian and 17th-century Spanish painting and a wonderful collection of Dutch masters. **Tate Britain** specializes in British paintings spanning all periods, while **Tate Modern** has displays of international modern art from 1900 to the present day. The **V&A** is strong on European art from 1500 to 1900 and British art of 1700–1900. The **Royal Academy** and the **Hayward Gallery** both have major temporary exhibitions. The **Courtauld Institute of Art Gallery** contains Impressionist and Post-Impressionist works, while the **Wallace Collection** has 17th-century Dutch and 18th-century French paintings. The **Dulwich Picture Gallery** includes works by Rembrandt, Rubens, Poussin and Gainsborough, while **Kenwood House** is home

Samson and Delilah (1620) by Van Dyck at the Dulwich Picture Gallery

to paintings by Reynolds, Gainsborough and Rubens in fine Adam interiors. The **Saatchi Gallery** is devoted to contemporary international art.

Ornate Drawing Room at the Wallace Collection

London's Best: Churches

London's churches have a special atmosphere
unmatched elsewhere in the city, and they can often
yield an intimate glimpse of the past. Many churches
have replaced earlier buildings in a steady succession
going back to pre-Christian times. Some began life in
outlying villages beyond London's fortified centre, and
were absorbed into suburbs when the city expanded in
the 18th century. The memorials in the capital's churches
and churchyards are a fascinating record of local life,
liberally peppered with famous names. A more detailed
overview of London's churches is on pages 50–51.

All Souls
This plaque comes from
a tomb in John Nash's
Regency church of 1824.

**Bloomsbury
and Fitzrovia**

St Paul's Covent Garden
Inigo Jones's Classical church
was known as "the handsomest
barn in England".

**Regent's Park
and Marylebone**

**Soho and
Trafalgar
Square**

St Martin-in-the-Fields
James Gibbs's church of
1722–6 was originally
thought "too gay" for
Protestant worship.

**South Kensington
and Knightsbridge**

**Piccadilly, Mayfair
and St James's**

**Whitehall
and
Westminster**

0 kilometres 1
0 miles 0.5

Westminster Cathedral
The Italian-Byzantine Catholic
cathedral's red-and-white brick
exterior conceals a rich interior
of multicoloured marbles.

Brompton Oratory
This sumptuous Baroque
church is decorated with
works by Italian artists.

Westminster Abbey
The famous abbey has the
most glorious medieval
architecture in London, and
highly impressive tombs
and monuments.

St Mary-le-Strand
Now on a traffic island, this ship-like church was built by James Gibbs in 1714–17 to a lively Baroque design, and features high windows and a rich interior.

St Mary Woolnoth
The jewel-like interior of Nicholas Hawksmoor's small Baroque church (1716–27) appears larger than the outside suggests

Smithfield and Spitalfields

Holborn and the Inns of Court

The City

Covent Garden and the Strand

Southwark and Bankside

South Bank

St Stephen Walbrook
Wren was at his best with this domed interior of 1672–7. Its carvings include Henry Moore's austere modern altar.

RIVER THAMES

St Paul's
At 110 m (360 ft) high, the dome of Wren's cathedral is the world's second-largest after St Peter's in Rome.

Temple Church
Built in the 12th and 13th centuries for the Knights Templar, this is one of the few circular churches to survive in England.

Southwark Cathedral
This largely 13th-century priory church was not designated a cathedral until 1905. It has a fine medieval choir.

Exploring Churches

The church spires that puncture London's skyline span nearly a thousand years of the city's history. They form an index to many of the events and periods that have shaped the city – the Norman Conquest (1066); the Great Fire of London (1666); the great restoration that followed it; the Regency period; the confidence of the Victorian era; and the devastation of World War II. Each has had its effect on the churches, many designed by the most influential architects of their times.

St Paul's, Covent Garden

Medieval Churches

The most famous old church to survive the Great Fire of 1666 is the superb 13th-century **Westminster Abbey**, the Coronation church, with its tombs of British monarchs and heroes. Less well known are the well-hidden Norman church of **St Bartholomew-the-Great**, London's oldest church (1123); the circular **Temple Church**, founded in 1160 by the Knights Templar; and **Southwark Cathedral**, set amid Victorian railway lines and warehouses. **Chelsea Old Church** is a charming village church near the river.

Churches by Jones

Inigo Jones (1573–1652) was Shakespeare's contemporary, and his works were almost as revolutionary as the great dramatist's. Jones's Classical churches of the 1620s and 1630s shocked a public used to conservative Gothic finery. By far the best-known is **St Paul's Church** of the 1630s, the centrepiece of Jones's Italian-style piazza in Covent Garden. **Queen's Chapel** was built in 1623 for Queen Henrietta Maria, the Catholic wife of Charles I. It was the first Classical church in England and has a magnificent interior but is, unfortunately, usually closed to the public.

Churches by Hawksmoor

Nicholas Hawksmoor (1661–1736) was Wren's most talented pupil, and his

Spires

Look out for London's richly decorated church steeples. Here are four of the city's most distinctive.

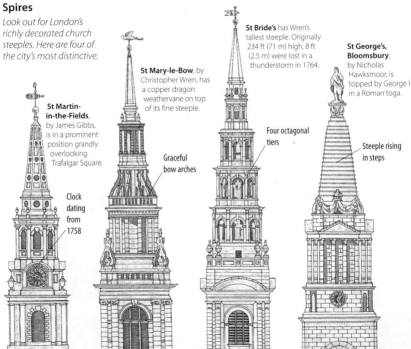

St Martin-in-the-Fields, by James Gibbs, is in a prominent position grandly overlooking Trafalgar Square.

Clock dating from 1758

St Mary-le-Bow, by Christopher Wren, has a copper dragon weathervane on top of its fine steeple.

Graceful bow arches

St Bride's has Wren's tallest steeple. Originally 234 ft (71 m) high, 8 ft (2.5 m) were lost in a thunderstorm in 1764.

Four octagonal tiers

St George's, Bloomsbury, by Nicholas Hawksmoor, is topped by George I in a Roman toga.

Steeple rising in steps

churches are among the finest Baroque buildings to be found in Britain.

St George's, Bloomsbury (1716–31) has an unusual centralized plan and a pyramid steeple topped by a statue of King George I. **St Mary Woolnoth** is a tiny jewel of 1716–27, and further east, **Christ Church, Spitalfields** is a Baroque tour-de-force of 1714–29.

Among Hawksmoor's East End churches are the stunning **St Anne's, Limehouse** and **St Alfege**, of 1714–17, which is across the river in Greenwich. The tower on this temple-like church was added later by John James in 1730.

Christopher Wren

Sir Christopher Wren (1632–1723) played an integral part in the restoration of London after the Great Fire of 1666. He devised a new city plan, replacing the narrow streets with wide avenues radiating from piazzas. His plan was rejected, but he was commissioned to build 52 new churches; 31 have survived various threats of demolition and the bombs of World War II, although six are shells. Wren's great masterpiece is the massive **St Paul's**, while nearby is splendid **St Stephen Walbrook**, his domed church of 1672–7. Other landmarks are **St Bride's**, off Fleet Street, said to have inspired the traditional shape of wedding cakes, **St Mary-le-Bow** in Cheapside and **St Magnus the Martyr** in Lower Thames Street. Wren's own favourite was **St James's, Piccadilly** (1683–4). Smaller gems are **St Clement Danes**, Strand (1680–82), and **St James, Garlickhythe** (1674–87).

St Anne's, Limehouse

Churches by Gibbs

James Gibbs (1682–1754) was more conservative than his Baroque contemporaries, such as Hawksmoor, and he also kept his distance from the Neo-Classical trend so popular after 1720. His idiosyncratic London churches were enormously influential. **St Mary-le-Strand** (1714–17) is an island church which appears to be sailing down the Strand. The radical design of **St Martin-in-the-Fields** (1722–6) predates its setting, Trafalgar Square, by a hundred years.

Regency Churches

The end of the Napoleonic Wars in 1815 brought a flurry of church building. The need for

churches in London's new suburbs fused with a Greek Revival. The results may lack the exuberance of Hawksmoor, but they have an austere elegance of their own. **All Souls, Langham Place** (1822–4), at the north end of Regent Street, was built by the Prince Regent's favourite, John Nash, who was ridiculed at the time for its unusual combination of design styles. Also worth visiting is **St Pancras**, a Greek Revival church of 1819–22, which is typical of the period.

Victorian Churches

London has some of the finest 19th-century churches in Europe. Grand and colourful, their riotous decoration is in marked contrast to the chaste Neo-Classicism of the preceding Regency era. Perhaps the best of the capital's late Victorian churches is

Brompton Oratory

Westminster Cathedral, a stunningly rich, Italianate Catholic cathedral built in 1895–1903, with architecture by J F Bentley and *Stations of the Cross* reliefs by Eric Gill. **Brompton Oratory** is a grand Baroque revival, based on a church in Rome and filled with magnificent furnishings from all over Catholic Europe.

Where to Find the Churches

London's Best: Parks and Gardens

Since medieval times, London has had large expanses of green. Some of these, such as Hampstead Heath, were originally common land, where smallholders could graze their animals. Others, such as Richmond Park and Holland Park, were royal hunting grounds or the gardens of large houses; several still have formal features dating from those times. Today you can cross much of central London by walking from St James's Park in the east to Kensington Gardens in the west. Purpose-built parks, like Battersea, and the botanic garden at Kew appeared later.

Hampst
and High

Hyde Park
The Serpentine is one of the highlights of a park which also boasts restaurants, an art gallery and Speakers' Corner.

Hampstead Heath
This breezy, vast, open space is located in north London. Nearby Parliament Hill offers views of St Paul's, the City and the West End.

Kensington Gardens
This plaque is from the Italian Garden, one of the features of this elegant park.

Kensington and Holland Park

South Kensington at Knightsbridg

Kew Gardens
The world's premier botanic garden is a must for anyone with an interest in plants, exotic or mundane.

Holland Park
The former grounds of one of London's grandest homes are now its most romantic park.

0 km   1
0 miles 0.5

Richmond Park
The biggest royal park in London remains largely unspoiled, with magnificent river views and a thriving deer population.

Regent's Park
In this civilized park, surrounded by fine Regency buildings, you can stroll around the rose garden, visit the open-air theatre, or simply sit and admire the view.

Queen Elizabeth Olympic Park
Beautifully landscaped wildflower gardens and children's play areas make the former Olympic site an appealing public space.

Bloomsbury
and Fitzrovia

egent's
ark and
rylebone

Smithfield
and
Spitalfields

Holborn
and the Inns
of Court

Soho and
Trafalgar
Square

The City

Piccadilly,
ayfair and
t James's

THAMES

South
Bank

Southwark
and Bankside

Whitehall
and
Westminster

elsea

Greenwich Park
Its focal point is the National Maritime Museum, well worth a visit for its architecture as well as its exhibits. There are also fine views.

Green Park
Its leafy paths are favoured by early-morning joggers from the Mayfair hotels.

Greenwich and
Blackheath

Battersea Park
Visitors can hire a rowing boat for the best view of the Victorian landscaping around the lake.

St James's Park
Located in the heart of the city, this park is a popular escape for office workers and has an abundance of wildfowl.

Exploring Parks and Gardens

London has one of the the world's greenest city centres, full of tree-filled squares and grassy parks. From the intimacy of the Chelsea Physic Garden to the wild, open spaces of Hampstead Heath, every London park has its own charm and character. For those looking for a specific outdoor attraction – such as sports, wildlife or flowers – here are some of the most interesting London parks.

Flower Gardens

The British are famed for their gardens and love of flowers and this is reflected in several of London's parks. Really keen gardeners will find all they ever wanted to know at **Kew Gardens** and the **Chelsea Physic Garden**, which is especially strong on herbs. Closer to the centre of town, **St James's Park** boasts some spectacular flowerbeds, filled with bulbs and bedding plants, which are changed every season. **Hyde Park** sports a magnificent show of daffodils and crocuses in the spring, while London's best rose garden is Queen Mary's in **Regent's**

Park. Kensington Gardens' flower walk has an exemplary English mixed border. There is also a delightful small 17th-century garden at the **Museum of Garden History**. **Battersea Park** also has a charming flower garden Indoor gardeners should head to the **Barbican Centre**'s well-stocked conservatory.

Formal Gardens

The most spectacular formal garden is at **Hampton Court**, which has a network of gardens from different periods, starting with Tudor. The gardens at **Chiswick House** remain dotted with their 18th-century statuary

Colourful flowerbeds at St James's Park

and pavilions. Other restored gardens include 17th-century **Ham House**, and **Osterley Park**, whose 18th-century layout was retraced through the art of dowsing. **Fenton House** has a really fine walled garden; **Kenwood**, with its woodland area, is less formal. The sunken garden at **Kensington Palace** has a formal layout; **Holland Park** has flowers around its statues.

Restful Corners

London's squares are cool, shady retreats, but many are reserved for key-holders, usually residents of the surrounding houses. Of those open to all, **Russell Square** is the largest and most secluded. **Berkeley Square** is open but barren. **Green Park** offers shady trees and deck chairs, right in central London. The Inns of Court provide some pleasant havens: **Gray's Inn** gardens, **Middle Temple** gardens and **Lincoln's Inn Fields**. **Grosvenor Square** is one of London's oldest Georgian

Sunken garden at Kensington Palace

Green London

In Greater London, there are 1,700 parks covering a total of 67 sq miles (174 sq km). This land is home to some 2,000 types of plant and 100 bird species. Trees help the city to breathe, manufacturing oxygen from the polluted air. Here are just a few of the species you are most likely to see in London.

The London plane, now the most common tree in London, grows along many streets.

The English oak grows all over Europe. The Royal Navy used to build ships from its wood.

squares, while **Soho Square** offers welcome respite from nearby busy Oxford Street.

Music in Summer

Stretching out on the grass or in a deckchair to listen to a band is a British tradition. Military and other bands give regular concerts throughout the summer at **St James's** and **Regent's Parks** and also at **Parliament Hill Fields**. The concert schedule will usually be found posted up close to the bandstand in the park.

Open-air summer festivals of pop and classical music are held in several parks (see p345).

Wildlife

There is a large and well-fed collection of ducks and other water birds, even including a few pelicans, in **St James's Park**. Duck lovers will also appreciate **Regent's, Hyde** and **Battersea Parks**, as well as **Hampstead Heath**. Deer roam in **Richmond** and **Greenwich Parks**. Captive animals can be found at **London Zoo**, in **Regent's Park**, as well as in aviaries or aquariums located at several parks and gardens, including **Kew Gardens** and **Syon House**.

Geese in St James's Park

Historic Cemeteries

In the late 1830s, private cemeteries were established around London to ease the pressure on the overcrowded and unhealthy burial grounds of the inner city. Today some of these, notably **Highgate Cemetery, Kensal Green Cemetery** (Harrow Road, W10) and **Brompton Cemetery** (Fulham Road, SW10), are worth visiting for their Victorian monuments. **Bunhill Fields** is an earlier burial site, first used during the plague of 1665.

Kensal Green cemetery

Boating pond at Regent's Park

Sports

Most parks have tennis courts, which normally have to be reserved in advance. Rowing boats may be hired at **Hyde, Regent's** and **Battersea Parks**, among others. There are athletics tracks at both Battersea Park and **Parliament Hill**. The public may swim at the ponds on **Hampstead Heath** and in the Serpentine in **Hyde Park**. Cycling is not universally encouraged in London's parks, but **Queen Elizabeth Olympic Park** is an exception. Sporting events are held here regularly and the Aquatics Centre is open to the public.

Where to Find the Parks and Gardens

The common beech has a close relation, the copper beech, with reddish-purple leaves.

The horse chestnut's hard round fruits are used by children for a game called conkers.

London's Best: Ceremonies

Much of London's rich inheritance of tradition and ceremony centres on royalty. Faithfully enacted today, some of these ceremonies date back to the Middle Ages, when the ruling monarch had absolute power and had to be protected from opponents. This map shows the venues for some of the most important ceremonies in London. For more details on these and other ceremonies turn to pages 58–9; information on all sorts of events taking place in London throughout the year can be found on pages 60–63.

St James's Palace and Buckingham Palace
Members of the Queen's Life Guard stand at the gates of these two palaces.

Bloomsbury and Fitzrovia

Soho and Trafalgar Square

South Kensington and Knightsbridge

Hyde Park
Royal Salutes are fired by guns of the King's Troop Royal Horse Artillery on royal anniversaries and ceremonial occasions.

Piccadilly, Mayfair and St James's

Whitehall and Westminster

Chelsea

Chelsea Hospital
In 1651 Charles II hid from Parliamentary forces in an oak tree. On Oak Apple Day, Chelsea Pensioners decorate his statue with oak leaves and branches.

Horse Guards
At Trooping the Colour, the most elaborate of London's royal ceremonies, the Queen salutes as a battalion of Foot Guards parades its colours before her.

The City and Embankment
At the Lord Mayor's Show a procession accompanies the newly elected Lord Mayor through the City, with events and celebrations throughout the day.

The Thames
The river is the venue for pageants and firework displays on ceremonial occasions, as well as the annual University Boat Race between Oxford and Cambridge.

Smithfield and Spitalfields

Holborn and the Inns of Court

Covent Garden and the Strand

The City

0 kilometres 1

0 miles 0.5

RIVER THAMES

Southwark and Bankside

South Bank

Tower of London
In the nightly Ceremony of the Keys, a Yeoman Warder locks the gates. A military escort ensures the keys are not stolen.

Houses of Parliament
The Queen travels to Westminster in the Irish State Coach for the annual State Opening of Parliament.

The Cenotaph
On Remembrance Sunday the Queen pays homage to the nation's war dead.

Attending London's Ceremonies

Royalty and commerce are the two principal sources of London's rich calendar of ceremonial events. Quaint and old-fashioned these events may be, but what may seem arcane ritual has real historical meaning – many of the capital's ceremonies originated in the Middle Ages.

A Queen's Guard in winter

Royal Ceremonies

Although the Queen's role is now largely symbolic, the Guard at Buckingham Palace still patrols the palace grounds. The impressive ceremony of **Changing the Guard** – dazzling uniforms, shouted commands, military music – consists of the Old Guard, which forms up in the palace forecourt, going off duty and handing over to the New Guard. The Guard comprises three officers and 40 men when the Queen is in residence, but only three officers and 31 men when she is away. The ceremony takes place in front of the palace. In another changeover ceremony, the Queen's Life Guards travel daily from Hyde Park Barracks to Horse Guards Parade.

Member of the Queen's Life Guards

The **Ceremony of the Keys** at the Tower of London is one of the capital's most historic ceremonies. After each of the Tower gates has been locked, the last post is sounded by a trumpeter before the keys are secured in the Queen's House.

The Tower of London and Hyde Park are also the scene of **Royal Salutes**, which take place on birthdays and other occasions throughout the year. At such times 41 rounds are fired in Hyde Park at noon, and 62 rounds at the Tower at 1pm. The spectacle in Hyde Park is a stirring one as 71 horses and six 13-pounder cannons swirl into place and the roar of the guns begins.

The combination of pageantry, colour and music makes the annual **Trooping the Colour** the high point of London's ceremonial year. The Queen takes the Royal Salute, and after her troops have marched past, she leads them to Buckingham Palace where a second march past takes place. The best place to watch this spectacle is from the Horse Guards Parade side of St James's Park. Bands of the Household Cavalry and the Foot Guards stage the ceremony

of **Beating Retreat** at Horse Guards Parade. This takes place annually on two successive evenings in June, leading up to Trooping the Colour. The spectacular **State Opening of Parliament**, when the Queen opens the annual parliamentary session in the House of Lords (usually in May), is not open to the general public, although it is televised. The huge royal procession, which moves from Buckingham Palace to Westminster, is, however, a magnificent sight, with the Queen travelling in the highly ornate Irish State Coach drawn by four horses.

Military Ceremonies

The Cenotaph in Whitehall is the setting for a ceremony held on **Remembrance Sunday** to give thanks to those who died fighting in any conflict from World War I onwards.

National Navy Day is commemorated by a parade down the Mall, followed by a service held at Nelson's Column in Trafalgar Square.

Royal Salute, Tower of London

Trooping the Colour

Silent Change ceremony at Guildhall for the new Lord Mayor

Ceremonies in the City

November is the focus of the City of London's ceremonial year. At the **Silent Change** in Guildhall, the outgoing Lord Mayor hands over symbols of office to the new Mayor in a virtually wordless ceremony. The following day sees the rumbustious **Lord Mayor's Show**. Accompanying the Lord Mayor in his gold state coach, a procession of bands, decorated floats and military detachments makes its way through the City, past Mansion House to the Law Courts, and back again along the Embankment. A day of events, including a river pageant, culminates in an evening firework display.

Many of the ceremonies that take place in the City are linked to the activities of the Livery Companies, and often mark key dates in the church calendar. Not all are open to the public. Those that are include the Worshipful Companies of **Vintners' and Distillers'** annual celebration of the wine harvest.

Lord Mayor's
chain of office

Name-Day Ceremonies

Every 21 May **King Henry VI**, who was murdered in the Tower of London in 1471, is still remembered by the members of his two famous foundations, Eton College and King's College, Cambridge, who meet for a ceremony at the Wakefield Tower where he was killed. **Oak Apple Day** commemorates Charles II's lucky escape from the Parliamentary forces of Oliver Cromwell in 1651. The King managed to conceal himself in a hollow oak tree, and today Chelsea Pensioners honour his memory by decorating his statue at Chelsea Royal Hospital with oak leaves and branches. On 18 December, the lexicographer **Dr Johnson** is commemorated in an annual service held at Westminster Abbey.

Informal Ceremonies

Each July, six guildsmen from the Company of Watermen compete for the prize in **Doggett's Coat and Badge Race**. In autumn, the **Pearly Kings and Queens**, representatives of working-class culture, meet at St Mary-le-Bow. In March children are given oranges and lemons at the **Oranges and Lemons service** at St Clement Danes church. In February, clowns take part in a service for **Joseph Grimaldi** (1779–1837) at the Holy Trinity Church in Dalston, E8.

Pearly Queen

Where to Find the Ceremonies

Beating Retreat
Horse Guards Parade *p84*, two successive evenings in June.

Ceremony of the Keys
Tower of London *pp158–61*, 9:30pm daily. Tickets from the Tower, but book well in advance.

Changing the Guard
Buckingham Palace *pp98–9*, Apr–Jul: 11:30am daily; Aug–Mar: alternate days. Horse Guards, Whitehall *p84*, 11am Mon–Sat, 10am Sun.

Doggett's Coat and Badge Race
From London Bridge to Cadogan Pier, Chelsea, July.

Dr Johnson Memorial
Westminster Abbey *pp80–83*, 18 Dec.

Joseph Grimaldi Memorial
Holy Trinity Church, Dalston E8, 7 Feb.

King Henry VI Memorial
Wakefield Tower, Tower of London *pp158–61*, 21 May.

Lord Mayor's Show
The City, second Sat in Nov.

Navy Day
Trafalgar Sq *p106*, 21 Oct.

Oak Apple Day
Royal Hospital *p201*, Thu after 29 May.

Oranges and Lemons Service
St Clement Danes *p142*, March.

Pearly Kings and Queens Harvest Festival
St Mary-le-Bow *p151*, autumn.

Remembrance Sunday
Cenotaph *p78*, Sun nearest 11 Nov.

Royal Salutes
Hyde Park *p213*, royal anniversaries and other state occasions.

Silent Change
Guildhall *p163*, second Fri in Nov.

State Opening of Parliament
Houses of Parliament *pp76–7*, May. Procession from Buckingham Palace to Westminster.

Trooping the Colour
Horse Guards *p84*, second Sat in Jun (rehearsals on previous two Sats). Tickets from Household Division, Horse Guards.

Vintners' and Distillers' Wine Harvest
St Olave's Church, Hart St EC3, second Tue in Oct.

LONDON THROUGH THE YEAR

Springtime in London carries an almost tangible air of a city waking up to longer days and outdoor pursuits. The cheerful yellow of daffodils studs the parks, and less hardy Londoners turn out for their first jog of the year to find themselves puffing in the wake of serious runners training for the London Marathon. As spring turns into summer, the royal parks reach their full glory as they, along with many other open spaces, host a season of musical festivals, open-air theatre, cinema screenings and summer food fiestas. As autumn takes hold, Londoners' thoughts turn to afternoons in museums, followed by tea and cake. The year draws to a close with Guy Fawkes fireworks, then Christmas markets and outdoor ice rinks. The official visitor organization Visit London, www.visitlondon. com *(see p358)*, and the listings magazines *(see p338)* have details of seasonal events.

Spring

The weather during the spring months may be raw, and an umbrella is a necessary precaution. Around Easter, Oxford and Cambridge universities compete in their annual boat race along the Thames, and marathon runners pound the streets. Footballers close their season in May with the FA Cup Final, while cricketers don their sweaters to begin theirs. Meanwhile, painters hope to have their works accepted by the Royal Academy.

Runners in the London Marathon pound the city's streets passing Tower Bridge

March
Head of the River Race *(Sat mid-Mar or early Apr)*. More than 400 teams row from Mortlake to Putney in a timed race on the ebb tide. A couple of weeks later, the more famous **Oxford and Cambridge boat race** *(Sat late Mar or early Apr)* takes place over the same route in the opposite direction. Riverside viewing spots and nearby pubs teem with spectators. **Spring Equinox celebration** *(21 Mar)*, Tower Hill EC3. Historic pagan ceremony with modern-day druids.

Easter
Good Friday and **Easter Monday** are public holidays. **Easter services** held at all London churches, including Westminster Abbey *(see pp80–83)*. Look out for kids' activities, such as Easter egg hunts, around the city, including at Kew Gardens *(see pp266–7)* and Greenwich *(see pp240–47)*.

April
Queen's Birthday gun salutes *(21 Apr)*, Hyde Park, Tower of London *(see p58)*. **London Marathon** *(Sun in Apr or May)*. Around 38,000 elite and novice athletes run the 42.2 km (26.2 mile) course from Blackheath to the Mall. Prime viewing spots at the start and finish and on Tower

The Holy Cross being carried through the streets during the Good Friday procession

Bridge are staked out hours before the race; canny spectators find a place near one of the Docklands Light Railway stations or join the crowds on the Embankment to cheer the now-weary runners on to the end.

May
First and last Mon are public holidays. **FA Cup Final**, football season's climax. **Beating the Bounds** *(Ascension Day)*, throughout the City. Children, clergy and locals from the City parishes use sticks to "beat" buildings that mark the parish boundaries. **Oak Apple Day** *(29 May)*, Royal Hospital, Chelsea *(see p59)*. **Covent Garden May Fayre and Puppet Festival** *(mid-May)*, St Paul's Church, Covent Garden *(see p118)*. **Chelsea Flower Show** *(5 days in late May)*, Royal Hospital, Chelsea. London's biggest, most spectacular horticultural event. **State Opening of Parliament** *(see p58)*.

Average Daily Hours of Sunshine

Hours

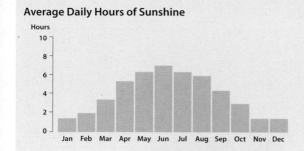

Sunshine Chart
London's longest and hottest days fall between May and August. In the height of summer, daylight hours can extend from well before 5am to after 9pm. Daytime is much shorter in the winter, but London can be stunning in the winter sunshine.

Summer

London's summer season is packed with indoor and outdoor events. The weather can be unreliable, but unless you are very unlucky there should be enough fine days to enjoy the great outdoors. There are traditional events, such as the Wimbledon tennis championships and the cricket test matches at Lord's and the Oval, as well as innovative arts seasons, such as those at the Southbank, and outdoor music festivals. Well out of view of the general public and prying photographers, the Queen holds garden parties for favoured subjects in the grounds of Buckingham Palace. The August public holiday weekend is marked by the Notting Hill Carnival, London's biggest street celebration.

June

Beating Retreat (see p58).
Coronation Day gun salutes (2 Jun), Hyde Park and Tower of London (see p58). **Art Antiques London** (mid-Jun), Kensington Gardens. Top dealers gather in a purpose-built pavilion opposite the Royal Albert Hall (see p209). **Trooping the Colour**, Horse Guards Parade (see p58). **Duke of Edinburgh's Birthday gun salutes** (10 Jun), Hyde Park and Tower of London (see p58). **Wimbledon Lawn Tennis Championships** (2 weeks in late Jun) The only major tournament held on grass. **Cricket test match**, Lord's Cricket Ground. **Open-air theatre season** (throughout the summer), stages in Regent's Park and Holland Park (see

Revellers at Notting Hill Carnival

p340). **Open-air concerts**, Kenwood, Hampstead Heath, Kew (see p345). Parks in and just outside the city host one-day music festivals and outdoor gigs. **Southbank summer season** (Jun–Sep). The Southbank Centre (see p344) hosts themed festivals including comedy and cabaret events. **Spitalfields Summer Festival** (Jun). Two weeks of classical concerts and talks at Christ Church (see p174), St Leonard's (see p175) and other nearby venues. **City of London Festival** (late Jun–mid-July),

various City venues. Arts and music festival with concerts in some of London's most beautiful churches.

July

Hampton Court Flower Show, Hampton Court Palace (see pp260–63). **Henry Wood Promenade Concerts (The Proms)** (late Jul–Sep), Royal Albert Hall (see p209). **Royal Academy of Arts Summer Exhibition** (Jun–Aug), Piccadilly (see p94). **Doggett's Coat and Badge Race**, a historic river-rowing contest between Thames watermen.

August

Screenings at Somerset House (2 weeks in Aug) (see p121). If the weather holds, this is the most glorious setting for viewing classic films. The **last Monday** in August is a public holiday. **Notting Hill Carnival** (late Aug holiday weekend). An internationally famous and well-attended Caribbean carnival that takes place throughout the area (see p223). Sunday is children's day while Monday is for adults – both days feature huge crowds, spectacular costumes and DJ sets.

Marching down the Mall for the finale of Trooping the Colour

Average Monthly Rainfall

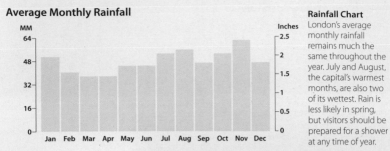

Rainfall Chart
London's average monthly rainfall remains much the same throughout the year. July and August, the capital's warmest months, are also two of its wettest. Rain is less likely in spring, but visitors should be prepared for a shower at any time of year.

Autumn

There is a sense of purpose about London in autumn. The build-up to the busiest shopping season and the start of the academic year inject some life into the colder months. Halloween, something of an import from the US, is now celebrated with costume parties and themed pub and club nights. A more traditional British night of revelry follows on 5 November, when bonfires and fireworks displays commemorate the failed conspiracy, led by Guy Fawkes in 1605, to blow up the Palace of Westminster. A few days later, the dead of conflicts from World War I onwards are honoured at a ceremony held at the Cenotaph in Whitehall.

September
Totally Thames *(Sep)*. This Thames-themed festival features a month of events

The season of promenade concerts reaches its climax on the Last Night of the Proms

alongside and on the river between Westminster Bridge and Southwark Cathedral. **Last Night of the Proms** *(mid-Sep)*, Royal Albert Hall *(see p209)*. Entertaining the masses with rousing classical hits and favourite British patriotic pieces. An open-air concert, "Proms in the Park", is held simultaneously in Hyde Park.

October
Pearly Harvest Festival
(first Sun). The festival begins at Guildhall Yard, from where a parade of Pearly Kings and Queens makes its way to St-Mary-le-Bow Church for the Harvest Festival service *(see p151)*. **Vintners' and Distillers' Wine Harvest** *(see p59)*.

November
Guy Fawkes Night *(5 Nov)*.
Listings magazines give

details of firework displays taking place across the city *(see p338)*; Alexandra Palace hosts a particularly excellent display. **Remembrance Day Service** *(see p58)*. **Lord Mayor's Show** *(see p59)*. **London to Brighton** veteran car rally *(first Sun)*. **Christmas lights** *(late Nov– 6 Jan)*. The West End, especially Regent Street, lights up during the festive season.

London-to-Brighton veteran car run

Fireworks explode on Guy Fawkes Night

Average Monthly Temperature

Temperature Chart
The chart shows the average minimum and maximum temperatures for each month. Top temperatures averaging 22° C (75° F) belie London's reputation for year-round chilliness, although November through to February can be extremely cold and icy.

Winter

Some of the most striking images of London are drawn from winter: paintings of frost fairs in the 17th and 18th centuries, when the River Thames froze over completely; and Claude Monet's views of the river and its bridges.

For centuries thick "pea-souper" fogs were an inevitable part of winter, until coal-burning in open grates was banned.

Christmas lights twinkle everywhere – from the West End shopping streets to the Christmas markets held in royal parks and along the South Bank.

Seasonal menus feature roast turkey, mince pies and Christmas pudding. Traditional shows in theatres include boisterous family pantomimes with their customary cross-dressing between the sexes (see p340) and popular ballets such as Swan Lake and The Nutcracker.

December
Oxford v Cambridge rugby union match Twickenham. **Spitalfields Music Winter Festival** (mid-Dec), Christ Church and other venues (see p174). **London International Horse Show** (late Dec), Olympia. Equestrian competition. **Christmas markets and ice**

Winter in the picturesque gardens of Kensington Palace

rinks Winter Wonderland in Hyde Park (see p213) is a vast festive market and fairground, with an ice rink, beer hall and German-style stalls. The South Bank has a Christmas market too, while Somerset House (see p121) has a great skating rink.

Christmas, New Year
25–26 Dec and **1 Jan** are public holidays. There is no public transport on Christmas Day.

Carol services (leading up to Christmas), Trafalgar Square (see p106), St Paul's (see pp152–5), Westminster Abbey (see pp80–83), St Martin-in-the-Fields (see p106) and many other churches. **Turkey auction** (24 Dec), Smithfield Market (see p168). **Christmas Day swim** Serpentine, Hyde Park (see p213). **New Year's Eve** (31 Dec) fireworks on the Thames, centred on the London Eye (see p193). Tickets must be purchased in advance for riverside viewing spots (www.London.gov.uk).

January
Sales (see p317). **New Year's Day Parade** ends at Parliament Square (see p78). **International Mime Festival** (late Jan), various venues. **Charles I Commemoration** (last Sun), procession from St James's Palace (see p95) to Banqueting House (see p84). **Chinese New Year** (late Jan–mid-Feb), Chinatown (see p112).

February
Queen's Accession gun salutes (6 Feb), 41-gun salute, Hyde Park; 62-gun salute, Tower of London (see p58). **Pancake races** (Shrove Tue), Brick Lane (see p174), Guildhall (see p163) and other locations.

Public Holidays
New Year's Day (1 Jan); **Good Friday**; **Easter Monday**; **May Day** (first Monday in May); **Whit Monday** (last Monday in May); **August Bank Holiday** (last Monday in Aug); **Christmas Day and Boxing Day** (25–26 Dec).

Christmas illuminations in Regent Street

A River View of London

Cruising down the Thames is one of the most interesting ways to experience London. Having served as the city's main commercial artery from Roman times to the 20th century, the river is packed with historical references, including the reconstruction of the Elizabethan Globe Theatre, royal palaces and parks, historic bridges and decommissioned power stations. Highlights also include excellent views of the ever-changing London skyline: look out for the Shard, the Gherkin and the Millennium Eye.

Passenger boat services cover about 50 kilometres (30 miles) of the Thames, from Hampton Court in the west to the Thames Barrier in the east. The most popular and best served section runs through the heart of the city from Westminster to Tower Bridge. Often accompanied by informative and witty commentary, a cruise along this fascinating stretch of the Thames should not be missed.

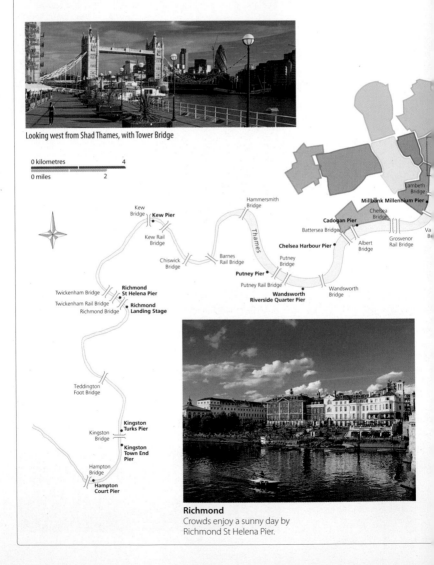

Looking west from Shad Thames, with Tower Bridge

0 kilometres 4
0 miles 2

Kew Bridge
Kew Pier
Kew Rail Bridge
Chiswick Bridge
Barnes Rail Bridge
Hammersmith Bridge
Thames
Millbank Millennium Pier
Lambeth Bridge
Chelsea Bridge
Cadogan Pier
Battersea Bridge
Chelsea Harbour Pier
Albert Bridge
Grosvenor Rail Bridge
Va
Bı
Putney Bridge
Putney Pier
Putney Rail Bridge
Wandsworth Riverside Quarter Pier
Wandsworth Bridge
Richmond St Helena Pier
Twickenham Bridge
Twickenham Rail Bridge
Richmond Bridge
Richmond Landing Stage

Teddington Foot Bridge

Kingston Turks Pier
Kingston Bridge
Kingston Town End Pier
Hampton Bridge
Hampton Court Pier

Richmond
Crowds enjoy a sunny day by Richmond St Helena Pier.

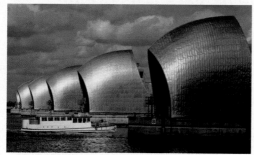

The Thames Barrier
Completed in 1982, the world's second largest movable flood barrier protects London from rising water levels. The massive steel gates have been raised over 100 times.

Riverside pubs
Beautifully preserved pubs, such as the Prospect of Whitby in Wapping, hug the river's banks.

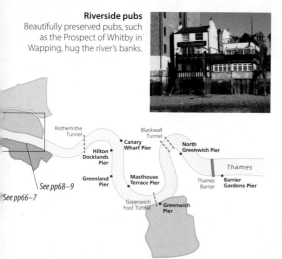

Cruise Operators

Bateaux London/ Catamaran Cruisers
Tel 020 7695 1800.
W bateauxlondon.com

City Cruises
Tel 020 7740 0400.
W citycruises.com

Crown River Cruises
Tel 020 7936 2033.
W crownrivercruise.co.uk

Thames Clippers
Tel 0870 781 5049.
W thamesclippers.com

Thames River Services
Tel 020 7930 4097.
W thamesriverservices. co.uk

Turks Launches
Tel 020 8546 2434.
W turks.co.uk

WPSA (Westminster Passenger Service Association [Upriver] Ltd)
Tel 020 7930 2062.
W wpsa.co.uk

Cruise Highlights

Most regular services run from April to September, with some routes having winter schedules. During the summer, sailings are frequent from Westminster and Embankment to Greenwich. The main commuter service, the Thames Clipper, runs regular services from Canary Wharf and Chelsea Harbour to the city's main termini (the latter Monday to Friday only), as well as daily trips from the London Eye to Greenwich. You can travel with an Oyster card (see p374) and most other services give a third off the ticket price to Travelcard holders (see p374).

Greenwich (see pp240–47)
Frequent services to Greenwich make a visit to this World Heritage Site, steeped in maritime history, an absolute must.
Operators: Bateaux London/ Catamaran Cruisers, City Cruises, Thames River Services.
Piers: Westminster, Waterloo, Embankment, Bankside, Tower.
Duration: 1 hr (Westminster).
Thames Barrier (see p253) Sail between the nine massive piers that raise the steel gates. Cruises to the barrier also pass the O2 Arena, formerly the Millennium Dome.
Operator: Thames River Services.
Piers: Westminster, Greenwich.
Duration: 30 mins (Greenwich).

Kew (see pp266–7) A cruise to Kew leaves the city behind after passing the Battersea Power Station.
Operator: WPSA (upriver only).
Piers: Westminster.
Duration: 1.5 hrs (Westminster).
Hampton Court (see pp260–63) Arrive at the Tudor bolthole Hampton Court in regal style, but be aware that the round trip from Westminster can take up to eight hours. Consider sailing from one of the piers upriver.
Operator: WPSA (upriver only), Turks Launches.
Piers: Kew, all Richmond and Kingston piers.
Duration: 2 hrs (Kew).

Westminster Bridge to Blackfriars Bridge

Until World War II, this stretch of the Thames marked the division between rich and poor London. On the north bank were the offices, shops, luxury hotels and apartments of Whitehall and the Strand, the Inns of Court and the newspaper district. To the south were smoky factories and slum dwellings. After the war, the Festival of Britain in 1951 started the revival of the South Bank (see pp188–95), which now has some of the capital's most interesting modern buildings.

Savoy Hotel
This hotel is on the site of a medieval palace (see p120).

Somerset House, built in 1786, houses an art gallery (see p121).

Shell Mex House
Built in 1931 on the site of the vast Cecil Hotel, this once housed offices for the oil company.

Embankment Gardens is the site of many open-air concerts held in the bandstand during summer (see p122).

Cleopatra's Needle was made in ancient Egypt and given to London in 1819 (see p122).

Charing Cross

Waterloo Bridge

Festival Pier

Embankment
Embankment Pier

Charing Cross
The rail terminus is encased in a Post-Modernist office complex (see p123).

The Southbank Centre was the site of the 1951 Festival of Britain and is London's most important arts complex. It is dominated by the Royal Festival Hall, the National Theatre and the Hayward Gallery (see p192).

London Eye Pier

Jubilee Gardens

The London Eye offers incredible views over London (see p193).

Hungerford Railway Bridge and Golden Jubilee Footbridges

The Banqueting House is one of Inigo Jones's finest works, built as part of Whitehall Palace (see p84).

The Ministry of Defence is a bulky white fortress completed in the 1950s.

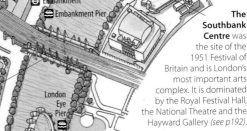

Westminster Pier

Westminster
Westminster Bridge

County Hall
This is home to the state-of-the-art Sea Life London Aquarium and its 350 species of fish.

Temple and the Inns of Court
These historic buildings have been the offices of
lawyers and barristers for over 500 years (see pp142–3).

St Paul's
Christopher Wren's
masterwork, finished in
1708, is still a prominent
feature of the London
skyline (see pp152–5).

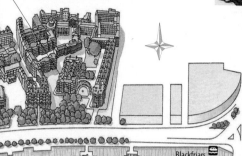

Blackfriars

Blackfriars
Millennium Pier

Blackfriars
Bridge

Millennium
Bridge

Gabriel's Wharf
Formerly home to
warehouses, this site
is now packed with
restaurants, boutiques
and cafés (see p195).

Tate Modern is
located in the old
Bankside power
station (see pp182–5).

Doggett's Coat and Badge
The modern pub here is
named after the world's oldest
rowing race.

Oxo Tower
The windows were designed
to spell the brand name of a
popular meat extract.

Blackfriars Bridge
The logo of a former railway
company adorns the bridge.

For keys to symbols see back flap

Southwark Bridge to St Katharine Docks

For centuries the stretch just east of London Bridge was the busiest part of the Thames, with ships of all sizes jostling for position to unload at the wharves on both banks. Then, in the 19th century, the construction of the docks to the east eased congestion. Today most landmarks on this section hark back to that commercial past.

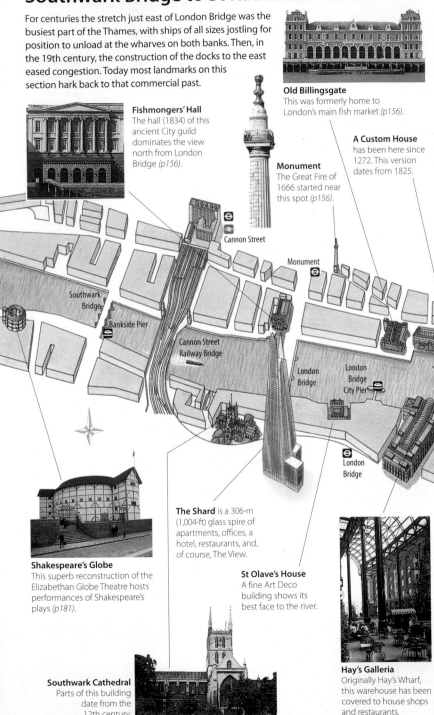

Old Billingsgate
This was formerly home to London's main fish market *(p156)*.

Fishmongers' Hall
The hall (1834) of this ancient City guild dominates the view north from London Bridge *(p156)*.

A Custom House
has been here since 1272. This version dates from 1825.

Monument
The Great Fire of 1666 started near this spot *(p156)*.

Cannon Street

Monument

Southwark Bridge

Bankside Pier

Cannon Street Railway Bridge

London Bridge

London Bridge City Pier

London Bridge

The Shard is a 306-m (1,004-ft) glass spire of apartments, offices, a hotel, restaurants, and, of course, The View.

St Olave's House
A fine Art Deco building shows its best face to the river.

Shakespeare's Globe
This superb reconstruction of the Elizabethan Globe Theatre hosts performances of Shakespeare's plays *(p181)*.

Southwark Cathedral
Parts of this building date from the 12th century.

Hay's Galleria
Originally Hay's Wharf, this warehouse has been covered to house shops and restaurants.

Tower of London
Look out for Traitors' Gate, where prisoners would be taken into the Tower by boat *(pp158–61)*.

Tower Bridge
It still opens to let tall ships pass, but not as often as it did when cargo vessels came through *(p157)*.

St Katharine Docks
Visitors come to London's only marina to admire the yachts and dine al fresco *(p162)*.

Tower Ilennium Pier

Tower Bridge

St Katharine's Pier

The stunning City Hall houses the Mayor and the governing offices.

Victorian warehouses on Butlers Wharf and Shad Thames have been converted into upmarket apartments and riverside restaurants.

HMS *Belfast*
This World War II cruiser has been a museum since 1971 *(p187)*.

St Saviour's Dock
A pedestrian bridge takes you over the old dock to more restored warehouses.

Aerial view of the City of London by night ▶

LONDON AREA BY AREA

WHITEHALL AND WESTMINSTER

Whitehall and Westminster have been at the centre of political and religious power in England for a thousand years. King Canute, who ruled at the beginning of the 11th century, was the first monarch to have a palace on what was then an island in the swampy meeting point of the Thames and its vanished tributary, the Tyburn. Canute built his palace beside the church that, some 50 years later,

Edward the Confessor would enlarge into England's greatest abbey, giving the area its name (a minster is an abbey church). Over the following centuries the offices of state were established in the vicinity. All this is still reflected in Whitehall's heroic statues and massive government buildings. To its north, Trafalgar Square marks the start of the West End entertainment district.

Sights at a Glance

Historic Streets and Buildings
1 Houses of Parliament pp76–7
2 Big Ben
3 Jewel Tower
5 Dean's Yard
7 Parliament Square
9 Downing Street
10 Churchill War Rooms
11 Banqueting House
12 Horse Guards Parade
14 Queen Anne's Gate
16 St James's Park Station
17 Blewcoat School

Churches, Abbeys and Cathedrals
4 Westminster Abbey pp80–83
6 St Margaret's Church
18 Westminster Cathedral
19 St John's Smith Square

Museums and Galleries
13 Household Cavalry Museum
15 Guards Museum
20 Tate Britain pp86–9

Monuments
8 Cenotaph

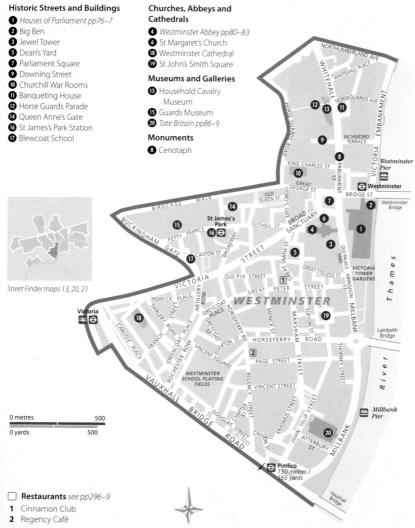

Street Finder maps 13, 20, 21

0 metres 500
0 yards 500

☐ **Restaurants** see pp296–9
1 Cinnamon Club
2 Regency Café

◀ The clock face on the Houses of Parliament

For keys to symbols see back flap

Street-by-Street: Whitehall and Westminster

Compared with many capital cities, London has little monumental architecture designed to overawe with pomp. Here, at the historic seat of both the government and the established church, it most closely approaches the broad, stately avenues of Paris, Rome and Madrid. On weekdays the streets are crowded with members of the civil service, as most of their work is based in this area. At weekends, however, it teems mainly with tourists, visiting some of London's most famous sights.

❿ ★ Churchill War Rooms
The meticulously preserved War Rooms were Winston Churchill's World War II headquarters.

The Treasury is where the nation's finances are administered.

Central Hall is a florid example of the Beaux Arts style, built in 1911 as a Methodist meeting hall. In 1946 the first General Assembly of the United Nations was held here.

❹ ★ Westminster Abbey
The Abbey is London's oldest and most important church.

❼ Parliament Square
Statues of famous statesmen, such as Benjamin Disraeli, Sir Winston Churchill and Nelson Mandela, stand here.

The Sanctuary was a medieval safe place for those escaping the law.

❻ St Margaret's Church
Society weddings often take place here, in Parliament's church.

❺ Dean's Yard
Westminster School was founded here in 1540.

Richard I's Statue, by Carlo Marochetti (1860), depicts the 12th-century *Coeur de Lion* (Lionheart).

❸ Jewel Tower
Kings once stored their most valuable possessions here.

The Burghers of Calais is a cast of Auguste Rodin's original in Paris.

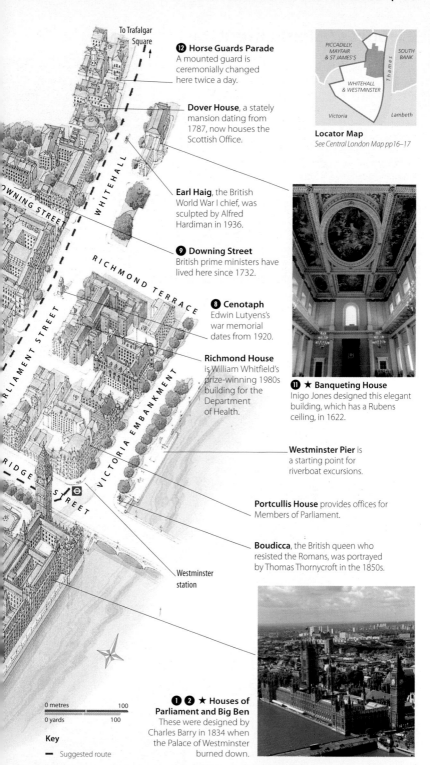

To Trafalgar Square

12 Horse Guards Parade
A mounted guard is ceremonially changed here twice a day.

Dover House, a stately mansion dating from 1787, now houses the Scottish Office.

WHITEHALL

Earl Haig, the British World War I chief, was sculpted by Alfred Hardiman in 1936.

RICHMOND TERRACE

9 Downing Street
British prime ministers have lived here since 1732.

8 Cenotaph
Edwin Lutyens's war memorial dates from 1920.

Richmond House is William Whitfield's prize-winning 1980s building for the Department of Health.

PARLIAMENT STREET

VICTORIA EMBANKMENT

BRIDGE STREET

Westminster station

Locator Map
See Central London Map pp16–17

PICCADILLY, MAYFAIR & ST JAMES'S

WHITEHALL & WESTMINSTER

SOUTH BANK

Thames

Victoria

Lambeth

11 ★ Banqueting House
Inigo Jones designed this elegant building, which has a Rubens ceiling, in 1622.

Westminster Pier is a starting point for riverboat excursions.

Portcullis House provides offices for Members of Parliament.

Boudicca, the British queen who resisted the Romans, was portrayed by Thomas Thornycroft in the 1850s.

0 metres 100
0 yards 100

Key
— Suggested route

1 2 ★ Houses of Parliament and Big Ben
These were designed by Charles Barry in 1834 when the Palace of Westminster burned down.

❶ Houses of Parliament

For over 500 years the Palace of Westminster has been the seat of the two Houses of Parliament, called the Lords and the Commons. The Commons is made up of elected Members of Parliament (MPs) of different political parties; the party – or coalition of parties – with the most MPs forms the Government, and its leader becomes prime minister. MPs from other parties make up the Opposition. Commons debates can become heated and are impartially chaired by an MP designated as Speaker. The Government formulates legislation which must be agreed to in both Houses before becoming law.

★ **Commons Chamber**
The room is upholstered in green. The Government sits on the left, the Opposition on the right, and the Speaker presides from a chair between them.

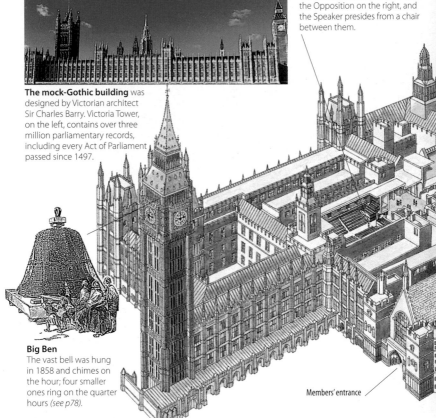

The mock-Gothic building was designed by Victorian architect Sir Charles Barry. Victoria Tower, on the left, contains over three million parliamentary records, including every Act of Parliament passed since 1497.

Big Ben
The vast bell was hung in 1858 and chimes on the hour; four smaller ones ring on the quarter hours *(see p78)*.

Members' entrance

KEY

① **Peers** are members of the House of Lords. They come from many walks of life and bring experience and knowledge from a wide range of professions. This is their lobby.

② **The Royal Gallery** is used for quiet work by members of the Lords, and occasional special events.

★ **Westminster Hall**
The only surviving part of the original Palace of Westminster dates from 1097; its hammerbeam roof is 14th-century.

Central Lobby
People who come to meet their MP wait here under a ceiling of rich mosaics.

VISITORS' CHECKLIST

Practical Information
London SW1
Map 13 C5. **Tel** 020 7219 4272 for general enquiries; 020 7219 4114 for tours (Sat year-round except Christmas recess; Mon–Fri summer and conference recesses; see below for recess dates).
parliament.uk/visiting.
Debates: Commons and Lords Visitors' Galleries **Open** check website for times. Gallery access: Cromwell Green entrance. UK residents can apply to their local MP for gallery tickets (needed only for Question Time). Galleries **Closed** Recesses: Easter, Whitsun, summer (late Jul–early Sep), conference (mid-Sep–mid-Oct), November (mid-Nov), Christmas.
tours and audioguides only.
see website.

Transport
Westminster. 3, 11, 12, 24, 53, 87, 88, 148, 159, 211, 453.
Victoria. Westminster Pier.

Peers' entrance

Cromwell Green (visitor) entrance

★ Lords Chamber
The room is upholstered in red and is similar in layout to the Commons, but has crossbenchers (non-party members). The Lord Speaker sits on the Woolsack.

1042 Work starts on first palace for Edward the Confessor

1550 St Stephen's Chapel becomes first Chamber of the House of Commons

1834 Palace destroyed by fire; only Westminster Hall and the Jewel Tower survive

1870 Present building, designed by Charles Barry, completed

1000 | 1200 | 1400 | 1600 | 1800 | 2000

1097–99 Westminster Hall built

The Mace: symbol of royal authority in the Commons and Lords.

1512 After a fire, palace stops being a royal residence

1605 Guy Fawkes and others try to blow up the king and Houses of Parliament

1642 Charles I tries to arrest five MPs but is forced to withdraw by the Speaker

1941 Chamber of House of Commons destroyed by World War II bomb

The world's most famous clock tower, which houses Big Ben

❷ Big Ben

Bridge St SW1. **Map** 13 C5. 🚇 Westminster. 📷 (UK residents only) 9am, 11am & 2pm Mon–Fri (also May–Sep: 4pm), except bank hols.

Big Ben is not the name of the world-famous four-faced clock in the 96 m (315 ft) tower that rises above the Houses of Parliament, but of the resonant 14-tonne bell on which the hours are struck, thought to be named after the Chief Commissioner of Works Sir Benjamin Hall. Cast at White-chapel in 1858, it was the second giant bell made for the clock, the first having become cracked during a test ringing. The clock is the largest in Britain, its four dials 7.5 m (23 ft) in diameter and the minute hand 4.25 m (14 ft) long, made in hollow copper for light-ness. It has kept exact time for the nation more or less continuously since it was first set in motion in May 1859, and has become a symbol of Britain the world over. The tower itself was renamed the Elizabeth Tower in 2012 in honour of Queen Elizabeth II in her Diamond Jubilee year.

❸ Jewel Tower

Abingdon St SW1. **Map** 13 B5. **Tel** 020 7222 2219. 🚇 Westminster. **Open** Apr–Sep: 10am–6pm daily; Oct 10am–5pm daily; Nov–Mar: 10am–4pm Sat & Sun. **Closed** 24 Dec–1 Jan. 🚫 🚫 ground floor only. 📷 🅦 **english-heritage.org.uk**

This and Westminster Hall *(see p76)* are the only remaining vestiges of the old Palace of Westminster. The tower was built in 1365 as a stronghold for Edward III's treasure and today houses a fascinating exhibition, "Parliament Past and Present", which relates the history of Parliament. The display on the upper floor is devoted to the history of the tower itself.

The tower served as the Weights and Measures office from 1869 until 1938 and another small display relates to that era. Alongside are the remains of the moat and a medieval quay.

❹ Westminster Abbey

See pp80–83.

❺ Dean's Yard

Broad Sanctuary SW1. **Map** 13 B5. 🚇 Westminster. Buildings **Closed** to the public.

An arch near the west door of the Abbey leads into this secluded grassy square, surrounded by a jumble of buildings from many different periods. A medieval house on the east side has a distinctive dormer window and backs

Entrance to the Abbey and cloisters from Dean's Yard

on to Little Dean's Yard, where the monks' living quarters used to be. Dean's Yard is private property. It belongs to the Dean and Chapter of Westminster and is close to Westminster School, whose former pupils include poet John Dryden and playwright Ben Jonson. Its scholars are, by tradition, the first to acknowledge a new monarch.

❻ St Margaret's Church

Parliament Sq SW1. **Map** 13 B5. **Tel** 020 7654 4840. 🚇 Westminster. **Open** 9:30am–3:30pm Mon–Fri, 9:30am–1:30pm Sat, 2–4:30pm Sun. 🕆 11am Sun. 📷 🚫 via North Door 🅦 **westminster-abbey.org/st-margarets**

Overshadowed by the Abbey, this late 15th-century church has long been a favoured venue for political and society weddings, such as Winston and Clementine Churchill's. Although much restored, the church retains some Tudor features, notably a stained-glass window commemorating the marriage of King Henry VIII and his first wife, Catherine of Aragon.

❼ Parliament Square

SW1. **Map** 13 B5. 🚇 Westminster.

Laid out in the 1840s to provide a more open aspect for the new Houses of Parliament, the square became Britain's first official roundabout in 1926. Today it is hemmed in by heavy traffic. Statues of statesmen and soldiers are dominated by Winston Churchill in his greatcoat, glowering at the House of Commons. On the north side, Abraham Lincoln stands in front of the mock-Gothic Middlesex Guildhall, completed in 1913.

❽ Cenotaph

Whitehall SW1. **Map** 13 B4. 🚇 Westminster.

This suitably bleak and pale monument, completed in 1920 by Sir Edwin Lutyens to commemorate the dead of

World War I, stands in the middle of Whitehall. On Remembrance Day every year – the Sunday nearest 11 November – the monarch and other dignitaries place wreaths of red poppies on the Cenotaph. This solemn ceremony, commemorating the 1918 armistice, honours those who have died while serving in the armed forces (see pp58–9).

The Cenotaph

⑩ Churchill War Rooms

Clive Steps, King Charles St SW1. **Map** 13 B5. **Tel** 020 7930 6961. ⊖ Westminster. **Open** 9:30am–6pm daily (last adm: 5pm). **Closed** 24–26 Dec. 🅿 🄰 🅰 🖃 📷 🖼 **iwm.org.uk**

This intriguing slice of 20th-century history is a warren of rooms below the Government Office building north of Parliament Square. This is where the War Cabinet – first under Prime Minister Neville Chamberlain, then his successor Winston Churchill – met during World War II, when German bombs were falling on London. The War Rooms include living quarters for key ministers and military leaders

Telephones in the Map Room of the Cabinet War Rooms

and a Cabinet Room, where many strategic decisions were taken. They are laid out as they were when the war ended, complete with period furniture, including Churchill's desk, communications equipment and maps for plotting military strategy. The Churchill Museum is a multimedia exhibit recording Churchill's life and career.

⑨ Downing Street

SW1. **Map** 13 B4. ⊖ Westminster. **Closed** to the public.

Sir George Downing (1623–84) spent part of his youth in the American colonies. He was the second graduate from the nascent Harvard College before returning to fight for the Parliamentarians in the English Civil War. In 1680, he bought some land near Whitehall Palace and built a street of houses. Four of these survive, though they are much altered. King George II gave No. 10 to Sir Robert Walpole in 1732. Since then it has been the official residence of the prime minister and contains offices as well as a private apartment. In 1989, for security reasons, iron gates were erected at the Whitehall end.

The famous front door of No. 10

No. 12, the Whips' Office, is where political campaigns are organized.

Government policy is decided in the Cabinet Room at No. 10.

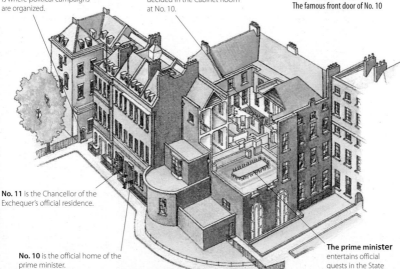

No. 11 is the Chancellor of the Exchequer's official residence.

No. 10 is the official home of the prime minister.

The prime minister entertains official guests in the State Dining Room.

❹ Westminster Abbey

The Abbey is world-famous as the resting place of Britain's monarchs, and as the setting for coronations and other great events, such as the marriage of Prince William in 2011. Within its walls can be seen some of the most glorious examples of medieval architecture in London. It also contains one of the most impressive collections of tombs and monuments in the world. Half national church, half national museum, the Abbey is part of British national consciousness.

★ **Flying Buttresses**
The massive flying buttresses help spread the great weight of the 31-m (102-ft) high nave.

North/Main Entrance
The stonework here, such as this carving of a dragon, is Victorian.

★ **West Front Towers**
These towers, completed in 1745, were designed by Nicholas Hawksmoor.

KEY

① **The North Transept** has three chapels on the east side containing some of the Abbey's finest monuments.

② **St Edward's Chapel** houses Edward the Confessor's shrine and the tombs of other English medieval monarchs.

③ **The South Transept** contains "Poets' Corner", where memorials to famous literary figures can be seen.

④ **Museum**

⑤ **The Cloisters**, built mainly in the 13th and 14th centuries, link the Abbey church with the other buildings.

★ **The Nave viewed from the West End**
At 10 m (35 ft) wide, the nave is comparatively narrow, but it is the highest in England.

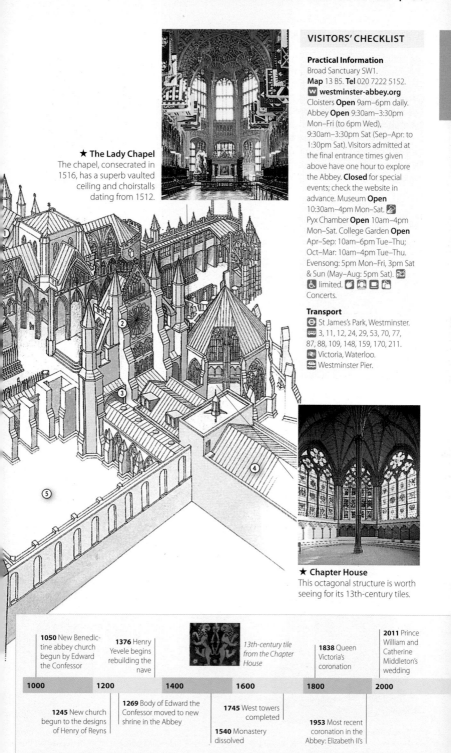

★ **The Lady Chapel**
The chapel, consecrated in 1516, has a superb vaulted ceiling and choirstalls dating from 1512.

VISITORS' CHECKLIST

Practical Information
Broad Sanctuary SW1.
Map 13 B5. **Tel** 020 7222 5152.
W **westminster-abbey.org**
Cloisters **Open** 9am–6pm daily.
Abbey **Open** 9:30am–3:30pm
Mon–Fri (to 6pm Wed),
9:30am–3:30pm Sat (Sep–Apr: to
1:30pm Sat). Visitors admitted at
the final entrance times given
above have one hour to explore
the Abbey. **Closed** for special
events; check the website in
advance. Museum **Open**
10:30am–4pm Mon–Sat.
Pyx Chamber **Open** 10am–4pm
Mon–Sat. College Garden **Open**
Apr–Sep: 10am–6pm Tue–Thu;
Oct–Mar: 10am–4pm Tue–Thu.
Evensong: 5pm Mon–Fri, 3pm Sat
& Sun (May–Aug: 5pm Sat).
limited. Concerts.

Transport
St James's Park, Westminster.
3, 11, 12, 24, 29, 53, 70, 77,
87, 88, 109, 148, 159, 170, 211.
Victoria, Waterloo.
Westminster Pier.

★ **Chapter House**
This octagonal structure is worth seeing for its 13th-century tiles.

1050 New Benedictine abbey church begun by Edward the Confessor
1376 Henry Yevele begins rebuilding the nave
13th-century tile from the Chapter House
1838 Queen Victoria's coronation
2011 Prince William and Catherine Middleton's wedding

1000 | 1200 | 1400 | 1600 | 1800 | 2000

1245 New church begun to the designs of Henry of Reyns
1269 Body of Edward the Confessor moved to new shrine in the Abbey
1745 West towers completed
1540 Monastery dissolved
1953 Most recent coronation in the Abbey: Elizabeth II's

A Guided Tour of Westminster Abbey

The Abbey's interior presents an exceptionally diverse array of architectural and sculptural styles. These range from the austere French Gothic of the nave to the stunning complexity of Henry VII's Tudor chapel and the riotous invention of the later 18th-century monuments. Many British monarchs were buried here; some of their tombs are deliberately plain, while others are lavishly decorated. There are also monuments to a number of Britain's greatest public figures – ranging from politicians to poets – crowded into the aisles and transepts.

② Grave of the Unknown Warrior
The body of an unknown soldier was brought from the battlefields of World War I and buried here in 1920. His grave commemorates all who have lost their lives in war.

Historical Plan of the Abbey

The first Abbey church was established as early as the 10th century, when St Dunstan brought a group of Benedictine monks to the area. The present structure dates largely from the 13th century; the new, French-influenced design was begun in 1245 at the behest of Henry III. Because of its unique role as the royal coronation church, the Abbey survived Henry VIII's mid-16th-century onslaught on Britain's monastic buildings.

Key

- ☐ Built between 1055 and 1350
- ■ Added from 1350 to 1420
- ☐ Built between 1500 and 1512
- ☐ Towers completed 1745
- ☐ Restored after 1850

The Jericho Parlour, added in the early 16th century, contains some fine panelling. It is closed to the public.

① Coronation Chair
Constructed in 1301, this chair has been used at every coronation since 1308.

Main entrance

The Choir houses a gilded 1840s screen, which contains remnants of the 13th-century original.

The Jerusalem Chamber has a 17th-century fireplace, fine tapestries and an interesting painted ceiling. It is closed to the public.

The Deanery, home of the Dean of Westminster, was once the monastic abbot's house. It is closed to the public.

Coronation

The Abbey has been the fittingly sumptuous setting for all royal coronations since 1066. The last occupant of the Coronation Chair was the present monarch, Elizabeth II. She was crowned in 1953 in the first televised coronation.

The Chapel of St John the Baptist is full of tombs dating from the 14th to the 19th centuries.

St Faith Chapel contains works of art that date back to the 13th century.

③ **The Nave**
The nave is 10.5 m (35 ft) wide and 31 m (102 ft) high. It took 150 years to build.

④ **Nightingale Memorial**
The North Transept chapels contain some of the Abbey's finest monuments – this one, by Roubiliac, is for Lady Elizabeth Nightingale (1761).

⑤ **Tomb of Elizabeth I**
Inside the Lady Chapel you will find Elizabeth I's (reigned 1558–1603) huge tomb. It also houses the body of her sister, "Bloody" Mary I.

⑥ **The Lady Chapel**
The undersides of the choirstalls, dating from 1512, are beautifully carved with exotic and fantastic creatures.

⑦ **The Chapel of St Edward the Confessor**
The shrine of the Saxon king Edward the Confessor and the tombs of many medieval monarchs are here.

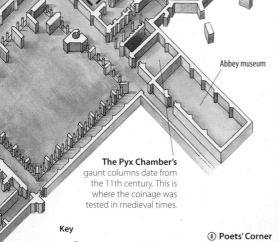

Abbey museum

The Pyx Chamber's gaunt columns date from the 11th century. This is where the coinage was tested in medieval times.

Key

— Tour route

Dean's Yard entrance

⑧ **Poets' Corner**
Take time to explore the memorials to countless literary giants, such as Shakespeare and Dickens, gathered here.

⓫ Banqueting House

Whitehall SW1. **Map** 13 B4. **Tel** 0844 482 7777; to check possible closures call 020 3166 6154). ⊖ Charing Cross, Embankment, Westminster. **Open** 10am–5pm daily (last adm 4:15pm). **Closed** public hols, 22 Dec–1 Jan; may close early for functions (see above). 🅿 ♿ Mon–Fri only. 🔲 📷 🌐 **hrp.org.uk**

This delightful building is of great architectural importance. It was the first in central London to embody the Classical Palladian style that designer Inigo Jones brought back from his travels in Italy. Completed in 1622, its disciplined stone façade marked a startling change from the Elizabethans' fussy turrets and unrestrained external decoration. It was the sole survivor of the fire that destroyed most of the old Whitehall Palace in 1698.

The ceiling paintings by Rubens, a complex allegory on the exaltation of James I, were commissioned by his son, Charles I, in 1630. This blatant glorification of royalty was despised by Oliver Cromwell and the Parliamentarians, who executed King Charles I on a scaffold outside Banqueting House in 1649. Only 11 years later, Charles II celebrated his restoration to the throne. The building is used for official functions.

Mounted sentries stationed outside Horse Guards Parade

⓬ Horse Guards Parade

Whitehall SW1. **Map** 13 B4. ⊖ Westminster, Charing Cross, Embankment. Changing the Guard: Mon–Sat 11am, Sun 10am. Daily inspection (front yard): 4pm daily. Trooping the Colour: *see Ceremonies pp56–9.*

The Changing the Guard ceremony takes place in what was Henry VIII's tiltyard (tournament ground) every morning. The elegant buildings, completed in 1755, were designed by William Kent. On the left is the Old Treasury, also by Kent, and Dover House, completed in 1758 and now used as the Scottish Office. Nearby is a trace of the "real tennis" court where Henry VIII is said to have played the

precursor of modern lawn tennis. On the opposite side, the view is dominated by the ivy-covered Citadel. This is a bomb-proof structure that was erected in 1940 beside the Admiralty. During World War II, it was used as a communications headquarters by the Navy.

⓭ Household Cavalry Museum

Horse Guards, Whitehall SW1. **Map** 13 B4. **Tel** 020 7930 3070. ⊖ Westminster, Charing Cross, Embankment. **Open** Apr–Oct: 10am–6pm daily, Nov–Mar: 10am–5pm daily. **Closed** Good Fri, 20 Jul, 24–26 Dec; in summer occasionally for ceremonies (phone to check). 🅿 ♿ 🔲 🌐 **household cavalrymuseum.co.uk**

A collection of artifacts and interactive displays cover the history of the senior regiments based at Horse Guards, from their role in the Battle of Waterloo to recent service in Afghanistan. Through a glass partition visitors can see the working stables, and kids (big and small) can try on uniforms.

⓮ Queen Anne's Gate

SW1. **Map** 13 A5. ⊖ St James's Park.

The spacious terraced houses at the west end of this well-preserved enclave date from 1704 and are notable for the ornate canopies over their front doors. At the other end are houses built some 70 years later, sporting blue plaques that record former residents, such as Lord Palmerston, the Victorian prime minister. It is rumoured that the British Secret Service, MI5, was formerly based in this unlikely spot. A small statue of Queen Anne stands in front of the wall separating Nos. 13 and 15. To the west, situated at the corner of Petty France, Sir Basil Spence's Home Office building (1976) is an architectural incongruity. Cockpit Steps, leading down to Birdcage Walk, mark the site of a 17th-century venue for the popular, blood-thirsty sport of cockfighting.

Panels from the Rubens ceiling, Banqueting House

⓯ Guards Museum

Birdcage Walk SW1. **Map** 13 A5.
Tel 020 7414 3428. 🚇 St James's Park.
Open 10am–4pm daily (last adm:
3:30pm). **Closed** Christmas, Jan &
ceremonies. 🎟 (free for under-16s). 📷
♿ 📷 🌐 **theguardsmuseum.com**

Entered from Birdcage Walk, the
museum is under the parade
ground of Wellington Barracks,
headquarters of the five Foot
Guards regiments. A must for
military buffs, the museum
illustrates various battles in
which the Guards have taken
part, from the English Civil
War (1642–8) to the present.
Weapons and row after row
of colourful uniforms are on
display, as well as a fascinating
collection of models.

⓰ St James's Park Station

55 Broadway SW1. **Map** 13 A5.
🚇 St James's Park.

The Underground station is built
into Broadway House, Charles
Holden's 1929 headquarters
for London Transport. It is
notable for its sculptures by
Jacob Epstein and reliefs by
Henry Moore and Eric Gill.

⓱ Blewcoat School

23 Caxton St SW1. **Map** 13 A5.
🚇 St James's Park. **Closed** to public
(Bridal shop by appt: 020 7222 2877).

This red-brick gem hemmed in
by the office towers of Victoria
Street was built in 1709 as a
charity school to teach pupils
how to "read, write, cast accounts

Statue of a Blewcoat pupil above the
Caxton Street entrance

Baroque interior of St John's Smith Square

and the catechism". All pupils
were boys until 1713, when
girls were admitted; they were
permitted to attend until 1876.
In 1899 it became an elementary
school, which it remained until
the mid 1920s. It was used as an
army store during World War II,
and was bought by the National
Trust in 1954; it now houses an
exclusive bridal shop.

⓲ Westminster Cathedral

Ashley Place SW1. **Map** 20 F1. **Tel** 020
7798 9055. 🚇 Victoria. **Open** 7am–
7pm Mon–Fri, 8am–7pm Sat & Sun.
🎟 for bell tower lift (9:30am–5pm
Mon–Fri, 9:30am–6pm Sat & Sun) and
exhibition. ℹ Check website for
details of Mass and services. ♿ 📷
📷 🌐 **westminstercathedral.org.uk**

One of London's rare Byzantine
buildings, the cathedral was
designed by John Francis
Bentley for the Catholic diocese
and completed in 1903 on the
site of a former prison. Its 87-m
(285-ft) high red-brick tower,
with horizontal stripes of white
stone, stands out on the skyline
in sharp contrast to the Abbey
nearby. A piazza on the north
side provides a good view of
the cathedral from Victoria
Street. The rich interior
decoration, with marble of
varying colours and intricate
mosaics, makes the domes
above the nave seem

incongruous. They were left
bare because the project ran
out of money. Eric Gill's dramatic
reliefs of the 14 Stations of the
Cross, created during World
War I, adorn the pier of the
nave, which is the widest in
Britain. The organ is one of the
finest in Europe, and there are
often free recitals on Sunday
afternoons at 4:45pm.

⓳ St John's Smith Square

Smith Sq SW1. **Map** 21 B1. **Tel** 020
7222 1061. 🚇 Westminster. **Closed** to
public except for concerts. Box office:
Open 10am–5pm Mon–Sat (to 6pm
on concert days). 📷 ♿ phone first.
📷 🌐 **sjss.org.uk**

Described by artist and art
historian Sir Hugh Casson as one
of the masterpieces of English
Baroque architecture, Thomas
Archer's plump church, with its
turrets at each corner, looks as if
it is trying to burst from the
confines of the square, and
rather overpowers the pleasing
18th-century houses on its
north side. Today it is principally
a concert hall. It has an accident-
prone history: completed in
1728, it was burned down in 1742,
struck by lightning in 1773 and
destroyed by a World War II bomb
in 1941. There is a reasonably
priced basement restaurant that
is open on weekdays for lunch
and on concert evenings.

⑳ Tate Britain

Tate Britain displays the world's largest collection of British art from the 16th to the 21st centuries. In the Clore Galleries are works from the magnificent Turner Bequest, left to the nation by the great landscape artist J M W Turner in 1851. The Clore Galleries have their own entrance, giving direct access to the Turner Collection and allowing a full appreciation of Sir James Stirling's Post-Modernist design for the building. The Tate often loans out or removes works for restoration, so the exhibits described here may not always be on display.

Main floor

★ **Three Studies for Figures at the Base of a Crucifixion** (c.1944, detail)
Francis Bacon's famous triptych encapsulates an anguished vision of human existence. When first displayed, its savagery deeply shocked audiences.

Lower floor

Manton entrance

Gallery Guide

Highlights from the collection are displayed chronologically around the outer perimeter of the galleries. More focused displays, "BP Spotlights", offer a detailed look at specific artists or themes. The Duveen Galleries showcase contemporary sculpture. Large retrospectives and themed temporary exhibits are shown either in the lower galleries or ground-floor east wing. Every other year, Tate Britain also exhibits the Turner Prize nominees.

★ **Ophelia** (1851–2)
Taken from Shakespeare's play *Hamlet*, the scene of the drowning of Ophelia by Pre-Raphaelite John Everett Millais is one of the most famous – and popular – paintings at Tate Britain.

The Saltonstall Family (c.1637)
David Des Granges's life-size family portrait includes the dead first Lady Saltonstall as the second shows off her new baby.

Henry Moore Galleries
This permanent display holds works by the sculptor.

Entrance to Clore Galleries

Rotunda

Stairs to lower floor
🖥 ✏ 🚻 ☕ 🍴

★ **Peace – Burial at Sea** (1842)
This is J M W Turner's tribute to his friend and rival David Wilkie. It was painted in 1842, the year after Wilkie died at sea.

Millbank entrance

The Art of Good Food

The lower floor of Tate Britain houses a café and an espresso bar, as well as a restaurant. Celebrated murals by Rex Whistler adorn the walls of the restaurant, telling the tale of the mythical inhabitants of Epicuriana and their expedition in search of rare foods. The extensive wine list has won awards. Open for lunch, weekend brunch and afternoon tea.

Key to Floorplan
- BP Walk Through British Art
- Duveen Galleries
- Clore Galleries
- Temporary exhibitions
- Non-exhibition space
- BP Spotlights
- Permanent displays

Exploring Tate Britain

Tate Britain draws its displays from the massive Tate Collection. The variety of works on show, combined with a rigorous programme of loan exhibitions and career retrospectives of British artists, results in a selection to suit all tastes – from Elizabethan portraiture to cutting-edge installation. The displays are changed frequently to explore many different aspects of the history and art of Britain from 1500 to the present day.

The Cholmondeley Ladies (c.1600–10), British School

BP Walk Through British Art (16th to Early 20th Centuries)

The national collection of British art has been hung in a continuous chronological display from the 1500s to the present day. This presentation allows viewers to observe a range of art from any one historical period, such as the Tudors and Stuarts, and see how British art has changed over the centuries. The walk comprises around 500 artworks in some 20 galleries. The galleries to the left of the main Duveen Galleries (if entering from the Millbank entrance) take you from the earliest paintings through to the 1910s.

Featured are important works by some of Britain's great 18th-century painters, including portraits and landscapes by Gainsborough, dramatic large-scale paintings in an idealized style by artists such as Benjamin West and society portraits by Joshua Reynolds, the head of the newly established Royal Academy.

Landscape painting lies at the heart of the revolution in British painting during the 19th century, when images of the countryside changed ideas not only about art, but about what it meant to be British.

The first half of the 19th century saw dramatic expansion and change in the arts in Britain. New themes began to emerge, and artists started working on a much larger scale as they competed for attention on the walls of public exhibitions. Monumental canvases by John Martin and Thomas Lawrence, plus celebrated works by David Wilkie are evidence of this. Storytelling was at the heart of Victorian art; the Victorians' belief in the power of art to convey moral messages produced such important works as Augustus Egg's series *Past and Present*.

Pre-Raphaelite and Idealist pieces are perhaps the most popular works at Tate Britain; key examples are John Everett Millais's *Ophelia*, which was completed in the mid-1880s, and William Holman Hunt's *Awakening Conscience*. Painting and sculpture from the late Victorian period includes the American artist John Singer Sargent's seductive *Mrs Carl Meyer and her Children*, and austere, haunting pieces by Gwen John.

20th-Century British Art

The modern section of Tate Britain begins towards the front of the gallery with the early 20th century. It includes Jacob Epstein's colossal alabaster sculpture of two wrestling figures, *Jacob and the Angel*. Work by other celebrated British sculptors, such as Barbara Hepworth and Henry Moore, can also be seen in this section. Moore is one of the few artists to have a room dedicated to his works in Tate Britain. Paintings by two of the most famous, and disturbing, modern British artists are also on display here: Francis Bacon, whose *Three Studies for Figures at the Base of a Crucifixion* (c.1944) depicts three mutant organisms in agony, confined in an apparently hostile and godless world; and Lucian Freud, with his early, unsettling portrait of his first wife, *Girl with a Kitten* (1947).

From the 1960s, Tate's funding for the purchase of works began to increase substantially, while artistic activity continued to pick up speed, encouraged by public support. As a result, the Tate has a particularly big collection of work from this period, which makes a frequent rotation of displays necessary. You are, however, likely to see iconic works of the period by artists such as Sir Peter Blake, Richard Hamilton and the early work of David Hockney.

The 1980s saw the emergence of provocative artists such as Gilbert & George, known as the Living Sculptures, whose photo installations, of which *England* is an example, are often concerned with identity, and Richard Long, who created a whole new approach to the relationship between art and landscape by importing the land itself into the gallery.

The following decade was dominated by the so-called Young British Artists (YBAs), who include Damien Hirst, perhaps the most notorious, as well as Tracey Emin and

Self-Portrait with Knickers (2000) by Sarah Lucas

Sarah Lucas, famed for their controversial installation and photgraphic work. Works from this period are well-represented in the gallery.

The frequently changing displays at Tate Britain include themed exhibitions as well as rooms devoted to single artists. The Contemporary British Art galleries reflect current developments in British art and are devoted to work by up-and-coming artists. Important newly acquired works are often featured.

Clore Galleries

The Turner Bequest comprises some 300 oil paintings, 300 sketchbooks, and about 20,000 watercolours and drawings left to the nation by the great landscape painter J M W Turner on his death in 1851. Turner's will had specified that a gallery be built to house his pictures and this was finally done in 1987 with the opening of the Clore Galleries. Most of the oil paintings are on show in the main galleries, while the watercolours are the subject of changing displays.

Upstairs in the Clore Galleries is a room dedicated to works by poet and artist William Blake, a seminal figure of the Romantic Age despite being largely unrecognized in his lifetime.

Temporary Exhibitions and the Turner Prize

Tate Britain is known for its large retrospectives of some of the biggest names in British art, including in recent years Barbara Hepworth, L S Lowry and Paul Nash. While these blockbusters have an entrance charge, smaller, changing exhibits in the "BP Spotlights" galleries are free, and focus on lesser-known artists, emerging artists, or a particular theme or movement. The elegant central spaces, the Duveen Galleries, are used to show special commissions of contemporary artists.

Tate also organizes the prestigious annual Turner Prize,

and hosts the exhibition in alternate years (other years it is shown in a gallery outside London). Representing all sections of the art world, artists are shortlisted on the basis of their work over the course of the preceding year. Works by all the artists shortlisted are exhibited, before a judging panel decides on the winner. Previous winners include film artist (and later Oscar winner) Steve McQueen and artist Grayson Perry. The prize has often been surrounded by controversy because of the often conceptual nature of the nominated works – for example, Damien Hirst's (1995) cow and calf, bisected and preserved in formaldehyde, Tracey Emin's dishevelled *My Bed* (1998) and Martin Creed's 2001 *Work No. 227*: an empty room in which the lights were turned on and off every five seconds.

Kids at the Tate

To encourage art appreciation from a young age, under-12s can visit any special exhibition at Tate Britain for free (when accompanied by an adult). Family-friendly events are held most weekends and you can pick up artist-designed, interactive kids' activity packs from the information points. Check the Tate website for details of events and also for its dedicated kids' zone, full of art-related games, films and fun.

Shipping at the Mouth of the Thames (c.1806–7) by J M W Turner

PICCADILLY, MAYFAIR AND ST JAMES'S

This is the part of London with the strongest royal connections. Next to Buckingham Palace itself are the former royal deer park of St James's and Green Park. To the north, Mayfair has the city's most exclusive streets and squares, filled with galleries, auction houses and gentlemen's clubs. St James's, redolent of the 18th century, still bristles with traditional gents' outfitters and other long-established, royal warrant-holding emporia; Piccadilly, the main artery of the West End, has the Ritz Hotel, the Royal Academy and luxury grocer Fortnum & Mason.

Sights at a Glance

Historic Streets and Buildings
1 Piccadilly Circus
4 Burlington Arcade
5 Ritz Hotel
6 Spencer House
7 St James's Palace
8 St James's Square
9 Royal Opera Arcade
10 Pall Mall
13 The Mall
14 Marlborough House
17 *Buckingham Palace pp98–9*
20 Wellington Arch
22 Shepherd Market
23 Grosvenor Square

Museums and Galleries
3 Royal Academy of Arts
11 Institute of Contemporary Arts
18 The Queen's Gallery
19 Royal Mews
21 Apsley House
24 Handel House Museum
25 Faraday Museum

Churches
2 St James's Church
15 Queen's Chapel

Parks and Gardens
12 St James's Park
16 Green Park

☐ Restaurants *see pp296–9*
1 Bellamy's
2 Bentley's Oyster Bar and Grill
3 Le Caprice
4 Cecconi's
5 Chisou
6 Cut at 45 Park Lane
7 Al Duca
8 Le Gavroche
9 Hakkasan Mayfair
10 Hard Rock Café
11 The Lanesborough
12 Murano
13 Nobu
14 Noura
15 La Petite Maison
16 El Pirata
17 Pollen Street Social
18 Rasa
19 The Ritz Restaurant
20 Scott's
21 The Square
22 Veeraswamy
23 The Wolseley

Street Finder, maps 12, 13

◀ Soldier taking part in the Changing the Guard ceremony

For keys to symbols *see back flap*

Street-by-Street: Piccadilly and St James's

As soon as Henry VIII built St James's Palace in the 1530s, the area around it became the centre of fashionable London, and it has remained so ever since. Its historic streets, squares and arcades attract a truly international – and extremely wealthy – set. The flagship stores of exclusive global brands sit alongside classic British names that have served royalty and aristocracy for centuries. The Royal Academy and many independent art galleries cluster nearby.

Piccadilly
The street derives its name from the ruffs, or "pickadills", worn by 17th-century dandies.

Albany
This mansion has been one of London's smartest addresses since it opened in 1803.

❸ ★ **Royal Academy of Arts**
Sir Joshua Reynolds founded the Academy in 1768. Now it mounts large popular exhibitions.

Fortnum & Mason
was founded in 1707 by one of Queen Anne's footmen (see p317).

❹ ★ **Burlington Arcade**
Uniformed beadles discourage unruly behaviour in this 19th-century mall.

❺ **Ritz Hotel**
Named after César Ritz, and opened in 1906, it still lives up to his name.

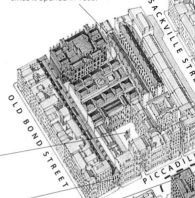

❻ **Spencer House**
An ancestor of Princess Diana built this house in 1766.

Clarence House was designed by John Nash for William IV, and is now Prince Charles's London home.

To The Mall

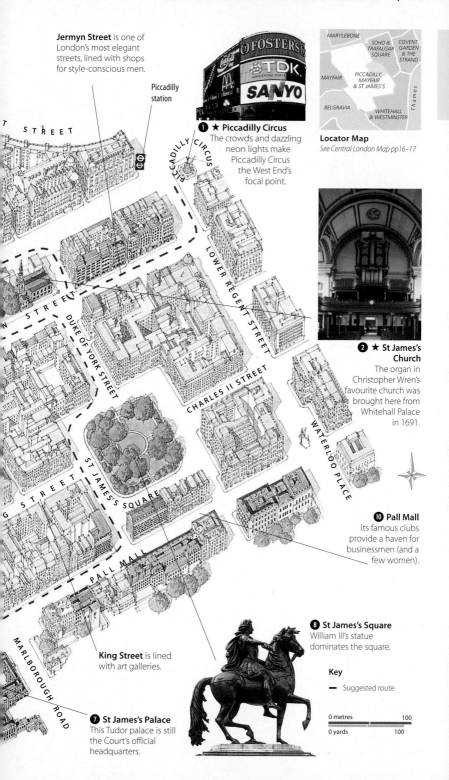

Jermyn Street is one of London's most elegant streets, lined with shops for style-conscious men.

Piccadilly station

Locator Map
See Central London Map pp16–17

❶ ★ Piccadilly Circus
The crowds and dazzling neon lights make Piccadilly Circus the West End's focal point.

❷ ★ St James's Church
The organ in Christopher Wren's favourite church was brought here from Whitehall Palace in 1691.

❿ Pall Mall
Its famous clubs provide a haven for businessmen (and a few women).

❽ St James's Square
William III's statue dominates the square.

Key

— Suggested route

King Street is lined with art galleries.

❼ St James's Palace
This Tudor palace is still the Court's official headquarters.

0 metres   100
0 yards   100

Alfred Gilbert's statue of *Eros* takes aim down Lower Regent Street

❶ Piccadilly Circus

W1. **Map** 13 A3. ⊖ Piccadilly Circus.

For years people have congregated beneath the symbolic figure of Eros, originally intended as an angel of mercy but renamed after the Greek god of love. Poised delicately with his bow, Eros has become almost a trademark for the capital. It was erected in 1892 as a memorial to the Earl of Shaftesbury, the Victorian philanthropist. Part of Nash's master plan for Regent Street, Piccadilly Circus has been considerably altered over the years and consists for the most part of shops. One shopping mall can be found behind the façade of the London Pavilion (1885), once a popular music hall. Piccadilly Circus has London's gaudiest array of neon advertising signs, marking the entrance to the city's lively entertainment district with its cinemas, theatres, nightclubs, restaurants and pubs.

❷ St James's Church

197 Piccadilly W1. **Map** 13 A3. **Tel** 020 7734 4511. ⊖ Piccadilly Circus. **Open** 8am–6:30pm daily. Food market 11am–5pm Mon, craft market 10am–6pm Wed–Sat, antiques market 10am–6pm Tue. ♿ 🖥 Concerts, talks, events. 🆆 sjp.org.uk

Among the many churches Wren designed *(see p51)*, this is said to be one of his favourites. It has

been altered over the years and was half-wrecked by a bomb in 1940, but it maintains its essential features from 1684 – the tall, arched windows, thin spire (a 1966 replica of the original) and a light, dignified interior. The ornate screen behind the altar is one of the finest works of the 17th-century master carver Grinling Gibbons, who also made the exquisite marble font, with a scene depicting Adam and Eve standing by the Tree of Life. Artist and poet William Blake and Prime Minister Pitt the Elder were both baptized here. More of Gibbons' carvings can be seen above the grandiose organ, made for Whitehall Palace chapel but installed here in 1691. The church now has a full calendar of events, and houses a popular café. A small market operates in the outer courtyard.

❸ Royal Academy of Arts

Burlington House, Piccadilly W1. **Map** 12 F3. **Tel** 020 7300 8000. ⊖ Piccadilly Circus, Green Park. **Open** 10am–6pm Sat–Thu, 10am–10pm Fri. **Closed** Good Fri, 24–26 Dec. 📷 for temporary exhibitions. 🎫 ♿ 📷 📷 🖥 📷 🆆 royalacademy.org.uk

The courtyard in front of Burlington House, one of the West End's few surviving mansions from the early 18th century, is often crammed with people waiting to get into one of the prestigious visiting art exhibitions on show at the Royal Academy (founded 1768). Every summer, its famous annual exhibition, which has now been held for over 200 years, shows around 1,200 new works. Any artist, established or unknown, may submit work.

The airy Sackler Galleries (1991), designed by Sir Norman Foster, hold visiting exhibitions. There are permanent items in the sculpture promenade outside the galleries, notably a Michelangelo relief of the *Madonna and Child* (1505). The exceptional permanent

Michelangelo's *Madonna and Child*

collection (not all on display) includes one work by each current and former Academician; the highlights are displayed in the Madejski Rooms. Two shops adjacent to the gallery exits sell merchandise inspired by the current exhibitions, as well as a great range of art books.

❹ Burlington Arcade

Piccadilly W1. **Map** 12 F3. ⊖ Green Park, Piccadilly Circus.

This is one of four 19th-century arcades of small shops that sell traditional British luxuries. (The Princes and Piccadilly Arcades are on the south side of Piccadilly, while the Royal Opera Arcade is off Pall Mall.) It was built for Lord Cavendish in 1819, who lived in Burlington House next door, to stop rubbish being thrown into what was then his side garden. The arcade is still patrolled by beadles, who make sure an atmosphere of refinement is maintained. They have authority to eject anyone who sings, whistles, runs or opens an umbrella; those powers are infrequently invoked now, perhaps because the dictates of commerce take precedence over those of decorum.

❺ Ritz Hotel

Piccadilly W1. **Map** 12 F3. **Tel** 020 7493 8181. ⊖ Green Park. **Open** to non-residents for tea or restaurant (book ahead). ♿ *(See p288).* 🆆 theritzlondon.com

César Ritz, the famed Swiss hotelier who inspired the

adjective "ritzy", had virtually retired by the time this hotel was built and named after him in 1906.

The colonnaded frontal of the imposing château-style building was meant to suggest Paris, where the very grandest and most fashionable hotels were to be found around the turn of the century. It maintains its Edwardian air of opulence and is a popular stop, welcoming those who are suitably dressed (no jeans or trainers; jacket and tie for men) for afternoon tea, with daily sittings in the Palm Court at 11:30am, 1:30pm, 3:30pm, 5:30pm and 7:30pm.

The exquisite Palm Room of Spencer House

❻ Spencer House

27 St James's Pl SW1. **Map** 12 F4. **Tel** 020 7514 1958 (Mon–Fri). 🚇 Green Park. **Open** Feb–Jul & Sep–Dec: 10:30am–5:45pm Sun (last adm: 4:45pm). **Closed** Jan & Aug. No children under 10. 🚫 📷 ♿ 🎥 compulsory. 🌐 **spencerhouse.co.uk**

This Palladian palace, built in 1766 for the first Earl Spencer, an ancestor of the late Princess of Wales, has been completely restored to its 18th-century splendour (thanks to an £18 million renovation project). It contains some wonderful paintings and contemporary furniture; one of the highlights is the beautifully decorated Painted Room. The house is open to the public – for guided tours only – and is also used for receptions and meetings.

❼ St James's Palace

Pall Mall SW1. **Map** 12 F4. 🚇 Green Park. **Closed** to the public. 🌐 **royal.gov.uk**

Built by Henry VIII in the late 1530s on the site of a former leper hospital, the palace was a primary royal residence only briefly, mainly during the reign of Elizabeth I and in the late 17th and early 18th centuries. In 1952, Queen Elizabeth II made her first speech as queen here, and foreign ambassadors are still officially accredited to the Court of St James's. Its northern gatehouse,

St James's
Tudor gatehouse

seen from St James's Street, is one of London's great Tudor landmarks. The palace buildings are now occupied by minor royals and privileged Crown servants.

❽ St James's Square

SW1. **Map** 13 A3. 🚇 Green Park, Piccadilly Circus.

London's squares, quadrangles of elegant homes surrounding gated landscaped gardens, are among the city's most attractive features. St James's, one of London's earliest, was laid out in the 1670s and lined by exclusive houses for those whose business made it vital for them to live near St James's Palace. Many of the buildings date from the 18th and 19th centuries and have had many illustrious residents. During World War II, Generals Eisenhower and de Gaulle both had headquarters here.

Today, No. 10 on the north side, Chatham House (1736), is home to the Royal Institute for International Affairs. In the northwest corner of the square is the London Library (1896), a private lending library founded in 1841 by historian Thomas Carlyle (see p200) and others. The lovely gardens in the middle contain an equestrian statue of William III, here since 1808.

Afternoon tea served in the opulent Palm Court of the Ritz

Royal Opera Arcade

⑨ Royal Opera Arcade

SW1. **Map** 13 A3. ⊖ Piccadilly Circus.

London's first shopping arcade was designed by John Nash and completed in 1818, behind the Haymarket Opera House (now called Her Majesty's Theatre). It beat the Burlington Arcade (see p94) by a year or so. The traditional shops that once used to be based here have since moved on: Farlows, selling shooting and fishing equipment, and the famous Hunter's green Wellington boots, is now nearby, at No. 9 Pall Mall.

The Duke of Wellington (1842), a frequent visitor to Pall Mall

⑩ Pall Mall

SW1. **Map** 13 A4. ⊖ Charing Cross, Green Park, Piccadilly Circus.

This dignified street is named for the game of palle-maille – a cross between croquet and golf – which was played here in the 17th century. For more than 150 years, Pall Mall has been at the heart of London's clubland. Here, exclusive gentlemen's clubs were formed to provide members with a refuge from their womenfolk.

The clubhouses now amount to a textbook of the most fashionable architects of the era. At the east end, on the left is the colonnaded entrance to No.

116, Nash's United Services Club (1827). This was the favourite club of the Duke of Wellington and now houses the Institute of Directors. Facing it, on the other side of Waterloo Place, is the Athenaeum (No. 107), designed three years later by Decimus Burton, and long the powerhouse of the British establishment. Next door are two clubs by Sir Charles Barry, architect of the Houses of Parliament (see pp76–7): the Travellers' is at No. 106 and the Reform at No. 104. The clubs' stately interiors are well preserved but only members and their guests are admitted.

⑪ Institute of Contemporary Arts

The Mall SW1. **Map** 13 B3. **Tel** 020 7930 3647. ⊖ Charing Cross, Piccadilly Circus. **Open** 11am–11pm Tue–Sun. (Exhibition space closes 6pm, 9pm Thu, bookshop 9pm.) **Closed** 1 Jan, 24–26 & 31 Dec, public hols. ♿ (cinema and lower gallery) phone first. 🖥 📺 Concerts, theatre, dance, lectures, films, exhibitions. 🅦 **ica.org.uk**

The Institute of Contemporary Arts (ICA) was established in 1947 to offer British artists some of the facilities available to artists at the Museum of Modern Art in New York. Originally on Dover Street, it has been situated in John Nash's Classical Carlton House Terrace (1833) since 1968. With its entrance on The Mall, this extensive warren contains a cinema, auditorium, bookshop, art gallery, bar and restaurant. It also hosts concerts and lectures. A modest fee applies to non-members, providing all-day access to most exhibitions and events.

Institute of Contemporary Arts, Carlton House Terrace

⑫ St James's Park

SW1. **Map** 13 A4. **Tel** 0300 061 2350. ⊖ St James's Park. **Open** 5am–midnight daily. 🌳 **Open** daily. ♿ 🅦 **royalparks.org.uk**

In summer, office workers sunbathe between the dazzling flowerbeds of the capital's most ornamental park. In winter, overcoated civil servants discuss affairs of state as they stroll by the lake and eye its resident ducks, geese and pelicans (who are fed at 2:30pm daily). Originally a marsh, the park was drained by Henry VIII and incorporated into his hunting grounds. On his return from exile in France, Charles II had it remodelled (probably by the French designer Andre Mollet) in the more continental style as pedestrian pleasure gardens, with an aviary along its southern edge (hence Birdcage Walk, the street where the aviary was). It is still a popular place to take the air, with an appealing view of Whitehall rooftops and an attractive central lake.

⑬ The Mall

SW1. **Map** 13 A4. ⊖ Charing Cross, Green Park, Piccadilly Circus.

This broad triumphal approach to Buckingham Palace was created by Aston Webb when he redesigned the front of the palace and the Victoria Monument in 1911. It follows the course of the old path at the edge of St James's Park, laid out in the reign of Charles II, when it became London's most fashionable promenade. On the flagpoles down both sides of The Mall national flags of foreign heads of state fly during official visits.

The annual London Marathon *(see p60)* finishes on The Mall, amid a mass of cheering crowds.

⑭ Marlborough House

Pall Mall SW1. **Map** 13 A4. **Tel** 020 7747 6491. ⊖ St James's Park, Green Park. **Open** only for group tours by prior arrangement.

Marlborough House was designed by Christopher Wren *(see p51)* for the Duchess of Marlborough and completed in 1711. It was substantially enlarged in the 19th century and used by members of the royal family. From 1863 until he became Edward VII in 1901, it was the home of the Prince and Princess of Wales and the social centre of London. An Art Nouveau memorial in the Marlborough Road wall of the house commemorates Edward's queen, Alexandra. The building now houses the Commonwealth Secretariat.

Queen's Chapel, built as a private place of worship for Charles I's Catholic queen

⑮ Queen's Chapel

Marlborough Rd SW1. **Map** 13 A4. ⊖ Green Park. **Open** for services only. ✝ Easter–Jul: 8:30am & 11:15am Sun.

This exquisite work of the architect Inigo Jones was built for Charles I's French wife, Henrietta Maria, in 1627. Originally intended to be part of St James's Palace, it was the first Classical church in England.

George III married his queen, Charlotte of Mecklenburg-Strelitz (who was to bear him 15 children), here in 1761. The interior, with its glorious 17th-century fittings – both Grinling Gibbons and Wren contributed to the decoration – is wonderful. It is only open for Sunday services in spring and summer.

⑯ Green Park

SW1. **Map** 12 E4. **Tel** 0300 061 2350. ⊖ Green Park, Hyde Park Corner. Ⓦ **royalparks.org.uk**

Once part of Henry VIII's hunting grounds, this was, like St James's Park, adapted for public use by Charles II in the 1660s and is a natural, undulating landscape of grass and trees (with a fine spring show of daffodils). It was a favourite site for duels during the 18th century: in 1771 the poet Alfieri was wounded here by his mistress's husband, Viscount Ligonier, but then rushed back to the Haymarket Theatre in time to catch the last act of a play. Today the park is popular with joggers.

⑰ Buckingham Palace

See pp98–9.

The impressive former royal residence, Marlborough House

⓱ Buckingham Palace

Buckingham Palace is both the office and official London residence of the British monarchy. It is also used for ceremonial state occasions, such as banquets for visiting heads of state. About 800 people work at the palace, including officers of the Royal Household and domestic staff.

John Nash converted the original Buckingham House into a palace for George IV (reigned 1820–30). Both he and his brother, William IV (reigned 1830–37), died before work was completed, and Queen Victoria was the first monarch to live at the palace. The present east front, facing The Mall, was added to Nash's conversion in 1913. The State Rooms are open to the public in summer.

Music Room
State guests are presented and royal christenings take place in this room, which boasts a beautiful, original parquet floor by Nash.

The Ballroom
The Victorian ballroom is used for state banquets and investitures.

The Queen's Gallery
Artworks from the Royal Collection (see p100), such as Canaletto's Rome: The Pantheon, are often on display.

KEY

① **The State Dining Room** is where meals that are less formal than state banquets are held.

② **The Blue Drawing Room** is decorated with imitation onyx columns, created by John Nash.

③ **The White Drawing Room** is where the royal family assemble before passing into the State Dining Room or Ballroom.

④ **The Green Drawing Room** is the first of the large and magnificent state rooms entered by guests of the Queen at royal functions.

⑤ **The Royal Standard** flies when the Queen is in residence.

Changing the Guard
Visitors can witness the Buckingham Palace grounds guard handing over duty regularly throughout the year in a colourful royal military ceremony (see pp56–9).

Who Lives in Buckingham Palace?

The palace is the London residence of the Queen and her husband, the Duke of Edinburgh. The Princess Royal, the Duke of York and the Earl of Wessex also have apartments here. About 50 domestic staff have rooms in the palace. There are more staff homes situated in the Royal Mews (see p100).

VISITORS' CHECKLIST

Practical Information
SW1. **Map** 12 F5.
Tel 020 7766 7300.
w royalcollection.org.uk
State rooms **Open** end July–end Aug: 9:30am–7:30pm daily; Sep: 9:30am–6:30pm daily (check online as times can vary). Changing the Guard: Apr–Jul: 11:30am daily; Aug–Mar: alternate days. Tickets not required. 🎫 ♿ prebook on 020 7766 7324. 📷 ✉

Transport
🚇 St James's Park, Victoria.
🚌 2B, 11, 16, 24, 25, 36, 38, 52, 73, 135, C1. 🚆 Victoria.

The Throne Room
In a room lit by seven magnificent chandeliers stand the thrones used by the Queen and the Duke of Edinburgh during her coronation.

View over The Mall
Traditionally, the royal family waves to crowds from the balcony.

The garden is a haven for wildlife and is overlooked by most of the lavishly decorated state rooms at the back of the palace. It is also the venue for royal garden parties, where guests enjoy tea and cakes.

⑱ The Queen's Gallery

Buckingham Palace Rd SW1. **Map** 12 F5. **Tel** 020 7766 7734. 🚇 St James's Park, Victoria. **Open** 10am–5:30pm daily (Aug & Sep: 9:30am–5:30pm). **Closed** between exhibitions; call or check website. 🖼️ 🔲 ♿ ✉️ 🅆 **royalcollection.org.uk**

The royal family possesses one of the finest and most valuable art collections in the world, rich in the work of old masters, including Vermeer and da Vinci. In 2002, the galleries were expanded in the most extensive addition to Buckingham Palace in 150 years, resulting in three and a half times more display space and an impressive entrance gallery with a striking columned portico.

The gallery has seven rooms, which host a rolling display programme of the Royal Collection's masterpieces. No items are on permanent display and changing exhibitions include fine art, porcelain, jewels, furniture and manuscripts.

Ceremonial harnesses and bridles on display at the Royal Mews

⑲ Royal Mews

Buckingham Palace Rd SW1. **Map** 12 E5. **Tel** 020 7766 7302. 🚇 St James's Park, Victoria. **Open** Apr–Oct: 10am–5pm daily; Nov, Feb–Mar: 10am–4pm Mon–Sat. Subject to closure at short notice (phone first). **Closed** Dec–Jan. 🖼️ 🔲 📷 Apr–Oct. ♿ 📷 🅆 **royalcollection.org.uk**

Fans of royal pomp will enjoy a visit to the Royal Mews. The stables and coach houses, designed by Nash in 1825, accommodate the horses and coaches used by the royal family on state occasions. Star

of the exhibit is the gold state coach built for George III in 1761, with fine panels by Giovanni Cipriani. Among the other vehicles are the Irish state coach, bought by Queen Victoria for the State Opening of Parliament; the open-topped 1902 royal landau, traditionally used to give the crowds the best view of newlywed royal couples; and the glass coach, also used for royal weddings. The newest coach is the Diamond Jubilee State Coach, built in 2012. Visitors may see carriages being prepared for use or limousines in action.

Some of the horses that pull the carriages are stabled in the mews and a guided tour includes a chance to view the 18th-century riding school where the horses are put through their paces. The elaborate harnesses the horses wear are also on display. There is also a shop selling royal souvenirs.

⑳ Wellington Arch

Hyde Park Corner SW1. **Map** 12 D4. **Tel** 020 7930 2726. 🚇 Hyde Park Corner. **Open** daily; Apr–Sep: 10am–6pm; Oct: 10am–5pm; Nov–March: 10am–4pm. **Closed** 1 Jan, Good Fri, 24–26 & 31 Dec. 📷 joint ticket with Apsley House available. ♿ limited. 📷 🅆 **english-heritage.org.uk**

After nearly a century of debate about what to do with the patch of land in front of Apsley House, Wellington Arch, designed by Decimus Burton, was erected in 1828 (and then

moved to its current position in the 1880s). The sculpture, by Adrian Jones, was added in 1912. Before it was installed Jones seated three people for dinner in the body of one of the horses.

The public now has access to exhibitions in the inner rooms of the arch. A viewing platform beneath the sculpture has great views over London.

Nike, winged goddess of victory, rides her chariot atop the Wellington Arch

㉑ Apsley House

Hyde Park Corner W1. **Map** 12 D4. **Tel** 020 7499 5676. 🚇 Hyde Park Corner. **Open** Apr–Oct: 11am–5pm Wed–Sun; Nov–Mar: 10am–4pm Sat & Sun (but check dates on website). **Closed** 1 Jan, 24–26 Dec. 📷 joint ticket with Wellington Arch available. ✉️ 🔲 📷 🅆 **english-heritage.org.uk**

Apsley House, or Number One London, as it is also known, at the southeast corner of Hyde Park, was completed by Robert Adam for Baron Apsley in 1778. Fifty years later it was enlarged and altered by the architect

Interior of Apsley House

The Rehearsal and Performance Room at the Handel House Museum

Benjamin Dean Wyatt to provide a grand home for the Duke of Wellington. His dual career as soldier and politician brought him victory against his arch-enemy Napoleon at Waterloo (1815) and two terms as prime minister (1828–30 and 1834). Against sumptuous silk hangings and gilt decoration is the duke's art collection: works by Goya, Velázquez, Titian and Rubens hang alongside displays of porcelain, silver and furniture. Ironically, the duke's memorabilia, including swords and medals, is dominated by Canova's colossal statue of Napoleon.

㉒ Shepherd Market

W1. **Map** 12 E4. ⊖ Green Park.

This attractive and bijou pedestrianized enclave of small shops, restaurants and outdoor cafés, between Piccadilly and Curzon Street, was named after Edward Shepherd, who built it in the mid-18th century. During the 17th century, the annual 15-day May Fair (from which the name of the area is derived) took place on this site, and today Shepherd Market is still very much the centre of Mayfair.

㉓ Grosvenor Square

W1. **Map** 12 D2. ⊖ Bond Street.

Mayfair has long been home to some of the grandest addresses in London, most notably in a series of prestigious squares, originally laid out in the early 18th century and still retaining many Georgian buildings. Grosvenor Square is the largest, and has long had connections with the USA, ever since John Adams lived at No. 9 between 1785 and 1789. The west side is dominated by the US Embassy, designed by Eero Saarinen in 1958. (In 2017 the embassy will move to a new, more secure building south of the river.) A handsome statue of Franklin D. Roosevelt stands at the centre of the square, with bronzes of Ronald Reagan and General Eisenhower nearer the embassy.

㉔ Handel House Museum

25 Brook St W1. **Map** 12 E2. **Tel** 020 7495 1685. ⊖ Bond Street. **Open** 11am–6pm Mon–Sat (to 8pm occasional Fri), noon–6pm Sun. ♿ 🅆 handelhouse.org

A pair of Georgian houses on Brook Street have a couple of notable, very different, musical connections. The composer George Frideric Handel lived at No. 25 from 1723 until his death in 1759, and his rooms have been restored to the early Georgian appearance they would have had during the composer's time, with portraits and musical instruments on display. The museum hosts changing exhibitions and regular recitals in an intimate performance space. In 1968, Jimi Hendrix moved into the attic apartment next door. These rooms were then used as offices by the museum, but have now also been lovingly restored to resemble Hendrix's former apartment, complete with 1960s decor.

㉕ Faraday Museum

The Royal Institution, 21 Albemarle St W1. **Map** 12 F3. **Tel** 020 7409 2992. ⊖ Green Park. **Open** 9am–6pm Mon–Fri. **Closed** 24 Dec–3 Jan. 🅀 ⬗ 🖥 📞 phone first. Lectures. 🅆 rigb.org

Michael Faraday was a 19th-century pioneer of the uses of electricity. Part of the Royal Institution, a body dedicated to scientific study, the museum includes a re-creation of Faraday's laboratory and some of his scientific apparatus and personal effects, as well as exhibits on the work of other great scientists.

Michael Faraday

SOHO AND TRAFALGAR SQUARE

First developed in the late 17th century, Soho was renowned for the extravagant parties thrown by its residents, and as the years have passed, it has consolidated its reputation as a centre for entertainment. Heaving with clubs, pubs, restaurants and cafés, the West End is where everyone heads for an evening out. Theatre buffs descend on the great playhouses of Shaftesbury Avenue and Charing Cross, while star-struck movie fans crowd on Leicester Square after enjoying a bite to eat in nearby Chinatown.

But the area is not just for night owls; Trafalgar Square, with its historic architecture and monuments, is home to two of the city's best galleries, the National Gallery, with its world-class collection of art, and the National Portrait Gallery, showcasing portraits of some of the country's prolific personalities.

Sights at a Glance

Historic Streets and Buildings
1. Trafalgar Square
2. Admiralty Arch
6. Leicester Square
8. Shaftesbury Avenue
9. Chinatown
10. Charing Cross Road
12. Soho Square
14. Carnaby Street

Shops and Markets
13. Berwick Street Market
15. Liberty

Churches
4. St Martin-in-the-Fields

Museums and Galleries
3. National Gallery pp108–11
5. National Portrait Gallery
16. Photographers' Gallery

Theatres
7. Theatre Royal Haymarket
11. Palace Theatre

Restaurants see pp296–9
1. Andrew Edmunds
2. Asia de Cuba
3. Barrafina
4. Bocca di Lupo
5. Brasserie Zedel
6. Dehesa
7. Gopals of Soho
8. Haozhan
9. Inamo
10. Kulu Kulu Sushi
11. Mildred's
12. Nopi
13. Patara
14. Princi
15. The Portrait
16. Refuel
17. Soho Joe
18. Tokyo Diner
19. Vasco and Piero's Pavilion
20. Yalla Yalla
21. Yauatcha

0 metres 250
0 yards 250

Street Finder maps 11, 12, 13

◀ Chinatown, Soho

For keys to symbols *see back flap*

Street-by-Street: Soho and Trafalgar Square

This area buzzes both day and night with crowds enjoying the numerous restaurants, cinemas, theatres and nightclubs. Broad avenues lined with regal office buildings converge at Trafalgar Square, a hub of the West End and popular meeting place for visitors to the city.

To Tottenham Court Road station

⑩ Charing Cross Road
Famous for specialist and second-hand bookshops.

⑧ Shaftesbury Avenue
Lined with theatres boasting popular permanent and new shows, this is the heart of London's theatreland.

⑨ ★ Chinatown
Chinese lanterns adorn this small district packed with restaurants and shops.

Notre Dame, once a theatre, was converted into a church in 1855. The Jean Cocteau murals inside date from 1960.

The Blue Posts pub stands on the site of a pick-up point for sedan chairs in the 18th century.

⑥ Leicester Square
A 19th-century statue of William Shakespeare overlooks the city's cinema district.

Key

— Suggested route

0 metres	100
0 yards	100

⑦ Theatre Royal Haymarket
It is graced by a John Nash portico.

The Hippodrome, a former nightclub, was once a variety theatre and is now a cabaret venue.

Cecil Court is lined with shops selling old books and prints.

Leicester Square station

Locator Map
See Central London Map pp16–17

BLOOMSBURY & FITZROVIA
HOLBORN & THE INNS OF COURT
SOHO & TRAFALGAR SQUARE
COVENT GARDEN & THE STRAND
Thames
PICCADILLY, MAYFAIR & ST JAMES'S
WHITEHALL & WESTMINSTER
SOUTH BANK

❹ ★ St Martin-in-the-Fields
James Gibbs's masterpiece inspired the US "colonial" style.

❺ ★ National Portrait Gallery
Portraits of prominent Britons from Tudor times to the present-day adorn the walls here.

❸ ★ National Gallery
Over 2,000 paintings are housed in this exceptional gallery.

DUNCANNON ST

STRAND

The Fourth Plinth
The empty plinth in the corner of Trafalgar Square hosts changing pieces by leading contemporary artists.

NORTHUMBERLAND AVE

TRAFALGAR SQUARE

CHARING CROSS

THE MALL EAST

COCKSPUR STREET

Nelson's Column

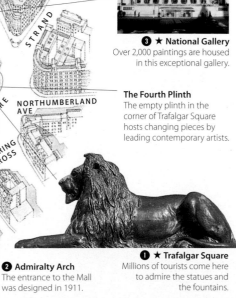

❷ Admiralty Arch
The entrance to the Mall was designed in 1911.

❶ ★ Trafalgar Square
Millions of tourists come here to admire the statues and the fountains.

❶ Trafalgar Square

WC2. **Map** 13 B3. ⊖ Charing Cross.

London's main venue for rallies and outdoor public meetings was conceived by John Nash and was mostly constructed during the 1830s. The 50-m (165-ft) column commemorates Admiral Lord Nelson, Britain's most famous sea lord, who died heroically at the Battle of Trafalgar in 1805. It dates from 1842; 14 stonemasons held a dinner on its flat top before the statue of Nelson was finally installed. Edwin Landseer's four lions guard its base. The north side of the square is now taken up by the National Gallery *(see pp108–11)*, with Canada House on the west side and South Africa House on the east. The restored Grand Buildings on the south side were built in 1880 as the Grand Hotel. Three plinths support statues of the great and the good, including King George IV; funds ran out before the fourth plinth, on the northwest corner, could be filled. It now hosts one of London's most idiosyncratic art displays, as artworks are commissioned specially for it, and change each year.

Nelson's statue overlooking the square

❷ Admiralty Arch

The Mall SW1. **Map** 13 B3. ⊖ Charing Cross.

Designed in 1911, this triple archway was part of Aston Webb's scheme to rebuild The Mall as a grand processional route honouring Queen Victoria. The arch effectively seals the eastern end of The Mall, although traffic passes through the smaller side gates, and separates courtly London from the hurly-burly of Trafalgar Square. The central gate is opened only for royal processions. There are plans to turn the Grade I-listed building into a five-star hotel.

Filming *Howard's End* at Admiralty Arch

❸ National Gallery

See pp108–11.

❹ St Martin-in-the-Fields

Trafalgar Sq WC2. **Map** 13 B3. **Tel** 020 7766 1100. ⊖ Charing Cross. **Open** daily. **Closed** for sightseeing during services (at which all are welcome). 🛈 daily; check website for details as times vary. ♿ 🔊 📷 🏛 London Brass Rubbing Centre **Open** 10am–6pm Mon–Wed, 10am–8pm Thu–Sat, 11:30am–5pm Sun (last brass rubbing entry 1 hr before close). Concerts: *See Entertainment p345.* 🌐 smitf.org

There has been a church on this site since the 13th century. Many famous people were buried here, including Charles II's mistress Nell Gwynne, and the painters William Hogarth and Joshua Reynolds. The present church was designed by James Gibbs and completed in 1726. In architectural terms it was one of the most influential ever built; it was much copied in the United States, where it became a model for the Colonial style of church-building. An unusual feature of St Martin's spacious interior is the royal box at gallery level on the left of the altar.

From 1914 until 1927 the crypt was used as a shelter for homeless soldiers and others; during World War II it was an air-raid shelter. Today it helps the homeless by providing a lunchtime soup kitchen. It also contains a café in the crypt, a religious bookshop, and the London Brass Rubbing Centre. Lunchtime and evening concerts are held in the church and in the café.

❺ National Portrait Gallery

2 St Martin's Place WC2. **Map** 13 B3. **Tel** 020 7306 0055. ⊖ Leicester Sq, Charing Cross. **Open** 10am–6pm Sat–Wed, 10am–9pm Thu & Fri. **Closed** 24–26 Dec. 🎟 for some special exhibitions. 🎦 ♿ Orange St entrance. 🔊 🖉 📷 🏛 🌐 npg.org.uk

Too often ignored in favour of the National Gallery next door, this fascinating museum recounts Britain's development through portraits of its main characters, giving faces to the names familiar from history books. The gallery's millennium development project, the Ondaatje Wing, which opened in May 2000, created 50 per

William Shakespeare portrait on display in the Ondaatje Wing

cent more exhibition and public space. There are pictures of kings, queens, poets, musicians, artists, thinkers, heroes and villains from all periods since the late 14th century. The oldest works, on the top floor, include a Hans Holbein cartoon of Henry VIII and paintings of some of his wives. Other important early portraits include one of Shakespeare (by John Taylor in 1651) and the Ditchley portrait of Elizabeth I. The collection runs roughly chronologically from the top floor down, with figures from the worlds of art, pop and politics of the 20th century represented on the first floor. Recent commissions are on the ground floor, which is also used for temporary exhibitions, such as the annual BP Portrait Award.

The gallery has a rooftop restaurant and an excellent shop selling books on art and literature, as well as an extensive range of cards, prints and posters featuring artworks from the main collection.

❻ Leicester Square

WC2. **Map** 13 B2. 🚇 Leicester Sq, Piccadilly Circus.

It is hard to imagine that this, the perpetually animated heart of the West End entertainment district, was once a fashionable place to live. Laid out in 1670 south of Leicester House, a long-gone royal residence, the square's occupants included the scientist Sir Isaac Newton and the artists Joshua Reynolds and William Hogarth. Reynolds made his fortune painting high society in his elegant salon at No. 46. Hogarth's house, in the southeast corner, became the Hôtel de la Sablionère in 1801, probably the area's first public restaurant.

In Victorian times, several popular music halls were established here, including the Empire (today the cinema on the same site perpetuates the name) and the Alhambra, replaced in 1937 by the Art Deco Odeon. A booth selling cut-price theatre tickets

(see p339) sits in the square. There is also a statue of Charlie Chaplin, which was unveiled in 1981. The Shakespeare statue dates from 1874.

Often crowded with visitors, the area around the Tube station can be very congested at times; the streets of Soho and Chinatown to the north can be a better bet for a meal or drink.

❼ Theatre Royal Haymarket

Haymarket SW1. **Map** 13 A3. **Tel** 020 7930 8800. 🚇 Piccadilly Circus. **Open** performances and guided tours (phone to book). 🚹 🌐 trh.co.uk

The fine frontage of this theatre, with its portico of six Corinthian columns, dates from 1821, when John Nash designed it as part of his plan for a stately route from Carlton House to Regent's Park. The interior is equally grand.

❽ Shaftesbury Avenue

W1. **Map** 13 A2. 🚇 Piccadilly Circus, Leicester Sq.

The main artery of London's theatreland, Shaftesbury Avenue has six theatres and three cinemas, all but one on its north side. This street was cut through an area of terrible slums between 1877 and 1886 in order to improve communications across the city's busy West End; it follows the route of a much earlier highway. It is named after the Earl of Shaftesbury (1801–85), whose attempts to improve housing conditions had helped some of the local poor. (The Earl is also commemorated by the Eros statue in Piccadilly Circus – see p94.) The Lyric Theatre, which was designed by C J Phipps, has been open for almost the same length of time as the avenue.

Multiplex cinemas, cafés and restaurants draw crowds to Leicester Square

❸ National Gallery

The National Gallery has flourished since its inception in the early 19th century. In 1824 the House of Commons was persuaded to buy 38 major paintings, including works by Raphael and Rubens, and these became the start of a national collection. Contributions by rich benefactors have today resulted in a collection of some 2,300 Western European paintings. The main gallery building was designed in Greek Revival style by William Wilkins and built in 1833–8. To its left lies the Sainsbury Wing, financed by the grocery family and completed in 1991.

Stairs and lift to lower galleries

★ **The Burlington House Cartoon** (c.1500)
The genius of Leonardo da Vinci glows through this chalk drawing of the Virgin and Child with St Anne and St John the Baptist.

Pigott Education Centre entrance

Stairs to lower floor

Link to main building

Stairs to lower floors

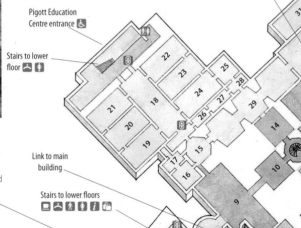

Doge Leonardo Loredan (1501–2)
Giovanni Bellini portrays this Venetian head of state as a serene father figure.

★ **The Baptism of Christ**
Piero della Francesca painted this tranquil masterpiece of early Renaissance perspective (1450s) for a church in his native Umbria.

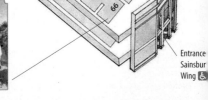

Entrance Sainsbur Wing

★ **Philip IV of Spain** (1631–2) One of Diego Velázquez's few signed paintings and the principal portrait of the king from that period.

★ **The Hay Wain** (1821) John Constable brilliantly caught the effect of distance and the changing light and shadow of a typically English cloudy summer day in this famous work.

VISITORS' CHECKLIST

Practical Information
Trafalgar Square WC2.
Map 13 B3.
Tel 020 7747 2885.
W nationalgallery.org.uk
Open 10am–6pm daily (9pm Fri).
Closed 24–26 Dec, 1 Jan.
Sainsbury Wing and Getty entrances. Major temporary exhibitions. Lectures, film presentations, exhibitions, special events.

Transport
Charing Cross, Leicester Sq, Piccadilly Circus. 3, 6, 9, 11, 12, 13, 15, 23, 24, 29, 88, 91, 139, 159, 176, 453. Charing Cross.

Central Hall

32 33 34 35 36 37 38 39 41 42 43 44 45 46

Getty entrance

Trafalgar Square entrance

At the Theatre (1876–7) Renoir was one of the greatest painters of the Impressionist movement. The theatre was a popular subject among artists of the time.

★ **The Ambassadors** The strange shape in the foreground of this Hans Holbein portrait (1533) is an anamorphic or distorted skull, a symbol of mortality.

Key to Floorplan
- 13th to 15th centuries
- 16th century
- 17th century
- 18th to early 20th centuries
- Special exhibitions
- Non-exhibition space

Gallery Guide
Most of the collection is housed on one floor divided into four wings. The paintings hang chronologically, with the earliest works (1250–1500) in the Sainsbury Wing. The North, West and East Wings cover 1500–1600, 1600–1700 and 1700–1900. Lesser paintings from all periods are on the lower floor.

Exploring the National Gallery

The National Gallery has over 2,300 paintings, most kept on permanent display. The collection ranges from early works by Cimabue, in the 13th century, to 19th-century Impressionists, but its particular strengths are in Dutch, early Renaissance Italian and 17th-century Spanish painting. The bulk of the British collections are housed in Tate Britain (see pp86–9), while Tate Modern specializes in international modern art (pp182–5).

The Adoration of the Kings (1564) by Pieter Bruegel the Elder

Early Renaissance (1250–1500): Italian and Northern European Painting

Three lustrous panels from the *Maestà*, Duccio's great altarpiece in Siena cathedral, are among the earliest paintings here. Other Italian works of the period include his outstanding *Madonna*.

The fine *Wilton Diptych* portraying England's Richard II is probably by a French artist. It displays the lyrical elegance of the International Gothic style that swept Europe.

Italian masters of this style include Pisanello and Gentile da Fabriano, whose *Madonna* often hangs beside another, by Masaccio – both date from the 1420s. Also shown are works by Masaccio's pupil, Fra Filippo Lippi, as well as Botticelli and Uccello. Umbrian paintings include Piero della Francesca's *Nativity* and *Baptism*, and there is an excellent collection of Mantegna, Bellini and other works from the Venetian and Ferrarese schools. Antonello da Messina's *St Jerome in his Study* has been mistaken for a Van Eyck; it is not hard to see why, when you compare it with Van Eyck's *Arnolfini Portrait*.

Important Netherlandish pictures, including some by Rogier van der Weyden and his followers, are also here, in the Sainsbury Wing.

St Jerome in his Study by Antonello da Messina (c.1475)

High Renaissance (1500–1600): Italian, Netherlandish and German Painting

Sebastiano del Piombo's *The Raising of Lazarus* was painted, with Michelangelo's assistance, to rival Raphael's great *Transfiguration*, which hangs in the Vatican in Rome. These and other well-known names of the High (or Late) Renaissance are extremely well represented. Exquisite Raphaels include the famous *Madonna of the Pinks*, only identified in the 1990s and bought by the gallery for £22 million in 2004. Look out for Leonardo da Vinci's charcoal cartoon of the *Virgin and Child*, and his second version of the *Virgin of the Rocks*. There are also tender and amusing works by Piero di Cosimo, and several Titians, including *Bacchus and Ariadne* – which the public found too bright and garish when it was first cleaned by the gallery in the 1840s.

The Netherlandish and German collections are weaker. Even so, they include *The Ambassadors*, a fine double portrait by Holbein; and Altdorfer's superb *Christ Taking Leave of his Mother*, bought by the gallery in 1980. There is also a Hieronymus Bosch of *Christ Mocked* (sometimes known as *The Crowning with Thorns*), and an excellent Bruegel, *The Adoration of the Kings*.

The Annunciation (early 1450s) by Fra Filippo Lippi

The Sainsbury Wing

Plans for the Sainsbury Wing, opened in 1991, provoked a storm of dissent. An incensed Prince Charles dubbed an early design "a monstrous carbuncle on the face of a much-loved friend". The final building, by Venturi, has drawn criticism from other quarters for being a derivative compromise.

Major temporary exhibitions are held here – check the gallery's website for details. Visitors can also find permanent collections on the Italian Renaissance.

Dutch, Italian, French and Spanish Painting (1600–1700)

The superb Dutch collection gives much of two rooms to Rembrandt. There are also works by Vermeer, Van Dyck (among them his equestrian portrait of King Charles I) and Rubens (including the popular *Chapeau de Paille*).

From Italy, the works of Carracci and Caravaggio are strongly represented, and Salvator Rosa has a glowering portrait entitled *Philosophy*.

French works on show include a magnificent portrait of Cardinal Richelieu by Philippe de Champaigne. Claude's seascape *Seaport with the Embarkation of the Queen of Sheba* hangs beside Turner's rival painting *Dido Building Carthage*, as Turner himself had instructed.

The Spanish collection has works by Murillo, Velázquez, Zurbarán and others.

Young Woman Standing at a Virginal (1670–72) by Jan Vermeer

The Scale of Love (1715–18) by Jean-Antoine Watteau

Venetian, French and English Painting (1700–1800)

One of the gallery's most famous 18th-century works is Canaletto's *The Stonemason's Yard*. Other Venetians here are Longhi and Tiepolo. The French collection includes Rococo masters such as Chardin, Watteau and Boucher.

Gainsborough's early work *Mr and Mrs Andrews* and *The Morning Walk* are favourites with visitors; his rival, Sir Joshua Reynolds, is represented by several of the portraits that secured his reputation. Hogarth's satirical *Marriage à-la-mode* series is another highlight.

English, French and German Painting (1800–1900)

The great age of 19th-century landscape painting is amply represented here, with fine works by Constable and Turner, including Constable's *The Hay Wain* and Turner's *The Fighting Temeraire*, as well as works by the French artists Corot and Daubigny.

Of Romantic art, there are Géricault's vivid works, *Horse Frightened by Lightning* and *A Shipwreck*, which possibly prefigures his *The Raft of the Medusa*. In contrast, the society portrait of *Madame Moitessier* by Ingres, though still Romantic, is more restrained and Classical.

Impressionists and other French avant-garde artists are well represented. Among the highlights are *The Water-Lily Pond* by Monet, Renoir's *At the Theatre* and Van Gogh's *Sunflowers*, not to mention one of Rousseau's famous jungle scenes, *Surprised!*, in which a tiger stalks explorers. In Seurat's *Bathers at Asnières* he did not originally use the pointillist technique he was later to invent, but subsequently reworked areas of the picture using dots of colour.

Sunflowers (1888) by Vincent van Gogh

9 Chinatown

Streets around Gerrard St W1. **Map** 13
A2. 🚇 Leicester Sq, Piccadilly Circus.

There has been a Chinese
community in London since
the 19th century. Originally it
was concentrated around the
East End docks at Limehouse,
where the opium dens of
Victorian melodrama were sited.
As the number of immigrants
increased in the 1950s, many
moved into Soho, where they
created an ever-expanding
Chinatown. It contains scores
of restaurants and aroma-filled
shops selling oriental produce.
Three Chinese arches straddle
Gerrard Street, where a vibrant,
colourful street festival, held in
late January or early February,
celebrates Chinese New
Year *(see p63)*.

Rows of jars containing Chinese sweets
in Chinatown

10 Charing Cross Road

WC2. **Map** 13 B2. 🚇 Leicester Sq.
See Shops and Markets pp316–17.

Once London's favourite street
for book lovers, with a clutch
of shops that were able to
supply just about any recent
volume, many of Charing Cross
Road's independent bookshops
have been forced to shut due
to rising rents. Several smaller,
second-hand bookshops
remain, however, including
Quinto & Francis Edwards
(see p326), which specializes
in antiquarian books, and a
good handful in nearby Cecil
Court. At the junction with
New Oxford Street rises the
1960s Centrepoint tower.
This junction is one of the key
sites for the huge Crossrail
underground rail project, so
expect traffic disruption.

Poster for the Palace Theatre, 1898

11 Palace Theatre

Shaftesbury Ave W1. **Map** 13 B2.
Tel Box office 0844 412 4656.
🚇 Leicester Sq. **Open** for performances only. *See Entertainment
pp340–41.* 🌐 nimaxtheatres.com/
palace-theatre

Most West End theatres are
disappointingly unassuming.
This one, which dominates the
west side of Cambridge Circus,
is a splendid exception, with its
terracotta exterior and opulent
furnishings. Completed as an
opera house in 1891, it became
a music hall the following year.
Now the theatre stages hit
shows such as *Spamalot* and
The Commitments; in 2016 it
premiered the eagerly awaited
Harry Potter and the Cursed Child,
based on a new J K Rowling story.

12 Soho Square

W1. **Map** 13 A1. 🚇 Tottenham
Court Rd.

Soon after it was laid out in 1681
this square enjoyed a brief reign
as the most fashionable address
in London. Originally it was called
King Square, after Charles II,
whose statue was erected in the
middle. The square had gone
out of fashion by the late 18th
century. Now surrounded by
bland office buildings, the
patches of green attract scores
of picnicking Soho office
workers at lunchtimes.

13 Berwick Street Market

W1. **Map** 13 A1. 🚇 Piccadilly Circus.
Open 9am–6pm Mon–Sat. *See Shops
and Markets p335.*

There has been a market here
since the 1840s. It was a Berwick
Street trader, Jack Smith, who
introduced grapefruit to London
in 1890. Today this is the West
End's best street market, at its
cheeriest and most crowded
during the lunch hour. The
freshest and least expensive
produce for miles around is to
be had here. There are also
some interesting shops, including Borovick's, which sells fabrics,
and a growing number of cafés
and restaurants. At its southern
end the street narrows into an
alley on which the famous strip
club Raymond Revuebar (in
retrospect, the comparatively
respectable face of Soho sleaze)
presented its "festival of erotica"
from 1958 to 2004.

Some of London's cheapest produce at Berwick Street Market

⑭ Carnaby Street

W1. **Map** 12 F2. ⊖ Oxford Circus.

During the 1960s this street was so much the hub of swinging London that the Oxford English Dictionary recognized the term "Carnaby Street" as meaning "fashionable clothing for young people". Today fashion shops can also be found on nearby streets such as Kingly Court and Fouberts Place.

⑮ Liberty

Regent St W1. **Map** 12 F2. ⊖ Oxford Circus. *See Shops and Markets p317.* 🌐 liberty.co.uk

Arthur Lasenby Liberty opened his first shop, selling oriental silks, on Regent Street in 1875.

Liberty's mock-Tudor façade

Among his first customers were the artists Ruskin and Rossetti. Soon Liberty prints and designs, by artists such as William Morris, epitomized the Arts and Crafts movement of the late 19th and early 20th centuries. They are still fashionable today.

The present purpose-built mock-Tudor building with its country-house feel dates from 1925.

Today the shop maintains its strong links with top quality craftsmanship of all kinds.

⑯ Photographers' Gallery

16-18 Ramillies St W1. **Map** 12 F1. ⊖ Oxford Circus. **Tel** 020 7087 9300. **Open** 10am–6pm Mon–Sat (till 8pm Thu), 11:30am–6pm Sun during exhibitions. 🚻 📷 after noon. 📷 📷 🌐 photonet.org.uk

This gallery exhibits work from both new and well-known photographers, as well as staging regular talks and events. The bookshop also sells cameras and prints.

The Heart of Soho

Old Compton Street is Soho's high street. Its shops and restaurants reflect the variety of people who have lived in the area over the centuries. These include many great artists, writers and musicians.

Maison Bertaux is known for producing delicious croissants and coffee and wonderful cakes.

Ronnie Scott's opened in 1959, and nearly all the big names of jazz have played here *(see pp347–9)*.

Bar Italia is a coffee shop situated under the room where John Logie Baird first demonstrated television in 1926. As a child, Mozart stayed next door with his family in 1764 and 1765.

The Coach and Horses pub has been a centre of bohemian Soho since the 1950s and is still popular.

Algerian Coffee Stores is one of Soho's oldest shops. Delicious aromas of the world's coffees fill the shop.

GREEK STREET

FRITH STREET

DEAN STREET

MOOR ST

OLD COMPTON STREET

WARDOUR STREET

ROMILLY STREET

Patisserie Valerie, now a chain, first opened in Soho in the 1920s.

St Anne's Church Tower is all that remains after a bomb destroyed the church in 1940.

The French House was frequented by Maurice Chevalier and General de Gaulle.

The Palace Theatre has hosted many successful musicals.

COVENT GARDEN AND THE STRAND

Site of a convent garden in medieval times, Covent Garden was laid out as an Italianate piazza in the 1630s by Inigo Jones, whose St Paul's Church still dominates the west side. The Piazza has been home to a market, in one form or another, since 1656. The elegant hall at its centre, dating from the 1830s, housed a produce market until 1974; now it is a bustling tourist magnet of shops, craft stalls and restaurants. The surrounding cobbled streets give the neighbourhood real charm, with traditional pubs tucked down alleyways and designer shops in converted warehouses. Particularly appealing are Neal's Yard, Floral Street and Seven Dials. Covent Garden is also synonymous with the Royal Opera House, while a parade of West End theatres lines the Strand and St Martin's Lane.

Sights at a Glance

Historic Streets and Buildings
- 1 The Piazza and Central Market
- 7 Neal Street and Neal's Yard
- 12 Savoy Hotel
- 14 Somerset House
- 16 Roman Bath
- 17 Bush House
- 20 Adelphi
- 21 Charing Cross

Museums and Galleries
- 3 London Transport Museum

Churches
- 2 St Paul's Church
- 13 Savoy Chapel
- 15 St Mary-le-Strand

Monuments and Statues
- 9 Seven Dials
- 18 Cleopatra's Needle

Famous Theatres
- 5 Theatre Royal Drury Lane
- 6 Royal Opera House
- 10 Wyndham's Theatre
- 11 Adelphi Theatre
- 22 The London Coliseum

Parks and Gardens
- 19 Victoria Embankment Gardens

Historic Pubs and Shopping Arcades
- 4 Lamb and Flag
- 8 Thomas Neal's

Restaurants see pp296–9
1. The 10 Cases
2. Atelier de Joël Robuchon
3. Belgo Centraal
4. Clos Maggiore
5. J Sheekey
6. The Northall
7. Rules
8. Sagar
9. Suda Thai
10. Terroirs
11. Thai Pot
12. Wahaca
13. Wild Food Café

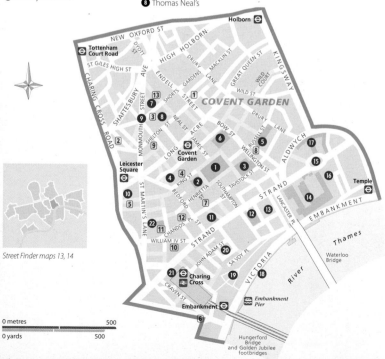

Street Finder maps 13, 14

0 metres 500
0 yards 500

◀ Enzo Piazotta's statue *The Young Dancer* (1988), Covent Garden

For keys to symbols *see back flap*

Street-by-Street: Covent Garden

Once an area of decaying streets and warehouses, Covent Garden came alive only when the fruit and vegetable market traders went about their business. After the market moved out in the 1970s, the area was renovated. Now, visitors, residents and street entertainers throng the Piazza, much as they would have done centuries ago.

❼ ★ Neal Street and Neal's Yard
A bright and colourful area of shops and cafés.

Covent Garden station

❽ Thomas Neal's
This airy complex houses designer shops and the Donmar theatre.

❾ Seven Dials
A replica of a 17th-century monument marks the junction.

Ching Court is a Post-Modernist courtyard by architect Terry Farrell.

St Martin's Theatre is home to the world's longest-running play: *The Mousetrap*.

Stanfords, established in 1852, is the largest map and guide retailer in the world *(see pp326–7)*.

❹ Lamb and Flag
Parts of this pub, one of London's oldest, date from 1623.

The Garrick Club is London's literary club.

New Row is lined with little shops and cafés.

Goodwin's Court is a charming, albeit small, alley lined with former Georgian shops.

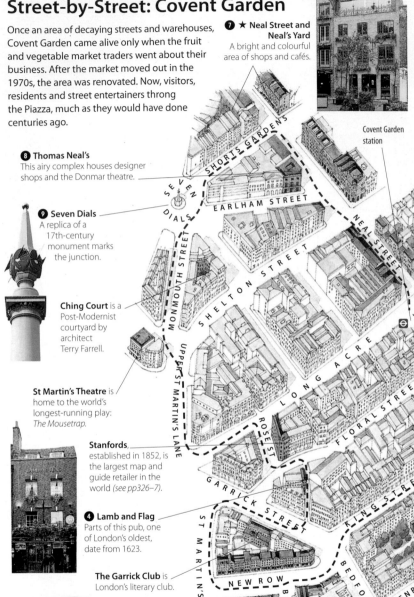

❶ ★ The Piazza and Central Market
Performers of all kinds – jugglers, clowns, acrobats and musicians – entertain the crowds in the square.

Locator Map
See Central London Map pp16–17

❻ Royal Opera House
Many of the world's greatest classical singers and dancers have appeared on its stage.

Bow Street Police Station housed London's first police force, the Bow Street Runners, in the 18th century. It closed in 1992.

❺ ★ Theatre Royal Drury Lane
A theatre has stood on this site since 1663, making it London's oldest theatre. The present theatre was built in 1812. It is owned by composer Andrew Lloyd Webber and stages popular musicals.

Boswells, now a coffee house, is where Dr Johnson first met his biographer, Boswell.

❸ ★ London Transport Museum
The history of the city's transport system is brought to life in this museum.

Jubilee Market sells clothes and bric-a-brac.

Key

— Suggested route

| 0 metres | 100 |
| 0 yards | 100 |

Rules is frequented by the rich and famous for its typically English food.

❷ ★ St Paul's Church
Despite appearances, Inigo Jones's church faces away from the Piazza – the entrance is through the churchyard.

❶ The Piazza and Central Market

Covent Garden WC2. **Map** 13 C2.
⊖ Covent Garden. ♿ but cobbled
streets. Street performers 10am–dusk
daily. *See Shops and Markets p319.*
Ⓦ **coventgardenlondonuk.com**

The 17th-century architect
Inigo Jones originally planned
this area to be an elegant
residential square, modelled
on the piazza of Livorno in
northern Italy. Today the
buildings on and around the
Piazza are almost entirely
Victorian. The covered central
market was designed by
Charles Fowler in 1833 for fruit
and vegetable wholesalers, the
glass and iron roof anticipating
the giant rail termini built later
in the century – for instance,
St Pancras *(see p134)* and
Waterloo *(see p195)*. It now
makes a magnificent shell for
an array of small shops selling
designer clothes, books, arts,
crafts, decorative items and
antiques, surrounded by
bustling market stalls
that continue south in
the neighbouring
Jubilee Hall, which
was built in 1903.

The colonnaded
Bedford Chambers, on
the north side, gives a
hint of Inigo Jones's plan,
although even they are
not original: they were
rebuilt and partially
modified in 1879.

Street entertainment
is a well-loved tradition
in the area; in 1662, diarist
Samuel Pepys wrote of
watching a Punch and
Judy show under the portico
of St Paul's Church.

A young street performer

West entrance to St Paul's

❷ St Paul's Church

Bedford St WC2. **Map** 13 C2. **Tel** 020
7836 5222. ⊖ Covent Garden. **Open**
8:30am–5pm Mon–Fri, some Sats
depending on events, 9am–1pm Sun.
🕊 1:20pm Tue & Wed, 11am Sun,
2nd Sun of the month 4pm evensong.
♿ Ⓦ **actorschurch.org**

Inigo Jones built this church
(completed in 1633) with the
altar at the west end, so as to
allow his grand portico, with
its two square and two
round columns, to face
east into the Piazza.
Clerics objected to
this unorthodox
arrangement, and the
altar was moved to its
conventional position at
the east end. Jones went
ahead with his original
exterior design. Thus the
church is entered from the
west, and the east portico is
a fake door, used now as
an impromptu stage for
street entertainers. In
1795, the interior was
destroyed by fire but was rebuilt
in Jones's airy, uncomplicated
style. Today the church is all that
is left of Jones's original plan for
the Piazza. St Paul's is known as

"The Actors' Church" and plaques
commemorate distinguished
men and women of the theatre.
A 17th-century carving by Grinling Gibbons on the west screen
is a memorial to the architect.

❸ London Transport Museum

The Piazza WC2. **Map** 13 C2. **Tel** 020
7379 6344. ⊖ Covent Garden.
Open 10am–6pm Sat–Thu,
11am–6pm Fri (last adm: 5:15pm).
♿ 📷 🏛 ♿ 🛍 book ahead.
Ⓦ **ltmuseum.co.uk**

You do not have to be a train
spotter or a collector of bus
numbers to enjoy this museum.
The intriguing collection is
housed in the picturesque
Victorian Flower Market, which
was built in 1872, and features
public transport from the past
and present.

The history of London's
transport is in essence a social
history of the capital. Bus, tram
and underground route patterns
first reflected the city's growth
and then promoted it; the
northern and western suburbs
began to develop only after their
Tube connections were built.
The museum houses a fine
collection of 20th-century
commercial art. London's bus
and train companies have
long been prolific patrons of
contemporary artists, and copies
of some of the finest posters on
display can be bought at the
well-stocked museum shop. They
include the innovative Art Deco
designs of E McKnight Kauffer, as
well as work by renowned artists
of the 1930s, such as Graham
Sutherland and Paul Nash.

A mid-18th-century view of the Piazza

This museum is excellent for children (and they can enter free of charge). There are plenty of hands-on exhibits, including a London bus and an Underground train that children can climb aboard and pretend to drive.

❹ Lamb and Flag

33 Rose St WC2. **Map** 13 B2. **Tel** 020 7497 9504. 🚇 Covent Garden, Leicester Sq. **Open** 11am–11pm Mon–Sat, noon–10:30pm Sun. *See Pubs and Bars p313.*

There has been an inn here since the 16th century, making the Lamb and Flag the oldest tavern in Covent Garden. Tucked away next to a narrow alleyway linking Garrick Street with Floral Street, the cramped bars are still largely unmodernized. A plaque concerns satirist John Dryden, who was attacked in the alley outside in 1679. He was set upon by hooligans sent by Charles II to uphold the honour of the Duchess of Portsmouth, one of his mistresses. Dryden had lampooned her in his verse. The upstairs bar is named after Dryden.

The pub is popular with both city centre workers and in-the-know tourists, who spill out into the alleyway.

❺ Theatre Royal Drury Lane

Catherine St WC2. **Map** 13 C2. **Tel** Box office 0844 412 4660; tours 0844 412 2957. 🚇 Covent Garden, Holborn. **Open** for tours and performances. 🎭 *See Entertainment p340* 🌐 theatreroyaldrurylane.co.uk

The first theatre on this site was built in 1663 as one of only two venues in London where drama could legally be staged. Nell Gwynne acted here. Three of the theatres built here since then burned down, including one designed by Sir Christopher Wren *(see p51)*. The present structure, by Benjamin Wyatt, was completed in 1812 and has one of the city's largest auditoriums. In the 1800s, it was famous for pantomimes – now

The Floral Hall, part of the Royal Opera House

it stages blockbuster musicals. It is called the Theatre Royal Drury Lane even though its entrance is on Catherine Street.

❻ Royal Opera House

Covent Garden WC2. **Map** 13 C2. **Tel** 020 7304 4000. 🚇 Covent Garden. **Open** for tours and performances (phone to check). *See Entertainment p344.* 🎭 🌐 roh.org.uk

Built in 1732, the first theatre on this site served as more of a playhouse, although many of Handel's operas and oratorios were premiered here. Like its neighbour the Theatre Royal Drury Lane, the building proved prone to fire and burned down in 1808 and again in 1856. The present opera house was designed in 1858 by E M Barry. John Flaxman's portico frieze, depicting tragedy and comedy, survived from the previous building of 1809.

The Opera House has had both high and low points during its history. In 1892, the first British performance of Wagner's Ring was conducted here by Gustav Mahler. Later, during World War I, the building was used as a storehouse by the government. Today, it is home to the Royal Opera and Royal Ballet companies – the best tickets can cost over £100 (though restricted-view tickets up in the "slips" can be had for as little as

£10). An extensive renovation project, completed in 1999, added a second auditorium, along with rehearsal rooms for the Royal Opera and Royal Ballet companies. Backstage tours are available.

❼ Neal Street and Neal's Yard

Covent Garden WC2. **Map** 13 B1. 🚇 Covent Garden. *See Shops and Markets p319.*

In this attractive street, former warehouses dating from the 19th century can be identified by the hoisting mechanisms high on their exterior walls. The buildings have been converted into shops, art galleries and restaurants. Off Neal Street in Short's Gardens is Neal's Yard Dairy, one of London's best cheese shops. Nearby, Neal's Yard itself is a bright and cheerful courtyard of independent restaurants and shops, most with vividly painted façades.

A specialist shop on Neal Street

Entrance to Thomas Neal's

➑ Thomas Neal's

Earlham St WC2. **Map** 13 B2.
🚇 Covent Garden, Leicester Sq.
Open 10am–7pm Mon–Sat, noon–
6pm Sun (individual shop times vary).
♿ ground floor only.

Located in an old converted
banana warehouse, this upscale
shopping complex offers an
interesting range of shops,
selling designer streetwear,
cosmetics, jewellery and
accessories. The Donmar
Warehouse theatre *(see p342)*
is also part of the complex,
staging must-see productions
such as *Coriolanus*.

➒ Seven Dials

Monmouth St WC2. **Map** 13 B2.
🚇 Covent Garden, Leicester Sq.

The pillar at this junction of seven
streets incorporates six sundials
(the central spike acted as a
seventh). It was installed in 1989
and is a copy of a 17th-century
monument. The original was
removed in the 19th century
because it had become a
notorious meeting place for
criminals, who operated in an
area that had become one of
London's most infamous slums.
    Today Seven Dials is a vibrant
shopping and dining area. The
cobbled streets and charming
hidden courtyards make the
neighbourhood particularly
attractive to wander around. Its
streets and alleyways are known
for one-off shops, boutiques,
high-end cosmetics stores,
restaurants and bars.

➓ Wyndham's Theatre

32 Charing Cross Rd, WC2. **Map** 13 B2.
Tel 0871 976 0072. 🚇 Leicester
Square. **Open** for performances only.
♿ 🌐 **wyndhams-theatre.com**
See Entertainment pp340–41.

Wyndham's Theatre opened its
doors in 1899 and takes its
name from Charles Wyndham
(1837–1919) – lauded as one of
the greatest actors of his day.
Designed by the architect
William Sprague, the Wyndham
was the first of seven theatres
he completed that year.
It boasts a Portland stone
exterior and a turquoise, cream
and gold interior decorated in
Louis XVI style, with a ceiling
painted in the style of Boucher.
    Many greats of British theatre
have graced the stage since
Wyndham himself: Vanessa
Redgrave, Sir Alec Guinness and
Sir John Gielgud among them.
It has also seen such talents as
Dame Judi Dench in *Madame de
Sade* and Jude Law as Hamlet.

⓫ Adelphi Theatre

Strand WC2. **Map** 13 C3. **Tel** 0844 412
4651. 🚇 Charing Cross, Embankment.
Open performances only. ♿
🌐 **adelphitheatre.co.uk**
See Entertainment pp340–41.

There has been a theatre on this
site since 1806, when the Sans
Pareil Theatre opened here.
It was set up by John Scott, a
wealthy tradesman, who was
helping to launch his daughter
on the stage. After several
refurbishments and name
changes, the current Adelphi
Theatre was remodelled in 1930
in Art Deco style by Ernest
Schaufelburg. His modernist
"straight-line" design resulted in
a building without curves. Note
the highly distinctive lettering
on the frontage, and the well-
kept lobby and auditorium,
with their stylized motifs.
    The Adelphi now stages a
variety of plays from *The Body-
guard*, featuring the music of
the late Whitney Houston, to
One Man, Two Guvnors, which
transferred to the Theatre Royal
Haymarket *(see p105)* in 2011.

⓬ Savoy Hotel

Strand WC2. **Map** 13 C2. **Tel** 020 7836
4343. 🚇 Charing Cross, Embankment.
🌐 **fairmont.com/savoy**

Pioneer of en-suite bathrooms
and electric lighting, the grand
Savoy was built in 1889 on
the site of the medieval Savoy
Palace. A £100 million lavish
refurbishment took place in
2008–10, incorporating both
the original Edwardian and the
later Art Deco style. The
forecourt is the only street
in Britain where traffic drives
on the right. Attached to the
hotel are the Savoy Theatre
built for the D'Oyly Carte opera,
famed for performing the
operas of Gilbert and Sullivan,
and the Simpson's-in-the-Strand
English restaurant.

Strand entrance to the Savoy Hotel

⓭ Savoy Chapel

Strand WC2. **Map** 13 C2. **Tel** 020
7836 7221. 🚇 Charing Cross,
Embankment. **Open** 9am–4pm
Mon–Thu. **Closed** Aug–Sep. 🕐 11am
Sun. 📷 💷 phone to book. 🌐
royalchapelsavoy.org

The first Savoy Chapel was
founded in the 16th century as the
chapel for the hospital set up by
Henry VII on the site of the old
Savoy Palace. Parts of the outside
walls date from 1512, but most of
the present building dates from
the mid-19th century. In 1890, it
was London's first church to be
electrically lit. It became the chapel
of the Royal Victorian Order in
1937, and is the Queen's private
chapel now. Nearby on Savoy Hill
were the first studios of the BBC.

⑭ Somerset House

Strand WC2. **Map** 14 D2. **Tel** 020 7845 4600. 🚇 Temple. Gallery & House **Open** 10am–6pm daily (last adm to galleries 5:30pm). **Closed** 1 Jan, 24–26 Dec. 🎫 free guided tours Tue, Thu and Sat. Ice rink: **Open** 2 months in winter. 🎫 call 0844 847 1520 for tickets. 🖥 🌐 **somersethouse.org.uk** Courtauld Institute of Art Gallery: **Tel** 020 7848 2777. 🎫 🖥 📷 ♿ 🌐 **courtauld.ac.uk** Embankment Galleries: 🎫 ♿ Tom's Kitchen: **Tel** 020 7845 4646.

This elegant Georgian building was the creation of Sir William Chambers. It was erected in the 1770s after the first Somerset House, a Renaissance palace built for the Duke of Somerset in the mid-16th century, was pulled down following years of neglect. The replacement was the first major building to be designed for use as government offices and has served to house the Navy Board (note that the classical grandeur of the Seamen's Waiting Hall and Nelson's Staircase are not to be missed), a succession of Royal Societies and, for a long time, the Inland Revenue. Today it is home to the Courtauld Institute of Art and its Gallery. The courtyard of Somerset House was closed to the public for nearly a century, but on the Inland Revenue's departure in 1997 it was rejuvenated, as part of a £48-million scheme. This created an attractive piazza with a 55-jet fountain. Films and concerts are often staged here in the summer, and for a few weeks in winter, there is an enchanting ice rink. From the courtyard, visitors can stroll through the South Building, where the highly regarded Tom's Kitchen restaurant overlooks the Thames, on to a riverside terrace that includes an open-air summer café and a restaurant, with pedestrian access to Waterloo Bridge and the South Bank.

Fountains at Somerset House

Located in Somerset House, but famous in its own right, is the spectacular **Courtauld Gallery**. Its exquisite collection of paintings has been displayed here since 1990 and owes its existence to the bequest of textile magnate and philanthropist Samuel Courtauld, one of the founders of the Art Institute. On display are works by Botticelli, Bruegel, Bellini and Rubens (including one of his early masterpieces, *The Descent from the Cross*), but it is the Courtauld's collection of Impressionist and Post-Impressionist paintings that draws the most attention. As well as works by Monet, Gauguin, Pissarro, Renoir and Modigliani, visitors can view Manet's *A Bar at the Folies-Bergères*, Van Gogh's *Self-Portrait with Bandaged Ear*, Cézanne's *The Card Players* and some evocative studies of dancers by Degas. In addition to its permanent collection, the Courtauld Institute hosts a series of world-class temporary exhibitions that take place throughout the year.

Also worth visiting are the modern, riverside **Embankment Galleries** occupying 750 square metres of exhibition space on the two lower floors of the south wing. The changing exhibition programme covers a broad range of contemporary arts, including photography, design, fashion and architecture.

Van Gogh's *Self-Portrait with Bandaged Ear* (1889) at the Courtauld

⑮ St Mary-le-Strand

Strand WC2. **Map** 14 D2. **Tel** 020 7836 3126. 🚇 Temple. **Open** 11am–4pm Tue–Thu, 10am–1pm Sun. 🕙 12:30pm Mon, Tue & Thu, 11am Sun. 📷 🌐 stmarylestrand.org

Now beached on a road island at the east end of the Strand, this pleasing church was consecrated in 1724. It was the first public building by James Gibbs, who designed St-Martin-in-the-Fields (see p106). Gibbs was influenced by Christopher Wren, but the exuberant external decorative detail here was inspired by the Baroque churches of Rome, where Gibbs studied. Its multi-arched tower is layered like a wedding cake, and culminates in a cupola and lantern. St-Mary-le-Strand is now the official church of the Women's Royal Naval Service.

St Mary-le-Strand

⑯ Roman Bath

5 Strand Lane WC2. **Map** 14 D2. **Tel** 020 7641 5264. 🚇 Temple, Embankment, Charing Cross. **Open** by appt only (1 week's notice required). 🚻 via Temple Pl.

This small bath may be seen from a full-length window on Surrey Street, by pressing a light switch on the outside wall. It is almost certainly not Roman, for there is no other evidence of Roman habitation in the

The north entrance of Bush House

immediate area. It is more likely to have been part of Arundel House, one of several palaces which stood on the Strand from Tudor times until the 17th century, when they were demolished for new building. In the 19th century the bath was open to the public for cold plunges, believed to be healthy.

⑰ Bush House

Aldwych WC2. **Map** 14 D2. 🚇 Temple, Holborn. **Closed** to the public.

Situated at the centre of the Aldwych crescent, this Neo-Classical building was first designed as manufacturers' showrooms by an American, Irving T Bush, and completed in 1935. It appears especially imposing when viewed from Kingsway, its dramatic north entrance graced with various statues symbolizing Anglo-American relations. From 1940 it was used as radio studios, and it served as the headquarters of the BBC World Service until 2012. To many Londoners it still symbolizes the BBC.

⑱ Cleopatra's Needle

Embankment WC2. **Map** 13 C3. 🚇 Embankment, Charing Cross.

Erected in Heliopolis in about 1500 BC, this incongruous pink granite monument is much older than London itself. Its inscriptions celebrate the deeds of the pharaohs of ancient Egypt. It was presented

to Britain by the then Viceroy of Egypt, Mohammed Ali, in 1819 and erected in 1878, shortly after the Embankment was built. It has a twin in New York's Central Park, behind the Metropolitan Museum of Art. The bronze sphinxes, added in 1882, are not Egyptian.

In its base is a Victorian time capsule of artifacts of the day, such as the day's newspapers, a rail timetable and photographs of 12 contemporary beauties.

⑲ Victoria Embankment Gardens

WC2. **Map** 13 C3. 🚇 Embankment, Charing Cross. **Open** 7:30am–dusk Mon–Sat, 9am–dusk Sun & public hols. 🚻 📷

This narrow sliver of a public park, created when the Embankment was built, boasts well-maintained flowerbeds, a clutch of statues of British worthies (including the Scottish poet Robert Burns) and, in summer, a season of concerts. Its main historical feature is the water gate at its northwest corner, which was built as a triumphal entry to the Thames for the Duke of Buckingham in 1626. It is a relic of York House, which used to stand on this site and was the home first of the Archbishops of York and then of the Duke. It is still in its original position and although the water used to lap against it, because of the Thames Embankment the gate is now a good 100 m (330 ft) from the river's edge.

Victoria Embankment Gardens

Dominating its neighbours, the office block above Charing Cross station

The façade of No. 7 Adam Street

⑳ Adelphi

Strand WC2. **Map** 13 C3. Ⓔ Embankment, Charing Cross. **Closed** to the public.

Adelphi is a pun on *adelphoi*, the Greek word for brothers – this area was once an elegant riverside residential development designed in 1772 by brothers Robert and John Adam. The name now refers to the Art Deco office block, its entrance adorned with N A Trent's heroic reliefs of workers at toil, which in 1938 replaced the Adams' much admired Palladian-style apartment complex. That destruction is now viewed as one of the worst acts of 20th-century official vandalism. A number of the Adams' surrounding buildings survive, notably No. 8, the ornate Royal Society for the encouragement of Arts, Manufactures & Commerce just opposite, which hosts many talks and events for its fellows and members of the public (see www.thersa.org). In the same exuberant idiom are Nos. 1–4 Robert Street, where Robert Adam lived for a time, and No. 7 Adam Street.

㉑ Charing Cross

Strand WC2. **Map** 13 C3. Ⓔ Charing Cross, Embankment.

The name derives from the last of 12 crosses erected by Edward I to mark the funeral route in 1290 of his wife, Eleanor of Castile, to Westminster Abbey. Today a 19th-century replica stands in the forecourt of Charing Cross station. Both the cross and the Charing Cross Hotel, built into the station frontage, were designed in 1863 by E M Barry, architect of the Royal Opera House *(see p119).*

Above the station platforms rises an assertive shopping centre and office block, completed in 1991. Designed by Terry Farrell, it resembles a giant ocean liner, with portholes looking on to Villiers Street, and is best seen from the river. The railway arches at the rear of the station have been modernized as a suite of small shops. From the station you can walk directly through to one of the Jubilee pedestrian bridges that run alongside the Hungerford rail bridge, crossing to the South Bank.

㉒ London Coliseum

St Martin's Lane WC2. **Map** 13 B3. **Tel** 020 7845 9300. Ⓔ Leicester Sq, Charing Cross. **Open** performances only. ♿ ▯ *See Entertainment p344.* Ⓦ eno.org

London's largest theatre and one of its most elaborate, this flamboyant building, topped with a large globe, was designed in 1904 by Frank Matcham and was equipped with London's first revolving stage. It was also the first theatre in Europe to have lifts. A former variety house, today it is the home of the English National Opera, and well worth visiting, if only for the Edwardian interior with its gilded cherubs and heavy purple curtains. In 2003, the original glass roof was restored, providing dramatic views over Trafalgar Square.

London Coliseum

BLOOMSBURY AND FITZROVIA

Since the beginning of the 20th century, Bloomsbury and Fitzrovia have been synonymous with literature, art and learning. The Bloomsbury Group of writers and artists were active from the early 1900s until the 1930s; the name Fitzrovia was invented by writers such as Dylan Thomas who drank in the Fitzroy Tavern. Bloomsbury still boasts the University of London, the British Museum and many fine Georgian squares. North of Bloomsbury, the former industrial hinterland of King's Cross is being transformed into one of the most exciting new districts in London.

Sights at a Glance

Historic Streets and Buildings
2 Bloomsbury Square
4 Russell Square
7 British Library
8 St Pancras International
9 Granary Square
14 Fitzroy Square
15 Charlotte Street

Museums
1 British Museum pp128–31
5 Charles Dickens Museum
6 Foundling Museum
12 Wellcome Collection
13 Grant Museum of Zoology
16 Pollock's Toy Museum

Churches
3 St George's, Bloomsbury
10 St Pancras Old Church and Garden
11 St Pancras Parish Church

Restaurants see pp301–2
1 Malabar Junction
2 Pied à Terre
3 Ragam
4 Roka
5 Salt Yard
6 Thai Metro

Street Finder maps 4, 5, 6, 13

0 metres   500
0 yards   500

BLOOMSBURY

◄ The Great Court at the British Museum

For keys to symbols see back flap

Street-by-Street: Bloomsbury

This so-called "brainy quarter" is dominated by the grand British Museum and, to its north, the main campus of University College London. The area is full of Georgian buildings (formerly the homes of some of London's prolific writers and greatest minds) and pretty squares, as well as a good handful of bookshops to browse.

The Senate House (1932) is the administrative headquarters of the University of London. It holds a priceless library.

Bedford Square is one of London's best-preserved Georgian squares.

❶ ★ British Museum
Designed in the mid-19th century, this popular museum attracts some five million visitors a year.

Key

— Suggested route

| 0 metres | 100 |
| 0 yards | 100 |

Museum Street is lined with small cafés and shops selling old books, prints and antiques.

Pizza Express occupies a charming and little-altered Victorian dairy.

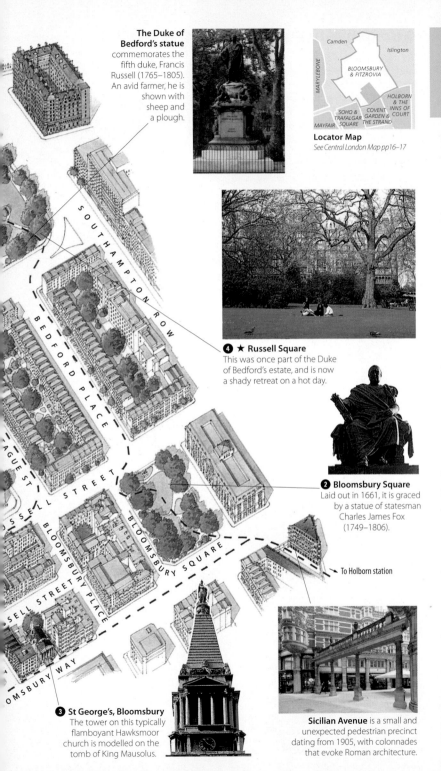

The Duke of Bedford's statue commemorates the fifth duke, Francis Russell (1765–1805). An avid farmer, he is shown with sheep and a plough.

Locator Map
See Central London Map pp16–17

❹ ★ **Russell Square**
This was once part of the Duke of Bedford's estate, and is now a shady retreat on a hot day.

❷ **Bloomsbury Square**
Laid out in 1661, it is graced by a statue of statesman Charles James Fox (1749–1806).

To Holborn station

❸ **St George's, Bloomsbury**
The tower on this typically flamboyant Hawksmoor church is modelled on the tomb of King Mausolus.

Sicilian Avenue is a small and unexpected pedestrian precinct dating from 1905, with colonnades that evoke Roman architecture.

❶ British Museum

The oldest public museum in the
world, the British Museum was
established in 1753 to house
the collections of the physician
Sir Hans Sloane (1660–1753), who
also helped create the Chelsea
Physic Garden *(see p201)*. Sloane's

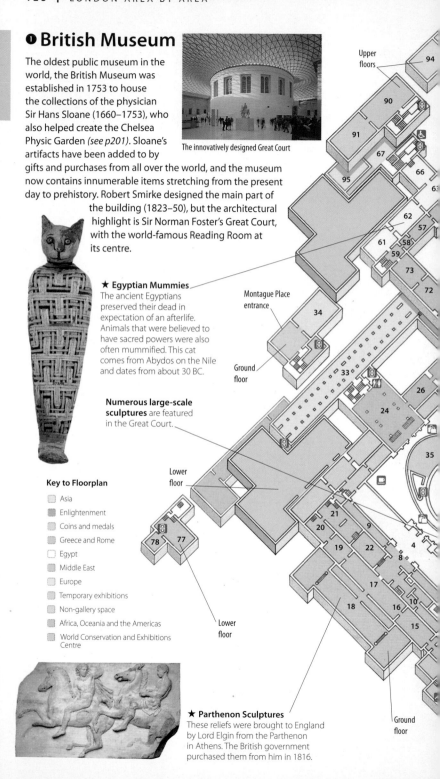

The innovatively designed Great Court

artifacts have been added to by
gifts and purchases from all over the world, and the museum
now contains innumerable items stretching from the present
day to prehistory. Robert Smirke designed the main part of
the building (1823–50), but the architectural
highlight is Sir Norman Foster's Great Court,
with the world-famous Reading Room at
its centre.

Upper
floors

94

90

91

67

66

95

63

62

57

61

58

59

73

72

★ **Egyptian Mummies**
The ancient Egyptians
preserved their dead in
expectation of an afterlife.
Animals that were believed to
have sacred powers were also
often mummified. This cat
comes from Abydos on the Nile
and dates from about 30 BC.

Montague Place
entrance

34

Ground
floor

33

26

24

35

**Numerous large-scale
sculptures** are featured
in the Great Court.

Lower
floor

Key to Floorplan

☐ Asia
☐ Enlightenment
☐ Coins and medals
☐ Greece and Rome
☐ Egypt
☐ Middle East
☐ Europe
☐ Temporary exhibitions
☐ Non-gallery space
☐ Africa, Oceania and the Americas
☐ World Conservation and Exhibitions
    Centre

78

77

21

20

9

19

22

4

8

17

10

18

16

15

Lower
floor

★ **Parthenon Sculptures**
These reliefs were brought to England
by Lord Elgin from the Parthenon
in Athens. The British government
purchased them from him in 1816.

Ground
floor

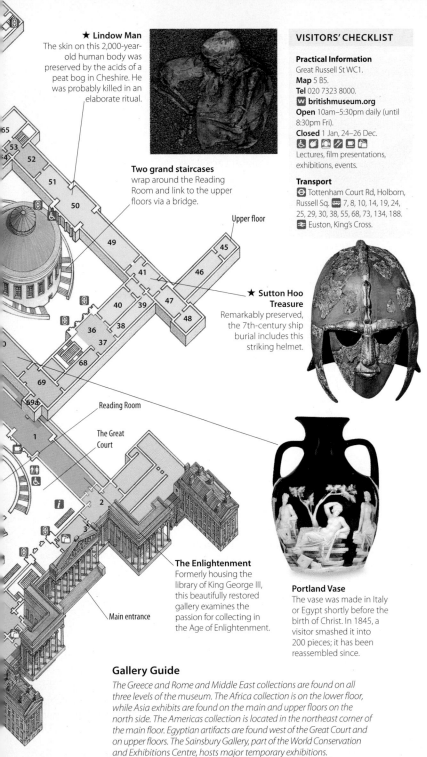

★ **Lindow Man**
The skin on this 2,000-year-old human body was preserved by the acids of a peat bog in Cheshire. He was probably killed in an elaborate ritual.

Two grand staircases
wrap around the Reading Room and link to the upper floors via a bridge.

Upper floor

★ **Sutton Hoo Treasure**
Remarkably preserved, the 7th-century ship burial includes this striking helmet.

Reading Room

The Great Court

The Enlightenment
Formerly housing the library of King George III, this beautifully restored gallery examines the passion for collecting in the Age of Enlightenment.

Main entrance

Portland Vase
The vase was made in Italy or Egypt shortly before the birth of Christ. In 1845, a visitor smashed it into 200 pieces; it has been reassembled since.

Gallery Guide

The Greece and Rome and Middle East collections are found on all three levels of the museum. The Africa collection is on the lower floor, while Asia exhibits are found on the main and upper floors on the north side. The Americas collection is located in the northeast corner of the main floor. Egyptian artifacts are found west of the Great Court and on upper floors. The Sainsbury Gallery, part of the World Conservation and Exhibitions Centre, hosts major temporary exhibitions.

Exploring the British Museum's Collections

The museum's immense hoard of treasure spans two million years of history and culture. Its 94 galleries, which stretch 2.5 miles (4 km), cover civilizations from ancient Egypt and Assyria to modern Japan.

1st-century BC bronze helmet dredged up from the Thames

Prehistoric and Roman Britain

Relics of prehistoric Britain are on display in six separate galleries. The most impressive items include the gold "Mold Cape", a ceremonial Bronze Age cape found in Wales; an antlered headdress worn by hunter-gatherers some 9,000 years ago; and "Lindow Man", a 1st-century AD sacrificial victim who lay preserved in a bog until 1984. Some superb Celtic metalwork is also on show, alongside the silver Mildenhall Treasure and other Roman pieces. The Hinton St Mary mosaic (4th century AD) features a roundel containing the earliest known British depiction of Christ.

Europe

The spectacular Sutton Hoo ship treasure, the burial hoard of a 7th-century Anglo-Saxon king, is on display in Room 41. This superb find, made in 1939, revolutionized our understanding of Anglo-Saxon life and ritual. The artifacts include a helmet and shield, Celtic hanging bowls, the remains of a lyre, and gold and garnet jewellery.

Adjacent galleries contain a collection of clocks, watches and scientific instruments. Some exquisite timepieces are on view, including a 400-year-old clock from Prague, designed as a model galleon;

in its day it pitched, played music, and even fired a cannon. Also nearby are the famous 12th-century Lewis chessmen. Baron Ferdinand Rothschild's (1839–98) remarkably varied treasures, largely from the Renaissance and known as the Waddesdon Bequest, are beautifully displayed in Room 2a.

Gilded brass late 16th-century ship clock from Prague

Ancient Near East

There are numerous galleries devoted to the Western Asian collections, covering 7,000 years of history. The most famous items are the 7th-century BC Assyrian reliefs from King Ashurbanipal's palace at Nineveh, but of equal interest are two large human-headed bulls from 7th-century BC Khorsabad, and the Black Obelisk of Shalmaneser III, which com-memorates the Assyrian king. The upper floors contain pieces from ancient Sumeria, part of the Oxus Treasure (which lay buried for over 2,000 years), and the museum's collection of clay

cuneiform tablets. The earliest of these are inscribed with the oldest known pictographs (c.3300 BC). Also of interest is a skull discovered in Jericho in the 1950s; augmented with shells and lime plaster, the skull belonged to a hunter who lived in the area some 7,000 years ago.

Ornamental detail from a Sumerian queen's lyre

Egypt

In Room 4 are Egyptian sculptures. These include a fine red granite head of a king, thought to depict Amenophis III, and a colossal statue of King Rameses II. Also on show is the Rosetta Stone, used by Jean-François Champollion (1790–1832) as a key for deciphering Egyptian hieroglyphs. An extraordinary array of mummies, jewellery and Coptic art can also be found upstairs. The various instruments that were used by embalmers to preserve bodies before entombment are all displayed. Room 61 houses paintings from the lost tomb-chapel of Nebamun.

Part of a colossal statue of Rameses II, the 13th-century BC Egyptian pharaoh

Greece and Rome

The Greek and Roman collections include the museum's most famous treasure, the Parthenon sculptures. These 5th-century BC reliefs were once part of a marble frieze that decorated the Parthenon, the temple to Athena on the Acropolis in Athens. Much of it was ruined in battle in 1687, and most of what survived was removed between 1801 and 1804 by the British diplomat Lord Elgin, and sold to the British nation. Other highlights include the Nereid Monument and sculptures and friezes from the Mausoleum at Halicarnassus.

Ancient Greek vase illustrating the mythical hero Hercules's fight with a bull

The beautiful 1st-century BC cameo-glass Portland Vase is located in the Roman Empire section.

Asia

The Chinese collection boasts fine porcelain and ancient Shang bronzes (c.1500–1050 BC). Particularly impressive are the ceremonial ancient Chinese bronze vessels, with their enigmatic animal-head shapes.

In the Sir Percival David gallery the Chinese ceramics date from the 10th to early 20th centuries. They range from delicate tea bowls to a model pond, which is almost a thousand years old.

Adjacent to these is one of the world's finest collections of sculpture from the Indian subcontinent. A major highlight is an assortment of sculpted reliefs, which once covered the walls of the Buddhist temple at Amaravati, and which recount stories from the life of the Buddha. A Korean section contains some gigantic works of Buddhist art.

The museum's collection of Islamic art, including a jade terrapin found in a water tank,

Statue of the Hindu god Shiva as Nataraja, or Lord of the Dance (11th century AD)

can be found in Room 34. Rooms 92 to 94 house the Japanese galleries, with a traditional teahouse in Room 92.

Africa

An interesting collection of African sculptures, textiles and graphic art can also be found in Room 25 on the lower floor of the museum. Famous bronzes from the Kingdom of Benin stand alongside modern African prints, paintings, drawings and colourful fabrics.

The Great Court and Reading Room

Surrounding the Reading Room of the former British Library, the £100-million Great Court opened to coincide with the new millennium. Designed by Sir Norman Foster, the court is covered by a tessellated glass roof, creating London's first indoor public square. The Reading Room is arguably one of the best-known libraries in the world, not least for the list of famous names who have studied here, including Karl Marx, Mahatma Gandhi and George Bernard Shaw. The interior was restored to its original design, and has been used for a variety of temporary exhibitions. However, further remedial work has necessitated closing it again; it may be worth checking in advance that it has reopened. From the outside, though, it remains an impressive sight, housed in a multi-level construction which partly supports the roof, and which also contains bookshops, cafés and restaurants.

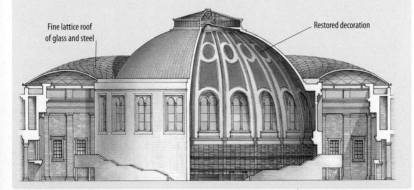
Fine lattice roof of glass and steel

Restored decoration

❷ Bloomsbury Square

WC1. **Map** 5 C5. 🌐 Holborn.

This is the oldest of the Bloomsbury squares. It was laid out in 1661 by the fourth Earl of Southampton, who owned the land. None of the original buildings survives and the square's shaded garden is encircled by a busy one-way traffic system. (There is a car park below the square that, unusually for central London, nearly always has a free space or two.)

The literary and artistic avant-garde Bloomsbury Group lived in the area during the early years of the last century. They included prominent figures such as novelists Virginia Woolf and E M Forster, biographer Lytton Strachey and artists Vanessa Bell, Duncan Grant and Dora Carrington. Look out for their individual plaques throughout the area (see p43).

The simple, tranquil interior of St George's church in Bloomsbury

❸ St George's, Bloomsbury

Bloomsbury Way WC1. **Map** 13 B1. **Tel** 020 7242 1979. 🌐 Holborn, Tottenham Court Rd, Russell Sq. **Open** 1–4pm daily (times may vary – call to check). 🕐 1:10pm Wed & Fri, 10:30am Sun. Recitals. 🔔 🎫 by appointment. 🅦 stgeorgesbloomsbury.org.uk

A slightly eccentric church, St George's was designed by Nicholas Hawksmoor, Wren's pupil, and completed in 1730. It was built as a place of worship for the prosperous residents of newly developed, fashionable Bloomsbury. The layered tower,

The flamboyant Russell Hotel on Russell Square

modelled on the tomb of King Mausolus (the original mausoleum in Turkey) and topped by a statue of George I, was for a long time an object of derision – the king was thought to be presented too heroically. In 1913, the funeral of Emily Davison, the suffragette who threw herself under King George V's horse, was held here.

Restored in 2006, it is now a thriving parish church, concert venue and community art centre.

❹ Russell Square

WC1. **Map** 5 B5. 🌐 Russell Sq. 🖥 **Open** 7:30am–10pm daily.

One of London's largest squares, Russell Square is a lively place, with a fountain, café and traffic roaring around its perimeter. The east side boasts perhaps the best of the Victorian grand hotels to survive in the capital. Charles Doll's Russell Hotel, which was opened in 1900, is a wondrous confection of red terracotta, with colonnaded balconies and prancing cherubs beneath the main columns. The exuberance is continued in the lobby, faced with marble of many colours.

The poet T S Eliot worked at the west corner of the square, from 1925 until 1965, in what were the offices of publishers Faber and Faber.

❺ Charles Dickens Museum

48 Doughty St WC1. **Map** 6 D4. **Tel** 020 7405 2127. 🌐 Chancery Lane, Russell Sq. **Open** 10am–5pm daily (last admission 4pm). **Closed** 1 Jan, 25 & 26 Dec, and occasionally Sat for events (phone to check). 🐾 🎫 🔔 ground floor only. 🎫 🖥 📷 🅦 dickensmuseum.com

The novelist Charles Dickens lived in this early 19th-century terraced house for three of his most productive years (from 1837 to 1839). *Oliver Twist* and *Nicholas Nickleby* were entirely written here, and *Pickwick Papers* was finished. Although Dickens had a number of London homes throughout his lifetime, this is the only one to have survived.

In 1923, it was acquired by the Dickens Fellowship and it is now a well-conceived museum with some of the principal rooms laid out exactly as they were in Dickens' time. Others have been adapted to display a varied collection of articles associated with him.

The museum houses over 100,000 exhibits, including manuscripts, paintings and personal items; papers and pieces of furniture from his other homes; and first editions of many of his best-known works.

❻ Foundling Museum

40 Brunswick Square WC1. **Map** 5 C4. **Tel** 020 7841 3600. ☻ Russell Square. **Open** 10am–5pm Tue–Sat, 11am–5pm Sun. **Closed** 1 Jan, 24–26 & 31 Dec. 🎭 🎟 🏛 ⬛ 📷 Coram's Fields: Guilford St WC1. **Open** 9am–dusk. 🅦 foundlingmuseum.org.uk

In 1722, Captain Thomas Coram, a retired sailor and shipbuilder recently returned from the Americas and horrified by the poverty on London's streets, vowed to establish a refuge for abandoned children, where they could be cared for, educated and placed in private homes. Assisted by his friend, the artist William Hogarth, and the composer George Frideric Handel, Coram worked tirelessly to raise funds for the refuge. Finally in 1739, after much petitioning of George II, he was granted a Royal Charter to establish a Foundling Hospital. Hogarth donated paintings to the hospital and other artists followed suit, creating Britain's first art gallery. The wealthy were encouraged to view the works of art and the children, in the hope that they would donate funds.

The first site of the hospital was at Hatton Garden, though it moved to near this site in 1745. The original buildings were demolished in the 1920s, with just the entrance arcades remaining, though the interiors of two of the 18th-century rooms were saved and installed in the new building.

On the ground floor, the story of the many children cared for in the Foundling Hospital is told. The nationally important collection of 18th-century paintings, sculpture, furniture and interiors is displayed on the first floor, and a room dedicated to Handel is on the top floor. The museum also has excellent temporary exhibitions and concerts.

Next to the museum, with its entrance on Guilford Street, is Coram's Fields, a unique park for children and young people (aged under 16). All adults, however, must be accompanied by children. It includes a youth centre, a city farm and a café.

Portrait of Captain Coram (1740) by William Hogarth

❼ British Library

96 Euston Rd NW1. **Map** 5 B3. **Tel** 01937 546 060. ☻ King's Cross St Pancras. Building and Treasures Gallery **Open** 9:30am–6pm Mon, Fri & Sat, 9:30am–8pm Tue–Thu, 11:30am–5pm Sun. Temporary exhibition galleries **Open** 9:30am–6pm Mon–Fri (to 8pm Tue), 9:30am–5pm Sat, 11am–5pm Sun. Regular events. 🎭 for some special exhibitions. 📷 twice daily; advance booking recommended. 🏛 🎟 ⬛ ✏ 📷 🅦 bl.uk

This late 20th-century building houses the national collection of books, manuscripts and maps, as well as the British Library Sound Archive. Designed in red brick by Sir Colin St John Wilson, it opened in 1997 after nearly 20 years of construction and despite controversial cost over-runs it is now widely admired. A copy of nearly every printed book in the UK is held here – more than 14 million – and can be consulted by those with a reader's ticket. There are also exhibition galleries open to all. In the Treasures Gallery, visitors may view some of the library's most precious items, including the Lindisfarne Gospels. Other rare volumes include a Gutenberg Bible and Shakespeare's First Folio.

❽ St Pancras International

Euston Rd NW1. **Map** 5 B2. **Tel** 020 7843 7688. ☻ King's Cross St Pancras. *See Getting to London p368.* 🅦 stpancras.com

St Pancras, the London terminal for Eurostar rail services to continental Europe, is easily the most spectacular of the three rail termini along Euston Road, thanks to the extravagant frontage, in red-brick ginger-bread Gothic, of the former Midland Grand Hotel, opened in 1874 as one of the most sumptuous hotels of its time. By 1935, now too expensive to run, it became office space. It was threatened with demolition in the 1960s but saved by a campaign led by the poet John Betjeman (there is a statue of him on the upper level of the station concourse). The hotel has since been restored.

The massive St Pancras Renaissance Hotel above St Pancras Station

St Martin's College of Art in its new home on Granary Square

❾ Granary Square

N1C. **Map** 5 B1 🚇 King's Cross St Pancras. Visitor centre: 11 Stable St. **Tel** 020 3479 1795. **Open** 10am–5pm Mon–Fri, 10am–4pm Sat 🎫 from the visitor centre; book online.
W **kingscross.co.uk**

The formerly drab area north of King's Cross station has been radically transformed into a cultural and social hub, with several major building projects still ongoing. The focus of the area is attractive Granary Square, which leads down to Regent's Canal. The square is dominated by magnificent fountains that dance to an ever-changing pattern of lights, a magnet for small children on hot days.

Adding to the appeal of this increasingly popular area are green spaces, such as Lewis Cubitt Park, just to the north of the square; exciting installations (including an outdoor swimming pond); a regular food market; and a number of good restaurants.

❿ St Pancras Old Church and Graveyard

Pancras Rd NW1. **Map** 5 A2. **Tel** 020 7424 0724. 🚇 King's Cross St Pancras. **Open** 9am–dusk daily (church until around 3pm; check in advance). ✝ 7pm Tue, 9:30am Sun. ♿ Recitals 1:15pm Thu. **W** **sosstpancras.org**

This site is thought to have been a place of Christian worship since the 4th century –

there are fragments of Roman tile embedded in one of the walls and some Norman masonry – though much of the church building dates from a substantial renovation in 1847.

St Pancras Old Church's graveyard, now a pleasant green space with a few monuments dotted around, was until the 1850s one of the largest burial sites in London. With the arrival of the railways, half the site was built over, and gravestones were moved – hence the remarkable sight of closely packed gravestones embedded into the base of a tree. This is the Hardy Tree, named after author Thomas Hardy, who worked as an architectural technician on the site. Sir John Soane (see pp140–41) designed his own family mausoleum, which is said to have inspired Sir Giles Gilbert Scott's design of London's famous and once-ubiquitous red telephone box.

Caryatids in classical Greek style support the portico of St Pancras Church

⓫ St Pancras Parish Church

Euston Rd NW1. **Map** 5 B3. **Tel** 020 7388 1461. 🚇 Euston. **Open** 8am–6pm Mon–Thu (check ahead. ✝ 8am, 10am & 6pm Sun. ♿ Recitals 1:15pm Thu.
W **stpancraschurch.org**

This is a stately Greek Revival church of 1822 designed by William Inwood and his son Henry, both great fans of Athenian architecture. The design is based on the Erechtheion at the Acropolis in Athens, and even the wooden pulpit stands on miniature Ionic columns of its own. The long galleried interior has a dramatic severity appropriate to the church's style. The female figures on the northern outer wall were originally taller than they are now: a chunk had to be taken out of the middle of each to make them fit under the roof they were meant to support.

The church hosts a festival of contemporary church music in May, and art exhibitions are sometimes mounted in the atmospheric crypt.

⓬ Wellcome Collection

183 Euston Rd NW1. **Map** 5 A4. **Tel** 020 7611 2222. 🚇 Euston, King's Cross, Warren St. **Open** 10am–6pm Tue–Sat (to 10pm Thu & first Fri of month), 11am–6pm Sun, noon–6pm public hols. **Closed** 1 Jan, 24–26 Dec. ♿ ⏺ 📷
W **wellcomecollection.org**

Sir Henry Wellcome (1853–1963) was a pharmacist, entrepreneur and collector. His passionate interest in medicine and its history, as well as ethnography and archaeology, led him to gather more than one million objects from around the world. The Wellcome Collection is a £30-million public venue used to house his vast collection. It also hosts events and exhibitions that explore medicine, art and the human condition.

Exhibits range from the bizarre to the beautiful, the ancient to the futuristic.

More than 900 objects are on permanent display, including a used guillotine blade and Napoleon's toothbrush. The Medicine Now exhibit includes works by contemporary artists created in response to current medical concerns, from swine flu to obesity. The Wellcome Library, on the upper floors, is the world's largest collection of books devoted to the history of medicine.

No. 29 Fitzroy Square, formerly the home of literary giants

⓭ The Grant Museum of Zoology

21 University St WC1. **Map** 5 A4. **Tel** 020 3108 2052. ⊖ Warren St, Goodge St, Russell Square **Open** 1–5pm Mon–Sat. ⓦ **ucl.ac.uk/museums**

The heart of Bloomsbury's university district can be found in Gower Street: on one side of the road is the Neo-Classical main building of University College London, designed by William Wilkins in 1827, and opposite is the original terracotta building of University College Hospital (now used by the university). UCL owns several museum collections, including the Grant Museum of Zoology, which was established in 1828. It houses around 68,000 specimens – animal skeletons, taxidermy, mounted insects and creatures preserved in jars (including a jar of 18 preserved moles) – in crowded wooden cases, making it an atmospheric, occasionally gruesome, insight into the world of 19th-century science and collecting. Other university museums include a large Egyptian collection in the Petrie Museum and an art gallery.

⓮ Fitzroy Square

W1. **Map** 4 F4. ⊖ Warren St, Great Portland St.

Designed by Robert Adam in 1794, the square's south and east sides survive in their original form, in dignified Portland stone. Blue plaques record the homes of many artists, writers and statesmen: George Bernard Shaw and Virginia Woolf both lived at No. 29 – although not at the same time. Shaw gave money to the artist Roger Fry to establish the Omega workshop at No. 33 in 1913. Here young artists were paid a fixed wage to produce Post-Impressionist furniture, pottery, carpets and paintings for sale to the public.

⓯ Charlotte Street

W1. **Map** 5 A5. ⊖ Goodge St.

As the upper classes moved west from Bloomsbury in the early 19th century, a flood of artists and European immigrants moved in, turning the area into a northern extension to Soho (see pp102–13). The artist John Constable lived and worked for many years at No. 76. The Fitzroy Tavern at No.16 was a popular drinking den for writers and artists, including Dylan Thomas, between the wars.

Some of the area's residents established small workshops to service the clothing shops on

Telecom Tower

Oxford Street and the furniture stores on Tottenham Court Road. Others set up reasonably priced restaurants. The street still boasts a great variety of eating places. It is overshadowed from the north by the 189-m (620-ft) Telecom Tower, built in 1964 as a vast TV, radio and telecommunications aerial (see p34).

⓰ Pollock's Toy Museum

1 Scala St W1 (entrance on Whitfield St). **Map** 5 A5. **Tel** 020 7636 3452. ⊖ Goodge St, Warren St, Tottenham Court Rd. **Open** 10am–5pm Mon–Sat. **Closed** public hols. 🚫 📷 ⓦ pollockstoys.com

Benjamin Pollock was a renowned maker of toy theatres in the late 19th and early 20th centuries, and counted the novelist Robert Louis Stevenson as an enthusiastic customer. The museum opened in Monmouth Street in Covent Garden in 1956 and relocated here in 1969. This is a child-sized museum created in two 18th- and 19th-century houses. The small rooms have been filled with a fascinating assortment of historic toys from all over the world. There are dolls, puppets, trains, cars, construction sets, a fine rocking horse and a splendid collection of mainly Victorian doll's houses. Parents beware – the exit leads you through a toyshop.

The attractive front of Pollock's Toy Museum

HOLBORN AND THE INNS OF COURT

This area was traditionally home to the legal and journalistic professions, but while the law is still practised here, in the Royal Courts of Justice and the Inns of Court, the national newspapers left Fleet Street in the 1980s. Several buildings here predate the Great Fire of 1666 (see pp26–7). These include the Old Curiosity Shop, the superb façade of Staple Inn and the interior of Middle Temple Hall. Two quirky collections stand on either side of Lincoln's Inn Fields: the Hunterian Museum of surgery and Sir John Soane's Museum, a treasure trove of art, antiquities and architectural models.

Sights at a Glance

Historic Buildings, Sights and Streets
- ② Lincoln's Inn
- ⑤ Old Curiosity Shop
- ⑦ Royal Courts of Justice
- ⑧ Law Society
- ⑩ Fleet Street
- ⑪ Temple
- ⑭ Dr Johnson's House
- ⑯ Holborn Viaduct
- ⑱ Hatton Garden
- ⑲ Staple Inn
- ㉑ Gray's Inn

Museums and Galleries
- ① Sir John Soane's Museum
- ④ Hunterian Museum

Churches
- ⑥ St Clement Danes
- ⑫ St Bride's
- ⑮ St Andrew, Holborn
- ⑰ St Etheldreda's Church

Monuments
- ⑨ Temple Bar Memorial

Parks and Gardens
- ③ Lincoln's Inn Fields

Pubs and Bars
- ⑬ Ye Olde Cheshire Cheese

Shops
- ⑳ London Silver Vaults

☐ Restaurants see pp301–2
1 The Chancery
2 De Palo's
3 Vanilla Black
4 The White Swan

Street Finder maps 6, 14

0 metres 500
0 yards 500

◄ Gothic façade of the Royal Courts of Justice

For keys to symbols see back flap

Street-by-Street: Lincoln's Inn

This is calm, dignified, legal London, packed with history and interest. Lincoln's Inn, adjoining one of the city's first residential squares, has buildings dating back to the late 15th century. Dark-suited lawyers carry bundles of briefs between their offices here and the Neo-Gothic Law Courts. Nearby is the Temple, another historic legal district, with a famous 13th-century round church.

❶ ★ Sir John Soane's Museum
The Georgian architect made this his London home and left it, with his collection, to the nation.

To Kingsway

LINCOLN'S INN FIELDS

LINCOLN'S INN FIELDS

Lincoln's Inn

❸ ★ Lincoln's Inn Fields
The mock-Tudor archway, leading to Lincoln's Inn and built in 1845, overlooks the Fields.

PORTSMOUTH ST

PORTUGAL STREET

CA

❺ Old Curiosity Shop
This is a rare 16th-century, pre-Great Fire building, which is now a shop.

❹ The Hunterian Museum forms part of the Royal College of Surgeons, designed in 1836 by Sir Charles Barry.

Key

 Suggested route

| 0 metres | 100 |
| 0 yards | 100 |

Twinings has been selling tea here since 1706. The doorway dates from 1787 when the shop (216 Strand) was called the Golden Lion.

The Gladstone Statue was erected in 1905 to commemorate William Gladstone, the Victorian statesman who served four terms as prime minister.

2 ★ Lincoln's Inn
The Court of Chancery sat here, in Old Hall, from 1835 until 1858. Sir John Taylor Coleridge, nephew of the poet, was a well-known judge of the time.

Locator Map
See Central London Map pp16–17

7 Royal Courts of Justice
The country's main court for civil cases and appeals was built in 1882. It is made out of 35 million bricks faced with Portland stone.

8 Law Society
Look for the gold lions on the railings of the Law Society's headquarters.

10 Fleet Street
For two centuries this was the centre of the national press. The newspaper offices moved out in the 1980s.

El Vino is a venerable wine bar where Fleet Street's journalists once mingled with barristers.

No. 17 Fleet Street has a superb half-timbered façade (1610) that survived the Fire. James I's eldest son, Prince Henry, had a room on the first floor of this former tavern.

6 St Clement Danes
Designed by Wren (1679), this is the Royal Air Force's church.

9 Temple Bar Memorial
A dragon marks where the City of London meets Westminster.

11 ★ Temple
This area was first home to the Knights Templar, who were based here in the 13th century.

The interior of the chapel in the grounds of Lincoln's Inn

❷ Lincoln's Inn

WC2. **Map** 14 D1. **Tel** 020 7405 1393.
🚇 Holborn, Chancery Lane.
Open Chapel: 9am–5pm Mon–Fri.
Other buildings: check website.
♿ 📷 First Fri of month 2pm.
w lincolnsinn.org.uk

Some of the buildings in
Lincoln's Inn, the best-preserved
of London's Inns of Court, go
back to the late 15th century.
The coat of arms above the
arch of the Chancery Lane
gatehouse is Henry VIII's, and
the heavy oak door is of the
same vintage. Shakespeare's
contemporary, Ben Jonson, is
believed to have laid some of
the bricks of Lincoln's Inn during
the reign of Elizabeth I. The
chapel is early 17th-century
Gothic. Women were not
allowed to be buried here until
1839, when the grieving Lord
Brougham petitioned to have
the rule changed so that his
beloved daughter could be
interred in the chapel, to wait
for him to join her.
   Lincoln's Inn has its share
of famous alumni. Oliver
Cromwell and John Donne,

❶ Sir John Soane's Museum

13 Lincoln's Inn Fields WC2. **Map** 14 D1.
Tel 020 7405 2107. 🚇 Holborn.
Open 10am–5pm Tue–Sat, 6–9pm
first Tue of month. **Closed** public hols,
24 Dec. ♿ limited – phone first. 📷
11:30am Tue & Fri, 3:30pm Wed & Thu,
11am Sat; groups book ahead. 📷
w soane.org

One of the most surprising
museums in London, this house
was left to the nation by Sir
John Soane in 1837, with a far-
sighted stipulation that nothing
at all should be changed. One
of Britain's leading 19th-century
architects, Soane was responsible
for designing Dulwich Picture
Gallery (see pp256–7). The son
of a bricklayer, he prudently
married the niece of a wealthy
builder, whose fortune he
inherited. He bought and
reconstructed No. 12 Lincoln's
Inn Fields, then No. 13, which he
and his wife moved into in 1813,
and later, in 1823–4, he rebuilt

No. 14, extending his museum
into the rear of this building.
Today, the collections are much
as Soane left them – an eclectic
gathering of beautiful, peculiar
and instructional objects.
   The building itself abounds
with architectural surprises and
illusions. In the main ground-
floor room, with its deep red
and green colouring, cunningly
placed mirrors play tricks with
light and space. The picture
gallery is lined with layers of
folding panels to increase its
capacity. The panels open out
to reveal galleried extensions to
the room itself. Among other
works here are many of Soane's
own exotic designs, including
those for Pitzhanger Manor (see
p264) and the Bank of England
(see p151). Here also is William
Hogarth's Rake's Progress series.
   In the centre of the basement,
an atrium stretches up to the
roof, the glass dome of which
lights galleries, on every floor,
laden with Classical statuary.

A glass dome allows light
into the basement.

A vast sarcophagus
(1300 BC) stands on the
floor of the basement.

the 17th-century poet, were both students here, as was William Penn, founder of the US state of Pennsylvania.

❸ Lincoln's Inn Fields

WC2. **Map** 14 D1. 🚇 Holborn. **Open** dawn–dusk daily. Public tennis courts.

This used to be a public execution site. Under the Tudors and the Stuarts, many religious martyrs, and those suspected of treachery to the Crown, perished here.

When the developer William Newton wanted to build here in the 1640s, students at Lincoln's Inn and other residents made him undertake that the land in the centre would remain a public area forever. Thanks to this early protest, tennis is played here throughout the summer, and lawyers read their briefs in the fresh air. For some years, it has also been the site of an evening soup kitchen for some of London's homeless.

Skeletons on display in the Hunterian Museum

❹ Hunterian Museum

35–43 Lincoln's Inn Fields, WC2. **Map** 14 D1. **Tel** 020 7869 6560. **Open** 10am–5pm Tue–Sat. **Closed** Good Friday, Easter Sat, 24 Dec–1 Jan 📷 1pm Wed, book in advance 📷 ♿ 🌐 **hunterianmuseum.org**

Inside the Royal College of Surgeons, the Hunterian Museum started life as the personal collection of John Hunter (1728–93), one of the leading teachers of surgery in his day, who amassed a large collection of human and animal anatomical specimens to aid his teaching. The museum was directly hit by a bomb in 1941 but of the collection of 14,000 objects, over 3,000 remain, including some of the most famous, such as the skeleton of Charles Byrne, the "Irish Giant" (somewhat controversially as Byrne wished to be buried at sea). It's not a museum for the squeamish, but the collection of surgical instruments and interactive displays on modern surgery are fascinating for those with an interest in the subject.

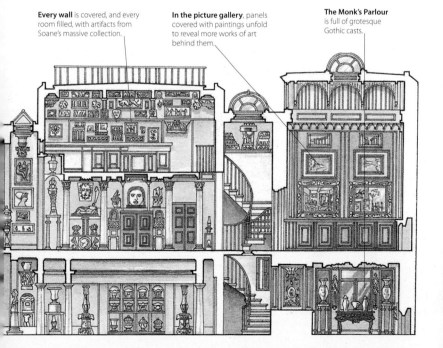

Every wall is covered, and every room filled, with artifacts from Soane's massive collection.

In the picture gallery, panels covered with paintings unfold to reveal more works of art behind them.

The Monk's Parlour is full of grotesque Gothic casts.

❺ Old Curiosity Shop

13–14 Portsmouth St WC2.
Map 14 D1. 🚇 Holborn.

Whether it inspired the Charles Dickens's 19th-century novel of the same name or not, the Old Curiosity Shop is a genuine 16th-century building and almost certainly the oldest shop in central London. With its wooden beams and over-hanging first floor, it gives a rare impression of a London streetscape from before the Great Fire of 1666. The Old Curiosity Shop maintains its retailing tradition, and currently operates as a handmade shoe shop. A preservation order guarantees the building's long-term future.

❻ St Clement Danes

Strand WC2. **Map** 14 D2. **Tel** 020 7242 8282. 🚇 Temple. **Open** 9am–4pm daily. **Closed** noon 25–27 Dec, pub hols. ♯ 12:30am Wed & Fri, 11am Sun. 🚻 See Ceremonies p59.
w raf.mod.uk/stclementdanes

Sitting proudly isolated on a traffic island, this wonderful church was designed by Christopher Wren in 1680. Its name derives from an earlier church built here by the descendants of Danish

The dragon, symbol of the City, at the entrance to the City at Temple Bar

invaders, whom Alfred the Great had allowed to remain in London in the 9th century. From the 17th to 19th centuries many people were buried here, and their memorial plaques are now in the crypt. The chain now hanging on the crypt wall was probably used to secure coffin lids against body snatchers who stole fresh corpses and sold them to the teaching hospitals. Outside, to the east, is a statue (1910) of Dr Johnson (see p144), who often came to services here.

Nearly destroyed during World War II, the church was rebuilt and became the central church of the Royal Air Force (RAF). The interior is dominated by RAF symbols, memorials and monuments.

The church bells ring to various tunes including that of the old English nursery rhyme "Oranges and Lemons" (though the carillon is currently under restoration).

❼ Royal Courts of Justice (the Law Courts)

Strand WC2. **Map** 14 D2. **Tel** 020 7947 6000. 🚇 Holborn, Temple, Chancery Lane. **Open** 9am–4:30pm Mon–Fri. **Closed** pub hols. 🚻 🛗 📷 call ahead 077 8975 1248.
w justice.gov.uk/courts

Knots of demonstrators and television cameras can often be seen outside this sprawling and fanciful Victorian Gothic building, waiting for the result of a contentious case. These are the nation's main civil courts, dealing with such matters as divorce, libel, civil liability and appeals. Cases involving criminal offences are dealt with at the Old Bailey (see p151), ten minutes' walk to the east. The public are admitted to all the court rooms and a list details which case is being heard in which court. The massive Gothic building was completed in 1882. It is said to contain 1,000 rooms and 5.6 km (3.5 miles) of corridors.

Ornate clock at the Victorian Gothic Royal Couts of Justice

❽ Law Society

113 Chancery Lane WC2. **Map** 14 E1. **Tel** 020 7242 1222. 🚇 Chancery Lane. **Closed** to the public.

The headquarters of the solicitors' professional body is, architecturally, one of the most interesting buildings in the legal quarter. The main part, dominated by four Ionic columns, was completed in 1832. More significant is the northern extension, an early work of Charles Holden, an Arts and Crafts enthusiast who later made his name as a designer of London Underground stations. In his window arches the four seated figures depict truth, justice, liberty and mercy.

The building is on the corner of Carey Street, the site of the bankruptcy court whose name, corrupted to "Queer Street", entered the language to describe a state of destitution.

❾ Temple Bar Memorial

Fleet St EC4. **Map** 14 D2. 🚇 Holborn, Temple, Chancery Lane.

The monument in the middle of Fleet Street dates from 1880 and marks the entrance to the City of London. On state occasions it is a long-standing tradition for the monarch to pause here and ask permission of the Lord Mayor to enter. Temple Bar, a huge archway designed by

William Capon's engraving of Fleet Street in 1799

Wren, used to stand here. It spent over a century in the grounds of a country estate in Hertfordshire before being erected near St Paul's Cathedral *(see pp152–5)* in 2004.

❿ Fleet Street

EC4. **Map** 14 E1. 🚇 Temple, Blackfriars, St Paul's.

England's first printing press was set up by William Caxton in the late 15th century. Some years later, his assistant began his own business in Fleet Street, and the area has been a centre of London's publishing industry ever since. Playwrights Shakespeare and Ben Jonson were patrons of the old Mitre tavern, now No. 37 Fleet Street. In 1702, the first newspaper, *The Daily Courant*, was issued from Fleet Street – conveniently placed for the City and Westminster, which were the main sources of news. Later the street became synonymous with the Press. The grand Art Deco building with Egyptian-style detail at No. 135 is the former headquarters of *The Daily Telegraph*. Next to the church of St-Dunstan-in-the-West (which largely dates from the 1830s) is a building adorned with the names of former newspapers.

The printing presses underneath the newspaper offices were abandoned in 1987, when new technology made it easy to produce papers away from the centre of town in areas such as Wapping and the Docklands. Today the newspapers have also

left Fleet Street, even though some of the journalists' traditional watering holes remain, such as Ye Olde Cheshire Cheese public house *(see p144)*, and the legendary El Vino wine bar, at the western end opposite Fetter Lane.

Effigies of Knights Templar from the era of the Crusades, in Temple Church

⓫ Temple

Inner Temple, King's Bench Walk EC4. **Map** 14 E2. **Tel** 020 7797 8241 (for tours). 🚇 Temple. **Open** 12:30–3pm Mon–Fri (grounds only). ♿ Middle Temple Hall, Middle Temple Lane EC4. **Tel** 020 7427 4800. **Open** 10am–noon Mon–Fri. **Closed** at short notice for functions. ♿ 📷 book ahead. ✉ Temple Church **Tel** 020 7353 8559. **Open** Mon–Fri; call ahead to check times. 🎵 🕊 1:15pm Thu, 8:30am & 11:15am Sun. 🅦 **templechurch.com**

This series of courtyards and buildings comprises two of the four Inns of Court: the Middle Temple and the Inner Temple. Lincoln's Inn *(see p140)* and Gray's Inn *(see p145)* complete the four.

The name derives from the Knights Templar, a chivalrous order that used to protect pilgrims to the Holy Land. The order was based here until it was suppressed by the Crown because its power was viewed as a threat. Initiations probably took place in the crypt of Temple Church and there are 13th-century effigies of Knights Templar in the nave.

Among some other ancient buildings is the Middle Temple Hall. Its fine Elizabethan interior survives – Shakespeare's *Twelfth Night* was performed here in 1601. Behind Temple, peaceful lawns stretch lazily down towards the Embankment.

⓬ St Bride's

Fleet St EC4. **Map** 14 F2. **Tel** 020 7427 0133. 🚇 Blackfriars. **Open** 8am–6pm Mon–Fri, 10am–6:30pm Sun (hours vary Sat). **Closed** pub hols. ♿ 📷 3pm Tue. 🕊 11am & 5:30pm Sun. 🎵 Concerts. 🅦 **stbrides.com**

St Bride's is one of Wren's best-loved churches. Its position just off Fleet Street has made it the traditional venue for memorial services to departed journalists. Wall plaques commemorate notable pressmen and women and printers. The marvellous octagonal layered spire has been the model for tiered wedding cakes since shortly after it was added in 1703. Bombed in 1940, the interior was faithfully restored after World War II. The fascinating crypt contains remnants of earlier churches on the site, and a section of Roman pavement.

Stonework at St Bride's, traditionally the "journalists' church"

Reconstructed interior of Dr Johnson's house

⑬ Ye Olde Cheshire Cheese

145 Fleet St EC4. **Map** 14 E1.
Tel 020 7353 6170. ⊜ Blackfriars.
Open 11am–11pm Mon–Fri,
noon–11pm Sat, noon–7pm Sun.
See Pubs and Bars pp312–15.

There has been an inn here for centuries and parts of this building date back to 1667, when the Cheshire Cheese was rebuilt after the Great Fire of 1666. The diarist Samuel Pepys often drank here in the 17th century, but it was Dr Samuel Johnson's *(see below)* association with "the Cheese" that made it a place of pilgrimage for the 19th-century literati. Novelists Mark Twain and Charles Dickens were frequent visitors. This is one of few pubs to have kept the 18th-century arrangement of small rooms with fireplaces, tables and benches, instead of knocking rooms into larger bars.

⑭ Dr Johnson's House

17 Gough Sq EC4. **Map** 14 E1.
Tel 020 7353 3745. ⊜ Blackfriars,
Chancery Lane, Temple. **Open** May–
Sep: 11am–5:30pm Mon–Sat; Oct–
Apr: 11am–5pm Mon–Sat.
Closed pub hols. 🎨 🔍 📷
🌐 **drjohnsonshouse.org**

The oft-quoted Dr Samuel Johnson was an 18th-century scholar famous for the many witty (and often contentious) remarks that his biographer, James Boswell, recorded and published. Johnson lived at 17 Gough Square from 1748 to 1759. He compiled the first definitive English dictionary (published in 1755) in the attic, where six scribes and assistants stood all day at high desks.

The house, built before 1700, retains some period features and is furnished with 18th-century pieces. There is a small collection of exhibits relating to Johnson and the times in which he lived, including a tea set belonging to his friend Mrs Thrale and pictures of Johnson and his contemporaries. There are also replica Georgian costumes for children to try on.

⑮ St Andrew, Holborn

5 St Andrew St EC4. **Map** 14 E1.
Tel 020 7583 7394. ⊜ Chancery Lane.
Open 9am–5pm Mon–Fri.
✝ 1:10pm Tue & Thu, 7pm Wed. ♿
🌐 **standrewholborn.org.uk**

The medieval church that stood here survived the Great Fire but in 1668, renowned architect Christopher Wren was asked to redesign it. The lower part of the tower is virtually all that remains of the earlier church. One of Wren's most spacious churches, it was gutted during World War II but faithfully restored as the church of the London trade guilds.

Benjamin Disraeli, the Jewish-born prime minister, was baptized here in 1817, at the age of 12. In the 19th century, a charity school was attached to the church.

⑯ Holborn Viaduct

EC1. **Map** 14 F1. ⊜ Farringdon, St Paul's, Chancery Lane.

This piece of Victorian ironwork was erected in the 1860s as part of a much-needed traffic scheme. It is best seen from Farringdon Street, which is linked to the bridge by a staircase. Climb up and see the statues of City heroes and bronze images representing Commerce, Agriculture, Science and Fine Arts.

Civic symbol on Holborn Viaduct

⑰ St Etheldreda's Church

14 Ely Place EC1. **Map** 6 E5. **Tel** 020 7405 1061. 🚇 Farringdon. **Open** 8am–5pm Mon–Sat, 8am–12:30pm Sun. 📷 🕐1pm Mon–Fri, 9am & 11am Sun. 🌐 **stetheldreda.com**

Built in 1290, this rare survivor is the oldest Catholic church in England. First the town chapel of the Bishops of Ely, who lived in the since demolished Ely House, the church passed through various hands over the centuries, including those of Sir Christopher Hatton, an Elizabethan courtier, who built Hatton House in the grounds and used the church crypt as a tavern. Rebuilt and restored several times, the church has some stunning stained-glass windows.

⑱ Hatton Garden

EC1. **Map** 6 E5. 🚇 Chancery Lane, Farringdon.

Named for Sir Christopher Hatton *(see above)*, Hatton Garden is the centre of London's diamond and jewellery district. Millions of pounds change hands daily in scores of small shops with sparkling window displays.
Running parallel to Hatton Garden is Leather Lane, which has a week-day market (10am–2pm Mon–Fri). The varied stalls sell a little of everything.

⑲ Staple Inn

Holborn WC1. **Map** 14 E1. 🚇 Chancery Lane.

This building was once the wool staple, where wool was weighed and taxed. The frontage overlooks Holborn and is the only real example of Elizabethan half-timbering left in central London. Although now much restored, it would still be recognizable by someone who had known it in 1586, when it was built. The shops at street level have the feel of the 19th century, and there are some 18th-century buildings in the courtyard.

Staple Inn, a survivor from 1586

⑳ London Silver Vaults

53–64 Chancery Lane WC2. **Map** 14 D1. **Tel** 020 7242 3844. 🚇 Chancery Lane, Holborn. **Open** 9am–5:30pm Mon–Fri, 9am–1pm Sat. 🌐 **thesilvervaults.com**

These silver vaults originate from the Chancery Lane Safe Deposit Company, established in the late 19th century. After descending a staircase you pass through steel security doors and reach a nest of underground shops sparkling

Coffee pot (1716): Silver Vaults

with antique and modern silverware. The best examples sell for many thousands of pounds but most shops also offer modest pieces at realistic prices.

㉑ Gray's Inn

Gray's Inn Rd WC1. **Map** 6 D5. **Tel** 020 7458 7800. 🚇 Chancery Lane, Holborn. Grounds **Open** noon–2:30pm Mon–Fri. ♿ 📷

This ancient legal centre and law school dates to the 14th century though it was largely rebuilt after damage inflicted during World War II. At least one of Shakespeare's plays *(A Comedy of Errors)* was first performed in Gray's Inn hall in 1594. The hall's 16th-century interior screen still survives. The young Charles Dickens was employed as a clerk here in 1827–8. The garden, known as "the Walks" and once a convenient site for staging duels, is open to lunchtime strollers for part of the year. The buildings may be visited only by prior arrangement.

THE CITY

The capital's financial district, the City of London (or just "the City"), is built on the site of the original Roman settlement. Much of the early City was obliterated by the Great Fire of 1666, though hints can be found in its still jumbled medieval street plan, with names such as Cheapside and Poultry. After the fire, rebuilding was rapid: Christopher Wren (see p51) rebuilt dozens of the city's churches, with his magnificent dome for St Paul's Cathedral rising above them all. These and the halls of the traditional guilds and livery companies are reminders of the City's long history. Now the spires and financial institutions stand alongside dour postwar office blocks and some extraordinary modern architecture, such as the Lloyd's building and the Gherkin.

Sights at a Glance

Historic Streets and Buildings
1 Mansion House
3 Royal Exchange
7 Old Bailey
8 Apothecaries' Hall
9 Fishmongers' Hall
12 Old Billingsgate
13 Sky Garden
15 Tower of London pp158–61
16 Tower Bridge
21 Lloyd's of London

Museums and Galleries
4 Bank of England Museum
22 Guildhall

Historic Markets
20 Leadenhall Market

Monuments
11 Monument

Churches and Cathedrals
2 St Stephen Walbrook
5 St Mary-le-Bow
6 St Paul's Cathedral pp152–5
10 St Magnus the Martyr
14 All Hallows by the Tower
18 St Helen's Bishopsgate
19 St Katharine Cree

Docks
17 St Katharine Docks

Restaurants see pp302–4
1 Goodman
2 Haz Plantation Place
3 The Restaurant at St Paul's Cathedral
4 Sauterelle

0 metres 500
0 yards 500

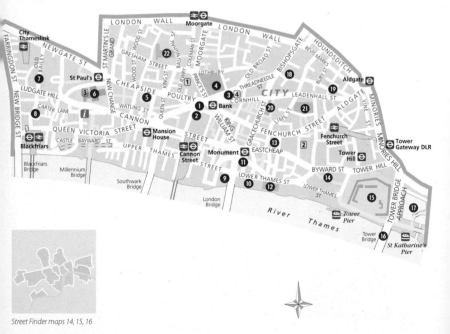

Street Finder maps 14, 15, 16

◀ South side view of St Paul's Cathedral with its impressive dome

For keys to symbols see back flap

Street-by-Street: The City

This is the business centre of London, home to vast financial institutions such as the Stock Exchange and the Bank of England. Alongside these 19th- and 20th-century buildings stand the architectural visions of Christopher Wren, England's most sublime and probably most prolific architect. After the Great Fire of 1666 he supervised the rebuilding of 52 churches within the area, and enough survive to testify to his genius.

❺ St Mary-le-Bow
Anyone born within earshot of the bells of this Wren church (the historic Bow Bells) is said to be a true Londoner or Cockney.

Temple Bar, the last remaining City gateway, formerly on Fleet Street, was installed here in 2004.

St Paul's station

Mansion House station

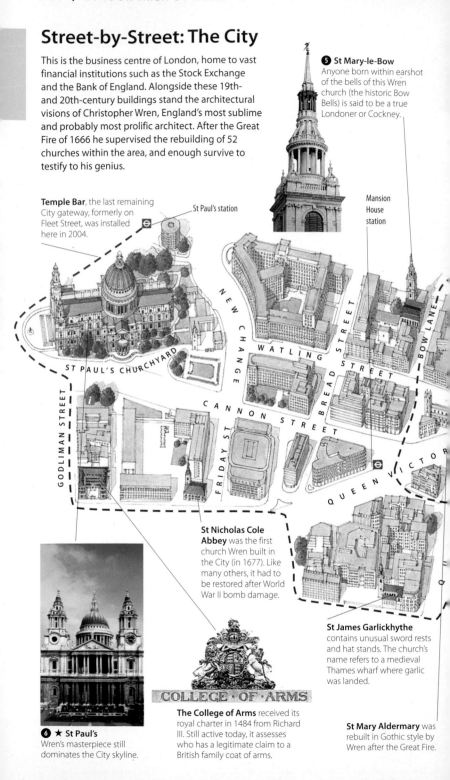

NEW CHANGE

WATLING STREET

BREAD STREET

BOW LANE

ST PAUL'S CHURCHYARD

GODLIMAN STREET

CANNON STREET

FRIDAY ST

QUEEN VICTOR

St Nicholas Cole Abbey was the first church Wren built in the City (in 1677). Like many others, it had to be restored after World War II bomb damage.

St James Garlickhythe contains unusual sword rests and hat stands. The church's name refers to a medieval Thames wharf where garlic was landed.

COLLEGE · OF · ARMS

The College of Arms received its royal charter in 1484 from Richard III. Still active today, it assesses who has a legitimate claim to a British family coat of arms.

❻ ★ St Paul's
Wren's masterpiece still dominates the City skyline.

St Mary Aldermary was rebuilt in Gothic style by Wren after the Great Fire.

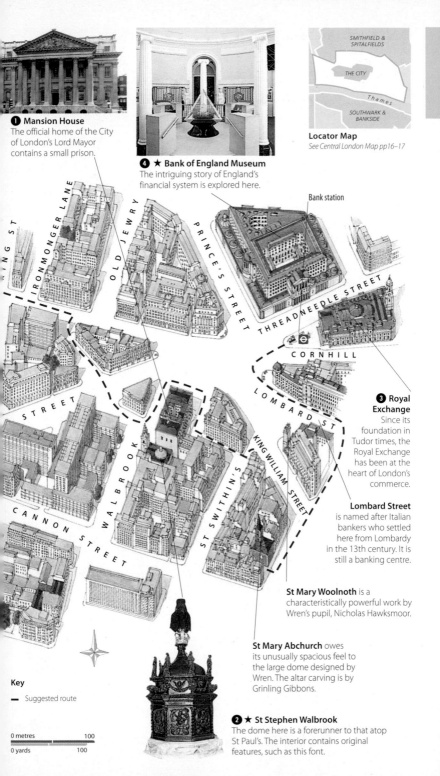

① Mansion House
The official home of the City of London's Lord Mayor contains a small prison.

④ ★ Bank of England Museum
The intriguing story of England's financial system is explored here.

Locator Map
See Central London Map pp16–17

Bank station

③ Royal Exchange
Since its foundation in Tudor times, the Royal Exchange has been at the heart of London's commerce.

Lombard Street
is named after Italian bankers who settled here from Lombardy in the 13th century. It is still a banking centre.

St Mary Woolnoth is a characteristically powerful work by Wren's pupil, Nicholas Hawksmoor.

St Mary Abchurch owes its unusually spacious feel to the large dome designed by Wren. The altar carving is by Grinling Gibbons.

② ★ St Stephen Walbrook
The dome here is a forerunner to that atop St Paul's. The interior contains original features, such as this font.

Key
— Suggested route

0 metres   100
0 yards   100

❶ Mansion House

Walbrook EC4. **Map** 15 B2. **Tel** 020 7626 2500. 🚇 Bank, Mansion House. **Open** to group tours only by appt or 1.45pm Tue on a first-come-first-served basis; check in advance, as tours can be cancelled. 🅿️ 🅿️
W cityoflondon.gov.uk

The official residence of the Lord Mayor was designed by George Dance the Elder and completed in 1758. The Palladian front with its six Corinthian columns is one of the most familiar City landmarks. The state rooms have a dignity appropriate to the office of mayor, one of the most spectacular being the 27-m (90-ft) Egyptian Hall. There is also an impressive collection of 17th-century Dutch art, including works by Frans Hals.

The cellars once housed 11 holding cells, a reminder of the building's other function as a magistrate's court; the Mayor is chief magistrate of the City during his year of office. Emmeline Pankhurst, who campaigned for women's suffrage in the early 20th century, was once held here.

Egyptian Hall in Mansion House

❷ St Stephen Walbrook

39 Walbrook EC4. **Map** 15 B2. **Tel** 020 7626 9000. 🚇 Bank, Cannon St. **Open** 10am–4pm Mon, Tue & Thu, 11am–3pm Wed, 10am–3:30pm Fri. ✝️ 12:45pm Thu, sung Mass. Organ recitals 12:30pm Fri. **W** ststephenwalbrook.net

The Lord Mayor's parish church was built by Christopher Wren in 1672–9 and it is considered the finest of his City churches *(see p51)*. The deep, coffered dome, with its ornate plasterwork, was a forerunner of St Paul's. St Stephen's airy columned interior comes as a surprise after its plain exterior. The font cover and pulpit canopy are decorated with exquisite carved figures that contrast strongly with the stark simplicity of Henry Moore's massive white stone altar (1972), installed in 1987.

However, perhaps the most moving monument of all is a telephone in a glass box. This is a tribute to Rector Chad Varah who, in 1953, founded the Samaritans, a volunteer-staffed telephone helpline for people in emotional need.

The church is also the home of the London Internet Church, which brings together people from all over the world to worship and discuss Christianity.

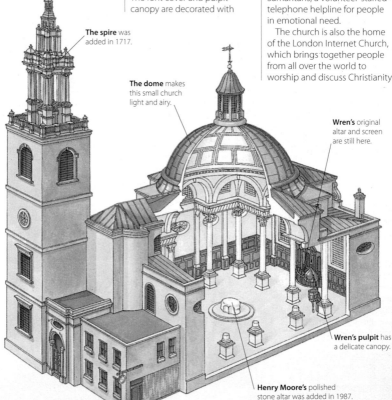

The spire was added in 1717.

The dome makes this small church light and airy.

Wren's original altar and screen are still here.

Wren's pulpit has a delicate canopy.

Henry Moore's polished stone altar was added in 1987.

❸ Royal Exchange

EC3. **Map** 15 C2. 🚇 Bank.
🌐 **theroyalexchange.co.uk**

Sir Thomas Gresham, an Elizabethan merchant and courtier, founded the Royal Exchange in 1565 as a centre for commerce of all kinds. The original building was centred on a vast courtyard where merchants and tradesmen did business. Queen Elizabeth I gave it its royal title and it is still one of the sites from which a new monarch is announced. Dating from 1844, this is the third splendid building on the site since Gresham's.

The building now contains a luxurious shopping centre with designer stores such as Hermès and Paul Smith, and an elegant central bar and café.

The façade of William Tite's Royal Exchange of 1844

The Duke of Wellington (1884), opposite the Bank of England

❹ Bank of England Museum

Bartholomew Lane EC2.
Map 15 B1. **Tel** 020 7601 5545.
🚇 Bank. **Open** 10am–5pm Mon–Fri.
Closed public hols. 🚻 phone first.
🎬 Films, lectures.
🌐 **bankofengland.co.uk**

The Bank of England was set up in 1694 to raise money for foreign wars. It grew to become Britain's central bank, and also issues currency notes. Sir John Soane (see pp140–41) was the architect of the 1788 bank building on this site, but only the exterior wall of his design has survived. The rest was destroyed in the 1920s and 1930s when the building was enlarged. There is now a reconstruction of Soane's

stock office of 1793. Glittering gold bars (which you can touch), silver-plated decoration and a Roman mosaic floor, which was discovered during the rebuilding, are among the items on display, along with a unique collection of banknotes. The museum illustrates the work of the Bank and the financial system.

❺ St Mary-le-Bow

(Bow Church) Cheapside EC2. **Map** 15 A2. **Tel** 020 7248 5139. 🚇 St Paul's, Mansion House. **Open** 7:30am–6pm Mon–Wed, 7:30am–6:30pm Thu, 7:30am–4pm Fri. 🔔 weekdays (see website for details). 📷 by arrangement. ♿ 🚻 🌐 **stmarylebow.co.uk**

The church takes its name from the bow arches in the Norman crypt. When Wren rebuilt the church (in 1670–80) after the Great Fire, he continued this pattern through the arches on the steeple. The weathervane, dating from 1674, is an enormous dragon.

The church was bombed in 1941, leaving only the steeple and two outer walls standing. It was restored in 1956–62, when the bells were recast and rehung. Bow bells have significance for Londoners: traditionally only those born within their sound can claim to be true Cockneys.

❻ St Paul's

See pp152–5.

❼ Old Bailey

EC4. **Map** 14 F1. **Tel** 020 7248 3277. 🚇 St Paul's. **Open** 9:55am–12:40pm & 1:55–3:40pm Mon–Fri (reduced times Aug; opening hours vary from court to court). **Closed** Easter, Christmas, New Year, public hols. ✉️ 🌐 **cityoflondon.gov.uk**

This short street has a long association with crime and punishment. The new Central Criminal Courts opened here in 1907 on the site of the infamous and malodorous Newgate prison (on special days in the legal calendar judges still carry small posies to court as a reminder of those times). Across the road, the Magpie and Stump served "execution breakfasts" until 1868, when mass public hangings outside the prison gates were stopped. Today, when the courts are in session, they are open to members of the public.

Old Bailey's rooftop Justice

❻ St Paul's Cathedral

Following the Great Fire of London in 1666, the medieval cathedral of St Paul's was left in ruins. The authorities turned to Christopher Wren to rebuild it, but his ideas met with considerable resistance from the conservative Dean and Chapter. Wren's 1672 Great Model plan was rejected and a watered-down plan was finally agreed in 1675. Wren's determination paid off, though: the cathedral is considered his greatest masterpiece.

Queen Anne's Statue
An 1886 copy of Francis Bird's 1712 original now stands on the forecourt.

Stone urn outside the South Transept

KEY

① **The West Porch**, approached from Ludgate Hill, is the main entrance to St Paul's.

② **The West Portico** comprises two tiers of columns rather than the single colonnade that Wren intended.

③ **The pediment** carvings, dating from 1706, show the Conversion of St Paul.

④ **The balustrade** along the top was added in 1718, against Wren's wishes.

⑤ **The lantern** weighs a massive 850 tonnes.

⑥ **The golden gallery** is at the highest point of the dome.

⑦ **The brick cone** located inside the outer dome supports the heavy lantern.

⑧ **The oculus** is an opening through which the lantern can be seen.

⑨ **The stone gallery** offers a splendid view over London.

⑩ **The upper screen wall** masks the flying buttresses.

⑪ **Flying buttresses** support the nave walls and the dome.

⑫ **The North and South Transepts** cross the nave in a medieval style that contrasts with Wren's original plan (see p154).

★ **The West Front and Towers**
The towers were not on Wren's original plan – he added them in 1707, when he was 75 years old. Both were designed to have clocks.

Main entrance

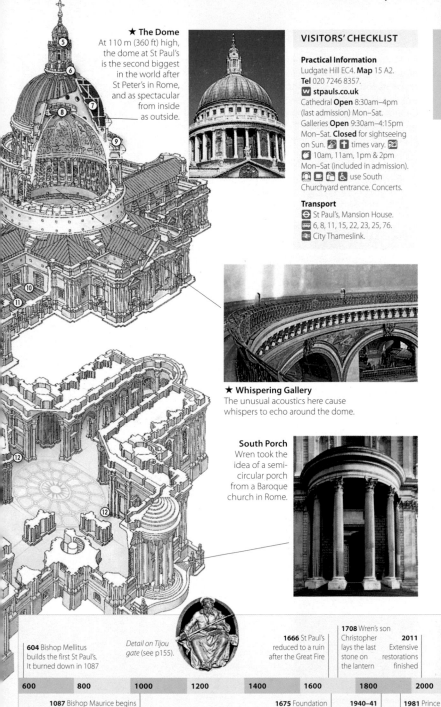

★ The Dome
At 110 m (360 ft) high, the dome at St Paul's is the second biggest in the world after St Peter's in Rome, and as spectacular from inside as outside.

VISITORS' CHECKLIST

Practical Information
Ludgate Hill EC4. **Map** 15 A2.
Tel 020 7246 8357.
[w] stpauls.co.uk
Cathedral **Open** 8:30am–4pm (last admission) Mon–Sat.
Galleries **Open** 9:30am–4:15pm Mon–Sat. **Closed** for sightseeing on Sun. 🅿 🕇 times vary. ✉ 10am, 11am, 1pm & 2pm Mon–Sat (included in admission). 🔲 🔲 🔲 🔲 use South Churchyard entrance. Concerts.

Transport
🅴 St Paul's, Mansion House.
🚌 6, 8, 11, 15, 22, 23, 25, 76.
🚆 City Thameslink.

★ Whispering Gallery
The unusual acoustics here cause whispers to echo around the dome.

South Porch
Wren took the idea of a semi-circular porch from a Baroque church in Rome.

604 Bishop Mellitus builds the first St Paul's. It burned down in 1087

Detail on Tijou gate (see p155).

1666 St Paul's reduced to a ruin after the Great Fire

1708 Wren's son Christopher lays the last stone on the lantern

2011 Extensive restorations finished

600	800	1000	1200	1400	1600	1800	2000

1087 Bishop Maurice begins Old St Paul's: a Norman cathedral of stone

1675 Foundation stone of Wren's design laid

1940–41 Slight bomb damage to the cathedral

1981 Prince Charles marries Lady Diana Spencer

A Guided Tour of St Paul's

Visitors to St Paul's will be immediately impressed by its cool, beautifully ordered and extremely spacious interior. The nave, transepts and choir are arranged in the shape of a cross, as in a medieval cathedral, but Wren's Classical vision shines through this conservative floorplan, forced on him by the cathedral authorities. Aided by some of the finest craftsmen of his day, he created an interior of grand majesty and Baroque splendour, a worthy setting for the many great ceremonial events that have taken place here. These include the funeral of Sir Winston Churchill in 1965 and the wedding of Prince Charles and Lady Diana Spencer in 1981.

The mosaics on the choir ceiling were completed in the 1890s by William Richmond.

② The North Aisle
As you walk along the North Aisle, look up: the aisles are vaulted with small domes mimicking those of the nave ceiling.

Key

— Tour route

① The Nave
Take in the full glory of the massive arches and the succession of saucer domes that open out into a huge space below the main dome.

⑨ South Aisle
From here the brave can ascend the 259 steps to the Whispering Gallery and test the acoustics.

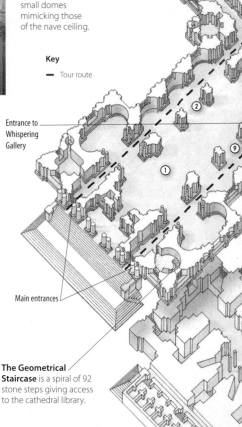

Entrance to Whispering Gallery

Main entrances

The Geometrical Staircase is a spiral of 92 stone steps giving access to the cathedral library.

⑧ Florence Nightingale's Memorial
Famous for her pioneering work in nursing standards, Florence Nightingale was the first woman to receive the Order of Merit.

⑦ Wren's Tomb
Wren's burial place is marked by a slab. The inscription states: "Reader, if you seek a monument, look around you."

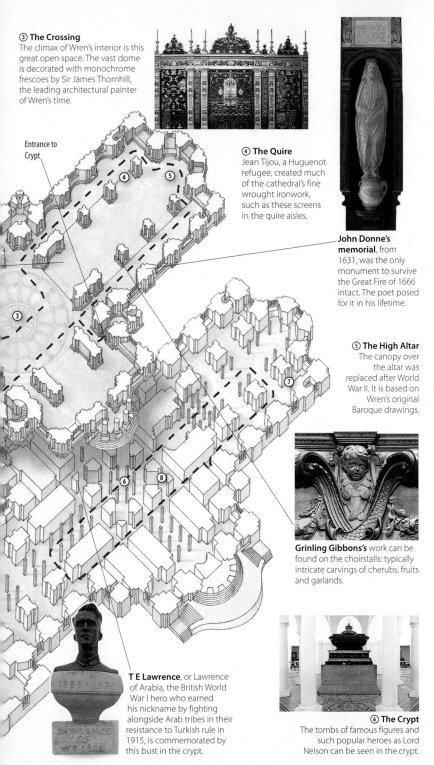

③ The Crossing
The climax of Wren's interior is this great open space. The vast dome is decorated with monochrome frescoes by Sir James Thornhill, the leading architectural painter of Wren's time.

Entrance to Crypt

④ The Quire
Jean Tijou, a Huguenot refugee, created much of the cathedral's fine wrought ironwork, such as these screens in the quire aisles.

John Donne's memorial, from 1631, was the only monument to survive the Great Fire of 1666 intact. The poet posed for it in his lifetime.

⑤ The High Altar
The canopy over the altar was replaced after World War II. It is based on Wren's original Baroque drawings.

Grinling Gibbons's work can be found on the choirstalls: typically intricate carvings of cherubs, fruits and garlands.

T E Lawrence, or Lawrence of Arabia, the British World War I hero who earned his nickname by fighting alongside Arab tribes in their resistance to Turkish rule in 1915, is commemorated by this bust in the crypt.

⑥ The Crypt
The tombs of famous figures and such popular heroes as Lord Nelson can be seen in the crypt.

Apothecaries' Hall, rebuilt in 1670

❽ Apothecaries' Hall

Blackfriars Lane EC4. **Map** 14 F2.
Tel 020 7236 1189. 🚇 Blackfriars.
Courtyard **Open** 9am–5pm Mon–Fri.
Closed pub hols, end Aug. Phone Hall
for appt to visit (groups only).
🅆 **apothecaries.org**

London has had livery companies, or guilds, to protect and
regulate specific trades since
early medieval times. The
Apothecaries' Society was
founded in 1617 for those who
prepared, prescribed or sold
drugs. It has some surprising
alumni, including Oliver Cromwell and the poet John Keats.
Now nearly all the members are
physicians or surgeons.

❾ Fishmongers' Hall

London Bridge EC4. **Map** 15 B3.
Tel 020 7626 3531. 🚇 Monument.
Closed to the public. Limited tours by
appt only. 🅆 **fishhall.org.uk**

This is home to the Fishmongers'
Company, which was established
in 1272. Its most illustrious
member was Lord Mayor
Walworth, who killed Wat Tyler,
leader of the Peasants' Revolt, in
1381 *(see p166)*. The company
still fulfils its original role; all the
fish sold in the City must be
inspected by company officials.

❿ St Magnus the Martyr

Lower Thames St EC3. **Map** 15 C3.
Tel 020 7626 4481. 🚇 Monument.
Open 10am–4pm Tue–Fri.
🕆 12:30pm Tue–Fri, 11am Sun. ♿
🅆 **stmagnusmartyr. org.uk**

There has been a church here
for over 1,000 years. Its patron
saint, St Magnus, Earl of the
Orkney Islands and a renowned

Norwegian Christian leader,
was brutally murdered in 1116.
When Christopher Wren built
this church in 1671–6, it was at
the foot of old London Bridge,
until 1738 the only bridge across
the River Thames in London.
Anyone going south from the
city would have passed under
Wren's magnificent arched porch
spanning the flagstones leading
to the old bridge.
 Highlights of St Magnus the
Martyr include the carved musical
instruments that decorate the
organ case. Wren's pulpit, with
its slender supporting stem,
was restored in 1924.

The altar of St Magnus the Martyr

⓫ Monument

Monument St EC3. **Map** 15 C2.
Tel 020 7626 2717. 🚇 Monument.
Open 9:30am–5:30pm daily (to
6:30pm Apr–Sep). **Closed** 1 Jan, 24–26
Dec. 📷 🅆 **themonument.info**

The column designed by
Christopher Wren to commemorate the Great Fire of London,
which devastated the original
walled city in September 1666, is
the tallest isolated stone column
in the world. It is 61.5 m (202 ft)
high and is said to be 61.5 m
west of where the fire started in
Pudding Lane. It was sited on the
direct approach to old London
Bridge, which was a few steps
downstream from the present
one. Reliefs around the column's
base show Charles II restoring
the city. The 311 steps to the

top lead to a viewing platform,
which was enclosed with
railings in 1842 after a suicide.
The views are spectacular.

⓬ Old Billingsgate

Lower Thames St EC3. **Map** 15 C3.
🚇 Monument. **Closed** to the public.

London's main fish market was
based here for 900 years, on one
of the city's earliest quays. During
the 19th and early 20th centuries,
400 tonnes of fish were sold
here every day, much delivered
by boat. It was London's noisiest
market, renowned, even in
Shakespeare's day, for foul
language. In 1982, the market
moved from this building (1877)
to the Isle of Dogs.

⓭ The Sky Garden

20 Fenchurch St EC3. **Map** 15 C2.
Tel 020 7337 2344. 🚇 Bank,
Monument. **Open** 10am–6pm
Mon–Fri (last adm 5pm), 11am–9pm
Sat & Sun (last adm 8pm). Advance
booking essential. ♿ 📷
🅆 **skygarden.london**

Completed in 2014, the Rafael
Viñoly-designed 20 Fenchurch
Street skyscraper is commonly
known as the "Walkie-Talkie",
thanks to its unusual shape. It
has been the most controversial
of London's modern towers, in
part because its shape and
position makes it particularly
obtrusive on the skyline. However,
it's one of the few with free,
straight-forward public access:
simply book a ticket online to
the Sky Garden, a large three-
level viewing deck at the top of
the building. Tickets are released
three weeks in advance, and go
quickly for popular times. There
is also the Sky Pod bar (pre-
booking advised) and some
pricey restaurants, but these
have more limited views.
 Thanks to its location, the Sky
Garden is a perfect place from
which to view London's other
mega-structures. To the south,
the Shard *(see p186)* stands
majestically alone. To the north
are Tower 42, formerly the
NatWest Tower (183 m/600 ft);
the immediately recognizable

"Gherkin" (180 m/590 ft), and the "Cheesegrater" or Leadenhall Building (224 m/738 ft). Over on Bishopsgate is Heron Tower, at 230 m (755 ft) currently the tallest building in the City.

Greenery flourishing in the Sky Garden, the top deck of the "Walkie-Talkie" building

⑭ All Hallows by the Tower

Byward St EC3. **Map** 16 D3. **Tel** 020 7481 2928. ⊖ Tower Hill. **Open** 8am–6pm Mon–Fri, 10am–5pm Sat & Sun (closed for sightseeing during services). **Closed** 26 Dec–2 Jan. ✝ 11am Sun. ♿ 🅿 available most weekdays Apr–Oct. 📷 🎧 🏛 for undercroft museum. 🅦 **allhallowsbythetower.org.uk**

The oldest church in the city, All Hallows by the Tower retains some of its original Saxon features – look for the arch in the southwest corner – plus a Roman pavement, which was discovered in the crypt in 1926.

The church has certainly played its part in history: located close to the Tower of London, it carried out temporary burials of those

Roman tile from All Hallows

executed on Tower Hill, including Thomas More, and it was from the church tower that Samuel Pepys watched the Great Fire consume London in 1666.

⑮ Tower of London

See pp158–61.

⑯ Tower Bridge

SE1 (main entrance north side; engine room entrance south side). **Map** 16 D3. **Tel** 020 7403 3761. ⊖ Tower Hill. The Tower Bridge Exhibition **Open** Apr–Sep: 10am–6pm daily; Oct–Mar: 9:30am–5:30pm daily (from noon 1 Jan). **Closed** 24–26 Dec. 🎧 🛗 ♿ 🏛 🅦 **towerbridge.org.uk**

Completed in 1894, this flamboyant piece of Victorian engineering quickly became a symbol of London. Its pinnacled towers and linking catwalk support the mechanism for raising the roadway when big ships have to pass through, or for special and historic occasions.

The bridge houses The Tower Bridge Exhibition, with interactive displays on the bridge's history, hair-raising views from the glass-floored catwalk and a close-up look at the steam engine which powered the lifting machinery until 1976, when the system was electrified.

Glass-floored walkways afford stunning views along the river and of the traffic passing below.

There are nearly 300 stairs to the top of the towers.

When raised, the bridge is 40 m (135 ft) high and 60 m (200 ft) wide. In its heyday, it was opened five times a day.

The Victorian winding machinery was powered by steam until 1976.

⓯ Tower of London

For much of its 900-year history, the Tower was an object of fear. Those who had committed treason or threatened the throne were held within its dank walls. A lucky few lived in comparative comfort, but the majority had to put up with appalling conditions. Many did not get out alive, and some were tortured before meeting violent deaths on nearby Tower Hill.

"Beefeaters"
Thirty-seven Yeoman Warders guard the Tower and live here.

★ The Jewel House
The magnificent Crown Jewels are housed here (see p160).

Queen's House
This is the official residence of the constables.

KEY

① **Beauchamp Tower** was used for high-ranking prisoners, who were often allowed to keep their own retinues of servants.

② **Tower Green** was where the aristocratic prisoners were executed, away from the ghoulish crowds on Tower Hill. But while only seven people died here – including two of Henry VIII's six wives – there were hundreds of public executions on Tower Hill.

③ **Wakefield Tower**, part of the Medieval Palace, has been carefully refurbished to match its original appearance in the 13th century.

④ **The Bloody Tower** is associated with the legend of the two princes and other deaths (see p161).

Main entrance

The Ravens

The Tower's most celebrated residents are a small colony of ravens. It is not known when they first settled here, but there is a legend that should they desert the Tower, the kingdom will fall. In fact, the birds have part of their wings trimmed on the right side, making full flight impossible. The Ravenmaster, one of the Yeoman Warders, looks after the birds. A memorial in the moat commemorates some of the ravens who have died at the Tower since the 1950s.

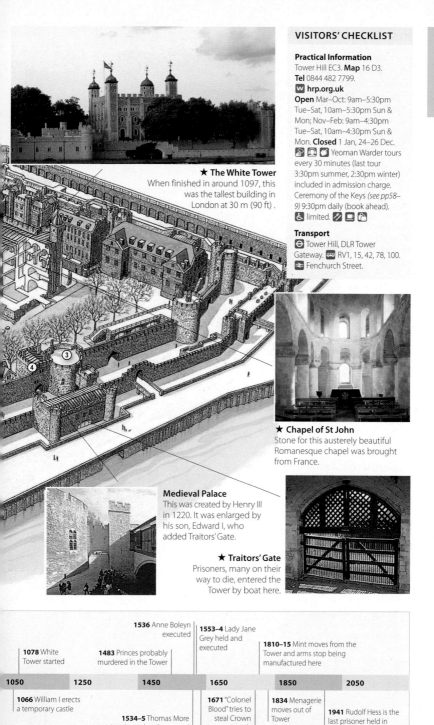

★ **The White Tower**
When finished in around 1097, this was the tallest building in London at 30 m (90 ft) .

VISITORS' CHECKLIST

Practical Information
Tower Hill EC3. **Map** 16 D3.
Tel 0844 482 7799.
W hrp.org.uk
Open Mar–Oct: 9am–5:30pm
Tue–Sat, 10am–5:30pm Sun &
Mon; Nov–Feb: 9am–4:30pm
Tue–Sat, 10am–4:30pm Sun &
Mon. **Closed** 1 Jan, 24–26 Dec.
Yeoman Warder tours
every 30 minutes (last tour
3:30pm summer, 2:30pm winter)
included in admission charge.
Ceremony of the Keys (see pp58–
9) 9:30pm daily (book ahead).
limited.

Transport
Tower Hill, DLR Tower
Gateway. RV1, 15, 42, 78, 100.
Fenchurch Street.

★ **Chapel of St John**
Stone for this austerely beautiful Romanesque chapel was brought from France.

Medieval Palace
This was created by Henry III in 1220. It was enlarged by his son, Edward I, who added Traitors' Gate.

★ **Traitors' Gate**
Prisoners, many on their way to die, entered the Tower by boat here.

1078 White Tower started
1483 Princes probably murdered in the Tower
1536 Anne Boleyn executed
1553–4 Lady Jane Grey held and executed
1810–15 Mint moves from the Tower and arms stop being manufactured here

1050 — 1250 — 1450 — 1650 — 1850 — 2050

1066 William I erects a temporary castle
1534–5 Thomas More imprisoned and executed
1671 "Colonel Blood" tries to steal Crown Jewels
1834 Menagerie moves out of Tower
1941 Rudolf Hess is the last prisoner held in Queen's House
1603–16 Walter Raleigh imprisoned in Tower

Inside the Tower

The Tower has been a tourist attraction since the reign of Charles II (1660–85), when both the Crown Jewels and the collection of armour were first shown to the public. They remain powerful reminders of royal might and wealth.

The Orb, symbolizing the power of Christ

The Crown Jewels

The Crown Jewels comprise the regalia of crowns, sceptres, orbs and swords used at coronations and other state occasions. They are impossible to price but their worth is irrelevant beside their enormous significance in the historical and religious life of the kingdom. Most of the Crown Jewels date from 1661, when a new set was made for the coronation of Charles II; Parliament had destroyed the previous crowns and sceptres after the execution of Charles I in 1649. Only a few pieces survived, hidden by the clergy of Westminster Abbey until the Restoration.

The Imperial State Crown, containing more than 2,800 diamonds, 273 pearls and other gems

The Coronation Ceremony

Many elements in this solemn and mystical ceremony date from the days of Edward the Confessor. The king or queen proceeds to Westminster Abbey, accompanied by objects of the regalia, including the State Sword, which represents the monarch's own sword. He or she is then anointed with holy oil, to signify divine approval, and invested with ornaments and royal robes. Each of the jewels represents an aspect of the monarch's role as head of the state and church. The climax comes when St Edward's Crown is placed on the sovereign's head; there is a cry of "God Save the King" (or Queen), the trumpets sound, and guns at the Tower are fired. The last coronation was Elizabeth II's in 1953.

The Crowns

There are ten crowns on display at the Tower. Many of these have not been worn for years, but the Imperial State Crown is in regular use. The Queen wears it at the Opening of Parliament (see p58). The crown was made in 1937 for George VI, and is similar to the one made for Queen Victoria. The sapphire set in the cross is said to have been worn in a ring by Edward the Confessor (ruled 1042–66).

The most recent crown is not at the Tower, however. It was made for Prince Charles's investiture as Prince of Wales at Caernarvon Castle in north Wales in 1969, and is kept at the Museum of Wales in Cardiff.

The Queen Mother's crown was made for the coronation of her husband, George VI, in 1937. It is the only one to be made out of platinum – all the other crowns on display at the Tower are made of gold.

Other Regalia

Apart from the crowns, there are other pieces of the Crown Jewels that are essential to coronations. Among these are three Swords of Justice, symbolizing mercy, spiritual and temporal justice. The Orb is a hollow gold sphere encrusted with jewels and weighing about 1.3 kg (3 lb). The Sceptre with the Cross contains the biggest cut diamond in the world, the 530-carat First Star of Africa. The rough stone it comes from weighed 3,106 carats.

The Sovereign's Ring, sometimes referred to as "the wedding ring of England"

Plate Collection

The Jewel House also holds a collection of elaborate gold and silver plates. The Maundy Dish is still used on Maundy Thursday when the monarch distributes money to elderly recipients. The Exeter Salt (a very grand salt cellar from the days when salt was a valuable commodity) was given by the citizens of the city of Exeter to Charles II; during the Civil War Exeter was a Royalist stronghold.

The Sceptre with the Cross (1660), reset in 1910 after Edward VII was presented with the First Star of Africa diamond

The hilt and solid-gold scabbard of the jewelled State Sword, one of the most valuable swords in the world

The White Tower

This is the oldest surviving building in the Tower of London, begun by William I in 1075 and completed before 1079. For centuries it served as an armoury, and much of the national collection of arms and armour is held here. "Fit for a King" showcases 500 years of royal arms and armour, while "Hands on History" allows visitors to get to grips with items of weaponry.

The "Power House" exhibition tells the stories of what went on behind the Tower's walls from 1100 to the present day, and brings to life the personalities that lived here.

The Royal Castle and Armour Gallery

These two chambers on the first floor were the main ceremonial rooms of the original Norman castle. The first one, to the east, is the smaller, probably an ante-chamber to the Banqueting Hall beyond, and contains exhibits setting out the history of the White Tower. It adjoins St John's Chapel, a rare example of a virtually intact early Norman chapel, with a a powerfully solid interior and little ornament-ation. Originally the two main rooms were twice their present height; a pitched roof was removed in 1490 to allow extra floors to be built on top. Suits of armour from Tudor and Stuart times are here, including three made for Henry VIII, one covering his horse as well. A suit made in Holland for Charles I is decorated in gold leaf.

Japanese armour presented to James I in 1613

The Ordnance Gallery

This and the temporary exhibition gallery next door were chambers created in 1490 when the roof was raised. They were used chiefly for storage, and in 1603 a new floor was installed to allow gun-powder to be kept here; by 1667 some 10,000 barrels of it were stored in the Tower. Among the displays are gilt panels and ornament from the barge of the Master of the Ordnance built in 1700.

The Small Armoury and Crypt

The room at the western end of the ground floor may originally have been a living area, and has traces of the oldest fireplaces known in England. Pistols, muskets, swords, pikes and bayonets are mounted on the walls and panels in elaborate symmetrical patterns based on displays in the Tower armouries in the 18th and 19th centuries. They were shown in the Grand Storehouse until it burned down in 1841. A collection of weapons taken from the men who planned to assassinate William III in 1696 is on show, and a wooden block made in 1747 for the execution of Lord Lovat – the last public beheading in England – is on the third floor. The crypt now houses a shop.

The Line of Kings

The Line of Kings, ten life-size carvings of prominent English Monarchs, wearing armour and seated on horseback, originated in Tudor times, when eight such figures adorned the royal palace at Greenwich. Two more had been added by the time they first appeared in the Tower in 1660, celebrating the Resto-ration of Charles II. In 1688, 17 new horses and heads were commissioned, some from the great carver Grinling Gibbons (the third from the left is reputed to be his work).

Henry VIII's armour (1540)

The Princes in the Tower

Now explored in a display in the Bloody Tower, one of the Tower's darkest mysteries concerns two boy princes, sons and heirs of Edward IV. They were put into the Tower by their uncle, Richard of Gloucester, when their father died in 1483. Neither was seen again and Richard was crowned later that year. In 1674, the skeletons of two children were found nearby.

The marina of the restored St Katharine Docks

⑰ St Katharine Docks

E1. **Map** 16 E3. **Tel** 020 7264 5287.
🚇 Tower Hill. ♿ 🚲 ✏ 🖥 🏠
🌐 **skdocks.co.uk**

This most central of all London's docks was designed by Thomas Telford and opened in 1828 on the site of St Katharine's Hospital. Commodities as diverse as tea, marble and live turtles (turtle soup was a Victorian delicacy) were unloaded here.

During the 19th and early 20th centuries, the docks flourished, but by the mid-20th century, cargo ships were delivering their wares in massive containers. The old docks became too small and new ones had to be built downstream. St Katharine's closed in 1968.

The redevelopment of St Katharine's has been one of the city's most successful, and the docks now boast commercial, residential and entertainment facilities, as well as a hotel and a marina. Old warehouse buildings have shops and restaurants on their ground floors, and offices above.

The dock is worth wandering through after visiting the Tower or Tower Bridge (see pp157–61). A weekly street food market is held here on Fridays from 11am to 3pm.

⑱ St Helen's Bishopsgate

Great St Helen's EC3. **Map** 15 C1.
Tel 020 7283 2231. 🚇 Liverpool St, Bank. **Open** 9:30am–12:30pm Mon–Fri; some afternoons (phone to check).
✝ 10:30am, 4pm & 6pm Sun (check website for weekday events). ♿
🌐 **st-helens.org.uk**

The curious appearance of this 13th-century church is due to its origins as two places of worship: one a parish church, the other the chapel of a long-gone nunnery next door. (The medieval nuns of St Helen's were notorious for their "secular kissing".) Among its monuments is the tomb of Sir Thomas Gresham, who founded the Royal Exchange (see p151).

⑲ St Katharine Cree

86 Leadenhall St EC3. **Map** 16 D1.
Tel 020 7488 4318. 🚇 Aldgate, Tower Hill. **Open** 9:30am–4pm Mon–Fri. ✝ 1:05pm Thu.
🌐 **sanctuaryinthecity.net**

A rare pre-Wren 17th-century church with a medieval tower, this was one of only eight churches in the City to survive the fire of 1666. Some of the elaborate plasterwork on and beneath the high ceiling of the nave portrays the coats of arms of the guilds, with which the church has special links. The

St Helen's Bishopsgate

17th-century organ, supported on magnificent carved wooden columns, was played by both Purcell and Handel.

⑳ Leadenhall Market

Whittington Ave EC3. **Map** 15 C2.
Tel 020 7332 1523. 🚇 Bank, Monument. **Open** 10am–6pm Mon–Fri. See Shops and Markets p337.
♿ 🌐 **cityoflondon.gov.uk**

There has been a food market here, on the site of the Roman forum (see pp20–21), since the Middle Ages. Its name comes from a lead-roofed mansion that stood nearby in the 14th century. Today's ornate Victorian covered shopping precinct was designed in 1881 by Sir Horace Jones, the architect of Billingsgate fish market (see p156). Leadenhall now has wine shops, cheesemongers, florists and food shops catering to city workers, along with several traditional pubs and wine bars. The area is busiest at breakfast and lunch time. At Christmas the decorated stores are an attractive sight.

The organ at St Katharine Cree

㉑ Lloyd's of London

1 Lime St EC3. **Map** 15 C2. **Tel** 020 7327 1000. 🚇 Bank, Monument, Liverpool St, Aldgate. **Closed** to the public. 🌐 **lloyds.com**

Lloyd's was founded in the late 17th century and takes its name from the coffee house where underwriters and shipowners used to meet to arrange marine insurance contracts. Lloyd's soon became the world's main insurer, issuing policies on everything from oil tankers to Betty Grable's legs.

The present building, by Sir Richard Rogers, dates from 1986 and is one of the most interesting modern buildings in London (see p34). Its exaggerated stainless steel external piping and high-tech ducts echo Rogers' forceful Pompidou Centre in Paris. Lloyd's is a far more elegant building and particularly worth seeing floodlit at night. Nearby is 30 St Mary Axe, otherwise known as "the Gherkin", one of the most recognizable land-marks on the London skyline.

㉒ Guildhall

Guildhall Yard EC2. **Map** 15 B1.
Tel 020 7332 1313. ⊖ St Paul's.
Great Hall **Open** 10am–4.30pm Mon–Sat (all year), also Sun in May–Sep (may close for events; call ahead to check).
Closed 1 Jan, 25 & 26 Dec. ☑ &
ⓦ **guildhall.cityoflondon.gov.uk**
St Lawrence Jewry **Open** 8am–5pm Mon–Fri. Guildhall Art Gallery and amphitheatre **Tel** 020 7332 3700.
Open 10am–5pm Mon–Fri, noon–4pm Sun. **Closed** 1 Jan, 24–26 Dec.
☑ for temporary exhibitions.
☑ & ☑ ⓦ **cityoflondon.gov.uk/ guildhallgalleries**

Guildhall has been the administrative centre of the City for at least 800 years. For centuries its Great Hall was used for trials and many people were condemned to death here,

Richard Rogers' Lloyd's building illuminated at night

including Henry Garnet, one of the Gunpowder Plot conspirators (see p26). The hall's 15th-century walls are 1.5 m (5 ft) thick, though its arched stone roof is a 20th-century replacement. Overlooking the hall from one end are the figures of legendary giants Gog and Magog, the guardians of the City (these are postwar reproductions of 18th-century models), while statues of notable figures such as Churchill and Nelson line the sides of the 46 m (150 ft) long hall. Each year, a few days

after the Lord Mayor's parade (see p59), the prime minister addresses a banquet here.

On the south side of Guildhall Yard is a Wren-designed church, St Lawrence Jewry, while on the east side is the Guildhall Art Gallery. The original gallery here was built in 1885 to house the art collection of the Corporation of London, but was destroyed in World War II. The present gallery houses the studio collection of 20th-century artist Sir Matthew Smith, portraits from the 16th century to the present day, a gallery of 18th-century works, including John Singleton Copley's *Defeat of the Floating Batteries at Gibraltar*, and numerous Victorian works.

In 1988, the foundations of a Roman amphitheatre were discovered beneath the gallery. Built in AD 70 and with a capacity of about 6,000 spectators, the arena would have hosted animal hunts, executions and gladiatorial combat. Access to the atmospheric ruins is through the art gallery.

The interior of the Guildhall Art Gallery

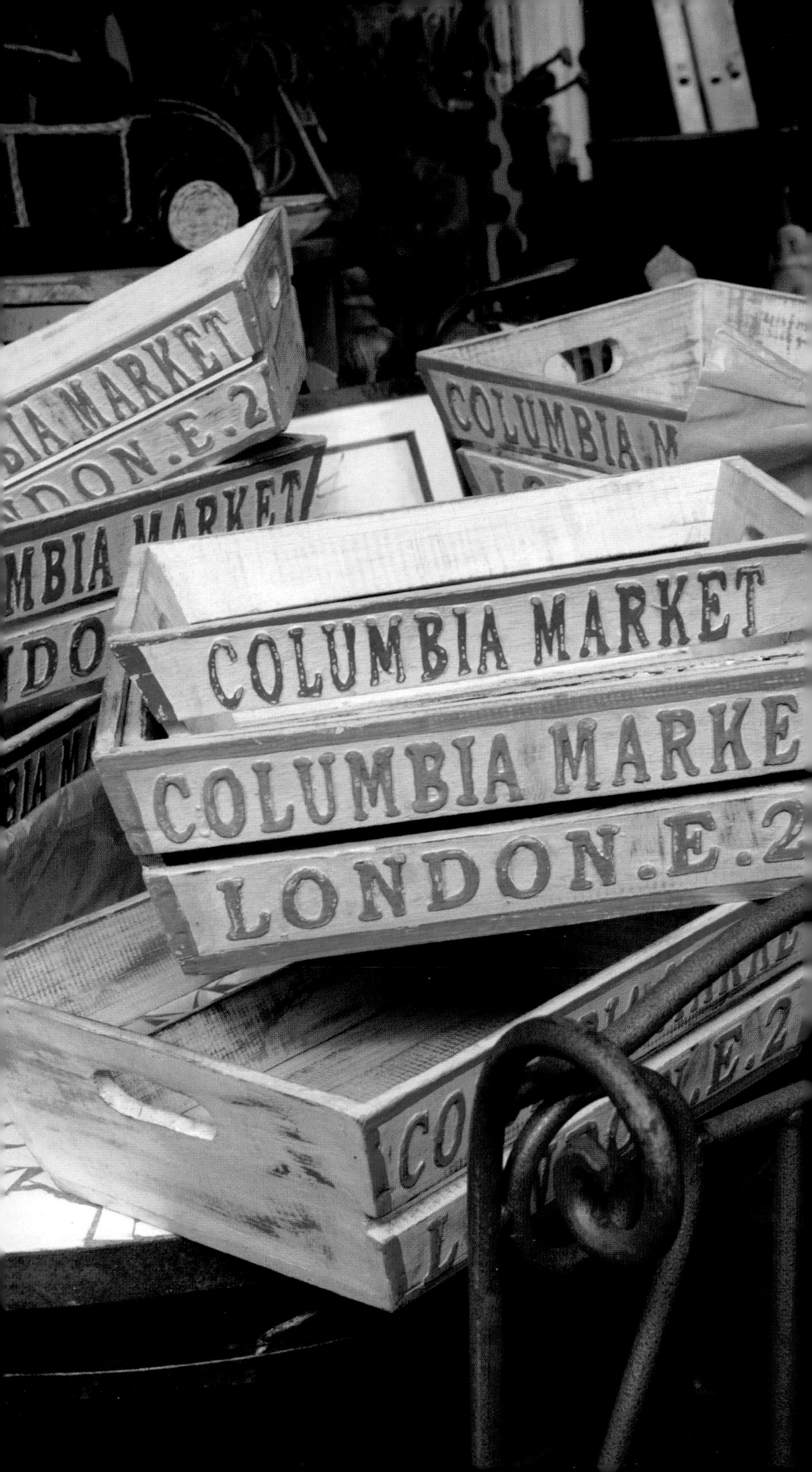
COLUMBIA MARKET
COLUMBIA MARKE
LONDON.E.2

SMITHFIELD AND SPITALFIELDS

These two areas, just north and east of the City walls, have long offered refuge to those who did not want to come under the City's jurisdiction, or were not welcome there: the French Huguenots in the 17th century and, in later times, other immigrants from Europe and then Asia. They founded small industries and brought with them their restaurants and places of worship, and as a result these are both vibrant, atmospheric quarters. London's traditional meat market still operates at Smithfield, while the markets of Spitalfields, Brick Lane and Columbia Road together form an essential Sunday destination, with their eclectic stalls, vintage fashions, food stands and beautiful blooms. While Smithfield tends to be quiet at weekends, Brick Lane and Spitalfields have a buzzing late-night scene.

Sights at a Glance

Historic Streets and Buildings
1 St John's Gate
2 Charterhouse
4 Cloth Fair
9 Barbican
11 Wesley's Chapel–Leysian Mission
16 Fournier Street
18 19 Princelet Street
19 Brick Lane
20 Dennis Severs' House

Museums and Galleries
6 Museum of London pp170–71
13 Whitechapel Gallery

Churches and Mosques
5 St Bartholomew-the-Great
7 St Botolph, Aldersgate
8 St Giles, Cripplegate
15 Christ Church, Spitalfields
17 London Jamme Masjid
21 St Leonard's Church

Cemeteries
10 Bunhill Fields

Markets
3 Smithfield Market
12 Petticoat Lane
14 Old Spitalfields Market
22 Columbia Road Market

Restaurants see pp302–4
1 L'Anima
2 Boho Mexica
3 The Boundary
4 Le Café du Marché
5 Carnevale
6 Cây Tre
7 Club Gascon
8 The Culpeper
9 Galvin la Chapelle
10 Hawksmoor
11 Pham Sushi
12 St John
13 Vinoteca

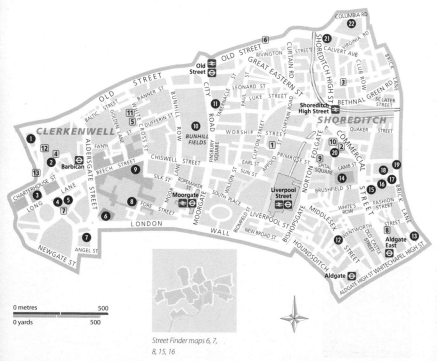

Street Finder maps 6, 7, 8, 15, 16

0 metres 500
0 yards 500

◄ Columbia Road flower and plant market

For keys to symbols see back flap

Street-by-Street: Smithfield

This area is among the most historic in London. It contains one of the capital's oldest churches, some rare Jacobean houses, vestiges of the Roman wall (near the Museum of London) and central London's only surviving wholesale food market.

Smithfield's long history is also bloody. In 1381, the rebel peasant leader Wat Tyler was killed here by an ally of Richard II as he presented the king with demands for lower taxes. Later, in the reign of Mary I (1553–8), scores of Protestant religious martyrs were burned at the stake here.

The Fox and Anchor pub is open from 7am for hearty breakfasts, washed down with ale by the market traders of Smithfield.

❸ ★ Smithfield Market
A contemporary print shows Horace Jones's stately building for the meat market when it was completed in 1867.

Key

— Suggested route

The Golden Boy of Pye Corner is a small statue commemorating the fact that the Great Fire was finally put out on Giltspur Street, saving buildings such as St Bartholomew-the-Great.

St Bartholomew-the-Less has a 15th-century tower and vestry. Its links to the hospital are shown by this early 20th-century stained glass of a nurse, a gift from the Worshipful Company of Glaziers.

St Bartholomew's Hospital (Bart's) has stood on this site since 1123. Some of the existing buildings date from 1759.

CHARTERHOUSE STREET

WEST SMITHFIELD

SMITHFIELD STREET

COCK LANE

SNOW HILL

GILTSPUR STREET

LON

0 metres   100
0 yards   100

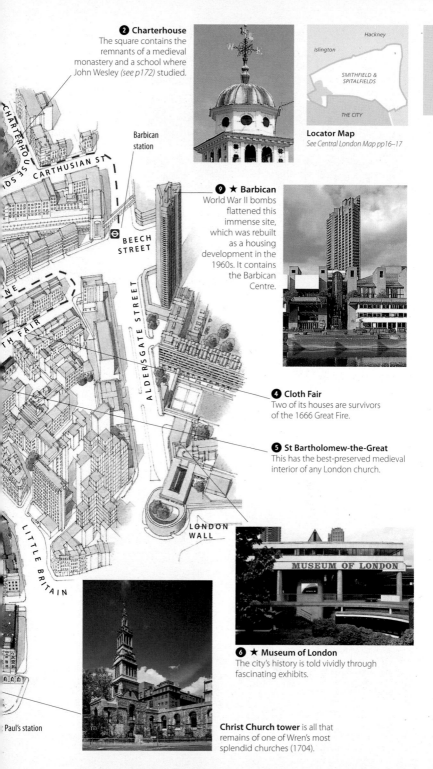

❷ Charterhouse
The square contains the remnants of a medieval monastery and a school where John Wesley *(see p172)* studied.

Locator Map
See Central London Map pp16–17

❾ ★ Barbican
World War II bombs flattened this immense site, which was rebuilt as a housing development in the 1960s. It contains the Barbican Centre.

❹ Cloth Fair
Two of its houses are survivors of the 1666 Great Fire.

❺ St Bartholomew-the-Great
This has the best-preserved medieval interior of any London church.

MUSEUM OF LONDON

❻ ★ Museum of London
The city's history is told vividly through fascinating exhibits.

Christ Church tower is all that remains of one of Wren's most splendid churches (1704).

Smithfield Market, now officially known as London Central Markets

❶ St John's Gate

St John's Lane EC1. **Map** 6 F4.
Tel 020 7324 4005. ⊖ Farringdon.
Open 10am–5pm Mon–Sat.
Closed Christmas week & bank
holiday weekends. 📷 11am, 2:30pm
Tue, Fri, Sat (donation). 📷 ♿ limited.
🅆 museumstjohn.org.uk

The Tudor gatehouse and parts
of the 12th-century church are
all that remain of the priory of
the Knights of St John, which
flourished here for 400 years
and was the precursor of the
St John Ambulance. Over the
years, the priory buildings have
had many uses, such as offices
for Elizabeth I's Master of the
Revels, a pub, and a coffee shop
run by the artist William
Hogarth's father. A museum of
the order's history has been
renovated, with support from
the Heritage Lottery Fund, to
create an exhibition space
showing hidden parts of the
gatehouse and a learning
space in the priory church.
The rest of the building can
be seen on guided tours.

❷ Charterhouse

Charterhouse Sq EC1. **Map** 6 F5.
⊖ Barbican. **Open** for 📷
2.15pm Tue–Thu and alternate
Sats, book well ahead (see
website for details).
🅆 thecharterhouse.org

The Tudor gateway on the
north side of the square
leads to the site of a former
Carthusian monastery, which
was dissolved under Henry
VIII. In 1611, the buildings
were converted into a hospital
for poor pensioners, and a
charity school – called
Charterhouse – whose pupils
included John Wesley (see
p172), writer William Thackeray
and Robert Baden-Powell,
founder of the Boy Scouts. In
1872, the school, now a top
boarding school, relocated
to Godalming in Surrey. Part
of the original site was
subsequently taken over by
St Bartholomew's Hospital
medical school. Some of
the old buildings remain,
including the chapel and
part of the cloisters. Today
Charterhouse is still home
to more than 40 pensioners,
who are supported by the
charitable foundation.

❸ Smithfield Market

Charterhouse St EC1.
Map 6 F5. ⊖
Farringdon, Barbican.
Open 2–9am Mon–
Fri. **Closed** public hols.
🅆 smithfieldmarket.
com

Animals have been
traded here since
the 12th century,
but the site was
granted its first
official charter in
1400. In 1648, it
was officially
established as a
cattle market and

Stone carving stands
atop Charterhouse

live cattle continued to be sold
here until the mid-19th century.
It now confines itself to wholesale trading in meat and poultry.
It was originally sited in Smithfield, outside the city walls.
Although moved to its present
location in Charterhouse Street
in the 1850s and called the
London Central Meat Market,
the original name stuck. The
old buildings are by Victorian
architect Horace Jones, but
there are 20th-century
additions. Some pubs in
the area keep market hours,
serving hearty breakfasts
from dawn. After much-
needed modernization, the
market is now one of the best
equipped meat markets in
the world. Visitors should aim
to arrive by 7am.

A 17th-century townhouse on
Cloth Fair

❹ Cloth Fair

EC1. **Map** 6 F5. ⊖ Barbican.

This attractive street is named
after the notoriously rowdy
Bartholomew Fair, which was
the main cloth fair in medieval
and Elizabethan England, held
annually at Smithfield until
1855. Nos. 41 and 42 are fine
examples of 17th-century
architecture and have
distinctive two-storey wooden
bay windows, although their
ground floors have since been
modernized. The former Poet
Laureate John Betjeman, who
died in 1984, lived at No. 43 for
most of his life.

❺ St Bartholomew-the-Great

West Smithfield EC1. **Map** 6 F5.
Tel 020 7600 0440. 🚇 Barbican.
Open 8:30am–5pm Mon–Fri (to 4pm mid-Nov–mid-Feb), 10:30am–4pm Sat, 8:30am–8pm Sun.
Closed Christmas week. 🕐 9am, 11am, 6:30pm Sun. 🅿 ♿ 📷 by appt. 🏪
🎵 Concerts. 🌐 **greatstbarts.com**

One of London's oldest churches, St Bart's was founded in 1123 by the monk Rahere, whose tomb is inside. A courtier of Henry I, he dreamed that the saint saved him from a winged monster.

The 13th-century arch used to be the door to the church until the nave of that earlier building was pulled down when Henry VIII dissolved the priory.

Today the arch leads from West Smithfield to the burial ground; the gatehouse above it is from a later period. The present building retains the crossing and chancel of the original, with its round arches and other fine Norman detailing. There are also some fine Tudor monuments. The artist William Hogarth was baptized here in 1697.

Parts of the church have been used for secular purposes. In 1725, US statesman Benjamin Franklin worked for a printer in the Lady Chapel. The church also featured in the films *Four Weddings and a Funeral*, *Shakespeare in Love* and *The Other Boleyn Girl*. The café in the cloisters is a peaceful spot.

❻ Museum of London

See pp170–71.

❼ St Botolph, Aldersgate

Aldersgate St EC1. **Map** 15 A1. **Tel** 020 7283 1670. 🚇 St Paul's, Barbican, Moorgate. **Open** 9am–3pm Mon–Fri. 🕐 1pm Tue & Thu, 10:30am Sun 🌐 **stbotolphs.org.uk**. ♿

A modest late Georgian exterior (completed in the late 18th century) conceals a flamboyant, well-preserved interior with a finely decorated plaster ceiling, a rich brown wooden organ case and galleries, and an oak pulpit resting on a carved palm tree. The original box pews have been kept in the galleries rather than in the body of the church. Some of the memorials come from a 14th-century church that originally existed on the site.

The former churchyard alongside was converted in 1880 into a green space known as Postman's Park, because it was used by workers from the nearby Post Office headquarters. In the late 19th century, the Victorian artist G F Watts dedicated one of the walls to a quirky collection of plaques that commemorate people – often children – who sacrificed their lives to save others. Each is remembered on a hand-painted tile. There are three St Botolph churches in the City; the other two can be found at Aldgate and in Bishopsgate.

❽ St Giles, Cripplegate

Fore St EC2. **Map** 7 A5. **Tel** 020 7638 1997. 🚇 Barbican, Moorgate. **Open** 11am–4pm Mon–Fri. 🕐 8:30am Mon–Thu, 10am & 4pm Sun. 📷 2–5pm Tue. ♿ 🌐 **stgilescripplegate.co.uk**

Completed in 1550, this church survived the ravages of the Great Fire in 1666, but was so

St Bartholomew's gatehouse

badly damaged by a World War II bomb that only the tower survived. St Giles was refurbished during the 1950s to serve as the parish church of the Barbican, and now stands awkwardly amidst the stark modernity of the area. It is one of the few UK churches to boast two complete organs.

Here, Oliver Cromwell married Elizabeth Bourchier in 1620 and the poet John Milton was buried in 1674. Well-preserved remains of London's Roman and medieval walls can be seen to the south.

St Giles, Cripplegate

❻ Museum of London

Opened in 1976 on the edge of the Barbican, this museum provides a lively account of London life from prehistoric times to the present day. Reconstructed interiors and street scenes alternate with displays of original domestic artifacts and items found on the museum's archaeological digs. The museum underwent a huge expansion in 2010; the latest addition is a specially built central space to display sections of the Thomas Heatherwick-designed Olympic 2012 torch.

★ **Marble Head of Serapis**
This statue of the Egyptian god of the underworld (2nd–3rd century) was discovered in the temple of Mithras.

Stairs to Galleries of Modern London

Oliver Cromwell's Death Mask
This plaster copy made from a wax impression is a permanent record of how he looked.

Boy's Leather Jerkin
This practical sleeveless jacket (c.1560), decorated with punched hearts and stars, would have been worn over a doublet for extra warmth.

Main entrance

Flint Hand Axe
Thousands of these cutting tools (c.350,000–120,000 BC) have been found in the gravels beneath modern London.

Key

- ☐ 450,000 BC–AD 50: London before London
- ☐ AD 50–410: Roman London
- ☐ AD 410–1558: Medieval London
- ☐ 1550s–1660s: War, Plague and Fire
- ☐ 1670s–1850s: Expanding City
- ☐ Victorian Walk
- ☐ Sackler Hall
- ☐ 1850s–1940s: People's City
- ☐ 1950s–Today: World City
- ☐ Inspiring London
- ☐ Linbury Gallery
- ☐ City Gallery
- ☐ Temporary Exhibitions
- ☐ London 2012 Cauldron: Designing a Moment

Gallery Guide

The galleries are laid out chronologically, starting on the entrance level with prehistory. Visitors can walk through Roman and medieval London galleries to the War, Plague and Fire gallery, which includes a special display on the Great Fire. On the lower level, they can learn about London from 1666 to the present day, and see the Lord Mayor of London's spectacular State Coach.

Tobacconist
The Victorian Walk uses several original shop fronts and objects to recreate the atmosphere of late 19th-century London.

VISITORS' CHECKLIST

Practical Information
London Wall EC2.
Map 15 A1.
Tel 020 7001 9844.
w museumoflondon.org.uk
Open 10am–6pm daily.
Closed 24–26 Dec. Induction loops fitted. Lectures, film presentations.

Transport
Barbican, St Paul's, Moorgate.
4, 8, 25, 56, 100, 172, 242, 521.
City Thameslink, Liverpool Street, Farringdon.

The Expanding City Gallery explores London after the Great Fire.

Ignazio Pluchino Shoes
The Sicilian opened his shoemaking business in London in 1900. He made high quality shoes for the wealthy.

Selfridges Lift
These bronze and cast iron Brandt Edgar lifts were installed in 1928.

Beatles Dress
Made in 1964, this cotton dress is printed with the Beatles' faces alongside a guitar that features their signatures.

★ **Lord Mayor's Coach**
Finely carved and painted, this gilded coach (c.1757) is paraded once a year during the Lord Mayor's Show *(see p59)*.

The Barbican Centre and surrounding residential blocks

⑨ Barbican

Silk St EC2. **Map** 7 A5. **Tel** 020 7638 8891. Barbican, Moorgate. Barbican Centre **Open** 9am–11pm Mon–Sat, 11am–11pm Sun, public hols. Art galleries: 10am–6pm daily (to 9pm Thu & Fri). Conservatory: 11am–5pm, most Suns (check website for days). induction loop. *See Entertainment pp345–8.* **barbican.org.uk**

An ambitious piece of 1960s city planning, this residential, commercial and arts complex was begun in 1962 on a site devastated by World War II bombs, and not completed for nearly 20 years. Residential tower blocks surround the Barbican Centre, a prestigious arts complex, which also includes an ornamental lake and fountains.

The old city wall turned a corner here and substantial remains of the fortifications are still clearly visible (particularly so from the Museum of London – *see pp170–71*). The word barbican means a defensive tower over a gate and in a sense the modern complex retains the air of a self-sufficient community, with formidable defences against the outside world. Obscure entrances and raised walkways remove pedestrians from the cramped bustle of the City, but, in spite of the signposts and yellow lines on the pavement, the complex can be difficult to navigate.

As well as two theatres and a concert hall, the Barbican Centre has two cinemas, two galleries and an excellent library. It is also home to the London Symphony Orchestra and the Guildhall School of Music and Drama. One of its more surprising features is a large conservatory; this tropical oasis, containing over 2,000 plants, makes a delightful refuge on a chilly afternoon.

⑩ Bunhill Fields

City Rd EC1. **Map** 7 B4. **Tel** 020 7374 4127 (City Gardens). Old Street. **Open** Apr–Sep: 8am–7pm (or dusk) Mon–Fri, 9:30am–7pm (or dusk) Sat, Sun & public hols; Oct–Mar: 8am–4pm Mon–Fri; 9:30am–4pm Sat, Sun & public hols. **Closed** 1 Jan, 25 & 26 Dec. Apr–Oct: 12:30pm Wed phone first. **cityoflondon.gov.uk**

This spot was first designated a cemetery after the Great Plague of 1665 *(see p27)*, when it was enclosed by a brick wall and gates. Twenty years later it was allocated to Nonconformists, who were banned from being buried in churchyards because of their refusal to use the Church of England prayer book.

William Blake's gravestone at Bunhill Fields

The cemetery is situated on the edge of the City, and shaded by large plane trees. There are monuments to the well-known writers Daniel Defoe, John Bunyan and William Blake, as well as to members of the Cromwell family. John Milton wrote his epic poem *Paradise Lost* while he lived in Bunhill Row, located on the west side of the cemetery.

Wesley's Chapel, with a museum to the Methodist church John Wesley founded

⑪ Wesley's Chapel–Leysian Mission

49 City Rd EC1. **Map** 7 B4. **Tel** 020 7253 2262. Old Street, Moorgate. **Open** 10am–4pm Mon–Sat. **Closed** between Christmas & New Year, public hols (except Good Friday). 9:45am (not 1st Sun of month), 11am Sun, 12:45pm Wed. groups book ahead. Free lunchtime recitals: Thu. **wesleyschapel.org.uk**

John Wesley, the founder of the Methodist church, laid this chapel's foundation stone in 1777. He preached here until his death in 1791, and is buried behind the chapel. Next door is the house where he lived, where some of his furniture, books and other possessions can be seen.

The chapel, adorned in spartan style, in accordance with Wesley's austere religious principles, has columns made from ships' masts. Baroness Thatcher, the first female British prime minister (1979–90), was married here. Beneath the chapel is a small museum devoted to the history of Methodism.

⑫ Petticoat Lane

Middlesex St E1. **Map** 16 D1. 🚇 Aldgate East, Aldgate, Liverpool St. **Open** Main market 9am–2pm Sun; smaller market on Wentworth St 8am–4pm Mon–Fri. *See Shops and Markets p337.*

In Queen Victoria's prudish reign, the name of this street, long famous for its market, was changed to the respectable but colourless Middlesex Street. That is still its official designation, but the old name, derived from the petticoats and lace sold here by the Huguenots who came from France, has stuck, and is now applied to the market held every Sunday morning in this and the surrounding streets. Numerous attempts were made to stop the market, but it was allowed by Act of Parliament in 1936. Though the street is not particularly attractive, having suffered wartime bomb damage, the lively market creates plenty of atmosphere. A great variety of goods is sold but there is still a bias towards clothing, especially leather coats. The atmosphere is noisy and cheerful, with Cockney stallholders making use of their wit to attract custom. There are scores of snack bars for pitstops.

⑬ Whitechapel Gallery

77–82 Whitechapel High St E1. **Map** 16 E1. **Tel** 020 7522 7888. 🚇 Aldgate East, Aldgate. **Open** 11am–6pm Tue–Sun, (to 9pm Thu). **Closed** 1 Jan, 24–26 Dec. 📷 occasionally for exhibitions. ♿ 🎁 💻 📷 Wide range of talks & events. 🆆 **whitechapelgallery.org**

A striking Art Nouveau façade by C Harrison Townsend fronts this light, airy gallery, founded in 1901 and expanded in the 1980s and again in 2007–9. Situated close to Brick Lane and the area's burgeoning art scene, this independent gallery was founded with the aim of bringing great art to the people of East London. Today it enjoys an international reputation for high-quality shows of major contemporary artists and for events, talks, live performances, films and art-themed evenings (especially on the first Thursday of each month, when many galleries in the area open late). In the 1950s and 1960s, the likes of Jackson Pollock, Anthony Caro, Robert Rauschenberg and John Hoyland all displayed their work here. In 1970 David

Whitechapel Gallery, expanded to include the former library next door

Hockney's first exhibition was held here. The gallery has a well-stocked arts bookshop and a relaxed café-bar.

⑭ Old Spitalfields Market

Commercial St E1. **Map** 8 D5. 🚇 Liverpool St, Aldgate. **Open** General market stalls: 10am–5pm Sun–Wed (from 9am Sun); antiques & vintage: 9am–5pm Thu; fashion & art: 10am–4pm Fri. Occasional themed market days: 11am–5pm Sat (check website listings). *See Shops and Markets p337.* 🆆 **oldspitalfieldsmarket.com**

Produce has been traded at Spitalfields market since 1682. In 1887 the original covered market buildings were completed, later expanded in the 1920s. The vegetable market moved out in 1991, after which today's version of the market – known for antiques, fashion, bric-a-brac and craft stalls – started to take shape. In the early 2000s, the 1920s western extension made way for offices and the rest was renovated and redeveloped. Now the market space is a mix of new units housing restaurants and shops and traditional market space. It's open during the week, but it is on Sundays that crowds come in search of vintage clothing and unique items. More new designers and unusual stalls abound in other nearby Sunday markets, particularly in the Old Truman Brewery off Brick Lane *(see p174).*

Bustling Petticoat Lane Market

⑮ Christ Church, Spitalfields

Commercial St E1. **Map** 8 E5. **Tel** 020 7377 6793. 🚇 Liverpool St. **Open** 10am–4pm Mon–Fri (unless in use as venue), 1–4pm Sun. 🕁 1:10pm Tue 8:30am & 10:30am Sun. 🚻 📷 book ahead. Concerts. 🔳 ccspitalfields.org

The finest of Nicholas Hawksmoor's six churches, Christ Church was commissioned by parliament in the Fifty New Churches Act of 1711, aimed at combating the threat of Nonconformism. It was intended to make a powerful statement in an area fast becoming a Huguenot stronghold. (The Protestant Huguenots had fled from persecution in Catholic France and came to Spitalfields to work in the local silkweaving industry.)

Completed in 1729, the building was mauled by alterations in the 1850s. By 1960 it was derelict, narrowly escaping demolition. In 1976 the Friends of Christ Church Spitalfields was formed to restore the building to its former glory – a goal achieved in 2004. The impression of size and strength created by its portico and spire is continued inside by such features as the high ceiling and the gallery. Now used for music events, it is one of the main venues for the Spitalfields music festivals in June and December.

Christ Church, Spitalfields, dominates the surrounding streets

Beautifully preserved 18th-century houses on Fournier Street

⑯ Fournier Street

E1. **Map** 8 E5. 🚇 Aldgate East.

The 18th-century houses on the north side of this street have attics with broad windows that were designed to give maximum light to the silk-weaving French Huguenot community who lived here. While the textile trade lives on in the area, still dependent on immigrant labour, Fournier Street itself has become a smart address for the art crowd.

⑰ London Jamme Masjid

59 Brick Lane E1. **Map** 8 E5. 🚇 Liverpool Street, Aldgate East. 🔳 bricklanejammemasjid.co.uk

The history of this Grade II-listed building reflects centuries of immigration in the area. Built in 1743 as a Huguenot chapel, it was a synagogue in the 19th century, a Methodist chapel in the early 20th century, and has been a mosque since 1976.

⑱ 19 Princelet Street

19 Princelet St E1. **Map** 8 E5. **Tel** 020 7247 5352. 🚇 Liverpool St. **Open** infrequently, check website for dates. 🔳 19princeletstreet.org.uk

This 1719 Huguenot silk merchant's house, with a Victorian synagogue hidden within, epitomizes the area's multicultural history. Now it exists as a museum of immigration, with exhibitions celebrating the Jewish and other peoples who arrived and settled in London's East End. It is hoped that, with funding this historic gem can be developed into a permanent centre.

⑲ Brick Lane

E1. **Map** 8 E5. 🚇 Liverpool St, Aldgate East, Shoreditch. Market **Open** dawn–noon Sun. *See Shops and Markets p335.* 🔳 bricklanemarket.com

Once a lane running through brickfields, Brick Lane has long been synonymous with the many curry houses that line it, and the British-Bangladeshi community that has long thrived here. Now the restaurants sit next to hip galleries and quirky boutiques. Shops and houses, some dating from the 18th century, have seen immigrants of many nationalities, and ethnic foods, spices, silks and saree are all on sale here. In the 19th century this was a predominantly Jewish quarter, and some Jewish shops remain, including a 24-hour bagel shop at No. 159.

On Sundays, a large market is held here and in the surrounding streets. At the northern end of Brick Lane is the Old Truman Brewery, a medley of 18th- and 19th-century industrial architecture, now home to an eclectic mix of bars, shops and markets: five separate markets at weekends sell food, vintage clothes and new fashions.

Authentic Indian pastries, biscuits and sweets for sale in Brick Lane

The grand bedroom of Dennis Severs' House

⑳ Dennis Severs' House

18 Folgate St E1. **Map** 8 D5. **Tel** 020 7247 4013. 🚇 Liverpool St. **Open** noon–4pm Sun, noon–2pm Mon, 5–9pm Mon & Wed (book ahead for evening visits). Private and group bookings welcome. 🏠
🌐 dennissevershouse.co.uk

At No. 18 Folgate Street, built in 1724, the late designer and performer Dennis Severs recreated a historical interior that takes you on a journey from the 17th to the 19th centuries. It offers what he called "an adventure of the imagination… a visit to a time-mode rather than… merely a look at a house". The rooms are like a series of *tableaux vivants*, as if the occupants had simply left for a moment. There is bread on the plates, wine in the glasses, fruit in the bowl; the candles flicker and horses' hooves clatter on the cobbles outside. This highly theatrical experience is far removed from more usual museum recreations and is not suitable for the under-12s. Praised by many, including artist David Hockney, it is truly unique. The house's motto is "you either see it or you don't".

Around the corner on Elder Street are two of London's earliest surviving terraces, where many of the Georgian red-brick houses have been carefully restored.

㉑ St Leonard's Church

Shoreditch High St E1. **Map** 8 D3.
Tel (box office) 020 7377 1362.
🚇 Old Street, Liverpool Street.
Open Mar–Oct: noon–2pm Mon–Fri.
✝ 10:30am Sun. ♿ Concerts and theatrical performances.
🌐 shoreditchchurch.org.uk

Standing as it does on the spot where several major Roman roads converged, this has been a site of worship for millennia. The Norman St Leonard's was the original "actors' church" and many famous names of Tudor theatre are buried in the crypt, including Richard Burbage, who played the first Hamlet, Macbeth and Romeo, and his brother Cuthbert, founder of the Globe Theatre.

Erected in 1736–40, the current Palladian-style church is the oldest building in Shoreditch. Its fine acoustics make it popular as a performance space with musicians.

㉒ Columbia Road Market

Columbia Rd E2. **Map** 8 D3.
🚇 Liverpool St, Old St, Bethnal Green.
Open 8am–3pm Sun. *See Shops and Markets p336.*

A visit to this flower and plant market is one of the most delightful things to do on a Sunday morning in London, whether you want to take advantage of the exotic species on offer or not – though it's hard to resist, as prices are competitive and the range impressive. Set in a well-preserved street of small Victorian shops, it is a lively, sweet-smelling and colourful event. Apart from the stalls, there are several shops selling, among other things, home-made bread and farmhouse cheeses, antiques and interesting objects, many flower-related. There are also cafés, a tapas bar and pubs to refuel at along the street.

Columbia Road flower market presents beautiful blooms on a Sunday morning

SOUTHWARK AND BANKSIDE

Southwark once offered an escape from the City, a place to indulge in the many forms of entertainment that were banned across the river. Borough High Street was lined with taverns: the medieval courtyards that still run off it mark where they stood. The George survives as the only galleried inn in London. Among the illicit pleasures that thrived here from the late 16th century were brothels, theatres, and bear and cock pits.

Shakespeare's company was based at the Globe Theatre, which has been rebuilt close to its original site. Today, the south bank of the river is an attractive riverside promenade that connects several of the city's major sights: the vast, ever-changing Tate Modern, standing opposite the Millennium Bridge; London's finest food market at Borough; and the Shard, the city's tallest building, with vertigo-inducing views from its pinnacle.

Sights at a Glance

Historic Streets and Areas
6 Cardinal's Wharf
13 Bermondsey Street
14 City Hall

Museums and Galleries
4 The Old Operating Theatre
7 Bankside Gallery
8 Tate Modern
11 Clink Prison Museum
12 The Shard

Cathedrals
1 Southwark Cathedral

Pubs
3 George Inn
10 The Anchor

Markets
2 Borough Market

Historic Ships
15 HMS *Belfast*

Theatres
5 Shakespeare's Globe
9 The Rose Playhouse

Restaurants *see pp304–5*
1 Champor-Champor
2 Dim T – London Bridge
3 José
4 Roast
5 Tapas Brindisa
6 Tito's Peruvian Restaurant
7 Wright Brothers
8 Zucca

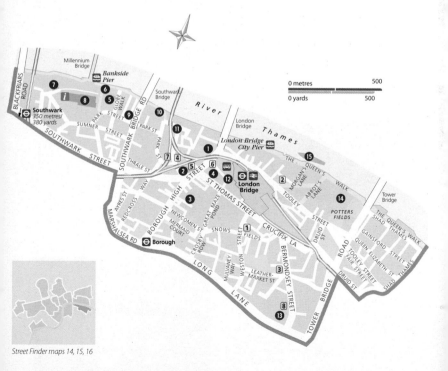

Street Finder maps 14, 15, 16

Street-by-Street: Southwark

From medieval times until the 18th century, Southwark
was a venue for the pursuit of illicit pleasures; south of the
Thames, it was out of the jurisdiction of the City authorities.
The 18th and 19th centuries brought docks, warehouses and
factories. A riverside walk here provides spectacular views of
St Paul's and takes in Tate Modern, a regenerated Borough
Market, the stunning recreation of Shakespeare's Globe
Theatre, and the Shard.

Southwark Bridge was opened in
1912 to replace a bridge of 1819.

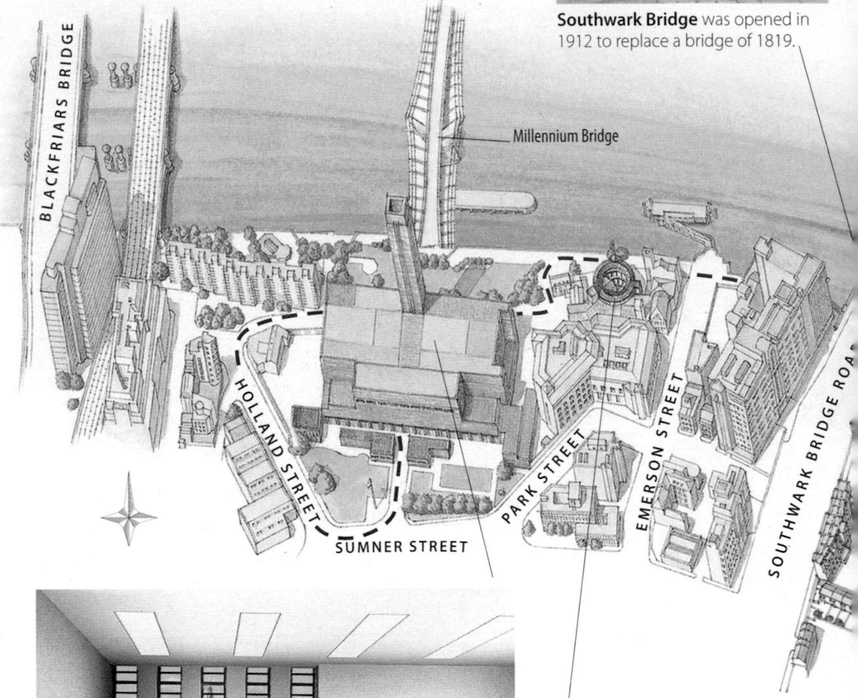

Millennium Bridge

BLACKFRIARS BRIDGE

HOLLAND STREET

SUMNER STREET

PARK STREET

EMERSON STREET

SOUTHWARK BRIDGE ROAD

Key

— Suggested route

0 metres 100
0 yards 100

⑧ ★ Tate Modern
The former Bankside Power Station
is now a spectacular space to
show off a huge collection of
contemporary art.

❺ ★ Shakespeare's Globe
This brilliant recreation of an
Elizabethan theatre has open-air
performances in the summer months
and an exhibition open all year round.

11 **Clink Prison Museum**
This museum, on the site of the notorious old prison, looks back at Southwark's colourful past.

10 **The Anchor**
For centuries this riverside pub has been a firm favourite.

The Hop Exchange
was where hops from Kent for brewing were traded; its pediment features carved scenes of the hop harvest.

Locator Map
See Central London Map pp16–17

THE CITY

Thames

SOUTHWARK & BANKSIDE

Elephant & Castle

14th-century rose window

The *Golden Hinde II* is a replica of Sir Francis Drake's galleon built in the 1970s; it sailed the globe for several decades before docking here.

1 ★ **Southwark Cathedral**
Despite major alterations, it still contains medieval elements.

London Bridge, in its various forms, was the only river crossing in London from Roman times until 1750. The present bridge, completed in 1972, replaced the one of 1831.

2 **Borough Market**
There has been a market on or near this site since 1276.

BANKEND

PARK STREET

CLINK STREET

STREET

CATHEDRAL STREET

MONTAGUE CLOSE

LONDON BRIDGE

STONEY

SOUTHWARK STREET

BOROUGH HIGH STREET

ST THOMAS STREET

The Shard

The War Memorial, commemorating soldiers who fell in World War I, was erected in 1924 on Borough High Street, where it has become a powerful landmark.

3 **George Inn**
This is London's only surviving traditional galleried inn.

THE GEORGE

❶ Southwark Cathedral

Montague Close SE1. **Map** 15 B3.
Tel 020 7367 6700. ⊖ London
Bridge. **Open** 8am–6pm Mon–Fri,
8:30am–6pm Sat & Sun. 🚹 daily
(check website). ♿ 🚻 📷
Concerts. 🇼 **cathedral.southwark.
anglican.org**

This church did not become a
cathedral until 1905. However,
some parts of it date back to the
12th century, when the building
was attached to a priory, and
many of its medieval features
remain. The memorials are
fascinating, including a late
13th-century wooden effigy
of a knight. John Harvard, the
first benefactor of Harvard
University, was baptized here
in 1607 and there is a chapel
named after him.

In 2000, the cathedral was
restored in a multi-million-
pound programme, which
included the addition of new
buildings housing a shop and
a refectory. The exterior has
been landscaped to create a
herb garden and an attractive
Millennium Courtyard that
leads to the riverside.

Southwark Cathedral's Shakespeare Window

❷ Borough Market

8 Southwark St SE1. **Map** 15 B4.
⊖ London Bridge. **Open** 10am–5pm
Wed–Thu, 10am–6pm Fri, 8am–5pm
Sat (some stalls also 10am–5pm Mon
& Tue). 🇼 **boroughmarket.org.uk**

Borough Market was once an
exclusively wholesale fruit and
vegetable market, which had
its origins in medieval times,
and moved to its current

The George Inn, now owned by the National Trust

atmospheric position beneath
the railway tracks in 1756.

An extremely popular fine
food market, it is known for
gourmet goods from Britain
and Europe, as well as quality
fruit and vegetables and
organic meat, fish and dairy
produce. A growing number
of hot food stalls, selling a
tempting array of dishes from
around the world, share the
space with produce stalls. It
is at its busiest on Fridays and
Saturdays, when stalls spread
out across the whole area. Food
demonstrations take place in
the glass atrium on Borough
High Street on Thursdays and
Fridays. The specialist food
shops and pubs on the streets
around the market are also well
worth checking out.

❸ George Inn

77 Borough High St SE1. **Map** 15 B4.
Tel 020 7407 2056. ⊖ London Bridge,
Borough. **Open** 11am–11pm Mon–Sat,
noon–10:30pm Sun. 🍷 *See Pubs and
Bars pp312–15.* 🇼 **nationaltrust.org.
uk/george-inn**

Dating from the 17th century,
this building is the only example
of a traditional galleried
coaching inn left in London and
is mentioned by Dickens in *Little
Dorrit.* It was rebuilt after the
Southwark fire of 1676 in a style
that dates back to the Middle
Ages. Originally, there would
have been three wings around a

courtyard where plays were
staged in the 17th century. In
1889, the north and east wings
were demolished, so there is
only one wing remaining.

The inn, now owned by the
National Trust, is still a working
pub. Perfect on a cold wet day,
the pub, spread over a series of
small rooms, has a well-worn,
comfortable atmosphere. In the
summer, the yard fills with
picnic tables.

Ancient remedies, the Old Operating Theatre

❹ The Old Operating Theatre

9a St Thomas St SE1. **Map** 15 B4.
Tel 020 7188 2679. ⊖ London Bridge.
Open 10:30am–5pm daily.
Closed 15 Dec–5 Jan. 📷 📷
♿ very limited (the museum is
upstairs). 🇼 **thegarret.org.uk**

St Thomas' Hospital, one of the
oldest in Britain, stood here
from its foundation in the
12th century until it was moved
west in 1862. At this time,
nearly all of its buildings were
demolished in order to make
way for the railway. The women's

operating theatre (the Old Operating Theatre Museum and Herb Garret) survived only because it had been constructed in a garret over the hospital church. The UK's oldest operating theatre, dating from 1822, it remained, bricked up and forgotten until the 1950s. It has now been fitted out just as it would have been in the early 19th century, before the discovery of either anaesthetics or antiseptics. Another section of the garret, which was once used by the hospital apothecary to store herbs, houses a collection of traditional herbs and remedies, plus displays of antiquated medicines.

Shakespeare's Henry IV, performed at the Globe Theatre around 1600

❺ Shakespeare's Globe

New Globe Walk SE1. **Map** 15 A3. **Tel** 020 7902 1400. Box Office: **Tel** 020 7401 9919. 🚇 Southwark, London Bridge. Exhibition **Open** 9am–5:30pm. 🅿 includes tour. 🎫 every 30 mins; Nov–May 9:30am–5:30pm, Apr–Oct 9:30am–12:30pm. **Closed** 24 & 25 Dec. Performances Apr–early Oct. ♿ 📷 🚻 📷 **w** shakespearesglobe.com

Built on the banks of the Thames, Shakespeare's Globe is an impressive reconstruction of the Elizabethan theatre where many of his plays were first performed. The circular wooden structure is open in the middle, leaving some of the audience exposed to the elements. Those holding seat tickets enjoy a roof over their heads. Performances (staged only in summer) are thrilling experiences, with top-quality acting. A second theatre,

the Sam Wanamaker Playhouse, is a splendidly atmospheric reproduction of a Jacobean indoor candle-lit theatre, with performances year-round.

The Globe has an exhibition covering the history of Elizabethan theatre in Southwark, the process of building the Globe and the exquisite costumes made for shows; you can also listen to classic performances of Shakespeare speeches.

❻ Cardinal's Wharf

SE1. **Map** 15 A3. 🚇 London Bridge.

A small group of 17th-century houses still survives here in the shadow of the Tate Modern gallery (see pp182–5). A plaque commemorates Christopher Wren's stay while St Paul's Cathedral (see pp152–5) was being built. He would have had a particularly fine view of the works. It is thought that the wharf got its name from Cardinal Wolsey, who was Bishop of Winchester in 1529.

❼ Bankside Gallery

48 Hopton St SE1. **Map** 14 F3. **Tel** 020 7928 7521. 🚇 Blackfriars, Southwark. **Open** 11am–6pm daily during exhibitions. **Closed** 1 Jan, 24–26 Dec. ♿ 📷 Lectures. **w** banksidegallery.com

This modern riverside gallery is the headquarters of two historic

View from the Founders' Arms

British societies, namely the Royal Watercolour Society and the Royal Society of Painter-Printmakers. The members of these societies are elected by their peers in a tradition that dates back over 200 years. The gallery's permanent collection is not on show here, but there are temporary displays of contemporary watercolours and original artists' prints. The exhibitions feature the work of both societies and many of the pieces on display are for sale. There is also a superb specialist art shop that sells both books and materials.

There is an unparalleled view of St Paul's Cathedral from the nearby pub, the Founders' Arms – built on the site of the foundry where the cathedral's bells were cast.

Row of 17th-century houses on Cardinal's Wharf

❾ Tate Modern

Looming over the southern bank of the Thames, Tate Modern, housed within the converted Bankside Power Station, is a dynamic space for one of the world's premier collections of contemporary art. Up until 2000, the Tate collection was shown at three galleries: Tate St Ives, Tate Liverpool and the former Tate Gallery, now Tate Britain (see pp86–9). With the addition of Tate Modern, space was made for a growing acquisition of contemporary art. Tate Modern continually re-hangs its collection, so works and exhibitions may differ. A vast extension, incorporating the power station's original tanks, opened in 2016.

Restaurants at Tate Modern
The kitchen and bar on level 6 of Tate Modern boast a view that's a veritable work of art in its own right, with floor-to-ceiling windows overlooking the Thames and St Paul's Cathedral. There are also cafés and restaurants on level 1 of the main building and level 9 of the extension.

The Turbine Hall
The massive scale of this space – it covers 3,300 sq m (35,520 sq ft) – presents an unusual challenge for the artists who install pieces here.

Key to Floorplan

- ▢ Turbine Hall
- ▣ Permanent collections (displays change frequently)
- ▣ Temporary exhibition space
- ▢ Non-exhibition space

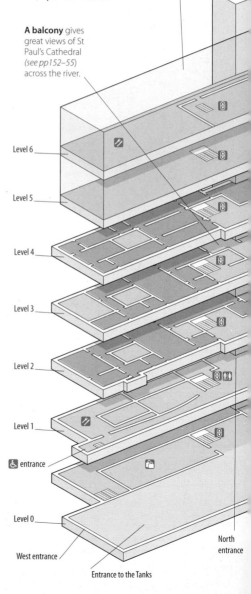

The "light beam", a two-storey glass box, allows light to filter into the upper galleries.

A balcony gives great views of St Paul's Cathedral (see pp152–55) across the river.

Level 6

Level 5

Level 4

Level 3

Level 2

Level 1

♿ entrance

Level 0

North entrance

West entrance

Entrance to the Tanks

Façade of Tate Modern
The imposing former power station is a recognizable building along the river. It is the perfect space to house its vast collection of contemporary art.

VISITORS' CHECKLIST

Practical Information
Bankside, SE1
Map 14 F3, 15 A3.
Tel 020 7887 8888.
w tate.org.uk
Open 10am–6pm Sun–Thu, 10am–10pm Fri–Sat.
Closed 24–26 Dec.
for special exhibitions only.

Transport
Blackfriars, Southwark.
45, 63, 100, 344, 381, RV1.

Interacting with Art
Tate Modern has won awards for its handheld multimedia guides, which present audio commentary alongside images, film clips and games. The gallery's latest digital project, Bloomberg Connects, enables members of the public to actively connect with art, artists and other visitors. A digital drawing bar on level 1 allows people to respond visually and see large-scale versions of their art projected on the wall. Visitors can compose captions to artworks, bringing their own experiences to bear.

Quattro Stagioni
(1993–4)
Cy Twombly's four paintings depict the changes of light and colour over the seasons.

★ Fish (1926)
Constantin Brâncuși attempted to portray the "spirit" of a fish in this abstract work constructed from bronze, metal and wood.

Gallery Guide
The main west entrance opens into the expansive, sloped Turbine Hall. From here, a flight of stairs leads to the café and foyer of level 1, or an escalator whisks visitors straight up to gallery level 2. The original power station, the Boiler House, features three floors of exhibition space for permanent and temporary exhibitions. Level 5 is members' access only, but a superb restaurant and spectacular city views can be found on level 6. The new ten-storey extension, the Switch House, adds more gallery space, performance areas in the Tanks, which lead off the turbine hall, and a rooftop terrace.

Exploring Tate Modern

Since its inception in 2000, Tate Modern has eschewed a traditional, chronological approach in favour of hanging its collections thematically, deliberately juxtaposing pieces from different eras and continents. Two floors of the main building, plus exhibition spaces in the ten-storey extension, are used to show displays from the collection, each space exploring the development of artistic movements or recurring themes in modern and contemporary art. Other spaces show temporary exhibitions (some with an exhibition charge). The focal point of the whole building is the vast Turbine Hall, often entirely taken over by a specially commissioned installation. Works shown on these pages are examples of what might be on display.

The Permanent Collections

The collections in Tate Modern comprise over 70,000 works of modern art by some of the most significant and well-known artists of the 20th and 21st century, from Pablo Picasso to Francis Bacon. The gallery continues to acquire new work by artists from across the globe and, as a result of an ever-expanding collection, displays are regularly rotated. This means that major works are not always guaranteed to be on show – always check online before visiting if there is a particular work you wish to see. In general, the best way to explore the gallery is to take one of the regular free guided tours (usually hourly 11am–3pm, check at the information desk) or pick up an audioguide.

By and large, the collections are displayed thematically. Located on floors 2 and 4 of the main building are four exhibition spaces comprising a series of rooms. Each space is dedicated to a particular art movement or theme, with various works exploring its origin and impact on modern art.

Making Traces, on floor 2, reviews the actions of artists and the marks they make while creating works. Mark Rothko's *Seagram murals* (1958–9) are at the heart of the exhibition. This series of canvasses had originally been commissioned by the opulent Four Seasons restaurant, located in the Seagram building in New York. The group of paintings, entitled *Red on Maroon* and *Black on Maroon*, are of open, rectangular, window-like forms and are sombre in mood. Rothko eventually decided to withhold the murals from the Four Seasons, considering the restaurant an inappropriate environment for the works. A number of the murals were presented to the Tate shortly before Rothko's death in 1970.

Section of *From the Freud Museum* (1991–6) by Susan Hiller

The Transformation of Bankside Power Station

This forbidding fortress was designed in 1947 by Sir Giles Gilbert Scott, the architect of Battersea Power Station, Waterloo Bridge and London's famous red telephone boxes. The power station is of a steel-framed brick skin construction, comprising over 4.2 million bricks. The Turbine Hall was designed to accommodate huge oil-burning generators and three vast oil tanks are still *in situ*. The power station itself was converted by Swiss architects Herzog and de Meuron who designed the two-storey glass box, or lightbeam, which runs the length of the building. This serves to flood the upper galleries with light and also provides wonderful views of London.

The three previously hidden tanks have been opened up for use as part of a vast extension. Maintaining a raw, industrial feel, they are used for performance works and installations. Rising 64.5 metres above the tanks (the original chimney is 99m) are another ten storeys, also designed by Herzog and de Meuron. The shape of the building is akin to a twisted trapezoid and the exterior is clad in a perforated brick lattice that complements the original power station. The extension is connected to the main building at levels 0 and 4, and topped with a roof terrace with views across London.

Roof terrace

Restaurant

2016 extension

Turbine Hall entrance

The Tanks

A 2D plan of the 2016 extension to Tate Modern

Dynamic Suprematism (1915 or 1916) by Kazimir Malevich

On the same floor is Citizens and States, which looks at the way artists explore and engage with political and social ideas. Pablo Picasso's *Weeping Woman* (1937) and Kazimir Malevich's *Dynamic Suprematism* (pictured) are examples of some of the works on display; there is a room dedicated to the German artist and activist Joseph Beuys (1921–86).

Floor 4, enlarged by 60 per cent by the 2016 extension, has two wings: Material Worlds and Media Networks. Material Worlds explores the different materials and textures used by artists. The wing features Marcel Duchamp's famous *Fountain* (a 1964 replica of the 1917 original). One of the artist's so-called "readymades", *Fountain* is a urinal purchased by Duchamp and designated a work of art. Media Networks looks at how artists have responded to mass media and the ever-evolving world of technology, and explores themes such as gender politics and the cult of celebrity. The collection includes works by Andy Warhol and Pablo Picasso, among others.

Artist Rooms celebrates individual artists with single rooms or tours devoted to their works. One such room is dedicated to Louise Bourgeois (1911–2010). Bourgeois's career spanned some 70 years and this exhibition highlights her later work, including her final vitrine, *Untitled 2010*, and several of her small sculptures. Other artists featured by Artist Rooms include Damien Hirst and Jeff Koons.

Special Exhibitions

To complement its permanent collection, Tate Modern presents a programme of exhibitions including five large shows a year (retrospectives of modern masters or surveys of important movements). The whole of the main building's level 3 is dedicated to temporary exhibitions.

Previous exhibitions have included retrospectives dedicated to Gilbert & George, Alexander Calder and Damien Hirst. An exploration of Henri Matisse's "cut-outs", which ran for nearly five months in 2015, brought together a huge number of the artist's works for the first time, and was the Tate Modern's most successful exhibition, attracting over half a million visitors.

Smaller-scale projects are dotted around the gallery. Works are sometimes shown in the restaurants and have even featured on the north-facing exterior of the gallery.

The Turbine Hall

Once a year, Tate Modern challenges an artist to create a work capable of occupying the vast five-storey Turbine Hall. This has resulted in a spectacular display of innovative sculptures and interactive works of art.

Untitled (1964) by Larry Bell

Louise Bourgeois was the first artist to exhibit here, with works that included her sculpture *Maman* (1999), a monumental steel spider. Others have included Olafur Eliasson's *The Weather Project* (2003), which lit the Turbine Hall with a giant glowing sun. In 2010, Chinese artist and activist Ai Weiwei's *Sunflower Seeds* filled the hall with 100 million hand-crafted porcelain seeds, and in 2012, Tate Modern staged its first live commission using non-actors – *These associations* created by Tino Sehgal. More performance pieces will feature in the Tanks, just off the Turbine Hall.

When there is no exhibition running, the space is occasionally used for smaller exhibitions and events, and even concerts.

Ai Weiwei holds painted ceramic "seeds" from his *Sunflower Seeds* installation (2010)

9 The Rose Playhouse

56 Park St SE1. **Map** 15 A3.
Tel 020 7261 9565. 🚇 London
Bridge. **Open** 10am–5pm Sat, plus
performances. 🏛 donation requested.
📷 w **rosetheatre.org.uk**

In 1989 the remains of the
Rose theatre, dating from
Elizabethan times, were
discovered during excavations
ahead of building work for
a new office block. The Rose,
built in 1587, was the first of
the Bankside theatres, and it
staged plays by Shakespeare
and Christopher Marlowe.
The site of the original Globe
theatre was just over the road
on Park Street (a plaque marks
the spot).

Preserved in a specially
designed space, with a new
building constructed overhead,
the archaeological remains are
submerged in water, with lights
indicating the shape of the
theatre. A small volunteer-run
exhibition tells the story of the
excavation, and the tmospheric
space is also sometimes used as
a small theatre.

Pub sign at the Anchor Inn, where a tavern
has stood for over 800 years

10 The Anchor

34 Park St SE1. **Map** 15 A3. **Tel** 020
7407 1577. 🚇 London Bridge.
Open 11am–11pm Mon–Wed, 11am–
midnight Thu–Sat, noon–11pm Sun.
♿ 🚻

This is one of London's most
famous riverside pubs. It dates
from after the Southwark fire of
1676, which devastated the
area *(see pp26–7)*. The present
building is 18th-century, but
traces of much earlier hostelries

The Shard, London's tallest building, soaring above Tower Bridge

have been found beneath it.
The inn was once connected
with a brewery across the road
that belonged to Henry Thrale,
a close friend of Dr Johnson
(see p144). When Thrale died in
1781, Johnson went to the
brewery sale and encouraged
the bidders with a phrase that
has passed into the English
language: "The potential of
growing rich beyond the
dreams of avarice."

11 Clink Prison Museum

1 Clink St SE1. **Map** 15 B3. **Tel** 020 7403
0900. 🚇 London Bridge. **Open** Jul–Sep:
10am–9pm daily; Oct–Jun: 10am–6pm
Mon–Fri, 10am–7:30pm Sat & Sun.
Closed 25 Dec. 🏛 📷 📹 for groups
(phone first). w **clink.co.uk**

The prison that was once
located here dates back to
the 12th century. It was owned
by successive Bishops of
Winchester, who lived in the
adjoining palace, of which all
that now remains is a lovely
rose window on Clink Street.
During the 15th century,
the prison became known
as the "Clink"; it closed down
in 1780.

The museum alongside
the palace remains illustrates
the history of the prison.
Tales are told of the inmates
incarcerated here, including
prostitutes, debtors and priests.
Visitors can handle instruments
of torture that leave little to the
imagination – a trip here is not
for the faint-hearted.

12 The Shard

London Bridge Street. **Map** 15 B4.
🚇 London Bridge. The View from the
Shard: Entrance via Joiner Street.
Tel 0844 499 7111. **Open** Apr–Oct:
10am–10pm daily; Nov–Mar:
10am–10pm Thu–Sat, 10am–7pm
Sun–Wed. **Closed** 25 Dec. 🏛 ♿ 📷
w **theviewfromtheshard.com**

Designed by Renzo Piano, the
Shard is the tallest building in
Western Europe and dominates
the London skyline. At 310 m
(1,016 ft) high with a crystalline
façade, the 95-storey building
houses offices, restaurants, the
five-star Shangri-La hotel,
exclusive apartments and the
country's highest observation
gallery, the View from the Shard.
Take a high-speed lift to the top
of the building for spectacular
unobstructed views of the
capital. There are two viewing
floors, the higher of which is
right among the "shards" with
the breeze blowing overhead.

13 Bermondsey Street

SE1. **Map** 15 C5. 🚇 London Bridge,
Borough. Market (Bermondsey
Square): **Open** 6am–2pm Fri. Fashion
and Textile Museum: 83 Bermondsey
St SE1. **Tel** 020 7407 8664. **Open**
11am– 6pm Tue–Sat (till 8pm Thu),
11am–5pm Sun. 🏛 ♿ 📹 on
request. 📷 📧 w **ftmlondon.org**

Bermondsey's winding streets
still hold traces of its historic
past in the form of medieval,
18th-century and Victorian
buildings. Today, Bermondsey
Street is home to galleries,

Market stalls in Bermondsey Square

coffee shops and a few excellent restaurants. The area is also famous for its antique market held in Bermondsey Square, at the bottom end of the street. Each Friday morning, seriously committed antiques dealers trade their latest acquisitions at Bermondsey. Trading starts at the crack of dawn, and the best bargains tend to go before most people are even awake. The **Fashion and Textile Museum** puts on a programme of exhibitions covering all aspects of fashion design, focusing on single designers or broader themes, and runs an education programme. Further along the street, White Cube Bermondsey is a major space for international contemporary art.

⑭ City Hall

The Queen's Walk SE1. **Map** 16 D4. **Tel** 020 7983 4000. ⊖ London Bridge. **Open** 8am–6pm Mon–Thu, 8:30am–5:30pm Fri. ♿ 📷
ⓦ london.gov.uk/city-hall

The Norman Foster-designed domed glass building just by Tower Bridge is the headquarters for London's Mayor and the Greater London Authority. Anyone can visit the building and walk up the sloping walkway to the second floor to look in on the assembly chamber, or sit in on Mayor's Question Time when assembly members interrogate the mayor on London issues, which takes place ten times a year on Wednesday mornings (check website for dates). Outside, the stone amphitheatre known as the Scoop hosts a range of free summer events, including plays, music and cinema screenings.

⑮ HMS Belfast

Morgan's Lane, Tooley St SE1. **Map** 16 D3. **Tel** 020 7940 6300. ⊖ London Bridge, Tower Hill. **Open** Mar–Oct: 10am–6pm daily (last adm 5pm); Nov–Feb: 10am–5pm (last adm 4pm). **Closed** 24–26 Dec. ♿ ♿ limited. 📷 📷 ⓦ iwm.org.uk/visits/hms-belfast

Originally launched in 1938 to serve in World War II, HMS *Belfast* was instrumental in the destruction of the German battle cruiser *Scharnhorst* in the battle of North Cape, and also played an important role in the Normandy Landings.

After the war, the battle cruiser, designed for offensive action and for supporting amphibious operations, was sent to work for the United Nations in Korea. The ship remained in service with the British navy until 1965.

Since 1971, the cruiser has been used as a floating naval museum. Part of it has been recreated to show what the ship, and life on board, was like in 1943, when it participated in sinking the German battle cruiser. Visitors can clamber down narrow ladders to the boiler and engine room, and experience what it was like in the gun turrets during a battle. Exhibits also explore the ship's history post-World War II, including during the Cold War.

The now-familiar sight of the naval gunship HMS *Belfast* on the Thames

SOUTH BANK

Following the Festival of Britain in 1951, the Southbank Centre grew up around the newly erected Royal Festival Hall. The architecture has been criticized over the years, especially the chunky concrete building that houses the Hayward Gallery, but now appears to be valued as an important part of London's river frontage. Popular with locals and tourists, the area is crowded with culture-seekers most afternoons and evenings, especially in summer and at Christmas when markets, pop-up venues and other attractions are installed. As well as the National and Old Vic theatres, the South Bank has concert halls, galleries and the BFI Southbank. In keeping with Festival of Britain tradition, the South Bank marked the new millennium with the raising of the world's highest observation wheel, the London Eye.

Sights at a Glance

Historic Streets and Buildings
- **9** Lambeth Palace
- **12** Gabriel's Wharf
- **13** Waterloo Station

Museums and Galleries
- **2** Hayward Gallery
- **7** Florence Nightingale Museum
- **8** Museum of Garden History
- **10** Imperial War Museum

Attractions
- **4** County Hall
- **5** London Dungeon
- **6** The London Eye

Theatres and Concert Halls
- **1** National Theatre
- **3** Royal Festival Hall
- **11** The Old Vic

Restaurants see pp304–5
1. Anchor and Hope
2. The Laughing Gravy
3. OXO Tower Restaurant
4. Ping Pong

Street Finder maps 13, 14, 21, 22

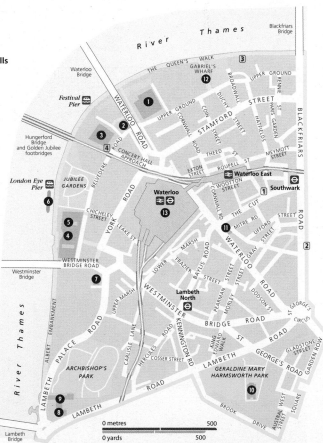

◄ The London Eye on the South Bank

For keys to symbols see back flap

Street-by-Street: Around the Southbank Centre

Originally this was an area of wharves and factories which was much damaged by bombing during World War II. It was chosen as the site of the 1951 Festival of Britain *(see p34)*, celebrating the centenary of the Great Exhibition *(see pp30–31)*. The Royal Festival Hall is the only building from 1951 to remain, but since then London's main arts centre has been created around it, including the national showcases for theatre, music and film, and a major art gallery.

To the Strand

❶ ★ National Theatre
Its three auditoriums offer a choice of plays ranging from the classics to the sharpest modern writing.

BFI Southbank, previously the National Film Theatre, was established in 1953 to show historic films *(see p343)*.

Festival Pier

The Queen Elizabeth Hall stages more intimate concerts than the Festival Hall. The adjoining Purcell Room is for chamber music *(see pp344–5)*.

❷ Hayward Gallery
The concrete exterior of this venue is well suited to many modern works.

❸ ★ Royal Festival Hall
The London Philharmonic is one of many world-class orchestras to perform here in the focal point of the Southbank Centre.

0 metres		100
0 yards		100

Hungerford Bridge was built in 1864 to carry both trains and pedestrians to Charing Cross. It now has two footbridges, the Golden Jubilee Bridges.

❻ ★ The London Eye
The world's tallest cantilevered observation wheel offers passengers a unique view of London.

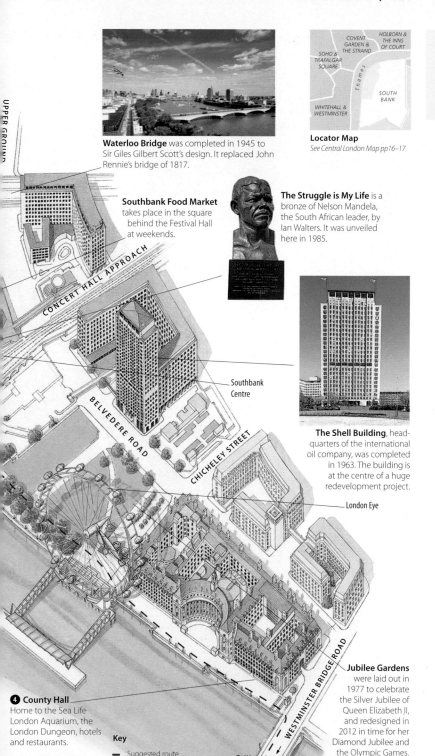

Waterloo Bridge was completed in 1945 to Sir Giles Gilbert Scott's design. It replaced John Rennie's bridge of 1817.

Locator Map
See Central London Map pp16–17

Southbank Food Market takes place in the square behind the Festival Hall at weekends.

The Struggle is My Life is a bronze of Nelson Mandela, the South African leader, by Ian Walters. It was unveiled here in 1985.

CONCERT HALL APPROACH

Southbank Centre

BELVEDERE ROAD

CHICHELEY STREET

The Shell Building, headquarters of the international oil company, was completed in 1963. The building is at the centre of a huge redevelopment project.

London Eye

WESTMINSTER BRIDGE ROAD

Jubilee Gardens were laid out in 1977 to celebrate the Silver Jubilee of Queen Elizabeth II, and redesigned in 2012 in time for her Diamond Jubilee and the Olympic Games.

4 County Hall
Home to the Sea Life London Aquarium, the London Dungeon, hotels and restaurants.

Key
— Suggested route

To Westminster station

The Royal Festival Hall and the London Eye

❶ National Theatre

South Bank SE1. **Map** 14 D3. **Tel** 020 7452 3000. 🚇 Waterloo. **Open** 9:30am–11pm Mon–Sat (walkway closes at 7:30pm), noon–6pm Sun (performance days). **Closed** Good Fri, 24 & 25 Dec, bank hols. 🔲 during performances. 📷 🔲 📷 ♿ 📷 daily, usually 9:45am (book in advance). *See Entertainment p340.* 🔳 **nationaltheatre.org.uk**

Even if you don't want to see a play, this complex is worth a visit, especially for a backstage tour. You can also get a glimpse of the backstage area from the Sherling High-Level Walkway (entrance near the Dorfman theatre), which runs above the prop-building areas.

Sir Denys Lasdun's building opened in 1976 after 200 years of debate: should there be a national theatre and, if so, where? The theatre company was formed in 1963, under Laurence (later Lord) Olivier. The largest of the three theatres is named after him; the others are the Dorfman and the Lyttleton.

❷ Hayward Gallery

South Bank SE1. **Map** 14 D3. **Tel** 020 7960 4200. 🚇 Waterloo. **Closed** temporarily for renovation. 📷 ♿ 🔲 📷 🔳 **southbankcentre.co.uk**

Though currently closed for repairs to its distinctive pyramidal glass roof panels, the Hayward Gallery, when open, is one of London's main venues for large art exhibitions. Its slabby grey concrete exterior is too starkly modern for some tastes, but for others it is an icon of 1960s Brutalist architecture. Hayward exhibitions cover classical and contemporary art, but the work of British contemporary artists is particularly well represented.

❸ Royal Festival Hall

South Bank SE1. **Map** 14 D4. **Tel** 0844 875 0073. 🚇 Waterloo. **Open** 10am–11pm daily. Poetry library: 11am–8pm Tue–Sun. **Closed** 25 Dec. 🔲 during performances. 📷 🔲 📷 ♿ Pre-concert talks, exhibitions, free concerts. *See Entertainment p344.* 🔳 **southbankcentre.co.uk**

This was the only structure for the 1951 Festival of Britain *(see p34)* designed for permanence. Sir Robert Matthew and Sir Leslie Martin's concert hall was the first major public building works undertaken in London following World War II. It has stood the test of time so well that many of the capital's major arts institutions have gathered round it, and the Grade I-listed building is today one of the world's leading performance venues. As well as the main auditorium, there is the Clore Ballroom; the main foyer area, which hosts a wide range of free concerts; the poetry library on Level 5; and also a gift shop, café, bar and the Skylon restaurant. In summer, temporary venues and bars are also installed on the riverside terrace.

❹ County Hall

Westminster Bridge Rd SE1. **Map** 13 C4. Aquarium **Tel** 0871 663 1678. 🚇 Waterloo. **Open** 10am–7pm daily (aquarium). **Closed** 25 Dec. 📷 ♿ 🔲 📷 🔳 **visitsealife.com/london**

Once the home of London's elected government, this imposing building now houses a leisure complex. The Sea Life London Aquarium and London Dungeon *(see below)* occupy the space alongside a hotel, several restaurants, and themed attractions such as Shrek's Adventure.

The Aquarium is home to myriad aquatic species from all over the world, including stingrays, turtles, jellyfish, starfish (which you can stroke) and penguins. There's a 25-m (82-ft) glass tunnel walkway through a tropical ocean environment, and a large tank housing numerous shark species, which you can view from several levels.

Shark in a tank at the Sea Life London Aquarium

❺ London Dungeon

Westminster Bridge Rd SE1. **Map** 13 C4. **Tel** 0871 423 2240. 🚇 Waterloo. **Open** 10am–5pm Mon–Fri (from 11am Thu), 10am–6pm Sat & Sun. Extended hours in school holidays. **Closed** 25 Dec. 📷 ♿ 🔲 📷 🔳 **thedungeons.com**

This scary attraction is a great hit with older children. It illustrates the most bloodthirsty events in British history with live actors and special effects. It is played strictly for terror, and screams abound during the 90-minute tour through gory scenes, recounting tales of such characters as Guy Fawkes and Jack the Ripper. Don't miss the Tyrant Boat Ride along a black River Thames to find out what happened to Anne Boleyn and her co-conspirators.

❻ The London Eye

The London Eye is a 135-m (443-ft) high observation wheel. Opened in 2000 as part of London's millennium celebrations, it immediately became one of the city's most recognizable landmarks, notable not only for its size, but for its circularity amid the block-shaped buildings flanking it. Thirty-two capsules, each holding up to 25 people, take a gentle 30-minute round trip. On a clear day, the Eye affords a 40-km (25-mile) view, which sweeps over the capital in all directions and on to the countryside beyond.

Houses of Parliament
Seventeen minutes into the flight, the spectacular aerial view of Westminster is a highlight.

The glass capsules are mounted on the outside of the rim, allowing unobstructed 360-degree views.

80 spokes made from 6 km (3.7 miles) of tensioned cable support the wheel.

Battersea Power Station
After 15 minutes, the distinctive white smokestacks of this old power station (now being redeveloped) are visible.

Two cables, 60 m (197 ft) in length, support the entire structure from concrete bases in Jubilee Gardens.

The wheel rim was floated down the Thames in sections and then assembled on site.

Buckingham Palace
Ten minutes into the journey, the Queen's official residence glides into view.

The Eye turns continuously and moves slowly enough that the capsules are boarded here while moving. The wheel is halted for those requiring assistance.

❼ Florence Nightingale Museum

2 Lambeth Palace Rd SE1. **Map** 14 D5.
Tel 020 7620 0374. ☻ Waterloo,
Westminster. **Open** 10am–5pm daily
(last adm 4:30pm). **Closed** 25 Dec
(and other dates; call to check). ⬚
⬚ ⬚ ⬚ Videos, lectures.
W florence-nightingale.co.uk

This determined woman
captured the nation's
imagination as the "Lady
of the Lamp", who nursed
the wounded soldiers of the
Crimean War (1853–6). She
also founded Britain's first
school of nursing at old St
Thomas' Hospital in 1860.

Sited near the entrance
to St Thomas' Hospital,
this museum gives an
account of Nightingale's
career through displays of
original documents and
personal memorabilia.
They illustrate her life
and the developments
she pioneered in
health care, until her
death in 1910 at the
age of 90.

Florence Nightingale

❽ Museum of Garden History

Lambeth Palace Rd SE1. **Map** 21 C1.
Tel 020 7401 8865. ☻ Waterloo,
Lambeth North, Westminster.
Closed for renovation until 2017;
check the website for updates.
W gardenmuseum.org.uk

Currently closed for renovation,
the world's first museum of
garden history is housed in the
restored church of St Mary of
Lambeth Palace, where it is set
around a central knot garden.
In the grounds are the tombs
of John Tradescant father and
son, who, as well as being
gardeners to Charles I and
Charles II, were adventurous
plant hunters and collectors of
curiosities. The tomb of William
Bligh of *The Bounty* can also be
seen here.

The museum presents a
history of gardening in Britain,
including objects collected by
the Tradescants, and an archive

of garden design. It also runs
a programme of exhibitions,
events and lectures and has
an excellent café.

❾ Lambeth Palace

SE1. **Map** 21 C1. **Tel** 0844 248 5134.
☻ Lambeth North, Westminster,
Waterloo, Vauxhall. **Open** for
guided tours only. ⬚ Thu & Fri
(booking essential).
W archbishopofcanterbury.org

This palace has housed
Archbishops of Canterbury
since the 13th century
and today remains the
Archbishop's official London
residence. The chapel and its
undercroft contain elements
from the 13th century, but
a large part of the rest
of the building is far
more recent. It has been
frequently restored,
most recently by Edward
Blore in 1828. The
Tudor gatehouse,
however, dates from
1485 and is one of
London's most
familiar riverside
landmarks. The
garden, planted
with many mature trees, is
occasionally open in summer,
while you can visit the palace
year-round by guided tour.

Until the first Westminster
Bridge was built, the horse
ferry that operated between
here and Millbank was a
principal river crossing. The
revenues from it went to the
Archbishop, who received
compensation when the
bridge opened in 1750.

The Tudor gatehouse of Lambeth Palace, a
familiar landmark along the Thames

❿ Imperial War Museum

Lambeth Rd SE1. **Map** 22 E1. **Tel** 020
7416 5000. ☻ Waterloo, Lambeth
North, Elephant & Castle. **Open**
10am–6pm daily. **Closed** 24–26 Dec.
⬚ for tours and some special
exhibitions. ⬚ booking required.
⬚ ⬚ ⬚ ⬚ Films, lectures.
W iwm.org.uk

This museum is not just
concerned with the engines of
modern warfare. Massive tanks,
artillery, bombs and aircraft are
on show in the main atrium, yet
some of the most fascinating
exhibits in the museum relate
more to the impact on the lives
of people at home than to the
business of fighting; one display
focuses on a London family's
experience of World War II,
including food rationing, air
raids, and the service of family
members at home and abroad.

On the ground floor, a major
permanent exhibition on World
War I includes a re-creation of
a trench, and many artifacts.
Other major permanent displays
include the Holocaust exhibition,
which tells the story of Nazi

Military aircraft at the Imperial War Museum

persecution of Jews before and during World War II; Secret War, which reveals the covert world of espionage, secret operations and the work of Britain's Special Forces; and a collection of Victoria Crosses and other medals, with tales of those who were awarded them. The museum also displays some of its impressive collection of wartime art, including John Singer Sargent's intensely moving World War I work *Gassed*, and contemporary commissions.

The museum is housed in part of what used to be the Bethlehem Royal Hospital for the Insane ("Bedlam"), built in 1811. It was not uncommon for people to visit to watch the antics of some of the patients. The hospital moved out to new premises in Surrey in 1930, leaving this vast building empty. Its two large flanking wings were pulled down and this central block converted into the museum, which moved here from its former South Kensington site in 1936.

The Old Vic theatre, rescued from the threat of closure in the 1990s

⓫ The Old Vic

Waterloo Rd SE1. **Map** 14 E4. **Tel** 0844 871 7628. 🚇 Waterloo. **Open** for performances and tours. 📷 Sat, book online or call 020 7928 2651. 🚻 contact the theatre in advance. 🚻 *See Entertainment pp340–42.*
🌐 oldvictheatre.com

This splendid building dates back to 1818, when it was opened as the Royal Coburg Theatre. In 1833, the name was changed to the Royal Victoria, in honour of the future queen. Shortly after this the theatre became a centre

for music hall, the immensely popular Victorian entertainment, which included singers and comedians. In 1912, Lillian Baylis became manager and from 1914 to 1923 she staged all of Shakespeare's plays here. The National Theatre *(see p192)* was founded in the 1960s and based at this site.

In 1997, a charitable trust, formed to secure the theatre's future. The Trust set up The Old Vic Theatre Company as resident company in 2003, with Kevin Spacey as its first artistic director. There are cheap seats for younger people and pantomimes at Christmas.

⓬ Gabriel's Wharf

56 Upper Ground SE1. **Map** 14 E3. 🚇 Waterloo. *See Shops and Markets pp316–37.*

This pleasant enclave of boutiques, craft shops and cafés was the product of a long and stormy debate over the future of what was once an industrial riverside area. Residents of Waterloo strongly opposed various schemes for office developments before a community association was able to acquire the site in 1984 and build cooperative housing.

Adjoining the market is a small garden and a riverside walkway with fine views of the City. The Oxo Tower to the east, built in 1928 to surreptitiously advertise a meat extract by means of its window shapes, now houses galleries and design shops on the lower floors and a restaurant and bar on the top floor.

The memorial to the dead of World War I at Waterloo Station

⓭ Waterloo Station

York Rd SE1. **Map** 14 D4. **Tel** 08457 484950. 🚇 Waterloo. *See Getting to London p368.*

The terminus for trains to southwest England, Waterloo station was originally built in 1848 but completely remodelled in the early 20th century, with the addition of a grand formal entrance at the northeast corner. Today the spacious concourse, including a mezzanine floor, is lined with clothing and gift shops, cafés and bars.

Towards the end of the 20th century the station was enlarged again to serve as London's first Channel Tunnel rail link to Europe. In autumn 2007, the Eurostar terminal moved from Waterloo station to its present home at St Pancras International *(see p133)*.

The area surrounding Waterloo, particularly Lower Marsh, is worth exploring: there are some great shops, pubs and restaurants to enjoy.

Warehouses painted with a tromp l'œil effect at Gabriel's Wharf

CHELSEA

The showy young shoppers who paraded along the King's Road from the 1960s until the 1980s have more or less gone, along with Chelsea's reputation for extreme behaviour, established by the bohemian Chelsea Set of writers and artists in the 19th century. Formerly a riverside village, Chelsea became fashionable in Tudor times. Henry VIII liked it so much that he built a small palace (long vanished) here. Artists, including Turner, Whistler and Rossetti, were attracted by the river views from Cheyne

Walk. The historian Thomas Carlyle and the essayist Leigh Hunt arrived in the 1830s and began a literary tradition continued by writers such as the poet Swinburne. Yet Chelsea has always had a raffish element, too: in the 18th century the pleasure gardens were noted for beautiful courtesans and the Chelsea Arts Club has held riotous balls for nearly a century. The Chelsea of today is home to expensive boutique shops, upmarket restaurants and exclusive residential areas.

Sights at a Glance

Historic Streets and Buildings
1 King's Road
2 Carlyle's House
5 Cheyne Walk
8 Royal Hospital
10 Sloane Square

Museums and Galleries
7 National Army Museum
9 Saatchi Gallery

Churches
3 Chelsea Old Church

Gardens
4 Roper's Garden
6 Chelsea Physic Garden

☐ **Restaurants** *see pp299–301*
1 Big Easy
2 Bluebird
3 Buona Sera Jam
4 Caraffini
5 Gallery Mess
6 Restaurant Gordon Ramsay

Street Finder maps 19, 20

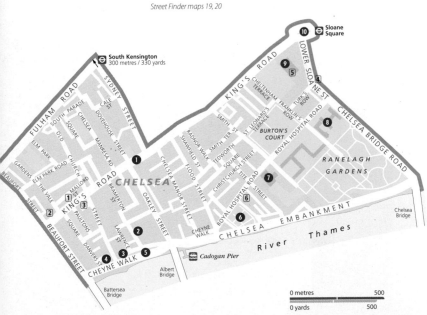

◀ A rustic garden at the Chelsea Flower Show

For keys to symbols *see back flap*

Street-by-Street: Chelsea

Once a peaceful riverside village, Chelsea has been fashionable since Tudor times, when Sir Thomas More, Henry VIII's Lord Chancellor, lived here. Artists such as Turner, Whistler and Rossetti were attracted by the views from Cheyne Walk, before a busy main road disturbed its peace. Chelsea's artistic connection was maintained by upscale galleries and antique shops, many of which have closed due to a rise in rents. Enclaves of 18th-century houses preserve a genteel atmosphere.

❶ King's Road
In the 1960s and 1970s this was the boutique-lined centre of fashionable London, and is still a main shopping street.

❷ Carlyle's House
The historian and philosopher lived here from 1834 until his death in 1882.

The Old Dairy, at 46 Old Church Street, was built in 1796, when cows still grazed in the surrounding fields. The tiling is original.

To King's Road

❸ Chelsea Old Church
Although severely damaged during World War II, it still holds some fine Tudor monuments.

❹ Roper's Garden
This features a sculpture by Jacob Epstein who had a studio here.

Thomas More, sculpted in 1969 by L Cubitt Bevis, gazes calmly across the river, near where he lived.

Key

— Suggested route

0 metres		100
0 yards		100

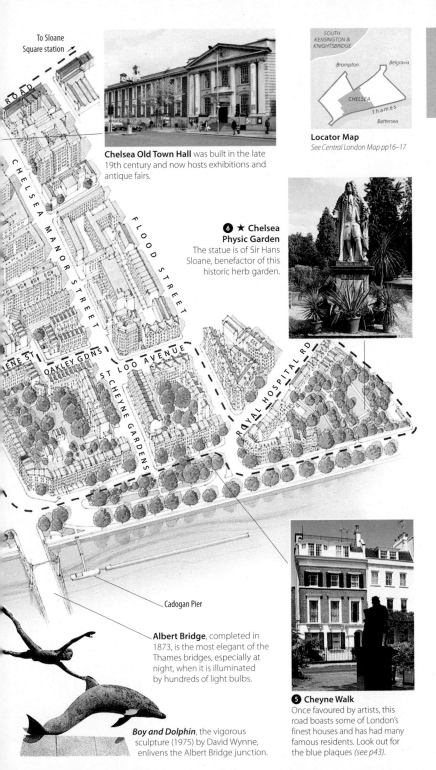

To Sloane Square station

Chelsea Old Town Hall was built in the late 19th century and now hosts exhibitions and antique fairs.

Locator Map
See Central London Map pp16–17

6 ★ Chelsea Physic Garden
The statue is of Sir Hans Sloane, benefactor of this historic herb garden.

Cadogan Pier

Albert Bridge, completed in 1873, is the most elegant of the Thames bridges, especially at night, when it is illuminated by hundreds of light bulbs.

Boy and Dolphin, the vigorous sculpture (1975) by David Wynne, enlivens the Albert Bridge junction.

5 Cheyne Walk
Once favoured by artists, this road boasts some of London's finest houses and has had many famous residents. Look out for the blue plaques (*see p43*).

The Pheasantry, King's Road

❶ King's Road

SW3 and SW10. **Map** 19 B3.
🚇 Sloane Square. *See Shops and Markets pp316–37.*

This is Chelsea's central artery, with a wealth of upmarket high street shops and smaller boutiques. The miniskirt revolution of the 1960s – the birth of so-called "Swinging London" – began here and so have many subsequent style trends, perhaps the most famous of them being punk.

Look out for the Pheasantry at No. 152, with its columns and statuary. It was built in 1881 as the shopfront of a furniture-maker's premises but now conceals a modern restaurant.

Once also a vibrant area for antiques, most of the Kings Road's merchants have packed up shop. Nearby Kensington Church Street is where to go to find high-quality art and antiques today.

❷ Carlyle's House

24 Cheyne Row SW3. **Map** 19 B4.
Tel 020 7352 7087. 🚇 Sloane Square, South Kensington. **Open** Mar–Oct: 11am–4:30pm Wed–Sun. 🅿 ✉
🆆 **nationaltrust.org.uk/ carlyleshouse**

The historian and founder of the London Library (*see St James's Square p95*), Thomas Carlyle moved into this modest 18th-century house in 1834, and wrote many of his best-known books here, notably *The French Revolution* and

Frederick the Great. His presence at this address made Chelsea more fashionable and the house became a mecca for some great literary figures. The novelists Charles Dickens and William Thackeray, poet Alfred Lord Tennyson and naturalist Charles Darwin were all regular visitors here. The house has been restored and looks as it would have done during Carlyle's lifetime.

Chelsea Old Church in 1860

❸ Chelsea Old Church

64 Cheyne Walk SW3. **Map** 19 A4.
Tel 020 7795 1019. 🚇 Sloane Square, South Kensington. **Open** 2–4pm Tue–Thu. 🅿 🕇 8am Thu, 8am, 10am, 11am, 12:15pm, 6pm Sun.
🆆 **chelseaoldchurch.org.uk**

Rebuilt after World War II, this square-towered building does not look old from the outside. However, early prints confirm that it is a careful replica of the medieval church that was largely destroyed by World War II bombs.

The glory of this church is its Tudor monuments. One to Sir Thomas More, who built a chapel here in 1528, contains an inscription he wrote (in Latin), asking to be buried next to his wife. Among other monuments is a chapel to Sir Thomas Lawrence, an Elizabethan merchant, and a 17th-century memorial to Lady Jane Cheyne, after whose husband Cheyne Walk was named. Outside the church is a statue in memory of Sir Thomas More, "statesman, scholar, saint", gazing piously across the river.

❹ Roper's Garden

Cheyne Walk SW3. **Map** 19 A4.
🚇 Sloane Square, South Kensington.

This is a small park outside Chelsea Old Church. It is named after Margaret Roper, Thomas More's daughter, and her husband William, who wrote More's biography. The sculptor Jacob Epstein worked at a studio on the site between 1909 and 1914, and there is a stone carving by him commemorating the fact. The park also contains a figure of a nude woman by Gilbert Carter.

❺ Cheyne Walk

SW3. **Map** 19 B4. 🚇 Sloane Square, South Kensington.

Until Chelsea Embankment was constructed in 1874, Cheyne Walk was a pleasant riverside promenade. Now it overlooks a busy road that has destroyed much of its charm. Many of the 18th-century houses remain, though, bristling with blue plaques celebrating some of the famous people who have lived in them. Most were writers and artists, including J M W Turner, who lived incognito at No. 119; George Eliot, who died at No. 4; and a clutch of writers (Henry James, T S Eliot and Ian Fleming) in Carlyle Mansions.

Statue of Thomas More on Cheyne Walk

❻ Chelsea Physic Garden

66 Royal Hospital Rd SW3.
Map 19 C4. **Tel** 020 7352 5646.
🚇 Sloane Square. **Open** Apr–Oct:
11am–6pm Tue–Fri & Sun; Nov–Mar:
9:30am–4pm Mon–Fri. Café and shop
closed winter, occasional late openings
summer. 🚫 ♿ call in advance.
📷 🖥 🏠 Gardening school.
🌐 **chelseaphysicgarden.co.uk**

Established by the Society of
Apothecaries in 1673 to study
plants for medicinal use, this
garden was saved from closure
in 1722 by a gift from Sir Hans
Sloane, whose statue adorns it.
Many new varieties have been
nurtured in its glasshouses,
including cotton sent to the
plantations of the southern
United States. Visitors to
London's oldest botanic
garden can see ancient trees
and one of Britain's first rock
gardens, installed in 1772.

❼ National Army Museum

Royal Hospital Rd SW3.
Map 19 C4. **Tel** 020 7730 0717.
🚇 Sloane Square. **Open**
Closed for refurbishment;
check website for special events
and reopening updates. ♿ 🖥
🏠 🌐 **nam.ac.uk**

Adjoining the Royal
Hospital in Chelsea is
the official museum
of the British Army,
with a collection that spans its
600-year history, including
many uniforms, paintings and
portraits. Since 2014, it has been
undergoing a major rebuilding
project during which it is closed
to the public.

❽ Royal Hospital

Royal Hospital Rd SW3. **Map** 20 D3.
Tel 020 7881 5516. 🚇 Sloane Square.
Open Museum, Chapel and Great Hall:
10am–4pm (no access to Hall noon–
2pm) Mon–Fri. **Closed** public hols,
functions (check first). 📷 10am &
1:30pm Mon–Fri, book in advance.
🏠 🌐 **chelsea-pensioners.co.uk**

This graceful complex was
commissioned by Charles II

Chelsea Physic Garden in autumn

from Christopher Wren in 1682
as a retirement home for old
or wounded soldiers, who
have been known as Chelsea
Pensioners ever since. The
hospital opened ten years
later and is still home to about
330 retired soldiers, whose
distinctive uniforms of
scarlet coats and tricorn
hats date from the
17th century. Flanking
the northern entrance
are Wren's two main
public rooms: the
chapel, notable for its
wonderful simplicity,
and the panelled Great
Hall, still used as the dining
room. A small museum
covers the history
of the Pensioners.
A statue of Charles II
by Grinling Gibbons
is to be found on the terrace
outside, from where there is a
fine view of Battersea Power
Station across the river.

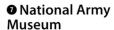
A Chelsea Pensioner in uniform

❾ Saatchi Gallery

Duke of York's HQ, King's Road SW3.
Map 19 C2. 🚇 Sloane Square.
Open 10am–6pm daily during
exhibitions. **Closed** for private
events. ♿ call in advance 020
7811 3085. 📷 🖥
🌐 **saatchigallery.coM**

Set up by advertising mogul
Charles Saatchi in order to
showcase his impressive
contemporary art acquisitions,
the Saatchi Gallery has moved
location several times in

London. Now, however, it is
firmly established in Chelsea at
the Duke of York's headquarters
building, which dates from
1801. Saatchi is perhaps best
known for his espousal, in the
1980s and 1990s, of the Young
British Artists movement led by
Damien Hirst. Today the range
of temporary exhibitions of
contemporary art is wide-
ranging and international in
scope, covering everything from
new Chinese artists to fashion
illustration and Pop Art.

Sloane Square fountain

❿ Sloane Square

SW1. **Map** 20 D2. 🚇 Sloane Square.

This pleasant small square
(rectangle to be precise) has a
paved centre with a flower stall
and a fountain depicting Venus.
Laid out in the late 18th century,
it was named after Sir Hans
Sloane, the wealthy physician
and collector who bought the
manor of Chelsea in 1712.
Opposite Peter Jones, the 1936
department store on the square's
west side, is the Royal Court
Theatre, which for over a century
has fostered new drama.

SOUTH KENSINGTON AND KNIGHTSBRIDGE

Packed with embassies and upmarket emporia, these are among London's most desirable and expensive areas. However, for visitors it is the three great museums – the Natural History Museum, the Science Museum and the Victoria and Albert – founded as

Victorian temples to learning that are the major draw. With Kensington Palace, the Royal Albert Hall and the Albert Memorial, there are some solidly royal connections here too, while Hyde Park and Kensington Gardens are among the city's prime green spaces.

Sights at a Glance

Historic Streets and Buildings
5 Royal College of Music
7 Royal College of Art
10 Kensington Palace
13 Speakers' Corner

Churches
4 Brompton Oratory

Museums and Galleries
1 Natural History Museum pp206–7
2 Science Museum pp210–11
3 Victoria and Albert Museum pp214–17
9 Serpentine Gallery

Parks and Gardens
11 Kensington Gardens
12 Hyde Park

Monuments
8 Albert Memorial
14 Marble Arch

Concert Halls
6 Royal Albert Hall

Shops
15 Harrods

Restaurants see pp299–301
1 Bar Boulud
2 Dinner
3 One-O-One
4 Zuma

Street Finder maps 10, 11, 19

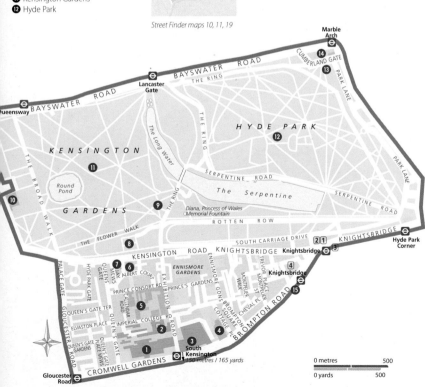

◀ The Royal Albert Hall and the Albert Memorial

For keys to symbols see back flap

Street-by-Street: South Kensington

A clutch of museums and colleges provides this area with its dignified character. The Great Exhibition of 1851 in Hyde Park was so successful that in the following years smaller exhibitions were held here, just to its south. By the end of the 19th century some of these had become permanent museums, housed in grandiose buildings celebrating Victorian self-confidence.

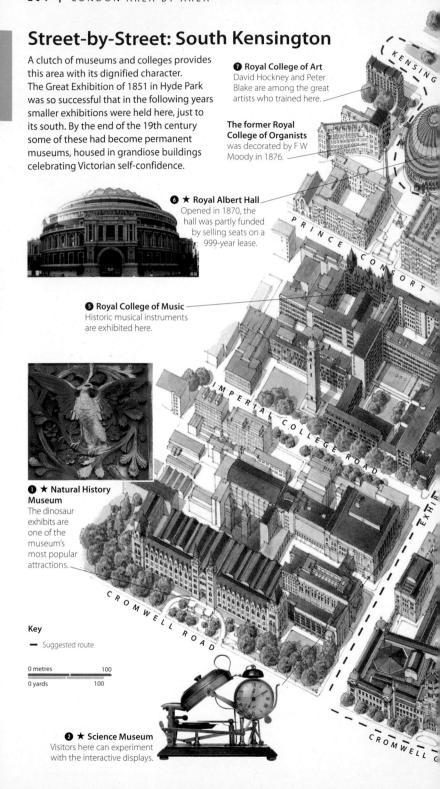

❼ Royal College of Art
David Hockney and Peter Blake are among the great artists who trained here.

The former Royal College of Organists was decorated by F W Moody in 1876.

❻ ★ Royal Albert Hall
Opened in 1870, the hall was partly funded by selling seats on a 999-year lease.

❺ Royal College of Music
Historic musical instruments are exhibited here.

❶ ★ Natural History Museum
The dinosaur exhibits are one of the museum's most popular attractions.

Key

━ Suggested route

0 metres	100
0 yards	100

❷ ★ Science Museum
Visitors here can experiment with the interactive displays.

The Albert Hall Mansions, built by Norman Shaw in 1879, started a fashion for red brick.

Locator Map
See Central London Map pp16–17

❽ Albert Memorial
This memorial was built to commemorate Queen Victoria's consort.

The Royal Geographical Society was founded in 1830. Scottish missionary and explorer David Livingstone (1813–73) was a member.

Imperial College, part of London University, is one of the country's leading scientific institutions.

❸ ★ Victoria and Albert Museum
A range of objects from around the globe illustrate a rich history of design and decoration.

Holy Trinity church dates from the 19th century and is located among cottages in a calm backwater.

❹ Brompton Oratory
The Oratory was built during the 19th-century Catholic revival.

Brompton Square, begun in 1821, established this as a fashionable residential area.

To Knightsbridge station

❶ Natural History Museum

Life on Earth and the Earth itself are vividly explained at the Natural History Museum. Using the latest interactive techniques alongside traditional displays, exhibits tackle such issues as how human beings evolved and how we can safeguard our planet. The vast museum building is a masterpiece in itself. It opened in 1881 and was designed by Alfred Waterhouse using revolutionary Victorian building techniques. It is built on an iron and steel framework concealed behind arches and columns, richly decorated with sculptures of plants and animals.

★ Mammals
The life-size model of a blue whale dwarfs everything else in this vast gallery.

The Darwin Centre features a futuristic cocoon in a glass atrium. It is home to 20 million insect and plant specimens and a research centre.

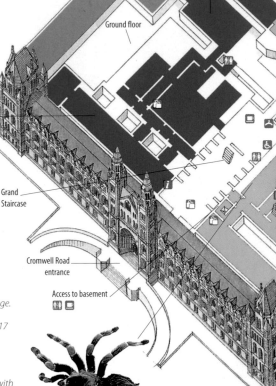

Ground floor

★ Dinosaurs
T Rex, one of the museum's impressively lifelike animatronic models, lurches and roars in this hugely popular gallery. More traditional exhibits of fossilized skeletons and eggs are also on display.

Grand Staircase

Cromwell Road entrance

Access to basement

Gallery Guide

The museum is divided into four zones: Blue, Green, Red and Orange.

The Hintze Hall is the grand centrepiece of the building. In 2017 its famous guardian, "Dippy" the Diplodocus skeleton cast, will be replaced by the real skeleton of a blue whale. Beyond, in the Blue Zone, Human Biology, together with Mammals, Dinosaurs and the Images of Nature, are to the left; Creepy Crawlies and Ecology to the right. On the first floor are Our Place in Evolution and The Vault.

The giant escalator in the Earth Hall leads through a stunning globe to Red Zone highlights The Power Within and Earth's Treasury.

Creepy Crawlies
This popular gallery celebrates arthropods – insects, crustaceans, centipedes and spiders, such as this tarantula.

Key to Floorplan

- Blue Zone
- Green Zone
- Red Zone
- Orange Zone

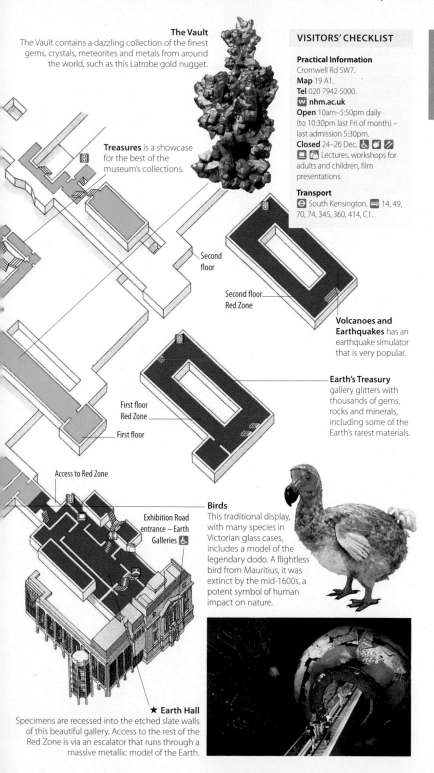

The Vault
The Vault contains a dazzling collection of the finest gems, crystals, meteorites and metals from around the world, such as this Latrobe gold nugget.

Treasures is a showcase for the best of the museum's collections.

Second floor

Second floor Red Zone

First floor Red Zone

First floor

Access to Red Zone

Exhibition Road entrance – Earth Galleries

Volcanoes and Earthquakes
has an earthquake simulator that is very popular.

Earth's Treasury
gallery glitters with thousands of gems, rocks and minerals, including some of the Earth's rarest materials.

Birds
This traditional display, with many species in Victorian glass cases, includes a model of the legendary dodo. A flightless bird from Mauritius, it was extinct by the mid-1600s, a potent symbol of human impact on nature.

★ Earth Hall
Specimens are recessed into the etched slate walls of this beautiful gallery. Access to the rest of the Red Zone is via an escalator that runs through a massive metallic model of the Earth.

❷ Science Museum

See pp210–11.

Kids captivated by the exhibits on display in the Science Museum

❸ Victoria and Albert Museum

See pp214–17.

❹ Brompton Oratory

Brompton Rd SW7. **Map** 19 A1. **Tel** 020 7808 0900. ⊖ South Kensington. **Open** 6:30am–8pm daily. ⊕ 11am Sun sung Latin Mass (see website for other times). ⊕ ⊕ ⊕ **bromptonoratory.com**

The Italianate Oratory is a rich (some think a little too rich) monument to the English Catholic revival of the late 19th century. The Oratory was established by John Henry Newman (who later became Cardinal Newman). Father Frederick William Faber (1814–63) had already founded a London community of priests at Charing Cross. The group had moved to Brompton, then an outlying London district, and this was to be its oratory. Newman and Faber (both Anglican converts to Catholicism) were following the example of St Philip Neri, who set up a community of city-based secular priests living without vows.

The present church was opened in 1884. Its façade and dome were added in the 1890s, and the interior has been progressively enriched ever since. Herbert Gribble, the architect, who was also a Catholic convert, was only 29 when he triumphed in the highly prestigious competition to design it. Inside, all the most eye-catching treasures predate the church – many of them were transported here from Italian churches. Giuseppe Mazzuoli carved the huge marble figures of the 12 apostles for Siena Cathedral in the late 17th century. The beautiful Lady Altar was originally created in 1693 for the Dominican church in Brescia, and the 18th-century altar in St Wilfrid's Chapel was actually imported from a church in Rochefort, Belgium.

The Oratory has always been famous for its splendid musical tradition.

❺ Royal College of Music

Prince Consort Rd SW7. **Map** 10 F5. **Tel** 020 7591 4300. ⊖ Knightsbridge, South Kensington. Museum of Music: **Tel** 020 7591 4842. **Open** Closed for renovation. ⊕ call 020 7591 4322 before visit. ⊕ ⊕ ⊕ **rcm.ac.uk**

17th-century viol at the Royal College of Music

Sir Arthur Blomfield designed the turreted Gothic palace, with Bavarian overtones, that has housed this distinguished institution since 1894. The college was founded in 1882 by George Grove, who also compiled the famous *Dictionary of Music*; pupils have included English composers Benjamin Britten and Ralph Vaughan Williams. The **Museum of Music** (closed for renovation until 2018) contains a variety of instruments from many parts of the world, together with portraits of great musicians and composers. Check the website for details of concerts and masterclasses hosted by the college.

The sumptuous interior of Brompton Oratory

Joseph Durham's statue of Prince Albert (1858) in front of the Royal Albert Hall

❻ Royal Albert Hall

Kensington Gore SW7. **Map** 10 F5.
Tel 020 7589 8212. ⊖ High St
Kensington, South Kensington.
Open for performances and guided
tours. 📷 🎫 daily; book online or by
phone. ♿ 🚻 🖥 *See Entertainment
pp344–5.* **W** **royalalberthall.com**

Designed by an engineer,
Francis Fowke, and completed
in 1871, this huge concert hall
was modelled on Roman
amphitheatres and is easier on
the eye than most Victorian
structures. On the red-brick
exterior the only ostentation is a
frieze symbolizing the triumph
of arts and science. The building
was planned as the Hall of Arts
and Science but Queen Victoria
renamed it to the Royal Albert
Hall, in memory of her husband,
when she laid the foundation
stone in 1868.

The hall is often used for
classical concerts, most
famously the "Proms", but it
also accommodates other large
gatherings, such as tennis
matches, comedy shows, rock
concerts, circus shows and
major business conferences.

❼ Royal College of Art

Kensington Gore SW7. **Map** 10 F5.
Tel 020 7590 4444. ⊖ High St
Kensington, South Kensington.
Open for exhibitions (phone or check
online) ♿ 🖥 📷 Lectures, events,
film presentations, exhibitions.
W **rca.ac.uk**

Sir Hugh Casson's mainly glass-
fronted building (1962) is in
stark contrast to the Victoriana
around it. The college was
founded in 1837 as a school
of design and practical art for
the manufacturing industries.
It became noted for modern art
in the 1950s and 1960s, when
David Hockney, Peter Blake and
Eduardo Paolozzi attended.

❽ Albert Memorial

South Carriage Drive, Kensington
Gdns SW7. **Map** 10 F5. ⊖ High St
Kensington, South Kensington. 📷
2pm & 3pm first Sun of the month,
Mar–Dec. **W** **royalparks.org.uk**

This grandiose but dignified
memorial to Queen Victoria's
beloved consort was completed
in 1876, 15 years after his death.
Albert was a German prince and
a cousin of Queen Victoria's.
When he died from typhoid in
1861, he was only 42 and they
had been happily married for 21
years, producing 9 children. It is
fitting that the monument is
near the site of the 1851 Exhibition *(see pp30–31)*; Albert was
closely identified with the
Exhibition and the scientific
advances it celebrated. The
statue, by John Foley, shows
him with an exhibition
catalogue on his knee.

The Queen chose Sir George
Gilbert Scott to design the
monument, which stands 55 m
(175 ft) high. It is loosely based
on a medieval market cross –
although considerably more
elaborate, with a black and
gilded spire, multi-coloured
marble canopy, stones, mosaics,
enamels, wrought iron and
nearly 200 sculpted figures. In
October 1998, the re-gilded
statue was unveiled by Elizabeth
II; it had been painted black
in 1915 to avoid attracting
attention during World War I.

Victoria and Albert at the Great
Exhibition opening (1851)

❷ Science Museum

Centuries of continuing scientific and technological development lie at the heart of the Science Museum's massive collection. The variety of objects displayed is magnificent: from steam engines to aeroengines; spacecraft to the first mechanical computers. Equally important is the social context of science – what discoveries and inventions mean for day-to-day life – and the process of discovery itself. The high-tech Wellcome Wing has interactive displays, an IMAX cinema, a 3D theatre and galleries devoted to new advances in science. The museum is undergoing renovations, so some floors may be closed and others may have temporary exhibitions.

Clockmakers' Museum
This collection of over a thousand watches, clocks and chronometers explores the history of timekeeping.

Agriculture
Original machinery and large-scale models provide an insight into working life on an arable farm.

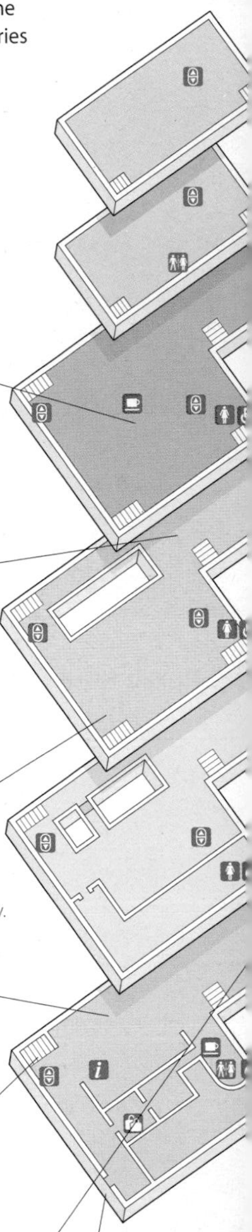

Media Space
looks at relationships between photography, science, art and technology.

★ The Energy Hall
Dedicated to steam power, this gallery includes the still-operational Harle Syke Mill Engine (1903).

Stairs to lower level 🛗 🚻

Key to Floorplan

- ▢ Basement
- ▢ Ground floor
- ▢ First floor
- ▢ Second floor
- ▢ Third floor
- ▢ Closed for renovation
- ▢ Wellcome Wing

Exploring Space
Rockets, satellites, space probes, landers and more.

Main entrance

★ **Flight and Fly Zone**
This gallery is packed with early flying contraptions, fighter planes and aeroengines, many of them suspended as if in mid-flight. Next door, the Fly Zone has flight simulators and other interactive aviation experiences.

VISITORS' CHECKLIST

Practical Information
Exhibition Rd SW7
Map 19 A1.
Tel 0870 870 4868.
W sciencemuseum.org.uk
Open 10am–6pm daily.
Closed 24–26 Dec. 🎟 some exhibitions, activities & IMAX cinema. 🔊 Lectures, films, workshops. 💻 📷

Transport
🚇 South Kensington. 🚌 9, 10, 14, 49, 52, 70, 74, 345, 360, 414, 430, 452, C1.

Atmosphere
This interactive gallery allows visitors to explore the science behind our changing climate – how it works, why it changes and what might happen in the future.

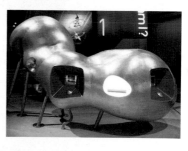

Escalator to IMAX cinema

★ **Who Am I?**
Find out what makes you unique and explore the science of being human. The exhibition utilizes intriguing objects, displays and hands-on exhibits.

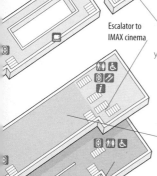

★ **Making the Modern World**
Apollo 10 took US astronauts around the moon in May 1969, and now forms part of this stunning gallery of museum highlights.

The Garden
Hands-on galleries specifically designed for younger children.

Gallery Guide

The Science Museum is spread over seven floors, balconies and mezzanine levels. The Wellcome Wing, offering four floors of interactive technology, is at the west end of the museum and is accessible from the ground floor and third floor of the main building. Power dominates the ground floor; here too are Exploring Space and Making the Modern World. The first floor has Challenge of Materials and Agriculture. On the second floor, a range of diverse galleries look at energy, mathematics and medicine. The third floor includes Flight and interactive galleries (undergoing renovation). The fourth and fifth floors (accessible only by one of the lifts) house the medical history galleries but are closed for renovation.

Statue of young Queen Victoria, by her daughter Princess Louise, outside Kensington Palace

🕘 Serpentine Gallery

Kensington Gdns and West Carriage Drive, W2. **Map** 11 A4. **Tel** 020 7402 6075. 🚇 Lancaster Gate, South Kensington. **Open** 10am–6pm Tue–Sun. **Closed** 1 Jan, 24–26, 31 Dec & between exhibitions. Lectures. ♿ 🎨 📷 art bookshop. 🌐 **serpentinegallery.org**

The Serpentine Gallery houses temporary exhibitions of major contemporary artists' work. This exciting gallery transforms its space to suit the exhibits. Every summer, a temporary pavilion (open daily) is commissioned from a major architect. A second building, the Serpentine Sackler Gallery, in a former gunpowder store a 5-minute walk from the main space, displays similarly ambitious exhibits. An extension, designed by Zaha Hadid, houses the Magazine restaurant.

🕙 Kensington Palace

Kensington Palace Gdns W8. **Map** 10 D4. **Tel** 0844 482 7777. 🚇 High St Kensington, Queensway, Notting Hill Gate. **Open** Mar–Oct: 10am–6pm daily; Nov–Feb: 10am–5pm daily; (last adm: 1 hr earlier). **Closed** 24–26 Dec. 🎨 🎧 🖼 📷 ♿ Exhibitions. 🌐 **hrp.org.uk**

Half of this spacious palace is used as royal apartments; the other half, which includes the 18th-century state rooms,

is open to the public. When William III and his wife Mary came to the throne in 1689, they bought a mansion, dating from 1605, and commissioned Christopher Wren to convert it into a royal palace. He created separate suites of rooms for the king and queen.

The palace has seen some important royal events. In 1714, Queen Anne died here from a fit of apoplexy brought on by overeating and, on 20 June 1837, Princess Victoria of Kent was woken at 5am to be told that her uncle William IV had died and she was now queen – the start of her 64-year reign. After the death in 1997 of Diana, Princess of Wales, the gold gates south of the palace became a focal point for mourners in their thousands, who turned the surrounding area into a field of bouquets.

Visitors can peek inside the King's and Queen's state apartments, the latter little changed since it was designed for Mary in the 17th century. The King's Staircase is particularly impressive, lavishly painted for George I by William Kent. Another exhibit examines the life of Queen Victoria. The palace also often displays clothes worn by many of the royals, including the Queen and Princess Diana.

🕚 Kensington Gardens

W8. **Map** 10 E4. **Tel** 0300 061 2000. 🚇 Bayswater, High St Kensington, Queensway, Lancaster Gate. **Open** 6am–dusk daily. 🌐 **royalparks.org.uk**

The former grounds of Kensington Palace became a public park in 1841. A small part of it has been dedicated as a memorial playground to Diana, Princess of Wales (see p223). The gardens are full of charm, starting with Sir George Frampton's statue (1912) of J M Barrie's fictional Peter Pan, the boy who never grew up, playing his pipes for the bronze fairies and animals that cling to the column below. Often surrounded by parents, nannies and their charges, the statue stands near the west bank of the Serpentine, not far from where Harriet, wife of the poet Percy Bysshe Shelley, drowned herself in 1816. Just north of here, in Hyde Park, are the ornamental fountains and statues, including Jacob Epstein's *Rima*, at the lake's head. George Frederick Watts' statue of a muscular horse and rider, *Physical Energy*, stands to the south. Not far away is a summer house designed by William Kent in 1735, and the

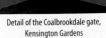

Detail of the Coalbrookdale gate, Kensington Gardens

Serpentine Gallery. The Round Pond, created in 1728 just east of the palace, is often packed with model boats navigated by children and older enthusiasts.

In the north, near Lancaster Gate, is a dogs' cemetery, started in 1880 by the Duke of Cambridge after the death of one of his pets.

Riding on Rotten Row, Hyde Park

⑫ Hyde Park

W2. **Map** 11 B3. **Tel** 0300 061 2000.
🚇 Hyde Park Corner, Knightsbridge, Lancaster Gate, Marble Arch. **Open** 5am–midnight daily. 🖳 Sports facilities. 🅦 **royalparks.org.uk**

The ancient manor of Hyde was part of the lands of Westminster Abbey seized by Henry VIII at the Dissolution of the Monasteries in 1536. It has remained a royal park ever since. Henry used it for hunting but James I opened it to the public in the early 17th century. The Serpentine, an artificial lake used for boating and bathing, was created when Caroline, George II's queen, dammed the flow of the Westbourne River in 1730.

In its time, the park has been a venue for duelling, horse racing, demonstrations and music. The 1851 Exhibition was held here in a vast glass palace (see pp30–31). There is a Princess Diana Memorial fountain to the south of the Serpentine. Hyde Park is the setting for one of the UK's largest Christmas markets, complete with an ice rink and funfair.

⑬ Speakers' Corner

Hyde Park W2. Map 11 C2.
🚇 Marble Arch.

An 1872 law made it legal to assemble an audience and address them on whatever topic you chose; since then this corner of Hyde Park has become the established venue for budding public speakers and a fair number of eccentrics. It is well worth spending time here on a Sunday: speakers from fringe groups and one-member political parties reveal their plans for the betterment of humanity while the assembled onlookers heckle them without mercy.

⑭ Marble Arch

Park Lane W1. **Map** 11 C2.
🚇 Marble Arch.

John Nash designed the arch in 1827 as the main entrance to Buckingham Palace. It was, however, too narrow for the grandest coaches and was moved here in 1851. Historically, only senior members of the royal family and one of the royal artillery regiments are allowed to pass under it.

The arch stands near the site of the old Tyburn gallows (marked by a plaque), where until 1783 the city's most notorious criminals were hanged in front of crowds of bloodthirsty spectators.

An orator at Speakers' Corner

⑮ Harrods

87–135 Brompton Rd, Knightsbridge SW1. **Map** 11 C5. **Tel** 020 7730 1234.
🚇 Knightsbridge. **Open** 10am–9pm Mon–Sat, 11:30am–6pm Sun. ✉ 🖉
🖳 ♿ See Shops and Markets p317.
🅦 **harrods.com**

London's most famous department store began in 1849 when Henry Charles Harrod opened a small grocery shop nearby on Brompton Road. By concentrating on good quality and impeccable service, the store soon became popular enough to expand.

It used to be claimed that Harrods could supply anything from a packet of pins to an elephant – not quite true today, but the range of stock is still vast. A dress code applies: shorts, bare midriffs and flip-flops are not permitted.

Harrods at night, lit by 11,500 lights

❾ Victoria and Albert Museum

The Victoria and Albert Museum (the V&A) contains one of the world's widest collections of art and design, ranging from early Christian devotional objects to cutting-edge furniture design. Originally founded in 1852 as the Museum of Manufactures to inspire design students, it was renamed by Queen Victoria in 1899 in memory of Prince Albert. The museum is undergoing a dramatic renovation, including work on a number of galleries, the facilities near the Exhibition Road entrance and the Sackler Education Centre, so expect some temporary closures.

British Galleries (1760–1900)
This charming sweet box (1770) is one of many pieces on display that were crafted in the workshops of Britain.

Silver Galleries
Pieces such as the Burges Cup (Britain, 1863) fill these galleries.

★ British Galleries (1500–1760)
Displays of evocative objects, such as this writing desk from King Henry VIII's court, illustrate Britain's fascinating history.

★ Fashion Gallery
European fashion, fabrics and accessories from 1750 to the present day are on display, including these gold 1920s Lilley & Skinner shoes.

Exhibition Road entrance

Key to Floorplan

- Level 0
- Level 1
- Level 2
- Level 3
- Level 4
- Level 6
- Henry Cole Wing
- Non-exhibition space
- Temporary exhibitions

Gallery Guide

The V&A has an 11-km (7-mile) layout spread over six levels, and the museum incorporates approximately 150 different galleries. The main floor, level 1, houses the China, Japan and South Asia Galleries, as well as the Fashion Gallery and the Cast Courts. The British Galleries are on levels 2 and 4. Level 3 contains the 20th Century Galleries and displays of silver, ironwork, paintings, photography and design works. The glass display is also on level 4. The Ceramics Galleries and Furniture are on level 6. European galleries from 300 to 1800 are on Level 0. On the ground floor, to the rear beyond the courtyard, are the beautiful café rooms, featuring designs by William Morris.

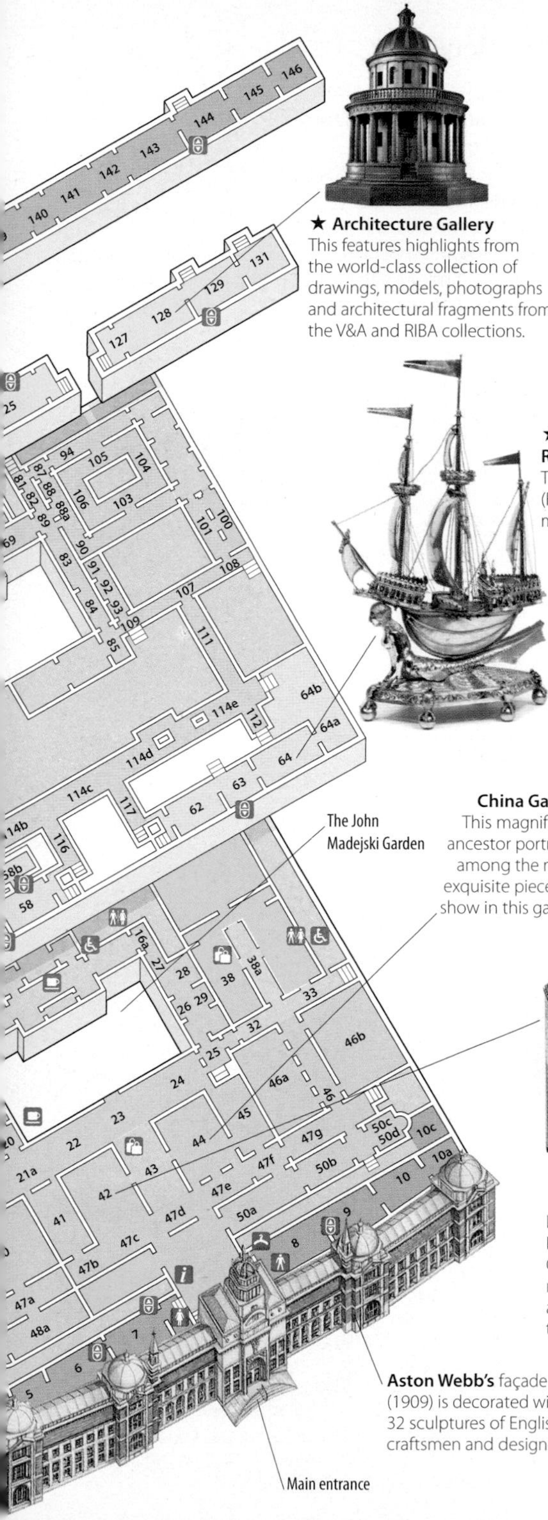

★ **Architecture Gallery**
This features highlights from the world-class collection of drawings, models, photographs and architectural fragments from the V&A and RIBA collections.

★ **Medieval and Renaissance Galleries**
The stunning Burghley Nef (France, 1527) is one of the many treasures in rooms 62–64.

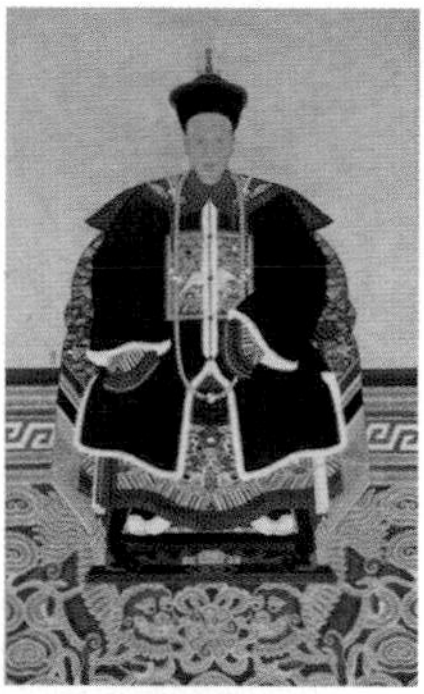

China Gallery
This magnificent ancestor portrait is among the many exquisite pieces on show in this gallery.

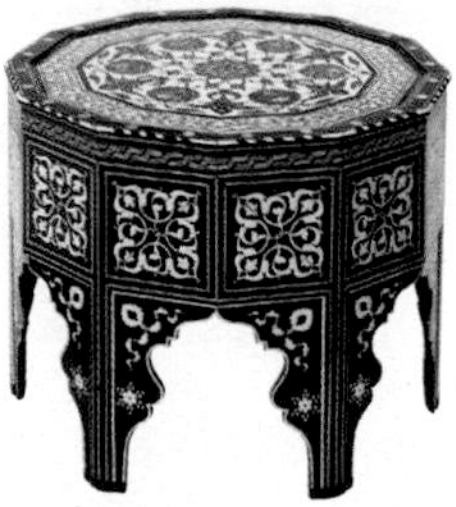

The John Madejski Garden

Islamic Middle East Gallery
On display are fantastic objects representing the finest in Islamic art and design, such as this 16th-century table from the Ottoman Empire.

Aston Webb's façade (1909) is decorated with 32 sculptures of English craftsmen and designers.

Main entrance

Exploring the V&A's Collections

The sheer size of the V&A means you should plan your visit carefully to avoid missing a highlight or an area of particular interest. The following sections list highlights but are by no means exhaustive. Be sure to visit the museum's original refreshment rooms off room 16a (one of which was designed by William Morris), now being used again as a café. If the weather is good, don't miss the John Madejski Garden. The Photographs galleries (rooms 38a and 100) display a changing selection of 300,000 photographs from 1856 to the present.

British Galleries

A sequence of grand rooms starting on level 2 and continuing on level 4 are devoted to the luxurious British Galleries. Covering design and decorative arts from 1500 to 1900, the galleries chart Britain's rise from obscure island to "workshop of the world". The galleries present the evolution of British design and the numerous influences, whether technological or aesthetic, it has absorbed from all over the world.

Beautiful textiles, furniture, costumes and household objects illustrate the tastes and lifestyles of Britain's ruling classes. Among the highlights are James II's wedding suit, the opulent State Bed from Melville House, and a number of carefully preserved period rooms, including the stunning Rococo Norfolk House Music Room. Discovery Areas give visitors a chance

Waistcoat (1734) in room 52b

to delve even deeper into the past by sporting a Tudor ruff or viewing 3D images through a Victorian stereoscope.

China, Japan and South Asia

The Jameel Gallery of Islamic Art was opened in July 2006 and houses a significant collection of more than 400 objects, including ceramics, textiles, carpets, metalwork, glass and woodwork. The exhibits date from the great days of the Islamic caliphate of the 8th and 9th centuries through to the years preceding World War I.

Middle Eastern art from Syria, Iraq, Iran and Egypt, and art from Turkey, is found in room 42. Beautifully crafted textiles and ceramics illustrate the Islamic influence on fine and decorative arts. A dramatic arc of burnished steel fins, representing the spine of a Chinese dragon, spans the China gallery

(room 44). Covering the millennia from 3000 BC to the present, the impressive collection includes a giant Buddha's head from 700–900 AD, a huge yet elegant Ming canopied bed, and rare jade and ceramics.

Japanese art is concentrated in the gallery in room 45, and is particularly notable for lacquer, Samurai armour and woodblock prints.

Gilt copper ice chest (Qing Dynasty 1700s), room 44

Architecture Gallery

The Architecture Gallery features highlights from the world-class collections of drawings, models, photographs and architectural fragments of the V&A and the Royal Institute of British Architects (RIBA) in both permanent displays and temporary exhibitions.

A superb collection of artifacts and illustrations spanning world cultures explores key themes, such as construction techniques and the role of public buildings. Don't miss the exquisitely detailed architectural scale models, including a traditional Japanese house, Modernist constructions from Ernö Goldfinger and others, and British designs such as Charles Barry's Gothic plans for the Palace of Westminster.

The Great Bed of Ware

Made from oak in around 1590, with inlaid and painted decoration, the Great Bed of Ware measures some 3.6 by 3.6 m (12 by 12 ft) and is 2.6 m (8 ft 9 inches) high. It is the V&A's most celebrated piece of furniture. Elaborately carved and decorated, the bed is a superb example of the art of the English woodworker. Its name derives from the town of Ware in Hertfordshire, about a day's ride north of London, where it resided in a number of inns. The Great Bed's enormous size made it an early tourist attraction, and no doubt interest was boosted by Shakespeare's reference to it in *Twelfth Night*, which he wrote in 1601.

Redecorated and refurbished, the bed is located in room 57.

Detail of the Ardabil Carpet (c.1539–40) in the Jameel Gallery of Islamic Art

Europe

Ten galleries, occupying an entire wing of the museum, house some of the world's greatest treasures of medieval and Renaissance Europe. Among the many remarkable exhibits are the notebooks of Leonardo da Vinci; sculptures by Italian masters such as Donatello and Giambologna, some in a Renaissance courtyard garden setting; the fine enamel Becket Casket (c.1180); and the reconstructed Santa Chiara Chapel, the only one of its kind outside Italy.

The Europe collection continues in the Level 0 galleries of the opposite wing, which cover the period 1600 to 1800, and include several re-created period rooms. Room 48a on the ground floor is dedicated to the famous Raphael cartoons – huge designs for tapestries planned for the Sistine Chapel, dating from 1515. The cartoons were acquired by Charles I.

Another of the most famous sights at the V&A are the extraordinary cast courts, which have been part of the museum since its founding. They house large plaster casts of major European sculptures, such as Rome's Trajan's Column (in two pieces) and a 5 m (16 ft) tall reproduction of Michaelangelo's *David*, created so that visitors to the museum could see these works without travelling.

Ruby glass flagon (c.1858–9)

Textiles and Fashion

The popular Fashion Gallery displays items from the largest and most comprehensive collection of dress in the world. Around 100 exhibits, spanning over three centuries, are arranged chronologically. They include a magnificent mantua from the 1760s; an 1850s wedding dress with veil and shoes; a Schiaparelli evening coat embroidered with a design by Jean Cocteau; and a punk outfit designed by Vivienne Westwood. Textiles are also found throughout the museum's collections; the Japanese galleries in particular have some exquisite kimonos and other traditional textiles.

Metalwork

This group of galleries is located on level 3. In the Silver Galleries, 3,500 pieces from 1400 to the present day are displayed in the beautifully refurbished Victorian rooms 65 to 69. Arms and armour, European metalwork from the 1500s to the present, and Islamic brass and bronze can be found in rooms 81, 82 and 87 to 89.

The Sacred Silver and Stained Glass galleries in rooms 83 and 84 display devotional treasures. The highlight of the Ironwork galleries, which are located

in rooms 113 to 114e, is the dazzling Hereford Screen designed by Sir George Gilbert Scott in 1862, and displayed at the International Exhibition of that year. The screen became the V&A's largest conservation project.

The Gilbert Collection of gold, silver, micromosaics and gold boxes, formerly housed at Somerset House, re-opened here in 2009.

Glass and Ceramics

The museum has the most comprehensive collection of glass and ceramics in the world. Examples of glass covering 2,000 years are largely housed in room 131, which has a stunning glass balustrade on the staircase and mezzanine by artist Danny Lane. Displays of international contemporary glass are on display in this room and in room 129.

The ceramics collection has an introductory gallery presenting the history and development of ceramics across the world. All of the major British pottery factories are represented

Stained-glass roundel illustrating *Susanna Accused by the Elders* (c.1520)

KENSINGTON AND HOLLAND PARK

The western and northern perimeters of Kensington Gardens make up a rich residential and commercial area. The shops on Kensington High Street are almost as smart as those in Knightsbridge, and Kensington Church Street is a good source of quality antiques. Around Holland Park are some magnificent late Victorian houses, two of them open to the public. But as you cross into Bayswater and Notting Hill, you enter a more vibrant, cosmopolitan part of London, with Queensway home to numerous Middle Eastern restaurants. Notting Hill is historically associated with London's African-Caribbean community; the area's flamboyant Carnival first took to the streets in 1966 and has been staged every year since on the last weekend in August *(see p61)*. Now that the area is fully gentrified, the elegant stucco terraces, market and independent shops attract an increasingly trendy set including a few famous names, as depicted in the eponymous film. Meanwhile, Portobello Road street market, selling everything from food to antiques, draws in tourists and Londoners from across the city at weekends.

Sights at a Glance

Historic Streets and Buildings
2 Holland House
3 Leighton House
5 18 Stafford Terrace
7 Kensington Square
8 Kensington Palace Gardens

Museums
4 Design Museum

Parks and Gardens
1 Holland Park
6 Kensington Roof Gardens
9 The Diana, Princess of Wales Memorial Playground

Markets
10 Portobello Road

Area of Interest
11 Notting Hill

Street Finder maps 9, 10, 17

□ **Restaurants** *see pp299–301*
1 Babylon at the Roof Garden
2 The Belvedere
3 Bill's
4 Ffiona's
5 Kensington Place
6 Kitchen W8

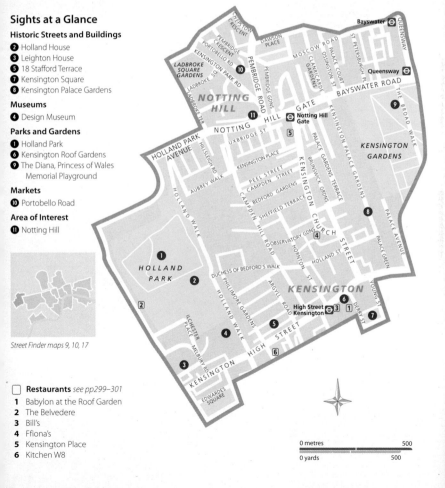

0 metres 500
0 yards 500

Street-by-Street: Kensington and Holland Park

Although now part of central London, as recently as the 1830s this was a country village of market gardens and mansions. Outstanding among these was Holland House; part of its grounds are now Holland Park. The area grew up rapidly in the mid-19th century and most of its buildings date from then – mainly expensive apartments, mansion flats and fashionable shops.

❷ Holland House
This rambling Jacobean mansion, started in 1605 and pictured here in 1795, was largely demolished in the 1950s.

❶ ★ Holland Park
Parts of the old formal gardens of Holland House feature in this delightful public park.

The Orangery, now a restaurant, has parts that date from the 1630s, when it was within the grounds of Holland House.

Melbury Road is lined with large Victorian houses. Many were built for fashionable artists of the time.

The Victorian letter box on the High Street is one of the oldest in London.

❸ ★ Leighton House
The house is preserved as it was when the Victorian painter Lord Leighton lived here.

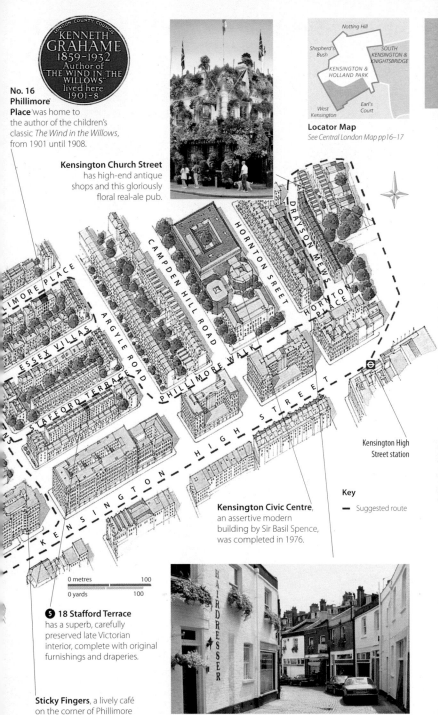

No. 16 Phillimore Place was home to the author of the children's classic *The Wind in the Willows*, from 1901 until 1908.

Kensington Church Street has high-end antique shops and this gloriously floral real-ale pub.

Locator Map
See Central London Map pp16–17

Key

— Suggested route

Kensington Civic Centre, an assertive modern building by Sir Basil Spence, was completed in 1976.

Kensington High Street station

0 metres 100
0 yards 100

5 18 Stafford Terrace has a superb, carefully preserved late Victorian interior, complete with original furnishings and draperies.

Sticky Fingers, a lively café on the corner of Phillimore Gardens, is owned by Bill Wyman, former guitarist of the Rolling Stones.

Drayson Mews is one of the quaint alleys that were built behind large town houses for the stabling of horses and coaches. Today most have been converted into small houses.

The café in Holland Park

❶ Holland Park

Abbotsbury Rd W14. **Map** 9 B5.
Tel 020 7361 3003 to book facilities.
🚇 Holland Park, High Street
Kensington, Notting Hill Gate. **Open**
7:30am–dusk daily (hours are flexible
depending on season). **Closed** 25
Dec. 🅿️ 🏢 Open-air opera, theatre,
dance. Information: **Tel** 020 7361 3570.
Art exhibitions Apr. *See Entertainment
pp340–41.* 🔲 **rbkc.gov.uk**

This small but delightful park,
more wooded and intimate
than the large royal parks to its
east (Hyde Park and Kensington
Gardens, *see pp212–13*), was
opened in 1952 on what
remained of the grounds of
Holland House – the rest had
been sold off in the late 19th
century for the construction of
new, large houses. The park still
contains some of the formal
gardens laid out in the early
19th century. There is also a
Japanese garden, created for
the 1991 London Festival of
Japan. The park is full of wildlife,
including peacocks.

❷ Holland House

Holland Park W8. **Map** 9 B5. 🚇
Holland Park, High Street Kensington.
Hostel **Tel** 020 7870 9629.
🔲 **safestay.com**

During its heyday in the 19th
century, this was a noted centre
of social and political intrigue.
Statesmen such as Lord
Palmerston mixed here with
the likes of the poet Lord Byron.
The Jacobean house suffered

heavy bomb damage during
World War II; the remains are
now used as a youth hostel.
  Outbuildings are put to
various uses: exhibitions are
held in the orangery and the
ice house, and the old Garden
Ballroom is now a restaurant.

❸ Leighton House

12 Holland Park Rd W14. **Map** 17 B1.
Tel 020 7602 3316. 🚇 High St Kensington. **Open** 10am–5:30pm Wed–
Mon (to 9pm select Thu). **Closed**
1 Jan, 25 Dec. 🅿️ 🎧 3pm Wed & Sun
or by appt for groups. 🏢 📷
Concerts, exhibitions, talks. 🔲 **rbkc.
gov.uk/leightonhousemuseum**

Built for respected Victorian
painter Lord Leighton in 1864–79,
the house has been preserved
with its opulent decoration as an
extraordinary monument to
Victorian aesthetics. The highlight
is the Arab Hall, added in 1879 to
house Leighton's collection of
Islamic tiles, some inscribed with
text from the Koran. There are
paintings and drawings displayed
including some by Edward Burne-
Jones, John Millais, G F Watts and
many works by Leighton himself.

Original tiling in Holland House

❹ Design Museum

Commonwealth Institute Building,
Kensington High St W8. **Map** 9 C5.
Tel 020 7940 8790. 🚇 High St
Kensington. **Open** check website.
🔲 **designmuseum.org**

This striking Grade II-listed
building with a tent-like parabolic
roof is the new home of the
Design Museum. The first in the
world to be devoted solely to
modern and contemporary
design, its frequently changing
exhibitions explore landmarks
in modern design history. It
embraces every area of design
from furniture and fashion to
household products.

❺ 18 Stafford Terrace

18 Stafford Terrace W8. **Map** 9 C5.
Tel 020 7602 3316 Mon–Fri; 020 7938
1295 Sat & Sun. 🚇 High St Kensington. **Open** 2–5:30pm Wed, Sat & Sun.
🅿️ 🎧 10:15am & 11:30am Wed, Sat &
Sun (costumed tour Sat); book ahead.
🏢 🔲 **rbkc.gov.uk/subsites/
museums.aspx**

The former home of Linley
Sambourne, 18 Stafford Terrace,
was built in about 1870. It has
undergone a major renovation
but remains much as Sambourne
furnished it – in the Victorian
manner, with Oriental ornaments
and heavy velvet drapes.
Sambourne was a cartoonist for
the satirical magazine *Punch*;
drawings cram the walls of the
house. Some rooms have William
Morris wallpaper *(see p253)*.

❻ Kensington Roof Gardens

99 Kensington High Street W8 (entrance in Derry Street). **Map** 10 D5. **Tel** 020 7937 7994; restaurant reservations 020 7268 3993. **Open** 9am–5pm daily (but call ahead, as often closed for private functions). Photo ID required. 🚫
W roofgardens.virgin.com

High above the bustle of Kensington High Street is one of London's best-kept secrets – a 6,000-sq m (1.5-acre) roof garden. First planted in the 1930s by the owners of Derry & Toms department store below (which now houses many different stores), the themed gardens are a lavish flight of fancy and feature a woodland garden, a Spanish garden (with palm trees) and a formal English garden (with a pond, live ducks and a pair of pink flamingos). Best of all, it's free to wander round, though there is no access when the gardens have been booked for events; there's also a restaurant, and a club night on Friday and Saturday.

❼ Kensington Square

W8. **Map** 10 D5. ⊖ High St Kensington.

This is one of London's oldest squares. It was laid out in the 1680s, and a few early 18th-century houses still remain. (Nos. 11 and 12 are the oldest.) The renowned philosopher John Stuart Mill lived at No. 18, and the Pre-Raphaelite painter and illustrator Edward Burne-Jones at No. 41.

❽ Kensington Palace Gardens

W8. **Map** 10 D3. ⊖ High St Kensington, Notting Hill Gate, Queensway.

This private road of luxury mansions occupies the site of the former kitchen gardens of Kensington Palace (see p212); its southern end is known as Palace Green. It is accessible to pedestrians but not cars, unless they have specific business. Many of the houses are occupied by embassies, though some have become private residences once again. It's said to be the most expensive street in London.

❾ The Diana, Princess of Wales Memorial Playground

Kensington Gardens. **Map** 10 E3. **Tel** 0300 061 2001. ⊖ Bayswater, Queensway. **Open** daily, Feb & late Oct: 10am–4:45pm; Mar & early Oct: 10am–5:45pm; Apr & Sep: 10am–6:45pm; May–Aug: 10am–7:45pm; Nov–Jan: 10am–3:45pm. **Closed** 25 Dec. 🖥 🚻
W royalparks.org.uk

The newest of Kensington Gardens' three playgrounds was opened in 2000. Located close to the Bayswater Road, on the site of an earlier playground funded by Peter Pan's creator, J M Barrie, it takes the boy who didn't want to grow up as its theme and is packed with novel ideas and activities including a beach cove with a 15-m (50-ft) pirates' galleon, a tree house with walkways, and a mermaid's fountain with a half-submerged slumbering crocodile (careful not to rouse him!). Though all children up to the age of 12 must be accompanied by an adult, staff are on hand to make sure the children are safe. Many features of the playground are accessible to children with special needs.

Antique shop on Portobello Road

❿ Portobello Road

W11. **Map** 9 C3. ⊖ Notting Hill Gate, Ladbroke Grove. Antiques market **Open** Main market 9am–5pm Fri & Sat; fruit & veg market 9am–5pm Mon–Wed & 9am–1pm Thu. Portobello Green Fri–Sun. *See also Shops and Markets p337.*

There has been a market here since 1837. Today the southern end consists almost exclusively of stalls that sell antiques, jewellery, souvenirs and other collectables – the busiest day is Saturday, when the antiques arcades are open. The market is extremely popular with tourists and tends to be very crowded. However, it is well worth visiting just to experience its bustling, cheerful atmosphere. If you are looking for bargains,, be warned – the stallholders have a sound idea of the value of what they are selling. Other markets run along the rest of the street on different days, with vintage and new clothes concentrated around Portobello Green, under the Westway near Ladbroke Grove Tube.

⓫ Notting Hill

W11. **Map** 9 C3. ⊖ Notting Hill Gate.

Now the home of Europe's biggest street carnival, most of this area was farmland until the 19th century. In the 1950s and 1960s, it became a centre for the Caribbean community, many of whom lived here when they first arrived in Britain. The carnival started in 1966 and takes over the area every August over the bank holiday weekend (see p61) when costumed parades meander through the streets.

Kensington Roof Gardens

REGENT'S PARK AND MARYLEBONE

The area south of Regent's Park, incorporating the medieval village of Marylebone, has London's highest concentration of quality Georgian housing, developed by Robert Harley, Earl of Oxford, in the 18th century.

Terraces by John Nash adorn the southern edge of Regent's Park, home to London's magnificent zoo and a delightful open-air theatre, while Marylebone High Street, with its independent shops, retains a village-like atmosphere.

Sights at a Glance

Historic Streets and Buildings
④ Harley Street
⑤ Portland Place
⑥ Broadcasting House
⑮ Cumberland Terrace

Museums and Galleries
⑩ Wallace Collection
⑪ Sherlock Holmes Museum

Churches and Mosques
③ St Marylebone Parish Church
⑦ All Souls, Langham Place
⑫ London Central Mosque

Parks and Gardens
② Regent's Park

Attractions
① Madame Tussauds
⑨ Wigmore Hall
⑭ London Zoo

Historic Hotels
⑧ Langham Hotel

Historic Waterways
⑬ Regent's Canal

Street Finder maps 3, 4, 12

☐ **Restaurants** see pp301–2
1 Galvin Bistrot de Luxe
2 Golden Hind
3 Orrery
4 The Providores and Tapa Room
5 Texture

0 metres 500
0 yards 500

◀ Georgian-style architecture, Regent's Park

For keys to symbols see back flap

Street-by-Street: Marylebone

South of Regent's Park lies the medieval village of
Marylebone (originally Maryburne, the stream by St Mary's
church). Until the 18th century it was surrounded by fields,
but these were built over as fashionable London drifted west.
In the mid-19th century, professional people, especially
doctors, used the spacious houses to receive wealthy clients.
The area has maintained both its medical connections and its
elegance. Marylebone High Street is full of interesting, high-
quality food and clothes shops, bookshops and cafés.

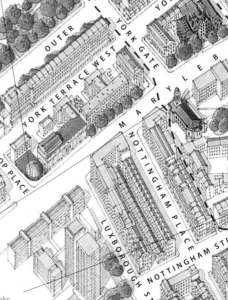

❷ ★ Regent's Park
John Nash laid out the royal
park in 1812 as a setting for
classically designed villas
and terraces.

**The Royal Academy of
Music**, England's first
music academy, was
founded in 1774. The
present brick building,
with its own concert
hall, is from 1911.

❶ ★ Madame Tussauds
This waxworks museum has been in
business since 1835 and remains one of
London's most popular attractions. It
moved to its present location in 1884.

To Regent's
Park

**❸ St Marylebone
Parish Church**
Poets Robert Browning
and Elizabeth Barrett
married in this church.

Baker Street
station

Marylebone High Street is lined with
attractive shops. At No. 83 is Daunt Books
with its galleried interior. On the corner
of Marylebone Lane, V V Rouleaux is a
gloriously colourful haberdashery shop.

Park Crescent's breathtaking façades by Nash have been preserved, although the interiors were rebuilt as offices in the 1960s. The crescent seals the north end of Nash's ceremonial route from St James's to Regent's Park, via Regent Street and Portland Place.

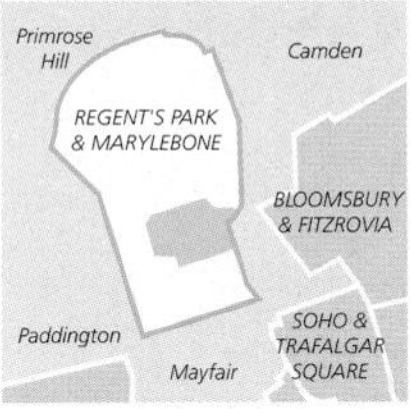

Locator Map
See Central London Map pp16–17

Primrose Hill

Camden

REGENT'S PARK & MARYLEBONE

BLOOMSBURY & FITZROVIA

Paddington

SOHO & TRAFALGAR SQUARE

Mayfair

Key

— Suggested route

| 0 metres | 100 |
| 0 yards | 100 |

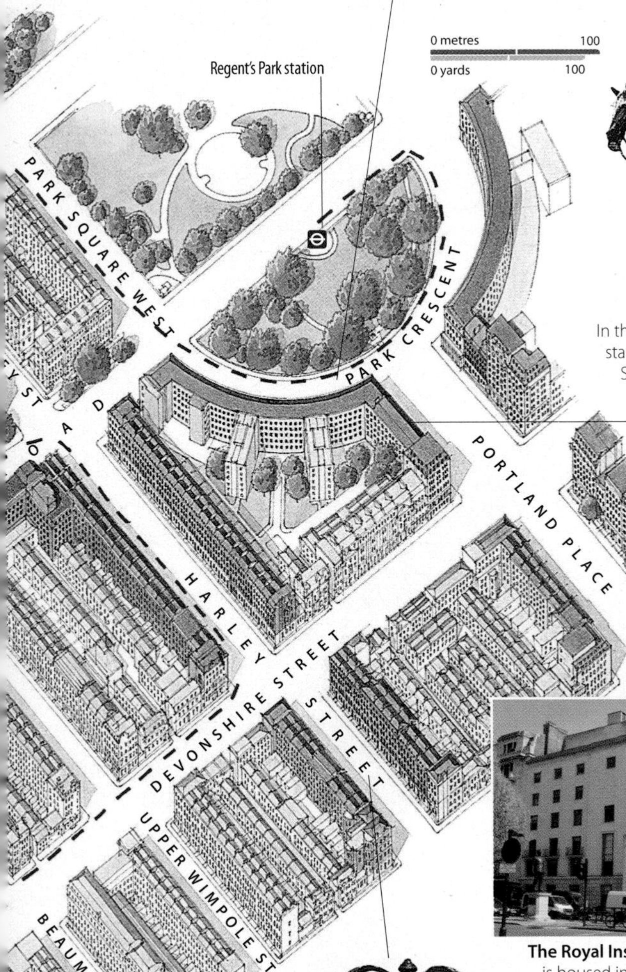

Regent's Park station

⑤ Portland Place
In the centre of this broad street stands a statue of Field Marshal Sir George Stuart White, who won the Victoria Cross for gallantry in the Afghan War of 1879.

PARK SQUARE WEST

PARK CRESCENT

PORTLAND PLACE

HARLEY STREET

DEVONSHIRE STREET

UPPER WIMPOLE ST

BEAUMONT STREET

The Royal Institute of British Architects is housed in a striking Art Deco building designed by Grey Wornum in 1934.

Nº 90A HARLEY STREET

④ Harley Street
Consulting rooms of eminent medical specialists have been located here for more than a century.

❶ Madame Tussauds

Marylebone Rd NW1. **Map** 4 D5. **Tel** 0871 894 3000. 🚇 Baker St. **Open** 9:30am–5:30pm Mon–Fri, 9am–6pm Sat & Sun (extended hours during peak holiday periods). **Closed** 25 Dec. 🎫 📷 🏬 ♿ phone first. 🌐 **madametussauds.com**

Madame Tussaud began her wax-modelling career rather morbidly, making death masks of many of the best-known victims of the French Revolution. In 1835 she set up an exhibition of her work in Baker Street, not far from the collection's present site.

The attraction still uses traditional wax-modelling techniques to recreate politicians, royals, actors, rock stars and sporting heroes, the displays changing fairly regularly to keep up with who's in and who's out in the world of modern celebrity.

The exhibition features "A-List Party", where visitors can "attend" a celebrity bash; "Film", devoted to Hollywood legends

Traditional wax-modelling at Madame Tussauds

and film characters such as Marilyn Monroe and ET; and "World Leaders", including Barack Obama, David Cameron and Nelson Mandela.

The "Culture" area has the likes of Shakespeare and Picasso, and the "Music Zone" includes Madonna, Rihanna and Lady Gaga. There are also sections dedicated to franchises such as Marvel and Star Wars, with detailed walk-in sets and a 4D Marvel film experience.

The Chamber of Horrors features gruesome episodes in the grim catalogue of crime and punishment: here visitors can recoil at the murderer Dr Crippen, and experience the chilly gloom of an east London street during Jack the Ripper's time in the late 19th century.

In the "Spirit of London" section visitors travel in stylized London taxi-cabs and participate in momentous events of the city, from the Great Fire of 1666 to 1960s Swinging London.

Ticket prices are fairly steep, but cheaper if you buy online in advance. Opting for timed tickets can help reduce queuing times.

Wax figure of Elizabeth II

Tulip time at Queen Mary's Gardens in Regent's Park

❷ Regent's Park

NW1. **Map** 3 C2. **Tel** 0300 061 2300. 🚇 Regent's Park, Baker St, Great Portland St. **Open** 5am–dusk daily. ♿ 🎭 Open air theatre *See Entertainment pp340–41*. *Zoo see p231*. Sports facilities. 🌐 **royalparks.org.uk**

This area of land became enclosed as a park in 1812. John Nash designed the scheme and originally envisaged a kind of garden suburb, dotted with 56 villas in a variety of Classical styles, and a pleasure palace for the Prince Regent. In the event only eight villas – but no palace – were built inside the park (three survive round the edge of the Inner Circle).

The boating lake, which has many varieties of water birds, is marvellously romantic, especially when music drifts across from the bandstand. Queen Mary's Gardens are a mass of wonderful sights and smells in summer, when visitors

can also enjoy a full programme of outdoor theatre, including Shakespeare, musicals and children's plays, at the **Open Air Theatre** nearby.

Nash's master plan for the park continues just beyond its northeastern edge in Park Village East and West. These elegant stucco buildings date from 1828.

The park is also renowned for its excellent sports facilities.

❸ St Marylebone Parish Church

Marylebone Rd NW1. **Map** 4 D5. **Tel** 020 7935 7315. 🚇 Regent's Park. **Open** 9am–5pm daily. ♿ 🚻 8:30 & 11am Sun. 📷 🌐 **stmarylebone.org**

This is where the poets Robert Browning and Elizabeth Barrett were married in 1846 after eloping from her strict family home on nearby Wimpole Street. The large, stately church by Thomas Hardwick was built in 1817 after the former church, where Lord Byron was christened in 1778, had become too small. Hardwick was determined that the same should not happen to his new church – so everything is on a grand scale.

Commemorative window in St Marylebone Parish Church

❹ Harley Street

W1. **Map** 4 E5. ⊖ Regent's Park, Oxford Circus, Bond St, Great Portland St.

The large houses on this late 18th-century street were popular with successful doctors and specialists in the middle of the 19th century, when it was a wealthy residential area. The medical practices stayed and lend the street an air of hushed order, unusual in central London. William Gladstone lived at No. 73 from 1876 to 1882 but there are very few private houses of apartments here now.

❺ Portland Place

W1. **Map** 4 E5. ⊖ Regent's Park, Oxford Circus.

The Adam Brothers, Robert and James, laid this street out in 1773. Only a few of the original houses remain, the best being Nos. 27 to 47 on the west side, south of Devonshire Street. John Nash added the street to his processional route from Carlton House to Regent's Park and sealed its northern end with Park Crescent.

The headquarters of the Royal Institute of British Architects (1934) at No. 66 is adorned with symbolic statues and reliefs. Its bronze front doors depict London's buildings and the River Thames.

❻ Broadcasting House

Portland Place W1. **Map** 12 E1. ⊖ Oxford Circus. **Open** daily for guided tours only. Pre-booking essential, via the website or call 0370 901 1227. No children under 9. 🅿 ♿ 🆆 **bbc.co.uk**

Broadcasting House was built in 1931 as a suitably modern Art Deco setting for the new medium of broadcasting. Its front, curving with the street, is dominated by Eric Gill's stylized relief of Shakespeare's Prospero and Ariel. As the invisible spirit of the air, Ariel was considered an appropriate personification of broadcasting. The character appears in two other sculptures on the western frontage, and again over the eastern entrance in "Ariel Piping to Children".

Broadcasting House is now the London headquarters of BBC news, radio, television and online departments. Fascinating tours of Broadcasting House are available, although not suitable for children under 9. Each tour is unique, as the itinerary depends on programming and events of the day.

A major refurbishment in 2011 created a public piazza, a BBC shop and a café that overlooks the central newsroom.

Relief on the Royal Institute of British Architects building, Portland Place

❼ All Souls, Langham Place

Langham Place W1. **Map** 12 F1. **Tel** 020 7580 3522. ⊖ Oxford Circus. **Open** 9:30am–5:30pm Mon–Fri, 9am–3pm & 5:30–8:30pm Sun. ✝ 9:30am, 11:30am, 6:30pm Sun. ♿ 🆆 **allsouls.org**

John Nash designed this church in 1824. Its quirky round frontage is best seen from Regent Street. When it was first built, the spire was ridiculed as it appeared too slender and flimsy.

The only Nash church in London, it had close links with the BBC, based across the street at Broadcasting House; the daily service, a stalwart of the radio schedule, was broadcast from here for many years.

❽ Langham Hotel

1 Portland Place W1. **Map** 12 E1. **Tel** 020 7636 1000. ⊖ Oxford Circus. 🆆 **langhamhotels.com**

This was London's grandest hotel on opening in 1865. The writers Oscar Wilde and Mark Twain, and composer Antonín Dvořák were among its many distinguished guests. It was, for a time, used by the BBC as a record library and as a venue for recording shows. It has since been restored, bringing it boldly into the 21st century with its luxurious rooms, chic Artesian bar and fine-dining restaurant, Roux at the Landau.

All Souls, Langham Place (1824)

❾ Wigmore Hall

36 Wigmore St W1. **Map** 12 E1. **Tel** 020
7258 8200. Box Office: **Tel** 020 7935
2141. ⊖ Bond St, Oxford Circus
♿ ⏎ *See Entertainment p345.*
🆆 **wigmore-hall.org.uk**

This appealing little concert hall
for chamber music was designed
by T E Collcutt, architect of the
Savoy hotel, in 1900. At first it
was called Bechstein Hall
because it was attached to the
Bechstein piano showroom; the
area used to be the heart of
London's piano trade. Opposite is
the Art Nouveau emporium built
in 1907 as Debenham and Free-
body's department store – now
Debenham's is on Oxford Street.

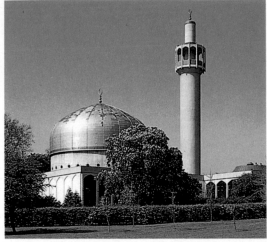

The Mosque on the edge of Regent's Park

Late 18th-century Sèvres porcelain vase,
Wallace Collection

❿ Wallace Collection

Hertford House, Manchester Sq W1.
Map 12 D1. **Tel** 020 7563 9500.
⊖ Bond St, Baker St. **Open**
10am–5pm daily. **Closed** 24–26 Dec.
Lectures. ♿ 🔊 ⏎ 📷 🏛
🆆 **wallacecollection.org**

This is one of the world's finest
private collections of art. It has
remained intact since it was
bequeathed to the government
in 1897 with the stipulation
that it should go on permanent
public display with nothing
added or removed. The product
of passionate collecting for four
generations of the Hertford

family, it is a must for anyone
with even a passing interest in
the progress of European art up
to the late 19th century. The
house itself is magnificent, with
dozens of rooms, including the
superb great gallery, rich with
period detail.

Among the 70 masterworks
are Frans Hals's *The Laughing
Cavalier*, Titian's *Perseus and
Andromeda* and Rembrandt's
Titus. There are superb portraits
by Reynolds, Gainsborough
and Romney. Other highlights
include Sèvres porcelain and
sculpture by Houdon and
Roubiliac. The fine European
and Oriental armour collection
is the second largest in the UK.

⓫ Sherlock Holmes Museum

221b Baker St NW1. **Map** 3 C4. **Tel** 020
7224 3688. ⊖ Baker St. **Open**
9:30am–6pm daily. **Closed** 25 Dec.
📷 🏛 🆆 **sherlock-holmes.co.uk**

Sir Arthur Conan Doyle's fictional
detective lived at 221b Baker
Street. This building, dating from
1815, has been converted to
resemble Holmes's flat, and is
furnished exactly as described
in the books. Visitors are greeted
by Holmes's "housekeeper" and
shown to his recreated rooms
on the first floor. The shop sells
souvenirs including short stories
and deerstalker hats.

⓬ London Central Mosque

146 Park Rd NW8. **Map** 3 B3. **Tel** 020
7724 3363. ⊖ Marylebone, St John's
Wood, Baker St. **Open** dawn–dusk
daily. ♿ 🏛 Lectures. 🆆 **iccuk.org**

Surrounded by trees on the
edge of Regent's Park, this large,
golden-domed mosque was
designed by Sir Frederick
Gibberd and completed in 1978.
Built to cater for the increasing
number of Muslim residents in
and visitors to London, the
mosque is capable of holding
1,800 worshippers. The main
hall of worship is a plain square
chamber with a domed roof
and a magnificent carpet.
Visitors must remove their shoes
before entering the mosque,
and women should remember
to cover their heads.

Conan Doyle's Sherlock Holmes

A boat trip on Regent's Canal

⓭ Regent's Canal

NW1 & NW8. **Map** 3 C1. **Tel** 020 7482 2660 (waterbus). 🚇 Camden Town, St John's Wood, Warwick Ave. Canal towpaths **Open** dawn–dusk daily. *See Six Guided Walks pp270–71.*
🔳 londonwaterbus.com

John Nash was extremely enthusiastic about this waterway, opened in 1820 to link the Grand Junction Canal, which ended at Little Venice in Paddington in the west, with the London docks at Limehouse in the east. He originally wanted the canal to run through the middle of his new Regent's Park, but was dissuaded by those who thought that the bargees' bad language would offend the genteel residents of the area. Perhaps this was just as well – the steam tugs that hauled the barges were dirty and sometimes dangerous. In 1874, a barge carrying

gunpowder blew up in the cutting by London Zoo, killing the crew, destroying a bridge, and terrifying the populace and the animals. After an initial period of prosperity for the canal, increasing competition from new railways saw it gradually slip into decline.

Today it has been revived as a leisure amenity; the towpath, now paved, is a pleasant walkway and short boat trips are offered between Little Venice and Camden Lock, with its huge crafts market. Visitors to the zoo can use the landing stage in the grounds.

⓮ London Zoo

Regent's Park NW1. **Map** 4 D2. **Tel** 0344 225 1826. 🚇 Camden Town. **Open** 10am–5:30pm (4pm Nov–Mar) daily (last admission 1 hr before closing). **Closed** 25 Dec. ♿ 🖥 📷 🍴 🔳 zsl.org

Opened in 1828, London Zoo has been one of London's biggest tourist attractions ever since, and is also a major research and conservation centre. The zoo has over 600 species of animal, from Sumatran tigers to bird-eating spiders. Exhibits include Penguin Beach; a gorilla kingdom; "meet the monkeys" where you can walk among dozens of spider

London Zoo's aviary, designed by Lord Snowdon (1964)

monkeys; an inventive, humid rainforest enclosure with sloths and anteaters; a lemur walk-through area; and an expanded home for the lions. Look out for feeding times for the day.

⓯ Cumberland Terrace

NW1. **Map** 4 E2. 🚇 Great Portland St, Regent's Park, Camden Town.

James Thomson is credited with the detailed design of this, the longest and most elaborate of the Nash terraces around Regent's Park. Its imposing central block of raised Ionic columns is topped with a decorated triangular pediment. Completed in 1828, it was designed to be visible from the palace Nash planned for the Prince Regent (later George IV). The palace was never built because the Prince was too busy with his plans for Buckingham Palace *(see pp98–9)*.

Nash's Cumberland Terrace, dating from 1828

HAMPSTEAD AND HIGHGATE

Two rather exclusive north London neighbour-hoods, set apart from the hurly-burly of the modern city, Highgate and Hampstead sit on either side of the vast, bucolic Hampstead Heath, arguably London's finest green space. Both have long been settlements – Hampstead is mentioned as far back as the 10th century – and both became fashionable retreats from the city, becoming essentially Georgian villages. There has been a settlement in Highgate since at least the early Middle Ages, when an important staging post on the Great North Road from London was established, with a gate to control access. Both also have illustrious literary and artistic connections, though Hampstead's have the edge, with the likes of John Keats having set up home there. But while they lived in Hampstead, many of the city's intellectuals are buried in Highgate's cemetery – not least Karl Marx, who is buried in the East Cemetery, though it is the West Cemetery that is the more atmospheric.

Sights at a Glance

Historic Streets and Buildings
1 Flask Walk and Well Walk
4 Church Row
5 Downshire Hill
13 Vale of Health

Museums and Galleries
2 Burgh House
3 Fenton House
6 Keats House
10 Kenwood House

Parks and Gardens
8 Hampstead Heath
9 Parliament Hill
12 The Hill Garden

Pubs and Bars
11 Spaniards Inn

Cemeteries
7 Highgate Cemetery

Restaurants see pp305–7
1 Jin-Kichi
2 Gaucho Hampstead
3 The Wells

Street Finder maps 1, 2

◀ Kenwood House on Hampstead Heath

For keys to symbols see back flap

Street-by-Street: Hampstead

Perched awkwardly on a hilltop, with its broad heath to the north, Hampstead has kept its village atmosphere and sense of being outside the city. This has attracted artists and writers since Georgian times and has made it one of London's most desirable residential areas. Its mansions and town houses are perfectly maintained and a stroll through Hampstead's narrow streets is one of London's quieter pleasures.

Old Bull and Bush
This pub on the edge of the Heath was a former haunt for writers and artists.

8 ★ Hampstead Heath
A welcome retreat from the city, its broad open spaces include bathing ponds, meadows and lakes.

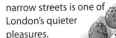

Grove Lodge was home to novelist John Galsworthy (1867–1933), author of *The Forsyte Saga*, for the last 15 years of his life.

Whitestone Pond takes its name from the old white milestone nearby. It is 7 km (4.5 miles) from Holborn *(see pp136–45).*

Admiral's House dates from about 1700. Built for a sea captain, its name derives from its external maritime motifs. No admiral ever actually lived in it.

Key

— Suggested route

0 metres	100
0 yards	100

3 ★ Fenton House
Summer visitors should seek out this late 17th-century house and its exquisite walled garden, which are well hidden in the jumble of streets near the Heath.

2 ★ Burgh House
Built in 1702 but much altered since, the house contains an intriguing local history museum and a café overlooking the small garden.

Locator Map
See Central London Map pp16–17

No. 40 Well Walk
is where artist John Constable lived while working on his many Hampstead pictures.

CHRISTCHURCH HILL

CANNON PLACE

NEW END SQUARE

NEW END

STREATLEY PLACE

WELL WALK

FLASK WALK

BACK LANE

STREET

HOLLY HILL

Hampstead station

HAMPSTEAD HIGH ST

CHURCH ROW

1 Flask Walk and Well Walk
An alley of charming specialist shops broadens into a residential village street.

The Everyman Cinema has been an arthouse cinema since 1933.

4 ★ Church Row
The tall houses are rich in original detail. Notice the superb ironwork on what is probably London's finest Georgian street.

Site of the well on Well Walk that provided Hampstead with its spa waters

❶ Flask Walk and Well Walk

NW3. **Map** 1 B5. 🚇 Hampstead.

Flask Walk is named after the Flask pub. Here, in the 18th century, the area's therapeutic spa water was put into flasks and sold to visitors or sent to London. The water, rich in iron salts, came from nearby Well Walk, where a disused fountain now marks the site of the well. The Wells Tavern, almost opposite the spring, was a hostelry that accommodated those who engaged in the illicit liaisons for which the spa became notorious.

There have been many notable residents of Well Walk, including artist John Constable (at No. 40), novelists D H Lawrence and J B Priestley, and the poet John Keats, before he moved to what is now Keats Grove (*see facing page*). At the High Street end, Flask Walk is narrow and lined with old shops. Beyond the Flask pub (note the Victorian tiled panels outside) it broadens into a row of Regency houses, one of which used to belong to the novelist Kingsley Amis.

❷ Burgh House

New End Sq NW3. **Map** 1 B4. **Tel** 020 7431 0144. 🚇 Hampstead. **Open** noon–5pm Wed–Sun (Sat ground floor art gallery & café only). Café 11am–5pm Wed–Fri, 9.30am–5pm Sat & Sun **Closed** Christmas week. 📷 📱 Music recitals. 🔳 burghhouse.org.uk

The last private tenant of Burgh House was the son-in-law of the writer Rudyard Kipling, who visited here occasionally in the last years of his life until 1936. After a period under the ownership of Hampstead Borough Council, the house was let to the independent Burgh House Trust. Since 1979, the Trust has run it as the Hampstead Museum, which illustrates the history of the area and concentrates on some of its most celebrated residents.

The museum owns a significant art collection, including works by the Bloomsbury Group painter Duncan Grant, along with furniture and archive material on the area. There is a display about Hampstead as a spa in the 18th and 19th centuries and exhibitions by contemporary local artists are often displayed in the ground-floor gallery.

The house itself was built in 1703 but is named after a 19th-century resident, the Reverend Allatson Burgh. It has been much altered inside, and today the marvellously carved staircase is a highlight of the interior. Also worth seeing is the music room, which was reconstructed in 1920 but contains 18th-century panelling from another house. In the 1720s, Dr William Gibbons, chief physician to the then thriving Hampstead spa, lived here.

Burgh House staircase

❸ Fenton House

20 Hampstead Grove NW3. **Map** 1 A4. **Tel** 020 7435 3471. 🚇 Hampstead. **Open** Mar–Oct: 11am–5pm Wed–Sun & public hols. 📷 📱 ground floor only. 📷 🔳 nationaltrust.org.uk/ fentonhouse

Built in 1686, this splendid William and Mary house is the oldest mansion in Hampstead. It contains several specialist exhibitions that are open to the public during the summer: the Benton-Fletcher collection of early keyboard instruments, which includes a harpsichord dating from 1612, said to have been played by Handel; and a fine collection of porcelain. The instruments are kept in full working order and are used for concerts

Fenton House's 17th-century façade

Personal items belonging to the poet John Keats can be seen at his former home

held in the house. The porcelain collection was largely accumulated by Lady Binning who, in 1952, bequeathed the house and its contents to the National Trust.

❹ Church Row

NW3. **Map** 1 A5. ⊖ Hampstead.

Church Row is one of the most complete Georgian streets in London. Much of its original detail has survived, notably the ironwork.

At the west end is St John's, Hampstead's parish church, built in 1745. The iron gates are earlier and come from Canons Park in Edgware. Inside the church is a bust of John Keats. John Constable's grave is in the churchyard, and many Hampstead luminaries are buried in the adjoining cemetery.

❺ Downshire Hill

NW3. **Map** 1 C5. ⊖ Hampstead.

A beautiful street of mainly Regency houses, Downshire Hill lent its name to a group of artists, including Stanley Spencer and Mark Gertler, who would gather at No. 47 between the two World Wars. The same house had been the meeting place of Pre-Raphaelite artists, among them Dante Gabriel Rossetti and Edward Burne-Jones. A more recent resident, at No. 5, was the

late Jim Henson, the creator of *The Muppets*.

The church on the corner (the second Hampstead church to be called St John's) was built in 1823 to serve the Hill's residents. Inside, it still has its original box pews.

❻ Keats House

Keats Grove NW3. **Map** 1 C5. **Tel** 020 7332 3868. ⊖ Hampstead, Belsize Park, Hampstead Heath Overground. **Open** Mar–Oct: 1–5pm Tue–Sun; Nov–Feb: 1–5pm Fri–Sun. **Closed** Good Fri, Christmas week. 🎫 🕐 3pm daily. ♿ ground floor only. 📷 Poetry readings, lectures. 🌐 **cityoflondon.gov.uk /keats**

Originally two semi-detached houses built in 1816, the smaller one became Keats' home in 1818, when a friend persuaded him to move in. Keats spent two productive years here: *Ode to a Nightingale,* perhaps his most celebrated poem, was said to have been written under a plum tree in the garden. The Brawne family moved into the larger house a year later and Keats became engaged to their daughter, Fanny. However, the marriage never took place: Keats died of consumption in Rome before two years had passed. He was only 25 years old.

A copy of one of Keats' love letters to Fanny, the engagement ring he offered her and a lock of her hair are among the mementos that are

exhibited at the house, which was first opened to the public in 1925. Visitors are also able to see facsimiles of some of Keats' manuscripts, part of a collection that serves as an evocative and memorable tribute to his life and work.

❼ Highgate Cemetery

Swain's Lane N6. **Tel** 020 8340 1834. ⊖ Archway. Eastern Cemetery: **Open** 10am–5pm Mon–Fri, 11am–5pm Sat & Sun (closes 4pm daily Nov–Feb). 🎫 check website for times. Western Cemetery: **Open** for tours only: 1:45pm Mon–Fri (advance booking essential), half-hourly 11am–3pm Sat & Sun (no advance booking at weekends; tickets on sale from 11am). No children admitted under 8 years. **Closed** 25 & 26 Dec & during funerals (phone to check). 📷 ♿ Eastern only. 🌐 **highgate-cemetery.org**

This Victorian gem, a Grade I-listed site, is divided into two parts. The western section opened in 1839. For many years it lay neglected, until a voluntary group, the Friends of Highgate Cemetery, prevented further decline. They have restored the Egyptian Avenue, a street of family vaults styled on ancient Egyptian tombs, and the Circle of Lebanon, more vaults in a ring, topped by a cedar tree.

In the eastern section lie Karl Marx, Herbert Spencer and novelist George Eliot (real name, Mary Anne Evans).

Graves at Highgate Cemetery

People relaxing in the open space of Hampstead Heath

❽ Hampstead Heath

NW3. **Map** 1 C2. **Tel** 020 7332 3322.
🚇 Belsize Park, Hampstead.
Open 24 hrs daily. Special walks on
Sundays. ♿ phone for disability
buggies: 020 7485 5757. 🖥 Concerts,
some children's activities in summer.
Sports facilities, bathing ponds. Sports
bookings **Tel** 020 7332 3773.
🌐 **cityoflondon.gov.uk**

Separating the hilltop villages
of Hampstead and Highgate,
the Heath embraces a variety of
landscapes – woods, meadows,
hills, ponds and lakes – which
attract a wealth of wildlife,
including bats and up to 180
species of birds. It covers an

area of 3 sq miles (8 sq km)
and remains uncluttered by the
haphazard buildings and
statues that embellish the
central London parks. Despite
attempts by local landowners to
encroach on the heath in the
19th century, it was protected
as public space in 1871. It is
now owned by the Corporation
of London and its open spaces
have become increasingly
precious to Londoners. There
are ponds for bathing and
fishing and, on three holiday
weekends – Easter, late spring
and late summer – the southern
part of the Heath is taken over
by a funfair (see pp60–63).

❾ Parliament Hill

NW5. **Map** 2 E4. **Tel** 020 7332 3773.
🚇 Belsize Park, Hampstead. ♿
Concerts, children's activities in
summer. Sporting facilities. 🖥

An unlikely but romantic
explanation for the area's name
is that it is where Guy Fawkes'
fellow plotters gathered on
5 November 1605 in the vain
hope of watching the Houses
of Parliament blow up after they
had planted gunpowder there
(see p26). More probably it was
a gun emplacement for the
Parliamentary side during the
Civil War 40 years later. The
gunners would have enjoyed a

❿ Kenwood House

Hampstead Lane NW3. **Map** 1 C1.
Tel 020 8348 1286. 🚇 Golders Green,
Archway, then 210 bus. Estate:
Open 10am–5pm daily. **Closed** 1 Jan,
24–26 & 31 Dec. 📷 selected Fridays.
🅿 ♿ ground floor. 🖥 🏛 Regular
events. 🌐 **english-heritage.org.uk**

This magnificent mansion, filled
with old master paintings, is
situated in landscaped grounds
high on the edge of Hampstead
Heath. There has been a house
here since 1616 – the present
one was remodelled by Robert
Adam in 1764 for the Earl of
Mansfield. Adam refitted
existing rooms and added to
the original building. Most of his

work has survived, the highlight
being the library. A Rembrandt
self-portrait is the star attraction
of the collection, and there are
also works by Vermeer, Turner,
Romney, Van Dyck, Hals and
Reynolds. The 2013 movie Belle
was inspired by Lord Mansfield's
mixed-race niece, Dido Belle,
who also lived here.

The orangery is now
used for occasional
concerts and recitals.

broad view across London; even today, when tall buildings intervene, it provides one of the most spectacular views over the capital. From here the dome of St Paul's is prominent. Parliament Hill is also a popular place for flying kites and sailing model boats on the boating pond.

The historic Spaniards Inn

⓫ Spaniards Inn

Spaniards Rd NW3. **Map** 1 B1.
Tel 020 8731 8406. ⊖ Hampstead,
East Finchley. **Open** noon–11pm Mon
& Tue, noon–midnight Wed–Sat,
noon–10:30pm Sun. &
Ⓦ **thespaniardshampstead.co.uk**

Dick Turpin, the notorious 18th-century highwayman, is said to have frequented this pub. When he wasn't holding up stagecoaches on their way to and from London, he stabled his horse, Black Bess, at the Kenwood stables. The building certainly dates from Turpin's

time and, although the bar downstairs has been altered frequently, the small upstairs Turpin Bar is original. A pair of guns over the bar were reputedly taken from anti-Catholic rioters, who came to Hampstead to burn the Lord Chancellor's house at Kenwood during the Gordon Riots of 1780. The landlord detained them by offering pint after pint of free beer, and when they were drunk, disarmed them.

Among the pub's noted patrons have been the poets Shelley, Keats and Byron, the actor David Garrick and the artist Sir Joshua Reynolds.

The tollhouse has been restored; it juts into the road so that, in the days when tolls were levied, traffic could not race past without paying.

⓬ The Hill Garden

North End Way NW3. **Map** 1 A2.
⊖ Hampstead, Golders Green.
Open dawn to dusk daily.

This charming garden was created by Edwardian soap manufacturer and patron of the arts Lord Leverhulme. It was originally the grounds to his house and is now part of Hampstead Heath. It boasts a raised pergola walkway, best seen in summer when the plants are in flower; the garden also has a beautiful formal pond.

Pergola walk at the Hill Garden

⓭ Vale of Health

NW3. **Map** 1 B3. ⊖ Hampstead.

This area was famous as a distinctly unhealthy swamp before it was drained in 1770; until then it was known as Hatches Bottom. Its newer name may derive from people fleeing here from cholera in London at the end of the 18th century. Alternatively, the name could have been the hype of a property developer when it was first recorded in 1801.

The poet James Henry Leigh Hunt put it on the literary map when he moved here in 1815 and played host to Coleridge, Byron, Shelley and Keats.

D H Lawrence lived here briefly and Stanley Spencer painted in a room above the Vale of Health Hotel, which was demolished in 1964.

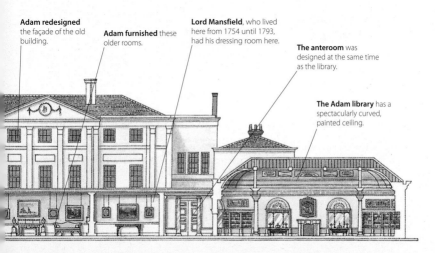

Adam redesigned the façade of the old building.

Adam furnished these older rooms.

Lord Mansfield, who lived here from 1754 until 1793, had his dressing room here.

The anteroom was designed at the same time as the library.

The Adam library has a spectacularly curved, painted ceiling.

GREENWICH AND BLACKHEATH

Best known as the place from which the world's time is measured, Greenwich marks the historic eastern approach to London by land and water. Exploring the Maritime Museum, the Queen's House, Royal Observatory, *Cutty Sark* and Old Royal Naval College can easily occupy a full day. The centre of Greenwich has a village feel, with charming shops and markets to explore.

Sights at a Glance

Historic Streets and Buildings
2 The Queen's House
7 Old Royal Naval College
9 Royal Observatory Greenwich
12 Croom's Hill

Museums
1 National Maritime Museum
4 Ranger's House – The Wernher Collection
5 *Cutty Sark*
13 The Fan Museum

Churches
3 St Alfege Church

Parks and Gardens
10 Greenwich Park
11 Blackheath

Walkway
6 Greenwich Foot Tunnel

Historic Pubs
8 Trafalgar Tavern

Restaurants *see pp305–7*
1 The Greenwich Union

| 0 metres | | 500 |
| 0 yards | | 500 |

Street Finder maps 23, 24

◄ View across to Canary Wharf from Greenwich Park

For keys to symbols *see back flap*

Street-by-Street: Greenwich

This historic town, with illustrious royal and naval connections, is a UNESCO World Heritage Site. In Tudor times it was the site of a palace much enjoyed by Henry VIII, near a fine hunting ground. The old palace is gone, leaving Inigo Jones's exquisite Queen's House, built for James I's wife. Museums, shops, cafés and markets, Wren's architecture and the magnificent Royal Park all make Greenwich an enjoyable day's excursion and it is best visited by river *(see pp64–5)*.

❻ Greenwich Foot Tunnel, leading to the Isle of Dogs, is one of two tunnels built solely for pedestrians.

Greenwich Pier is a boarding point for boats to Westminster, the O2 and the Thames Barrier.

❺ Cutty Sark
Clipper ships such as this once traded across the oceans. The impressively restored *Cutty Sark* has been raised to allow visitors to explore above and below decks.

Greenwich Market
This market, in the heart of Greenwich, sells crafts, antiques and books.

To Cutty Sark DLR

❸ St Alfege Church
There has been a church here since 1012.

Locator Map
See Greater London Map pp14–15

❼ ★ **Old Royal Naval College**
Wren's stately structure was built in two halves so that the Queen's House would keep its river view.

George II Statue
Sculpted by John Rysbrack in 1735, this statue depicts the king as a Roman emperor.

The Painted Hall
contains 18th-century murals by Sir James Thornhill, who painted the interior of the dome of St Paul's Cathedral.

R O A D

❷ ★ **The Queen's House**
On his return from Italy, this was the first building Inigo Jones designed in the Palladian style.

Key

— Suggested route

❶ **National Maritime Museum**
Real and model boats, paintings and instruments such as this 18th-century compass illustrate naval history.

0 metres	100
0 yards	100

❶ National Maritime Museum

Romney Rd SE10. **Map** 23 C2. **Tel** 020 8858 4422. 🚇 Cutty Sark DLR. 🚆 Greenwich. **Open** 10am–5pm daily. **Closed** 24–26 Dec. 🏛 special exhibitions. 🖼 ♿ 💻 📷 Lectures. 🌐 **rmg.co.uk**

The sea has always played an important role in British history, and this museum – built in the 19th century as a school for sailors' children – celebrates this seafaring heritage, from early British trade and empire to the exploratory expeditions of Captain Cook, and from the Napoleonic Wars through to the modern day.

The Sammy Ofer wing, the biggest development in the museum's history, boasts "the Wave", a 20-m (65-ft) audiovisual installation in which images and films from the museum's vast archives unfurl in dramatic, thematic journeys.

The Nelson gallery looks at the course of British maritime history over the tumultuous 18th century, a period when seafaring heroes were national celebrities. A star exhibit is the uniform that Lord Horatio Nelson was wearing when he was shot at the Battle of Trafalgar in October 1805.

Rather more spectacular is the royal barge built for Prince Frederick in 1732, decorated with gilded mermaids and his Prince of Wales's feathers on the stern. Throughout the museum there are numerous activities for children, such as navigating a ship around the world on the Great Map.

Prince Frederick's barge at the National Maritime Musueum

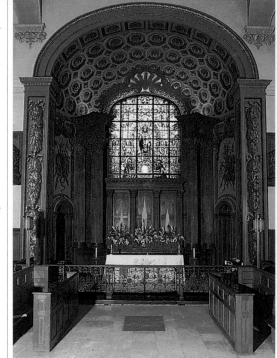

St Alfege's altar, with rails attributed to Jean Tijou

❷ The Queen's House

Romney Rd SE10. **Map** 23 C2. **Tel** 020 8858 4422. 🚇 Cutty Sark DLR. 🚆 Greenwich. **Open** 10am–5pm daily. **Closed** 24–26 Dec. 🖼 ♿ 💻 📷 🌐 **rmg.co.uk**

The Queen's House was designed by Inigo Jones and completed in 1637. It was originally intended to be the home of Anne of Denmark, wife of James I, but she died while it was still being built and it was finished for Charles I's queen consort, Henrietta Maria. She fell in love with it and called it her house of delights. After the Civil War it was briefly occupied by Henrietta as dowager queen, but was not much used by the royal family after that.

From 1821 to 1933 the Royal Hospital School was housed here, and in the late 20th century the building was refurbished. Period highlights include the square Great Hall, the King's and Queen's Presence Chambers and the spiral cantilevered "tulip staircase", which curves sinuously upwards without a central support. The staircase is reputed to be haunted. The house also displays the art collection of the National Maritime Museum.

❸ St Alfege Church

Greenwich Church St SE10. **Map** 23 B2. **Tel** 020 8853 0687. 🚇 Cutty Sark DLR. **Open** 11am–4pm Mon–Fri, 10am–4pm Sat, noon–4pm Sun. ✝ 8am, 10am Sun. ♿ if accompanied. Concerts. 🌐 **st-alfege.org**

This is one of Nicholas Hawksmoor's most distinctive and powerful designs, with its gigantic columns and pediments topped by urns. It was completed in 1714 on the site of an older church, which marked the martyrdom of St Alfege, the then Archbishop of Canterbury, killed on this spot by Danish invaders in 1012. A second church here was the site of Henry VIII's baptism in 1491 and of 16th-century composer and organist Thomas Tallis's burial in 1585. Today a stained-glass window commemorates Tallis.

Some of the carved wood inside is by Grinling Gibbons, but much of it was badly damaged by a World War II bomb and has been restored. The wrought iron of the altar and gallery rails is original, attributed to Jean Tijou.

❹ Ranger's House – the Wernher Collection

Chesterfield Walk, Greenwich Park SE10. **Map** 23 C4. **Tel** 020 8294 2548. ⊖ Cutty Sark DLR. ⇌ Blackheath. **Open** by guided tour only. 🎧 📷 Apr–Sep, several weekly. ♿ 📷 🌐 **english-heritage.org.uk**

The Wernher Collection is located in Ranger's House (1688), an elegant building southeast of Greenwich Park *(see p247)*. It is an enchanting array of over 650 pieces accumulated by South African mine owner Sir Julius Wernher in the late 19th century. The collection is displayed in 12 rooms and includes paintings, jewellery, furniture and porcelain. Highlights include Renaissance masterworks by Hans Memling and Filippo Lippi, over 100 Renaissance jewels, and an opal-set lizard pendant jewel. The tour ends with the magnificent sculpture of a woman and angel by Bergonzoli.

Opal-set lizard pendant at the Wernher Collection

The Greenwich Foot Tunnel is lined with 200,000 ceramic tiles

❺ Cutty Sark

King William Walk SE10. **Map** 23 B2. **Tel** 020 8858 4422. ⊖ Cutty Sark DLR. ⇌ Greenwich Pier. **Open** 10am–5pm daily (last adm 4:30pm). **Closed** 25 & 26 Dec. 🎧 **Tel** 020 8312 6608. 💻 📷 ♿ book ahead. 🌐 **rmg.co.uk**

This majestic vessel is a survivor of the clippers that crossed the Atlantic and Pacific oceans in the 19th century. Launched in 1869 as a tea carrier, it was something of a speed machine in its day, winning the annual clippers' race from China to London in 1871 in just 107 days. It made its final voyage in 1938 and was put on display here in 1957. In 2006 the *Cutty Sark* was closed to visitors for renovation work, which suffered a major setback in May 2007 when the ship was severely damaged by fire. It was reopened by the Queen in spring 2012, fully restored and slightly raised in a glass enclosure. You can explore the cargo decks and sleeping quarters below deck. There are interactive displays on navigation and life on board.

❻ Greenwich Foot Tunnel

Between Greenwich Pier SE10 and Isle of Dogs E14. **Map** 23 B1. ⊖ Island Gardens, Cutty Sark DLR. ⇌ Greenwich Pier. **Open** 24hrs daily. ♿ when lifts operating.

This 370-m (1,200-ft) long tunnel was opened in 1902 to allow south London

labourers to walk to work in Millwall Docks. Today it is worth crossing for the wonderful views, back across the river, of Christopher Wren's Royal Naval College and of Inigo Jones's Queen's House.

Matching round red-brick terminals, with glass domes, mark the top of the lift shafts on either side of the river. Both ends of the tunnel are close to stations on the Docklands Light Railway (DLR), with trains to Canary Wharf *(see p253)*, Limehouse, East London, Tower Hill and Lewisham. Although there are security cameras, the tunnel can be eerie at night.

A late 19th-century figurehead in the *Cutty Sark*

❼ Old Royal Naval College

King William Walk SE10. **Map** 23 C2. **Tel** 020 8269 4799. 🚇 Cutty Sark DLR, Greenwich DLR. 🚉 Greenwich, Maze Hill. Chapel, Hall and Discover Greenwich visitor centre: **Open** 10am–5pm daily. **Closed** 24–26 Dec & some Sat. Grounds: **Open** 8am–11pm daily. Chapel: 🕂 6:30pm Mon, 1.05pm Wed, 11am Sun. 🖥 talks in Painted Hall 11:45am, 12:45pm, 2:45pm & 3:45pm daily, guided walks daily from visitor centre. ♿ ⬚ 🖥 📷 🆆 **ornc.org**

These ambitious buildings by Christopher Wren were built on the site of the old 15th-century royal palace, where Henry VIII, Mary I and Elizabeth I were born. The west front was completed by Vanbrugh. The Painted Hall, Chapel, Discover Greenwich Visitor Centre – with displays on the history of the area and its buildings – and grounds are open to the public.

Wren's Chapel was destroyed by fire in 1779. The present Greek Revival interior, by James Stuart, is light and airy. The Painted Hall was opulently decorated by Sir James Thornhill in the early 18th century. The huge ceiling painting is the largest figurative painting in the country.

❽ Trafalgar Tavern

Park Row SE10. **Map** 23 C1. **Tel** 020 8858 2909. 🚇 Cutty Sark DLR, Greenwich DLR. **Open** noon–11pm Mon–Thu, noon–midnight Fri & Sat, noon–10pm Sun. ♿ *See Pubs and Bars pp312–15.* 🆆 **trafalgartavern.co.uk**

This charming panelled pub was built in 1837 and quickly became

Thornhill's painting of King William III in the Painted Hall of the Old Royal Naval College

established, along with other waterside inns in Greenwich, as a venue for "whitebait dinners". Government ministers, legal luminaries and the like would arrive from Westminster and Charing Cross by water on celebratory occasions and feast on the tiny fish. The last such meeting was held here in 1885. Whitebait still features on the pub restaurant's menu, when in season, although they are no longer fished from the Thames.

This was another of Charles Dickens's haunts. He drank here with one of the best-known illustrators of his works, George Cruickshank.

In 1915, the pub became an institution for old merchant seamen. It was restored in 1965 after a spell of being used as a social club for working men.

❾ Royal Observatory Greenwich

Greenwich Park SE10. **Map** 23 C3. **Tel** 020 8858 4422. 🚇 Cutty Sark DLR. 🚉 Greenwich. **Open** 10am–5pm daily (last adm: 4:30pm). **Closed** 24–26 Dec. 🎟 for Flamsteed House and Planetarium shows (last show 4pm). 🔊 ✉ ♿ 📷 🆆 **rmg.co.uk**

The meridian (0° longitude) that divides the Earth's eastern and western hemispheres passes through here, and millions of visitors have taken the opportunity to be photographed standing with a foot on either side of it. In 1884, Greenwich Mean Time became the basis of time measurement for most of the world.

The original building, Flamsteed House, was designed by Christopher Wren. Above one of the building's two turrets is a ball on a rod, which has dropped at 1pm every day since 1833 so that sailors on the Thames could set their clocks by it. The house now contains a display of John Harrison's marine timekeepers and the original instruments of several Astronomers Royal, such as Edmond Halley. John Flamsteed was the first Astronomer Royal, appointed by Charles II, and this was the official government observatory from 1675 until 1948, when the lights of London

Trafalgar Tavern viewed from the Thames

became too bright and the astronomers moved to darker Sussex. There is also a state-of-the-art planetarium here, the only one in London, and free exhibits on space exploration and the Big Bang in the Astronomy Centre in the south building.

A rare 24-hour clock at the Royal Observatory Greenwich

❿ Greenwich Park

SE10. **Map** 23 C3. **Tel** 0300 061 2380. 🚇 Cutty Sark DLR, Greenwich DLR. 🚃 Greenwich, Maze Hill, Blackheath. **Open** from 6am until 6pm–9:30pm depending on season. 🅿 ♿ Children's shows, playground, boating lake and sports facilities. 🆆 royalparks.org.uk

Originally the grounds of a royal palace and still a Royal Park, Greenwich Park was enclosed in 1433 and its brick wall built in the reign of James I. Later, in the 17th century, the French royal landscape gardener André Le Nôtre, of Versailles and Fontainebleau fame, was invited to redesign the park. The broad avenue, rising south up the hill, was part of his plan.

There are great river views from the hilltop and on a fine day, most of London can be seen. In 2012, the park hosted the London Olympic equestrian events.

To the south of the park, on the edge of the park's rose garden, is the Ranger's House (1688), which now houses the art collection of Julius Wernher *(see p245)*. From here the walk to the charming village of Blackheath is flat, compared with the steep walk down the hill to Greenwich town.

Ranger's House in Greenwich Park

⓫ Blackheath

SE3. **Map** 24 D5. 🚃 Blackheath.

This open heath used to be a rallying point for large groups who were entering London from the east, including Wat Tyler's band of rebels at the time of the Peasants' Revolt in 1381.

Blackheath is also the place where King James I of England (James VI of Scotland) introduced the game of golf from his native Scotland to the then largely sceptical English.

Today the heath is well worth exploring for the stately Georgian houses and terraces that surround it. The prettily named Tranquil Vale to the south of the heath is Blackheath village's main shopping strip.

⓬ Croom's Hill

SE10. **Map** 23 C3. 🚇 Cutty Sark DLR, Greenwich DLR. 🚃 Greenwich.

Croom's Hill is one of the best kept 17th- to early 19th-century streets in London. The oldest buildings are at the Blackheath end: the original Manor House of 1695; No. 68, from about the same date; and No. 66, the oldest of all (c. 1630). The actor Daniel Day Lewis grew up in No. 6.

⓭ The Fan Museum

12 Croom's Hill SE10. **Map** 23 B3. **Tel** 020 8305 1441. 🚃 Greenwich. **Open** 11am–5pm Tue–Sat, noon–5pm Sun. **Closed** 1 Jan, 24–26 Dec. 📷 no flash. 📷 by appt. ☕ Afternoon tea Tue, Fri, Sat & Sun (booking advised Tue & Sun) ♿ Lectures, fan-making workshops first Sat of the month. 🆆 thefanmuseum.org.uk

One of London's most unusual museums – the only one of its kind in the UK – this opened in 1991. It owes its existence and appeal to the enthusiasm of Helene Alexander, whose personal collection of about 4,000 fans from the 17th century onwards has been augmented by donations. A small permanent exhibition looks at types of fans and fan-making, while the large collection is rotated in temporary displays. On some days, afternoon tea is served in the pretty orangery at the back.

Stage fan used in a D'Oyly Carte operetta

FURTHER AFIELD

Many of the great houses originally built as country retreats for London's high and mighty were overrun by sprawling suburbs in the Victorian era. Grandest of the survivors is Hampton Court, a royal palace since Henry VIII's time, but there are others that have become interesting, often eclectic museums and galleries. For a green escape from the city, try Richmond Park, or Kew Gardens, with its unrivalled international collection of plants.

Sights at a Glance

Historic Streets and Buildings
5 Alexandra Palace
9 Sutton House
20 Charlton House
21 Eltham Palace
29 Hampton Court pp260–63
30 Ham House
31 Orleans House Gallery
32 Marble Hill House
34 Syon House
36 Osterley Park House
37 Pitzhanger Manor House and Gallery
40 Strand on the Green
41 Chiswick House
43 Fulham Palace

Modern Architecture
15 Canary Wharf
19 The O2 Arena
44 Chelsea Harbour

0 kilometres   5

0 miles   3

Markets
2 Camden Market

Museums and Galleries
3 Freud Museum
6 The Jewish Museum
8 Geffrye Museum
10 V&A Museum of Childhood
14 Museum of London Docklands
16 William Morris Gallery
22 Horniman Museum
23 Dulwich Picture Gallery
26 Wimbledon Lawn Tennis Museum
27 Wimbledon Windmill Museum
35 Musical Museum
38 London Museum of Water & Steam
42 Hogarth's House

Parks and Gardens
24 Battersea Park
28 Richmond Park
39 Kew Gardens pp266–7

Churches and Temples
4 BAPS Shri Swaminarayan Mandir
11 St Mary, Rotherhithe
12 St Anne's, Limehouse
25 St Mary's, Battersea

Historic Districts
7 Islington
33 Richmond

Modern Technology
17 Emirates Air Line Cable Car
18 Thames Barrier

Sports Grounds
1 Lord's Cricket Ground
13 Queen Elizabeth Olympic Park pp254–5

Key
▪ Main sightseeing areas
▬ Motorway
▬ Main road
▭ Minor road

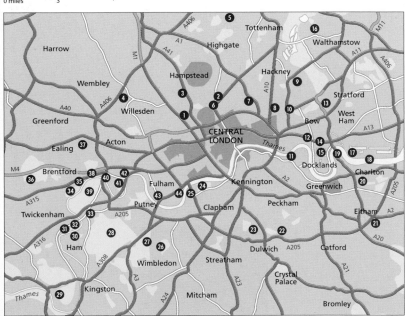

All the sights in this section lie inside the M25 motorway (see pp14–15).

◀ Red deer, frequently spotted in Richmond Park

For keys to symbols see back flap

North of the Centre

❶ Lord's Cricket Ground

NW8. **Map** 3 A3. **Tel** 020 7616 8595. MCC Museum: 020 7616 8658. 🚇 St John's Wood. **Open** Tours daily every hour: Jan–Mar 11am–2pm; Apr–Oct 10am–3pm; Nov & Dec 10am–2pm. Pre-booking recommended. No tours on major match days. **Closed** 25 & 26 Dec (and occasional other days). 🚫 museum free for match ticket holders. ♿ 📷 *See Entertainment pp350–51.* 🌐 lords.org

You can visit the headquarters of Britain's chief summer sport on regular guided tours that take in the honour boards, dressing rooms and the MCC Museum, which is full of memorabilia from cricketing history, including a stuffed sparrow killed by a cricket ball, as well as the Ashes. This tiny urn contains, supposedly, the burned remains of a cricket bail signifying "the death of English cricket" after a notable defeat by Australia. It is still the object of ferocious competition between the two national teams. The museum explains the history of the game, and mementos of notable cricketers make it a place of pilgrimage for devotees of the sport.

Professional cricketer Thomas Lord moved his ground here in 1814. The Pavilion (1890), from which women were excluded until 1999, is late Victorian.

❷ Camden Market

NW1. 🚇 Camden Town, Chalk Farm. **Open** 10am–6pm daily.

Camden Market is really a series of interconnected markets stretching along Chalk Farm Road and Camden High Street. Packed with shoppers at the weekends, most of the shops and some of the stalls are also open on weekdays. Many units are housed in restored Victorian buildings alongside Camden Lock and the canal. Some of the more interesting stalls are in the Stables Market towards the Chalk Farm end. The first market

here was a crafts market at Camden Lock in 1975. Today, all the markets sell a wide range of goods, from crafts and street fashion to new-age remedies, and there are plenty of food stalls, particularly near the lock and in the Stables Market.

❸ Freud Museum

20 Maresfield Gdns NW3. **Tel** 020 7435 2002. 🚇 Finchley Rd. **Open** noon–5pm Wed–Sun. **Closed** 1 Jan, 24–26 Dec. 🚫 no flash. ♿ limited. 📷 Events. 🌐 freud.org.uk

In 1938 Sigmund Freud, the founder of psychoanalysis, fled from Nazi persecution in Vienna to this Hampstead house. Making use of the possessions he brought with him, his family recreated the atmosphere of his Vienna consulting rooms. After Freud died in 1939 his daughter Anna (who was a pioneer of child psychoanalysis) kept the house as it was and in 1986 it was opened as a museum dedicated to Freud. The most famous item is the couch on which patients lay for analysis. A series of 1930s home movies shows cheerful moments with his dog as well as

The meticulously preserved consulting rooms in the Freud Museum

The lavish exterior of the BAPS Shri Swaminarayan Mandir

footage of Nazi attacks on his apartment. The bookshop has a large collection of his works.

❹ BAPS Shri Swaminarayan Mandir

105–119 Brentfield Rd, Neasden NW10. 🚇 Harlesden Station, then bus 224 (or Stonebridge Park and bus 112) **Tel** 020 8965 2651. **Open** Mandir and Haveli: 9am–11am, 11:45am–12:15pm, 4pm-6pm (to 5pm Sat) daily 📷 arrange in advance. 🚫 for museum. ✉ ♿ 📷 🌐 londonmandir.baps.org

Right out in northwest London, not far from Wembley Stadium, stands one of the most incongruous – and beautiful – religious buildings in the city, often known simply as the Neasden Temple. The intricately carved Hindu temple was completed in 1995, after a small army of volunteers from the local community banded together to raise funds and build it. Thousands of tonnes of Bulgarian limestone and Italian Carrara marble were shipped to India to be carved, then assembled on site like a giant jigsaw, largely by volunteers. The result is a staggeringly detailed, intricately carved temple. Make sure you visit when the inner hall is open (it closes for prayers several times a day; check website) when you can inspect some of the carving close-up. The complex also includes a Haveli, the cultural education centre, the interior of which features yet more beautiful carving, this time from Burmese teak and English oak. Leave any large bags at the security desk across the road, dress modestly (with your shoulders, upper arms and knees covered) and remove your shoes when you enter the main building (cloakrooms are provided).

There's a small museum on Hinduism, with a video about the temple's construction.

❺ Alexandra Palace

Alexandra Palace Way N22.
🚉 Alexandra Palace. 🚇 Wood Green, then bus W3. **Tel** 020 8365 2121. ♿
🏢 ⛸ Ice rink **Open** 11am–1:30pm & 2–5:30pm Mon–Fri, 10:30am–12:30pm & 2–4:30pm Sat & Sun, plus weekend evening sessions and special events.
🚣 Boat hire: Apr–Oct 11am–6pm.
🌐 **alexandrapalace.com**

Built as the People's Palace in 1873, Alexandra Palace has a slightly chequered history – it has burned down twice, once just 16 days after it opened, again in 1980. From 1936 until 1956 the BBC's television studios were housed at Alexandra Palace, and in 1936 the first television transmission took place from here (there are plans afoot to re-create the BBC studios in the eastern end of the palace). Affectionately known as Ally Pally, the large, ornate Victorian halls now host a wide variety of events, from trade and antiques fairs to large-scale concerts. Set in 80 hectares (196 acres) of parkland, the building sits majestically exposed on a hill, so the views are spectacular, and it's a good spot for fireworks and funfairs. There's a permanent ice rink and the grounds have a ten-hole pitch-and-putt golf course, boating lake and playgrounds. Check the website for details of events.

❻ The Jewish Museum

129–31 Albert St NW1. **Map** 4 E1. **Tel** 020 7284 7384. 🚇 Camden Town.
Open 10am–5pm Sat–Thu, 10am–2pm Fri. **Closed** Jewish hols, 25 & 26 Dec. 🏢 ♿ 🖥 (not Sat). 📷
🌐 **jewishmuseum.org.uk**

London's Jewish Museum was founded in 1932 in Bloomsbury, and over its history has occupied several locations – at one point it was split between two sites, in Finchley and Camden. In 2007 the museum celebrated its 75th anniversary with the commencement of works to bring the two collections together in a single building. Opened in 2010, the museum has large galleries, education facilities and hands-on displays for children.

Celebrating Jewish life in Britain from the Middle Ages onwards, the museum is packed with memorabilia. It also has important collections

Jewish Bakers' Union banner, c.1926, in the Jewish Museum, Camden

of Jewish ceremonial objects and some illuminated marriage contracts. The highlight is a 17th- or 18th-century Venetian synagogue ark. There is also an exhibition on the Holocaust.

❼ Islington

N1. **Map** 6 E1. 🚇 Angel, Highbury & Islington.

Islington was once a highly fashionable spa, but the rich began to move out in the late 18th century, and the area deteriorated rapidly. During the 20th century, writers such as Evelyn Waugh, George Orwell and Joe Orton lived here. Now Islington has again returned to fashion as one of London's first areas to become gentrified, with many young professionals buying and refurbishing old houses.

An older relic is Canonbury Tower, the remains of a medieval manor house converted into apartments in the 18th century. Writers such as Washington Irving and Oliver Goldsmith lived here and today it houses the Tower Theatre.

On Islington Green, there is a statue of Sir Hugh Myddleton, who built a canal through Islington in 1613 to bring water to London from Hertfordshire; today a landscaped walk along its banks runs between Essex Road and Canonbury stations. Chapel Market takes place close to Angel Tube (*see p336*), and there are antique shops at Camden Passage. The N1 Centre is a shopping and cinema complex.

Alexander Palace, a landmark in television broadcasting history

East of the Centre

❽ Geffrye Museum

136 Kingsland Rd E2. **Tel** 020 7739
9893. ⊖ Hoxton. **Open** 10am–5pm
Tue–Sun & public hols. **Closed** 1 Jan,
Good Fri, 24–26 Dec. Garden **Open**
Apr–Oct. 🎟 tours of restored
almshouse on selected days; check
website. 🔲 🚻 🔲 ▨ 📷
Exhibitions & events.
🌐 **geffrye-museum.org.uk**

This delightful museum is housed
in a set of 18th-century almshouses, one of which has been
restored to its original appearance.
The almshouses were built in
1715 on land bequeathed by Sir
Robert Geffrye, a 17th-century
Lord Mayor of London. Inside,
you take a trip through a series of
11 rooms decorated in different
period styles, each providing an
insight into the domestic interiors
of the urban middle classes. The
historic room settings begin with
Elizabethan (which contains
magnificent panelling) and run
chronologically through various
major styles, including High
Victorian, while an attractive
extension houses more modern
settings, such as an example of

1990s "loft living". Each room
contains superb examples of
British furniture of the period.
Outside, a series of garden
"rooms" show the designs and
planting schemes popular in
urban gardens between the
16th and 20th centuries.

❾ Sutton House

2–4 Homerton High St E9. **Tel** 020 8986
2264. ⊖ Bethnal Green then bus 253.
Open noon–5pm Wed–Sun. **Closed**
Christmas, Jan. ▨ 🚻 limited. 📷 at
weekends, phone first. 🔲 📷 Regular
events. 🌐 **nationaltrust.org.uk**

One of the few London Tudor
merchants' houses to survive
in something like its original
form, Sutton House was built in
1535 for Ralph Sadleir, a courtier
to Henry VIII. It was owned by
several wealthy families before
becoming a girls' school in the
17th century. In the 18th
century, the front was altered,
but the Tudor fabric remains
surprisingly intact, including
original brickwork, fireplaces
and panelling.

❿ V&A Museum of Childhood

Cambridge Heath Rd E2. **Tel** 020
8983 5200. ⊖ Bethnal Green.
Open 10am–5:45pm daily (to 9pm
first Thu of month). **Closed** 1 Jan,
24–26 Dec. 🚻 🔲 📷 Workshop,
children's activities.
🌐 **vam.ac.uk/moc**

After the success of the Victoria
and Albert Museum in South
Kensington *(see pp214–17)*,
an idea was mooted to open
similar museums in other
parts of the city. Only one
was opened: the Bethnal
Green Museum, in 1872.
    Over time the museum
gradually evolved into today's
Museum of Childhood, officially
re-opening as such in 1974.
With an array of toys, games,
lavish dolls' houses, model
trains and costumes, dating
from the 16th century to the
present day, the museum
has the largest collection of
childhood-related objects
in the UK.
    There are plenty of activities
to keep children amused,
including story-telling, arts and
crafts, and fun trails.

⓫ St Mary, Rotherhithe

St Marychurch St SE16. **Tel** 020
7394 3394. ⊖ Rotherhithe.
Open 9am–6pm daily.
🕍 10am & 6pm Sun. 🚻
🌐 **stmaryrotherhithe.org**

St Mary was built in 1715 on
the site of a medieval church.
It has nautical connotations,
most notably a memorial
to Christopher Jones, captain
of the *Mayflower*, on which
the Pilgrim Fathers sailed
from the westcountry port of
Plymouth to North America. The
communion table is made from
the timbers of the *Temeraire*, a
warship whose final journey to
the breaker's yard at Rotherhithe
was evocatively recorded in
Turner's painting at the National
Gallery *(see pp108–11)*.
    The church also contains a
fine example of 18th-century
organ building by John Byfield.

A typical Victorian-era room at the Geffrye Museum

⓬ St Anne's, Limehouse

3 Colt St E14. **Tel** 020 7987 1502.
🚇 Westferry DLR. 🕐 10:30am & 6pm
Sun. 🎵 Concerts, lectures;
see website for details.
🅦 stanneslimehouse.org

Designed by Nicholas Hawksmoor,
St Anne's was built between
1714 and 1727. Its 40-m (130-ft)
tower was a land-mark for ships
using the East End docks and
still has the highest church
clock in London. The interior,
damaged by fire in 1850, was
subsequently Victorianized.

⓭ Queen Elizabeth Olympic Park

See pp254–5.

⓮ Museum of London Docklands

No. 1 Warehouse, West India Quay E14.
Tel 020 7001 9844. 🚇 Barbican,
St Paul's. **Open** 10am–6pm daily.
Closed 24–26 Dec. ♿ 🚫 🖥 📷
🅦 museumoflondon.org.uk/
docklands

Occupying a late Georgian
warehouse, this museum tells
the story of London's docks and
their links from Roman times to
the present. A highlight is the
recreation of the dark and
dangerous "Sailortown" of
Wapping in the 1850s.

⓯ Canary Wharf

E14. 🚇 Canary Wharf or West India
Quay DLR. ♿ 🚫 🖥 📷

London's most ambitious
commercial development
opened in 1991, when the
first tenants moved into the
50-storey Canada Tower. At
250 m (800 ft), it dominates the
city's eastern skyline. The tower
stands on what was the West
India Dock, closed, like all the
London docks, between the
1960s and the 1980s, when
trade moved down-river to
Tilbury. Today, Canary Wharf is
thriving, with a major shopping
complex and restaurants.

⓰ William Morris Gallery

Lloyd Park, Forest Rd E17. **Tel** 020 8496
4390. 🚇 Walthamstow Central.
Open 10am–5pm Wed–Sun. **Closed**
25 & 26 Dec, 1 Jan. ♿ 🖥
📷 Lectures. 🅦 wmgallery.org.uk

The most influential designer
of the Victorian era, born in
1834, lived in this 18th-century
house as a young man in
1848–56. It is now a beguiling
and well-presented museum
giving a full account of William
Morris the artist, designer, writer,
craftsman and socialist.

It has examples of his work
and that of other members of
the Arts and Crafts movement –
tiles by William de Morgan, and
paintings by members of the
Pre-Raphaelite Brotherhood.

Interactive exhibits introduce
visitors to techniques such as
hand-printing and dyeing.

⓱ Emirates Air Line Cable Car

Western Gateway E16/Edmund Halley
Way SE10. 🚇 Royal Victoria DLR,
North Greenwich. **Open** 7am–9pm
Mon–Fri, 8am–9pm Sat, 9am–9pm
Sun (to 8pm winter). 🚫
🅦 emiratesairline.co.uk

Connecting the Royal Victoria
Dock and The O2, this cable car
provides spectacular views over
the river during the 5-minute trip.

Intricate detail visible on a William Morris
tapestry (1885)

⓲ Thames Barrier

Unity Way SE18. **Tel** 020 8305 4188.
🚆 Charlton, Woolwich Arsenal (south
side); Silvertown (north side). Visitor
centre **Open** 10:30am–5pm Thu–Sun
(last adm 4:30pm). **Closed** 25 Dec–
1 Jan. 🚫 ♿ 🖥 📷 exhibition.

In 1236, the Thames rose so high
that people rowed across Westminster Hall; London flooded
again in 1663, 1928 and in 1953.
Something had to be done, and
in 1965 the Greater London
Council invited proposals.
The Thames Barrier was opened
in 1984. It is 520 m (1,700 ft)
across. Its 10 gates swing up to
1.6 m (6 ft) above the level
reached by the tide in 1953, and
have been used over 100 times.
Some boat tours *(see p379)* go as
far as the barrier. There's a small
visitor centre on the south side.

Unique structure of the O2 Arena

⓳ The O2 Arena

North Greenwich SE10. **Tel** 020 8463
2000 or 0844 856 0202 (to book
tickets). 🚇 North Greenwich.
Open 9am–late. Up at the O2
(climbing) **Tel** 020 8463 2680.
🅦 theo2.co.uk

The former Millennium Dome
was the focal point of Britain's
celebration of the year 2000.
Controversial from its earliest
days, it is nonetheless a
spectacular feat of engineering.
Its canopy is made from 100,000
sq m (109,000 sq yards) of
Teflon-coated spun glass-fibre,
and is supported by over 70 km
(43 miles) of steel cable rigged
to twelve 100-m (328-ft) masts.

Now one of London's largest
concert venues, the O2 also
has bars, restaurants, a cinema
and IndigO2, a smaller venue.
You can also don climbing
gear and ascend the outside
along a long, bouncy walkway
to the very top.

⓭ Queen Elizabeth Olympic Park

As the only city to have hosted the Olympic Games three times – in 1908, 1948 and 2012 – London is justifiably proud of its place in Olympic history. The main site for the 2012 Olympics and Paralympics was a 225-hectare (560-acre) area of land stretching along the River Lea in east London, which was previously a fairly bleak former industrial area. The main attractions today are immediately familiar to anyone who watched the events: a series of large, functional but striking venues dotted amid meandering waterways and surrounded by quintessentially English wildflower gardens. Renamed the Queen Elizabeth Olympic Park to commemorate the Queen's Diamond Jubilee in 2012, the site has been transformed into a permanent leisure attraction. Renovation continues around the periphery, but there is plenty to see and do, particularly if you catch one of the numerous events hosted here, including big sporting events and live music, or go equipped to try out some sports.

KEY

① **Lee Valley Hockey and Tennis Centre**

② **Mountain bike trails**

③ **Olympic Rings**

④ **Wetlands Walk**

⑤ **Underpass** to Stratford International station

Waterways and Wetlands
There are 6.5 km (4 miles) of waterways, including stretches of the River Lea and its tributaries and sections of canal. In the north of the park a wetland area known as the Waterglades has been created, complete with wetland plants to attract wildlife.

← Hackney Wick station

Copper Box Arena
An indoor arena that hosted the handball and modern pentathlon fencing during the Games now hosts numerous indoor sporting events.

Olympic Stadium
Substantially redesigned since the Games, the stadium now hosts sporting and music events. It is the home of West Ham United FC and also the National Competition Centre for athletics in the UK.

Lee Valley VeloPark
The Velodrome is now the hub of a large cycling activity centre, which also has BMX and road tracks and mountain-bike trails. Visitors can book taster sessions.

VISITORS' CHECKLIST

Practical Information
E20. **Tel** 0800 0722 110.
Park: **Open** 24 hrs daily; information point 10am–3pm daily. 🖥️ ♿ 🆆 queen elizabeth-olympicpark.co.uk
🚤 boat tours Apr–Sep: daily, Mar: Sat & Sun, Oct–Feb: select days. **Tel** 0845 116 2012. ♿ 🆆 leeandstortboats.co.uk

ArcelorMittal Orbit: **Open** Apr–Sep: 10am–6pm daily; Oct–Mar: 10am–4pm daily. ♿ 🆆 arcelormittalorbit.com

Aquatics Centre: **Tel** 020 8536 3150. **Open** 6am–10:30pm daily; check online for timings of swimming sessions and events. ♿ 🆆 londonaquaticscentre.org

Lee Valley VeloPark: **Tel** 03000 030 613. **Open** 9am–10pm Mon–Fri, 8am–10pm Sat, 8am–8pm Sun. Book taster sessions online in advance. ♿ 🆆 visitleevalley.org.uk

Transport
🚆 Stratford. 🚆 Pudding Lane. Ⓔ Hackney Wick. 🚌 308, 339 388, D8.

Tumbling Bay Playground
The best of several playgrounds in the park has sandpits and water features, a treehouse and wobbly bridges. The neighbouring Timber Lodge Café has outdoor seating, and is a good spot for families.

London Aquatics Centre
Architect Zaha Hadid was inspired by the movement and flow of water for her sweeping, curved design for the Aquatics Centre. Everyone can swim in the pools here: a 50-m competition pool, plus training and diving pools.

ArcelorMittal Orbit
Designed by artist Anish Kapoor, this is one of the most recognizable landmarks in the park. The twisting steel tower is part sculpture, part viewing platform and part fairground attraction for adults and kids: a hair-raising 178-m (580-ft) slide will be added in 2016.

South of the Centre

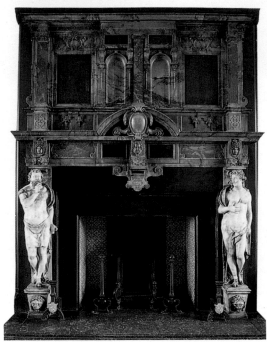

A Jacobean fireplace at Charlton House

⑳ Charlton House

Charlton Rd SE7. **Tel** 020 8856 3951.
🚈 Charlton. **Open** for prebooked
tours, exhibitions and special events
only, call to check. Peace Garden:
Open 10am–5pm daily (until dusk
in winter). **Closed** public hols. 🗂
group tours available, book ahead.
♿ limited. 🖥 9am–4pm Mon–Fri.
W **charlton-house.org**

Completed in 1612 for Adam
Newton, tutor to Prince Henry,
Charlton House has good river
views and is the best-preserved
Jacobean mansion in London –
well worth the tricky journey for
enthusiasts of that period. It is
now used as a community centre
and library, but many of the
original ceilings and fireplaces
survive, as does the carved main
staircase. Parts of the wood
panelling, too, are original, and
the ceilings have been restored
using the original moulds. The
grounds contain a summer
house reputedly designed by
Inigo Jones, and a mulberry tree
said to have been planted by

James I in 1608. Visitors can walk
around the gardens, including
the Peace Garden.

㉑ Eltham Palace

Court Yard SE9. **Tel** 020 8294 2548.
🚈 Eltham then a 15-minute walk.
Open Apr–Sep: 10am–6pm Sun–Thu;
Oct: 10am–5pm Sun–Thu; Nov–Mar:
10am–4pm Sun (plus extra days
during school holidays). **Closed** 1 Jan,
25, 26 & 31 Dec. 🦌 🍴 ♿ 🛍 ⊘
🖥 🗂 W **english-heritage.org.uk**

This unique property lets visitors
relive the grand life of
two very different
eras. In the 14th
century, English
kings spent
Christmas in a
splendid palace
here. The Tudors
used it as a base
for deer-hunting
but it fell in to ruin
after the Civil
War (1642–8).
In 1935

Stephen Courtauld, of the
wealthy textile family, restored
the Great Hall and, next to it, he
built a house described as "a
wonderful combination of Hollywood glamour and Art Deco
design". It has been superbly
restored – especially the circular
glass-domed entrance hall – and
is open to the public along with
the Great Hall, the carp-filled
moat and the 1930s garden.

㉒ Horniman Museum

100 London Rd SE23. **Tel** 020 8699
1872. 🚈 Forest Hill. Gardens: **Open**
7:15am–sunset Mon–Sat, 8am–sunset
Sun. Museum: **Open** 10:30am–5:30pm
daily. Animal Walk: **Open** 12:30–4pm
daily. **Closed** 24–26 Dec. 🖥 🗂 ♿
Events & activities. W **horniman.ac.uk**

Frederick Horniman, the tea
merchant, had this museum
built in 1901 to house the curios
he had collected on his travels
in the 1860s. It features a music
gallery, aquarium, world culture
displays and a natural history
gallery that contains a remarkable
collection of taxidermy and
skeletons, including the famous
Horniman Walrus. The gardens
have a Victorian conservatory, a
bandstand, a formal sunken
garden and a small petting zoo.

㉓ Dulwich Picture Gallery

College Rd SE21. **Tel** 020 8693 5254.
🚈 West Dulwich, North Dulwich.
Open 10am–5pm Tue–Fri, 11am–5pm
Sat, Sun & bank hol Mon (last adm
4:30pm). **Closed** Mon, 1 Jan, 25 & 26
Dec. 🦌 🍴 3pm Sat & Sun. ♿ 🖥
🗂 W **dulwichpicturegallery.org.uk**

Rembrandt's *Jacob III de Gheyn* at
Dulwich Picture Gallery

England's oldest public
art gallery, which
opened in 1817 was
designed by Sir
John Soane (*see
pp140–41*). Its
imaginative use of
skylights made it
the prototype of
most art galleries
built since. It was
commissioned
to house the
royal collection

of the King of Poland when he was forced to abdicate in 1795. The superb collection has works by Rembrandt (his *Jacob III de Gheyn* has been stolen from here four times), Canaletto, Poussin, Watteau, Claude, Murillo, Raphael and Gainsborough. The building houses Soane's mausoleum to Desenfans and Bourgeois, the art dealers who built the collection.

㉔ Battersea Park

Albert Bridge Rd SW11. **Map** 19 C5. **Tel** 020 8871 7530. 🚇 Sloane Sq then bus 137. 🚃 Battersea Pk. **Open** 6:30am–10:30pm daily. 🚻 📵 Sports facilities. *See Six Guided Walks pp272–3.* 🌐 **batterseapark.org**

This was the second public park created to relieve the growing urban stresses of Victorian Londoners (the first was Victoria Park in the East End). It opened in 1858 on the former Battersea Fields, a swampy area notorious for vice, centred on the Old Red House, a disreputable pub.

The new park was immediately popular, especially for its manmade boating lake, with its romantic rocks, gardens and waterfalls. In 1985, a peace pagoda was unveiled, a 35-m (100-ft) high monument built by Buddhist nuns and monks. There are also an excellent children's zoo (entry fee), a playground, sports activities and an art gallery, the Pumphouse.

Peace Pagoda, Battersea Park

Tennis racket and net from 1888, Wimbledon Lawn Tennis Museum

㉕ St Mary's, Battersea

Battersea Church Rd SW11. **Tel** 020 7228 9648. 🚇 Sloane Sq then bus 19 or 219. **Open** by arrangement. 🕍 8:30am Mon–Wed; 8:30am, 11am & 6:30pm Sun. 🚻 Concerts. 🌐 **stmarysbattersea.org.uk**

There has been a church here since at least the 10th century. The present brick building dates from 1775, but the 17th-century stained glass, commemorating Tudor monarchs, comes from the former church. In 1782, the poet and artist William Blake was married in the church. Later, J M W Turner painted views of the Thames from the church tower. Benedict Arnold, who served George Washington in the American War of Independence, is buried in the crypt.

㉖ Wimbledon Lawn Tennis Museum

Church Rd SW19. **Tel** 020 8247 3142; tours 020 8946 6131. 🚇 Southfields. **Open** Apr–Sep: 10am–5:30pm; Oct–Mar: 10am–5pm daily (during championships, ticket holders only). **Closed** 1 Jan, 24–26 Dec. 🚫 🚻 📷 book ahead. 📵 📷 🌐 **wimbledon. com/museum**

Even those with only a passing interest in the sport will find plenty to enjoy here. The museum explores tennis's development from its invention in the 1860s as a diversion for country house parties to the sport it is today. Equipment and tennis fashion from the Victorian era are on display and visitors can

watch clips and recent matches in the video theatre. Tours include a visit to Centre Court.

㉗ Wimbledon Windmill Museum

Windmill Rd SW19. **Tel** 020 8947 2825. 🚇 Wimbledon then 30-minute walk. **Open** Apr–Oct: 2–5pm Sat, 11am–5pm Sun & public hols (Nov– Mar: groups only, by arrangement). 🚻 📷 📵 🌐 **wimbledonwindmill.org.uk**

Built in 1817, the mill on Wimbledon Common now houses a museum exploring windmills, rural life and local history. Boy Scout founder Robert Baden-Powell wrote part of *Scouting for Boys* here in 1908.

St Mary's, Battersea

West of the Centre

Ham House

❷❽ Richmond Park

Kingston Vale SW15. **Tel** 0300 061 2200. 🚇 🚈 Richmond then bus 65 or 71. **Open** 7am–dusk (from 7:30am in winters) daily. 🚻 ♿ 🅿️
w royalparks.org.uk

In 1637, Charles I built a 13-km (8-mile) wall round to enclose the royal park as a hunting ground. Today the park is a national nature reserve and deer still graze warily among the chestnuts, birches and oaks, no longer hunted but still discreetly culled. They have learned to coexist with the thousands of human visitors who stroll here on fine weekends.

In late spring, the park's highlight is the Isabella Plantation with its spectacular display of azaleas, while the nearby Pen Ponds are popular with optimistic anglers. (Adam's Pond is for model boats.) The rest of the park is covered with heath, bracken and trees (some of them hundreds of years old). Richmond Gate, in the northwest corner, was designed by the landscape gardener Capability Brown in 1798. Nearby is Henry VIII Mound, where in 1536 the

Deer in Richmond Park

king, staying in Richmond Palace, awaited the signal that his former wife, Anne Boleyn, had been executed. The Palladian White Lodge, built in 1729, is home to the Royal Ballet School.

❷❾ Hampton Court

See pp260–63.

❸❶ Ham House

Ham St, Richmond. **Tel** 020 8940 1950. 🚇 🚈 Richmond then bus 65 or 371. **Open** Mar–early Oct: noon–4pm daily; mid-Oct–Feb: for tours only (arrange in advance). **Closed** 1 Jan, 25–26 Dec. 🎫 📷 by appt. ♿ partial. 📷 📷 Gardens, café and shop: **Open** 10am–5pm daily.
w nationaltrust.org.uk

This magnificent house by the Thames was built in 1610, but its heyday came when it was home to the Duke of Lauderdale, confidant to Charles II and Secretary of State for Scotland. His wife, the Countess of Dysart, inherited it from her father, who had been Charles I's "whipping boy" (he took the punishment for the future king's misdemeanours). From 1672, the Duke and Countess modernized the house, and it was regarded as one of Britain's finest. The garden has been restored to its 17th-century form.

On some days in summer, a foot passenger ferry runs from

here to Marble Hill House and Orleans House at Twickenham.

❸❶ Orleans House Gallery

Orleans Rd, Twickenham. **Tel** 020 8831 6000. 🚇 🚈 St Margaret's or Richmond then bus 33, 90, 290, R68 or R70. **Open** 10am–5pm Tue–Sun. **Closed** between exhibitions, and occasionally for private events; 1 Jan, Good Fri, 24–26 Dec. Gardens **Open** 9am–dusk daily. ♿ ground floor. 📷 📷 **w** richmond.gov.uk/orleans_house_gallery

This gallery is on the site of the original Orleans House, named after Louis Philippe, Duke of Orleans, who lived there from 1815 to 1817. The Octagon Room was designed by James Gibbs for James Johnson in 1720. The gallery hosts temporary exhibitions throughout the year.

Marble Hill House

❸❷ Marble Hill House

Richmond Rd, Twickenham. **Tel** 020 8892 5115. 🚈 St Margaret's. **Open** Apr–Oct: by guided tour only, Sat & Sun (several daily, phone or visit website to check). **Closed** Nov–Mar. 📷 ♿ restricted. 🎫 📷 📷 Park: **Open** daily 7am–7pm.
w english-heritage.org.uk

Built in 1729 for George II's mistress, Henrietta Howard, the house and its grounds have been open to the public since 1903. Fully restored to its Georgian appearance, the house has a collection of paintings by William Hogarth and a view of the river and house in 1762 by Richard Wilson, who is widely regarded as the father of English landscape painting. The café is especially good.

A Richmond lane

㉝ Richmond

SW15. ⊖ ≋ Richmond.

This attractive London suburb took its name from the palace that Henry VII built here in 1500. Many early 18th-century houses survive near the river and off Richmond Hill, notably Maids of Honour Row, which was built in 1724. The beautiful view of the river from the top of the hill has been captured by many artists, and remains largely unspoiled.

㉞ Syon House

London Rd, Brentford. **Tel** 020 8560 0882. ⊖ Gunnersbury then bus 237 or 267. House: **Open** mid-Mar–Oct: 11am–5pm Wed–Thu, Sun & public hols. **Closed** Nov–mid-Mar. Gardens: **Open** mid-Mar–Oct: 10:30am–5pm daily. **Closed** Nov–mid-Mar. 🅿 ⬚ 🖼 📷 ⬚ 🖼 ♿ gardens only. ⓦ syonpark.co.uk

The Earls and Dukes of Northumberland have lived here for 400 years – it is the only large mansion in the London area still in hereditary ownership. The interior was remodelled in

1761 by Robert Adam and is considered one of his masterpieces. The five Adam rooms house original furnishings and a collection of old master paintings.

The 200-acre (80-ha) park, landscaped by Capability Brown, includes a lovely 40-acre (16-ha) garden with more than 200 species of rare trees. The park's Great Conservatory inspired Joseph Paxton's designs for the Crystal Palace *(see pp30–31).*

㉟ Musical Museum

399 High St, Brentford. **Tel** 020 8560 8108. ≋ Kew Bridge. ⊖ Gunnersbury, South Ealing then bus 237 or 267. **Open** 11am–5pm Fri– Sun & bank hol Mon. 🅿 ♿ 🔊 📷 ⬚ 🖼 ⓦ musicalmuseum.co.uk

The collection is arranged over three floors and comprises chiefly large instruments, including player (automatic) pianos and organs, miniature and cinema pianos, and what is thought to be the only surviving self-playing Wurlitzer organ in Europe.

Drawing room, Osterley Park House

㊱ Osterley Park House

Jersey Rd, Isleworth. **Tel** 020 8232 5050. ⊖ Osterley. **Open** Mar & Oct noon–4pm Wed–Sun; Apr–Sep: 11am–5pm Wed–Sun; first 2 weeks Dec: noon–4pm Sat & Sun. 🅿 ⬚ 🖼 Garden: **Open** 10am–5pm daily. Park: **Open** 7am–6pm (later in summer). ⓦ nationaltrust.org.uk/osterley

Osterley is ranked among Robert Adam's finest works, and its colonnaded portico and elegant library ceiling show why. Much of the furniture is by Adam; the garden and temple are by William Chambers, architect of Somerset House.

Robert Adam's Red Drawing Room at Syon House

㉙ Hampton Court

Hampton Court was not originally built as a royal palace but begun in 1514 by Cardinal Wolsey, Henry VIII's Archbishop of York, as his riverside country house. Later, in 1528, in the hope of retaining royal favour, Wolsey offered it to the king. After the royal takeover, Hampton Court was twice rebuilt and extended, first by Henry himself and then, in the 1690s, by William and Mary, who employed Christopher Wren as architect.

There is a striking contrast between Wren's Classical royal apartments and the Tudor turrets, gables and chimneys elsewhere. The inspiration for the gardens as they are today comes largely from the time of William and Mary, who created a vast, formal Baroque landscape, with radiating avenues of majestic limes and many collections of exotic plants.

★ The Maze
Lose yourself in one of the garden's most popular features.

Main entrance

★ The Great Vine
The vine was planted in the 1760s, and in the 19th century produced up to 910 kg (2,000 lb) of black grapes.

The Pond Garden
This sunken garden was once a pond to store fresh fish for Henry VIII's court.

KEY

① River boat pier
② Royal Tennis Court
③ Privy Garden
④ River Thames

★ The Mantegna Gallery
Andrea Mantegna's nine canvases depicting *The Triumphs of Caesar* (c.1484–1505) are housed here.

Broad Walk
A contemporary print shows the East Front and the Broad Walk during the reign of George II (1727–60).

Long Water
An artificial lake runs parallel to the Thames, from the Fountain Garden across the Home Park.

Fountain Garden
Some of the clipped yews here were planted in the reign of William and Mary.

The East Front
The windows of the Queen's Drawing Room, designed by Wren, overlook the central avenue of the Fountain Garden.

Exploring the Palace

As a historic royal palace, Hampton Court bears traces of many of the kings and queens of England from Henry VIII to the present day. The building itself is a harmonious blend of Tudor and English Baroque architecture. Inside, visitors can see the Great Hall, built by Henry VIII, as well as the state apartments of the Tudor court. Many of the Baroque state apartments, including those above Fountain Court, are decorated with furniture, tapestries and old masters from the Royal Collection.

Tudor Chimneys
Ornate chimneys, some original, some careful restorations, adorn the roof of the Tudor palace.

★ Chapel Royal
The Tudor chapel was re-fitted by Wren except for the carved and gilded vaulted ceiling.

★ Great Hall
The stained-glass window in the Tudor Great Hall shows Henry VIII flanked by the coats of arms of his six wives.

KEY

① **Haunted Gallery**

② **Queen's Presence Chamber**

③ **Queen's Guard Chamber**

④ **Wren's east façade**

★ Clock Court
Anne Boleyn's gatehouse, adorned with the Astronomical Clock, created by Henry VIII in 1540, is the entrance to Clock Court.

King's Great Bedchamber
William III bought the crimson bed from his Lord Chamberlain.

Cardinal Wolsey

Thomas Wolsey (c.1475–1530), simultaneously a cardinal, Archbishop of York and chancellor, was, after the king, the most powerful man in England. However, when he was unable to persuade the pope to allow Henry VIII to divorce his first wife, Catherine of Aragon, Wolsey fell from royal favour. He died while making his way to face trial for treason.

Queen's Gallery
This marble chimneypiece by John Nost was moved from the King's Great Bedchamber to the Queen's Gallery.

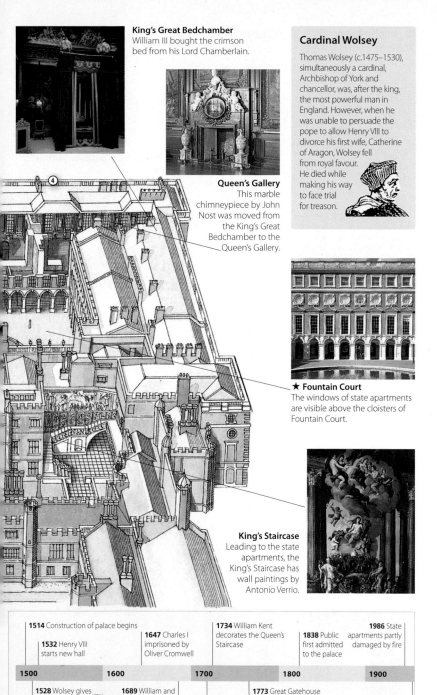

★ Fountain Court
The windows of state apartments are visible above the cloisters of Fountain Court.

King's Staircase
Leading to the state apartments, the King's Staircase has wall paintings by Antonio Verrio.

1514 Construction of palace begins

1532 Henry VIII starts new hall

1647 Charles I imprisoned by Oliver Cromwell

1734 William Kent decorates the Queen's Staircase

1838 Public first admitted to the palace

1986 State apartments partly damaged by fire

1500	1600	1700	1800	1900

1528 Wolsey gives the palace to Henry VIII

Henry VIII painted by Hans Holbein

1689 William and Mary move to Hampton Court

c.1727 Queen's Apartments are finally completed

1773 Great Gatehouse reduced by two storeys

1992 Damaged apartments are reopened

③⑦ Pitzhanger Manor House and Gallery

Mattock Lane W5. **Tel** 020 8567 1227. 🚇 Ealing Broadway. **Open** House closed for refurbishment until 2018. Park: 7:30am–dusk daily; café: 8am–6pm Mon–Fri, 8:30am– 6pm Sat & Sun (till 5pm in winter). **Closed** public hols. ♿ Exhibitions. 🌐 **pitzhanger.org.uk**

Sir John Soane, architect of the Bank of England *(see p151)*, designed this manor house, completed in 1803, as his own country residence. There are clear echoes of his elaborately constructed town house in Lincoln's Inn Fields *(see pp140–41)*. Soane retained two of the principal formal rooms: the drawing room and the dining room, designed in 1768 by George Dance the Younger, with whom Soane had worked before establishing his own reputation.

A sympathetic 20th-century extension houses a gallery (currently closed for refurbishment). The gardens, which were bought by Soane in 1800 along with the house, have been a public park since 1901. The section behind the house has been restored to how it would have looked in Soane's time, and there's an attractive café. It offers a welcome contrast to the bustle of nearby Ealing.

③⑧ London Museum of Water & Steam

Green Dragon Lane, Brentford. **Tel** 020 8568 4757. 🚇 Kew Bridge, Gunnersbury then bus 65, 237 or 267. **Open** 11am–4pm Tue–Sun & bank hol Mon (engines operate at weekends at set times – check website for details). 📷 🍴 book ahead. ♿ Sat & Sun. 📷 ♿ 🌐 **waterandsteam.org.uk**

This 19th-century water pumping station near the north end of Kew Bridge is now a museum of steam power and water. Its main exhibits are five giant Cornish beam engines that pumped water here from the river, to be distributed across London. The earliest engines, dating from 1820, are similar to those built to pump water out of Cornish mines. Visitors can see them working at weekends and on public holidays. The Waterworks gallery tells the story of London's water supply, in lots of interactive detail, and there's a fun outdoor area, Splash Zone, where younger children can play with the water features.

Miniature train, London Museum of Water & Steam

③⑨ Kew Gardens

See pp266–7.

City Barge, Strand on the Green

④⓪ Strand on the Green

W4. 🚇 Gunnersbury then bus 237 or 267. 🚢 Kew Bridge.

This charming Thames-side walk passes fine 18th-century houses as well as more modest cottages once inhabited by fishermen. The oldest of its three pubs is the City Barge, parts of which date from the 15th century; the name is older and derives from the time when the Lord Mayor's barge was moored on the Thames outside.

④① Chiswick House

Burlington Lane W4. **Tel** 020 8995 0508. 🚇 Chiswick. **Open** Apr–Oct: 10am–6pm (to 5pm Oct) Sun–Wed & bank hols. 📷 🍴 for groups, book in advance. ♿ phone ahead. 📷 Gardens **Open** 7am–dusk daily (free admission). 📷 8:30am–6pm Apr–Oct, to 1hr before garden closes in winter. 🌐 **chgt.org.uk**

Completed in 1729 to the design of its owner, the third Earl of Burlington, this is a fine

Chiswick House

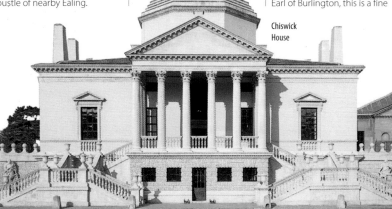

example of a Palladian villa. Burlington revered Palladio and his disciple Inigo Jones, and statues of both stand outside. Built around a central octagonal room, the house is packed with references to ancient Rome and Renaissance Italy, as is the garden.

Chiswick was Burlington's country residence and this house was built as an annexe to a larger, older house (since demolished). It was designed for recreation and entertaining – Lord Hervey, Burlington's enemy, dismissed it as "too little to live in and too big to hang on a watch chain". Some of the ceiling paintings are by William Kent, who also contributed to the garden design.

The house was an asylum from 1892 until 1928, when a long process of restoration began. The layout of the garden, now a public park, is much as Burlington designed it.

Plaque on Hogarth's House

㊷ Hogarth's House

Hogarth Lane W4. **Tel** 020 8994 6757. ⊖ Turnham Green. **Open** noon–5pm Tue–Sun & bank hol Mon. **Closed** 1 Jan, Good Fri, Easter Sun, 24–26 Dec. ♿ ground floor only. 📷
ⓦ **hounslow.info/arts/ hogarthshouse**

When the painter William Hogarth lived here from 1749 until his death in 1764, he called it "a little country box by the Thames" and painted bucolic views from its windows – he had moved here from Leicester Square *(see p107)*. Today, traffic roars by along the Great West Road on its way to and from Heathrow Airport. In an environment as hostile as this, and following years of neglect

and then bombing during World War II, the house has done well to survive. It has now been turned into a small museum and gallery, which is filled mostly with engraved copies of the moralistic cartoon-style pictures with which Hogarth made his name. Salutary tales, such as *The Rake's Progress* (in Sir John Soane's Museum – *see pp140–41*), *Marriage à la Mode, An Election Entertainment* and many others, can all be seen here.

㊸ Fulham Palace

Bishops Ave SW6. **Tel** 020 7736 3233. ⊖ Putney Bridge. **Open** Summer: 12:30–4:30pm Mon–Thu, noon–5pm Sun & bank hol Mon; Winter: 12:30–3:30pm Mon–Thu, noon–4pm Sun. **Closed** Good Fri, 25 & 26 Dec. Park **Open** daylight hours daily. ♿ 🚗 2–3 times each month; check website for days and times. 📷 Events, concerts, lectures. ⓦ **fulhampalace.org**

The home of the Bishops of London from the 8th century until 1973, the oldest surviving parts of Fulham Palace date from the 15th century. The palace stands in its own landscaped gardens northwest of Putney Bridge. A restoration project completed in 2007 revealed a grand, long-hidden Rococo ceiling.

The Belvedere takes centre stage at Chelsea Harbour

㊹ Chelsea Harbour

SW10. ⊖ Fulham Broadway. ♿ Exhibitions. 📷 📷

This is an impressive development of modern apartments, shops, offices, restaurants, a hotel and a marina. It is near the site of Cremorne Pleasure Gardens, which closed in 1877 after more than 40 years as a venue for dances and circuses. The centrepiece is the Belvedere, a 20-storey apartment tower with an external glass lift and a pyramid roof, topped with a golden ball on a rod that rises and falls with the tide.

Fulham Palace's entrance, which dates from Tudor times

㊴ Kew Gardens

The Royal Botanic Gardens, Kew, the most complete public gardens in the world, are a World Heritage Site. Their reputation was first established by Sir Joseph Banks, the British naturalist and plant hunter, who worked here in the late 18th century. The former royal gardens were given to the nation in 1841 and now display about 30,000 plants. Garden enthusiasts will want a full day to visit. Kew is also a centre for scientific research.

Princess Augusta
King George III's mother established the first garden on a 9-acre (3.6-ha) site here in 1759.

★ Pagoda
William Chambers' pagoda, built in 1762, reflects the fashion of the time.

KEY

① Cherry Walk

② The Temperate House (closed for renovation)

③ Waterlily Pond

④ Queen Charlotte's Cottage

⑤ River Thames

⑥ Sackler Crossing

⑦ Marianne North Gallery

⑧ King William's Temple

⑨ Azalea Garden

⑩ Climbers and Creepers soft play area

⑪ Kew Palace

⑫ Nash Conservatory

⑬ The Orangery restaurant

⑭ Duke's Garden

⑮ Princess of Wales Conservatory
Encompassing ten climatic zones, this glasshouse contains cacti, giant waterlilies and orchids.

⑯ Davies Alpine House

⑰ Rock Garden

⑱ Winter Garden

⑲ Campanile

⑳ Rose Garden

㉑ Crocus carpet

㉒ Temple of Bellona

Lion Gate entrance

★ Rhizotron and Xstrata Treetop Walkway
This 200-m (660-ft) walkway meanders through the tree canopy and offers fine views.

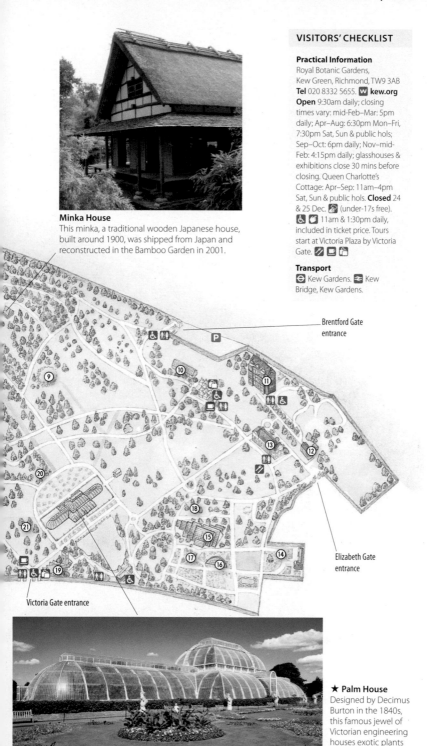

Minka House
This minka, a traditional wooden Japanese house, built around 1900, was shipped from Japan and reconstructed in the Bamboo Garden in 2001.

Practical Information
Royal Botanic Gardens,
Kew Green, Richmond, TW9 3AB
Tel 020 8332 5655. **W** kew.org
Open 9:30am daily; closing
times vary: mid-Feb–Mar: 5pm
daily; Apr–Aug: 6:30pm Mon–Fri,
7:30pm Sat, Sun & public hols;
Sep–Oct: 6pm daily; Nov–mid-
Feb: 4:15pm daily; glasshouses &
exhibitions close 30 mins before
closing. Queen Charlotte's
Cottage: Apr–Sep: 11am–4pm
Sat, Sun & public hols. **Closed** 24
& 25 Dec. (under-17s free).
11am & 1:30pm daily,
included in ticket price. Tours
start at Victoria Plaza by Victoria
Gate.

Transport
Kew Gardens. Kew
Bridge, Kew Gardens.

Brentford Gate
entrance

Elizabeth Gate
entrance

Victoria Gate entrance

★ Palm House
Designed by Decimus
Burton in the 1840s,
this famous jewel of
Victorian engineering
houses exotic plants
in tropical conditions.

SIX GUIDED WALKS

London is an excellent city for walkers. Although it is much more spread out than most European capitals, many of the main tourist attractions are fairly close to each other *(see pp16–17)*. Central London is full of parks and gardens *(see pp52–5)*, and there are also several walk routes plotted by the tourist board and local history societies. These include footpaths along canals and the Thames, and the Silver Jubilee Walkway. Planned in 1977 to commemorate the Queen's Silver Jubilee, the walk runs for 19 km (12 miles) between Lambeth Bridge in the west and Tower Bridge in the east; Visit London *(see p358)* has maps of the route, which is marked by silver-coloured plaques sunk into the pavement at intervals.

Each of the 16 areas described in the *Area by Area* section of this book has a short walk marked on its *Street-by-Street* map. These walks will take you past many of the most interesting sights in that area. On the following 12 pages are routes for six walks that take you through areas of London not covered in detail elsewhere. These range from the bustling, fashionable King's Road *(see pp272–3)* to the wide open spaces of riverside Richmond and Kew *(see pp274–5)*.

Several companies offer guided walking tours of London. Most of these have themes, such as ghosts, Jack the Ripper or Shakespeare's London. Check listings magazines *(see p338)* for details.

The Six Walks

This map shows the location of the six guided walks in relation to the main sightseeing areas of London.

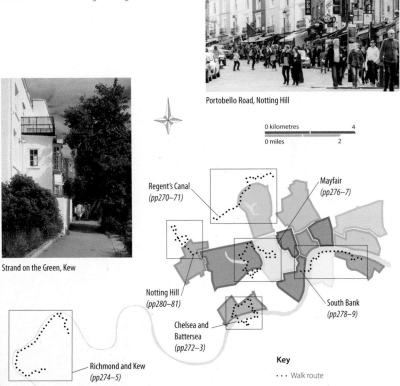

Portobello Road, Notting Hill

Strand on the Green, Kew

Regent's Canal *(pp270–71)*

Mayfair *(pp276–7)*

Notting Hill *(pp280–81)*

South Bank *(pp278–9)*

Chelsea and Battersea *(pp272–3)*

Richmond and Kew *(pp274–5)*

0 kilometres 4
0 miles 2

Key

··· Walk route

◀ Traditional narrow boats on Regent's Canal, Little Venice

A Two-Hour Walk Along the Regent's Canal

Master builder John Nash wanted the Regent's Canal to pass through Regent's Park, but instead it circles north of the park. Opened in 1820, it is long defunct as a commercial waterway but very popular with cyclists and walkers. This walk starts at Little Venice and ends at Camden Lock Market, diverting briefly to take in the view from Primrose Hill. For more details on the sights near Regent's Canal, see pages 224–31.

③ Houseboat on the canal

③ Houseboats moored at Little Venice

From Little Venice to Lisson Grove

At Warwick Avenue station ①, take the left-hand exit and walk straight to the traffic lights by the canal bridge at Blomfield Road. Turn right and descend to the canal through an iron gate ② opposite No. 42, marked "Lady Rose of Regent". The pretty basin with moored narrow boats is Little Venice ③. At the foot of the steps, turn left to walk back beneath the blue iron bridge ④. You soon have to climb up to street level again because this stretch of the towpath is reserved for access to the barges. Cross Edgware Road and walk down Aberdeen

Place. When the road turns to the left by a pub, Crocker's Folly ⑤, follow the signposted Canal Way down to the side of some modern flats. Continue your route along the canal towpath, crossing Park Road at street level. The scenery along this stretch is unremarkable, but it is not long before a splash of green to your right announces that you are now walking alongside Regent's Park ⑥.

Regent's Park

Soon you see four mansions ⑦. A bridge on huge pillars marked "Coalbrookdale" ⑧

Key

• • • Walk route

0 metres	500
0 yards	500

carries Avenue Road into the park. Cross the next bridge, with London Zoo ⑨ on your right, then turn left up a slope. A few steps later, take the right fork, and turn left to cross Prince Albert Road. Turn right before entering Primrose Hill through a gate ⑩ on your left.

Primrose Hill

From here, there is a view of the zoo aviary ⑪, designed by Lord

⑦ Mansion with riverside gardens

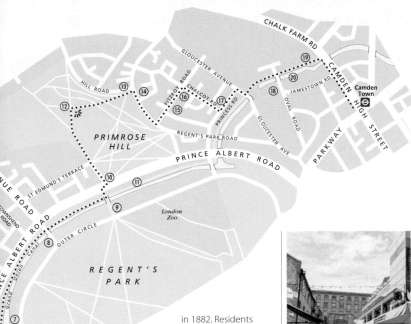

Camden's huge street market is one of the most popular in the country

Snowdon and opened in 1965. Inside the park, keep to the left-hand path that climbs to the top of the hill. Soon you fork right to the summit, which offers a fine view of the city skyline. A viewing panel ⑫ helps identify the landmarks but it does not include the 1990 skyscraper at Canary Wharf, with its pyramid crown, on the left. Descend on the left, making for the park gate at the junction of Regent's Park Road and Primrose Hill Road.

Towards Camden

Almost opposite the gate is the Queens ⑬, a Victorian pub, and just to the left is No. 122 Regent's Park Road ⑭. This was for 24 years the home of the Communist philosopher Friedrich Engels; he was often visited there by his friend Karl Marx.

Turn right and walk down Regent's Park Road for 135 m (150 yd) then turn left up Fitzroy Road. On the right, between Nos. 41 and 39, is the entrance to Primrose Hill Studios ⑮, built

in 1882. Residents have included the conductor Sir Henry Wood and renowned book illustrator Arthur Rackham.

Continue down Fitzroy Road past No. 23 ⑯, once home to the poet W B Yeats, then go right into Chalcot Road and left down Princess Road, past a Victorian boarding school ⑰. Turn right and rejoin the canal down steps across Gloucester Avenue. Turn left under the railway bridge and past the Pirate Castle ⑱, a water sports centre. Cross a humpback bridge and enter Camden Lock Market ⑲ (see

pp335–6) through an arch on your left. After browsing there, you can take the water bus ⑳ back to Little Venice or turn right into Chalk Farm Road and walk up to Camden Town Underground station.

Kayaking on the canal at Camden Lock

For keys to symbols *see back flap*

A Three-Hour Walk in Chelsea and Battersea

This delightful circular walk ambles through the grounds of the Royal Hospital and across the river to Battersea Park, with its romantic Victorian landscaping. It then returns to the narrow village streets of Chelsea and the stylish shops on the King's Road. For more detail on sights in Chelsea, see pages 196–201.

③ Royal Hospital

Sloane Square to Battersea Park

From the station ①, turn left and walk down Holbein Place. The Renaissance painter's connection with Chelsea stems from his friendship with Sir Thomas More, who lived nearby. Pass the cluster of antique shops ② as you turn on to Royal Hospital Road. Enter the grounds of the Royal Hospital ③, designed by Christopher Wren, and turn left into Ranelagh Gardens ④. The small pavilion by John Soane ⑤ displays a history of the area as Georgian pleasure gardens – it was the most fashionable meeting place for London society. Leave the gardens for fine views of the

⑥ Charles II statue at the Royal Hospital

hospital and Grinling Gibbons's bronze of Charles II ⑥. The granite obelisk ⑦ commemorates the 1849 battle at Chilianwalla, in what is now Pakistan, and forms the centrepiece of the main marquee at the Chelsea Flower Show (see p60).

Battersea Park

When crossing the Chelsea Bridge ⑧ (1937), look up to see four gilded galleons on top of the pillars at each end. Turn into Battersea Park ⑨ (see p257), one of London's liveliest, and follow the main path along the river to enjoy the excellent views of Chelsea. Turn left at the Buddhist Peace Pagoda ⑩ to enter the main part of the park.

Past the bowling greens are Henry Moore's sculpture of *Three Standing Figures* ⑪ (1948) and the lake, a favoured spot for wildfowl. (There are boats for hire.) Just beyond the sculpture, head northwest and, after crossing the central avenue, fork right and make for the wooden gate into the rustic Old English Garden ⑫. Leave the garden by the metal gate and return to Chelsea via the Victorian Albert Bridge ⑬.

0 metres 500
0 yards 500

Key

• • • Walk route

Tips for Walkers

Starting point: Sloane Square.
Length: 4 miles (6.5 km).
Getting there: Sloane Square is the nearest Tube. There are frequent buses 11, 19, 22 and 349 to Sloane Square and along the King's Road. Royal Hospital grounds are open 10am–6pm Mon–Sat, 2–6pm Sun.
Stopping-off points: There is a café in Battersea Park, by the lake. Cheyne Walk Brasserie, on Cheyne Walk, serves upmarket Provençal food. There are plenty of pubs, restaurants and sandwich shops to be found along the King's Road. The Chelsea Farmers Market on Sydney Street has several cafés.

⑫ Old English Garden in Battersea Park

⑬ Albert Bridge

Thomas Carlyle statue ⑮

Place ㉒ has retained much of its original character. Where Glebe Place meets the King's Road are three early 18th-century houses ㉓. Cross Dovehouse Green, which used to be a burial ground, to Chelsea Farmers Market ㉔, an enclave of cafés and craft shops.

The King's Road

Leave the market on Sydney Street and cross into the garden of St Luke's Church ㉕, where Charles Dickens was married in 1836. The walk then winds through quaint back streets until it rejoins the King's Road ㉖ (see p200), which was very fashionable in the 1960s. On the left is The Pheasantry ㉗. Look down the side streets on both left and right to see Wellington Square ㉘, then Royal Avenue ㉙, intended as a triumphal way to the Royal Hospital, and Blacklands Terrace ㉚, where book-lovers will want to visit John Sandoe's shop. The Duke of York's Territorial Headquarters ㉛ (1803) on the right – now home to the Saatchi Gallery – marks the approach to Sloane Square ㉜ and the Royal Court Theatre (see Sloane Square p201).

The Backstreets of Chelsea

Over the bridge is David Wynne's sculpture of a boy and dolphin ⑭ (1975). Pass the sought-after residences on Cheyne Walk and the statues of historian Thomas Carlyle ⑮ and Sir Thomas More ⑯ – this area was renowned for gatherings of intellectuals. Past Chelsea Old Church ⑰ is Roper's Gardens ⑱

with its carving by Jacob Epstein. Just beyond these is the medieval Crosby Hall ⑲. On Justice Walk ⑳ are two early Georgian houses – Duke's House and Monmouth House. Turn left to pass the site of the Chelsea porcelain factory ㉑, which used to make highly fashionable (and today highly collectable) wares in the late 18th century. Glebe

㉜ Royal Court Theatre

A 90-Minute Walk Around Richmond and Kew

This delightful riverside walk begins in historic Richmond, by
the remains of Henry VII's once splendid palace, and ends at
Kew, Britain's premier botanic garden. For more detail on the
sights in Richmond and Kew, turn to pages 258–67.

The river at low tide

Richmond Green

From Richmond station ①,
proceed to Oriel House ②, which
is practically opposite. Take the
alleyway beneath it, and turn left
towards the red-brick and
terracotta Richmond Theatre ③,
built in 1899. The remarkable
Edmund Kean, whose brief,
meteoric career in the early 19th
century had a lasting impact on
English acting, was closely
associated with the previous
theatre on the site. Opposite is
Richmond Green ④. Cross it
diagonally and go through the
entrance arch ⑤ of the old
Tudor palace, which is adorned
with the arms of Henry VII.

Richmond

Richmond owes much of its
importance – as well as its
name – to Henry, victor of the
Wars of the Roses and the first
Tudor monarch. On becoming
king in 1485 he spent a lot of
time at an earlier residence on
this site, Sheen Palace, dating
from the 12th century. The
palace burned down in 1499
and Henry had it rebuilt,
naming it Richmond after the
town in Yorkshire where he held
an earldom. In 1603, Henry's
granddaughter, Elizabeth I, died
here. The houses inside the
archway on the left contain
remnants, much modified, of

the 16th-century buildings.
Leave Old Palace Yard at the
right-hand corner ⑥, following
a sign "To the River", and turn
left to pass the White Swan pub
⑦. At the river, go right along
the towpath under the iron
railway bridge and then the
concrete Twickenham Bridge
⑧, completed in 1933, to reach
Richmond Lock ⑨, with its cast-
iron footbridge built in 1894.
The Thames is tidal as far as
Teddington, some 3 miles
(5 km) upstream, and the lock
is used to make the river
continuously navigable.

The Riverside

Do not cross the bridge but
continue along the wooded
path by the river to Isleworth Ait
⑩, a large island where herons
may be standing warily on the
riverbank. Just beyond it, on the
far shore, is All Saints' Church ⑪,
whose 15th-century tower has
survived several rebuildings,
most recently in the 1960s.
Further round the inlet, Isleworth
⑫, once a small riverside village
with a busy harbour, is now a
dormitory suburb of central
London. Here, there is river traffic
to watch: barges, yachts and, in
summer, the passenger boats
that ply upriver to Hampton
Court (see pp260–63). Rowers
are out at most times of year,

training for races. The most
prestigious occasions are the
Henley Regatta in July and the
Oxford v Cambridge Boat Race,
every spring from Putney
to Mortlake (see p60).

③ Richmond Theatre

Key

••• Walk route

Kew

After a while, the appearance of iron railings on your right marks where Old Deer Park ⑬ turns into Kew Gardens ⑭ (officially called the Royal Botanic Gardens – see pp266–7). There used to be a riverside entrance for visitors arriving on foot or by water, but the gate ⑮ is now

⑲ Kew Palace in Kew Gardens

out in the 18th century. Just beyond are modern waterside apartments at Brentford ⑰. This was originally an industrial suburb, sited where the Grand Union Canal runs into the Thames, and its residential potential has only recently been exploited. You can pick out the tall chimney of the waterworks ⑱, now a museum dedicated to steam power. On the right, behind the Kew Gardens car park, there is a view of Kew Palace ⑲, now fully restored and open to the public.

Beyond the car park, leave the river by Ferry Lane, which leads to Kew Green ⑳. You could spend the rest of the day in Kew Gardens or cross Kew Bridge and turn right on to Strand on the Green ㉑, a fine riverside walkway with atmospheric pubs, the oldest of them the City Barge ㉒. Head south down Kew Road, then turn left at Kew Gardens Road to reach Kew Gardens Underground station (District line).

Tips for Walkers

Starting point: Richmond station.
Length: 3 miles (5 km).
Getting there: Richmond Underground or railway station. Buses 391 and R68 come here from Kew.
Stopping-off points: There are many cafés, pubs and tearooms in Richmond. The famous Maids of Honour tearoom is at Kew, and Kew Grill is one of several good eateries on Kew Green.

closed and the nearest entrance is to the north, near the car park.

Across the river, there are magnificent views of Syon House ⑯, seat of the Dukes of Northumberland since 1594. Part of the present house dates from the 16th century but it was largely redesigned by Robert Adam in the 1760s. You are looking at it across the garden Capability Brown laid

The riverbank between Richmond and Kew

For keys to symbols see back flap

A Two-Hour Walk Through Mayfair to Belgravia

This walk takes you from Green Park to Hyde Park, through the hearts of Mayfair and Belgravia, two of London's most elegant Georgian residential districts. It includes a bracing stroll through Hyde Park and, if you're feeling energetic, a row on the Serpentine.

⑦ L'Artiste Musclé restaurant, Shepherd Market, Mayfair

Green Park to Berkeley Square

Exit Green Park station ① following the signs for Piccadilly North. With Green Park opposite you, turn left. Pass Devonshire House ②, a 1920s office block that replaced the 18th-century mansion designed by William Kent. Only Kent's gates survive, now at the park entrance across Piccadilly. Turn left and walk up Berkeley Street to Berkeley Square ③. To the south, the remains of Lansdowne House by Robert Adam are now occupied by an advertising agency ④. There are still a few splendid 18th-century houses to the west, including No. 45 ⑤,

home of the soldier and governor, Lord Clive of India.

Mayfair

Keep to the south of the square and turn into Charles Street, noting the evocative lampholders at Nos. 40 and 41 ⑥. Turn left into Queen Street and cross Curzon Street to enter Shepherd Market ⑦ (see p101) through Curzonfield House alleyway. Turn right up a pedestrian-only street then right onto Hertford Street, passing the Curzon Cinema ⑧ on the corner of Curzon Street. Here you are almost facing Crewe House ⑨, built in 1730 by Edward Shepherd, who also laid out the market.

Turn left and walk up Curzon Street, then turn right onto Chesterfield Street. A left turn at Charles Street brings you to Red Lion Yard ⑩, where a pub stands opposite one of the few weatherboarded buildings in the West End. Turn right into Hay's Mews and left up Chesterfield Hill. Cross Hill Street and South Street and head left until you reach an alley leading to the peaceful haven of Mount Street Gardens ⑪. The gardens back on to the Church of the Immaculate Conception ⑫. Cross the garden and turn left onto Mount Street; then right onto South Audley Street and left at Grosvenor Square ⑬ into Upper Grosvenor Street, passing to the left of the US Embassy. Look out for the statue of Franklin D Roosevelt. Turn

Tips for Walkers

Starting point: Green Park station.
Length: 5 km (3 miles).
Getting there: Green Park is on the Victoria, Jubilee and Piccadilly underground lines. Hyde Park Corner is on the Piccadilly line.
Stopping-off points: There are numerous pubs, cafés and restaurants in the area. Serpentine Bar and Kitchen on the Serpentine is open 8am–7pm.

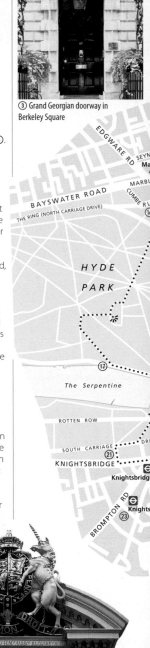

③ Grand Georgian doorway in Berkeley Square

Royal coat of arms above the door of Auckley House

right up Park Lane and walk along what was once the city's most desirable residential street, before the traffic got so heavy ⑭. At the end you can see Marble Arch (see p213).

Hyde Park

Enter the pedestrian subway ⑮ at exit No. 6 and follow signs for Park Lane West Side, exit No. 5. You will emerge at Speakers' Corner ⑯ (see p213), where on Sundays anyone can make a speech on any topic. Cross Hyde

⑰ The Serpentine, on a fine day

Park (see p213) south–southwest, enjoying the views on all sides, and make for the boat house ⑰ on the Serpentine (an artificial lake created by Queen Caroline in 1730), where you can rent a rowing boat. Turn left and follow the path to Serpentine Bar and Kitchen ⑱ for refreshments. From there, take the stone bridge ⑲ and cross Rotten Row ⑳, where the very wealthy

exercise their horses. Leave the park at Edinburgh Gate ㉑.

Knightsbridge

Cross Knightsbridge and, resisting the temptations of two of London's great department stores – Harvey Nichols ㉒ and Harrods ㉓ (see p213) on Brompton Road – head down Sloane Street to turn left at Harriet Street. At Lowndes Square, turn right and leave the square on the far side, turning left into Motcomb Street. On your left is the Pantechnicon, an eccentric structure fronted by colossal Doric columns, built in 1830.

Belgravia

Turn left out of the arcade onto Kinnerton Street, which boasts one of London's smallest pubs, the Nag's Head ㉔. A pretty mew runs off to the left of this street at its northern end; look for Ann's Close and Kinnerton Place North. Almost opposite the latter, the street makes a sharp right turn to emerge into Wilton Place opposite St Paul's Church (1843). Turn right here and follow Wilton Crescent round to the left before turning left into Wilton Row, where there is another small pub, the Grenadier ㉕, once the officers' mess of the Guards' barracks and reputedly frequented by the Duke of Wellington. Up Old Barracks Yard to the right of the pub there are some old officers' billets and a worn stone said to have been used by the Iron Duke when mounting his horses. The alley leads to a T-junction. To finish the walk, turn left and walk around the building in front of you to reach Knightsbridge. Turn right and continue to Hyde Park Corner station.

Key

••• Walk route

| 0 metres | 400 |
| 0 yards | 400 |

For keys to symbols see back flap

㉖ Once the officers' mess, now the Grenadier pub, Belgravia

A 90-Minute Walk Along the South Bank

The Riverside Walk along the South Bank from Westminster Bridge (see p189) via Bankside to Southwark Cathedral is one of the most entertaining excursions in town. From County Hall to Shakespeare's Globe, the South Bank's well-known music, theatre and film venues, the shops and galleries of Gabriel's Wharf and the Oxo Tower, there's something for everyone. For more details on the sights in Southwark and Bankside, see pages 176–87.

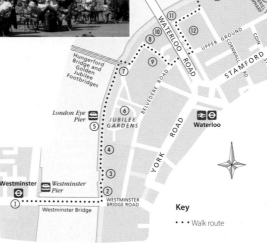

⑭ Cafés and shops at Gabriel's Wharf

p343), where films are shown throughout the day. Outside its lively café, rows of tables stacked with second-hand books shelter beneath the bridge. The National Theatre ⑫ (see p192) has exhibitions and musical events as well as a good bookshop. You can see into the set-building areas from the windows at the back and the walkway near the Dorfman Theatre. Several of the theatre's restaurants, cafés and bars offer outside seating overlooking the

The Southbank Centre

Begin at Westminster station ① by the statue of the Iceni warrior Queen Boudicca (or Boadicea), and walk over Westminster Bridge. Once on the south side ②, there is a fine view back over the river to the Houses of Parliament (see pp76–7). The main building on this side is the former County Hall ③, now offering a range of entertain-ment (see p192), the highlight being the Sea Life London Aquarium ④, a fascinating underwater world. For the best city view, the London Eye ⑤ (see p193) is

Tips for Walkers

Starting point: Westminster Bridge.
Length: 2.75 km (1.75 miles).
Getting there: Westminster Underground station on the District, Circle and Jubilee lines.
Stopping off points: All the South Bank's art centres have cafés, bars and restaurants. There are places to eat in Gabriel's Wharf and great food stalls at Borough, where there is also Brindisa for tapas and a good pub, the Rake.

beside Jubilee Gardens ⑥, where buskers and mime artists perform. Walk past Hungerford Bridge ⑦ with its Golden Jubilee footbridges either side and trains to Charing Cross Station, on the site of the former Hungerford market. Ahead is the Southbank Centre ⑧ (see pp190–91), the capital's main arts showcase. Music and exhibitions fill the Royal Festival Hall ⑨ (see p192), created for the Festival of Britain in 1951. Next are the Queen Elizabeth Hall ⑩ and Hayward Gallery (see p192). Moving on along the Riverside Walk, past Waterloo Bridge, you reach BFI Southbank ⑪ (see

Key

• • • Walk route

River

Waterloo Bridge

THE ... **QUEEN'S** ...

⑬

⑭ **GABRIEL'S WHARF**

DUCHY

⑪

WATERLOO ROAD

⑩

⑫

UPPER GROUND

COIN

⑧

⑨

CORNWALL RD

STAMFORD ST

Hungerford Bridge and Golden Jubilee Footbridges

⑦

BELVEDERE ROAD

London Eye Pier

⑥

⑤ **JUBILEE GARDENS**

ROAD

⊞ ⊟ **Waterloo**

④

③

YORK

Westminster ⊟ ⊟ **Westminster Pier**

②

①

WESTMINSTER BRIDGE ROAD

Westminster Bridge

View from the Oxo Tower ⑮

Brutalist architecture of the Hayward Gallery, South Bank

(see p181). A tour around the theatre is the next best thing to attending a performance.

Bankside

Bankside becomes more cramped here, as the historic streets pass The Anchor ㉕ riverside pub to reach the Clink Prison Museum ㉖ (see p186), on the site of one of London's first lock-ups. The Rose Window on Clink Street ㉗ is all that is left of the Bishop of Winchester's Palace. At St Mary Ovarie Dock, climb aboard a replica (1973) of Golden Hinde II ㉘, in which the Elizabethan buccaneer

South Bank. Past the London Studios (ITV) ⑬ is Gabriel's Wharf ⑭ (see p195), a pleasant diversion with its art and craft shops and lively cafés.

Following the Queen's Walk

The next landmark you come to is the Oxo Tower ⑮, a red-brick industrial building with galleries and independent designer shops. The top of the tower provides an excellent, free view of the city. Pass by Sea Containers House ⑯, decorated with gold trimmings (built as a hotel, but now offices), and Doggett's Coat and Badge pub ⑰ (see p67), then walk under Blackfriars Bridge ⑱, emerging by the remaining piers and railway emblem of a former bridge. Alongside Blackfriars Bridge is Blackfriars railway station, its platforms looking onto the river. On the right, opposite the Founders Arms ⑲, is the esteemed Bankside Gallery ⑳ (see p181), which has regular

exhibitions of its members' work. Behind it on Holland Street is Marcus Campbell, an excellent art bookshop, a stone's throw from Tate Modern ㉑ (see pp182–5), the best free show on the river. Drop in for a coffee if nothing else. The Millennium Bridge ㉒ leads over to St Paul's (see pp152–5) and the City. Its architect Sir Christopher Wren had a house in Cardinal's Wharf ㉓, where he had a good view of it. Next door to his house is Shakespeare's Globe theatre ㉔

Sir Francis Drake became the second man to circumnavigate the world. Southwark Cathedral ㉙ (see p180) is a quiet place to end the walk, with a good tea shop. Or, if you still feel energetic, explore Borough Market ㉚ (see p180) overlooked by London's highest landmark, The Shard ㉛. Either ascend to the top (see p187) or have a drink in one of the stylish bars, such as Aqua Shard on level 31, before heading to the Tube or train at London Bridge station ㉜.

㉑ Tate Modern: a vast space for contemporary British art

A Two-Hour Walk Around Notting Hill

This walk centres on Portobello Road, the city's most famous antiques and bric-a-brac shopping area, in one of the ultra-fashionable parts of London. Great for original souvenirs, the neighbourhood is fascinating at any time, though the streets are busiest on Fridays and Saturdays, when all the shops are open and the market stalls set up *(see page 337)*. This is the heart of Notting Hill, renowned for its lively carnival.

in the street. At Colville Terrace ⑩, the daily fruit and vegetable market begins. On the left is the Electric Cinema ⑪, said to be the oldest working cinema in Britain (1910), and certainly one of the most delightful. If there is no film showing, you can go in and try the comfortable armchair seats and sofas.

⑤ Bright paintwork on Portobello Road

Around Notting Hill
Turn left down Blenheim Crescent to find The Notting Hill Bookshop ⑫,

Portobello Road

Leaving Notting Hill Gate Tube station ①, follow the signs to Portobello Road *(see p223)*, taking Pembridge Road ②. Intriguing shops here include Retro Woman ③ (Nos. 20 and 32) and Retro Man ④ (No. 34) for period clothes and accessories. At the Sun in Splendour pub ⑤, turn left into Portobello Road. No. 22, among the attractively painted terraced houses on the right, was where George Orwell lived in 1927 before his writing career began ⑥. Cross

Chepstow Villas ⑦ and the serious antique shops begin. Near the Portobello Arcade ⑧, signposted with a large teapot, is Portobello Gold (Nos. 95–7), a guest house where Bill, Hillary and Chelsea Clinton dropped in for a beer and a snack in 2000. At No. 115 ⑨ is a plaque to June Aylward who opened the first antique shop

⑪ The Electric Cinema, the UK's oldest working cinema

Tips for Walkers

Starting point: Notting Hill Gate station.
Length: 3 km (2 miles).
Getting there: Notting Hill underground station on Central, District and Circle lines.
Stopping-off points: The area is known for its pubs and restaurants. Try Ottolenghi's Patisserie at 63 Ledbury Rd for superb pastries or the café at Books for Cooks, 4 Blenheim Crescent. Arancina, 19 Pembridge Rd, near Notting Hill Gate Tube station, is good for a quick slice of pizza and other Italian snacks.

formerly The Travel Bookshop, a location of the 1999 film *Notting Hill*, starring Hugh Grant and Julia Roberts. Books for Cooks ⑬ (No. 4) stocks thousands of cookbooks, from which recipes are prepared and served in the inhouse café. Head back to Portobello Road and pass the local Salvation Army centre ⑭. Beyond the Westway flyover, other sections of the market operate on Fridays, Saturdays and Sundays: Portobello Green market ⑮ has vintage fashions and bric-a-brac (with new fashions on Saturdays); Acklam Village Market ⑯, 4–8 Acklam Road, is the place to

㉒ Ottolenghi Patisserie display

Saints' Church ⑱ has a glassed-in shrine to Our Lady of Walsingham (a pilgrimage destination in the county of Norfolk) – an unusual feature in a Protestant church. Just beyond the red-brick Tabernacle Arts Centre ⑲, where Pink Floyd performed in 1966, is My

Beautiful Laundrette ⑳, named after the successful 1986 film. Turn right into Ledbury Road to find high fashion shops. At the end of the road is the still-functioning Westbourne Grove Church ㉑. As you are passing No. 63, try the delicious pastries in Ottolenghi Patisserie ㉒. Turn right into Westbourne Grove for more stylish shopping. Dinny Hall ㉓ at No. 200 stocks award-winning jewellery. Just opposite is the renowned florist Wild at Heart ㉔, full of beautiful bouquets. On the far side is the Oxfam charity shop ㉕, where the bargains reflect the good taste of the locals. Head back to Portobello Road ㉖ to return to Notting Hill Gate Tube station.

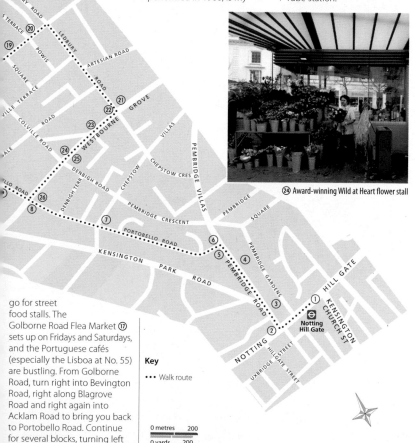

㉔ Award-winning Wild at Heart flower stall

go for street food stalls. The Golborne Road Flea Market ⑰ sets up on Fridays and Saturdays, and the Portuguese cafés (especially the Lisboa at No. 55) are bustling. From Golborne Road, turn right into Bevington Road, right along Blagrove Road and right again into Acklam Road to bring you back to Portobello Road. Continue for several blocks, turning left on Talbot Road, where All

Key

••• Walk route

0 metres 200
0 yards 200

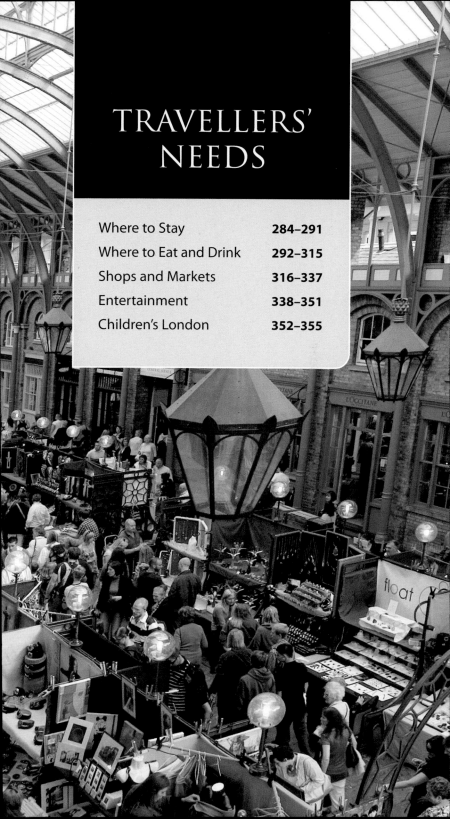

TRAVELLERS' NEEDS

WHERE TO STAY

The high cost of accommodation in London is one of the biggest drawbacks for visitors. At the top end of the market, there is no shortage of expensive pedigree hotels, such as Claridge's and the Ritz. Mid-range hotels, while there are many, tend to be slightly further out from the centre, and budget hotels are few and far between, thanks to rising property prices. However, there are ways to stay in the capital without breaking the bank. Low-cost hotel chains have establishments in convenient locations throughout the city, many concentrated in the centre of town, offering good-quality accommodation at affordable prices. If you don't need a hotel's facilities, consider self-catering apartments or private homes *(see pp286–7)*, an increasingly popular option available at a wide range of prices. The accommodation choices on the pages that follow offer something to suit a range of budgets and tastes, and represent the very best places to stay in and just outside of the city.

Where to Look

The hotel listings in this guide have been divided into six key areas of London, covering a broader span of the capital than the sightseeing sections of this guide. The most expensive hotels tend to be in smart West End areas such as Mayfair and Belgravia. Often large and opulent, with uniformed staff, they are great for those seeking luxury accommodation. Slightly smaller hotels, nonetheless providing superb comfort and service, can be found in South Kensington or Holland Park.

The streets off Earls Court Road are full of hotels at the lower end of the price range. Several of the big railway stations are in locations well served with budget hotels. Try Ebury Street near Victoria, or Sussex Gardens near Paddington. Close to Euston or Waterloo and in the City and Docklands, well-known hotel chains cater for travellers at a range of prices.

There are also inexpensive hotels in London's suburbs, such as Ealing, Hendon, Richmond or Harrow (such hotels are listed within the Further Afield category). From here, you can get into town on public transport, including suburban rail line services. Be sure to check the times of the last train service leaving central London.

If you get stranded at an airport or have to catch an early morning flight, check-in to a hotel near the airport *(see p373)*. For further information, advice and reservation services, go to www.visitlondon.com, which publishes several annually updated booklets on the different types of accommodation in Greater London.

Discount Rates

Prices in the capital tend to stay high all year round, but there are bargains to be found. Online price comparison sites will often provide you with the best deals on hotel rooms and package deals. Many hotels, especially the chains, also offer reduced rates for weekends and special breaks *(see p286)*. Others work on a more ad hoc basis, depending on how busy they are. It is always worth trying to negotiate a discount, especially if it is off-season.

Hidden Extras

Read the small print carefully. Most hotels quote room rates rather than rates per person, but not all. Service charges and VAT are usually included in the quoted price but in some cases they are added on later, which means that the final bill can come as a shock to visitors. Also be aware of high mark-ups on telephone calls made in your hotel room and additional fees for Wi-Fi access. Breakfast may not be included in room rates, though it generally is in cheaper hotels. Most hotels expect visitors to vacate rooms by noon (sometimes earlier) on the day of departure and may charge extra for late checkout.

Comfortable foyer area in Charlotte Street hotel *(see p288)*

◀ Apple Market, Covent Garden Piazza

Attractive façade of the London Bridge hotel *(see p289)*

Single travellers are usually charged a supplement and end up paying about 80 per cent of the double room rate, even if they are occupying a single room – so don't accept anything substandard.

Tipping is expected in the more expensive hotels, but there is no need to tip staff other than porters, except perhaps a helpful concierge for arranging theatre tickets or phoning for taxis.

Facilities

Room sizes in London hotels tend to be on the small side whatever the price range, but the majority of hotels provide telephones, televisions and private baths or showers in all their rooms. At the top end of

The Ritz *(see p288)* on Piccadilly, one of London's most exclusive hotels

the scale, hotels compete to offer the very latest sound and video systems, computer equipment and high-tech gadgetry. Most hotel rooms come equipped with Wi-Fi.

How to Book

It is always advisable to book your accommodation well in advance. Direct bookings can be made by phone, via the hotel website booking form or by email. This generally entails giving a guarantee: either a credit card number from which a cancellation fee can be deducted, or a one-night deposit (some hotels will expect more for longer stays). Don't forget that if you do cancel, part or even all of the room price may be charged unless the hotel can re-let the accommodation. Insurance cover is advised.

Online booking is the easiest way to book hotels, with the best prices often only available via the internet. Many hotels have their own online advance purchase rate while internet travel sites, holiday retailers and hotel wholesalers such as Expedia (www.expedia.co.uk) and Travel Republic (www.travelrepublic.co.uk) quote good rates, particularly if you book a hotel and flight together.

The visitlondon.com website has an excellent guide to finding accommodation in London, from self-catered apartments and budget hostels to luxury hotels. To make a booking by phone, call 020 3564 5657. The British Hotel Reservation Centre in Victoria railway station is also useful. A number of commercial booking agencies operate from booths in the major railway stations, charging a small fee to personal callers. Avoid unidentified touts, who often hang around at railway and coach stations offering cheap accommodation.

Special Breaks

Many travel agencies carry brochures from the major hotel chains listing special offers, which are usually costed on a

Impeccably stylish interior at Hotel 41 *(see p290)*

minimum two-night stay. Some are extraordinarily good value compared to the usual tariff. For most leisure travellers or families with children, this is the best way to get value for money out of London hotels.

City-break packages are organized by specialist operators, ferry companies and airlines, and some hotels. Sometimes the same hotel may feature in several brochures at differing prices and with different perks. It's worth asking the hotel directly what special rates they offer. As previously mentioned, online travel websites are also an excellent source for great-value holiday packages.

Disabled Travellers

Information about wheelchair access is based largely on hotels' own assessments, so disabled travellers should always confirm when booking whether an establishment is suitable. If forewarned, many hotels will go out of their way to help. The nationwide **Tourism for All** scheme provides details on accommodation standards and facilities for elderly visitors or those with mobility problems. For information on hotels that meet the three-tier "National Accessible Standard", contact **DisabledGo** or Tourism For All. A guide book for people with access needs, Open Britain, can be obtained from **Disability Rights UK**.

Opulent bathroom at The Goring *(see p290)*

Travelling with Children

London hotels are very welcoming to children and many provide cots, high-chairs, babysitting services (always ensure sitters have had a DBS – Disclosure and Barring Service – check) and special meal arrangements. Ask whether the hotel offers special deals for children – some have special rates, or allow children to stay free of charge in their parents' room. Self-catering flats and private homes are also great options for families as these are more affordable and have far more space than a hotel room.

Self-Catering Flats

Many agencies offer self-catering accommodation in flats, usually for stays of a week or more. Prices, depending on size and location, start at about £300 per week. Some luxury apartment complexes are fully serviced, so you don't need to cook, shop or clean. **Bridge Street Global Hospitality** has over 550 London apartments in smart locations. It caters mainly for corporate and professional travellers, but its properties can be rented for short-term lets whenever they are available.

The **Landmark Trust** rents accommodation in historic or unusual buildings. These include a house in Hampton Court *(see pp260–63)* and two in a pretty 18th-century terrace in the City: one of these was the home of the late Poet Laureate, Sir John Betjeman. A handbook of Landmark Trust properties is available for a charge via their website.

Staying in Private Homes

A number of agencies organize stays in private homes; several are registered with Visit London. Prices depend on location, starting at around £25 per person per night. Sometimes you will enjoy family hospitality, but this isn't guaranteed, so enquire when you book. Many private homes are situated on the outskirts of the city, so consider travel costs when planning your trip; depending on the length of your stay, these are still often the more affordable option.

Airbnb offers accommodation for one night's stay or longer in private homes in London. Deposits may be requested and cancellation fees imposed. **TripAdvisor** and **Roomorama** also offer similar holiday rental services.

The Bed & Breakfast and Homestay Association (BBHA) is an umbrella organization for several reputable agencies whose properties are inspected regularly. **Uptown Reservations** arranges B&B stays in interesting, London homes which have been chosen for their welcome,

security and comfort. Prices start at £125 per night for a double room. It works in tandem with **Wolsey Lodges**, a nationwide consortium of distinctive private homes, often of historic or architectural interest, offering individual hospitality.

Chain Hotels

Chain hotels are an important feature of the London hotel market. Though they can lack character, they offer some of the best-value accommodation in town. Some also offer particular facilities; **Novotel**, for example, caters for both business guests and families. Other good-value chains include **Express by Holiday Inn** and **easyHotel**. **Travelodge** and **Ibis** also have affordable rooms in key locations in the capital. For basic yet contemporary rooms, **Tune** has several hotels. **Premier Inn** offers competitive "saver rates" when booking directly through their website.

Budget Accommodation

Despite the high cost of many London hotels, budget accommodation does exist and many options can be found in the listings *(p291)*. While private accommodation and chain hotels offer cheap rates with good amenities, hostels are another inexpensive option, particularly for those travelling alone. Dormitory accommodation and youth hostels can be booked through Visit London's hotel reservation centre at Victoria Station for a small fee

Imaginative dining suite at W *(see p288)*

plus a refundable deposit. Some private hostels near Earl's Court charge little more than £10 a night for a dormitory bed with breakfast. The **London Hostels Association** has a selection of reasonably priced accommodation throughout central London. The **Youth Hostels Association** (YHA) runs seven hostels in London. There is no age limit, though non-members pay a joining fee. Of the seven, two are located in the heart of London. The Oxford Street hostel is actually in Noel Street, Soho, while the London St Paul's hostel is located near St Paul's Cathedral (see pp152–5). One of the most popular hostels is Holland House, a Jacobean mansion in Holland Park. The easiest way to book a bed online is through the **Hostelling International** (HI) website, which offers a range of global hostels to stay at.

At the top end of the market, the Mandarin Oriental Hyde Park (see p288)

Many student rooms are available at Easter and from July to September. Some of these are in central locations such as South Kensington. **London University Rooms** arranges stays in halls, or, if you need a room in a hurry, King's College or Imperial College may be able to find you one.

Recommended Hotels

The hotels on pages 288–91 include a wide variety to suit all tastes and budgets. Boutique hotels, which often have small, uniquely decorated rooms, have been included, as have character hotels, which are full of charm and usually family-run. There are also B&Bs, guesthouses and apartments, as well as pubs and restaurants with rooms.

They are first listed according to theme, and then alphabetically by area. Most of the hotels are spread across the main tourist areas, although a number that are located further afield are included if they offer particularly good value for money, facilities, service and charm.

Where a hotel has an exceptional feature, such as great-value rates or spectacular views, it has been highlighted as a DK Choice.

DIRECTORY

Reservations and Information

British Hotel Reservation Centre
Victoria railway station,
East Concourse SW1V 1JU.
Tel 020 7828 1027.
w weknowlondon.com
w visitlondon.com

Disabled Travellers

DisabledGo
Tel 0845 270 4627.
w disabledgo.com
Disability Rights UK
Ground Floor CAN
Mezzanine 49–51 East Rd
N1 6AH. **Tel** 020 7250 8181.
w disabilityrightsuk.org
Tourism For All
7A Pixel Mill, 4 Appleby
Rd, Kendal, Cumbria LA9
6ES. **Tel** 0845 124 9971;
+44 1539 726 111
(overseas).
w tourismforall.org.uk

Self-Catering

Bridge Street Global Hospitality
Tel 020 7792 2222.
w bridgestreet.com

Landmark Trust
Shottesbrooke, Maidenhead, Berks SL6 3SW.
Tel 01628 825925.
w landmarktrust.org.uk

Stays in Private Homes

Airbnb
w airbnb.com
At Home in London
70 Black Lion Lane W6
9BE. **Tel** 020 8748 2701.
w athomeinlondon.co.uk
Bed & Breakfast & Homestay Association
8 Kelso Place W8 5OP.
Tel 020 7937 2001.
w bbha.org.uk
Uptown Reservations
8 Kelso Place W8 5QD.
Tel 020 7937 2001.
w uptownres.co.uk
Roomorama
w roomorama.co.uk
TripAdvisor Rentals
w tripadvisor.co.uk/rentals
Wolsey Lodges
9 Market Place, Hadleigh,
Ipswich, Suffolk IP7 5DL.
Tel 01473 822058.
w wolseylodges.com

Chain Hotels

Express by Holiday Inn
Tel 08714234876.
w hiexpress.co.uk/London
easyHotel
w easyhotel.co.uk
Ibis
w ibis.com/hotel-directory/gb/europe/united-kingdom/london/london-hotel.htm
Novotel
w novotel.com
Premier Inn
Tel 0871 527 9222.
w premierinn.com/en/london-hotels.html
Travelodge
Tel 0871 984 8484.
w travelodge.co.uk/uk/London/hotels-in-london
Tune
w tunehotels.com

Hostels

Hostelling International
2nd Floor Gate House,
Fretherne Rd, Welwyn

Garden City, Herts AL8 6RD.
Tel 01707 324170.
w hihostels.com
London Hostels Association
53 Eccleston Sq SW1V
1PG. **Tel** 020 3642 4535.
w lhalondon.com
Youth Hostels Association
Trevelyan House, Dimple
Rd, Matlock, Derbyshire
DE4 3YH. **Tel** 01629
592700.
w yha.org.uk

University Rooms

Imperial College Summer Accommodation Centre
Sherfield Building, Level
3 SW7 2AZ.
Tel 020 7594 9507.
w imperial.ac.uk/visit/summer-accommodation
King's Conference & Vacation Bureau
Tel 020 7848 1700.
w kingsvenues.com
London University Rooms
w universityrooms.com/en/city/London/home

Where to Stay

Luxury

Westminster and the West End

The Athenaeum   £££
116 Piccadilly W1J 7BJ
Tel 020 7499 3464   **Map** 12 E4
W athenaeumhotel.com
An established hotel, but with up-to-date, airy bedrooms and family-friendly apartments. Great on-site spa.

Leicester House   ££
1 Leicester Street WC2H 7BL
Tel 020 3301 8020   **Map** 13 A2
W leicesterhouse.com
Dine at the sumptuous restaurant and stay in one of the calm, white, minimalist rooms.

Claridge's   £££
49 Brook Street W1K 4HR
Tel 020 7629 8860   **Map** 12 E2
W claridges.co.uk
One of London's greats; seamless service and understated luxury in a dazzling Art Deco building. Perfect for a special occasion.

Covent Garden   £££
10 Monmouth Street WC2H 9HB
Tel 020 7806 1000   **Map** 13 B2
W firmdalehotels.com/london/covent-garden-hotel
A vibrant, sexy and designer-dressed hotel from the Firmdale stable. Combines old-world style with metropolitan chic.

Flemings Hotel and Apartments   £££
7–12 Half Moon Street W1J 7BH
Tel 020 7499 0000   **Map** 12 E4
W flemings-mayfair.co.uk
This tranquil oasis is stylish without being too precious. Choose between charming rooms and apartments.

Four Seasons Hotel London at Park Lane   £££
Hamilton Place W1J 7DR
Tel 020 7499 0888   **Map** 12 E4
W fourseasons.com/london
Sumptuously glossy and in a fantastic location, this hotel boasts immaculate service. It also has a stunning glass-walled rooftop spa.

The Ritz   £££
150 Piccadilly W1J 9BR
Tel 020 7493 8181   **Map** 12 F3
W theritzlondon.com
Perfectly preserved in its original Louis XVI style; glamour and glitz rolled into one. Don't miss the famous afternoon tea.

W   £££
10 Leicester Square W1D 6QF
Tel 020 7758 1000   **Map** 13 A2
W wlondon.co.uk
All glass outside, sleek and bright inside, this luxury global brand hotel is the ultimate in cool.

Bloomsbury and Regent's Park

Charlotte Street   £££
15–17 Charlotte Street W1T 1RJ
Tel 020 7806 2000   **Map** 13 A1
W firmdalehotels.com/london/charlotte-street-hotel
The groovy favourite of media folk, with lively public areas and a stylish private cinema.

The Langham   £££
1c Portland Place W1B 1JA
Tel 020 7636 1000   **Map** 12 E1
W langhamhotels.com
A grande dame hotel with an Eastern look. Rooms have a relaxing private-home feel.

The City and the East End

Boundary Rooms   ££
2–4 Boundary Street E2 7DD
(entrance in Redchurch Street)
Tel 020 7729 1051   **Map** 8 D4
W theboundary.co.uk
A converted Victorian warehouse in trendy Shoreditch is the setting for Terence Conran's hotel. It exudes style, from the retro cellar bar to each perfectly designed bedroom. All rooms are bespoke and decorated with designer objects. Don't miss the spectacular views from the rooftop brasserie, which hums on summer weekends.

Individually designed room at Charlotte Street hotel

Shoreditch Rooms   ££
Ebor Street E1 6AW
Tel 020 7739 5040   **Map** 8 D4
W shoreditchhouse.com
An imaginatively renovated warehouse, home to 26 bright, fresh-looking bedrooms decorated in a New England vintage style.

Kensington and Chelsea

The Capital   ££
22–24 Basil Street SW3 1AT
Tel 020 7589 5171   **Map** 11 C5
W capitalhotel.co.uk
All the luxury and service of a grand hotel, but much more intimate and personal. The bedrooms are a good size and traditionally elegant.

Belgraves   £££
20 Chesham Place SW1X 8HQ
Tel 020 7858 0100   **Map** 20 D1
W thompsonhotels.com/hotels/london/belgraves-london
New York "boho" in Belgravia, with bold, eclectic design. There's a terrace with a retractable roof, a buzzy lobby and superb restaurant.

The Halkin by COMO   £££
5 Halkin Street SW1X 7DJ
Tel 020 7333 1100   **Map** 12 D5
W comohotels.com/thehalkin
Welcoming service, fresh flowers, soft lighting and luxurious beds – the perfect place to chill out.

The Levin   £££
28 Basil Street SW3 1AS
Tel 020 7589 6286   **Map** 11 C5
W thelevinhotel.co.uk
A little gem; from the pistachio-coloured reception to the gorgeous, cosy bedrooms.

Mandarin Oriental Hyde Park   £££
66 Knightsbridge SW1X 7LA
Tel 020 7235 2000   **Map** 11 C5
W mandarinoriental.com/london
Mandarin Oriental is a byword for luxury and impeccable Eastern-style service, and this vast Edwardian red-brick pile is no exception. Blending old and new, it has traditional bedrooms with mahogany furniture and marble fireplaces.

The studio suite at the W hotel, Leicester Square

Royal Garden £££
2–24 Kensington High Street W8 4PT
Tel *020 7937 8000* **Map** 10 D5
W royalgardenhotel.co.uk
A 1960s hotel favoured by celebrities and well-suited to families. Go for a room with an unrivalled park view. Service throughout is courteous and very efficient.

Boutique

Westminster and the West End

The Arch ££
50 Great Cumberland Place W1H 7FD
Tel *020 7724 4700* **Map** 11 C2
W thearchlondon.com
Cleverly converted from a terrace of town houses. Bedrooms are stylishly decorated with warm-coloured fabrics and handprinted wallpaper. The restaurant is popular with guests and locals.

Bloomsbury and Regent's Park

Megaro, King's Cross ££
Belgrove Street WC1H 8AB
Tel *020 7843 2222* **Map** 5 C3
W hotelmegaro.co.uk
A buzzing urban hang-out with striking contemporary rooms. Conveniently located close to King's Cross and St Pancras

Montagu Place ££
2–3 Montagu Place W1H 2ER
Tel *020 7467 2777* **Map** 11 C1
W montagu-place.co.uk
Go for a "Comfy", "Swanky" or "Fancy" room. An intimate hotel that stands out from the crowd, with plentiful facilities.

No. Ten Manchester Street ££
10 Manchester Street W1U 4DG
Tel *020 7317 5900* **Map** 12 D1
W tenmanchesterstreethotel.com
A handsome Edwardian town house with a gentleman's club feel. All-weather cigar terrace and comfy bar.

The City and the East End

The Hoxton ££
81 Great Eastern Street EC2A 3HU
Tel *020 7550 1000* **Map** 7 C4
W thehoxton.com
The earlier you book this hip hotel, the less you pay. The vast open-plan lobby has a real buzz.

King's Wardrobe by Bridge Street ££
6 Wardrobe Place EC4V 5AF
Tel *020 7792 2222* **Map** 14 F2
W bridgestreet.com/The_Kings_
Wardrobe_by_BridgeStreet_
Worldwide.htm
Flagship building with apartments, ranging from studios to three bedrooms, all well equipped.

The Zetter Townhouse ££
49–50 St John's Square EC1V 4JJ
Tel *020 7324 4567* **Map** 6 E2
W thezettertownhouse.com
Get your toothpaste and Champagne from the same vending machine at this hip hotel with playful touches. Ultra cool and very welcoming.

Threadneedles £££
5 Threadneedle Street EC2R 8AY
Tel *020 7657 8080* **Map** 15 B2
W hotelthreadneedles.co.uk
A converted bank, this boutique-style hotel has immaculate service and luxurious rooms. A spectacular glass dome crowns the reception area.

Southwark and the South Bank

Bermondsey Square ££
Bermondsey Square, Tower Bridge Road SE1 3UN
Tel *020 7378 2450* **Map** 16 D4
W bermondseysquarehotel.co.uk
Treat yourself to a loft suite and hot tub with a view at this wittily furnished hotel.

DK Choice

London Bridge ££
8–18 London Bridge Street SE1 9SG
Tel *020 7855 2200* **Map** 15 B4
W londonbridgehotel.com
Through the handsome 19th-century entrance, a modern lobby sets the scene for this hip yet intimate four-star hotel. The bedrooms are stylishly decorated, each with a black-and-white bathroom. There's also a well-equipped gym, three restaurant/bars and great weekend rates.

Kensington and Chelsea

The Ampersand ££
10 Harrington Road SW7 3ER
Tel *020 7589 5895* **Map** 19 A2
W ampersandhotel.com
The decor is inspired by nearby museums, with rooms themed around music, science and nature.

Baby ABode Sydney House ££
9–11 Sydney Street SW3 6PU
Tel *020 7376 7711* **Map** 19 A3
W abodehotels.co.uk/chelsea
A chic bolthole; pale pistachio walls, blonde wood floors and Frette linen sheets.

myhotel Chelsea ££
35 Ixworth Place SW3 3QX
Tel *020 7225 7500* **Map** 19 B2
W myhotels.com/my-hotel-chelsea
Designed along Feng Shui principles; you feel a sense of wellbeing as soon as you arrive.

Grand Plaza Serviced Apartments ££
42 Prince's Square W2 4AD
Tel *020 7985 8000* **Map** 10 D2
W grand-plaza.co.uk
Snug studios for couples; airy apartments for groups. Access to the square's gardens is a big plus.

Space Apart Hotel ££
36–37 Kensington Gardens Square W2 4BQ
Tel *020 7908 1340* **Map** 10 D2
W aparthotel-london.co.uk
Practical, comfortable apartments with funky details; a good choice for families.

For more information on types of hotel *see page 287*

Further Afield

Avo   £
82 Dalston Lane E8 3AH
Tel *020 3490 5061*
🌐 avohotel.com
DVDs for rent, memory-foam
beds and a host of thoughtful
extras at this trendy crash pad.

High Road House   ££
162–170 Chiswick High Road W4 1PR
Tel *020 8742 1717*
🌐 highroadhouse.co.uk
Enjoy breakfast in the brasserie,
after a night in a chic,
Scandinavian-inspired room.

Rafayel on the Left Bank   ££
34 Lombard Road SW11 3RF
Tel *020 7801 3600*
🌐 hotelrafayel.com
Large relaxing rooms, a spa
and conscientious staff
single out this eco-friendly
Battersea hotel.

**Town Hall Hotel and
Apartments**   ££
8 Patriot Square E2 9NF
Tel *020 7871 0460*
🌐 townhallhotel.com
Edwardian architecture, Art Deco
interiors and hip furnishings –
a winning combination.

Character

Westminster and the West End

Dean Street Townhouse   ££
69–71 Dean Street W1D 3SE
Tel *020 7434 1775*   **Map** 13 A1
🌐 deanstreettownhouse.com
A dynamic hotel with its Georgian
heritage intact. Lively restaurant
and charming bedrooms.

The Fox Club   ££
46 Clarges Street W1J 7ER
Tel *020 7495 3656*   **Map** 12 E3
🌐 foxclublondon.com
Decorated with eye-catching
fabrics, this charming hotel is
open to non-club members.

Hazlitt's   ££
6 Frith Street W1D 3JA
Tel *020 7434 1771*   **Map** 13 A2
🌐 hazlittshotel.com
Furnished with antiques, busts
and prints, this is a distinctive
hotel with bags of charm.

The Orange   ££
37 Pimlico Road SW1W 8NE
Tel *020 7881 9844*   **Map** 20 D2
🌐 theorange.co.uk
Calls itself a "Public House and
Hotel", but really it's a rustic
restaurant with four cosy rooms.

The polished, elegant exterior and lobby
of the Stafford London

Hotel 41   £££
*41 Buckingham Palace Road
SW1W 0PS*
Tel *020 7300 0041*   **Map** 20 E2
🌐 41hotel.com
A stunning hotel with a clubby
atmosphere, black-and-white
bedrooms and dark wood.

The Goring   £££
Beeston Place SW1W 0JW
Tel *020 7396 9000*   **Map** 20 E1
🌐 thegoring.com
There are liveried doormen and a
lovely private garden at this great
English institution. It's where the
Duchess of Cambridge – then
Kate Middleton – stayed the
night before her wedding.

The Stafford London   £££
16–18 St James's Place SW1A 1NJ
Tel *020 7493 0111*   **Map** 12 F4
🌐 thestaffordlondon.com
A class act. Traditional English
country house furnishings and
an American Bar.

Bloomsbury and Regent's Park

Durrants   ££
26–32 George Street W1H 5BJ
Tel *020 7935 8131*   **Map** 12 D1
🌐 durrantshotel.co.uk
An English classic, from the
venerable panelled entrance
to the tiny snug bar. The
uniformed staff and Edwardian
lobby set the scene for the rest
of the hotel.

Montague on the Gardens   ££
15 Montague Street WC1B 5BJ
Tel *020 7637 1001*   **Map** 5 B5
🌐 montaguehotel.com
Modern, chic and charming, with
attentive, helpful staff. Located
close to the British Museum.

Rough Luxe   ££
1 Birkenhead Street WC1H 8BA
Tel *020 7837 5338*   **Map** 5 C3
🌐 roughluxehotel.co.uk
This quirky hotel boasts original
art and a touch of luxury.

The City and the East End

DK Choice

The Rookery   ££
*12 Peter's Lane, Cowcross Street
EC1M 6DS*
Tel *020 7336 0931*   **Map** 6 F5
🌐 rookeryhotel.com
A romantic venue, The Rookery
consists of three restored
18th-century houses, crammed
with curiosities. Its seductive
bedrooms have antique beds
and bathrooms with roll-top
baths. Downstairs in the foyer
you'll find an open fire.

Kensington and Chelsea

The Gore   ££
190 Queen's Gate SW7 5EX
Tel *020 7584 6601*   **Map** 10 F5
🌐 gorehotel.com
A hotel that explodes with
character; pictures jostle for wall
space; bedrooms are all unique.

Twenty Nevern Square   ££
20 Nevern Square SW5 9PD
Tel *020 7565 9555*   **Map** 17 C2
🌐 20nevernsquare.com
Some deliciously over-the-top
rooms at this calm refuge with
colonial and Asian decor.

Vancouver Studios   ££
30 Prince's Square W2 4NJ
Tel *020 7243 1270*   **Map** 10 D2
🌐 vancouverstudios.co.uk
Elegant modern studios in a
stylish town house, each has a
mini-kitchen with all accessories.

Further Afield

The Alma   £
499 Old York Road, SW18 1TF
Tel *020 8870 2537*
🌐 almawandsworth.com
A Victorian tavern, now one of
Wandsworth's new-breed pub-
restaurants, with 23 rooms.

Bingham   ££
*61–63 Petersham Road, Richmond-
Upon-Thames, Surrey TW10 6UT*
Tel *020 8940 0902*
🌐 thebingham.co.uk
A Georgian town house overlooking the Thames, with a great
restaurant. Located close to
Richmond's shops.

Fox and Grapes ££
9 Camp Road SW19 4UN
Tel *020 8619 1300*
W foxandgrapeswimbledon.co.uk
This chic getaway offers small but
comfy rooms above a gastropub.

The Rose and Crown ££
*199 Stoke Newington Church Street
N16 9ES*
Tel *020 7923 3337*
W roseandcrownn16.co.uk
Stay in a king-sized room above
this classic oak-panelled pub.

Bed & Breakfast

Westminster and the West End

Luna Simone £
47–49 Belgrave Road SW1V 2BB
Tel *020 7834 5897* **Map** 20 F2
W lunasimonehotel.com
Family-run since the 1980s;
home-cooked English breakfast.

Lime Tree ££
135–137 Ebury Street SW1W 9QU
Tel *020 7730 7865* **Map** 20 E2
W limetreehotel.co.uk
Great value, family-run venture.
The rooms boast original 18th-
century features.

The Sumner ££
54 Upper Berkeley Street W1H 7QR
Tel *020 7723 2244* **Map** 11 C1
W thesumner.com
A Georgian town house full of
warmth and charm. Elegantly
decorated throughout.

Bloomsbury and Regent's Park

22 York Street ££
22 York Street W1U 6PX
Tel *.0207 224 2990* **Map** 3 B5
W 22yorkstreet.co.uk
This Georgian terraced house is
filled with character. Rooms are
cosy and individually decorated.

Arosfa ££
83 Gower Street WC1E 6HJ
Tel *020 7636 2115* **Map** 5 A5
W arosfalondon.com
Guests are made to feel like part
of the family at this simple B&B.

Kensington and Chelsea

Hyde Park Rooms £
137 Sussex Gardens W2 2RX
Tel *020 7723 0225* **Map** 11 A1
W hydeparkrooms.com
No-frills rooms (some not en-
suite), all kept admirably spick
and span. Generous breakfasts.

Rhodes £
195 Sussex Gardens W2 2RJ
Tel *020 7262 0537* **Map** 11 A1
W rhodeshotel.com
A warm welcome is assured at
this eclectic hotel. The Super
Deluxe rooms have spa baths.

Amsterdam ££
7 Trebovir Road SW5 9LS
Tel *020 7370 5084* **Map** 17 C3
W amsterdam-hotel.com
A prize-winning B&B with pastel
rooms and apartments. The
garden is perfect in summer.

Aster House ££
3 Sumner Place SW7 3EE
Tel *020 7581 5888* **Map** 19 A2
W asterhouse.com
A peaceful, eco-friendly
sanctuary. Victorian architecture
and traditional furnishings.

Budget

Bloomsbury and Regent's Park

No. 5 Doughty Street ££
5 Doughty Street WC1N 2PL
Tel *020 7373 9120* **Map** 6 D4
W blueprintlivingapartments.com/
no-5-doughty-street
Apartments with pizzazz;
Blueprint Living's complex offers
comfort at reasonable rates.

The City and the East End

**Premier Inn London City
(Tower Hill)** £
24 Prescot Street E1 8BB
Tel *0871 527 8646* **Map** 16 E2
W premierinn.com/en/hotel/
LONCIT/london-city-tower-hill
Plain but pleasant rooms with
comfortable king-size beds.
Bathrooms have power showers.

Kensington and Chelsea

DK Choice

London House Hotel £
*781 Kensington Gardens Square
W2 4DJ*
Tel *0203 788 1814* **Map** 10 D2
W londonhousehotels.com
A smart and stylish hotel
with contemporary decor
throughout, this place is
excellent value for money.
Rooms range from a small
single to the family suite. Great
location close to Paddington
station and Hyde Park.

Southwark and the South Bank

Tune – Westminster £
*118–120 Westminster Bridge Road
SE1 7RW*
Tel *020 7633 9317* **Map** 14 D5
W tunehotels.com
London outpost of a modest
Asian chain. Smart, simple,
spotless accommodation.

**Premier Inn London
County Hall** ££
County Hall, Belvedere Road SE1 7PB
Tel *0871 527 8648* **Map** 13 C5
W premierinn.com/en/hotel/
LONCOU/london-county-hall
Spacious, noise-insulated
bedrooms, some with
river views.

Further Afield

Shandon House Hotel £
*36–38 Church Road,
Richmond- Upon-Thames
TW9 1UA*
Tel *020 8940 5000*
W shandonhouse.com
Modern, clean and affordable
accommodation in one
of London's more genteel
areas.

The traditional interior of the Arosfa B&B

For more information on types of hotel *see page 287*

WHERE TO EAT AND DRINK

Hailed as the world's dining capital, London bursts at the seams with thousands of restaurants, cafés, food markets and gastro-pubs. Perennial favourites and Michelin-starred stalwarts rub shoulders with a burgeoning street food scene, and pop-ups showcase the latest foodie trends. The city thrives on an extraordinary culinary diversity. With a long tradition of Indian, Chinese,

French and Italian restaurants, eating out in London can nowadays take you on a gastronomic journey around the world. Dine on dim sum, feast on Middle Eastern favourites, tuck into a multi-course Italian extravaganza: whatever your tastes, the city has somewhere on every corner to satiate your appetite and the listings on the following pages highlight some of the very best.

Diners at a Leon restaurant *(see p309)*

London Restaurants

The broadest choice of restaurants can be found in Covent Garden, Piccadilly, Mayfair, Soho and Leicester Square, grouped in the listings under Westminster and the West End. Kensington and Chelsea also offer a good range of restaurants, as does Bloomsbury and Regent's Park. In central London, Southwark and the South Bank is always buzzing, with a large variety of riverside restaurants. The City and the East End is home to a wide range of chic and contemporary eateries, and there is a fair selection of highly commended restaurants to be found further afield.

Londoners have long had a tremendously cosmopolitan appetite and visitors will find international favourites presented in every imaginable way. For fine-dining fans, the city boasts an impressive array of restaurants overseen by world-class chefs, such as Angela Hartnett's Italian-inspired Murano *(see p299)* and the Michelin-starred Marcus Wareing at the Berkeley

(see p301). Those who prefer something a little more informal are well served by an assortment of restaurants that buzz with happy patrons tucking into an eclectic menu of British and international classics.

With an international community, the city is home to plenty of restaurants dedicated to specific cuisines. Indian, French, Mexican, Korean: whatever your tastes, the huge range on offer means there is always something different to taste and enjoy. And such is the variety of London's food scene that those with specific requirements need not fear missing out: vegetarians will find at least one option on most menus and should look out for one of the growing number of specialist veggie restaurants (some of which are listed on the following pages).

Other Places to Eat

As well as excellent restaurants, London also has a dynamic café scene, with light meals readily available throughout the day. Visitors on a budget looking for

a simple, tasty meal should head to one of the good-quality chains that have branches all over the capital. They offer a variety of cuisines, such as burgers, pizza, pasta and tapas, and often have seating for large groups. Gastropubs and wine bars are continuingly popular and both serve anything from standard British dishes to Thai curries and more imaginative international food, complemented by global wine lists. For a selection of mainly informal places to eat and drink, including pubs, see pages 308–15.

Tips on Eating Out

Most London restaurants serve lunch between noon and 2:30pm, with dinner from 6:30pm until 11pm, which usually means that last orders are taken at 11pm. Even after

A revolution in "pub grub" has made London's pubs an attractive dining option

Entrance to the Gallery Mess *(see p300)* at the Saatchi Gallery

midnight you can usually find somewhere open to grab a snack. Some restaurants may close for either lunch or dinner at weekends, so it is always best to check opening times first. Many restaurants and some cafés and brasseries serve alcohol without restriction.

If you plan to eat out on a Sunday be aware that many pubs and restaurants (including some fine-dining establishments) serve only a traditional British Sunday lunch (typically a roasted meat with vegetables).

Most formal restaurants insist on a smart-casual dress code (no jeans, trainers or shorts). Some insist on a jacket; a few on jacket and tie.

Booking is advisable, especially at gourmet restaurants and between Friday and Sunday. Smoking is banned in all London pubs and restaurants.

Price and Service

As London is one of the world's most expensive cities, restaurant prices can often seem exorbitant to visitors, with an average three-course meal and a few glasses of house wine at a medium-priced central London restaurant costing around £40–£60 per person. Many restaurants have set-price menus which are generally significantly less expensive than ordering à la carte. Similarly, various West

End restaurants serve pre-theatre set menus (typically from around 5:30–6pm). Prices may be lower (around £20–£30 a head) at smaller, more modest restaurants, wine bars and pubs.

Before ordering, check the small print on the menu. Prices may include an optional service charge (10–15 per cent). If this isn't included, you may be asked to "add gratuity" when paying with a card machine, though there is some argument that a cash tip is more likely to find its way into the staff's pockets.

Eating with Children

Many London restaurants, particularly chain restaurants and fast-food establishments, welcome children. A few venues, such as The Rainforest Café on Shaftesbury Avenue, create a unique dining experience especially for kids.

With the growing trend for a more informal style of dining, more restaurants, including those at the top end of the market, have become child-friendly, offering children's menus, smaller portions and high chairs. Some provide colouring books and even put on live entertainment to keep the little diners happy. See page 353 for suggested places that cater particularly for children.

Recommended Restaurants

The restaurants on pages 296–307 of this guide cover a comprehensive range of cuisines suited to those on different budgets. With such an eclectic mix of restaurants on offer, the listings showcase the best of their kind, from Spanish tapas bars to formal fine-dining establishments. Where a restaurant is in some way exceptional – perhaps for its exquisite food, good-value menu or family-friendly facilities – it has been highlighted as a DK Choice.

The listings have been divided into six key areas of London, covering a broader span of the capital than the 14 areas within the *Area by Area* section: Westminster and the West End, Kensington and Chelsea, Bloomsbury and Regent's Park, Southwark and the South Bank, the City and the East End; there are also a number further afield that merit a special trip out of the city. Within these areas, places are listed alphabetically in each of the three price categories.

Everywhere listed here offers sit-down meals. If you are looking for a light bite in a more informal setting, see pages 308–15 for dependable food chains, gastropubs, street food markets and cafés.

Bibendum, a popular choice for sophisticated French cuisine *(see p301)*

The Flavours of London

Reflecting the capital's multicultural population and cosmopolitan nature, the dishes on London's menus take inspiration from all parts of the globe and draw on a rich range of flavours. Middle Eastern mezze, aromatic Chinese dim sum, spicy Indian curries: all are as familiar on the city's dining tables as the ubiquitous meat and two veg. Despite the representation of global cuisines, "modern British cooking" best describes much of what's on offer in the city, with restaurants reviving the country's classic dishes using home-grown ingredients and cooking international favourites in a truly British style.

Chef and customer at Clerkenwell's St John restaurant

The Marketplace

Nowhere better exemplifies the city's love affair with good food than Borough Market (see p335). Its busy stalls offering both regional and continental food are a microcosm of what Londoners today like to eat. There is produce from all over Britain – English and Irish cheeses, Scottish beef, Welsh lamb, Devon cider, Suffolk oysters – as well as from the rest of the world. Visitors can snack as they browse, on anything from Cornish scallops to grilled Spanish chorizo.

Modern British Food

London menus will often detail the provenance of ingredients with obvious pride. Ancient or "rare" breeds of cattle are name-checked, such as Gloucester Old Spot pork. Once-overlooked, old-fashioned ingredients like rhubarb and black (blood) pudding are being used in creative new ways. Seasonal and organic produce is also taking centre stage. The new breed of gastropubs were among the first to adopt these

Dorstone (Dorset)   Waterloo (Berkshire)   Blue Stilton

Ashdown (Sussex)   Golden Cross (Sussex)

Selection of English farmhouse cheeses

Traditional English Food

Though global cuisine is now a firm fixture on the London food scene, traditional English dishes are still readily available. Classics such as roast beef, fish and chips, and shepherd's pie have been given a makeover and can be found in many restaurants in the capital as well as in informal gastropubs. For an archetypal national dish, head out early for a "full English breakfast": an assortment of fried sausages, eggs, bacon, tomatoes, mushrooms and toast. Popular snacks include pasties and sausage rolls, which can be picked up from food stands and bakeries. For those with a sweet tooth, look out for old-fashioned puddings such as treacle tart, jam roly-poly (suet sponge and jam), spotted dick (suet sponge and currants) and fruit crumbles with custard. Teatime may be a thing of the past but many top hotels and boutique cafés offer "cream teas" with scones topped with clotted cream and strawberry jam, cakes and cucumber sandwiches.

Fish and Chips Battered cod or plaice and chips served with tartare sauce. A side order of mushy peas is popular.

Bountiful vegetable stall at London's Borough Market

trends, offering good, imaginative, well-prepared and sensibly priced food, as well as fine wines and beers, in the relaxed surroundings of the traditional London pub.

London's historic seafood favourites – cockles in vinegar, whelks and jellied eels – are increasingly hard to find but, as capital of an island nation, the city offers many fine fish restaurants. Many places selling seafood, from restaurants to market stalls, are conscious of the environment and advocate sustainable fishing, so patrons should look out for seafood sourced from approved suppliers. As a consequence, it's very likely that you'll spot local catches such as bream, bass, sole and gurnard on the menu alongside cod and haddock. Salmon is often billed as wild and scallops as diver-caught.

International Flavours

Such is the diversity of the city's restaurants that there really is something for everyone in London. Britain has long had a love affair with both Asian and Indian food, and some of the best examples of each can be found across the capital. While chicken tikka masala has been voted the nation's favourite dish (invented here, the legend goes, to satisfy the national passion for

Market stall-holders offering prepared food follow high hygiene standards

gravy by pairing tandoori dry-roasted meat with a mild, creamy sauce), regional Indian food is now to the fore, notably southern cuisine strong on coconut, fish and fruits. Spanish and Mexican-style tapas and Mediterranean and Middle Eastern-style mezze are all prominent, and no area is without its Italian ristorante. Street food stalls and markets provide a taste of the global flavours prevalent across the city and while there is a variety of foods everywhere, there are pockets of London dominated by a particular cuisine.

WHERE TO EAT

Asian Chinatown in Soho is, of course, home to an impressive collection of Chinese restaurants, but also offers excellent Japanese and Vietnamese food.

Indian Southall in Ealing is home to the largest Indian community in London.

Caribbean Traditional Caribbean dishes such as curried goat, plantain and jerk chicken, are cooked to perfection in Brixton, south London.

Spanish Tapas restaurants are increasingly popular in the West End, serving a taste of the Mediterranean in small dishes.

Italian Possibly one of London's most popular cuisines, an array of traditional Italian restaurants surrounds St Peter's Italian Church near Holborn.

Shepherd's Pie Minced lamb slow-cooked with diced vegetables, topped off with creamy mashed potato.

Roast Beef Horseradish sauce is a traditional accompaniment, as are crisp Yorkshire puddings made of batter.

Eton Mess Named for the elite public school, a crushed mix of fresh strawberries, whipped cream and meringue.

Where to Eat and Drink

Westminster and the West End

Belgo Centraal
Belgian £
Map 13 B2
50 Earlham Street WC2H 9LJ
Tel *020 7813 2233*
A bustling branch of a quirky chain, where staff dress as monks. Team the excellent lobster or *moules frites* with a Trappist beer.

Brasserie Zedel
French £
Map 13 A2
20 Sherwood Street W1F 7ED
Tel *020 7734 4888*
This authentic French-styled restaurant complete with a cocktail bar is a diner's delight. Excellent well-priced dishes and frequent live jazz.

Kulu Kulu Sushi
Japanese £
Map 13 A2
76 Brewer Street W1F 9TU
Tel *020 7734 7316*
Sit on a stool in the bar area and help yourself to tasty sushi and sashimi from a conveyor belt. Perfect for a quick bite.

Princi
Italian £
Map 13 A2
135 Wardour Street W1F 0UT
Tel *020 7478 8888*
A stylish Milan import. Help yourself to handmade bread, wood-fired pizzas and mouthwatering pastries; eat at communal tables or at the gleaming counters.

Regency Café
British £
Map 21 A2
17–19 Regency Street SW1P 4BY
Tel *020 7821 6596*
A 1950s-style "caff", featured in the movie *Layer Cake*. Heavenly hash browns and eggs Benedict for breakfast or brunch.

DK Choice

Sagar
Indian Vegetarian £
Map 13 C2
31 Catherine Street WC2B 5JS
Tel *020 7836 6377*
Subtle flavours distinguish a broad range of dishes from South India at this simple, canteen-style restaurant. Curries are freshly made and the lunch *thali* (selection of small dishes) not only tastes good, it's also great value for money. Don't overlook the delicious crispy *dosas* (potato-filled pancakes). Efficient, friendly service.

Soho Joe
Mediterranean £
Map 13 A1
22–5 Dean Street W1D 3RY
Tel *07534 134398*
Thin-crust pizzas are the stars of the show at this great-value Italian. Pasta, burgers and toasted sandwiches also feature.

Tokyo Diner
Japanese £
Map 13 B2
2 Newport Place WC2H 7JJ
Tel *020 7287 8777*
Authentic food, including katsu curry, sushi and bento boxes, at this functional three-storey diner. Strictly no tipping.

Wahaca
Mexican £
Map 13 B3
66 Chandos Place WC2N 4HG
Tel *020 7240 1883*
Colourful and cool, this is the original branch of a chain serving a seasonal menu of tasty Mexican street food. No bookings.

The 10 Cases
British ££
Map 13 B1
16 Endell Street WC2H 9BD
Tel *020 7836 6801*
Outstanding wines – ten reds,

Price Guide
For a three-course meal per person, including tax, service, and half a bottle of house wine.

£	under £30
££	£30–£60
£££	Over £60

ten whites – plus three choices per course at this exciting restaurant. British cooking with European overtones.

Andrew Edmunds
European ££
Map 13 A2
46 Lexington Street W1F 0LW
Tel *020 7437 5708*
A tiny, candlelit, romantic retreat. Imaginative dishes, including well-balanced seafood and game, feature on a daily-changing menu.

Barrafina
Spanish tapas ££
Map 13 A2
54 Frith Street W1D 4SL
Tel *020 7440 1456*
Take pot luck at this hip joint – there are just 23 bar stools and no reservations. Fabulous, intensely flavoured tapas.

Bocca di Lupo
Italian ££
Map 13 A2
12 Archer Street W1D 7BB
Tel *020 7734 2223*
A small place (only 14 tables) with a big Italian heart. Chef Jacob Kennedy specializes in robust, little-known traditional regional recipes.

Chisou
Japanese ££
Map 12 F2
4 Princes Street W1B 2LE
Tel *020 7629 3931*
Unfussy decor teamed with delectable sushi at this bona fide Japanese bistro. There's also a mind-blowing selection of saké.

DK Choice

Clos Maggiore
European ££
Map 13 B2
33 King Street WC2E 8JD
Tel *020 7379 9696*
For a magical experience, try for a table in the courtyard conservatory at Clos Maggiore, with its blossom-laden branches. On balmy evenings, the roof is opened to the stars, while a fire is lit when it's chilly – sheer romance. French regional food inspires the modern European cooking. Fixed-price pre- and post-theatre menus are quite a bargain.

The traditional dining rooms of Clos Maggiore

The tables double up as touch-screen menus at Asian-inspired Inamo

Dehesa
Tapas   ££
Map 12 F2
25 Ganton Street W1F 9BP
Tel *020 7494 4170*
A buzzy vibe paired with stand-out tapas. Make sure you taste its famous charcuterie and signature dish – stuffed courgette flower.

Al Duca
Italian   ££
Map 13 A3
4–5 Duke of York Street SW1Y 6LA
Tel *020 7839 3090*   **Closed** *Sun*
A reasonably priced and popular local. Using the freshest of ingredients, classic Italian dishes are given a modern twist.

Gopals of Soho
Indian   ££
Map 13 A2
12 Bateman Street W1 5TD
Tel *020 7434 1621*
Come to this traditional family-run curry house for the intense flavours of the expertly spiced food. Excellent vegetarian *thalis*.

Haozhan
Chinese   ££
Map 13 A2
8 Gerrard Street W1D 5PJ
Tel *020 7434 3838*
Try delicate black cod dumplings or wasabi prawns – a world away from the standard sweet-and-sour staples.

Hard Rock Café
American   ££
Map 12 E4
150 Old Park Lane W1K 1QZ
Tel *020 7514 1700*
Try American classics at this legend with its fascinating collection of rock memorabilia. Still rocking after more than 40 years.

Inamo
Asian fusion   ££
Map 13 A2
134–6 Wardour Street W1F 8ZP
Tel *020 7851 7051*
An Oriental eatery with a difference. Order your meal on a touch-screen pad and play games while you wait.

Mildred's
Vegetarian   ££
Map 13 A2
45 Lexington Street W1F 9AN
Tel *020 7494 1634*   **Closed** *Sun*
Drawing on a range of cuisines, the inspired vegetarian dishes at this popular restaurant are fit to convert the most confirmed carnivore. Try the ale and porcini mushroom pie. No bookings.

Nopi
Middle Eastern   ££
Map 12 F2
21–2 Warwick Street W1B 5NE
Tel *020 7494 9584*
Cookery writer Yotam Ottolenghi's grown-up restaurant. A blend of aromatic flavours, bold colours and exciting textures in dishes designed for sharing. The menu changes according to the season.

The Northall
British   ££
Map 13 B3
Corinthia Hotel, 10 Northumberland Avenue WC2N 5AE
Tel *020 7321 3100*
Accomplished cooking by head chef Garry Hollihead, served in a vast dining room. Try the set Theatre Menu before or after a show at the nearby Playhouse.

Noura
Lebanese   ££
Map 20 E1
16 Hobart Place SW1W 0HH
Tel *020 7235 9696*
Exceptional *mezzes* and kebabs at the flagship of an award-winning chain. Classy decor and a tempting menu with plenty to choose from.

Patara
Thai   ££
Map 13 A2
115 Greek Street W1D 4DP
Tel *020 7437 1071*
An enticing all-rounder, spread over two dimly lit, romantic floors. Specialities include several prawn dishes, each an explosion of flavour.

El Pirata
Tapas   ££
Map 12 E4
5–6 Down Street W1J 7AQ
Tel *020 7491 3810*   **Closed** *Sun*
There's a deft hand in the kitchen at this lively, laid-back restaurant. All the classic Spanish and Portuguese favourites are on offer.

DK Choice

The Portrait
British   ££
Map 13 B3
National Portrait Gallery, 2 St Martin's Place WC2H 0HE
Tel *020 7312 2490*
Spot London's famous monuments from a window seat at this top-floor restaurant. The excellent food served here is contemporary British: the seabass with marsh samphire stands out. The main dining area is smart and modern, in complete contrast to the historical surroundings. Before or after your meal, be sure to take a turn around the splendid National Portrait Gallery.

Rasa
Indian   ££
Map 12 E2
6 Dering Street W1S 1AD
Tel *020 7629 1346*   **Closed** *Sun*
Unusual and exquisitely fragrant specialities from Kerala, each served on a huge fresh banana leaf. The choice of vegetarian and fish dishes is exceptional. Rasa's original branch can be found in Stoke Newington, north London.

Refuel
British   ££
Map 13 A2
The Soho Hotel, 4 Richmond Mews W1D 3DH
Tel *020 7559 3007*
Rub shoulders with the glitterati at this stylish media-land hang-out. A diverse menu of modern European cuisine. Great service.

Suda Thai
Thai   ££
Map 13 B2
St Martin's Courtyard, 23 Slingsby Place WC2E 9AB
Tel *020 7240 8010*
Award-winning Thai restaurant with plenty of choice. Opt for a selection of Small Bites and Small Bowls to share.

Terroirs
Mediterranean   ££
Map 13 B3
5 William IV Street WC2N 4DW
Tel *020 7036 0660*   **Closed** *Sun*
An impressive selection of wines, teamed with wholesome organic food (pork, snails, lentils, mush-rooms and charcuterie). Reminiscent of a Parisian wine bar.

For more information on types of restaurants *see page 293*

The elegant afternoon tea at The Wolseley

Thai Pot ££
Thai **Map** 13 B2
1 Bedfordbury WC2N 4BP
Tel *020 7379 4580* **Closed** *Sun &
bank hol Mon*
Thai staples full of fragrant
flavour. Dashes of warm colour
jazz up the sleek, contemporary
decoration.

Vasco and Piero's Pavilion ££
Italian **Map** 13 A2
15 Poland Street W1F 8QE
Tel *020 7437 8774* **Closed** *Sun*
Home-made pasta is used in
their own excellent recipes, often
with truffles when in season.
Umbrian specialities, such as pork
and lentils, are favourites.

Wild Food Café ££
Vegetarian **Map** 13 B1
14 Neals Yard WC2H 9DP
Tel *020 7419 2014*
Watch your food prepared right
in front of you in this cool and
quirky café. They proudly use
locally sourced produce, so
be sure to ask for the week's
specials. There's always a choice
of vegan dishes.

The Wolseley ££
European **Map** 12 F3
160 Piccadilly W1J 9EB
Tel *020 7499 6996*
The glorious 1920s Wolseley
Motors car showroom makes a
stunning home for this glamorous
café/restaurant. The afternoon
tea is legendary.

Yalla Yalla ££
Lebanese **Map** 13 A2
1 Green's Court W1F 0HA
Tel *020 7287 7663*
Be transported to Beirut at this
little gem, where the spicy street
food packs a punch. Heartier
meals are also on offer.

Asia de Cuba £££
Fusion **Map** 13 B2
45 St Martin's Lane WC2N 4HX
Tel *020 7300 5588*
Combines Latin and Asian
cuisine, served sharing-style in a
high-energy, sophisticated and
yet relaxed environment.

Atelier de Joël Robuchon £££
French **Map** 13 B2
13–15 West Street WC2H 9NE
Tel *020 7010 8600*
Try for a front-row seat at the
Japanese-inspired counter in
this contemporary Michelin-
starred temple to modern
French cuisine.

Bellamy's £££
French **Map** 12 E3
18 Bruton Place W1J 6LY
Tel *020 7491 2727* **Closed** *Sun*
Patrons can dine in the quietly
traditional dining room or the
clubby Oyster Bar. Exclusively
French wines accompany a well-
executed menu.

Bentley's Oyster Bar and Grill £££
Seafood **Map** 12 F3
11 Swallow Street W1B 4DG
Tel *020 7734 4756* **Closed** *Sun*
A civilized island of calm, in
business since 1916. Chef
Richard Corrigan's inventive
creations keep it firmly on the
map. There are plenty of meat
dishes if you're not in the mood
for seafood.

Le Caprice £££
International **Map** 12 F3
*Arlington House, Arlington Street
SW1A 1RJ*
Tel *020 7629 2239*
Classy, yet vibrant rendezvous for
media types, where everyone is
made to feel like a star by the
delightful staff. Bistro food.

Cecconi's £££
Italian **Map** 12 F3
5A Burlington Gardens W1S 3EP
Tel *020 7434 1500*
Expect handmade pasta and the
freshest ingredients. Gets busy at
peak times, so try to book in
advance if you can.

Cinnamon Club £££
Indian **Map** 21 B1
*The Old Westminster Library,
30–32 Great Smith Street SW1P 3BU*
Tel *020 7222 2555* **Closed** *Sun*
Delicately spiced North Indian
cuisine, using the freshest
ingredients. Housed in a former
library with an atmosphere of
hushed sophistication.

DK Choice

CUT at 45 Park Lane £££
Steakhouse **Map** 12 D4
45 Park Lane W1K 1PN
Tel *020 7493 4554*
US celebrity chef Wolfgang
Puck's first European venture is
a paradise for carnivores.
Choose a raw cut from a platter
brought to your table before it
is whisked away and expertly
cooked. Grand surroundings
and well-informed waiters.

Le Gavroche £££
French **Map** 12 D2
43 Upper Brook Street W1K 7QR
Tel *020 7408 0881* **Closed** *Sun*
Come to Michel Roux Jr's
flagship restaurant for
exceptional haute cuisine and
supremely professional service.
The set lunch is well priced.

Hakkasan Mayfair £££
Chinese **Map** 12 E3
17 Bruton Street W1J 6QB
Tel *020 7907 1888*
Glitzy, adeptly lit showcase for
exquisite Cantonese cuisine,
including some of the finest dim
sum you're likely to taste.

DK Choice

J Sheekey £££
Fish and seafood **Map** 13 B2
28–32 St Martin's Court WC2N 4AL
Tel *020 7240 2565*
London's finest fish restaurant
dates back to the 1890s. The
wonderfully varied menu
consists of responsibly sourced
fish, oysters and shellfish. Most
fun is to sit on a high stool at
the horseshoe-shaped bar for
the signature oysters and
Champagne. Or dine in the
elegant banquette seating area
and admire the open kitchen.

The Lanesborough £££
Italian   Map 12 D5
*The Lanesborough Hotel, Hyde Park
Corner SW1X 7TA*
Tel *020 7333 7254*
If you're celebrating, push
the boat out and order the
impressive seven-course tasting
menu. The Venetian-style dining
room is sumptuous, and is lit
by a glass-domed roof during
the day and elegant chandeliers
at night.

Murano £££
European   Map 12 E3
20 Queen Street W1J 5PP
Tel *020 7495 1127*   **Closed** *Sun*
The clue is in the name: celebrated
chef Angela Hartnett's sublime
cooking is Venetian influenced.
Nothing disappoints at this
Michelin-starred restaurant, from
amuse-bouches to *petits fours*.

Nobu £££
Japanese   Map 12 E4
*Metropolitan Hotel W1,
19 Old Park Lane W1K 1LB*
Tel *020 7447 4747*
Sample beautifully prepared
sashimi, tempura and many
more contemporary, ground-
breaking dishes at this Japanese
restaurant. The seafood and fish
are of the highest quality.

La Petite Maison £££
French   Map 12 E2
53–54 Brook's Mews W1K 4EG
Tel *020 7495 4774*
Come to this exhilarating spot in
a group; the small Mediterranean
dishes and southern French
flavours combine seasonal
ingredients and are perfect
for sharing.

Pollen Street Social £££
British   Map 12 F2
10 Pollen Street W1S 1NQ
Tel *020 7290 7600*   **Closed** *Sun*
Opened by Gordon Ramsay
protégé Jason Atherton in 2011,
this Michelin-starred restaurant
focuses on British-sourced
ingredients and seasonal
produce. The food is ravishing
– and there are menus for vegetarians and vegans. The set-
menu is reasonably priced.

The Ritz Restaurant £££
British   Map 12 F3
150 Piccadilly W1J 9BR
Tel *020 7300 2370*
The world-renowned Piccadilly
hotel boasts a glamorous dining
room decorated with ceiling
frescoes, marble columns and
floor-to-ceiling windows. The
impressive cuisine is classic and
based on British ingredients.

Rules £££
British   Map 13 C2
35 Maiden Lane WC2E 7LB
Tel *020 7836 5314*
Robust British food in an opulent
setting – rib of beef, oysters and
game from its own country
estate – at the capital's oldest
restaurant, established in 1798.

Scott's £££
Fish and seafood   Map 12 D3
20 Mount Street W1 2HE
Tel *020 7495 7309*
Join the league of celebrities
who have dined here, including
Marilyn Monroe. Its sensational
seafood makes it as popular as
ever. The roasted shellfish platters
are outstanding.

The Square £££
French   Map 12 E3
6–10 Bruton Street W1J 6PU
Tel *020 7495 7100*
A luxurious haunt of wine-lovers
and foodies alike. All down to its
encyclopedic wine list and
complex, wonderful food.

Veeraswamy £££
Indian   Map 12 F3
*Victory House, 99 Regent Street
W1B 4RS*
Tel *020 7734 1401*
There's a mix of contemporary
and classic cooking at this
London institution, which opened
in 1926.

Yauatcha £££
Chinese   Map 13 A2
15 Broadwick Street W1F 0DL
Tel *020 7494 8888*
A reinterpretation of a traditional
Chinese teahouse, serving sublime
dim sum and, as a surprise bonus,
exquisite European-style pâtisserie.

Kensington
and Chelsea

DK Choice

Alounak £
Persian   Map 10 D2
44 Westbourne Grove W2 5SH
Tel *020 7229 4158*
Queues often snake down the
street, so popular is this
bazaar-style café. It specializes
in deliciously light Middle
Eastern food at low prices.
Inside, it's all bare wood tables
and exposed brick walls.
There's no wine on sale, so
bring your own. The presence
of so many Iranians dining
here speaks for itself.

Buona Sera Jam £
Italian   Map 19 A4
289 King's Road SW3 5EW
Tel *020 7352 8827*
A lively trattoria that's fun for
all the family. You have to climb
miniature ladders to reach the
top-tier tables. The pizzas
are terrific.

Café Mona Lisa £
French   Map 18 E5
417 King's Road SW10 0LR
Tel *020 7376 5447*
A much-loved neighbourhood
café with friendly service and a
warm feel. Specials chalked up
on the blackboards are always
a good option.

Jak's £
Mediterranean   Map 19 B2
77 Walton Street SW3 2HT
Tel *020 7584 3441*
Choose from an array of healthy,
organic dishes and tempting
desserts and eat in the
diminutive country-style
back room.

Raison d'Etre £
European   Map 18 F2
18 Bute Street SW7 3EX
Tel *020 7584 5008*   **Closed** *Sun*
They bake their own bread at
this very French, very popular
café. Sandwiches, filled with
super fresh ingredients, are
delicious.

The Abingdon ££
International   Map 17 C1
54 Abingdon Road W8 6AP
Tel *020 7937 3339*
A converted pub with a refined
feel. Try to secure one of the
comfortable booths for high-end,
brasserie-style food.

The sleek interior of Hakkasan Mayfair, in
one of London's most exclusive areas

For more information on types of restaurants *see page 293*

Bar Boulud £££
French   **Map** 11 C5
Mandarin Oriental Hyde Park,
66 Knightsbridge SW1X 7LA
Tel *020 7201 3899*
The look is chic but the mood
relaxed at US star chef Daniel
Boulud's London venture.
A French-inspired bistro with
unforgettable terrines.

The Belvedere £££
French   **Map** 9 B5
Holland Park (off Abbotsbury Road)
W8 6LU
Tel *020 7602 1238*
Enjoy modern European fare in
a sumptuous former ballroom
overlooking lawns and flower
gardens. A treat, whether you
eat inside or out.

Big Easy £££
American   **Map** 19 A4
332–334 King's Road SW3 5UR
Tel *020 7352 4071*
Specializing in lobster, ribs and
great live music, this restaurant is
always heaving and has a terrific
atmosphere. Book ahead to avoid
disappointment.

Bill's £££
European   **Map** 10 D5
Kensington Arcade, 123 Kensington
High Street W8 5SF
Tel *020 7937 1482*
From small beginnings as a
grocery shop, Bill's has grown
into a much-loved restaurant
chain, with delicious meals
served throughout the day.

Bluebird £££
European   **Map** 19 A4
350 King's Road SW3 5UU
Tel *020 7559 1000*
This ever-popular restaurant
serves light British dishes made
from seasonal ingredients. It has
a café, bar, a food store and a
wine cellar.

Caraffini £££
Italian   **Map** 20 D3
61–3 Lower Sloane Street
SW1 8DH
Tel *020 7259 0235*   **Closed** *Sun &*
bank hol Mon
This old favourite is still hopping
at lunchtimes. Plump for the
lobster taglierini or one of
the specials.

Chez Patrick £££
French   **Map** 18 D1
7 Stratford Road W8 6RF
Tel *020 7937 6388*
Front-of-house owner Patrick gives
excellent advice on ordering at
this intimate restaurant. Classic
French recipes, mostly fish,
flawlessly executed.

E&O £££
Asian fusion   **Map** 9 A2
14 Blenheim Crescent W11 1NN
Tel *020 7229 5454*
Dine on dim sum, tempura, sushi
or sashimi in glossy black
surroundings. Specials might
include pad thai or crispy sea
bass. Dim sum is available all day
at the bar.

The Enterprise £££
European   **Map** 19 B2
35 Walton Street SW3 2HU
Tel *020 7584 3148*
A humble local pub that has
been converted into a well-
groomed restaurant/bar.
Don't miss the impeccably
cooked squid and courgette
tempura starter.

Ffiona's £££
British   **Map** 10 D4
51 Kensington Church Street W8 4BA
Tel *020 7937 4152*
Patrons are made to feel right at
home by the friendly staff here.
The menu is full of home-cooked
favourites; definitely worth
visiting for the Sunday roast.

Gallery Mess £££
European   **Map** 19 C2
Saatchi Gallery, Duke Of York's HQ,
King's Road SW3 4RY
Tel *020 7730 8135*
A great spot for lunch after an
exhibition. Try for the most
attractive tables, in the airy
cloister, which overlook a leafy
square. Appetizing lunches.

Hunan £££
Chinese   **Map** 20 D2
51 Pimlico Road SW1W 8NE
Tel *020 7730 5712*   **Closed** *Sun*
Taiwanese tapas-size portions
keep arriving at your table, as
fiery or mild as you like, until
you're full. Try the signature dish
of hearty broth with minced
pork, mushroom and ginger.

Kensington Place £££
Fish   **Map** 9 C4
201 Kensington Church Street
W8 7LX
Tel *020 7727 3184*
Fresh decoration and a classic
menu, including superb beer-
battered fish and chips, game
and steaks at this famous
goldfish bowl brasserie.

Kitchen W8 £££
British   **Map** 17 C1
11–13 Abingdon Road W8 6AH
Tel *020 7937 0120*
A benchmark for quality: head
chef Philip Howard's creative
Michelin-starred cooking
served in a sleek, comfortable

Oriental minimalist decor at the stylish
Asian fusion restaurant E&O

environment. And it won't
break the bank.

Maroush £££
Lebanese   **Map** 19 B1
38 Beauchamp Place SW3 1NU
Tel *020 7581 5434*
The perfect spot for a late-
night bite; tender, tasty grilled
dishes are available till 5am.
Fine dining on the first floor.
Branches on Edgware Road
and Vere Street have belly
dancing and live music.

Le Metro at the Levin Hotel £££
British   **Map** 11 C5
28 Basil Street SW3 1AS
Tel *020 7589 6286*
A basement brasserie with
delectable food and the
ambience of a contemporary
European tearoom. It has comfy
banquettes and an open kitchen.
Feels like a well-kept secret.

The Painted Heron £££
Indian   **Map** 19 A5
112 Cheyne Walk SW10 0DJ
Tel *020 7351 5232*
Not a run-of-the-mill Indian
restaurant. A smartly modern
room is the setting for succulent
dishes using unconventional
ingredients, such as game, wild
sea trout, black cod and soft-
shell crab. Spicing is complex
but not overstated. For the
health conscious, there's a
vegetarian menu based on
Ayurvedic principles.

La Poule au Pot £££
French   **Map** 20 E2
231 Ebury Street SW1W 8UT
Tel *020 7730 7763*
Full of romance and rustic
French charm, which
complements the honest
cooking. All the classics are
on the menu, such as boeuf
bourguignon and tarte tatin.

Rossopomodoro
Italian   ££
          Map 18 F4
214 Fulham Road SW10 9NB
Tel *020 7352 7677*
Sourcing their ingredients and cooking knowledge directly from Naples, this branch of the family-friendly chain brings a little bit of Italy into the heart of Chelsea. Pizzas are cooked in a spectacular golden-tiled, wood-fired oven. Check out the seasonal menus.

DK Choice

Babylon at the Roof Garden
British   £££
        Map 10 D5
99 Kensington High Street W8 5SA
Tel *020 7368 3993*
The "hanging gardens" overlooked by this fashionable restaurant sprawl high above the street. Eat here and explore three themed areas filled with trees, flamingos and a fish-stocked stream. Enjoy the modern British cuisine and the panorama. Best in summer, when you can dine al fresco on the terrace (though always book ahead).

Bibendum
French   £££
        Map 19 A2
Michelin House, 81 Fulham Road SW3 6RD
Tel *020 7581 5817*
Seasonal food, assiduous service and Michelin House's Art Nouveau stained glass as a stunning backdrop. Head chef Matthew Harris produces classic French food with a strong British influence and 21st-century style.

Blakes
Asian   £££
        Map 18 F3
33 Roland Gardens SW7 3PF
Tel *020 7370 6701*
Fans, orchids and Oriental touches decorate this seductive downstairs sanctuary. The imaginative menu mingles Mediterranean and Eastern flavours. Specials include angel-hair pasta with black truffle.

Dinner
by Heston Blumenthal   £££
British   Map 11 C5
Mandarin Oriental Hyde Park, 66 Knightsbridge SW1X 7LA
Tel *020 7201 3833*
London's most hyped restaurant showcases this celebrity chef's inspired take on classic cuisine. Blumenthal is well known for his innovative recipes and visitors won't be disappointed. Only for those with deep pockets, but unforgettable.

Launceston Place
British   £££
        Map 18 E1
1a Launceston Place W8 5RL
Tel *020 7937 6912*
Imaginative modern cooking in a series of traditional, carpeted rooms: an oasis of calm, where patrons can dine in style. The menu features British classics given a flamboyant twist.

The Ledbury
European   £££
        Map 9 C2
127 Ledbury Road W11 2AQ
Tel *020 7792 9090*
Possibly London's most happening restaurant, the realm of thrilling Australian chef Brett Graham. Expect two-Michelin-starred culinary fireworks.

Marcus
European   £££
        Map 12 D5
The Berkeley Hotel, Wilton Place SW1X 7RL
Tel *020 7235 1200*   **Closed** *Sun*
Sample delectable cooking from superstar chef Marcus Wareing in the dining rooms of the Berkeley Hotel. Two Michelin stars attest to the genius behind the sophisticated fine dining.

One-0-One
Fish and seafood   £££
        Map 11 C5
Sheraton Park Tower Hotel, 101 Knightsbridge SW1X 7RN
Tel *020 7290 7101*
Seafood's the thing at this exquisite restaurant. Try Norwegian halibut or crab in stunning recipes from head chef Pascal Proyart, or the signature crab risotto.

Restaurant Gordon Ramsay £££
French   Map 19 C4
68 Royal Hospital Road SW3 4HP
Tel *020 7352 4441*   **Closed** *Sat & Sun*
Standards remain high at this triple-Michelin-starred shrine to haute cuisine. Eye-wateringly expensive, but worth a treat.

Zuma
Japanese   £££
        Map 11 B5
5 Raphael Street SW7 1DL
Tel *020 7584 1010*
Spot the celebrities at this cool joint, drawn – like everyone – by the divine robata-grilled dishes, tempura, nigiri sushi and sashimi.

Bloomsbury and Regent's Park

Golden Hind
British   £
        Map 12 E1
73 Marylebone Lane W1U 2PN
Tel *020 7486 3644*   **Closed** *Sun*
Devotees claim its fish and chips are unequalled. A welcoming, no-frills family-run place with no licence, but minimal corkage. The home-made fishcakes make an enticing alternative.

DK Choice

Thai Metro
Thai   £
        Map 5 A5
38 Charlotte Street W1T 2NN
Tel *020 7436 4201*
The exemplary Thai cooking at this down-to-earth corner café has made it a smash hit. Choose carefully if you can't take your curries too hot: some of the specialities are guaranteed to make you sweat. Service is speedy and efficient, and the bill shouldn't be a nasty shock.

Burger and Lobster
American   ££
        Map 12 F1
6 Little Portland Street W1W 7JF
Tel *020 7907 7760*
An arty American-style diner with a simple menu: a choice between a burger and lobster, with a selection of bespoke drinks designed to complement both. No reservations.

Rustic charm and traditional French cuisine at La Poule au Pot

For more information on types of restaurants *see page 293*

The Chancery   £££
European   Map 14 E1
9 Cursitor Street EC4A 1LL
Tel *020 7831 4000*   **Closed** *Sun*
A small legal-land treasure,
tempting for lazy lunches.
Fabulous hake, muntjac and
slow-cooked pork belly. Well-
priced too.

Galvin Bistrot de Luxe   ££
French   Map 3 C5
66 Baker Street W1U 7DJ
Tel *020 7935 4007*
You could be in Paris in the
Galvin brothers' high-class bistro.
Beautifully cooked classics in a
room bristling with happy
customers: this is top quality
French cuisine at affordable prices.

Malabar Junction   ££
South Indian   Map 13 B1
107 Great Russell Street WC1B 3NA
Tel *020 7580 5230*
This glass-roofed restaurant is
decorated with wood floors and
wicker chairs. The menu features
specialities from Kerala, all tender,
fragrant and skilfully prepared.

Ragam   ££
South Indian   Map 4 F5
57 Cleveland Street W1T 4JN
Tel *020 7636 9098*
Not much to look at, but this
veteran offers Keralan specialities
zinging with aromatic flavour.
The filled pancakes are
guaranteed to wow. Choose from
side dishes such as beetroot *baji*
or spinach with lentils.

DK Choice

Salt Yard   ££
Tapas   Map 5 A5
54 Goodge Street W1T 4NA
Tel *020 7637 0657*   **Closed** *Sun*
Fans claim this go-to place
offers the best tapas in London.
What's unique is the
combination of Spanish and
Italian cuisines. Fresh, top-
quality ingredients are centre
stage in such delights as duck
and spinach *gnocchetti* and
the signature courgette flowers
stuffed with goat's cheese
and drizzled with honey.
Always heaving.

Vanilla Black   ££
Vegetarian   Map 14 E1
17–18 Tooks Court EC4A 1LB
Tel *020 7242 2622*   **Closed** *Sun*
Exciting and exquisitely
presented vegetarian dishes in
an elegant setting. Deliciously
inventive, the meals prepared
here are proof positive that you
don't need meat.

Diners enjoying lunch on the outdoor
decking at Clerkenwell Kitchen

The White Swan   ££
British   Map 14 E1
108 Fetter Lane EC4A 1ES
Tel *020 7242 9696* **Closed** *Sat & Sun*
You'll find this place above a
no-nonsense pub. The room's
light and sunny, the cooking
sophisticated, with gourmet
twists on pub classics.

Orrery   £££
French   Map 4 D5
*55–7 Marylebone High Street
W1U 5RB*
Tel *020 7616 8000*
Outstanding modern cuisine
on the first floor of a converted
stable block. Great attention
to detail in both cooking and
service. Ask for a table beside
the arched windows.

Pied à Terre   £££
French   Map 5 A5
34 Charlotte Street W1T 2NH
Tel *020 7636 1178*   **Closed** *Sun*
Adventurous and impeccable
food tops the bill at this discreet
haven. A comfortable dining
room and friendly staff.

The Providores and Tapa Room
£££
International fusion   Map 4 D5
109 Marylebone High Street W1U 4RX
Tel *020 7935 6175*
The global fusion food has won
plaudits at this showcase
establishment. For lighter fare,
try the downstairs tapas bar.

Roka   £££
Japanese   Map 5 A5
37 Charlotte Street W1T 1RR
Tel *020 7580 6464*
Sit at the wood counter in this
goldfish bowl restaurant, graze
on luscious sushi and watch the
chefs at the robata grill.

Texture   £££
European   Map 11 C2
34 Portman Street W1H 7BY
Tel *020 7224 0028* **Closed** *Mon & Sun*
Bold, experimental cookery from
Icelandic chef Agnar Sverrisson.
Expect to find cod, lamb and
herbs from his homeland.

The City and the East End

Cây Tre   £
Vietnamese   Map 7 A4
301 Old Street EC1V 9LA
Tel *020 7729 8662*
The menu's short, but dishes
are authentic and high quality.
Surprises include Cornish
scallops and anchovied chicken
wings, plus unusual combinations
like the beef *carpaccio* and
tamarind soup special.

Clerkenwell Kitchen   £
British   Map 6 E4
27–31 Clerkenwell Close EC1R 0AT
Tel *020 7101 9959* **Closed** *Sat & Sun,
Mon–Fri pm*
Organic produce, gutsy home
cooking and appealingly modern
brick-and-wood surroundings.
Open at lunchtimes only.

Kolossi Grill   £
Greek   Map 6 E4
56–60 Rosebery Avenue EC1R 4RR
Tel *020 7278 5758*   **Closed** *Sun*
Home-made Cypriot classics
have been served in this cosy,
unpretentious restaurant for
more than 50 years. Service is
warm and friendly.

Lahore Kebab House   £
Pakistani   Map 16 E1
2–10 Umberston Street E1 1PY
Tel *020 7481 9737*
A traditional but spartan Pakistani
spot, open late and with the
kitchen on view. Spiced curries
and kebabs set tastebuds
tingling in this warehouse-style
space. Bring your own alcohol.

The smart interior of Salt Yard, serving
Spanish and Italian tapas

De Palo's £
Italian Map 14 F2
8 Bride Court EC4Y 8DU
Tel *020 7583 8440* **Closed** *Sat & Sun*
Fresh ingredients and authentic
Sicilian flavours are the stars at
this intimate, family-owned
restaurant. Try the amazing
tortiglioni special.

Tayyabs £
Punjabi Map 16 F1
83 Fieldgate Street E1 1JU
Tel *020 7247 6400*
A local favourite serving delicious
spiced curries and sizzling mixed
grills. Be sure to book ahead to
avoid the very long queues.

Boho Mexica ££
Mexican Map 8 D5
151–3 Commercial Street E1 6BJ
Tel *020 7388 8418*
Authentic Mexican dining
experience with a friendly staff,
a lively atmosphere and huge
selection of dishes.

DK Choice

Brawn ££
French Map 8 E3
49 Columbia Road E2 7RG
Tel *020 7729 5692*
Big, bold, full-bodied flavours
can be found in abundance in
Brawn's seasonal cuisine. Dishes
you might find on the daily
menu are venison pie, pig's
trotters and ceps with
Bordelaise sauce. Accompany
your choice with one of the
many organic wines. The
industrial-rustic dining room
oozes with charm.

Le Café du Marché ££
French Map 6 F5
22 Charterhouse Square EC1M 6DX
Tel *020 7608 1609* **Closed** *Sun*
Very French; a hideaway with
accomplished classic cooking
and a simple, stylish look.

Carnevale ££
Vegetarian Map 7 A4
135 Whitecross Street EC1Y 8JL
Tel *020 7250 3452* **Closed** *Sun*
Stellar culinary creations in a
modest little café. Delicious
Middle Eastern-inspired risottos,
casseroles and curries.

The Culpeper ££
British Map 8 D5
40 Commercial Street E1 6LP
Tel *020 7247 5371*
Head up to the first floor of this
pub for an intimate three-course
meal (the menu changes daily);
on the next floor up you will
find a rooftop garden, which

Contemporary dining area, L'Anima

is where many of the menu's
ingredients are grown.

The Gate ££
Vegetarian Map 6 E2
370 St John Street EC1 4NN
Tel *020 7278 5483*
An award-winning menu draws
on influences from all over the
world. The best place in town for
a vegetarian weekend brunch.

Haz Plantation Place ££
Turkish Map 15 C2
6 Mincing Lane EC3M 3BD
Tel *020 7929 3173* **Closed** *Sun*
Order the marvellous *mezze* for a
range of authentic dishes, or try
the perfectly cooked tuna steak
with home-made chilli sauce.
The set menus are a bargain for
the City.

The Peasant ££
British Map 6 E2
240 St John Street EC1V 4PH
Tel *020 7336 7726*
Finely executed brasserie
cooking in an agreeable Victorian
pub dining room. Enjoy the
Chilean chef's first-rate pub food
in the cavernous bar below.
Splendid Sunday roasts.

Pham Sushi ££
Japanese Map 7 A4
159 Whitecross Street EC1Y 8JL
Tel *020 7251 6336* **Closed** *Sun*
Exquisite sushi, sashimi, tempura
and California rolls, all so fresh
and full of flavour, you hardly
notice the uninspiring interior.

**The Restaurant at St Paul's
Cathedral** ££
British Map 15 A1
St Paul's Cathedral EC4M 8AD
Tel *020 7248 2469*
Have a substantial or a light
lunch or a slap-up tea in the
beautifully lit crypt. Imaginative
seasonal menus of fine British
produce are served daily.

DK Choice

Vinoteca ££
European Map 6 E2
7 St John Street EC1M 4AA
Tel *020 7253 8786* **Closed** *Sun*
Admirers come from far
and wide to this Farringdon
wine bar, with its list of
300 outstanding wines and
excellent modern European
cuisine. Pairing suggestions are
made for every dish. Arrive early
for dinner; reservations are only
accepted for lunch.

L'Anima £££
Italian Map 7 C5
1 Snowden Street EC2A 2DQ
Tel *020 7422 7000* **Closed** *Sun*
The food served at this award-
winning restaurant is as elegant
as the simple setting. Stunning
recipes inspired by cuisine from
southern Italy, including Sicily
and Sardinia.

The Boundary £££
French Map 8 D4
2 Boundary Street E2 7DD
Tel *020 7729 1051*
Faultless modern versions of
traditional recipes are served at
style guru Terence Conran's sexy,
subterranean hideout. Staff
are very attentive.

Club Gascon £££
French Map 14 F1
57 West Smithfield EC1A 9DS
Tel *020 7600 6144* **Closed** *Sun*
Dinner here is an experience
to savour. Try the creamy
signature *foie gras*, paired with
a recommended wine.

Galvin La Chapelle £££
French Map 8 D5
35 Spital Square E1 6DY
Tel *020 7299 0400*
Once a school and parish hall,
this converted mansion now
houses an impressive restaurant.

For more information on types of restaurants *see page 293*

Goodman   £££
Steakhouse   **Map** 15 B1
11 Old Jewry EC2R 8DU
Tel *020 7600 8220* **Closed** *Sat & Sun*
Melt-in-the-mouth steaks are the
staple at this all-American
steakhouse. You can see the
meat dry-ageing in the kitchen.

DK Choice

Hawksmoor   £££
Steakhouse   **Map** 16 E1
157 Commercial Street E1 6BJ
Tel *020 7426 4850*
Hailed as serving the best
steak in the country, this is
one of a handful of branches
around the city and a must-visit
for ardent carnivores. Patrons
dine on astonishing, dictionary-
thick steaks, produced from
traditionally reared Longhorn
cattle, dry-aged and cooked
simply on a charcoal grill –
scrumptious.

Sauterelle   £££
French   **Map** 15 C2
The Royal Exchange EC3V 3LR
Tel *020 7618 2480* **Closed** *Sat & Sun*
Stylish cuisine in a captivating
setting: on a mezzanine over-
looking the glorious courtyard of
the Grade I-listed Neo-Classical
Royal Exchange.

St John   £££
British   **Map** 6 E2
26 St John Street EC1M 4AY
Tel *020 7251 0848*
Not for the squeamish. Fergus
Henderson's celebrated – and
unique – kitchen makes the
most of offal, including heart,
lung, kidney and more obscure
animal parts.

Southwark and the South Bank

Anchor and Hope   £
British   **Map** 14 E4
36 The Cut SE1 8LP
Tel *020 7928 9898* **Closed** *Sun pm*
Turn up with a good appetite.
Large portions of such gutsy fare
as calves' brains, pumpkin risotto
and braised venison.

Dim T – London Bridge   £
Asian fusion   **Map** 16 D4
*2 More London Place, Tooley Street
SE1 2DB*
Tel *020 7403 7000*
Be creative by choosing from a
range of noodles, toppings and
sauces to make your own dish.
Fun for the family, plus
spectacular river views.

Impressive view of St Paul's Cathedral from the OXO Tower Restaurant

The Laughing Gravy   £
British   **Map** 14 F3
154–156 Blackfriars Road SE1 8EN
Tel *020 7998 1707*
A laid-back restaurant, with a
more lively bar, housed in an old
foundry building. A well-chosen
wine list complements the menu.

Ping Pong   £
Chinese   **Map** 14 D4
*Festival Terrace, Southbank Centre
SE1 8XX*
Tel *020 7960 4160*
A cool, contemporary restaurant
serving dim sum close to the
South Bank. There's a huge
selection of cocktails too.

Champor-Champor   ££
Fusion   **Map** 15 C4
62–4 Weston Street SE1 3QJ
Tel *020 7403 4600*
The name means "mix and
match" – a perfect depiction of its
exotic, yet wacky decoration, and
Malaysian-Thai cuisine.

José   ££
Spanish   **Map** 15 C4
104 Bermondsey Street SE1 3UB
Tel *020 7403 4902*
Team extraordinarily good
Barcelona-style tapas with a
choice from the varied list
of sherries and wines. An
authentic experience.

Tapas Brindisa   ££
Spanish   **Map** 15 B4
18–20 Southwark Street SE1 1TJ
Tel *020 7357 8880*
Hearty flavours steal the show at
this animated tapas bar. Fantastic
Serrano hams, Cantabrian
anchovies and piquillo peppers.

Tito's Peruvian Restaurant   ££
Peruvian   **Map** 15 B4
*4–6 London Bridge Street
SE1 9SG*
Tel *020 7407 7787*
Drink a pisco sour while you wait
for robust and spicy regional

dishes, many meat-based, at this
brightly lit local favourite.

**Wright Brothers Oyster and
Porter House**   ££
Seafood   **Map** 15 B3
11 Stoney Street SE1 9AD
Tel *020 7403 9554*
Fast food with a difference:
market-fresh fish and shellfish
from Cornwall. The oysters are
sublime. Very informal.

Zucca   ££
Italian   **Map** 15 C4
184 Bermondsey Street SE1 3TQ
Tel *020 7378 6809* **Closed** *Mon*
All white, hard edged and über
cool, with an open kitchen
and mind-blowing menu.
Excellent pasta – including
fennel and lemon tagliatelle –
and polenta.

DK Choice

**OXO Tower Restaurant, Bar
and Brasserie**   £££
European   **Map** 14 E3
*Oxo Tower Wharf, Barge House
Street SE1 9GY*
Tel *020 7803 3888*
Whether you're lunching or
dining, the eighth-floor view
will take your breath away;
colourful by day, glittering by
night. Eat on the terrace in
summer, but when it's cold, the
picture windows bring the
outside in. Choose between the
relaxed brasserie and the
sophisticated restaurant, both
serving modern British classics.

Roast   £££
British   **Map** 15 B3
*The Floral Hall, Stoney Street
SE1 1TL*
Tel *020 3006 6111*
A smart, light-filled, modern
dining room in the eaves of Floral
Hall. Come for a whopping
breakfast or succulent roasts.

The relaxed dining area of The Laughing Gravy, in Southwark

Further Afield

Anarkali £
Indian
303–305 King Street W6 9NH
Tel *020 8748 1760*
A Hammersmith restaurant in a class of its own. Unique, subtle spicing and a great choice for vegetarians. Delightful service.

DK Choice

Brady's £
British
39 Jew's Row SW18 TB
Tel *020 8877 9599* **Closed** *Sun*
"The best fish and chips in London", assert enthusiasts of this cheerful Wandsworth bistro with a suitably seaside atmosphere. Choose from line-caught fresh fish, battered or grilled, with perfect chips – crunchy outside and fluffy inside – a pint of prawns, or smoked salmon. Finish with a traditional English dessert of treacle tart or apple crumble.

Gem £
Turkish **Map** 6 F1
265 Upper Street N1 2UQ
Tel *020 7359 0405*
Gem by name and by nature. Fragrant *mezze* at bargain prices in a charming white-painted room decorated with Kurdish farm implements. The speciality is the wonderful *qatme* (stuffed Kurdish bread). No bookings.

The Greenwich Union £
British **Map** 23 B3
56 Royal Hill SE10 8RT
Tel *020 8692 6258*
A local landmark, this pub showcases a unique range of beers. Menus recommend ale pairings for each delicious traditional dish.

Mamuśka £
Polish
16 Elephant and Castle SE1 6TH
Tel *020 3602 1898*
This cheerful restaurant serves authentic Polish favourites. The menu changes regularly but stalwarts include excellent *pierogi* and *schabowy*. There is plenty for vegetarians and meat-eaters alike.

Mandalay £
Burmese **Map** 3 A5
444 Edgware Road W2 1EG
Tel *020 7258 3696* **Closed** *Sun*
This basic eatery is an ideal introduction to Burmese food, best-described as a fusion of Chinese, Indian and Thai cuisines.

Taiwan Village £
Taiwanese **Map** 17 A5
85 Lillie Road SW6 1UD
Tel *020 7381 2900* **Closed** *Mon*
Dishes draw on regional cuisines, including those from Taiwan, Hunan and Szechuan. If you are hungry, opt for the "set feast".

Zumbura £
Indian
36 Old Town SW4 0LB
Tel *020 7720 7902*
Off the beaten tourist track, this place serves up authentic Punjabi food (don't miss the comforting gourd and lentil dish, *ghiya channa daal*) in a wonderfully stylish setting; the owners were previously interior designers. Sip top-notch cocktails and sample a range of delicious tasting dishes.

Buen Ayre ££
Steakhouse **Map** 8 F1
50 Broadway Market E8 4QJ
Tel *020 7275 9900*
A back-to-basics Hackney hotspot where Argentine steak and grilled meats are the order of the day. The wine list is huge.

DK Choice

Canton Arms ££
British **Map** 21 C4
177 South Lambeth Road SW8 1XP
Tel *020 7582 8710*
In a culinary desert, this stand-out gastropub is worth crossing the river for. Its style is plain and countrified – bar at the front, restaurant at the back – and the food is knock-out: gutsy, meaty flavours, interesting textures and combinations. Bookings cannot be made in advance, so head there in good time to avoid disappointment.

The Depot ££
British
Tideway Yard, 125 Mortlake High Street SW14 8SN
Tel *0844 288 0726*
A tranquil riverside setting and superior cooking have made this brasserie a hit. Try for a window table or enjoy the outdoor dining terrace in the summer.

Emile's ££
European
98 Felsham Road SW15 1DQ
Tel *020 8789 3323* **Closed** *Sun*
A Putney treasure; good food in an unfussy room. A black-board, brought to your table, displays the seasonal menu.

Argentine grill and steakhouse, Buen Ayre

For more information on types of restaurants *see page 293*

A selection of tempting salads on display at Ottolenghi

The Glasshouse   ££
European
14 Station Parade, Kew TW9 3PZ
Tel *020 8940 6777*
Asian overtones jazz up the
contemporary European food at
this light, urban, award-winning
restaurant. An impressive wine
list complements the menu.
Comfortable, relaxed and
excellent value for money.

Indian Zing   ££
Indian
236 King Street W6 0RF
Tel *020 8748 5959*
A noteworthy wine list and
contemporary Indian cuisine,
prepared with panache at this
upmarket gem.

Inn at Kew Gardens   ££
British
*Kew Gardens Hotel, 292 Sandycombe
Road, Kew TW9*
Tel *020 8940 2220*
Perfectly located beside Kew
Gardens, this lovel hostelry has
great ales and moreish gastro
food. The menu changes on a
monthly basis to make the most
of seasonal produce.

Jin-Kichi   ££
Japanese   **Map** 1 A4
73 Heath Street NW3 6UG
Tel *020 7794 6158*   **Closed** *Mon*
A tiny piece of Tokyo in
Hampstead, with a grill as a
focus, well-spaced tables,
efficient service and sublime
sushi. The food is authentic
and delicious.

Kennington Tandoori   ££
Indian   **Map** 22 E1
313 Kennington Road SE11 4QE
Tel *020 7735 9247*
A calm refuge serving some of
the best curries in London,
according to aficionados.
Novel dishes are mixed in
with the classics.

Khan's   ££
Indian
159 Lavender Hill SW11 5QH
Tel *020 7978 4455*
Low-fat, colouring-free authentic
curries with a sufficiently broad
menu to appeal to a range
of palates. Takeaway also
available to those staying locally.

Lamberts   ££
British
*2 Station Parade, Balham
High Road SW12 9AZ*
Tel *020 8675 2233*   **Closed** *Mon*
Harmonious cuisine, top-notch
organic ingredients and
comfortable, easy surroundings.
Classic favourites sit side by
side with modern variations.
The wine list excels and prices
are sensible.

Lobster Pot   ££
French   **Map** 22 D3
3 Kennington Lane SE11 4RG
Tel *020 7582 5556* **Closed** *Mon & Sun*
Walk through the door and you're
in Brittany, complete with piped

Fine dining establishment Chez Bruce,
Wandsworth Common

seagulls. Try the eight-course
"surprise" menu. Book ahead.

Manor   ££
British   **Closed** *Mon, Sun
eve, Tue lunch*
148 Clapham Manor Street SW4 6BX
Tel *020 7720 4662*
The decor may be casual but
the food is innovative, exciting
and worth making the trip out
of the city for. Choose the
tasting menu (there's one for
vegetarians, too) and enjoy an
evening of modernist cooking.

North China   ££
Chinese
305 Uxbridge Road W3 9QU
Tel *020 8992 9183*
A family affair set up in 1976 by
the current owner's father, this
tasteful little restaurant offers
mouthwatering dishes with
specialities from both north and
south China.

Ottolenghi   ££
Mediterranean   **Map** 6 F1
287 Upper Street N1 2TZ
Tel *020 7288 1454*
The Islington flagship restaurant
of a popular chain and sister to
the exquisite Nopi *(see p297)*.
Vegetables are given top billing
(though there is a selection of
meat dishes) and served in a
tasty Mediterranean and Middle
Eastern fashion.

El Parador   ££
Tapas   **Map** 4 F2
245 Eversholt Street NW1 1BA
Tel *020 7387 2789*
A small, family-run Spanish
restaurant. Simplicity is the
keynote here, both in the sunny
decoration – yellow walls,
terracotta floor, wooden chairs –
and market-fresh ingredients.

Le Sacré Coeur   ££
French   **Map** 6 E1
18 Theberton Street N1 0QX
Tel *020 7354 2618*
Montmartre comes to Islington
in this cosy Parisian spot. Classic
French style, with poster-lined
walls, wooden beams, blue-
and-white checked tablecloths
and superior traditional dishes.
Unfailingly friendly service.

Le Salon Privé   ££
French
43 Crown Road, St Margarets TW1
Tel *020 8892 0602*
The best of French bistrot
cooking with fresh seasonal
ingredients. This charming
local establishment has an
intimate atmosphere and a
great wine list.

Singapore Garden££
Singaporean
83 Fairfax Road NW6 4DY
Tel *020 7328 5314*
A jovial Swiss Cottage veteran serving the best soft-shelled crabs, with chillies and garlic, you're likely to taste. Also recommended is the beef *rendang* (slow cooked beef in thick coconut sauce).

Tatra££
Polish
24 Goldhawk Road W12 8DH
Tel *020 8749 8193*
This Shepherd's Bush local blends the most appetizing tastes from Eastern Europe. At dinner, be prepared: sampling the flavoured vodka is almost compulsory.

Trinity££
British
4 The Polygon SW4 0JG
Tel *020 7622 1199*
The wonderfully complex flavours of Adam Byatt's cooking draw people to this Clapham restaurant. Smoked rabbit leg, roast cod and pan-fried sea bream are satisfying specialities. Exemplary service.

Le Vacherin££
French
76–7 South Parade W4 5LF
Tel *020 8742 2121*
A neighbourhood bistro with a refined, intimate air. It boasts a sure hand in the kitchen and old-fashioned service. The set menu affords good value.

The Wells££
British   **Map** 1 B4
30 Well Walk NW3 1BX
Tel *020 7794 3785*
Take a ramble on Hampstead Heath before heading to this

Prime grilled meats served up at Gaucho, which has branches across the capital

splendid gastropub. Modern European specialities are on the menu in the dining room, with traditional bar snacks downstairs. Enjoy the pretty terrace when the weather is good. Busy at weekends.

DK Choice

Chez Bruce£££
British
2 Bellevue Road SW17 7EG
Tel *020 8672 0114*
Bruce Poole's modern British food has strong classical French notes with an emphasis on offal, fish and remarkable flavour combinations. Specialities include home-made charcuterie and bread, and slow-cooked meats. Overlooking Wandsworth Common, this light, refined restaurant has maintained a reputation for its food, wine and service.

Gaucho – Hampstead£££
Steakhouse   **Map** 1 A4
64 Heath Street NW3 1DN
Tel *020 7431 8222*
A destination for carnivores: hearty steaks are cooked on a genuine Argentinian *asado* barbecue at the north London outpost of this stylish chain of restaurants. As well as an à la carte menu, there is a tasting menu and a "carnivore's feast".

DK Choice

River Café£££
Italian
Thames Wharf, Rainville Road W6 9HA
Tel *020 7386 4200*
First-rate seasonal ingredients, cooked simply, is Ruth Rogers' ethos at her famous Hammersmith eatery – one of the first in London to make the sourcing of sustainable ingredients a priority. It is sophisticated, in a canteen style, with a wood-burner and open kitchen. The rustic Italian meals rarely disappoint and sit alongside the more refined dishes on the menu. A pricey option, but worth every penny.

La Trompette£££
French
5–7 Devonshire Road W4 2EU
Tel *020 8747 1836*
Sister of the Chez Bruce *(see above)* outlet, La Trompette is perfectly placed close to the botanic gardens in Kew. The menu at Bruce Poole's Chiswick outpost has roots in regional France. Defined by charcuterie and *confits*; rounded off with comforting desserts. Relaxed and excellent value for money.

The sunny outdoor terrace at the River Café

For more information on types of restaurants *see page 293*

Light Meals and Snacks

When you want to make the most of the available sightseeing time, it doesn't always make sense to sit down for a lengthy restaurant meal. Or perhaps you don't have the budget or the appetite for a three-course affair. London has an abundance of eateries for every taste and occasion – many of them unmissable institutions – from traditional fish-and-chip and pie-and-mash shops to elegant tearooms and cool cafés.

Breakfast

A good breakfast prepares you for a solid day's sightseeing, and the "full English" *(see p294)* is always a good start. Many hotels serve this classic British meal to residents and non-residents, and there are plenty of "greasy spoons" (traditional cafés) around the city with the artery-clogging morning meal on the menu.

Though a little pricey, **Simpson's-in-the-Strand** offers an old-fashioned breakfast menu (as well as classic lunchtime and dinner roasts) in a historic panelled dining room. A breakfast staple is the egg: scrambled, poached, fried, boiled, most menus are dominated by this simple ingredient and it continues to feature during brunch, an increasingly popular meal in the city. The spacious, modern restaurant in the back of popular French grocer/delicatessen **Villandry** serves one of the best on Saturday and Sunday.

American restaurants such as **Joe Allen** and **Christopher's** also offer brunch; or head for well-heeled Westbourne Grove, where it's a weekend ritual at relaxed eateries such as **202**. **The Breakfast Club**, a trendy diner with a few branches around the city, serves a variety of breakfast-style meals all day, but for a more sophisticated experience, **34 Mayfair** is certainly worth a visit. **The Riding House Café** has a scrumptious weekend brunch, as does **Duck & Waffle**, which serves delicious dishes with stunning views of the city from its 40th-floor restaurant.

For continental breakfasts comprising pastries and a coffee, there is a huge array of independent cafés to choose from, as well as dependable chains. The elegantly old-world **The Wolseley** in Piccadilly serves croissants, brioches and cooked breakfasts in opulent surroundings but those who want something simpler should pick from any of the coffee shops listed below.

Coffee and Tea

For a cappuccino or espresso at any time of day, step into round-the-clock Soho stalwart **Bar Italia**, which also serves a range of pastries and paninis; it's a legendary late-night pit-stop, full of colourful characters. There is no shortage of coffee-bar chains, but one of the best is Caffè Nero, which dispenses authentic Italian coffee at reasonable prices across town.

If you're out shopping, many of London's department stores have their own cafés: Harvey Nichols has one of the most stylish, while Selfridges has a branch of the cool Moroccan tearoom Momo. In Portobello Market, quaint tearoom **Still Too Few**, below the antique shop of the same name, serves tea, sandwiches and cakes to bric-a-brac hunters on Saturdays. Superb coffee (and cakes) can also be found at the **Monmouth Coffee House** in Covent Garden.

Patisseries such as **Maison Bertaux** and **Patisserie Valerie** are a delight, with mouth-watering window displays of French pastries, and **Paul** offers delicious tarts and other treats in a Parisian-café atmosphere. **The Wolseley** has an all-day café menu of sandwiches and salads. If you're strolling in picturesque Little Venice, **Café Laville** commands a spectacular view over Regent's Canal. **Bluebird**, Terence Conran's multi-faceted food centre in the converted 1920s Bluebird motor garage on the King's Road, has a café with tables on its cobbled forecourt, as well as a more formal restaurant, bar and market.

No visit to London would be complete without afternoon tea. Top hotels such as **The Ritz** and **Brown's** offer pots of your choice of tea, scones with jam and cream, thin cucumber sandwiches and delicious cakes galore. For a relaxed treat in the beautiful Kensington Gardens, there's nothing to beat **The Orangery**. Its selection of English teas and cakes tastes even better in the elegant surroundings of Sir John Vanbrugh's 18th-century building. **Fortnum & Mason** *(see p317)* serves both afternoon and high teas. In Kew, the **Maids of Honour** tearoom offers pastries reputedly enjoyed by Henry VIII. For a more modern experience, **Sketch** offers exquisite contemporary confections in a restyled Georgian room.

Museum and Theatre Cafés

Most museums and galleries have cafés, including the Royal Academy, Tate Modern (with wonderful views over the Thames), the National Portrait Gallery and the British Museum. BFI Southbank has the buzzing **Riverfront Bar & Café**, much frequented by cinephiles, while St Martin-in-the-Fields church in Trafalgar Square, famous for its concerts, has the capacious self-service **Café in the Crypt**.

Although some of these tend to be slightly expensive, their locations often justify the cost. The stunning interiors of **Benugo**, the café found in the original Morris, Gamble and Poynter rooms of the Victoria & Albert Museum, are definitely worth the price of a cup of tea and a sandwich.

Lunches

For those on the go, there is a plethora of sandwich chains with branches throughout the city: **Pret a Manger** serves a good range of prepacked sandwiches, salads, cakes and soft drinks, and **Eat** offers a daily-changing menu of interesting soups and salads made using seasonal ingredients, as well as sandwiches made with home-made breads and tortilla wraps.

Healthy fast-food chain **Leon** offers a great range of lunchtime alternatives to the sandwich, such as curry pots, salads and wraps. **Itsu** and **Wasabi** are also excellent for the health-conscious luncher, with a range of Asian-inspired soups, salads and sushi. Supermarkets are also a good choice for those on a budget as they often offer a lunchtime meal deal: look out for branches of Tesco, Sainsbury's and Marks & Spencer.

Delis

With Londoners becoming more and more interested in high-quality foods from small producers in Britain and abroad, there has been a boom in stylish delis, many of which provide seating so that you can sample their wares on site. **Minkies** deli in north London is renowned for its award-winning food. The chic **Luigi's** in the south sells delicious Italian fare, from fresh pasta to farmhouse cheeses, freshly roasted vegetables and salads, while deli/cheese shop **La Fromagerie** in Marylebone has a large communal table in the back for light bites. The family-run delicatessen/lunchroom **Paul Rothe & Son**, which opened in the early 1900s, serves sandwiches and soups among shelves of "British and foreign provisions".

Diners and Burger Joints

London is full of American-style fast-food joints, serving burgers, fries, fried chicken, apple pie, milk shakes and cola, particularly around Soho, Leicester Square, Shaftesbury Avenue and Covent Garden. Time-honoured establishments include family favourite **Maxwell's** in Covent Garden, the **Hard Rock Café** and the fun, 1950s-kitsch **Ed's Easy Diner**, but thanks to the continuing vogue for retro burger eateries, choices are plentiful. **GBK** (Gourmet Burger Kitchen) and **Byron** (both with several branches) are two of the best, while **Lucky 7** and **The Diner** serve up burgers and breakfasts in a dice-and-cards-themed setting, complete with vinyl-seated booths and blaring rock'n'roll.

The **Electric Diner** in Notting Hill is open from 8am until late at night and offers French-American diner-style fare throughout the day, both at the bar and in booths. For great-tasting burgers made with high quality all-British ingredients, visit **Honest Burgers**, which has several locations across London, and also offers gluten-free burger buns. Covent Garden's **Shake Shack** has a more extensive menu, complete with frozen custard shakes and even snacks for dogs.

Pizza and Pasta

Italian food has now become a staple of the British diet. Street-side stands offer variable quality, but there are decent well-established chains with several branches, including **Ask**. **Pizza Express** offers thin-crust pizzas that are a step up from the norm. Try the elegant Georgian townhouse outlet on Chelsea's King's Road, or the branch in Soho that plays live jazz. **Kettners**, also part of the group, offers casual, inexpensive Soho eating in a legendary old dining room with a Champagne bar.

The **Carluccio's** chain, which has a branch with alfresco tables in pedestrianized St Christopher's Place, serves good-quality, freshly made pastas and salads. Inexpensive pasta is also served at bustling trattorias such as **Pollo** in Soho. **Marine Ices** near Camden Market serves great pizza and pasta in addition to its famous ice cream (*see* Street Food, *pp310–11*). From humble beginnings in street markets and roving food vans, **Franco Manca**, **Pizza Pilgrims** and **Homeslice** have taken up permanent residency around the city, the last providing tasty wood-fired pizzas and the first two specializing in authentic Neapolitan sourdough pizzas.

Food in Pubs

Perhaps the biggest – and most popular – change in the London dining scene has been the transformation of the food found in pubs. Before the early 1990s, most pubs that provided food at all offered a pretty simple range of salads and sandwiches, put together with no great imagination.

The rapid rise of the gastropub, in which the food has equal billing with the beer selection, steadily made the pub a viable dining option. Grilled steaks, fresh fish or English classics like sausage and mash have been reinvigorated by the use of first-rate, seasonal or organic ingredients and the menus have become increasingly sophisticated, mixing Mediterranean, Asian and other global influences.

The neighbourhood gastropub has become an essential London institution. Some have separate dining rooms while others have retained the traditional pub style, where you order at the bar from a chalkboard menu. All tend to be more relaxed than formal restaurants, but they can get busy, so book in advance. Among the best are **The Eagle**, **The Engineer**, **The Lansdowne**, **The Jugged Hare** and the **Wells Tavern** (*see pp312–15*).

Fish and Chips

Fish and chips is typically considered the national dish of Britain, with a "chippy" serving a choice of fish (typically cod) deep-fried in batter, accompanied by chips (thicker cut than French fries). A range of accompaniments includes baps (soft bread rolls) for a "chip buttie" (a chip sandwich), mushy peas, pickled eggs or onions. Four of the best places for such fare are the **North Sea Fish Restaurant**, **Rock & Sole Plaice**, **Faulkner's** and **Fish Central**. Such is its popularity, fish and chips is increasingly available on the menu in smart restaurants and chains such as **Fish!**

Noodle Bars

Popular chain **Wagamama** still draws queues for its good-value noodles and other Asian dishes in airy yet basic environs; customers sit at long communal tables. **Dim T**

serves dim sum and mix-and-match noodles, meats and toppings in a modern café setting. In Soho, **Tuk Tuk** noodle bar serves up a range of Thai noodle dishes, and is open until late. Nearby **Tonkotsu** is famed for its tasty ramen noodles, while **Taro** is a busy Japanese diner offering inexpensive sushi, ramen and teriyaki. Family-run restaurant **Viet Pho** is small but certainly worth a visit for authentic Vietnamese cuisine.

A Taste of the East End

In the East End, Jewish bakeries such as **Brick Lane Beigel Bake** are open 24 hours a day. Fresh plain bagels, with a wide range of fillings, are available here.

The East End also has the largest number of pie and mash shops, which provide an inexpensive and satisfying "nosh-up" of jellied eels and potatoes, or meat pie with mash and liquor (green parsley sauce). Two classic venues, both on Bethnal Green Road, are **G Kelly** and **S&R Kelly**; or try **Manze's** on Tower Bridge Road. For the real East End experience, you should wash you meal down with a mug of strong, hot tea.

Street Food

Street food markets have become increasingly popular in London, and have gone far beyond the traditional roasted chestnuts sold on London's

DIRECTORY

Breakfast

202
202 Westbourne Grove W11. **Map** 9 C2.

34 Mayfair
34 Grosvenor Square W1. **Map** 12 D2.

The Breakfast Club
33 D'Arblay St W1. **Map** 13 A2.

Christopher's
18 Wellington St WC2. **Map** 13 C2.

Duck and Waffle
Heron Tower, 110 Bishopsgate EC2. **Map** 15 C1.

Joe Allen
13 Exeter St WC2. **Map** 13 C2.

The Riding House Café
43–51 Great Titchfield St W1. **Map** 12 F1.

Simpson's-in-the-Strand
100 Strand WC2. **Map** 13 C2.

Villandry
170 Great Portland St W1. **Map** 4 F5.

The Wolseley
100 Piccadilly W1. **Map** 12 F3.

Coffee and Tea

Bar Italia
22 Frith St W1. **Map** 13 A2.

Bluebird Café
350 King's Rd SW3. **Map** 19 A4.

Brown's
47 Maddox St W1. **Map** 12 F2.

Café Laville
Little Venice Parade, 453 Edgware Rd W2.

Fortnum & Mason
181 Piccadilly W1. **Map** 12 F3.

Maids of Honour
288 Kew Rd, Richmond, Surrey.

Maison Bertaux
28 Greek St W1. **Map** 13 A1.

Monmouth Coffee House
27 Monmouth St WC2. **Map** 13 B2.

The Orangery
Kensington Palace, Kensington Gardens W8. **Map** 10 D3.

Patisserie Valerie
17 Motcombe St, Belgravia SW1. **Map** 12 D5.

Paul
29 Bedford St WC2. **Map** 13 B2.

The Ritz
150 Piccadilly W1. **Map** 12 F3.

Sketch
9 Conduit St W1. **Map** 12 F2.

Still Too Few
300 Westbourne Grove W11. **Map** 9 B2.

Museum and Theatre Cafés

Benugo
Victoria & Albert Museum, Cromwell Road SW7. **Map** 19 A1.

Café in the Crypt
St Martin-in-the-Fields, Duncannon St WC2. **Map** 13 B3.

Riverfront Bar & Kitchen
BFI Southbank, South Bank SE1. **Map** 14 D3.

Lunches

(All have several branches around the city)

EAT
12 Oxo Tower Wharf, Barge House St SE1. **Map** 14 E3.

Itsu
31 Broadwick St W1. **Map** 13 A2.

Leon
275 Regent St W1. **Map** 12 F1.

Pret a Manger
88 Strand WC2. **Map** 13 C3.

Wasabi
388 Strand WC2. **Map** 13 C2.

Delis

La Fromagerie
2–6 Moxon St W1. **Map** 4 D5.

Luigi's
349 Fulham Rd SW6. **Map** 18 F4.

Minkies
Chamberlayne Rd NW10.

Paul Rothe & Son
35 Marylebone Lane W1. **Map** 12 D1.

Diners and Burger Joints

Byron
11 Haymarket SW1. **Map** 13 A3.
(One of several branches.)

The Diner
190 Shaftesbury Ave WC2. **Map** 13 B1.
(One of several branches.)

Ed's Easy Diner
12 Moor St W1. **Map** 13 B2.

street corners. They epitomize all that is great about London's food scene: culinary delights from all over the world standing shoulder to shoulder, offering locals and visitors alike a choice like no other.

Borough Market stalls are exceptionally good for street food: **Bread Ahead** makes an excellent range of fresh loaves and exquisite sweet doughnuts, while **The German Deli** grills up bratwursts at lunchtime; **Horn OK Please** provides a vegetarian option with spicy Indian dishes to go.

The Global Kitchen in Camden Lock serves up some of the finest street food in the capital, including Lebanese falafel, French crêpes, Jamaican jerk chicken, Japanese sushi,

Turkish wraps, Mexican chilli, American BBQ, Mediterranean salads and Malaysian dishes, to name but a few of the appetizing options.

The Real Food Market champions small producers and hosts street food markets and festivals throughout the year. Market locations vary so check the website to find out where they're setting up next. **Street Feast** similarly takes over London during the summer months; look out for the Dalston Yard festival, which serves an eclectic range of delicious and artisanal foods from gourmet burgers and grilled cheese toasties to cream-filled cupcakes and home-made gelato. Be sure to seek out B.O.B's Lobster

there for fresh and succulent lobster rolls. **KERB** markets are held in a few locations around the city including Paddington (monthly) and by the Gherkin (weekly). KERB's traders rotate so check the website to see what's on offer when you visit – favourites include Anna Mae's unique take on macaroni cheese and Batch Bakery's oozing chocolate brownies.

Next to Royal Festival Hall, the **Southbank Centre Food Market** is home to a variety of international favourites including Greek-style wraps, curries, paellas, sweet treats and tasty ingredients to take home. It is open on Fridays, Saturdays and Sundays, from lunchtime to early evening.

DIRECTORY

Electric Diner
191 Portobello Rd W11.
Map 9 B2.

GBK
13–14 Maiden Lane, WC2.
Map 13 C2.
(One of several branches.)

Hard Rock Café
150 Old Park Lane W1.
Map 12 E4.

Honest Burgers
4A Meard St W1. **Map** 13 A2. *(One of several branches.)*

Lucky 7
127 Westbourne Park Rd W2. **Map** 9 C1.

Maxwell's
8 James St WC2. **Map** 13 C2.

Shake Shack
24 Market Building, The Piazza WC2. **Map** 13 C2.

Pizza and Pasta

Ask
56–60 Wigmore St W1.
Map 12 D1.
(One of several branches.)

Carluccio's
St Christopher's Place W1.
Map 12 E2.
(One of several branches.)

Franco Manca
98 Tottenham Court Rd W1. **Map** 5 A5.
(One of several branches.)

Homeslice
13 Neal's Yard WC2.
Map 13 B1.

Marine Ices
61 Chalk Farm Rd NW1.

Kettner's
29 Romilly St W1.
Map 13 A2.

Pizza Express
30 Coptic St WC1.
Map 13 B1.
(One of several branches.)

Pizza Pilgrims
11 Dean St W1.
Map 13 A1.
(One of several branches.)

Pollo
20 Old Compton St W1.
Map 13 A2.

Fish and Chips

Faulkner's
424–6 Kingsland Rd E8.

Fish!
Borough Market SE1.
Map 15 B4.

Fish Central
149–155 Central St EC1.
Map 7 A3.

North Sea Fish Restaurant
7–8 Leigh St WC1.
Map 5 B4.

Rock & Sole Plaice
47 Endell St WC2.
Map 13 B1.

Noodle Bars

Dim T
32 Charlotte St W1.
Map 13 A1.

Taro
59–61 Brewer St W1.
Map 13 A2.

Tuk Tuk
Old Compton St W1.
Map 13 A2.

Tonkotsu
63 Dean St W1.
Map 13 A1.
(One of several branches.)

Viet Pho
34 Greek St W1.
Map 13 A2

Wagamama
101 Wigmore St W1.
Map 12 D1.
(One of several branches.)

A Taste of the East End

Brick Lane Beigel Bake
159 Brick Lane E1.
Map 8 E5.

G Kelly
526 Roman Rd E3.
Map 8 D4.

S&R Kelly
284 Bethnal Green Rd E2.
Map 8 F3.

Manze's
87 Tower Bridge Rd SE1.
Map 16 D5.

Street Food

Bread Ahead
Borough Market SE1.
Map 15 B4.

The German Deli
Borough Market SE1.
Map 15 B4.

The Global Kitchen
Camden Lock NW1.

Horn OK Please
Borough Market SE1.
Map 15 B4.

KERB
Various locations.
w kerbfood.com

The Real Food Market
Various locations.
w realfoodfestival.co.uk

Southbank Centre Food Market
Sutton Walk SE1.
Map 14 D4.

Street Feast – Dalton Yard
Hartwell St E8.
(One of several locations.)

London Pubs and Bars

Affectionately known as a "pub", "boozer" or "the local", a public house was originally just that – a house in which the public could eat, drink and even stay the night. Large inns with courtyards, such as the George Inn, were originally stopping points for horse-drawn coach services. Their names have hung on signs outside since 1393, when King Richard II decreed that they should replace the usual bush outside the door. As most people were illiterate, names that could easily be illustrated were chosen, such as the Rose & Crown, coats of arms (Freemasons' Arms), historical figures (Princess Louise) or heraldic animals (Red Lion). Some pubs stand on historic public house sites, for example the Ship, the Lamb and Flag, and the City Barge. However, many of the finest ones date from the emergence of "gin palaces" in the late 1800s, where Londoners took refuge from the misery of their poverty amid lavish interiors with elaborate decoration. Since the 1990s cocktail-bar boom and the rise of the gastropub, the traditional pub has been given an image makeover, restoring the British institution's popularity with a fashionable crowd.

Rules and Conventions

Visitors to London have long been bemused by early pub closing times, which made a night out a bit tricky – an after-theatre nightcap, for example, was usually out of the question outside of your hotel. In theory, reforms to the licensing laws, which came into effect in 2005, mean pubs can now stay open up to 24 hours, as long as they obtain permission from their local authority, and many extend their hours beyond the standard 11am–11pm.

You must be aged at least 18 to buy or drink alcohol, and at least 14 to enter a pub without an adult. Children can be taken into pubs that serve food, or may use outside areas. Order drinks at the bar and pay when you are served; tips are not customary unless you are served food and drink at a table. "Last orders" are usually called 10 minutes before closing, then "time" is called, and a further 20 minutes is then allowed for finishing drinks. Smoking is banned in all pubs and clubs, though some have outdoor smoking areas.

British Beer

The most traditional beers are available in various strengths and styles, and are flat (not fizzy) and served only lightly cooled. The spectrum of bottled beers goes from "light" ale, through "pale", "brown", "bitter" and the strong "old". A sweeter, lower-alcohol alternative is shandy, a classic mixture of draught beer or lager and lemonade. Many traditional methods of brewing and serving beer have been preserved over the years, and there is a great variety of "real ales" in London pubs.

The main London brewers are Young's (try their strong "Winter Warmer" beer), Meantime and Fuller's. Competing with these city stalwarts is an increasing number of microbreweries, championing "craft beers". Beavertown, Kernel, Camden Town Brewery and Brixton Brewery are just some of the many brewing up around the capital. The Scottish craft beer company **Brewdog** has a number of pubs around the city, serving up a good variety of beers, as does the **Craft Beer Co.** On Saturdays, beer connoisseurs should head to the "Bermondsey Beer Mile", home to half a dozen or so microbreweries mostly nestled in the railway arches under the tramline.

Other Pub Drinks

Cider is another traditional English alcoholic drink found in every pub. Made from apples, it comes in a range of strengths and degrees of dryness. Blended Scotch whisky and malt whiskies are also staples, as is gin, usually drunk with tonic water. During the winter, mulled wine (warm and spicy) or hot toddies (brandy or whisky with hot water and sugar) may be served and in summer many Brits enjoy a pitcher of Pimms (a fruit cup, or punch, usually served with a garnish of summer fruits). Non-alcoholic drinks are also always available.

Historic Pubs

Many pubs have a fascinating history and decor, whether it is a beamed medieval snug or an extraordinary Arts and Crafts interior, as at the **Black Friar**, a must-see temple to imbibing, featuring bronze bas reliefs and an intimate, marble-and-mosaic chamber at the back. While many of the gin palaces of the 19th century have been revamped or abandoned, there are some notable survivors. At the **Prince Alfred** in Maida Vale, the bar is divided by "snobscreens", a feature that enabled the upper set to enjoy a drink without mixing with their servants. The semicircular **Viaduct Tavern**, opposite the Old Bailey, ablaze with mirrors, chandeliers and etched glass, is a suitably stately setting for distinguished barristers and judges, while the **Princess Louise** retains its magnificent central mahogany bar, complete with original clock, moulded ceiling and vivid wall tiles. Less grand but just as lovingly decorated is the tiny, tiled **Dog & Duck** in Soho – but you may have to battle for a seat or (in warm weather) stand outside with its many devotees. Many pubs have strong literary associations, such as the **Fitzroy Tavern**, a meeting place for writers and artists in the 1930s and 40s, including Dylan Thomas, George Orwell and Augustus John. **Ye Olde Cheshire Cheese** is associated with Dr Johnson, while Charles Dickens frequented the **Trafalgar Tavern** and Oscar Wilde often went to **The Salisbury**. Samuel Pepys witnessed the Great Fire of London from the **Anchor**, on the river at Bankside. The less literary **Old Bull and Bush** in north London was the subject of a well known old music-hall song, while the 17th-century **Lamb and Flag** – one of central London's few surviving timber-framed buildings down an alleyway – was known as the Bucket of Blood because it was the venue for bare-knuckle prize fights. Some pubs have sinister associations; for example, some of Jack the Ripper's victims were found near the **Ten Bells**. Dick Turpin, the 18th-century highwayman, took refreshment at the **Spaniards Inn** in north London, and the **French House** in Soho was a meeting point for the French Resistance during World War II.

Pub Entertainment

Fringe theatre productions (see p338) are staged at the **King's Head**, the **Latchmere**, and at the Gate Theatre above the **Prince Albert**. Some pubs have live music: there is excellent modern jazz at the **Bull's Head** in Barnes and a wide variety of music styles at the popular **Spice of Life**. The diminutive **Golden Eagle**, on a winding backstreet in Marylebone, is a rare central London piano pub, with nostalgic singalongs a few nights a week.

Outdoor Drinking

Most pubs with outdoor seating tend to be located slightly outside the city centre. The **Freemasons Arms**, for example, near Hampstead Heath, has a very pleasant garden, as does the **Hampshire Hog** in

Hammersmith. Some pubs enjoy riverside locations with fine views, from the **Prospect of Whitby** in Wapping and the **Grapes** in Limehouse to the **White Cross** in Richmond. There is an array of bars and restaurants along the South Bank, including the **Queen Elizabeth Roof Garden and Bar** which overlooks the river.

Gastropubs

Emerging in the early 1990s, the gastropub offers patrons the chance to enjoy a drink or sit down to a good meal – or both. Among the first was **The Eagle**, which offers gourmet dishes from the open kitchen that occupies half of the bar. Some, like **The Lansdowne** in Primrose Hill and the **Wells Tavern** in Hampstead, have dedicated upstairs dining rooms as well as laid-back neighbourhood pub rooms where you can eat and drink.

TV foodie Roxy Beaujolais serves simple bistro dishes in a tiny, quirky old pub, the **Seven Stars**, near the Royal Courts of Justice. The **Cow** is known for its oysters and Guinness, while the **Chapel** and the **Fire Station** are popular with both drinkers and diners. The **Norfolk Arms** is a traditional-looking pub on the corner of Leigh Street and Sandwich Street, and serves a delicious selection of Mediterranean tapas. For an authentic British Sunday roast, head to **The Lady Ottoline** in Bloomsbury or **The Engineer**, just north of Regent's Park in Primrose Hill, an ideal retreat from Camden Market. The smart **Jugged Hare** in Clerkenwell has wonderful game dishes in season and has a set pre- and post-theatre menu handy for those taking in a show at the Barbican.

Bars

London's bar scene has been gradually transformed since the mid-1990s; up until then, the choice was limited to either hotel bars, wine bars or pubs.

Propelled by a cocktail revival, as well as the fact that eating and drinking out is now deeply ingrained in daily London life, new bars are opening all the time. Eagerly sought out by style-conscious connoisseurs, the latest watering holes are now as much a talking point as new restaurants.

Soho and Covent Garden are brimming with bars, but to sample the hottest places, head either east or west. In the past decade, Shoreditch has been transformed from a no-go area to an evening destination, which is spilling into neighbouring Bethnal Green. One of the earliest pioneers, the basement lounge, no-frills **Electricity Showrooms** in Shoreditch, is still hopping. The chic and cosy **Whistling Shop** serves unconventional cocktails in a dimly lit setting. The hip **Book Club** is an eclectic space in which to eat, drink and enjoy events, from arts and science to crafts and DIY.

Across town in Notting Hill, sip good-value Scorpion Bowls and Zombies in the kitsch tiki-lounge ambience of **Trailer Happiness** or go for classic and more inventive cocktails at **Gate**, which has a lively atmosphere. The area's stylish bars contrast with the down-to-earth pubs frequented by the market traders, such as the bustling **Portobello Star**.

If you want to stick to the centre of town, fashionable options include the **Lab Bar**, which serves excellent cocktails, especially Latin American drinks such as caipirinhas and mojitos, or **Aqua Spirit**, a bar with a rooftop terrace behind Oxford Circus. South of the river, the **Fridge Bar** in Brixton has DJs playing decent hip-hop and deep house with lots of dancing and drinking.

Many restaurants feature excellent bars. The bar at **Green's Restaurant and Oyster Bar** is a very special place to go, to drink Champagne and eat oysters and lobster in elegant surroundings. **Smiths of Smithfield**, opposite the famous meat market, has a large, industrial-style café/bar at ground level, and a sleek cocktail and Champagne bar on the next floor, topped by two restaurants upstairs; nearby, **St John** has a stylish bar serving excellent wine and bar food. A drink in the bar is the less expensive way to experience the **Criterion** brasserie's sumptuous, gilded neo-Byzantine decor. Contemporary Chinese restaurant **Hakkasan** serves exotic cocktails flavoured with the likes of ginger and lemongrass in its glamorous Oriental-style bar.

Specialist Bars

Aficionados of particular spirits are well served in London. Scottish restaurant **Boisdale**'s Macdonald Bar boasts 170 Scotch malt whiskies (and an impressive selection of Cuban cigars), while the **Rockwell**, an upscale bar in the Trafalgar Hotel, offers London's largest bourbon selection. **Salt** is a slick, modern whisky bar, and **Dirty Martini** in Covent Garden offers a range of bespoke cocktails – its happy hour includes half-price martinis. Mexican bar/restaurant **La Perla** is nearby and has an extensive range of tequilas for your shooting pleasure.

Chain Bars

Halfway between a bar and a pub, with large windows and white walls, London's chain bars may not be the most exciting places to drink, but they are a reliable option and some find them more inviting than dark pubs. Filled with chunky wood furniture, **All Bar One** is very popular. **Pitcher & Piano** has sofas and blonde wood surrounds, while the **Slug & Lettuce** chain features paintings on the walls and quiet rooms for talking. **Be At One** specializes in cocktails and even offers master classes. Branches of **Browns Bar & Brasserie** are often located in grand buildings, decorated with modern twists.

DIRECTORY

Soho & Piccadilly

Admiral Duncan
54 Old Compton St W1.
Map 13 A2.

Aqua Spirit
240 Regent St W1.
Map 12 F2.

Balans
60 Old Compton St W1.
Map 13 A2.

Brewdog
113 Bayham St NW1.
Map 12 F1.
(One of several branches.)

Compton's of Soho
51–53 Old Compton St W1.
Map 13 A2.

Criterion
224 Piccadilly W1.
Map 13 A3.

Dog & Duck
18 Bateman St W1.
Map 13 A2.

The Edge
11 Soho Square W1.
Map 13 A1.

The French House
49 Dean St W1.
Map 13 A1.

Hakkasan
8 Hanway Place W1.
Map 13 A1.

Lab Bar
12 Old Compton St W1.
Map 13 A2.

Long Bar
50 Berners St W1T.
Map 12 F1.

Pitcher & Piano
69 Dean St W1.
Map 13 A1.

Rupert Street
50 Rupert St W1.
Map 13 A2.

Spice of Life
6 Moor St W1.
Map 13 B2.

Mayfair & St James's

Be At One
20 Great Windmill St W1.
Map 13 A2.
(One of several branches.)

Browns Bar & Brasserie
47 Maddox St W1.
Map 12 F2.

Claridge's
Brook St W1.
Map 12 E2.

Rivoli Bar
Ritz Hotel,
150 Piccadilly W1.
Map 12 F3.

Salt
82 Seymour St W2.
Map 11 C2.

Slug & Lettuce
19 Hanover St W1.
Map 12 F2.
(One of several branches.)

Trader Vic's
The London Hilton,
22 Park Lane W1.
Map 12 D3.

Covent Garden & Strand

American Bar
The Savoy, Strand WC2.
Map 13 C2.

Brasserie Max
Covent Garden Hotel,
10 Monmouth St WC2.
Map 13 B2.

The Craft Beer Co
168 High Holborn WC1.
Map 13 B1.
(One of several branches.)

Dirty Martini
11–12 Russell St WC2.
Map 13 C2.

Ku Bar
30 Lisle St WC2.
Map 13 A2.

La Perla
28 Maiden Lane WC2.
Map 13 C2.

Lamb and Flag
33 Rose St WC2.
Map 13 B2.

Rockwell Bar
The Trafalgar, 2 Spring
Gardens SW1.
Map 13 B3.

The Salisbury
90 St Martin's Lane WC2.
Map 13 B2.

Seven Stars
53–54 Carey St WC2.
Map 14 D1.

Bloomsbury & Holborn

Fitzroy Tavern
16 Charlotte St W1.
Map 13 A1.

The Lady Ottoline
11a Northington St WC1.
Map 6 D5.

Norfolk Arms
28 Leigh St WC1.
Map 5 B4.

Princess Louise
208 High Holborn WC1.
Map 13 C1.

Scarfes Bar
Rosewood London, High
Holborn WC1. **Map** 13 C1.

The City & Clerkenwell

All Bar One
103 Cannon St EC4.
Map 15 A2.
(One of several branches.)

Hotel Bars

London's hotel bars continue to offer an elegant setting for classic and innovative cocktails, with **The Blue Bar** at the Berkeley Hotel and the **Long Bar** at the Sanderson Hotel prime examples. The **American Bar** at the Savoy, decorated in an Art Deco style, has a pianist, a terrific atmosphere and classic cocktails (try the signature White Lady or the Dry Martini, which the bar introduced to Britain), while another Jazz Age gem, the **Rivoli Bar** at The Ritz, has been resplendently restored. **Claridge's Bar** offers excellent Champagne cocktails (among other concoctions) in a glamorous, contemporary-classic setting. **Trader Vic's** in the Park Lane Hilton provides an exotic tropical setting in which to enjoy an amazing range of rum cocktails.

Scarfes Bar, in the Rosewood London, is a lively bar with a traditional soul, evoking the atmosphere of a London gentlemen's club with a roaring fire at one end and wooden bar running along the other. Warm, intimate and sophisticated, with plush furniture and handwoven rugs on a parquet floor, **Brasserie Max** in the Covent Garden Hotel is always buzzing and is very popular with theatre and film people.

Gay Bars

Old Compton Street in Soho has a well-established gay scene. Tables spill out onto the pavements and there is a lively, friendly atmosphere. **Compton's of Soho**, a busy pub, is across the road from the gay bar and eatery **Balans** and close to the well-known gay pub **The Admiral Duncan**. **The Edge** is a sprawling bar and club over four floors, while **Rupert Street** is a stylishly low-key option for a relaxed drink. The **Ku Bar & Club** is a popular lesbian hangout, while, away from the West End, the **Royal Vauxhall Tavern** hosts Duckie's outrageous cabaret and DJs on Saturday nights.

DIRECTORY

Black Friar
174 Queen Victoria St EC4. **Map** 14 F2.

The Book Club
100 St Leonard St EC1. **Map** 7 C5.

The Eagle
159 Farringdon Rd EC1. **Map** 6 E4.

The Jugged Hare
49 Chiswell St EC1. **Map** 7 B5.

Smiths of Smithfield
67–77 Charterhouse St EC1. **Map** 6 F5.

St John
26 St John St EC1. **Map** 6 E2.

Ten Bells
84 Commercial St E1. **Map** 8 D5.

Viaduct Tavern
126 Newgate St EC1. **Map** 14 F1.

Whistling Shop
63 Worship St EC2. **Map** 7 C4.

Ye Olde Cheshire Cheese
145 Fleet St EC4. **Map** 14 E1.

Southwark & South Bank

Anchor
34 Park Street SE1. **Map** 15 A3.

Fire Station
150 Waterloo Rd SE1. **Map** 14 E4.

George Inn
77 Borough High St SE1. **Map** 15 B4.

Queen Elizabeth Roof Garden Bar & Café
Southbank Centre, Belvedere Rd SE1. **Map** 14 D4.

Knightsbridge & Belgravia

Blue Bar
The Berkeley, Wilton Place SW1. **Map** 12 D5.

Boisdale
15 Eccleston St SW1. **Map** 20 E1.

Green's Restaurant & Oyster Bar
36 Duke St SW1. **Map** 12 F3.

Hampstead, Primrose Hill & Marylebone

Chapel
48 Chapel St NW1. **Map** 3 B5.

The Engineer
65 Gloucester Ave NW1. **Map** 4 D1.

Freemasons Arms
32 Downshire Hill NW3. **Map** 1 C5.

Golden Eagle
59 Marylebone Lane W1. **Map** 12 D1.

The Lansdowne
90 Gloucester Ave NW1. **Map** 4 D1.

Old Bull and Bush
North End Way NW3. **Map** 1 A3.

Spaniards Inn
Spaniards Rd NW3. **Map** 1 A3.

The Wells Tavern
30 Well Walk NW3. **Map** 1 B4.

Bayswater & Notting Hill

The Cow
89 Westbourne Park Rd W11. **Map** 9 B1.

The Gate
87 Notting Hill Gate W11. **Map** 9 C3.

Portobello Star
171 Portobello Rd W11. **Map** 9 B2.

Prince Albert
11 Pembridge Rd W11. **Map** 9 C3.

Trailer Happiness
177 Portobello Rd W11. **Map** 9 B2.

Further Afield

Bull's Head
373 Lonsdale Rd SW13.

City Barge
27 Strand-on-the-Green W4.

Electricity Showrooms
39A Hoxton Square N1. **Map** 7 C3.

Fridge Bar
1 Town Hill Parade SW2.

Grapes
76 Narrow St E14.

Hampshire Hog
227 King St W6.

King's Head
115 Upper St N1. **Map** 6 F1.

Latchmere
503 Battersea Park Rd SW11.

Prince Alfred
5a Formosa St W9.

Prospect of Whitby
57 Wapping Wall E1.

Royal Vauxhall Tavern
372 Kennington Lane SE11. **Map** 22 D3.

Trafalgar Tavern
Park Row SE10.

White Cross
Water Lane, Richmond-Upon-Thames.

SHOPS AND MARKETS

London offers a shopping experience like no other. From luxurious department stores such as Liberty, Harrods and Fortnum & Mason to the many bustling street markets, this is one of the most lively and exuberant shopping scenes in the world. No matter what you are looking for, there is a place to find it. At the top end, head to the designer shops of Knightsbridge with their stunning window displays, or indulge in the luxurious shopping experience provided by the stores on Regent Street, where ultramodern shops sit comfortably alongside the old-fashioned emporia. Oxford Street boasts a plethora of stores showcasing the latest in high street fashion: Topshop's flagship branch is definitely worth a visit. For more bespoke finds, head to specialist boutiques, such as those found in Notting Hill and Covent Garden. Bargain-hunters will find a wealth of inexpensive goods in the thriving markets, which often exude a carnival atmosphere; pick up a vintage piece in Camden Market or browse for bric-a-brac or handmade jewellery on legendary Portobello Road.

When to Shop

In London, standard opening hours are from 10am to 5:30 or 6pm, Monday to Saturday. Sundays and public holidays see shorter trading hours, usually from 11am to 4pm or 12pm to 5pm. Many stores across the city, however, operate longer hours from Monday to Saturday; some in Oxford Street and Covent Garden, for example, open before 10am and close their doors at 9pm.

Street market opening times vary: some may operate daily whereas others will only set up once a week (see pp335–7 for details of specific markets).

How to Pay

Most stores and retail chains accept all major credit cards, including MasterCard, American Express, Diners Club, Japanese Credit Bureau and Visa. However, smaller independent shops may take Visa and MasterCard only, and street market stalls often do not have card payment facilities, so it is always worth carrying cash or keeping an eye out for an ATM. Most shops no longer accept payment by personal cheque, and their use is likely to be phased out completely by 2018. Some major stores accept Euros.

Bags from two of the most famous West End shops

Rights and Services

On a defective purchase, you usually get a refund, if proof of purchase is produced and the goods are returned. This isn't always the case with sales goods, so check the store policy. Most large stores, and some small ones, will pack goods up for you and send them anywhere in the world.

VAT Exemption

VAT (Value Added Tax) is a sales tax of 20%, which is charged on virtually all goods sold in Britain. The exceptions are books, some food and children's clothes. VAT is mostly included in the advertised or marked price, although business suppliers, including some stationers and electrical goods shops, often charge separately.

Non-European Union visitors to Britain who stay no longer than three months may claim back VAT. If you plan to do so, carry your passport when shopping. You must complete a form in the store when you buy the goods and then give a copy to Customs when leaving the country. The tax refund may be returned by cheque or refunded to your credit card (though there may be a service charge for the latter). Most stores have a minimum purchase threshold (often £50 or £75). If you arrange to have your goods shipped directly home from the store, VAT should be deducted before you pay.

Harrods' elaborate Edwardian tiled food hall

Twice-Yearly Sales

The traditional sale season runs from Boxing Day (26 December) until February, and again from June to July, when shops slash their prices and sell off unwanted stock. The department stores have some of the best reductions and it is not uncommon for queues to form outside long before opening.

Best of the Department Stores

The king of London's department stores is **Harrods**, with over 300 departments specializing in fashion, luxury items, beauty and homeware, and a staff of 5,000. The spectacular food hall decorated with Edwardian tiles sells fish, cheese, fruit and vegetables. **Harvey Nichols** boasts fashion and beauty collections, with emphasis placed on British, European and American designers and brands. The food hall, opened in 1992, is one of London's most stylish.

Selfridges, on Oxford Street, has a wide choice of labels, a great lingerie department and a section devoted to emerging designers. High-street concessions on the ground-floor cater to young women. It also has a food hall featuring global delicacies.

John Lewis in Oxford Street and its partner Peter Jones in Sloane Square are royal warrant holders, meaning they supply goods to members of the royal family. Both have an excellent selection of fashion, homeware and haberdashery. **Liberty** *(see p113)*, housed in an impressive mock-Tudor building near Carnaby Street, is renowned for its floral and graphic prints, which were first developed in the late 19th century. **Fortnum & Mason** began as a grocery store and, though it gradually evolved into a department store with classic fashion and luxury items, it continues to boast an impressive food section. Continuously popular are Fortnum's tins of biscuits and tea, and its luxury picnic hampers.

For affordable fashion, head to high-street favourite **Debenhams**, which champions British designers at reasonable prices. As other department stores, it also has beauty and homeware collections.

Marks & Spencer

Marks & Spencer (M&S) has come a long way since 1882, when the Russian emigré Michael Marks had a single stall in Leeds' Kirkgate market with the sign, "Don't ask the price – it's a penny!" It now has more than 800 stores worldwide and most stock is "own label". Marks & Spencer's underwear in particular is a staple of the British wardrobe. The food department has a great range of everyday items. The Oxford Street branches at the Pantheon (near Oxford Circus) and Marble Arch are best for clothes and household goods.

Some well-known names in British clothes design

Markets

As well as offering a wealth of delights for the discerning bargain hunter, London's thriving markets also provide an atmospheric glimpse into the past, with many dating back to medieval times.

Soak up the rich colours, aromas and flavours at specialist food stalls, browse quaint antique shops for curios or pick up a retro bargain at one of the many vintage clothes outlets. Early risers have a better chance of finding a bargain *(see also pp335–7)*.

Doorman at Fortnum & Mason

Penhaligon's for scents *(see p329)*

London's Best: Shopping Streets and Markets

London's best shopping areas range from the elegance of Knightsbridge, where porcelain, jewellery and couture fashion come at the highest prices, to colourful markets such as Brick Lane, Spitalfields and Portobello. Meccas for those who enjoy searching for a bargain, London's markets also reflect the vibrant street life engendered by its enterprising multicultural community. The city is fertile ground for specialist shoppers: there are streets crammed with antique shops, antiquarian booksellers and art galleries. Turn to pages 320–35 for more detail on shops, grouped according to category.

Kensington Church Street
Home to over 60 antique dealers and one of the largest selections of art and antiques in London *(see p219)*.

Regent's Park and Marylebone

Portobello Road Market
Over 1,000 stalls sell *objets d'art*, jewellery, medals, paintings and silverware – plus fresh fruit and vegetables *(see p337)*.

| 0 kilometres | 1 |
| 0 miles | 0.5 |

See inset map

South Kensington and Knightsbridge

Kensington and Holland Park

Piccadilly Mayfair and St James

Knightsbridge
Exclusive designer clothing is on sale here, at Harrods as well as smaller stores *(see p213)*.

Chelsea

King's Road
A centre for avant-garde fashion in the 1960s and 1970s, the street is now home to chain stores and designer shops. This area also has upmarket antique shops *(see p200)*.

London's West End Shops

Oxford Street is sometimes called London's High Street and many of the shops that line it are branches of national or international chains. The big department stores such as Selfridges and John Lewis line this street, as do smaller shops selling clothes and tourist souvenirs. On Regent Street, Piccadilly and Bond Street, prices rise and shoppers search for specialized purchases among the designer clothes shops, jewellers and art and antique dealers, while Carnaby Street has a more eclectic vibe.

Bloomsbury and Fitzrovia

Smithfield and Spitalfields

Covent Garden and the Strand

Holborn and the Inns of Court

The City

South Bank

Southwark and Bankside

Whitehall and Westminster

RIVER THAMES

Brick Lane Market
In this East End street, everything from old books to new trainers is on sale (see p335).

Columbia Road Flower Market
Lined with independent art and antique shops, Columbia Road hosts a wonderful flower market every Sunday (see p336).

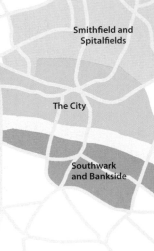

Covent Garden and Neal Street
Street entertainers perform in this lively and historic market. The specialist shops of Neal Street are nearby (see p119).

Charing Cross Road
Shops selling old and new books line this street and the nearby Cecil Court (see p326).

Clothes

Traditional British tailoring, international haute couture, vintage fashion, the latest high street trends: the fashion capital of the UK has it all. London's clothing stores, much like its restaurants, reflect the city's diverse styles and culture, and there really is something to suit every taste. Visit the stylish stores of British designers such as Vivienne Westwood and Stella McCartney or wander through the hugely popular high-street chains, which have perfected the art of mimicking catwalk trends – and offering them at a reasonable price. For unique fashion, London's boutiques are second to none and there is always a bargain to be found at vintage stores and market stalls.

Traditional Clothing

British tailoring and fabrics are world-renowned for their high quality. In Savile Row, you can follow in the sartorial footsteps of Winston Churchill and the Duke of Windsor, among other dapper luminaries, and have a suit made to measure or buy one off the peg. Established in 1806, **Henry Poole** was the first tailor in the Row. At **H Huntsman & Sons**, you can choose from three options – bespoke, custom-made and ready-to-wear. The bespoke suits are painstakingly hand-stitched on the premises, which partly explains the exorbitant £3,000-plus price tag. In addition to making suits to order, **Gieves & Hawkes** has two ready-to-wear lines.

Competing with the distinguished and traditional line-up are fashion-conscious tailors, known for modern cuts and vibrant fabrics, including **Ozwald Boateng** and **Richard James**.

Jermyn Street is famous for smart shirts. At venerable shops such as **Turnbull & Asser** or the family-run **Harvie & Hudson**, you can either have them custom-made or choose the less expensive standard-sized options. Many manu-facturers, including the popular shirt chain **Thomas Pink**, also sell a variety of classic women's blouses.

Several bastions of classic British style have completely reinvented themselves as fashion labels. **Burberry** is the best example of this, although it still does a brisk trade in its famous trenchcoats, checked clothing (for children too) and distinctive accessories. **Daks** is also a good choice for classic raincoats, suits and accessories for both sexes, giving traditional British styles a modern twist. **Dunhill** specializes in

immaculate, if expensive, menswear and accessories, while at the **Crombie** outlet, you can buy the famous fitted overcoat that was given the company name. The menswear emporium **Hackett** caters to a younger, yet still conservative, clientele. Designers **Margaret Howell** and **Nicole Farhi** create updated versions of relaxed British country garments for men and women, such as knitwear, tweeds and sheepskin coats. You can still find a more traditional, smart country look in the Regent Street, Piccadilly or Knightsbridge areas; the classic Barbour wax jacket, for example, can be found at Harrods and Liberty (see p317). **Cordings**, established 1839, is good for country-gent/-lady gear, such as check shirts, moleskin trousers and Covert coats.

While **Liberty** (see p317) now has a good selection of

Size Chart

For Australian sizes follow British and American convention

Children's clothing

British	2–3	4–5	6–7	8–9	10–11	12	14	14+ (years)
American	2–3	4–5	6–6X	7–8	10–12	14	16 (size)	
Continental	2–3	4–5	6–7	8–9	10–11	12	14	14+ (years)

Children's shoes

British	7½	8	9	10	11	12	13	1	2
American	7½	8½	9½	10½	11½	12½	13½	1½	2½
Continental	24	25½	27	28	29	30	32	33	34

Women's dresses, coats and skirts

British	6	8	10	12	14	16	18	20
American	4	6	8	10	12	14	16	18
Continental	32	34	36	38	40	42	44	46

Women's blouses and sweaters

British	30	32	34	36	38	40	42
American	6	8	10	12	14	16	18
Continental	34	36	38	40	42	44	46

Women's shoes

British	3	4	5	6	7	8
American	5	6	7	8	9	10
Continental	36	37	38	39	40	41

Men's suits

British	34	36	38	40	42	44	46	48
American	34	36	38	40	42	44	46	48
Continental	44	46	48	50	52	54	56	58

Men's shirts

British	14	15	15½	16	16½	17	17½	18
American	14	15	15½	16	16½	17	17½	18
Continental	36	38	39	41	42	43	44	45

Men's shoes

British	7	7½	8	9	10	11	12
American	7½	8	8½	9½	10½	11	11½
Continental	40	41	42	43	44	45	46

contemporary designers, it still uses its patterned prints to make blouses and stylish men's shirts, as well as scarves and ties. Floral print dresses and feminine blouses can be found at **Laura Ashley**, although the store has introduced more contemporary looks as well.

Modern British Design and Street Fashion

London designers are known for their eclectic, irreverent style. Grand dames **Vivienne Westwood** and Zandra Rhodes have been on the scene since the 1970s – the latter opened the **Fashion and Textile Museum** in southeast London in 2003. It features 3,000 of her own garments as well as examples by other influential fashion figures. Many British designers of international stature have their flagship stores in the capital, including **Paul Smith** and **Stella McCartney**, both of whom showcase their collections in fabulous townhouses, and the late **Alexander McQueen**, with an upscale showcase in Bond Street. Young home-grown talent such as Alice Temperley, whose feminine frocks are beloved by the London party set, Eley Kishimoto, characterized by bold prints, and avant-garde design duo Boudicca, can be found in the capital's boutiques.

Selfridges (see p317) also has an impressive selection of emerging designers. **Dover Street Market**, conceived by Comme des Garçons' Rei Kawakubo, revives the age-old tradition of the covered clothes market, but in a much more upmarket milieu. Its four minimalist floors showcase a varied array of goods, from glitzy shoes by king of the platform Terry de Havilland to cool art books and vintage and contemporary designer clothes.

If you want to take home a bit of British design, but can't afford the high prices, it's worth visiting **Debenhams** (see p317), which has harnessed the talents of numerous leading designers, including Jasper Conran, Matthew Williamson, Julien Macdonald and Ben De Lisi, to create cheaper collections exclusive to the department store. Young designers often start out with a stall on Portobello Road or Old Spitalfields Market (see p337), both good sources of interesting clothing. There are also a few good designer sale shops: **Paul Smith Sale Shop** is located in central London, while those looking for **Burberry** bargains at its factory outlet will have to travel a bit further afield to the East End. For those willing to travel further, **Bicester Village** is an excellent discount shopping centre with mid- to high-end stores.

Boutiques

London is home to an extensive variety of boutiques – hot new shops crop up and, it must be said, close down with dizzying regularity. The mother of them all is **Browns**. Established in the 1970s, it occupies several storefronts in South Molton Street and stocks a wide selection of international labels. But the highest concentration of boutiques is in Notting Hill, near the intersection of Westbourne Grove and Ledbury Road. Because of the numerous cafés in the area, and the relaxed, affluent atmosphere away from the crowded West End shopping districts, it's an extremely pleasant place to browse.

JW Beeton embodies quirky British style, while **Matches**, which also has outposts in Richmond and Wimbledon, dominates Ledbury Road with three separate shops – one for both sexes, another just for women, plus one specializing in frocks by Diane von Furstenberg. Like Browns in the West End, Matches stocks international designer labels, including Balenciaga, Fendi and Chloé, interspersed with a variety of British talent such as Giles Deacon, Bella Freud and Jade Jagger. **Question Air**

and **Feathers** also stock designer labels, while **Aimé** specializes in French clothes and homewares. A short walk away in a quiet residential street, celebrity favourite **The Cross** is a delightfully understated little shop, packed with women's fashion, cute children's clothes and toys, toiletries and unusual accessories. **The Dispensary** in Kensington Park Road is much loved by locals for its Notting Hill style. Primrose Hill, Islington, Soho and the streets radiating off Seven Dials near Covent Garden are also dotted with independent fashion shops. **Diverse**, in Islington, caters for both sexes with a great selection of iconic labels and collections from new designers.

Chain Stores and Street Fashion

In Britain, cutting-edge styles are no longer, as they once were, the exclusive preserve of the rich. "High-street" stores have never been better, both in terms of quality and design. Moreover, the cheaper versions of all the latest styles appear in the shops, almost as soon as they have been sashayed down the catwalk. **Oasis** and **Topshop** have both won celebrity fans for their up-to-the-minute, young womenswear. The latter, which proudly claims to be "the world's largest fashion store", is a complete mine of inexpensive clothes and beautiful accessories; there is even an in-store "boutique" with the latest collections by hip designers, and a vintage section as well.

The upmarket chains **Jigsaw**, **Karen Millen** and **Whistles** are more expensive with the emphasis on beautiful fabrics and shapes which, while stylish, don't slavishly copy the catwalk. **Jigsaw Junior**, available in larger branches, offers delectable mini versions of its designs for girls. **Reiss** and **Ted Baker** are popular with trend-conscious young men, though they also have good women's collections.

More unique shops can be found in and around Newburgh Street, behind Carnaby Street.

Vintage Fashion

The city offers a vast hunting ground for aficionados of vintage style, ranging from market stalls to exclusive shops showcasing immaculately preserved designerwear. Head east for funky emporia such as **Rokit**, which also has branches in Camden and Covent Garden, in addition to a huge warehouse, **Beyond Retro**. Grays Antique Market (see p336) covers all bases with the award-winning Vintage Modes, spanning the styles of the past century, as well as fashion-conscious Advintage, run by a former department-store personal shopper. Glamorous evening gowns and pin-up lingerie for the girls, flashy Hawaiian shirts and novelty bar accessories for the guys, can be found at fashionistas' favourite **Rellik** in Kensington. Vintage and antique dealers often have beautiful pieces for sale in Alfie's Antique Market.

For mint-condition 1930s bias-cut silk slips and 1920s flapper dresses, head to **Annie's Vintage Clothes** in Camden Passage. **Absolute Vintage**'s flagship store, on Hanbury Street, has great vintage items Be warned, neither of these shops is cheap.

Knitwear

Traditional British knitwear is still hugely popular, from Fair Isle jumpers to Aran knits. The best places for these are in Piccadilly, Regent Street and Knightsbridge. Heritage label **Pringle** has been revitalized with more contemporary shapes and vivid colours. Luxurious casual labels **Joseph** and **The White Company** feature modern chunky knits, while **John Smedley** concentrates on simple designs in fine-gauge wool and sea island cotton. For cashmere, **N. Peal**, which has both men's and women's shops at opposite ends of the Burlington Arcade, has a great

selection of luxury jumpers, cardigans and accessories. While the popular chain **Brora** offers an affordable range of contemporary, Scottish cashmere for the entire family. **Marilyn Moore** designs hip interpretations of classic knitwear.

Underwear and Lingerie

Marks & Spencer (see p317) is the most popular source of reasonably priced basics; it now has several fashionable lingerie lines as well. **Agent Provocateur**, founded by designer Vivienne Westwood's son and his wife, oozes retro pin-up glamour, from the slightly kinky pink uniforms worn by the staff to its nostalgically seductive bra sets. **Tallulah Lingerie** sells wispy negligées, hand-made silk undergarments and sumptuous bridal lingerie. For top quality bras head to **Rigby and Peller**. This British institution holds a royal warrant and has experts on hand to help you find the perfect lingerie for your shape. **Myla** is a good choice for luxury lingerie and tasteful nightwear

Children's Clothes

You can get traditional hand-smocked dresses and romper suits from Liberty, **Caramel Baby & Child** and **Rachel Riley**, which stock smocks, gowns and tweed coats. Burberry's New Bond Street store has a children's section showcasing adorable mini macs, kilts and other items featuring the famous check. **Trotters** offers everything from shoes and clothes to haircuts, while the **Little White Company** makes pretty dresses and smart sweaters, amongst others, in pure cotton and wool. They also sell delightful bedding and sleepwear. **JoJo Maman Bébé** caters for new-borns to six year olds with cute corduroy dresses, skirts and trousers, and nautical-inspired tops and bottoms.

Shoes

Some of the most famous names in the footwear industry

are based in Britain. If you have a few thousand pounds to spare, you can have a pair custom-made by the royal family's shoemaker, **John Lobb**. Ready-made, traditional brogues and Oxfords are the mainstay of **Church's Shoes**, while **Oliver Sweeney** gives classics a contemporary edge. For traditional, bench-made shoes at bargain prices, it's worth travelling further afield to Battersea and splurging at the **Shipton & Heneage** outlet. It offers an exceptionally wide range of Oxfords, Derbys, loafers and boots crafted in the same Northamptonshire factories as some of the most celebrated names, for considerably lower prices; the out-of-the-way location keeps costs down.

Fans of the Fab Four can s tep into their idols' shoes: **Anello & Davide** designed the original Beatle Boot and still sells bespoke shoes in a range of materials. **The British Boot Company** in Camden has a wide range of Dr Martens, which were originally designed as hard-wearing work boots but soon adopted by fans of rock 'n' roll and punk music.

Jimmy Choo and **Manolo Blahnik**, two celebrated shoe designers, remain popular with women worldwide, and both have stores in central London.

French Soles produces stunning, quality ballet flats and pumps in numerous colours and materials, while **Emma Hope** in Sloane Square is best known for simple, timeless shapes embellished with embroidery or beadwork. **Gina**, also in Sloane Square, produces luxury footwear for women.

Less expensive, yet good quality designs can be found on the high street in **Hobbs** or **Clarks**, while **Aldo, Office** and **Schuh** focus on styles for a younger crowd.

The Natural Shoe Store, a Covent Garden institution of more than 30 years' standing, sells what its name says – shoes crafted from natural products. Vegan shoes and Birkenstocks are among its top sellers.

DIRECTORY

Traditional Clothing

Burberry
21–23 New Bond St W1.
Map 12 F2.
Tel 020 7980 8425.

Cordings
19–20 Piccadilly W1.
Map 13 A3.
Tel 020 7734 0830.

Crombie
48 Conduit St W1.
Map 12 F2.
Tel 020 7434 2886.
(One of two branches.)

Daks
10 Old Bond St W1.
Map 12 F3.
Tel 020 7409 4040.

Dunhill
48 Jermyn St W1.
Map 12 F3.
Tel 020 7290 8609.

Gieves & Hawkes
1 Savile Row W1.
Map 12 E3.
Tel 020 7432 6403.

H Huntsman & Sons
11 Savile Row W1.
Map 12 F3.
Tel 020 7734 7441.

Hackett
87 Jermyn St SW1.
Map 13 A3.
Tel 020 7930 1300.
(One of several branches.)

Harvie & Hudson
96–97 Jermyn St SW1.
Map 12 F3.
Tel 020 7839 3578.
(One of three branches.)

Henry Poole & Co
15 Savile Row W1.
Map 12 F3.
Tel 020 7734 5985

Laura Ashley
House of Fraser, 318
Oxford St W1.
Map 12 F1.
Tel 0344 800 3752.
(One of several branches.)

Liberty
Regent St W1.
Map 12 F2.
Tel 020 7734 1234.

Margaret Howell
34 Wigmore St W1.
Map 12 E1.
Tel 020 7009 9009.

Nicole Farhi
25 Conduit St W1.
Map 10 F2.
Tel 020 7499 8368.
(One of several branches.)

Ozwald Boateng
30 Savile Row W1.
Map 12 F3.
Tel 020 7440 5237.

Richard James
29 Savile Row W1.
Map 12 F2.
Tel 020 7434 0171.

Thomas Pink
85 Jermyn St SW1.
Map 12 F3.
Tel 020 7930 6364.
(One of several branches.)

Turnbull & Asser
71–72 Jermyn St SW1.
Map 12 F3.
Tel 020 7808 3000.

Modern British Design and Street Fashion

Alexander McQueen
4–5 Old Bond St W1.
Map 12 F3.
Tel 020 7355 0088.

Bicester Village
50 Pingle Drive, Bicester,
Oxfordshire OX26 6WD.
Tel 1869 366266.

Burberry Factory Shop
29–31 Chatham Place E9.
Tel 020 8328 4287.

Debenhams
334–348 Oxford St W1.
Map 12 E2.
Tel 08445 616 161.

Dover Street Market
17–18 Dover Street W1.
Map 12 F3.
Tel 020 7518 0680.

Fashion and Textile Museum
83 Bermondsey St SE1.
Map 15 C4.
Tel 020 7407 8664.

Paul Smith
Westbourne House, 120 &
122 Kensington Park Rd
W11. **Map** 9 B2.
Tel 020 7727 3553.
(One of several branches.)

Paul Smith Sale Shop
23 Avery Row W1.
Map 12 E2.
Tel 020 7493 1287.

Selfridges
400 Oxford St W1.
Map 12 D2.
Tel 0870 837 7377.

Stella McCartney
30 Bruton St W1.
Map 12 E3.
Tel 020 7518 3100.

Vivienne Westwood
44 Conduit St W1.
Map 12 F2.
Tel 020 7439 1109.

Boutiques

Aimé
32 Ledbury Rd W11.
Map 9 C2.
Tel 020 7221 7070.

Browns
23–27 South Molton St
W1. **Map** 12 E2.
Tel 020 7514 0016.

The Cross
141 Portland Rd W11.
Map 9 A3.
Tel 020 7727 6760.

Diverse
294 Upper St, Islington
N1. **Map** 6 F1.
Tel 020 7359 8877.

Feathers
176 Westbourne Grove
W11. **Map** 9 C2.
Tel 020 7243 8800.

JW Beeton
48–50 Ledbury Road W11.
Map 9 C2.
Tel 020 7229 8874.

Matches
60–64 Ledbury Rd W11.
Map 9 C2.
Tel 020 7221 0255.

Question Air
28 Rosslyn Hill NW3.
Map 1 C5.
Tel 020 7435 9921.
(One of several branches.)

Chain Stores and Street Fashion

The Dispensary
200 Kensington Park Rd
W11. **Map** 9 B2.
Tel 020 7727 8797.

Hobbs
84–88 King's Rd SW3.
Map 19 C2.
Tel 020 7581 2914.
(One of several branches.)

Jigsaw
6 Duke of York Sq, Kings
Rd SW3. **Map** 19 C2.
Tel 020 7730 4404.
(One of several branches.)

Karen Millen
247 Regent St W1. **Map**
12 F1. **Tel** 020 7629 1901.
(One of several branches.)

Oasis
12–14 Argyll St W1.
Map 12 F2.
Tel 020 7434 1799.
(One of several branches.)

Reiss
Kent House, 14–17
Market Place W1.
Map 12 F1.
Tel 020 7637 9112.
(One of several branches.)

DIRECTORY

Ted Baker
9–10 Floral St WC2.
Map 13 C2.
Tel 020 7836 7808.
(One of several branches.)

Topshop
Oxford Circus W1.
Map 12 F1.
Tel 0844 848 7487.
(One of several branches.)

Whistles
12–14 St Christopher's Pl
W1. **Map** 12 D1.
Tel 020 7487 4484.
(One of several branches.)

Vintage Fashion

Absolute Vintage
15 Hanbury St E1.
Map 8 E5.
Tel 020 7247 3883.

**Annie's Vintage
Clothes**
12 Camden Passage N1.
Map 6 F1.
Tel 020 7359 0796.

Beyond Retro
110–112 Cheshire St E2.
Map 8 E4.
Tel 020 7613 3636.

Rellik
8 Golborne Gardens W10.
Tel 020 8962 0089.

Rokit
101 & 107 Brick Lane E1.
Map 8 E4.
Tel 020 7375 3864.
(One of three branches.)

Knitwear

Brora
81 Marylebone High St
W1. **Map** 4 D5.
Tel 020 7224 5040.
(One of several branches.)

John Smedley
24 Brook St W1.
Map 12 E2.
Tel 020 7495 2222.

Joseph
299 Fulham Rd SW10.
Map 18 F3.
Tel 020 7352 6776.
(One of several branches.)

Marilyn Moore
7 Elgin Crescent W11.
Map 9 B2.
Tel 020 7727 5577.

N. Peal
Burlington Arcade,
Piccadilly, W1.
Map 12 F3.
Tel 020 7499 6485.

Pringle Scotland
94 Mount St W1.
Map 12 D3.
Tel 020 3011 0031.

The White Company
Unit 5, Slingsby Pl, St
Martin's Courtyard WC2.
Map 13 B2.
Tel 020 8166 0200.

Underwear and Lingerie

Agent Provocateur
6 Broadwick St W1.
Map 13 A2.
Tel 020 7439 0229.
(One of several branches.)

Myla
Cabot Place West E14.
Tel 020 7519 6867.
(One of several branches.)

Rigby & Peller
22A Conduit St W1.
Map 12 F2.
Tel 020 7491 2200.

Tallulah Lingerie
65 Cross St, Islington N1.
Map 6 F1.
Tel 020 7704 0066.

Children's Clothes

Caramel Baby & Child
4 Denman Place W1.
Map 13 A2.
Tel 020 7287 2622.
(One of several branches.)

JoJo Maman Bébé
12 Cale St SW3.
Map 19 B3.
Tel 020 7589 9593.
(One of several branches.)

Little White Company
90 Marylebone High St W1.
Map 4 D5.
Tel 020 7486 7550.

Rachel Riley
82 Marylebone High St
W1. **Map** 4 D5.
Tel 020 7935 7007.

Trotters
34 King's Rd SW3.
Map 19 C2.
Tel 020 7259 9620.

Shoes

Aldo
3–7 Neal St WC2.
Map 13 B1.
Tel 020 7836 7692.
(One of several branches.)

Anello & Davide
15 St Alban's Grove W8.
Map 10 E5.
Tel 020 7938 2255.

**The British Boot
Company**
5 Kentish Town Rd NW1.
Map 4 F1.
Tel 020 7485 8505.

Church's Shoes
108–10 Jermyn St SW1.
Map 12 F3.
Tel 020 7930 8210.

Clarks
119 Oxford St W1.
Map 13 A1.
Tel 020 7437 2593.
(One of several branches.)

Emma Hope
53 Sloane Sq SW1.
Map 19 C2.
Tel 020 7259 9566.
(One of two branches.)

French Soles
6 Ellis St SW1.
Map 19 C2.
Tel 020 7730 3771.

Gina
189 Sloane St SW1.
Map 19 C1.
Tel 020 7235 2932.

Hobbs
124 Long Acre WC2.
Map 13 B2.
Tel 020 7836 0625.
(One of several branches.)

Jimmy Choo
27 New Bond St W1.
Map 12 F2.
Tel 020 7493 5858.

John Lobb
88 Jermyn St SW1.
Map 12 F3.
Tel 020 7930 8089.

Manolo Blahnik
49–51 Old Church St,
Kings Road SW3.
Map 19 A4.
Tel 020 7352 8622.

Office
57 Neal St WC2.
Map 13 B1.
Tel 020 7379 1896.
(One of several branches.)

Oliver Sweeney
5 Conduit St W1.
Map 12 F2.
Tel 020 7491 9126.

Schuh
200 Oxford St W1.
Map 13 A1.
Tel 020 3355 9914.
(One of several branches.)

Shipton & Heneage
117 Queenstown Rd SW8.
Map 20 E5.
Tel 020 7738 8484.

**The Natural Shoe
Store**
70 Neal St WC2.
Map 13 B1.
Tel 020 7240 2783.

Specialist Shops

London may be famed for grand department stores such as Harrods, but there are many specialist shops which should also figure on the visitor's itinerary. Some have expertise built up over a century or more, while others are new and fashionable, or cater to the whims of eccentric collectors. Whether you are looking for traditional British products and food, high-tech gadgets, or the latest trends in music, London has a wide range of stores to suit everyone's tastes.

Food

Britain's reputation for terrible food is proving hard to shake off but, in reality, the national cuisine has improved immeasurably, and London has become one of the culinary capitals of the world. There is a huge interest in local and organic produce, as well as delicacies imported from all over Europe. This is reflected in the growing number of food markets, the biggest being Borough Market (see p335). Specialities that are well worth sampling include a variety of chocolates, biscuits, preserves, cheeses and teas (see pp292–3).

The food halls of Fortnum & Mason, Harrods and Harvey Nichols (see p317) are good outlets for all of these, but it's also worth visiting the gastro-nomic gems dotted around town. Of these, **A Gold**, housed in an atmospheric old milliner's shop near Spitalfields Market, specializes in traditional foods from across Britain. Its goods, including cheeses, sausages, jams, baked goods, English wines and mead, are advertised on chalkboards. **Paxton & Whitfield**, a delightful shop dating from 1797, stocks more than 300 cheeses, including baby Stiltons and Cheshire truckles, along with pork pies, biscuits, oils and preserves.

The shelves of tiny **Neal's Yard Dairy** groan with huge British farmhouse cheeses. **Paul Rothe & Son** is a family-run deli that has hardly changed since it opened more than a century ago. Besides selling "British and foreign provisions", such as preserves, old-fashioned sweets and biscuits, the white-coated proprietors also serve morning toast and sandwiches on proper china. For traditional English chocolates, such as violet or rose creams and after-dinner mints in beautiful gift boxes, head for **Charbonnel et Walker** in Royal Arcade off Bond Street. It has been in business for more than 100 years, and holds royal warrants. True chocoholics will be in their element at **Hotel Chocolat**'s shop/café, with a vast selection to choose from. Also committed to "real" chocolate, **Rococo** is well-known for its unique blue-and-white Victorian-style packaging.

Drinks

Tea, the most British of drinks, comes in all kinds of flavours. Fortnum & Mason's traditional teas come in appealingly refined gift selections. **The Tea House** is packed with myriad varieties from classic to creative (such as "summer pudding"), colourful souvenir tins and teapots. **Postcard Teas** is another specialist retailer of high-quality teas.

The quaint 19th-century **Algerian Coffee Stores** manages to pack more than 140 varieties of coffee and 200 teas into its small shop. Family business **HR Higgins** sells fine coffees and teas from around the world. Attractive gift sets are available and you can try before you buy in the coffee room downstairs.

Whisky lovers should head to **The Vintage House**, which displays the widest array of single malts in England, including some very old bottles. **Berry Bros & Rudd** is one of the oldest wine merchants in the world, still trading in wines, fortified wines and spirits from its ancient, panelled shop in St James's. In contrast, the **Wine Rooms**, with locations in both Fulham and Kensington, offer excellent wine tastings and have a vast selection of wines to try and buy in a sleek and modern setting.

One-Offs

Many of London's quirky old specialist shops have closed due to rising rents, but there are still some fascinating anachronisms, as well as interesting newcomers, to be found across the city. A large number of specialist traders operate from stalls in antiques markets such as Alfie's and Portobello Road (see p337), where you can find everything from old military medals to commemorative china and vintage luggage. A notable survivor is **James Smith & Sons**, the largest and oldest umbrella shop in Europe, which first opened for business in 1830. Behind its mahogany and glass-panelled façade lies an array of high-quality umbrellas and walking sticks, including the once ubiquitous city gent brolly.

Halcyon Days specializes in little enamelled copper boxes, the delightful products of a revived 18th-century English craft. Top-quality wooden chess sets and boards, including an ornamental design featuring Sherlock Holmes characters, are available at **Chess & Bridge Ltd**. **VV Rouleaux** is festooned with every imaginable type of ribbon and flamboyant trimming.

The young and young at heart will enjoy **Honeyjam**, which sells traditional toys and games for all ages. **Benjamin Pollock's Toyshop** does a nifty line in miniature self-assembly paper theatres, as well as other traditional toys and antique teddies. **The Old Cinema** in Chiswick specializes in quirky vintage furniture.

At **The Bead Shop** in Covent Garden, you will find two floors stocked with thousands of items from Swarovski crystals to glass, pewter and stirling silver beads.

Fans of *Doctor Who* and all things science fiction will love **ScifiCollector** on the Strand. It stocks a huge range of toys and merchandise, including items inspired by the time-travelling Time Lord, *Red Dwarf* and *Star Trek*. There is also a section for first day covers, stamp sheets and signed items. Special events held at the store include appearances by science fiction authors, artists and actors.

Books and Magazines

Though bookshops no longer thrive as they used to, plenty can still be found across the capital. Once a bookshop haven, Charing Cross Road *(see p112)* has a few stalwarts including **Quinto & Francis Edwards**, which has a good selection covering travel, natural history, naval and military history, and art and literature, and **Any Amount of Books**, a shop with an eclectic mix of secondhand fiction and non-fiction.

Charing Cross Road is also home to the flagship branch of **Foyles**. Spread across four floors, this impressive store stocks over 200,000 different titles. There is also a jazz shop and café *(see below)*, an art gallery and real live piranhas in the children's department. **Grant & Cutler**, within the store, is an unrivalled source of foreign books and DVDs. Over in Piccadilly, the flagship store of **Waterstones** (which has branches across the city) rivals Foyles for its vast collection. With over eight miles of shelving space, it is Europe's largest bookshop.

Just off Charing Cross Road is Cecil Court *(see p105)*, a charming pedestrian alleyway lined with dealers specializing in everything from illustrated children's books to modern first editions. **Watkins Books**

focuses on mind, body and soul, while **Marchpane** dedicates itself to Lewis Carroll and his *Alice in Wonderland*, as well as other British children's classics – keep an eye out for signed copies of the *Harry Potter* books. **Storey's Ltd** is an antiquarian bookshop specializing in engraved prints and maps.

London's oldest bookshop is **Hatchards** in Piccadilly. Operating since 1797, this historic store is a holder of three royal warrants. It stocks new fiction and non-fiction, and often hosts author signings. The beautiful Edwardian **Daunt Books** in Marylebone has a soaring, galleried back room devoted entirely to travel titles and, unusually, related fiction organized by country. It is worth a visit for its stunning interior alone.

Globe trotters should head to **Stanfords** *(see p116)* in Long Acre, which stocks guides to nearly every part of the world. It also has a great range of maps. More travel books can be found at the **Notting Hill Bookshop**, made famous by the Hugh Grant and Julia Roberts film. Also in Notting Hill is **Books for Cooks**, complete with café and test kitchen *(see p281)*.

Magma, a short walk from Charing Cross Road, is excellent for design subjects and avant-garde illustrated books. Graphic novels and American and European comics are the speciality at **Gosh!** and **Orbital Comics**, while fantasy and science fiction abound at the world-famous **Forbidden Planet**. Stocking all of the latest comic and graphic novels, this megastore also offers a huge range of merchandise and hosts signings with leading science fiction and fantasy authors. For gay writing, visit the pioneering **Gay's The Word**, near Russell Square. The best selection of books on movies is found at the **Cinema Store**.

The French Bookshop in South Kensington is stocked

with best-selling French titles. If you are looking for newspapers and magazines from abroad, **Capital Newsagents** stocks, among others, American, Italian, French, Spanish and Middle Eastern publications. **Gray's Inn News** is also worth a visit for European titles. For those with a keen interest in vintage magazines, there are more than 200,000 in the basement of **Vintage Magazines** in Soho, dating from the early 1900s all the way through to the present day. There are also all manner of movie and popular culture memorabilia and gifts on the ground floor of the shop.

CDs and Records

As one of the world's greatest centres of recorded music, London has an excellent selection of record shops catering to fans of all musical styles. **Fopp** sells a wide range of music from pop to punk to easy listening, and their Covent Garden branch stocks a comprehensive range.

Small specialist shops tend to cater to the more esoteric tastes. **Rough Trade** was at the centre of the emerging punk scene and still sniffs out interesting indie talent today. It has a live music venue in east London. For jazz, check out **Ray's Jazz**, which is now housed in Foyles' bookshop along with a café where you can chill out to the vibe.

Secializing in jazz since 1974, **Honest Jon's** also offers various types of music in both vinyl and CD format. In particular, it carries an extensive selection of soul and reggae. **Flashback Records** sells rare, hard to find music and collectable records, from reggae to pop.

There is a high concentration of indie vinyl and CD shops in and around Berwick Street. **Sister Ray** is the largest indie record store in the West End. For 12-inch singles, the medium of club and dance music, one of the top places to go is **Phonica** in Soho.

DIRECTORY

Foods

A Gold
42 Brushfield St E1.
Map 8 D5.
Tel 020 7247 2487.

Charbonnel et Walker
1 Royal Arcade, 28 Old
Bond St W1. **Map** 12 F3.
Tel 020 7491 0939.

Hotel Chocolat Café
163 Kensington High St
W8. **Map** 9 C5.
Tel 020 7938 2144.

Neal's Yard Dairy
17 Short's Gardens WC2.
Map 13 B2.
Tel 020 7240 5700.

Paul Rothe & Son
35 Marylebone
Lane W1. **Map** 12 E1.
Tel 020 7935 6783.

Paxton & Whitfield
93 Jermyn St SW1.
Map 12 F3.
Tel 020 7930 0259.

Rococo
321 King's Rd SW3.
Map 19 A4.
Tel 020 7352 5857.

Drinks

**Algerian Coffee
Stores**
52 Old Compton St W1.
Map 13 A2.
Tel 020 7437 2480.

Berry Bros & Rudd
3 St James's St SW1.
Map 12 F4.
Tel 020 7396 9600.

HR Higgins
79 Duke St W1.
Map 12 D2.
Tel 020 7629 3913.

Postcard Teas
9 Dering St W1.
Map 12 E2.
Tel 020 7629 3654.

The Tea House
15A Neal St WC2.
Map 13 B2.
Tel 020 7240 7539.

The Vintage House
42 Old Compton St W1.
Map 13 A2.
Tel 020 7437 5112.

The Wine Rooms
129 Kensington Church St
W8. **Map** 10 D4.
Tel 020 7727 8142.
871–3 Fulham Road SW6.
Tel 020 7042 0440.

One-Offs

The Bead Shop
21a Tower St WC2.
Map 13 B2.
Tel 020 7240 0931.

**Benjamin Pollock's
Toyshop**
44 The Market, Covent
Garden Piazza WC2.
Map 13 C2.
Tel 020 7379 7866.

Chess & Bridge Ltd
44 Baker St W1. **Map** 12
D1. **Tel** 020 7486 7015.

Halcyon Days
14 Brook St W1.
Map 12 E2.
Tel 020 7629 8811.

Honeyjam
2 Blenheim Crescent W11.
Map 9 A2.
Tel 020 7243 0449.

James Smith & Son
53 New Oxford St WC2.
Map 13 B1.
Tel 020 7836 4731.

The Old Cinema
160 Chiswick High St W4.
Tel 020 8995 4166.

ScifiCollector
79 Strand WC2.
Map 13 C3.
Tel 020 7836 2341.

VV Rouleaux
102 Marylebone Lane W1.
Map 4 D5.
Tel 020 7224 5179.

Books and Magazines

Any Amount of Books
56 Charing Cross Road
WC2. **Map** 13 B2.
Tel 020 7836 3697.

Books for Cooks
4 Blenheim Crescent W11.
Map 9 B2.
Tel 020 7221 1992.

Capital Newsagents
115 Tottenham Court Rd.
Map 4 F4.
Tel 020 7388 9107.

Cinema Store
Unit 4B, Upper St Martin's
Lane WC1. **Map** 13 B2.
Tel 020 7379 7838.

Daunt Books
83–4 Marylebone High St
W1. **Map** 4 D5.
Tel 020 7224 2295.

Forbidden Planet
179 Shaftesbury Ave W1.
Map 13 B1.
Tel 020 7420 3666.

Foyles
107 Charing Cross Rd
WC2. **Map** 13 B1.
Tel 020 7437 5660.
(One of several branches.)

The French Bookshop
28 Bute St SW7.
Map 18 F2.
Tel 020 7584 2840.

Gay's The Word
66 Marchmont St WC1.
Map 5 B4.
Tel 020 7278 7654.

Gosh!
1 Berwick St W1.
Map 13 B1.
Tel 020 7636 1011.

Gray's Inn News
50 Theobalds Rd WC1.
Map 6 D5.
Tel 020 7405 5241.

Hatchards
187 Piccadilly W1.
Map 12 F3.
Tel 020 7439 9921.

Magma
8 Earlham St WC2.
Map 13 B2.
Tel 020 7240 8498.

Marchpane
16 Cecil Court WC2.
Map 13 B2.
Tel 020 7836 8661.

**Notting Hill
Bookshop**
13 Blenheim Crescent W11.
Map 9 A2.
Tel 020 7229 5260.

Orbital Comics
8 Great Newport St WC2.
Map 13 B2.
Tel 020 7240 0591.

**Quinto & Francis
Edwards**
72 Charing Cross Rd WC2.
Map 13 B1.
Tel 020 7379 7669.

Stanfords
12–14 Long Acre WC2.
Map 13 B2.
Tel 020 7836 1321.

Waterstones
203/206 Piccadilly W1.
Map 13 A3.
Tel 020 7851 2400.
(One of several branches.)

Watkins Books
19–21 Cecil Court WC2.
Map 13 B2.
Tel 020 7836 2182.

Vintage Magazines
39–43 Brewer St W1.
Map 13 A2.
Tel 020 7439 8525.

CDs and Records

Flashback Records
50 Essex Rd N1.
Map 6 F1.
Tel 020 7354 9356.

Fopp
1 Earlham St WC2.
Map 13 B2.
Tel 020 7845 9770.
(One of several branches.)

Honest Jon's
278 Portobello Rd W10.
Map 9 B2.
Tel 020 8969 9822.

Phonica
51 Poland St W1.
Map 12 F1.
Tel 020 7025 6070.

Ray's Jazz
107 Charing Cross Rd
WC2.
Map 13 B1.
Tel 020 7437 5660.

Rough Trade
130 Talbot Rd W11.
Map 9 C1.
Tel 020 7229 8541.

Sister Ray
34–35 Berwick St W1.
Map 13 A1.
Tel 020 7734 3297.

Storey's Ltd
1 & 3 Cecil Court WC2.
Map 13 B2.
Tel 020 7836 3777.

Gifts and Souvenirs

London is a wonderful place to shop for gifts. It boasts an impressive array of original ceramics, jewellery, perfume and glassware, exotic merchandise from around the world, including jewellery from India and Africa, stationery from Europe and kitchenware from France and Italy. The elegant, Regency-period Burlington Arcade (see p94), the largest of several covered shopping arcades in central London, is known for its high-quality clothes, antique and new jewellery, leather goods and other items, many of which are made in the UK. It is also a real boon when the famously unpredictable weather turns nasty.

Shops at the big museums, such as the Victoria and Albert (see pp214–17), the Natural History (see pp206–7) and the Science Museum (see pp210–11), often have unusual items to take home as mementoes, while Contemporary Applied Arts and the market in Covent Garden Piazza (see p118) sell a range of British pottery, knitwear, pictures, clothing and other crafts. To buy all your gifts under one roof, go to Liberty (see p113), where beautiful stock from the world over fills every department, and the classic Liberty prints feature on many goods.

Gift Shops

If the phrase "gift shop" conjures up images of tacky tourist souvenirs, think again. A number of interesting shops bringing together a variety of goods under one roof has sprung up in the capital. **Eightsq** in Spitalfields is a delightful store with an irresistible collection covering everything from elegant furniture to interesting accessories. Best-sellers include hand-painted furniture, organic cotton baby clothes and tote bags. A short walk away, **Story**, in a beautifully preserved 18th-century residential street, looks more like a gallery space than a shop. It has an eclectic mix of items, including vintage dresses, organic bath products and modern and classic furnishings.

Across town in Notting Hill, **Brissi** is a lovely emporium kitted out with beautifully crafted household items, including elegant furniture and lamps, stylish mirrors and lighting. It also stocks fashion accessories for women, such as sun hats, tote bags and flip-flops in summer.

The **Design Museum Shop** is a museum gift shop with a difference. It stocks Post-Modern toys, games and innovative – and in some cases surprisingly affordable – accessories for home and office by big design names such as Arne Jacobsen, Tord Boontje and Eames. There are some wonderfully witty items, such as shoe-shaped shoe brushes and a doorstop in the form of a figure holding it open.

CultureLabel, which works with a plethora of museums and galleries, sells an eclectic range of items. **House of Hackney**, though specializing in clothes and interiors, has a great range of traditional British items perfect for gifts.

Jewellery

There are styles to suit every taste, from the fine traditional jewellery found in the exclusive shops of Bond Street to unusual pieces by independent designers in areas like Covent Garden (see pp114–23), Gabriel's Wharf (see p195) and Camden Lock (see pp335–6). Antique jewellery can be found in Hatton Garden and the Silver Vaults (see p145). The Crown Jeweller, **Garrard**, in Albemarle Street, has been designing jewellery since 1735. Be warned, the spectacular creations have price tags to match the plush store interior.

Asprey sells updated classics, while **Butler & Wilson** specializes in reproductions of vintage jewellery and accessories. **Nude Jewellery London**, tucked away in Mayfair's Shepherd Market, deals mainly in handmade pieces, and **Kabiri**, with a store in Marylebone and a concession in Selfridges, aims to bring works of previously unseen jewellery designers to London. **Assya** is a boutique jewellery store selling precious and semi-precious pieces. It is designed as a boudoir, so customers can try on a gorgeous array of jewellery, have a drink and relax. The husband and wife duo **Wright & Teague** design covetable modern silver and gold charm bracelets and necklaces, among other things.

The **Victoria & Albert** museum shop sells modern replicas of historic British designs, as does the shop at the British Museum (see pp128–31). Liberty (see p113) stocks a wide range of attractive jewellery as well.

Hats

Traditional men's headgear, from flat caps to trilbies and top hats, can be found at **Edward Bates**. Venerable hatter **Lock & Co**, founded in 1676, caters for both men and women, while Swaine Adeney Brigg sells hats by **Herbert Johnson**, who specializes in military wear.

Philip Treacy is Britain's most celebrated milliner and his fabulous creations are on display at his shop on Elizabeth Street and in upmarket department stores. Established name **Stephen Jones** also has some very eye-catching styles, while **Jane Taylor's** beautifully made designs range from cute cloches to extravagant Ascot confections. **Fred Bare's** funky, affordable designs can be found on Columbia Road on Sundays when the weekly flower market is in bloom, or from high-end department stores.

Bags and Leather Goods

Traditional British luggage, bags and small leather goods can be found in the streets and arcades off Piccadilly. **Swaine Adeney Brigg** sells umbrellas, hats, classic bridle-leather bags, old-fashioned walking sticks and other accoutrements for the country gent and lady. Well known for its classic, hard-wearing bags and luggage is upmarket **Mulberry**. Established in 1971, its modern interpretations of English country clothes and accessories are sought after by fashion folk as well as anyone who appreciates fine quality.

The ultimate luxury is **Connolly**, a name famous for crafting sleek leather interiors for Rolls-Royce. Its swish shop sells items that hark back to the golden age of motoring, such as leather driving jackets and shoes, magnificent tool cases and smart luggage, bound diaries and other extravagant home accessories and clothes.

J&M Davidson, owned by an Anglo-French couple, produces beautifully crafted, slightly retro bags, belts and small leather goods, often in unusual colours. The shop in Notting Hill also stocks a line of clothes and homeware. In Piccadilly, **Bill Amberg**'s shop sells simple, contemporary bags in various types of leather, suede and other skins, plus gloves, wallets, leather boxes and unusual items such as a stylish leather and sheepskin baby papoose.

Lulu Guinness and **Anya Hindmarch** both bring British wit and eccentricity to their handbags. Guinness's elaborate designs have included a bag in the shape of a flowerpot topped with red roses and a circular purse resembling an old-fashioned rotary telephone dial; she also produces many London-themed items. Hindmarch is famous for personalized, digitally printed photo bags, but also produces classic leather ones. For less expensive but high quality bags, purses and wallets, try **Radley**.

Scarves

The luxury French designer store **Hermès** sells beautiful silk and cashmere scarves, often using vibrant colours. Of course, Liberty's famous print scarves are perennially popular. Small, stylish department store **Fenwick** is known for its accessories, which includes a wide array of interesting scarves by the likes of Pucci and Missoni, as well as bags, hats and a huge range of hair decorations. The **V&A Museum** shop has a good selection of scarves, including William Morris print silk scarves and stunning replica scarves inspired by V&A collections. N. Peal (*see p322*) has an extensive choice of cashmere scarves and shawls.

Perfumes and Toiletries

Many British perfumeries use recipes that are hundreds of years old. **Floris** and **Penhaligon's**, for example, still manufacture the same flower-based scents and toiletries for men and women that they sold in the 19th century. The same goes for men's specialists **Truefitt & Hill** and **George F Trumper**, where you can buy some wonderful reproductions of antique shaving equipment as well. Chemist and perfumer **DR Harris** has been making its own range of toiletries for over two centuries; it's worth stopping by just to see the old-fashioned shop.

Neal's Yard Remedies employs traditional herbal and floral remedies as bases for its natural, therapeutic products. The fragrances, skincare range and candles of **Jo Malone** use such delicious aromas as herbs, fruit, even coffee, as well as traditional floral essences. The products all come in simple yet sophisticated packaging. If you're looking for an unusual scent, head to **Miller Harris**; Grasse-trained perfumer Lyn Harris creates fragrances with remarkable depth, which come in boxes decorated with botanical prints. **Content** is an organic skincare boutique store that sells an advanced range of beauty products, cherry-picked from around the globe. It also has a naturopathic clinic and beauty salon, making it one of London's leading organic and natural apothecaries.

Space NK stocks the best and the most up-to-date collection of beauty products from around the world, along with its popular own-brand range. **The Body Shop** uses recyclable plastic packaging for its affordable natural cosmetics and toiletries, and encourages staff and customers alike to take an interest in environmental issues. **Molton Brown** sells a range of cosmetics, body and haircare products in branches throughout London. **Kiehl's** American luxury toiletries and skincare brand has its own store in Covent Garden.

Stationery

For luxurious writing paper and desk accessories, try the Queen's stationer, **Smythson** of Bond Street. The little bound notebooks and address books embossed with a wide selection of amusing and practical titles, such as "Travel Notes" and "Blondes, Brunettes, Redheads" make great gifts and souvenirs. Fortnum & Mason (*see p317*) does handsome leather-bound diaries, blotters and pencil holders, while Liberty embellishes desk accessories with its famous Arts and Crafts prints. **The Wren Press** creates high quality and prestigious stationery, including bespoke letterheads and unique invitations. It also holds two royal warrants.

Aspinal of London, known for its fine leather goods, such as hand-crafted wallets and purses, handbags and travel bags, also produces leather-bound high-end stationery. Beautiful photo albums, diaries, iPad and iPhone cases and sleeves, pencil cases and even leather-encased tape measures are sold out of their Marylebone store, alongside all manner of other leather and non-leather gifts, such as silk and cashmere scarves.

Shepherd's Bookbinders stocks a range of handmade and decorative papers. Its marbled paper can make a glorious giftwrap for that very special present. Finally, for greeting cards, pens, gift wrapping paper and general stationery, pop into one of the many branches of **Paperchase** scattered around the city.

Interiors

Wedgwood still makes the famous pale blue Jasper china that Josiah Wedgwood designed in the 18th century. You can buy this and Irish Waterford crystal in many large department stores. For a fine variety of original pottery, visit **Contemporary Ceramics**, the gallery of the Craft Potters Association, or go to **Contemporary Applied Arts**. **Mint's** hand-picked selection of unique furniture, home accessories, china and glassware by established names and up-and-coming design talent is a pleasure to browse. Large interior furnishing stores **Heal's** and the **Conran Shop** have a great selection of stylish, modern accessories for the home. Those with more traditional tastes may prefer **Thomas Goode**, presided over by courteous tail-coated staff, which sells exquisite china, glassware, crystal, linen and gifts, including some antique pieces.

Check out **Graham & Green**, and its huge array of attractive – and affordable – items from around the globe, ranging from Moroccan tea glasses to Mongolian cushions and pretty nightwear. **Labour & Wait** is a wonderful source of solid, functional British items for home and garden, such as old-fashioned stainless

DIRECTORY

Gift Shops

Brissi
196 Westbourne Grove W11. **Map** 10 B2.
Tel 020 7727 2159.

Design Museum Shop
Commonwealth Institute Buiding, Kensington W14.
Map 9 C5.

Eightsq
Market Street, Spitalfields E1. **Map** 8 D5.
Tel 020 7375 0060.

Labour & Wait
85 Redchurch St E2.
Map 8 E4.
Tel 020 7729 6253.

Story
4 Wilkes St E1. **Map** 8 E5.
Tel 020 7377 0313.

Jewellery

Asprey
167 New Bond St W1.
Map 12 F3.
Tel 020 7493 6767.

Assya London
53 Ledbury Rd W11.
Map 9 C2.
Tel 020 7243 1687.

Butler & Wilson
20 South Molton St W1.
Map 12 E2.
Tel 020 7409 2955.

Garrard
24 Albemarle St W1.
Map 12 F3.
Tel 020 7518 1070.

Kabiri
37 Marylebone High St W1. **Map** 4 D5.
Tel 020 7317 2150.

Nude Jewellery
36 Shepherd Market, Mayfair W1. **Map** 12 E4.
Tel 020 7629 8999.

Wright & Teague
35 Dover St W1.
Map 12 F3.
Tel 020 7629 2777.

Hats

Edward Bates
73 Jermyn St SW1.
Map 13 A3.
Tel 020 7734 4707.

Fred Bare
118 Columbia Rd E2.
Map 8 E3.
Tel 020 7229 6962.

Herbert Johnson
7 Piccadilly Arcade SW1.
Map 12 F3.
Tel 020 7409 7277.

Jane Taylor
3 Filmer Mews SW6.
Map 17 B5.
Tel 020 7392 2333.

Lock & Co
6 St James's St SW1.
Map 12 F4.
Tel 020 7930 8874.

Philip Treacy
69 Elizabeth St SW1.
Map 20 E2.
Tel 020 7730 3992.

Stephen Jones
36 Great Queen St WC2.
Map 13 C1.
Tel 020 7242 0770.

Bags and Leather Goods

Anya Hindmarch
15–17 Pont St SW1.
Map 20 D1.
Tel 020 7838 9177.

Bill Amberg
2 Lonsdale Rd NW6.
Map 9 B2.
Tel 020 8960 2000.

Connolly
4 Clifford St W1.
Map 12 F2.
Tel 020 7439 2510.

J&M Davidson
97 Golborne Rd W10.
Tel 020 8969 2244.

Lulu Guinness
3 Ellis St SW1.
Map 19 C2.
Tel 020 7823 4828.

Mulberry
50 New Bond St W1.
Map 12 E2.
Tel 020 7491 3900.

Radley
37 Floral St WC2. **Map** 13 B2. **Tel** 020 7379 9709.

Swaine Adeney Brigg
7 Piccadilly Arcade SW1.
Map 12 F3.
Tel 020 7409 7277.

Scarves

Fenwick
63 New Bond St W1.
Map 12 E2.
Tel 020 7629 9161.

Hermès
179 Sloane St SW1.
Map 11 C3.
Tel 020 7823 1014.
(One of several branches.)

V&A
V&A Museum, Cromwell Rd SW7.
Map 19 A1.
Tel 020 7942 2696.

Perfumes and Toiletries

The Body Shop
66, 268 & 374 Oxford St W1.
Map 12 D2–F1.
Tel 020 7323 2183.

Content
14 Bulstrode St W1.
Map 12 D1.
Tel 020 3075 1006.

DR Harris
52 Piccadilly W1.
Map 12 F3.
Tel 020 7499 2939.

steel kettles, Welsh blankets and Guernsey sweaters. **David Mellor** is famous for his streamlined modern cutlery designs, while **Divertimenti** sells all manner of kitchen equipment and has a pleasant café at the back.

Emma Bridgewater has chunky mugs, crockery and tea towels, which are decorated with traditional motifs and amusing mottoes. **The Cloth Shop** in Notting Hill stocks beautiful new and antique British wool and cashmere blankets and throws, as well as cottons, velvets and soft furnishings. **Cath Kidston** designs fresh, nostalgic,

English-style prints which adorn everything from humble household items to fashion accessories. There's a huge range of pretty, giftable goods, including toiletries, ironing-board covers, laundry bags, eiderdowns, clothes for women and children, bags, china and stationery.

Several interiors stores on Upper Street in affluent Islington offer an impressive cache of gifts. **After Noah** is a big warehouse-like space bursting with vintage and retro-look items, including Bakelite rotary telephones, old metal tins and street signs, classic board games

and a huge assortment of children's toys. There is another branch in King's Road and a concession in Harvey Nichols *(see p317)*.

The modern interiors emporium **Aria** has two stores close to each other. One of these concentrates entirely on furniture and housewares by designers such as Alessi and Philippe Starck, while its satellite across the street sells gifts, including stationery, frames, bags and jewellery. Just nearby, on Upper Street, is the contemporary-design heavyweight **twentytwentyone** It also has a great selection of vintage items.

DIRECTORY

Floris
89 Jermyn St SW1.
Map 13 A3.
Tel 020 7930 2885.

George F Trumper
9 Curzon St W1.
Map 12 E3.
Tel 020 7499 1850.

Jo Malone
23 Brook St W1.
Map 12 E2.
Tel 0370 192 5771.

Kiehl's
29 Monmouth St WC2.
Map 13 B1.
Tel 020 7240 2411.

Miller Harris
21 Bruton St W1.
Map 12 E3.
Tel 020 7629 7750.

Molton Brown
227 Regent St W1.
Map 12 F2.
Tel 020 7493 7319.
(One of several branches.)

Neal's Yard Remedies
15 Neal's Yard WC2.
Map 13 B1.
Tel 020 7379 7222.

Penhaligon's
13 Market Building,
Covent Garden
Piazza WC2.
Map 13 C2.
Tel 020 3040 3030.

Space NK
131 Westbourne Grove
W2. **Map** 9 C2.
Tel 020 7727 8063.

Truefitt & Hill
71 St James's St SW1.
Map 12 F3.
Tel 020 7493 2961.

Stationery

Aspinal of London
46 Marylebone High St W1.
Map 4 D5.
Tel 020 7224 0413.

Asprey
167 New Bond St W1.
Map 12 F3.
Tel 020 7493 6767.

Paperchase
213 Tottenham Court Rd
W1. **Map** 5 A5.
Tel 020 7467 6200.
(One of several branches.)

Shepherd's Bookbinders
30 Gillingham St SW1.
Map 20 F2.
Tel 020 7233 9999.

Smythson
40 New Bond St W1.
Map 12 E2.
Tel 020 7629 8558.

The Wren Press
1 Curzon St W1.
Map 12 D2.
Tel 020 7351 5887.

Interiors

After Noah
121 Upper St N1.
Map 6 F1.
Tel 020 7359 4281.

Aria
Barnsbury Hall, Barnsbury
St N1. **Map** 6 F1.
Tel 020 7704 6222.

Cath Kidston
51 Marylebone High St W1.
Map 4 D5.
Tel 020 7935 6555.

The Cloth Shop
290 Portobello Rd W10.
Map 9 A1.
Tel 020 8968 6001.

Conran Shop
Michelin House, 81
Fulham Rd SW3.
Map 19 A2.
Tel 020 7589 7401.

Contemporary Applied Arts
89 Southwark St SE1.
Map 14 F3.
Tel 020 7436 2344.

Contemporary Ceramics
63 Great Russell St WC1.
Map 13 B1.
Tel 020 7242 9644.

David Mellor
4 Sloane Sq SW1.
Map 20 D2.
Tel 020 7730 4259.

Divertimenti
33–34 Marylebone High
St W1. **Map** 4 D5.
Tel 020 7581 8065.

Emma Bridgewater
81a Marylebone High St.
Map 4 D5.
Tel 020 7486 6897.
779 Fulham Road.
Map 17 C5.
Tel 020 7371 5264.

Graham & Green
4 Elgin Crescent W11.
Map 9 B2.
Tel 020 7243 8908.

Heal's
196 Tottenham Court Rd
W1. **Map** 5 A5.
Tel 020 7636 1666.

Mint
2 North Terrace SW3.
Map 19 A1.
Tel 020 7225 2228.

Thomas Goode
19 South Audley St W1.
Map 12 D3.
Tel 020 7499 2823.

twentytwentyone
274 Upper St N1.
Map 6 F1.
Tel 020 7288 1996.

Waterford Wedgwood
Sold at John Lewis, 300
Oxford St W1.
Map 12 E1.
Tel 0844 693 1765.

Art and Antiques

London's art and antique shops are spread across the length and breadth of the capital. While the more fashionable and expensive dealers are mainly concentrated in a relatively small area bounded by Mayfair and St James's, other shops and galleries catering to more modest budgets are scattered over the rest of the city. Whether your taste is for old masters or young modern artists, Boule or Bauhaus, you are bound to find something of beauty in London that is within your financial means.

Mayfair

Cork Street is the centre of the British contemporary art world and is home to a plethora of galleries, many of which have launched the careers of major British artists.

The first gallery to open in the street was the **Mayor Gallery**, famous for Dada and Surrealism. The biggest name to look out for, however, is **Waddington Custot Galleries**. It regularly exhibits works by major twentieth-century artists, such as Henri Matisse and Peter Blake. A stop here is a must – though pieces are understandably priced highly.

Redfern Gallery shows mainstream modern art while **Flowers Central**, part of a growing modern gallery chain, has some unusual British pieces. A couple of doors down, **Browse and Darby Gallery** sells 19th- and 20th-century British and French paintings, as well as contemporary works.

Also look into Clifford Street, where **Maas Gallery** excels in Victorian masters, and Sackville Street for **Henry Sotheran**'s rare books and prints. On Albemarle Street, the **Albemarle Gallery** specializes in contemporary prints and sculptures, showcasing the works of international and British artists. Established and up-and-coming talents are featured in the gallery's frequent installations.

Nearby, New Bond Street is the centre of the fine antiques trade in London. If it's Turner watercolours or Louis XV furniture you're after, this is the place. A walk up from Piccadilly takes you past **Richard Green**

and the **Fine Art Society**, among other extremely smart galleries. For jewellery and objets d'art visit **David Aaron Ancient Art** and **Grays Antique Market** *(see p336)*; for silver, go to **S J Phillips**; and for 18th-century British furniture and art, try **Mallett Antiques**.

Also on New Bond Street are two of the big London auction houses, **Bonhams** and **Sotheby's** *(see p333)*.

North of Mayfair, on a quiet Marylebone Street, is the **Lisson Gallery**, which often features cutting-edge installations. **Thompson's Gallery** has locations in Marylebone and the City, selling a diverse mix of appealing if somewhat mainstream current British art.

Even if you are not a buyer, these galleries are fascinating places to visit, so don't be afraid to walk in – you can learn more from an hour spent here than you can from weeks of studying text books.

St James's

South of Piccadilly lies a maze of 18th-century streets. This is gentlemen's club country *(see Pall Mall p96)* and the galleries mostly reflect the traditional nature of the area. At the centre is Duke Street, home of old master dealers **Johnny van Haeften** and **Derek Johns**. Nearby, on King Street, you will find the main salerooms of **Christie's**, the well-known auction house where Van Goghs and Picassos change hands for millions. On the corner of Bury Street, celebrating past masculine pleasures is the sophisticated **Pullman Gallery**, which

specializes in automobile art and collectables, racy cigarette cases, vintage cocktail shakers and other bar accessories.

Walk back up Bury Street past several interesting galleries, including the **Tryon Gallery** for traditional British sporting pictures and fine sculptures. Also duck into Ryder Street to take in **Chris Beetle**'s gallery of works by illustrators and caricaturists.

Knightsbridge

If you walk around to the back of Harrods *(see p317)*, you'll find the beginning of pretty Walton Street, which is lined with art galleries, traditional interiors shops and boutiques. As you would expect in this exclusive area, prices are high. On nearby Brompton Road, the **Crane Kalman** gallery shows an enticing variety of contemporary art. Motcomb Street houses some notable galleries, including the fascinating **Mathaf Gallery**, which features 19th-century British and European paintings of the Arab world.

Pimlico Road

The antique shops that line this road tend to cater predominantly for the pricey requirements of the interior decorator. This is where to come if you are searching for an Italian leather screen or a silver-encrusted ram's skull. **Westenholz** specializes in 18th and 19th century decorative furniture and has some delightful pieces. While he doesn't deal in antiques, the Queen's nephew, furniture designer **Viscount Linley** produces some beautiful pieces that could pass as such, as well as contemporary designs. The finely crafted accessories, such as inlaid wooden boxes and frames, make great gifts.

East and West London

London's East End is a growth area for contemporary art. **Flowers East** in Kingsland

Road represents sculptors, painters and photographers. There is a cluster of art dealers and galleries in **The Tea Building** on nearby Shoreditch High Street. **The Approach** combines an upstairs gallery with a good pub, frequented by local artists. The **Hundred Years Gallery** in Hoxton frequently shows the work of internationally emerging artists.

On the other side of the river in southeast London, **Purdy Hicks**, based in a converted warehouse near Tate Modern, is great for contemporary British painting. The **Oxo Tower Wharf**, in a landmark Thameside building topped by a good restaurant, is a hive of creativity, housing over 30 design and craft studios. You can find everything from handwoven textiles and jewellery to homewares and fashion. Among the highlights are Black + Blum's innovative, affordable interior designs – for example, a lamp in the shape of a reading figure, made up of a lightbulb "holding" a book shade. Bodo Sperlain focuses on modern tableware and Studio Fusion works with different materials to produce innovative jewellery and silverware.

There are some interesting contemporary galleries in the vicinity of Portobello Road and Westbourne Grove. **East West Gallery** is great for contemporary art, **Themes & Variations**, combines striking postwar and contemporary furniture and decorative art, and **Gallery 85** boasts a range of the finest antiques, including some exceptional Meissen porcelain.

A browse along Kensington Church Street in west London will take you to a concentration of small antiques emporia that has everything from Arts and Crafts furniture to Staffordshire pottery dogs.

North London

High-profile American dealer Larry Gagosian contributed to the regeneration of famously sleazy King's Cross by opening his second gallery here, in a capacious former garage. Expect world-class contemporary names and lesser-known artists at **Gagosian Gallery**. **Victoria Miro**'s massive Victorian warehouse in Islington is a showcase for British as well as young international talent.

Affordable Art

For the chance to acquire a work by what could become one of the big names of the future, visit the **Contemporary Art Society**. Its annual ARTFutures market showcases the work of more than 100 artists, at prices from £100 to well into the thousands.

Open seven days a week all year round, **Will's Art Warehouse** in Putney sells pieces for between £50 and £3,000. This friendly gallery has a wide variety of art and holds a new exhibition every six weeks. The owner founded the aptly named Affordable Art Fair, which takes place twice a year in Battersea Park.

Photography

The largest collection of original photographs for sale in the country is to be found in the print sales room of the **Photographers' Gallery**. It displays work from emerging global talents and established artists, as well as works from its historical archives over its three floors of exhibition space.

Atlas Gallery is one of the foremost galleries in London dealing exclusively with fine art photography. It is the official gallery for Magnum photographs. **Hamiltons Gallery** is worth visiting, especially during its major exhibitions.

Michael Hoppen's three-floor space in Chelsea shows both vintage and current works. If you want to take home a piece of London's rock 'n' roll heritage, the **Rock Archive**, near Camden Passage in Islington, is a great source of limited-edition photographic prints of British music legends such as Paul Weller posing with Pete Townshend or Mick Jagger jamming with Ronnie Wood.

Bric-a-Brac and Collectables

For smaller, more affordable pieces, it's worth going to one of the established London markets, such as Portobello Road (see p337), Camden Passage (see p336) or Bermondsey (see p335), which is the main antiques market, catering to the trade. Grays Antique Market (see p336) has some great specialist dealers, but the prices are a bit higher than elsewhere given the location, while further afield, Greenwich Market (see p336) is well worth a rummage and may throw w up some bargains. Many high streets out of the city centre have covered markets of specialist stalls.

Alfies Antique Market is London's largest indoor market for antiques and collectables. The dealers are experienced specialists, and anyone interested in 20th-century design and vintage fashion especially will enjoy browsing the eclectic stock here.

Auctions

If you are confident enough, auctions are a much cheaper way to buy art or antiques, but be sure to read the small print in the catalogue, which usually costs around £15. Bidding is simple – you need to register, take a number, then raise your hand when the lot you want comes up. The auctioneer will see your bid. It's as easy as that, and can be great fun.

The main auction houses in London are **Christie's Fine Art Auctioneers**, **Sotheby's Auctioneers** and **Bonhams**. Don't forget Christie's saleroom in Kensington, which deals with art and antiques for a more modest budget. Bonhams' second London saleroom in Knightsbridge also holds weekly auctions of affordable antiques and collectables.

DIRECTORY

Mayfair

Albemarle Gallery
49 Albemarle St W1.
Map 12 F3.
Tel 020 7499 1616.

Browse and Darby Gallery
19 Cork St W1.
Map 12 F3.
Tel 020 7734 7984.

David Aaron Ancient Art
22 Berkeley Square W1.
Map 12 E3.
Tel 020 7491 9588.

Fine Art Society
148 New Bond St W1.
Map 12 E2.
Tel 020 7629 5116.

Flowers Central
21 Cork St W1.
Map 12 F3.
Tel 020 7439 7766.

Grays Antique Market
58 Davies St & 1–7 Davies Mews W1.
Map 12 E2.
Tel 020 7629 7034.

Henry Sotheran
2 Sackville St W1.
Map 12 F3.
Tel 020 7439 6151.

Lisson Gallery
29 & 52–4 Bell St NW1.
Map 3 B5.
Tel 020 7724 2739.

Maas Gallery
15a Clifford St W1.
Map 12 F3.
Tel 020 7734 2302.

Mallett Antiques
37 Dover St W1S.
Map 12 F3.
Tel 020 7499 7411.

Mayor Gallery
22a Cork St W1.
Map 12 F3.
Tel 020 7734 3558.

Redfern Gallery
20 Cork St W1.
Map 12 F3.
Tel 020 7734 1732.

Richard Green
33 & 147 New Bond St.
Map 12 E2.
Tel 020 7499 4738.

S J Phillips
139 New Bond St W1.
Map 12 E2.
Tel 020 7629 6261.

Thompson's Gallery
15 New Cavendish St W1.
Map 4 E5.
Tel 020 7935 3595.

Waddington Custot Galleries
11, 12 & 34 Cork St W1.
Map 12 F3.
Tel 020 7851 2200.

St James's

Chris Beetle
8 & 10 Ryder St SW1.
Map 12 F3.
Tel 020 7839 7551.

Derek Johns
12 Duke St SW1.
Map 12 F3.
Tel 020 7839 7671.

Johnny van Haeften
13 Duke St SW1.
Map 12 F3.
Tel 020 7930 3062.

Pullman Gallery
14 King St SW1.
Map 12 F4.
Tel 020 7930 9595.

Tryon Gallery
7 Bury St SW1.
Map 12 F3.
Tel 020 7839 8083.

Knightsbridge

Crane Kalman
178 Brompton Rd SW3.
Map 19 B1.
Tel 020 7584 7566.

Mathaf Gallery
24 Motcomb St SW1.
Map 12 D5.
Tel 020 7584 2396.

Pimlico Road

Linley
60 Pimlico Rd SW1.
Map 20 D2.
Tel 020 7730 7300.

Westenholz
297 Lillie Rd SW6.
Map 17 A5.
Tel 020 7386 1888.

East and West

The Approach
1st Floor, 47 Approach Rd E2. **Tel** 020 8983 3878.

East West Gallery
8 Blenheim Cres W11.
Map 8 D4.
Tel 020 7229 7981.

Flowers East
82 Kingsland Rd E2.
Tel 020 7920 7777.

Gallery 85
85 Portobello Rd W11.
Map 9 A1.
Tel 020 7243 6365.

Hundred Years Gallery
13 Pearson St E2.
Map 8 D2.
Tel 020 3602 7973.

Oxo Tower Wharf
Bargehouse St SE1.
Map 14 E3.
Tel 020 7021 1600.

Purdy Hicks
65 Hopton St SE1.
Map 14 F3.
Tel 020 7401 9229.

The Tea Building
56 Shoreditch High St E1.
Map 8 D4.
Tel 020 7101 2020.

Themes & Variations
231 Westbourne Grove W11.
Map 9 B2.
Tel 020 7727 5531.

North

Gagosian Gallery
6–24 Britannia St WC1.
Map 5 C3.
Tel 020 7841 9960.

Victoria Miro
16 Wharf Rd N1.
Map 7 A2.
Tel 020 7336 8109.

Affordable Art

Contemporary Art Society
59 Central St EC1.
Map 7 A3.
Tel 020 7017 8400.

Will's Art Warehouse
180 Lower Richmond Rd SW15. **Tel** 020 8246 4840.

Photography

Atlas Gallery
49 Dorset St W1.
Map 3 C5.
Tel 020 7224 4192.

Hamiltons Gallery
13 Carlos Place W1.
Map 12 E3.
Tel 020 7499 9493.

Michael Hoppen
3 Jubilee Place SW3.
Map 19 B3.
Tel 020 7352 3649.

Photographers' Gallery
16–18 Ramilies St W1.
Map 12 F1.
Tel 020 7087 9300.

Rock Archive
Image Space Gallery, 199 Bishopsgate EC2M.
Map 8 D5.
Tel 020 7267 4716.

Bric-a-Brac and Collectables

Alfies Antique Market
13–25 Church St NW8.
Map 3 A5.
Tel 020 7723 6066.

Auctions

Bonhams Auctioneers
Montpelier St SW7.
Map 11 B5.
Tel 020 7393 3900.
101 New Bond St W1.
Map 12 E2.
Tel 020 7447 7447.

Christie's Fine Art Auctioneers
8 King St SW1.
Map 12 F4.
Tel 020 7839 9060.
85 Old Brompton Rd SW7.
Map 18 F2.
Tel 020 7930 6074.

Sotheby's Auctioneers
34–35 New Bond St W1.
Map 12 E2.
Tel 020 7293 5000.

Markets

Even if you're not looking for cut-price cabbages or a silk sari, it's worth paying a visit to one of London's crowded, colourful markets. Many mix English traditions with those of more recent immigrants, creating an exotic atmosphere and a fascinating patchwork of merchandise. At some, the seasoned Cockney hawkers have honed their sales patter to an entertaining art, which reaches fever pitch just before closing time as they advertise ever-plummeting prices. Keep your wits about you and your hand on your bag and join in the fun.

Archway Market

Holloway Rd N19. 🚇 *Archway.*
🚌 *4; 17, 41, 43, 143, 271.* **Open** *noon–6pm Thu, 10am–5pm Sat.*
This young and growing market is one of North London's best kept secrets. Its speciality traders are committed to offering shoppers things great produce, including organic cheeses, breads and cakes, gourmet pickles and chutneys, farm-pressed juices and much more. Tasty lunch options include Breton crêpes, spicy curries and organic hot dogs. Several craft stalls sell unusual objects and gifts.

Bermondsey Market (New Caledonian Market)

Long Lane and Bermondsey St SE1.
Map *15 C5.* 🚇 *London Bridge, Borough.* **Open** *6am–2pm Fri. Starts closing midday. See pp186–7.*
Bermondsey is the gathering point for London's antique traders every Friday. Serious collectors start early and scrutinize the paintings, the silver and the vast array of old jewellery. Browsers might uncover some interesting curiosities but most bargains go before 9am.

Berwick Street Market

Berwick St W1. **Map** *13 A1.*
🚇 *Piccadilly Circus, Leicester Sq.*
Open *9am–6pm Mon–Sat. See p112.*
The spirited costermongers of Soho's Berwick Street sell some of the cheapest and most appealing fruit and vegetables in the West End. Spanish black radish, star fruit and Italian plum tomatoes are among the produce you might find here, plus a variety of nuts and sweets. The market is good for fabrics and cheap household goods too, as well as leather handbags. Separated from Berwick Street by a passageway is the quieter Rupert Street market, where stallholders sell very reasonably priced street fashion.

Borough Market

Southwark St SE1. **Map** *15 B4.*
🚇 *London Bridge, Borough.* **Open** *10am–5pm Wed & Thu, 10am–6pm Fri, 8am–5pm Sat; for lunch: 10am–5pm Mon & Tue. See p180.*
On one of London's most ancient trading sites, Borough has for many years been a wholesale market catering to the restaurant and hotel trade. Open to the public from Wednesday to Saturday, the award-winning market has a reputation as London's premier centre for fine foods, selling a vast array of British and international foodstuffs. Among the cornucopia is organic meat, fish and produce, top-quality handmade cheeses, breads, sweets and chocolates, plus coffees, teas and also soaps. It's a favourite foraging ground for the city's celebrity chefs.

Brick Lane Market

Brick Lane E1. **Map** *8 E5.*
🚇 *Shoreditch, Liverpool St, Aldgate East.* **Open** *11am–6pm Sat, 10am–5pm Sun. See pp174–5.*
This massively popular East End jamboree is at its best around its gloriously frayed edges. Pick through the mish-mash of junk sold on Bethnal Green Road or head east on Cheshire Street, past the new outcrop of fashionable home-design and gift shops, to explore the indoor stalls, packed with tatty furniture and old books. Much of the action takes place in cobbled Sclater Street and the plots on either side. Here, you'll find everything from fresh shellfish and trainers to old power tools and new bicycles. Further south on Brick Lane itself, the trendy boutiques and cafés give way to spice shops and curry restaurants in this centre for London's Bangladeshi community.

Brixton Market

Electric Ave SW9. 🚇 *Brixton.*
Open *8am–6pm Mon, Tue, Thu–Sat, 8am–3pm Wed.*

This lively market lies at the heart of London's Caribbean community, so expect a wonderful assortment of Afro-Caribbean food, from goats' meat, pigs' feet and salt fish to plantain, yams and breadfruit. As well as fresh produce, stalls are laden with crafts, fabrics, children's toys and secondhand vinyl. On the third Saturday of the month the market is taken over by vintage clothes, jewellery and furniture. In nearby Brixton Village and Market Row there is an abundance of street food restaurants and cafés, serving everything from Neapolitan pizzas to bowls of delicious ramen.

Broadway Market

Broadway Market, between Andrews Rd & Westgate St E8. 🚌 *236, 394.*
Open *7:30am–7pm Sat.*
Although this market is a bit tricky to get to because it's not served by the Tube, it's worth getting a bus from Islington or walking from Bethnal Green Tube. One of London's oldest, Broadway Market had gone into decline until its rebirth as a popular organic farmers' market. On Saturdays, the historic street running between London Fields and the Regent's Canal comes alive with around 40 stalls selling fruit and vegetables, cheeses, baked goods, meats and confectionery. Also lining Broadway Market are some interesting, arty shops, catering to the young creative types who have been colonizing this part of Hackney over the past couple of decades. Black Truffle (No. 4) stocks a range of accessories made by independent designers – both local and international – while textile designer Barley Massey sells her own unusual designs and those of others at Fabrications (No. 7). L'Eau à la Bouche (No. 35-37) is a deli offering everthing from charcuterie to fruit tarts. When it's time to refuel, duck into the Dove pub (No. 24–28) for a choice of Belgian beers.

Camden Lock Market

Chalk Farm Road NW1. 🚇 *Camden Town.* **Open** *9:30am–6pm daily.*
Camden Lock Market has grown swiftly since its opening in 1974, spreading along Chalk Farm Road and Camden High Street. Crafts, new and second-hand street fashion, wholefoods, books, records and antiques make up most of what's on offer. Its setting alongside the Regent's Canal is a bonus, too. Often, young people come here simply to enjoy the vibrant atmosphere, especially at weekends when Camden Lock is abuzz with activity *(see p250).*

Camden Passage Market

Camden Passage N1. **Map** *6 F1.*
Ⓔ *Angel.* **Open** *9am–6pm Wed & Sat,
10am–6pm Fri, 11am–6pm Sun.*

Camden Passage is a quiet walkway
where cafés nestle among bijou
antique shops. Prints, silverware,
19th-century magazines, jewellery
and toys are among the many
collectables on offer. Don't miss the
tiny shops tucked away in the
atmospherically poky Pierrepont
Arcade; one is precariously stacked
with 18th- and 19th-century
porcelain; another specializes in
antique puzzles and games. The
passage is also lined with shops –
Annie's Vintage Clothes is known for
pristine 1920s–40s frocks, while
Origin sells classic 20th-century
furniture. There's a specialist book
market on Thursdays.

Chapel Market

Chapel Market N1. **Map** *6 E2.*
Ⓔ *Angel.* **Open** *9am–6pm Tue–Sat,
8:30am–4pm Sun.*

This is one of London's most
traditional and exuberant street
markets, and is best visited on
weekends. Its produce is second
to none: the fruit and vegetables
are varied and cheap, the fish
stalls are the finest in the area,
and there are also stalls selling
European delicacies and cheeses.
Visitors will also find a wealth of
bargain household goods.

Church Street Market

Church St NW8 and Bell St NW1.
Map *3 A5.* Ⓔ *Edgware Rd.*
Open *8am–6pm Mon–Sat.*

Like many of London's markets,
Church Street reaches a crescendo
at the weekend. On Friday and
Saturday, stalls selling cheap
clothes, household goods, fish,
cheese and antiques join the
everyday fruit and vegetable stalls.
Alfies Antique Market (Nos. 13–25)
houses around 100 dealers selling
everything from jewellery to
furniture. There is also a cluster of
interesting stand-alone antique
furniture shops, including James
Worrall Antiques (No. 2), showcasing
beautiful pieces from all over Europe.

Columbia Road Market

Columbia Rd E2. **Map** *8 D3.*
Ⓔ *Shoreditch, Old St.*
Open *8am–3pm Sun. See p175.*

This is the perfect place to come
to buy greenery and blossoms,
or just to enjoy the fragrances
and colours. Cut flowers, plants,
shrubs, seedlings and pots are all

sold at about half their normal prices
on a Sunday morning in this
charming Victorian street. (In
December, as you might expect,
there's a brisk trade
in Christmas trees.) There is also a
selection of vintage and modern
china for sale, and alongside the
market are some lovely shops that
keep market hours, such as Angela
Flanders' pretty perfumerie (No. 96),
Glitterati for vintage jewellery and
watches (No. 148), and leather
specialists Kaye Symons (No. 144).
When you're shopped out, take tea
at Treacle (No. 110–112), which turns
out cute retro cupcakes and classic
jam sponge cakes, plus cups of
proper tea to wash them down.
Alternatively, snack on deep-fried
prawns from hole in the wall, Lee's
Seafoods (No. 134).

Earlham Street Market

Earlham St WC2. **Map** *13 B2.*
Ⓔ *Covent Garden.* **Open** *10am–4pm
Mon–Sat.*

Radiating off Seven Dials *(see p120)*,
this market is a small affair. Several
stalls sell a range of items from
second-hand clothes to fashion
jewellery and accessories.

East Street Market

East St SE17. Ⓔ *Elephant and Castle.*
Open *8am–5pm Tue–Fri,
8am–6:30pm Sat, 8am–2pm Sun.*

East Street Market, also known
as The Lane or East Lane, is best
visited on a Sunday. More than
250 stalls fill the narrow street and
a small plant and flower market
is set up on Blackwood Street.
The majority of traders sell clothes,
accessories and household goods,
although there is plenty of local
and Afro-Caribbean produce, fish
and other delicacies. Charlie Chaplin
(see p33) was born in this street
and was inspired by characters
he encountered in the area.

Gabriel's Wharf and Riverside Walk Markets

*56 Upper Ground and Riverside Walk
SE1.* **Map** *14 E3.* Ⓔ *Waterloo. Gabriel's
Wharf* **Open** *11am–6pm Tue–Sun;
Riverside Walk* **Open** *noon–7pm Sat &
Sun. See p195.*

At Gabriel's Wharf, little shops filled
with ceramics, paintings and
jewellery surround a bandstand
where jazz groups sometimes play
in the summer. A few stalls are set up
around the courtyard, selling ethnic
clothing and handmade jewellery

and pottery. On Riverside Walk, a
book market stands under Waterloo
Bridge, with rows of tables laden
with new and secondhand books,
including much sought-after
Penguin paperbacks.

Grays Antique Market

58 Davies St & 1–7 Davies Mews W1.
Map *12 E2.* Ⓔ *Bond St.* **Open**
10am–6pm Mon–Fri, 11am–5pm Sat.

Conveniently sited in the West End,
Grays probably isn't the place to bag
a bargain – the liveried doorman is a
tip-off that this place is posh – but it
makes a pleasant place to browse.
There are some lovely pieces here,
from costume jewellery and
fabulous vintage fashion to enamel
boxes and modern first editions from
the bookseller Biblion.

Greenwich Market

College Approach SE10. **Map** *23 B2.*
🚆 *Greenwich.* Ⓔ *Cutty Sark DLR.*
Open *10am–5:30pm Tue–Sun.*

Situated in the maritime town of
Greenwich, this covered market is
packed with up to 120 stalls. Loosely
divided into two sections, one side
devotes itself to unique crafts,
wooden toys, clothes, handmade
jewellery and accessories, and much
more. The other does a storming
trade in street food. Ethiopian
curries, roasted meats, gluten-free
chocolate brownies, the freshest
sushi: no one will be left wanting.
Surrounding the market are vintage
shops, a pub, children's stores and an
excellent sweet shop.

Jubilee and Apple Markets

Covent Gdn Piazza WC2. **Map** *13 C2.*
Ⓔ *Covent Gdn.* **Open** *Apple Market:
10:30am–6pm daily (to 7:30pm Thu);
Jubilee Market: 5am–5pm Mon,
10:30am–7pm Tue–Fri, 10am–6pm
Sat & Sun.*

In the centre of bustling Covent
Garden, both the Apple and Jubilee
markets sell crafts and designs. The
Apple Market, inside the Piazza
where the original fruit and
vegetable market was housed *(see
p118)*, has knitwear, jewellery and
novelty goods. The Piazza is also
home to a plethora of shops, cafés
and restaurants. Jubilee Hall sells
antiques on Monday, crafts at the
weekend, and a large selection of
clothes, handbags, cosmetics and
tacky mementos in between.
The East Colonnade Market also
has a variety of stalls, selling
handmade soaps to hand-knitted
children's clothing.

Leadenhall Market

Whittington Ave EC3. **Map** *15 C2.*
🅴 *Bank, Monument.* **Open** *10am–6pm Mon–Fri. See p162.*

There has been a marketplace on this site since medieval times, but the present spectacular glass-roofed structure was built in 1881. Leadenhall Market traditionally sold fish, meat and poultry, but only fishmonger HS Linwood & Sons remains. The smart red and green façades now bear the names of upmarket clothing chains, restaurants, pubs and gift shops. Leadenhall does, however, retain something of its reputation as a centre for fine food. More than a dozen stalls set up shop on the cobblestones beneath this dramatic structure Monday to Friday from 10am to 6pm, selling European cheeses, cured meats, baked goods, condiments and other gourmet delicacies.

Leather Lane Market

Leather Lane EC1. **Map** *6 E5.*
🅴 *Farringdon, Chancery Lane.*
Open *10am–2pm Mon–Fri.*

This ancient street, originally called Leveroun Lane, has played host to a market for over 300 years. The history of the lane, however, has nothing to do with leather. Stalls here sell cut-price high-street clothes, plus shoes, bags, jewellery and accessories. All are well worth a browse.

Marylebone Farmers' Market

Cramer St car park, behind Marylebone High St W1. **Map** *4 D5.* 🅴 *Baker St, Bond St.* **Open** *10am–2pm Sun.*

There are many farmers' markets across the city, enabling farmers and other producers to sell directly to the public. Locations include Islington Green and the car park behind Waterstones, Notting Hill, but Marylebone is the largest and most central, offering seasonal fruit and veg, dairy products, fish, meat, breads, preserves and sauces. There is also a line-up of excellent gourmet shops in adjacent Moxon Street, including a renowned rare-breed pork butcher, the Ginger Pig, and La Fromagerie delicatessen with its extensive cheese cave.

Old Spitalfields Market

Commercial St E1. **Map** *8 D5.*
🅴 *Aldgate East, Liverpool St.*
Open *10am–5pm Mon–Wed, 9am–5pm Thu & Sat, 10am–4pm Fri, 11am–5pm Sun. See p173.*

The main market is on a Sunday, and is a mecca for those interested in the latest street fashion trends. Many young designers have stalls, and prices are also reasonable. The stalls are of mixed quality, so you have to search for the gems. The organic food stalls and a selection of cafés make it a good brunch venue. A varying number of stalls are open during the week.

Petticoat Lane Market

Middlesex St E1. **Map** *16 D1.*
🅴 *Liverpool St, Aldgate, Aldgate East.*
Open *9am–2pm Sun (Wentworth St 10am–4:30pm Mon–Fri). See p173.*

Probably the most famous of all London's street markets, Petticoat Lane continues to attract many thousands of visitors and locals every Sunday. The prices may not be as cheap as elsewhere, but the sheer volume of leather goods, clothes (Petticoat Lane's traditional strong point), watches, cheap jewellery and toys more than make up for that. A variety of fast-food sellers do a brisk trade catering for the bustling crowds that throng the market on a weekend.

Piccadilly Crafts Market

St James's Church, Piccadilly W1.
Map *13 A3.* 🅴 *Piccadilly Circus, Green Park.* **Open** *antiques: 10am–6pm Tue. Arts and crafts: 10am–6pm Wed–Sat.*

Many of the markets in the Middle Ages were held in churchyards and Piccadilly Crafts Market has rekindled that ancient tradition. It is aimed mostly at visitors rather than locals, and the merchandise ranges from tacky T-shirts to wooden toys. All are spread out in the shadow of Wren's beautiful church *(see p94).*

Portobello Road Market

Portobello Rd W10. **Map** *9 C3.*
🅴 *Notting Hill Gate, Ladbroke Grove.*
Open *antiques and junk: 5:30am–5:30pm Sat. General market: 9am–6pm Mon–Wed, 9am–1pm Thu, 9am–7pm Fri & Sat. See p223.*

Portobello Road is really three or four markets rolled into one. The Notting Hill end has more than 1,000 stalls in numerous arcades and on the street itself, displaying a variety of jewellery, old medals, paintings and silverware. Most stalls are managed by experts, so bargains are very rare. Further down the gentle hill, antiques give way to fruit and vegetables. The next transformation comes under the Westway flyover, where young fashion designers sell inexpensive creations alongside second-hand clothes, record and food stalls on Fridays and Saturdays. It's also worth venturing into the covered Portobello Green market, which has an interesting mix of small shops selling everything from avant-garde fashion to kitsch cushions and lingerie. From this point on, the market becomes increasingly shabby.

Ridley Road Market

Ridley Rd E8. 🚆 *Dalston.*
Open *6am–6pm Mon–Thu, 6am–7pm Fri & Sat.*

Early last century, Ridley Road was a centre of the Jewish community. Since then, Asians, Greeks, Turks and West Indians have also settled in the area and the market is a lively celebration of this cultural mix. Highlights include the 24-hour bagel bakery, shanty-town shacks selling green bananas and reggae records, colourful drapery stalls, and cheap fruit and vegetables.

Roman Road Market

Roman Rd, between Parnell Rd and St Stephen's Rd E3. 🅴 *Bethnal Green.* 🚌 *8.* **Open** *10am–4pm Tue & Thu, 9am–5pm Sat. Farmers' market 1st Sat of month.*

This lively market established in the 19th century has a real East End flavour and traditionally sells everything from cheap bedding and fashion to cut-price cleaning products and fruit and veg. Chances are that you'll be treated to some colourful Cockney patter from the stallholders trying to drum up custom. As well as the standard market traders, some more unusual vendors, street entertainers and special events add variety to the mix; you could find yourself tempted by handmade jewellery, vintage clothes or antiques.

Shepherd's Bush Market

Goldhawk Rd W12. 🅴 *Goldhawk Rd, Shepherd's Bush.*
Open *9am–6pm Mon–Sat.*

A focal point for many local ethnic communities, this rambling market contains an impressive volume of eclectic wares. West Indian food, Afro wigs, Asian spices, exotic fish, rugs and other household goods are just some of the attractions. There are acres of cheap clothing for every occasion, from floral flannel nighties and men's suits to clubwear and elaborately beaded wedding gowns. Cheap fabric stalls are a highlight of the Shepherd's Bush Market, and there is even an on-site tailor and barber.

ENTERTAINMENT

London has the enormous, multi-layered variety of entertainment that only the great cities of the world can provide. Theatre fans can spend the evening in the company of Shakespeare's Hamlet, sit mesmerized during a reworking of a classic play or sing along to everyone's favourite showtunes at a West End musical. There's a healthy, innovative fringe theatre scene too, plus world-class ballet and opera in fabled venues such as Sadler's Wells, the Royal Opera House and the Coliseum. Enjoy a piece of contemporary dance or try out your own dance moves at one of the city's many nightclubs. Music fans are spoiled with a variety of venues hosting the best of all genres, be it classical, jazz, rock or pop, while dedicated movie buffs have hundreds of different films to choose from each night, shown in large, multiscreen complexes or excellent small independent cinemas. Sports fans can watch a game of cricket at Lords, cheer on oarsmen on the Thames or eat strawberries and cream at Wimbledon. Those feeling sporty themselves can try horse riding along Rotten Row in Hyde Park or follow in the footsteps of Olympians at the Queen Elizabeth Park. There are festivals and celebrations to attend, and there's plenty for children to do, too – in fact, there's plenty for everyone to do. Whatever you want, you'll be sure to find it on offer in London; it's just a question of knowing where to look.

Top: performers at the Theatre Royal Drury Lane; Above left: visitors enjoying the view at the National Theatre on the South Bank; Above right: the Theatre Royal Haymarket

Information Sources

For details of events in London, check out **Time Out London**'s website. *Time Out* also publishes a free comprehensive listings and review magazine every Tuesday, which can be picked up at most Tube and train stations. The weekday commuter newspapers the *Metro* (morning) and the *Evening Standard* are both free and give brief daily listings. National newspapers are a useful source, too. *The Independent* has daily listings and a weekly round-up section titled "The Information". It also reviews a different arts sector every day. *The Guardian* has daily arts reviews in its G2 section and weekly listings in "The Guide" on Saturday. *The Independent, Guardian* and *The Times* all have lists of ticket availability.

Specialized news sheets, brochures and advance listings are distributed free in the foyers of theatres, concert halls, cinemas and arts complexes such as the South Bank and Barbican. Transport for London Visitor Centres and hotel foyers often have the same publications. Fly posters advertise forthcoming events on billboards everywhere.

The **Society of London Theatre** (SOLT) publishes an informative free broadsheet every fortnight, available in many theatre foyers. It provides invaluable information about what's on but tends to concentrate on mainstream theatres. SOLT's website provides full details of current productions plus news, interviews, access information and online ticket booking. The **London Theatre** website showcases a range of performances in the capital, with reviews, news, tickets and theatre seating plans.

Café sign advertising free live music

Booking Tickets

Some of the more popular shows and plays in London's West End – starring big-name actors, for instance – can be totally booked out weeks and even months ahead. Though this isn't the norm for every show – and tickets are often available on the day – it is always best to book tickets in advance, especially if you are keen to see a particular show.

Tickets can be bought from the theatre box office in person, by telephone or online. Box offices are usually open from 10am to 8pm and accept payment by cash and credit card. Theatre websites will usually show the seating plan with available seats and prices highlighted. To reserve seats by telephone, call the box office and have your debit or credit card ready. Some venues have separate phone numbers for your credit card bookings and some don't accept credit cards at all, so always check. Pre-booked tickets can be collected at the theatre or posted to you – tickets are often not posted until nearer the show run. Remember to take your payment card with you if you are collecting from the theatre.

Tickets are also available from agencies, such as Ticketmaster. Always compare prices, try to avoid agencies in bureaux de

Line-up from the Royal Ballet, on stage at Covent Garden

Palace Theatre plaque

change, and do not be tempted to buy from ticket touts or unofficial Internet sources.

Many venues sell unclaimed or returned tickets on the day of the performances; ask at the box office for queuing times.

Discounted Tickets

The **TKTs** booth in Leicester Square has been in operation since 1980 and is a great place to find discounted tickets for big West End shows, plays, operas and ballets. It sells on-the-day tickets, sometimes for half the price. It opens Monday to Saturday 10am–7pm and 11am–4:30pm on Sundays.

Many theatres release a set amount of tickets for as little as £10, so it is worth signing up to theatre mailing lists. A number of reduced-price tickets are usually available to those under 25. The Globe *(see p181)*

reserves 700 standing tickets for every performance for £5 only.

Get Into London Theatre runs an annual ticket promotion during January and February, where tickets are available for a plethora of shows for £10–£40.

Disabled Visitors

Many London venues are old buildings and were not originally designed with disabled visitors in mind, but a lot of facilities have been updated, particularly to give access to those using wheelchairs, or for those with hearing difficulties.

Telephone the box office prior to your visit to reserve the special seating places or equipment, which are often limited. Special discounts may be available; for details and information on facilities, visit **Artsline**'s website.

DIRECTORY
Listings and Booking

Artsline
W artsline.org.uk

Get Into London Theatre
W getintolondontheatre.co.uk

London Theatre
W londontheatre.co.uk

Society of London Theatre (SOLT)
W officiallondontheatre.co.uk

Time Out London
W timeout.com/london

TKTs Leicester Square
W tkts.co.uk

The TKTs booth in Leicester Square

Theatres

London offers an extraordinary range of theatrical entertainment – this is one of the world's great stages, and, at its best, standards are extremely high. Despite their legendary reputation for reserve, the British are passionate about theatre and there is an abundance of plays and shows performed around the capital: you can stroll along a street of West End theatres and find a sombre Samuel Beckett, Brecht or Chekhov play showing next door to some absurdly frothy farce like *No Sex Please, We're British!* Whether you are a fan of Shakespeare or musicals, there is something here for you.

West End Theatre

There is a distinct glamour to the West End theatres. Perhaps it is the glittering lights of the foyer and the impressively ornate interiors, or maybe it is their hallowed reputations – but whatever it is, the old theatres retain a magic all their own.

The West End's billboards always feature a generous sprinkling of world-famous performers such as Judi Dench, Benedict Cumberbatch, Kenneth Branagh and Nicole Kidman.

The major commercial theatres cluster along Shaftesbury Avenue and Haymarket and around Covent Garden and Charing Cross Road. Unlike the national theatres, most West End theatres survive only on profits; they do not receive any state subsidy. They rely on an army of ever-hopeful "angels" (financial backers) and producers to keep the old traditions alive.

Many theatres are historical landmarks, such as the classic **Theatre Royal Drury Lane**, established in 1663 *(see p119)*, and the elegant **Theatre Royal Haymarket** – both superb examples of early 19th-century buildings. Another to note is the **Palace** *(see p112)*, with its terracotta exterior and imposing position right on Cambridge Circus.

National Theatres

The **National Theatre** is based in the Southbank Centre *(p192)*. Here, the large, open-staged Olivier, the proscenium-staged Lyttelton and the small, flexible Cottesloe host every kind of production from large, extravagant works to small, one-man shows. The complex is also a lively social centre. Enjoy a drink before your play begins; watch the crowds and the river drift by; wander round the many free art exhibitions; relax during the free early evening concerts in the foyer or browse through the theatre bookshop.

The **Royal Shakespeare Company** is one of Britain's leading theatre companies. With an unparalleled reputation for its dramatic interpretation of the works of Shakespeare, the world renowned ensemble continually attracts big crowds to its performances. Although its official home since the 19th century has been in Stratford-upon-Avon, the company has maintained a regular London presence since the 1960s. Previously located at the Barbican Centre, the RSC enjoys regular London seasons in the West End, at the Novello Theatre and other smaller venues. To find out where the RSC is performing in London, call their ticket hotline.

National Theatre

(Lyttelton, Cottesloe, Olivier) Southank Centre SE1. **Map** 14 D3. **Tel** 020 7452 3000. W **nationaltheatre.org.uk**

Royal Shakespeare Company

Tel 0844 800 1110 (tickets, information). W **rsc.org.uk**

Pantomime

Should you happen to be visiting London between December and February, one thing not to miss is a trip to the pantomime. Guaranteed to entertain all the family, "panto" is an absurd tradition in which major female characters are played by men and male characters by women. The audience is encouraged to participate, by shouting out traditional panto cheers. The shows are usually based on children's stories such as Cinderella, Peter Pan and Snow White and the Seven Dwarfs, and more often than not feature British celebrities from the world of television and music. Whatever adults may think of it, children love the experience.

Open Air Theatre

A performance of one of Shakespeare's airier creations, such as *A Midsummer Night's Dream,* takes on an atmosphere of pure enchantment among the green vistas of **Regent's Park** *(see p228)*. Lavish opera productions are staged during the summer months in **Holland Park** *(see p222)*. Wear warm clothing, take a blanket and, to be safe, an umbrella. Refreshments are available, or you can take a picnic.

Open-air performances of a different kind can be experienced at **Shakespeare's Globe** on Bankside *(see p181)*. This authentic reproduction of an Elizabethan playhouse, open to the skies – but with protected seating – is open to visitors all year round but only puts on performances in the summer months.

Holland Park Theatre

Holland Park. **Map** 9 B4. **Tel** 020 7361 3570. **Open** Jun–Aug. W **operahollandpark.com**

Open Air Theatre

Inner Circle, Regent's Park NW1. **Map** 4 D3. **Tel** 0844 826 4242. **Open** Jun–Sep. W **openairtheatre.org**

Shakespeare's Globe

New Globe Walk SE1. **Map** 15 A3. **Tel** 020 7401 9919. **Performances** Apr–Oct. W **shakespearesglobe.com**

DIRECTORY

West End Theatres

Adelphi ⑬
Strand WC2.
Tel 020 3725 7060.

Aldwych ⑱
Aldwych WC2.
Tel 0845 200 7981.

Ambassadors ㉖
West St WC2.
Tel 0844 811 2334.

Apollo ㉜
Shaftesbury Ave W1.
Tel 0844 482 9671.

Cambridge ㉔
Earlham St WC2.
Tel 0844 412 4652.

Criterion ⑦
Piccadilly Circus W1.
Tel 020 7839 8811.

Dominion ㉓
Tottenham Court Rd.
Tel 0844 847 1775.

Duchess ⑯
Catherine St WC2.
Tel 0844 482 9672.

Duke of York's ③
St Martin's Lane WC2.
Tel 0844 871 3051.

Fortune ⑳
Russell St WC2.
Tel 0844 871 7627.

Garrick ④
Charing Cross Rd WC2.
Tel 0844 482 9673.

Gielgud ㉛
Shaftesbury Ave W1.
Tel 0844 482 5141.

Harold Pinter ⑧
Panton St SW1.
Tel 0844 871 7627.

Her Majesty's ⑩
Haymarket SW1.
Tel 0844 412 4653.

Lyceum ⑮
Wellington St WC2.
Tel 0844 844 0005.

Lyric ㉝
Shaftesbury Ave W1.
Tel 0844 482 9674.

New Leicester Square Theatre ⑤
Leicester Pl W1.
Tel 020 7734 2222.

New London ㉑
Drury Lane WC2.
Tel 020 7242 9802.

Noel Coward ①
St Martin's Lane WC2.
Tel 0844 482 5138.

Novello ⑰
Aldwych WC2.
Tel 0844 482 5170.

Palace ㉘
Shaftesbury Ave W1.
Tel 0844 482 9676.

Phoenix ㉗
Charing Cross Rd WC2.
Tel 020 7438 9600.

Piccadilly ㉞
Denman St W1.
Tel 0844 412 6666.

Playhouse ⑫
Northumberland Ave WC2.
Tel 0844 871 7631.

Prince Edward ㉙
Old Compton St W1.
Tel 0844 482 5151.

Prince of Wales ⑥
Coventry St W1.
Tel 0844 482 5115.

Queen's ㉚
Shaftesbury Ave W1.
Tel 0844 482 5160.

Shaftesbury ㉒
Shaftesbury Ave WC2.
Tel 020 7379 5399.

St Martin's ㉕
West St WC2.
Tel 0844 499 1515.

Theatre Royal Drury Lane ⑲
Catherine St WC2.
Tel 0844 412 4660.

Theatre Royal Haymarket ⑨
Haymarket SW1.
Tel 020 7930 8890.

Trafalgar Studios ⑪
Whitehall SW1.
Tel 0844 871 7632.

Vaudeville ⑭
Strand WC2.
Tel 0844 482 9675.

Wyndham's ②
Charing Cross Rd WC2.
Tel 0844 482 5138.

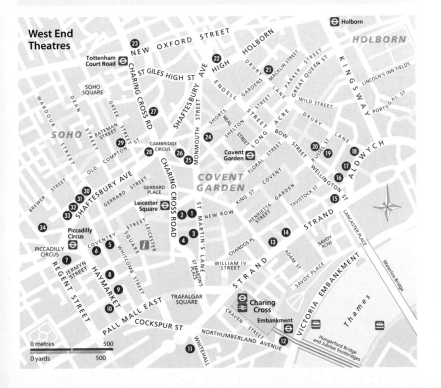

West End Theatres

Fringe Theatre

London's fringe theatre acts as an outlet for new, adventurous plays produced by a variety of writers from different cultures and backgrounds – works by Irish writers appear regularly, as do plays by Caribbean and Latin American authors and feminist and gay writers.

The plays are usually staged in tiny theatres based in pubs, such as the **Gate Theatre** above the Prince Albert pub in Notting Hill, the **King's Head** in Islington and the **Latchmere** pub in Battersea, or in warehouses and spare space in larger theatres, such as the **Donmar Warehouse** and the **Lyric**.

Venues like the **Bush Theatre**, the **Almeida** and the **Jerwood Theatre Upstairs** at the Royal Court have earned their reputations for discovering outstanding new works, some of which have subsequently transferred successfully to the West End.

Foreign-language plays are sometimes performed at national cultural institutes; for example, you might be able to catch Molière at the **Institut Français** or Brecht at the **Goethe Institute**; check the listings magazines.

For alternative stand-up comedy and cabaret, where you can encounter the sharp edge of satire with its brash, newsy style, try the **Comedy Store**, the birthplace of so-called "alternative" comedy, or the **Hackney Empire**, a former Victorian music hall that showcases local talent and hosts theatre, music and comedy events.

Budget Tickets

There is a wide range of prices for seats in London theatres. The cheaper West End tickets, for example, can cost under £10, whereas the best seats for musicals hover around £35–50. However, it is usually quite possible to obtain cheaper tickets.

"tkts" (see p339) is the only official discount theatre ticket shop in London, and sells tickets on the day of the performance for a wide range of mainstream shows. Located on the south side of Leicester Square, the booth is open Monday to Saturday 10am–7pm for matinee and evening shows, and Sunday 11am–4:30pm for matinees only. Payment is by cash or credit card, and there is a strict limit of four tickets per purchase, and a small service charge.

You can sometimes get reduced-price seats for matinee performances, press and preview nights – it is always worth checking with the box office to see what they currently have on offer.

Choosing Seats

If you go to the theatre in person or book online, you will be able to see the theatre's seating plan and note where you can get a good view at an affordable price. If you book by telephone, you should note the following: stalls are in front of the stage and expensive. The back stalls are slightly cheaper; dress, grand or royal circles are above the stalls and cheaper again; the upper circle or

balcony offer the cheapest seats but you will have to climb several flights of stairs; the slips are seats that run along the edges of the theatre; boxes are the most expensive option.

It is also wise to bear in mind that some of the cheap seats have a restricted view.

Theatre Tours

Those intrigued by what goes on behind the scenes should try a backstage tour. The National Theatre (see p340) organizes tours of its three stages – Lyttleton, Olivier and Cottesloe – as well as the workshops and dressing rooms. The London Palladium also offers a backstage guided tour complete with an account of the theatre's history.

Haunted Theatres

Many of London's oldest theatres are reputed to be haunted; however, the two most famous spectres haunt the Garrick and the Duke of York's (see p341). The Garrick is heavily atmospheric and the ghost of Arthur Bourchier, a manager at the turn of the 20th century, is reputed to make fairly regular appearances. He hated critics and many believe he is still trying to frighten them away. The Duke of York's theatre is said to be haunted by Violet Melnotte, an actress manager during the 1890s, who was famed for her extremely fiery temper.

Cinemas

If you can't find a movie you like in London, then you don't like movies. The huge choice of British, American, foreign-language, new, classic, popular and special-interest films makes London a major international film centre, with about 250 different films showing at any one time. There are about 50 cinemas in the centre of London alone, many of them ultramodern multiscreened complexes. The big commercial chains show current blockbusters and a healthy number of independent cinemas throughout the city offer some inventive programming drawing on the whole history of film.

West End Cinemas

"West End" is a loose term for the main cinemas in the West End of London, which show new releases, such as the **Odeon Leicester Square**, but it also includes the cinemas found in Chelsea, Fulham and Notting Hill. Programmes begin around midday and are then repeated every two or three hours, with the last show around 9pm; there are often late-night screenings on Fridays and Saturdays.

Tickets tend to be expensive, but admission is often cheaper for afternoon performances or on Mondays. Reservations are recommended.

BFI London IMAX

Boasting the largest cinema screen in Britain, the BFI IMAX regularly shows the latest Hollywood blockbusters alongside more alternative films and documentaries. It also has a programme of educational films that benefit from appearing on the big screen, including trips under the sea and into space.

Independent Cinemas

These cinemas often show foreign-language and slightly more offbeat art films and sometimes change programmes daily or even several times each day. Some cinemas show two or three films, often on the same theme.

The best of the "indies" include the **Prince Charles**, just by Leicester Square, the **Everyman** in locations across north London, the ICA in the Mall, the **Picturehouse** chain, with cinemas across London, and the BFI Southbank.

In summer, outdoor screenings take place in parks, up on rooftops and in other inspired locations, such as Somerset House (see p121).

BFI Southbank

Formerly known as the National Film Theatre, BFI Southbank is located in the Southbank Centre. It has four cinemas of its own, which together offer a huge and diverse selection of films, both British and international. It also holds regular screenings of rare and restored films and television programmes.

Foreign-Language Films

These are screened at a number of repertory and independent cinemas, including the **Prince Charles**, the **Curzon Soho** in Shaftesbury Avenue, the **Curzon Bloomsbury** and **Ciné Lumière**. Films are shown in the original language, with English subtitles.

Film Certificates

Children are allowed to go to a cinema unaccompanied by an adult to films which have been awarded either a U (universal) or a PG (parental guidance advised) certificate for viewing. Children must be accompanied by an adult to view a film rated 12A.

With other films, the numbers 12, 15 or 18 quite simply denote the minimum ages allowed for admission to the cinema.

London Film Festival

The most important cinema event in Britain is held every autumn, when hundreds of films – some of which will have already won awards abroad – from a number of countries are screened. The BFI Southbank, several of the repertory cinemas and some of the big West End cinemas take part in the festival. Details are published in listings magazines. Tickets are quite hard to come by but some "tandby tickets may be available to the public 30 minutes before a screening.

Cinema Addresses

BFI London IMAX
Waterloo Rd SE1.
Map 14 D4.
Tel 0330 333 7878.

BFI Southbank
Southbank Centre
SE1.
Map 14 D3.
Tel 020 7928 3232.

Ciné Lumière
Institut Français, 17
Queensberry Pl SW7.
Map 18 F2.
Tel 020 7871 3515.

Curzon Bloomsbury
Brunswick Sq WC1.
Map 5 C4.
Tel 0330 500 1331.

Curzon Soho
93–107 Shaftesbury
Ave W1.

Map 13 B2.
Tel 0330 500 1331.

Everyman
Hollybush Vale NW3.
Map 1 A5.
Tel 0871 906 9060.

Odeon Leicester Square
Leicester Sq, WC2.
Map 13 B2.
Tel 0333 006 7777.

Prince Charles
Leicester Pl, WC2.
Map 13 B2.
Tel 020 7494 3654.

Picturehouse
Branches across London.
W picturehouses.com

Opera, Classical and Contemporary Music

Opera has had a somewhat elitist reputation in Britain. However, televised concerts and free outdoor events in Hyde Park and the Covent Garden Piazza have greatly increased its popularity. London is home to five world-class orchestras and a veritable host of smaller music companies and contemporary music ensembles; it also houses three permanent opera companies and numerous smaller opera groups and leads the world with its period orchestras. It is a major centre for the classical recording industry, which helps to support a large community of musicians and singers. Mainstream, obscure, traditional and innovative music are all to be found in profusion. Following is a list of venues showcasing opera, classical and contemporary music. Check listings (see p338) for events occuring during your visit.

Royal Opera House
Floral Street WC2. **Map** 13 C2. **Tel** 020 7304 4000. See p119. **W** roh.org.uk
The building, with its elaborate red, white and gold interior, is the home of the Royal Opera and the Royal Ballet, but visiting opera and ballet companies also perform here. Many productions are shared with foreign opera houses, so check that you haven't already seen the same production at home. Works are always performed in the original language, English translations flashed up above the stage.

Seats are usually booked well in advance, particularly if major stars such as Placido Domingo or Anna Netrebko are performing. Tickets range from about £5 to £200 or more for world-class performers. The cheapest seats tend to go first, although a number of these tickets are reserved for sale on the day. Some of the cheaper seats have extremely restricted views. Standing passes can often be obtained right up to the time of a performance. Standby information is available on the day, and there are often concessions on tickets.

London Coliseum
St Martin's Lane WC2. **Map** 13 B3. **Tel** 0871 911 0200 (24 hrs), 020 7845 9300 (booking). See p123. **W** eno.org
The Coliseum, built in the early 1900s, is home to the English National Opera (ENO). The company's hallmarks are performances in English, high musical standards and a permanent ensemble complemented by guest appearances. Productions range from the classic to the adventurous. For weekday performances, there are 500 prebookable seats at £10 and under.

Southbank Centre
Southbank Centre SE1. **Map** 14 D4. **Tel** 0844 875 0073. See pp190–91. **W** southbankcentre.co.uk
The Southbank Centre includes the **Royal Festival Hall (RFH)**, the **Queen Elizabeth Hall** and the **Purcell Room**. There are nightly performances, mostly of classical music, interspersed with opera, jazz, ballet and modern dance seasons, as well as festivals of contemporary and ethnic music. The largest concert hall on the South Bank is the Royal Festival Hall. Built in the 1950s, it is considered one of the best modernist structures in London. The airy halls outside the auditorium house exhibitions and there are a number of cafés, and a book and music shop.

The Purcell Room is comparatively small and tends to host chamber and contemporary music in addition to many debut recitals. The Queen Elizabeth Hall lies somewhere in between. It stages medium-sized ensembles whose audiences, while too large for the Purcell Room, would not fill the Festival Hall. The hall is undergoing renovation until 2017 and performances will be staged at St John's Smith Square (see p345).

London Music Festivals

The BBC-run Promenade concerts are mostly held at the Royal Albert Hall (see p345) between July and September. More than 70 concerts feature soloists, orchestras and conductors from around the world, performing a wide repertoire, from much-loved classics to newly commissioned pieces. Every concert is broadcast live both on the radio and online. Tickets are best bought in advance, but 500 standing or "promming" places are sold on the day, one and a half hours before the performance. The City of London Festival is held annually in June and July, when churches and public buildings in the City host a range of varied musical events. Venues such as the Tower of London (see pp158–9) and Goldsmiths' Hall lend a special atmosphere to the events. Many concerts are free. For more details, contact the information office (0845 401 5040) from May onwards.

Resident orchestras at the Southbank Centre include the world-class London Philharmonic Orchestra and the Philharmonia Orchestra. The Royal Philharmonic and the BBC Symphony Orchestra are frequent visitors, along with leading ensembles and soloists such as Angela Gheorghiu, Mitsuko Uchida, Stephen Kovacevich and Anne-Sofie von Mutter. World-renowned conductors who have appeared here include Daniel Barenboim, Kurt Masur and Simon Rattle.

The Academy of St Martin-in-the-Fields, the London Festival Orchestra, the London Classical Players and the London Mozart Players all have regular seasons. The often controversial Opera Factory makes several appearances throughout the year, performing modern interpretations of the classics.

There are also frequent free foyer concerts, and throughout the summer the centre is well worth visiting.

Barbican Concert Hall
Silk Street EC2. **Map** 7 A5. **Tel** 020 7638 8891. *See p172.* W **barbican.org.uk**
The Barbican is the home of the London Symphony Orchestra (LSO). Classical concerts are performed by the resident LSO and the BBC Symphony Orchestra, as well as many other visiting orchestras and ensembles, as part of the Barbican's own international concert seasons. The concert hall also hosts performances of contemporary music, including jazz, blues and world music.

Royal Albert Hall
Kensington Gore SW7. **Map** 10 F5. **Tel** 020 7589 8212. *See p209.* W **royalalberthall.com**
Each year the Royal Albert Hall hosts over 300 concerts and events, from ballet to rock and concerts. From mid-July to mid-September, it is devoted to the Henry Wood Promenade Concerts, the "Proms". Organized by the BBC, the season features performances by orchestras and soloists *(see p344)*. Tickets for the Proms can be bought on the day of performance or booked in advance. Long queues build up early in the day and keen fans – Promenaders– take cushions to sit on. Tickets sell out weeks ahead for the "Last Night of the Proms", which has become a national institution.
The hall is also open for tours that take you on a journey through its extraordinary history.

Handel House Museum
25 Brook St W1. **Map** 12 E2. **Tel** 020 7495 1685. *See p101.* W **handelhouse.org**
Located in the finely restored Georgian house where George Frideric Handel lived from 1723 until his death in 1759, the Handel House Museum provides an intimate venue for perfor- mances. Thursday night recitals of Baroque music using period instruments are held in the pan-elled rehearsal and performance room, where Handel himself would have entertained his guests. Concert tickets include access to the museum. Check the website for more details.

Outdoor Music
London has many outdoor musical events in summer. Many royal parks, palaces, stately homes, National Trust properties and council parks host a range of music festivals and performances throughout summer. Arrive early as the concerts are popular, particularly if fireworks are to accompany the music. Take a sweater and a picnic. Purists beware – people walk around, eat and talk throughout and the music is amplified so it can be a little distorted. These events sell out fast and it's best to book tickets in advance.
Venues include Hyde Park *(see p213)*, Marble Hill House in Twickenham *(see p258)* Kenwood House *(see pp239–9)*, Crystal Palace Park and Holland Park *(see p222)*.

Wigmore Hall
36 Wigmore St W1. **Map** 12 E1. **Tel** 020 7935 2141. *See p230.* W **wigmore-hall.org.uk**
Because of its excellent acoustics, the Wigmore Hall is a favourite with visiting artists, and attracts international names such as Andreas Scholl and András Schiff. It hosts a concert most evenings, broadcasts live on BBC radio on Monday lunchtimes and has a Sunday morning concert from September to July.

St Martin-in-the-Fields
Trafalgar Sq WC2. **Map** 13 B3. **Tel** 020 7766 1100. *See p106.* W **smitf.org**
This elegant Gibbs church on the corner of Trafalgar Square hosts over 350 performances every year. Orchestras as dispa- rate as the Belmont Ensemble and the London Oriana Choir provide evening concerts. The choice of each programme is partly dictated by the religious year; for example, Bach's *St John Passion* is played at Ascensiontide. Visitors can enjoy, among other events, an evening concert held by candlelight or a free lunchtime concert (Mondays, Tuesdays and Fridays).

St John's Smith Square
Smith Sq SW1. **Map** 21 B1. **Tel** 020 7222 1061. *See p85.* W **sjss.org.uk**
This converted Baroque church has good acoustics and seating. It hosts concerts by groups such as the Academy of Ancient Music, the London Mozart Players, the Monteverdi Choir and Polyphony. The concert period runs from September to mid-July.

Broadgate Arena
3 Broadgate EC2. **Map** 7 C5. W **broadgate.co.uk**
This open-air venue in the City offers a summer season of lunchtime concerts, with varied programmes from up-and-coming musicians.

Music Venues

Orchestral
Barbican Concert Hall
Broadgate Arena
Queen Elizabeth Hall
Royal Albert Hall
Royal Festival Hall
St Martin-in-the-Fields
St John's Smith Square

Chamber and Ensemble
Barbican Concert Hall
Broadgate Arena
Handel House Museum
LSO St Luke's
Purcell Room
Royal Festival Hall foyer
St Martin-in-the-Fields
St John's Smith Square
Wigmore Hall

Soloists and Recitals
Barbican Concert Hall
Handel House Museum
Purcell Room
Royal Albert Hall
St Martin-in-the-Fields
St John's Smith Square
Wigmore Hall

Children's
Barbican Concert Hall
Royal Festival Hall

Free
Barbican Concert Hall
Royal Festival Hall foyer
Royal National Theatre foyer
St Martin-in-the-Fields (lunchtime)

Early Music
Purcell Room
Wigmore Hall

Contemporary Music
Barbican Concert Hall
Southbank Centre

Dance

An array of London venues including the Royal Opera House, the London Coliseum, Sadler's Wells and The Place theatre all regularly host performances by both London-based dance companies and those visiting from around the world, from the classic Bolshoi Ballet to the innovative Jaleo Flamenco. There are also performances at the Southbank Centre and other arts centres across the city. Companies specialize in a range of styles from classical ballet to mime, jazz, experimental and world dance. With the exception of the resident ballets, most companies have short seasons, seldom lasting longer than a fortnight and often less than a week – check listings for details *(see p338)*.

Ballet

The **Royal Opera House** *(see p119)* and the **London Coliseum** in St Martin's Lane are by far the best venues for classical ballet, providing a stage for visiting foreign companies. The Opera House is home to the world-class Royal Ballet, which performs an extensive repertory. Book well in advance for classics such as *Swan Lake* and *Giselle*. The company also performs some contemporary ballet; triple-bill performances provide a mixture of new and old, and seats are normally quite readily available.

The English National Ballet holds its summer season at the **London Coliseum**. Under artistic director Tamara Rojo, prima ballerina, the ballet performs both classical and contemporary productions. **Sadler's Wells**, though primarily dedicated to contemporary dance, hosts some classical productions.

Contemporary

Sadler's Wells in Islington, near Angel, has a proud reputation as the host of contemporary dance companies from around the world and has been active, in one form or another, since the 18th century. There are regular visits from such luminaries as the Nederlands Dance Theatre and the Alvin Ailey Company from New York. The innovative English ensemble Rambert has a regular, twice-yearly slot at the theatre – usually in May and November. The **Peacock Theatre** (the West End home of Sadler's Wells) features performances of popular dance styles such as salsa and hip hop, and even hosts contemporary circus dance groups.

The Place is a hub of activity: it is home to the London Contemporary Dance School and a dance theatre that stages some 200 performances a year. A purpose-built space in Deptford, south London, the **Laban Theatre** presents a rich and diverse mix of dance, music and physical theatre.

Other venues include the **Institute of Contemporary Arts** (ICA) *(see p96)* and the **Chisenhale Dance Space**, a centre for small companies currently regarded as being on the experimental fringes.

World Dance

World dance is well represented in the capital and visiting groups perform traditional dance from all over the world. Both **Sadler's Wells** and the **Riverside Studios** (reopening in 2018 following redevelopment) are major venues, while companies specializing in specific dance styles, including Indian and Far Eastern, have seasons at the Southbank Centre, often in the **Queen Elizabeth Hall**. Check listings magazines for details.

Dance Festivals

London has two major contemporary dance festivals each year featuring many different companies. Spring Loaded runs from February to April, while Dance Umbrella runs from early October to early November. Listings magazines carry all the details. Other smaller festivals include Almeida Dance, from the end of April to the first week of May at the **Almeida Theatre**, and The Turning World, a festival in April and May showcasing dance from all over the world.

Dance Venues

Almeida Theatre
Almeida St N1.
Tel 020 7359 4404.
W almeida.co.uk

Chisenhale Dance Space
64 Chisenhale Rd E3.
Tel 020 8981 6617.
W chisenhaledance space.co.uk

ICA
Carlton House Terrace, The Mall SW1.
Map 13 A4.
Tel 020 7930 3647.
W ica.org.uk

Laban Theatre
Creekside SE8.
Map 23 A2.
Tel 020 8463 0100.

London Coliseum
St Martin's Lane WC2.
Map 13 B3.
Tel 020 7845 9300.
W eno.org/London-Coliseum

Peacock Theatre
Portugal St WC2. **Map** 14 D1. **Tel** 020 7863 8222.
W peacocktheatre.com

The Place
17 Duke's Rd WC1. **Map** 5 B3. **Tel** 020 7121 1100.
W theplace.org.uk

Queen Elizabeth Hall
Southbank Centre SE1.
Map 14 D4.
Tel 0844 875 0073.
W southbankcentre.co.uk

Riverside Studios
Crisp Rd W6.
Tel 020 8237 1000.
W riverside studios.co.uk

Royal Opera House
Floral St WC2. **Map** 13 C2.
Tel 020 7304 4000.
W roh.org.uk

Sadler's Wells
Rosebery Ave EC1.
Map 6 E3.
Tel 020 7863 8198.
W sadlerswells.com

Rock, Pop, Jazz and World Music

Rock giants, pop divas, jazz legends: London has hosted them all and the city continues to draw the biggest names in music while nurturing acts that could be the next big thing. There may be as many as 80 listed concerts on an ordinary weeknight: rock or reggae, folk or soul, all tastes are catered for and in venues all over the city. In addition to gigs, music festivals are held across the capital in parks, pubs, halls and stadiums. Check the listings websites and magazines (see p338) and keep your eyes open for publicity posters and flyers.

Major Venues

Global superstars such as Beyoncé, the Rolling Stones and Taylor Swift inevitably include a night or two in London while on tour. More often than not the **O2 Arena** in Greenwich, the indoor **Wembley Arena** and the **Eventim Apollo** are the venues of choice, or, if the performers are looking for something a little more elegant, the grand **Royal Albert Hall**.

The **O2 Academy Brixton** and **The Forum** are next in prominence and size. Each can accommodate an audience of well over 2,000 people, and for many Londoners these former cinemas are the capital's best venues, with seating upstairs, standing room downstairs and accessible bars.

Rock and Pop

The capital has a healthy and diverse rock and pop scene. In Camden, **Koko** has hosted some of the biggest names in music including Coldplay, Katy Perry and Madonna. It has a busy calendar of gigs featuring up-and-coming bands and current favourites. Nearby, **The Underworld** promotes alternative music. Though a relatively small venue, it has hosted artists such as Radiohead and the Foo Fighters. The venue is also home to two nightclubs. Once upon a time, Jimi Hendrix and Led Zeppelin took to the stage at the **Roundhouse** in Chalk Farm. In its current incarnation, this excellent venue features a programme of acts that range from pop princess Ellie Goulding to metalheads Opeth. The venue is a Grade II-listed former railway repair shed and the main concert space has an impressive domed ceiling. Just up the road is **Barfly**, which some refer to as a music institution. It is a popular choice for those looking for the latest rock and indie bands – some of the biggest names in rock played early gigs here. They also took to the stage at **The Garage** at Highbury Corner, another favourite venue of rock fans.

Those looking for somewhere a little different should check out the events list at the **Union Chapel** in Islington. A working church with stunning Gothic achitecture, this award-winning venue has hosted a variety of acts including Tom Jones and Billy Bragg.

The **O2 Shepherd's Bush**, like its sister venue in Brixton, is a safe bet for chart-toppers, music legends and fresh talent. Mumford & Sons, Pearl Jam and Prince have all entertained the crowds here.

Lastly, pubs and clubs across the capital regularly host live acts – always check listings when you visit to catch an evening of great music.

Jazz

The number of jazz venues in London continues to grow – both the music and the lifestyle which are romantically imagined to go with it are popular once again. **Ronnie Scott's** in the West End is still the pick of the vintage crop, and since the 1950s, many of the finest performers in the world have come to play here, including Ella Fitzgerald, Nina Simone and Curtis Mayfield. The **100 Club** in Oxford Street is another very popular venue for confirmed jazz fans. Jazz and food have formed a partnership at venues such as the largely vegetarian **Jazz Café**, the branch of **Pizza Express** on Dean Street and the **Mau Mau Bar** on Portobello Road.

The **Southbank Centre** (see pp190–91) and the **Barbican** (see p169) schedule formal jazz concerts and free jazz in the foyers.

World Music

World music encompasses different styles of music from around the globe. It includes, though is by no means limited to, African, Latin and South American music. The popularity of traditional musical styles has even sparked a revitalization of British and Irish folk music. **Cecil Sharp House** has regular shows for folk purists, while the **ICA** (see p96) hosts a range of acts. **Cargo** in Shoreditch has an eclectic programme of live music that includes African beats and Latin funk. Hot Latin nights are held at **Salsa!** on Charing Cross Road, and laid-back vibes pervade the **Notting Hill Arts Club**. For the widest selection of African sounds and food in town, try visiting the **Africa Centre** in Covent Garden. The **Barbican Centre** and the Southbank Centre's **Royal Festival Hall** and **Queen Elizabeth Hall** all include world music on their programmes.

London's large West Indian community has contributed to a lively reggae scene. At the **Notting Hill Carnival** (see p61), in late August, many top bands perform free. Reggae has now become integrated with the mainstream rock music scene, and bands appear at most of London's rock venues.

Clubs

The old cliché that London dies when the pubs shut no longer holds true. Europe has long scoffed at Londoners going to bed at 11pm when the night is only just beginning in Paris, Madrid and Rome, but London has caught on at last and you can revel all night if you want to. The best clubs are not all confined to the city's centre – initial disappointment that your hotel is a half-hour Tube ride from Leicester Square can be offset by the discovery of a trendy club right on your doorstep.

Practical Information

Fashions and club nights change very rapidly and nightspots open and close down all the time. Some of the best club nights are one-nighters – check listings magazines *(see p338)*. Be aware that most clubs have bouncers on the door who may check your ID, look inside your bag (for security reasons) and ensure that your attire conforms with the club dress code. If you are heading out to a particular club, it's worth doing a bit of research before you go.

A few clubs require that you arrange membership 48 hours in advance, and you may also find that you have to be introduced by a member. Again, check these details in listings magazines. Groups of men may not be welcome, so split up before going in; expect to queue to get in. Entrance fees may seem reasonable, but drinks tend to be overpriced.

Opening times are usually 10pm–3am Monday to Saturday, although many clubs stay open until 6am at the weekend and some open on Sunday from about 8pm to midnight.

Mainstream

London offers a broad selection of nightclubs that cater for all musical tastes and budgets.

Most of the more upmarket nightclubs in London, for example **Annabel's**, have a strict members-only policy; they require nominations by current members and have long waiting lists, so unless you mix in privileged circles you are unlikely to get in.

Traditional disco-type clubs include the **Café de Paris**, where you can dine and boogie the night away. For those keen on samba and Latin beats **Guanabara** in Covent Garden is friendly, unpretentious and fun.

Further north, the **Forum** hosts popular club nights, which feature classic soul, funk and R&B. Similar clubs are **East Village** in Shoreditch and the **Tattershall Castle**, a disco boat moored on the bank of the Thames.

Fashionable Venues and Club Nights

London is easily one of the most innovative club capitals in the world and there are plenty of venues that explain why. **Heaven**, the city's best-known gay club, hosts an excellent house night. With its huge dance floor, excellent lasers, sound systems and lightshows it's very popular, so start queuing early. **The Roxy** in Soho is a relaxed club and bar playing a mixture of indie, electronic and pop. The **Ministry of Sound** is a New York-style club that set the pattern for others to follow, hosting some of the world's best-known DJs. If you are feeling energetic, club nights are also run at the **Queen of Hoxton** in trendy Shoreditch. Try **XOYO** also in Shoreditch, or the cavernous, warehouse-style **Egg** near King's Cross for funky house, electro and old skool, and for die-hard clubbers there's always **Fabric**. **Electric Brixton**, formerly the much-loved Fridge, hosts club events and live music.

As with many clubs, **Bar Rumba** has different themes on different evenings. One of the most popular is salsa night and the club runs dance classes

for those wishing to perfect their moves. **Cargo**, with a calendar of live acts, features some of London's funkiest sounds. **93 Feet East** showcases a variety of live music and club nights from indie and rock to techno beats.

In Kensington, **The Roof Gardens** is London's only roof-top private members club. It opens on Friday and Saturday nights, admits over-21s only and has a "no effort, no entry" dress code. Apply for entry via the website, www. roofgardensclub.com.

LGBT

London's best-known gay bars and late-night clubs can be found in Soho. One of the most popular clubs is **The Village** on Wardour Street, which has disco nights on Thursday and Friday, and podium dancers every Saturday. The iconic **G-A-Y Bar** is renowned for its mixed gay nights. In Piccadilly, **The Electric Carousel** (a reincarnation of Soho's legendary Madame Jojo's) is a fabulous whirl of glittering colour and extreme high camp. **Heaven**, with its huge dance floor, bar and video lounge under the arches at Charing Cross station, continues to draw big crowds.

South of the river, Vauxhall is home to several clubs that stay open until the early hours. Though not technically a club, the **Royal Vauxhall Tavern** is an institution and is worth visiting for its cabaret events alone.

Casinos

To gamble in London, you must be a member, or at least the guest of a member, of a licensed gaming club. Most clubs are happy to let you join but membership must be arranged 48 hours in advance. Many will let you in to use facilities other than the gambling tables until about 4am, when most close. Many clubs also have "hostesses" – beware the cost of their company.

DIRECTORY

Major Music Venues

Eventim Apollo
Queen Caroline St W6.
Tel 0844 249 4300 (tickets),
020 8563 3800 (venue).

The Forum
9–17 Highgate Rd NW5.
Tel 020 7428 4080.

O2 Academy Brixton
211 Stockwell Rd SW9.
Tel 0844 477 2000.

O2 Arena
Peninsula Square SE10.
Tel 020 8463 2000.

Royal Albert Hall
See p209.

SSE Arena, Wembley
Empire Way, Wembley,
Middlesex HA9.
Tel 0844 815 0815, 0844
824 4824.

Rock and Pop Venues

Barfly
49 Chalk Farm Rd NW1.
Map 4 F1.
Tel 020 7424 0800.

Koko
1a Camden High St NW1.
Map 4 F2.
Tel 0870 432 5527.

The Garage
20–22 Highbury Corner, N5.
Tel 0844 847 1678.

O2 Shepherd's Bush Empire
Shepherd's Bush Green
W12.
Tel 0844 477 2000.

The Roundhouse
Chalk Farm Rd NW1.
Tel 0300 678 9222

The Underworld
174 Camden High St NW1.
Map 4 F1.
Tel 020 7482 1932.

Union Chapel
The Vestry, Compton
Ave N1.
Tel 020 7226 1686.

Jazz Venues

100 Club
100 Oxford St W1.
Map 13 A1.
Tel 020 7636 0933.

Barbican Hall
See p172.

Jazz Café
5 Parkway NW1.
Map 4 E1.
Tel 020 7485 6834.

Mau Mau Bar
265 Portbello Rd W11.
Map 9 A1.
Tel 020 7229 8528.

Pizza Express
10 Dean St W1.
Map 13 A1.
Tel 0845 602 7017.

Ronnie Scott's
47 Frith St W1.
Map 13 A2.
Tel 020 7439 0747.
W ronniescotts.co.uk

Royal Festival Hall
See p192.

World Music

Africa Centre
38 King St WC2.
Map 13 C2.
Tel 020 7836 1973.

Barbican Centre
See p172.

Cargo
83 Rivington St EC2.
Map 7 C3.
Tel 020 7739 3440.

Cecil Sharp House
2 Regent's Park Rd NW1.
Map 4 D1.
Tel 020 7485 2206.

ICA
See p96.

Notting Hill Arts Club
21 Notting Hill Gate W11.
Map 9 C3.
Tel 020 7460 4459.

Queen Elizabeth Hall
Southbank Centre SE1.
Map 14 D4.
Tel 020 7960 4200.

Royal Festival Hall
See p192.

Salsa!
96 Charing Cross Rd WC2.
Map 13 B1.
Tel 020 7379 3277.

Clubs

93 Feet East
150 Brick Lane E1.
Map 8 E4.
Tel 020 7770 6006.

Annabel's
44 Berkeley Sq W1.
Map 12 E3.
Tel 020 7629 1096.

Bar Rumba
36 Shaftesbury Ave WC2.
Map 6 E2.
Tel 020 7287 6933.

Café de Paris
3 Coventry St W1.
Map 13 A3.
Tel 020 7734 7700.

Cargo
89 Rivington St EC2.
Map 7 C3.
Tel 020 7739 3440.

East Village
89 Great Eastern St EC2.
Map 7 C4.
Tel 020 7739 5173.

Egg
200 York Way N7.
Map 5 C1.
Tel 020 7871 7111.

Electric Brixton
Town Hall Parade, Brixton
Hill SW2.
Tel 020 7274 2290.

The Electric Carousel
215–217 Piccadilly W1.
Map 13 A3.
Tel 020 7734 3040.

Fabric
77a Charterhouse St EC1.
Map 6 F5.
Tel 020 7336 8898.

G-A-Y Bar
30 Old Compton St W1.
Map 13 A2.
Tel 020 7494 2756.

Guanabara
Drury Lane WC2.
Map 13 C1.
Tel 020 7242 8600.

Heaven
Under the Arches, Villiers
St WC2.
Map 13 C3.
Tel 020 7930 2020.

Ministry of Sound
103 Gaunt St SE1.
Tel 020 7740 8600.

Queen of Hoxton
1 Curtain Rd EC2.
Map 7 C3.
Tel 020 7422 0958.

Tattershall Castle
Victoria Embankment
SW1.
Map 13 C3.
Tel 020 7839 6548.

The Roof Gardens
99 Kensington High St
W8.
Map 10 D5.
Tel 020 7937 7994.

The Roxy
3–5 Rathbone Place W1.
Map 13 A1.
Tel 020 7255 1098.

Royal Vauxhall Tavern
372 Kennington Lane
SE11.
Map 21 C3.
Tel 020 7820 1222.

The Village
81 Wardour St W1.
Map 13 A2.
Tel 020 7478 0530.

XOYO
32–37 Cowper St EC2.
Map 7 B4.
Tel 020 7608 2878.

Sport

The range of sports on offer in London is quite phenomenal. Should you feel the urge to watch a game of medieval tennis or go scuba-diving in the city centre, you've come to the right place. More likely, you'll just want to watch a football or rugby match, or play a set of tennis in a park. With far more public facilities than most European capitals, London is the place to enjoy cheap, accessible sport. To top if off, sports fan can relive the Olympics at the Queen Elizabeth Park, where venues built for the 2012 Games, including the Aquatics Centre and Olympic Stadium, are open to the public.

Athletics

Athletes will find a good choice of running tracks, often with free admission. **Linford Christie Stadium** has good facilities; **Regent's Park** is free; try also **Parliament Hill Fields**. For a sociable jog, meet the **Mornington Chasers** in Kentish Town, Camden, on Tuesdays at 7pm.

Cricket

Five-day test matches and one-day internationals are played in summer at **Lord's** (see p250) and the **Kia Oval**, near Vauxhall. Tickets for the first four days of tests and for one-day games are hard to get, but you may get in on the last day and see a thrilling finish. When Middlesex and Surrey play county games at these grounds, there are always seats.

Football (Soccer)

This is the most popular spectator sport in Britain, its season running from August to May, with matches at weekends and on weekday evenings. It is the most common topic of conversation in pubs, where games are often shown live on TV. Premier League and FA Cup games are frequently sold out in advance. London's top clubs include **Arsenal, Chelsea, West Ham** and **Tottenham Hotspur**.

Golf

There are no golf courses in central London, but a few are scattered around the outskirts. The most accessible public courses are **Hounslow Heath, Chessington** (nine holes, train from Waterloo) and **Richmond Park** (two courses, with lessons available). If you didn't pack your clubs, sets can be hired at a reasonable price.

Greyhound Racing

At a night "down the dogs", you can follow the races on a screen in the bar, stand by the track or watch from the comfort of the restaurant (book in advance) at **Romford Stadium** or the **Greyhound Stadium** in Wimbledon.

Horse Racing

High-class flat racing in summer and steeplechasing in winter can be seen at **Ascot, Kempton Park** and **Sandown Park**, which are all less than an hour from central London by train. Britain's most famous flat race, the Derby, is run at **Epsom** in June.

Horse Riding

For centuries, fashionable riders have exercised their steeds in Hyde Park; **Ross Nye** will provide you with a horse so that you can follow a long tradition.

Ice-Skating

Ice-skaters should head for London's best-known rink, **Queens**. The most attractive ice rinks, open only in winter, are at **Somerset House** (see p121) and at the **Tower of London** (see pp158–61).

Rugby Union

International matches are played at **Twickenham Rugby Football Ground**. The season runs from September to April and you can watch "friendly" weekend games at local grounds. Top London teams **Saracens** and **Rosslyn Park** can be seen at their own grounds outside the centre of town.

Squash

Squash courts tend to be busy, so try to book at least two days ahead. Many sports centres have squash facilities and will hire out equipment. Try **Swiss Cottage Leisure Centre** and the **Oasis Sports Centre**.

Swimming

The best indoor pools include **Chelsea Sports Centre**, the **Oasis** and **Porchester Centre**; for outdoor swimming, try **Hampstead and Highgate Ponds** (two separate ponds for men and women and one mixed) and the Oasis. Out of town, the **London Aquatics Centre** at the Queen Elizabeth Olympic Park (see pp254–5), purpose-built for the 2012 Games, has world-class facilities, a state-of-the-art gym and a full programme of activities.

Tennis

There are hundreds of tennis courts in London's public parks, most of them cheap to hire and easily reserved. It can be busy in the summer, so book your court two or three days ahead. You must supply your own racquet and balls. Good public tennis courts include those at **Holland Park** and **Parliament Hill**.

Tickets for the Centre Court of the **All England Lawn Tennis Club** at Wimbledon are hard to obtain – it is possibly easier to enter the tournament as a player. Try queueing overnight, or queue for return tickets after lunch on the day – for a bargain price, you can still enjoy a good four hours of tennis (see p61).

Traditional Sports

An old London tradition is the University Boat Race, held in March or April, when teams from Oxford and Cambridge row from Putney to Mortlake *(see p60)*; a newer tradition is the London Marathon, which is run from Greenwich to The Mall at Westminster *(see p60)* on an April Sunday. You can watch croquet at **Dulwich Croquet Club** and medieval (real) tennis at **Queen's Club**.

Water Sports

There are facilities for a wide variety of water sports at the **Docklands Sailing & Watersports Centre**. You can choose from sports such as windsurfing, dinghy sailing, powerboating, waterskiing and canoeing. Rowing boats are also available for hire by the hour on the calmer, central London waters of the **Serpentine** in Hyde Park and **Regent's Park Lake**.

Working Out

Most sports centres have gymnasiums, work-out studios and health clubs. If you are a member of the YMCA, you'll be able to use the excellent facilities at the **Central YMCA**. **Jubilee Hall Clubs** and the **Oasis Sports Centre** both offer a variety of aerobic classes, keep-fit and weight training. For those who have overdone it, the **Chelsea Sports Centre** has a sports injury clinic.

DIRECTORY

All England Lawn Tennis and Croquet Club
Church Rd, Wimbledon SW19. **Tel** 020 8944 1066.

Arsenal (Emirates) Stadium
Ashburton Grove N7.
Tel 020 7619 5000.

Ascot Racecourse
Ascot, Berkshire.
Tel 0844 346 3000.

Central YMCA
112 Great Russell St WC1.
Map 13 B1.
Tel 020 7343 1844.

Chelsea Football Club
Stamford Bridge SW6.
Tel 0871 984 1955.

Chelsea Sports Centre
Chelsea Manor St SW3.
Map 19 B3.
Tel 020 7352 6985.

Chessington Golf Course
Garrison Lane, Surrey.
Tel 020 8391 0948.

Docklands Sailing & Watersports Centre
235a Westferry Rd E14.
Tel 020 7537 2626.
W dswc.org

Dulwich Croquet Club
Giant Arches Rd, off Burbage Rd SE24.
W dulwichcroquet.com

Epsom Racecourse
Epsom Downs, Surrey.
Tel 01372 726 311.

Greyhound Stadium
Plough Lane, Wimbledon SW17. **Tel** 020 8946 8000.

Hampstead and Highgate Ponds
Mixed: off East Heath Rd NW3. **Map** 1 C4.
Men's and Women's: Millfield Lane N6. **Map** 2 E3.
Tel 020 7485 3873.

Holland Park Public Tennis Courts
1 Ilchester Place W8.
Map 9 B5.
Tel 020 7602 2226.

Hounslow Heath Golf Course
Staines Rd, Middlesex TW4.
Tel 020 8570 5271.

Jubilee Hall Clubs
30 The Piazza, Covent Garden WC2.
Map 13 C2.
Tel 020 7836 4007.

Kempton Park
Sunbury on Thames, Middx.
Tel 01932 782 292.

Kia Oval
Kennington Oval SE11.
Map 22 D4.
Tel 0844 375 1845.

Linford Christie Stadium
Du Cane Rd W12.
Tel 020 3772 8260.

London Aquatics Centre
Queen Elizabeth Olympic Park E20.
Tel 020 8536 3150.

Lord's Cricket Ground
St John's Wood NW8.
Map 3 A3.
Tel 020 7616 8500.

Mornington Chasers
W chaser.me.uk

Oasis Swimming Pool & Sports Centre
32 Endell St WC2.
Map 13 B1.
Tel 020 7831 1804.

Parliament Hill
Highgate Rd NW5.
Map 2 E5.
Tel 020 7332 3773.

Porchester Centre
Queensway W2.
Map 10 D1.
Tel 020 7792 2919.

Queen's Club (Real Tennis)
Palliser Rd W14.
Map 17 A3.
Tel 020 7385 3400.

Queens Ice Skating Club
17 Queensway W2.
Map 10 E2.
Tel 020 7229 0172.

Regent's Park and Lake
Regent's Park NW1.
Map 3 C3.
Tel 0300 061 2300, 020 7724 4069 (boat hire).

Richmond Park Golf
Roehampton Gate, Priory Lane SW15.
Tel 020 8876 3205.

Romford Stadium
London Road, Essex RM7.
Tel 01708 762 345.

Rosslyn Park Rugby
Priory Lane, Upper Richmond Rd SW15.
Tel 020 8876 1879.

Ross Nye Stables
8 Bathurst Mews W2.
Map 11 A2.
Tel 020 7262 3791.

Sandown Park Racecourse
Esher, Surrey.
Tel 01372 464 348.

Saracens Rugby Football Club
5 Vicarage Rd, Watford, Hertfordshire, WD1.
Tel 01727 792 800.

Serpentine
Hyde Park W2.
Map 11 B4.
Tel 020 7262 1330 (boat hire).

Somerset House
Strand WC2.
Map 14 D2.
Tel 0844 847 1520.

Swiss Cottage Leisure Centre
Adelaide Rd NW3.
Tel 020 7974 2012.

Tottenham Hotspur FC
White Hart Lane, 748 High Rd N17.
Tel 0344 499 5000.

Twickenham Rugby Ground
Whitton Rd, Twickenham, Middlesex.
Tel 020 8892 8877.

West Ham United
Boleyn Ground, Green St, Upton Park E13.
Tel 0871 529 1966.

CHILDREN'S LONDON

London is as much of a treat for children as it is for adults. Besides the traditional ceremonies and favorite famous buildings, there are plenty of attractions to avoid any cries of boredom. Museums and galleries are packed with workshops, hands-on experiments, and interactive displays that are not only educational but also heaps of fun. The South Bank is lined with historic sights, crowd-pleasing street performers, and family-friendly restaurants. For entertainment away from the hustle and bustle, there is a plethora of royal parks, some only a few minutes from the city center, as well as playgrounds, sports centers, farms, and zoos. Best of all, there's no need to spend a fortune to have fun. For even more family-friendly ideas, see DK's *Family Guide to London*.

Practical Advice

A little planning is the key to a successful London outing with children. Check the opening hours of the places you plan to visit in advance and work out your journey carefully using the Tube map at the end of this book. If you are traveling with very young children, remember that there are very likely to be lines at the Underground stations or bus stops near popular sights. These will be long during peak hours, so buy your tickets, Travelcard, or Oyster Card in advance *(see p374)*. Children under 11 are entitled to free Tube, bus, and DLR travel provided they are traveling with an adult who has a valid ticket or Oyster card. Child fares are in effect for all children between the ages of 11 and 15. Consider also swapping the Tube for a riverboat or even hopping aboard a double-decker sightseeing bus to take in some of the city's attractions

The Natural History Museum ranks among London's top children's attractions

while traveling from one area to another.

Visiting all the exhibitions and museums as a family is fairly inexpensive as the majority of London's principal museums have no entry charge. Many also offer complimentary or low-priced children's tours, trails, story-telling sessions, and workshops. For those where you do have

to pay, an annual family season ticket, usually for two adults and up to four children, is available. In some cases you can even buy a family ticket that covers a group of museums.

There are always lots of organized activity programs going on across London during the long summer school vacation (July to the beginning of September). For tips and ideas, check out *Time Out London's* "kids' hot list" for events happening in the capital at the time of your visit.

Be prepared for changeable weather: raincoats and umbrellas are essential, even in summer, when you may also need sunscreen. In winter, bring warm clothes and comfy shoes with non-slip soles.

Children and the Law

Only people over 18 can drink or buy alcohol. In restaurants, the law is a little more relaxed: those over 16 can drink wine or beer with their meal, but you still have to be over 18 to be served spirits. Many pubs, particularly gastropubs, welcome children, and some offer kids' menus as well as a selection of toys or activity sheets. This is less common in more traditional "drinking" pubs, where children may not necessarily be welcome. Those heading to the movies should check the film classification; some are classed as unsuitable for children.

If you want to travel by car, you must use seat belts, and children less than 4 ft 5 inches (135 cm) tall or under 12 years will need a special car seat.

Taking a break during a visit to the zoo

Eating Out with Children

The variety of cuisines available in the city is vast and there is plenty to suit kids with adventurous tastes: enjoy a trip to the orange-lantern-filled Chinatown, tuck into a *thali* at an authentic Indian curry house, or share a selection of Spanish tapas, perfect for those wanting to try a little of everything.

They may not be the most imaginative choice, but chain restaurants are guaranteed to be a safe option for families, with highchairs, easy-wipe surfaces, suitable good-value food, friendly staff, and no exorbitant prices. Some places also provide activity sheets with puzzles to solve and pictures to color in. A few of the best, all with branches across the city, include Gourmet Burger Kitchen (GBK) and Byron for good-quality burgers, and Ask, Pizza Express, and Carluccio's for popular Italian meals. There's a branch of family favorite **Giraffe** at the Southbank Centre *(see below)*. For more options, and more contact details for places mentioned here, see the Light Meals and Snacks section on pp308–11.

For a totally different and fun-filled family dining experience, **The Rainforest Café** is most certainly worth a visit. The restaurant, complete

All branches of the cheerful Giraffe chain have an excellent children's menu

with gift shop, is designed as an Amazonian jungle with lifelike moving animals and the sounds of tropical thunderstorms. Those who want to make a night of it might enjoy a visit to **All Star Lanes**, an American-style diner complete with bowling alleys. The kids' deal – main meal, drink, dessert, and game of bowling – makes for a reasonably priced evening.

Combine a family-friendly meal with an evening's entertainment at All Star Lanes

Useful Addresses

All Star Lanes
Bloomsbury Place WC1.
Tel 020 7025 2676.
(One of several branches.)

Giraffe
Riverside Level 1, Southbank Centre SE1.
Tel 020 7042 6900.
(One of several branches.)

The Rainforest Café
20 Shaftesbury Avenue W1D.
Tel 020 3326 6390.

In England it is illegal to smoke in a vehicle carrying anyone under 18.

The South Bank

With a walkway that stretches virtually unbroken along the Thames from Tower Bridge *(see p157)* to the London Eye *(see p193)*, the South Bank, with its many attractions, is the perfect destination for families seeking a fun day out. It is also conveniently sandwiched between London Bridge and London Waterloo train stations.

By London Bridge, bustling Borough Market *(see p180)* makes a perfect stop for lunch or a snack. Worth a visit are two very different ships, both moored nearby: HMS *Belfast* *(see p187)* and the replica of the *Golden Hinde II* *(see p179)*.

A little farther along the river, Shakespeare's Globe *(see p181)* has monthly children's workshops during theater

season, and the towering Tate Modern *(see pp182–5)* offers art trails and challenges for kids.

Nearby the London Eye, street performers entertain the crowds and there is a weekly food market behind Royal Festival Hall *(see p311)*. The London Aquarium *(see p192)* provides close-up encounters with sea life from starfish to sharks. The London Dungeon *(see p192)*

takes older kids with a strong stomach on a grisly tour of the most bloodthirsty events in British history.

The Southbank Centre itself *(see pp190–91)* is home to the National Theatre, the British Film Institute (BFI), and the Royal Festival Hall. The center offers a huge program of events all through the year, as well as family-friendly restaurants.

The London Eye, providing views across the city

Shopping

Don't miss **Hamleys** toy shop or **Harrods'** Toy Kingdom, both of which have shelves of toys, books and games. Kids will be just as awestruck at the smaller but specialized **Benjamin Pollock's Toy Shop**. Bookshops such as Waterstones and Foyles have excellent children's sections and often organize readings and signings by children's authors.

For souvenirs, there are many shops and stands all over London, which are great for buying children a memento from their trip. Museum gift shops are filled with toys, clothes and stationery.

Useful Numbers

Benjamin Pollock's Toy Shop
44 The Market, Royal Opera House WC2. **Tel** 020 7379 7866.

Foyles
107 Charing Cross Road WC2H 0DT. **Tel** 020 7437 5660.
(One of several branches.)

Hamleys
188–196 Regent St W1.
Tel 0870 333 2455.

Harrods
87–135 Brompton Road SW1.
Tel 020 7730 1234.

Waterstones
203/206 Piccadilly W1J 9HD.
Tel 020 7851 2400.
(One of several branches.)

Letting off steam before visiting the nation's treasure house, the British Museum

Museums and Galleries

The museums and galleries of London are so packed full of interesting artifacts and interactive displays that it's unlikely you'll have to drag reluctant children around an assortment of lifeless, stuffy exhibits.

The Science Museum *(see pp210–11)*, with hundreds of working models, is one of London's best attractions for children – its hands-on galleries in the basement, including the much-loved Launch Pad, will help keep them amused for hours. Equally popular is the Natural History Museum *(see pp206–7)*, which explores life on earth with dinosaur models, a giant whale and an examination of the human body. Both museums hold sleepovers once a month.

The British Museum *(see pp128–31)* has fabulous treasures from all over the world, including the fascinating Egyptian

A familiar face at Hamleys toy shop

collection, and the Horniman Museum *(see p254)* has an eclectic array of objects including a collection of taxidermy and skeletons.

On the north side of Tower Bridge is the Tower of London *(see pp158–61)*, with suits of armour built for knights and monarchs and, of course, the Crown Jewels. Armoury and weapons, including aircraft and the tools of modern warfare, can be seen at the National Army Museum *(see p201)* and the Imperial War Museum *(see pp194–5)*. At the London Transport Museum *(see p118)*, kids can dress up in historical costumes and play on real buses and trams in the family play-zone, "All Aboard". The V&A Museum of Childhood *(see p252)*, the children's branch of the V&A located in east London, has a fascinating collection of children's toys from throughout history.

Madame Tussauds *(see p228)*, the world-famous wax museum, lets kids get up close to their celebrity heroes.

Children's Theatre

London is home to a plethora of theatres, including some for children. **The Polka Theatre** offers the best range of children's theatre, and has workshops during the school holidays. **The Unicorn Theatre** is also highly

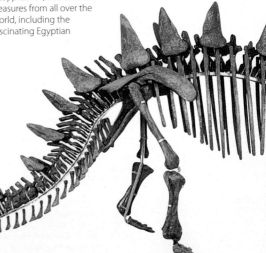

acclaimed, and the **Little Angel Theatre** and the **Puppet Barge**, moored in Little Venice, specialize in puppet shows. For older kids who aspire to the stage, the Royal National Theatre *(see p192)*, the Royal Opera House *(see p119)*, Sadler's Wells *(see p346)* and the Theatre Royal Drury Lane *(see p119)* offer tours.

During **Kids Week**, which runs throughout August, kids aged under 16 go free at participating theatres when accompanied by a fee-paying adult.

Useful Numbers

Kids Week
🖥 kidsweek.co.uk

Little Angel Theatre
Tel 020 7226 1787.

Polka Theatre
Tel 020 8543 4888.
🖥 polkatheatre.com

Puppet Barge
Tel 020 7249 6876.
🖥 puppetbarge.com

Unicorn Theatre
Tel 020 7645 0560.
🖥 unicorntheatre.com

Puppets at the Little Angel Theatre

Tuojiangasaurus skeleton at the Natural History Museum

Giraffes at London Zoo, in Regent's Park

The Great Outdoors

London is fortunate to have many parks and open spaces *(see pp52–5)*. Most local parks will include conventional playgrounds for children, many with modern, safe equipment. Young children will particularly enjoy the Diana Memorial Playground in Kensington Gardens *(see p223)*, which features a huge Peter Pan-inspired wooden pirate ship for kids to play on and explore. Coram's Fields *(see p133)* in Bloomsbury is another delightful park, with a farmyard, paddling pool and sports pitches.

Animal-lovers will enjoy a trip to the Children's Zoo in Battersea Park *(see p257)* (coincide a visit with feeding time) or to London Zoo and Regent's Canal *(see p231)*. The canal is also home to Camley Street Natural Park, a beautiful reserve that has butterflies, bats and birds. Vauxhall City Farm has kids' clubs and riding lessons available for all abilities.

The city's parks are ideal for a picnic lunch and bit of respite. Feed the ducks at St James's Park or hire a boat on the lakes at Regent's Park and Hyde Park. The Serpentine lido in Hyde Park is the perfect place to enjoy a swim in the summertime and there is a separate area and paddling pool for children.

All of the large parks make perfect places for a good walk or cycle ride and bicycles are easy to hire *(see p375)* – though cyclists should be sure to watch out for pedestrians and remember that some paths may be out of bounds.

Sports

For sports enthusiasts, there is plenty to see and do across the capital. Sports centres *(see pp350–51)* often have special clubs to occupy children of every age. Battersea Park Millennium Arena is one of many parks that has an athletics track and sports facilities; most parks also have tennis courts available for hire.

One of London's greatest sporting facilities is the Queen Elizabeth Olympic Park *(see pp254–5)*, which was built for the Games in 2012. It is now home to a huge range of activities: go for a swim in the world-famous Aquatics Centre, play a game of hockey or climb the wall in the Tumbling Bay play area. Older children are also able to cycle inside the Velodrome, or attempt the mountain bike course in the Lee Valley VeloPark.

Other sporting must-visits in London include Twickenham Rugby Football Ground *(see p351)*, Lord's Cricket Ground *(see p250)*, the Wimbledon Lawn Tennis Museum *(see p255)* and Chelsea Football Stadium *(see p351)*. All are open most of the year and offer exciting behind-the-scenes tours.

Sports facilities and green spaces at the Queen Elizabeth Olympic Park

SURVIVAL GUIDE

PRACTICAL INFORMATION

London has responded well to the demands of modern tourism. The range of facilities on offer to travellers, from ATMs and medical clinics to boutique hotels and late-night transport, continues to expand. Whether you find London an expensive city will depend on the exchange rate between the pound and your own currency. It is known for high hotel prices, but even here there are good mid-range and budget options (see pp284–7). You need not spend a lot on food, if you choose carefully and make the most of the range London has to offer; for the price of a single meal at some West End restaurants, you could eat enjoyably for several days (see pp308–11). The following tips will help you make the most of your visit.

Crossing the Millennium Bridge

When to Go

London's weather is famously changeable, but in general it is chilly from November to February, and warmest from June to August (see p63). It can rain at any time of year. Extremes of temperature are rare, so there is no time of year when London closes down and everyone goes on holiday. Many concerts and exhibitions take place in winter and spring, but there are plenty of events during the summer too, such as the BBC Proms and open-air theatre seasons. In short, there's plenty to see all year round (see pp60–63).

Visas and Passports

Citizens of European Union countries may enter the UK for an unlimited period with a passport or national identity card. Visitors from the United States, Canada, Australia and New Zealand need only a full passport for tourist and business stays of up to six months, but on arrival they must fill in an Immigration Card, which is given out on incoming flights. Citizens of some countries may require a visa; details can be found in the Visa Services section of the **UK Border Agency** (UKBA) website. The UK is not signed up to the Schengen open-borders agreement operated by most EU countries. Hence, visitors arriving from France or any other Schengen country must still pass through immigration checks when entering the UK.

The UKBA has a strict points-based visa system under which anyone from any non-EU country (including the USA, Canada, Australia and New Zealand) entering Britain for any purpose other than pure tourism or short business trips (this includes students on short study-abroad programmes) must obtain a visa before travelling. The visa system is complicated and detailed, so check well in advance; details are on the UKBA website.

Travel Safety

Visitors can get up-to-date travel safety information from the Foreign and Commonwealth Office in the UK, the State Department in the US and the Department of Foreign Affairs and Trade in Australia.

Customs Information

EU residents may carry any amount of goods between EU countries without paying duty, as long as the goods are for their personal use. Customs officers may question whether large amounts of any item are genuinely for your own use.

Examples of amounts usually accepted are: up to 3,200 cigarettes and up to 90 litres of wine. For travellers arriving from outside the EU, stricter allowances apply. Visitors not resident in the EU can reclaim the Value Added Tax (VAT) on many goods when they leave Britain, but note that the items must have been bought from a shop operating the VAT Retail Export Scheme. Ask the retailer for the correct form, which has details on how to obtain your refund; these can also be found on the UKBA website under "Travel and Customs".

Tourist Information and Tours

Visit London is the city's central tourism service and is a key source of information. Tourist Information Centres can be found all over London (www.visitlondon.com has a full list). The City of London Information Centre, located by St Paul's Cathedral, provides leaflets on attractions, tours, museums, walks and public transport. Others can be found at main rail stations. The centres sell travelcards and **London Pass** (see p359) discount cards, provide currency exchange and distribute Visit London's handy free monthly magazine, London Planner.

For comprehensive listings information – including art, cinema, music, theatre and nightlife – visit the websites of **LondonNet** and *Time Out London*, London's leading

Signpost

Double-decker sightseeing boat on the Thames

listings magazine. Guided tours are an effective way to explore the city; a trip in an open-top double-decker bus makes a good introduction. **Original London Sightseeing Tours** and **Big Bus Tours** are the main companies offering hop-on, hop-off services, with tickets valid for 24 or 48 hours. Other tour companies include **London Walks**, which offers over 40 different routes, and **London Duck Tours**, which take in the sights on road and by river. To find a private tour guide for a specific interest, contact the **Association of Professional Tourist Guides**. For river cruises and commuter services, *see page 65*. The major sights are often crowded and have long queues. Museums and galleries get particularly busy at weekends and on late-opening nights, so try to visit midweek.

Admission Prices

Admission to the main collections of London's major public museums and galleries is free, but you will pay to see temporary exhibits. Private museums and other attractions have admission charges; they vary greatly, but for adults most are between £5 and £15. There are often reduced prices for seniors, students and children.

If you aim to do lots of sightseeing, you can cut costs with a **London Pass**, a card that gives you free entry and fast-track admission at many attractions. Cards are valid for 1, 2, 3 or 6 days and can be combined with a Travelcard. A London Pass can be bought in advance from www.visit london.com and mailed to your home or collected from a tourist centre.

Opening Hours

Opening times for individual sights are listed in the *Area by Area* section of this book. Core visiting times are 10am to 5pm or 6pm daily; last admission is usually 1 hour before closing time. Most of the big museums have at least one late-opening day each week. Opening hours are often shorter on Sundays and public holidays. Some smaller attractions are closed on Mondays.

Social Customs and Etiquette

Londoners are known for queueing – whether for theatre tickets, taxis or takeaways. Things aren't quite as genteel as they used to be, but in general, anyone barging in will still encounter frosty glares.

Casual clothing is accepted in most restaurants, and only a few upscale establishments still require men to wear a jacket and tie.

The religious pattern of London reflects the city's huge ethnic diversity: all of the world's major faiths are represented here. Smoking is forbidden in all public indoor spaces. Some hotels still designate bedrooms for smokers, but it's best to double check when booking.

Tipping

It is usual to tip in restaurants, hotels, hairdressers and taxis, but not for bar service in pubs. Many restaurants add a service charge – usually 12.5 per cent – to the bill, in which case an extra tip is not necessary. Be wary of places that add a service charge, then encourage you to add a "gratuity" when you pay by credit card. In taxis, tip around 10 per cent; for hotel porters, £1 is usually sufficient.

Travellers with Disabilities

Access to transport and attractions, and services for wheelchair users and others with mobility problems is continually improving. The Visit London website has a guide to access and services. **Transport for London** (TfL) produces a *Getting Around London* guide, which can be downloaded from the TfL or Visit London websites, and is available free from Underground stations. **Artsline** gives information on facilities at cultural events and venues.

Nearly all London buses have wheelchair-access ramps, and all licensed taxis and some minicabs are wheelchair-accessible. The huge task of improving access to the entire Underground network is ongoing and TFL maps show accessible stations. Most museums and theatres have accessible facilities, but hotels with fully adapted rooms are scarce.

Disabled drivers with a blue badge allowing free parking should note that in four London boroughs – the City, Westminster, Kensington & Chelsea, and Camden – it allows you to park only in designated blue-badge bays.

London bus with ramp for easy wheelchair access

The Natural History Museum, a great day out for all the family

Travelling with Children

Under Transport for London's "Kids Go Free" scheme, travel is free on buses, the Underground, DLR and trains within London for all children aged under 11 accompanied by an adult (up to four children per adult). Children aged 11–15 can also travel free, with or without an adult, on all buses, and for reduced prices on the Underground and DLR (see p374); the Zip Oyster 11–15 Identity Card can be ordered online and collected at a tourist information centre on arrival in London. See the Visit London and Transport for London websites for more detail.

Most museums and attractions have reduced prices for children under 11 and at many places entry is free for under-5s. Many also sell good-value family tickets. Plenty of restaurants welcome children, and a number of hotels have family rooms; the Novotel chain represents particularly good value for families.

London is a child-friendly city. A huge variety of entertainment and activities is on offer, and many museums have special kids' programmes (see pp352–5). There are dozens of parks, many of them with playground facilities. The Visit London website's "Family" pages are a useful source of information. Time Out London has a "Kids" section covering current attractions.

Senior Travellers

Over-60s can enjoy reduced admission prices at most museums and attractions. You may be asked to show photo ID. Free travel on the Tube, rail and ferry services is only available to residents but most bus passes can be used across the city.

Gay and Lesbian Travellers

London has a huge and diverse gay scene. Its core is Soho – it even has a (non-official) **LGBT Tourist Office**, which offers advice on everything from the best gay bars to useful support groups. It's hard to keep track of everything going on, but the **Pink News** and **Gay London** websites, and Time Out London have up-to-date information.

Travelling on a Budget

London can be a very expensive city, but sightseeing costs can be reduced with the London Pass (see p359), and remember that admission to London's largest museums is free. To get

around town by public transport, always buy a Travelcard rather than single tickets; for trips out of town, the coach is much cheaper than the train, especially when booked in advance. Discounted theatre tickets can be bought at the **TKTS** booth in Leicester Square, and many theatres have cheap-ticket nights.

London has plenty of budget restaurants and cafés, and even quite grand restaurants offer accessibly priced lunch menus. As well as dorm-style hostels, there are no-frills budget hotels with private rooms, some ensuite, for under £50 (see pp286–7). There's also a growing trend for spare-room lets and "couch surfing" via the **Airbnb** website.

Students pay lower admission to many exhibitions, and holders of an **ISIC** (International Student Identity Card) or IYTC (International Youth Travel Card) are eligible for a range of other discounts. A **Hostelling International** card is also handy for lower rates at hostels and other discounts.

Electricity

The voltage in London is 240V AC, and plugs have three square pins. Visitors will need plug adaptors for appliances, and with any older North American 110V equipment you may also need a transformer.

Conversion Chart

Officially the metric system is used, but imperial measures are still common.

Imperial to metric
1 inch = 2.5 centimetres
1 foot = 30 centimetres
1 mile = 1.6 kilometres
1 ounce = 28 grams
1 pound = 454 grams
1 pint = 0.6 litre
1 gallon = 4.6 litres

Metric to imperial
1 millimetre = 0.04 inch
1 centimetre = 0.4 inch
1 metre = 3 feet 3 inches
1 kilometre = 0.6 mile
1 gram = 0.04 ounce
1 kilogram = 2.2 pounds

International Student Identity Card (ISIC)

Time

London is on Greenwich Mean Time (GMT) during the winter months, five hours ahead of Eastern Standard Time and ten hours behind Sydney. From late March to late October, clocks are set forward 1 hour to British Summer Time (equivalent to Central European Time). At any time of year, you can check the correct time by dialing 123 on a BT landline to contact the 24-hour automated Speaking Clock service (note that there is a charge for this service).

Responsible Tourism

London has set itself ambitious targets for improving the urban environment and reducing energy use. **Thames 21**, for example, is an environmental charity which involves the local community in schemes to help keep the river Thames clean and clear.

The **Green Tourism Business Scheme** awards Green Tourism badges to businesses in the UK that meet the highest environ-

Green Tourism badge

mental standards. These standards ensure that each business is committed to sustainable tourism and dedicated to minimizing its damage to the environment. See the website for green accommodation options. Recycling bins, which separate paper and plastic, are widely used and many shoppers carry reusable cloth bags to avoid charges for plastic bags.

DIRECTORY

Visas and Passports

UK Border Agency
W ukba.homeoffice.
gov.uk

Embassies and Consulates

Australian High Commission
Australia House, The Strand WC2. **Map** 13 C2.
Tel 020 7379 4334.
W uk.embassy.gov.au

Canadian High Commission
1 Grosvenor Square W1.
Map 12 D2. **Tel** 020 7258 6600. W unitedking
dom.gc.ca

New Zealand High Commission
80 Haymarket SW1. **Map** 13 A3.**Tel** 020 7930 8422.
W nzembassy.com/
united-kingdom

United States Embassy
24 Grosvenor Square W1.
Map 12 D2.
Tel 020 7499 9000.
W usembassy.org.uk

Travel Safety

UK Foreign and Commonwealth Office
W gov.uk/foreign-travel-
advice

US Department of State
W travel.state.gov/

Australia Department of Foreign Affairs and Trade
W dfat.gov.au/
smartraveller.gov.au/

Tourist Information

Association of Professional Tour Guides
Tel 020 7611 2545.
W guidelondon.org.uk

Big Bus Tours
Tel 020 7808 6753.
W eng.bigbustours.com

City of London Information Centre
St. Paul's Churchyard EC4.
Map 15 A2.

London Duck Tours
W londonducktours.
co.uk

LondonNet
W londonnet.co.uk

London Pass
W londonpass.com

London Walks
W walks.com

Original London Sightseeing Tour
W theoriginaltour.com

Time Out London
W timeout.com/
london

Transport for London
W tfl.gov.uk

Visit London
W visitlondon.com

Religious Services

Anglican (Episcopalian)
St Paul's Cathedral EC4.
Map 15 A2.
W stpauls.co.uk

Catholic
Westminster Cathedral, Victoria St SW1. **Map** 20 F1. W westminster
cathedral.org.uk

Evangelical Alliance
UK Resource Centre, 176 Copenhagen St N1.
Map 6 D1.
W eauk.org

Jewish
Liberal Jewish Synagogue, 28 St John's Wood Rd NW8.
Map 3 A3. W ljs.org

United Synagogue (Orthodox)
735 High Rd N12.
W theus.org.uk

Muslim
Islamic Cultural Centre, 146 Park Rd NW8.
Map 3 B3.
W iccuk.org

Travellers with Disabilities

Artsline
W artsline.org.uk

Transport for London
Tel 0343 222 1234 (24 hours).
W tfl.gov.uk

Gay & Lesbian Travellers

Gay London
W gaylondon.com

LGBT Tourist Information Office
25 Frith St W1.
Map 13 B2.
W gaytouristoffice.
co.uk

Pink News
W pinknews.co.uk

Travelling on a Budget

Airbnb
W airbnb.com

Hostelling International
W hihostels.com

ISIC (International Student Identity Card)
W isiccard.com

TKTS (Discount Theatre Tickets)
Leicester Square WC2.
Map 13 B2. W tkts.co.uk

Responsible Tourism

Thames 21
W thames21.org.uk

Tourism Business Scheme
Tel 01738 632 162.
W greenbusiness.co.uk

Personal Security and Health

London is a large city which, like any other, has had its share of urban problems. It has also been a terrorist target, and London life is sometimes disrupted by security alerts. Nearly all of these turn out to be false alarms, but they should always be taken seriously. Never hesitate to approach one of London's many police officers for assistance – they are trained to help the public with problems.

Mounted police

Police

If you are robbed, or are the victim of any other kind of crime, report it to the police as soon as possible. Patrolling police officers are generally fairly easy to find in central London, but if you cannot find one, call or go to the nearest police station – these are listed on the **Metropolitan Police** website; alternatively, your hotel should be able to advise. Note that the **City of London Police** is a separate force, with its own website. Police stations are also shown on the Street Finder maps towards the end of this book (pp382–419).

When you report a crime, police will take a statement from you, and you will need to list any lost or stolen items.

What to be Aware of

It is unlikely that your stay in London will be blighted by crime. Even in run-down parts of town, the risk of having your pocket picked or bag stolen is not particularly great. It is actually more likely to happen in the middle of heaving shopping crowds in areas like Oxford Street or Camden Lock, or perhaps on a packed Underground platform.

As in any big city, the risk of being a victim of street crime can be further reduced by following a few sensible precautions. Make sure your possessions are adequately insured before you travel. Do not carry all your valuables around with you, but take only as much cash as you need, and leave the rest in a hotel safe or a locked suitcase.

Avoid poorly lit or isolated places like backstreets, parks and unstaffed railway stations at night. To be extra careful, try to travel around in a group at night.

In crowds, be aware of anyone standing especially close. Keep bags zipped up; keep a hand on your bag when walking along; and never leave bags unattended in any public place – they may be stolen or considered a security threat. When you sit at a table, especially outdoors, always keep your bag within reach and in sight – preferably on your lap or on the table – and never leave it on the ground or hanging on the back of a chair.

In an Emergency

In a serious emergency, you can call 999 – or the European emergency number 112 – to summon police, fire or ambulance services. Note that this is only for genuine emergencies, so if

your problem is less serious, it is better to contact a police station or hospital directly.

Lost and Stolen Property

Although you should report thefts, or loss of any property, to the police, be warned that it's unlikely that they will be able to recover any of it for you. However, they will give you a copy of your police statement, which you will need to make an insurance claim.

Traffic police officer

If you lose anything on buses, Underground and DLR trains or in taxis (black cabs), it should eventually reach the **Transport for London Lost Property Office** in Baker Street. You can also enquire about lost items online, through the TfL website (under "Useful Contacts"). It will usually take a few days for items to reach the office, so if you notice the loss the same day, try to enquire about it at the station nearest to where you lost it, or at the nearest police station. Items lost on riverboats or in minicabs should be held by the individual companies. For property lost on national rail services, you will need to contact the individual trainline operator.

Hospitals and Pharmacies

All European Union nationals with a European Health Insurance Card (EHIC), as well as citizens of some other countries with special agreements with the UK (Australia and New Zealand among them), can obtain free treatment from the British **National Health Service (NHS)**. Visitors from other non-EU countries should have full medical cover as part of their travel insurance, and if necessary make use of an NHS or private hospital (such as

Pharmacy sign

Typical London police car

London ambulance

London fire engine

attention, ask your hotel to recommend a doctor, or go to the nearest NHS health centre (doctor's surgery) or hospital Accident & Emergency (A&E) department. Not all hospitals have A&E departments, but those that do are listed on the NHS and Visit London websites, and in local phone books. In many cases, the simplest thing may be to call **NHS 111**, a free advice service for non-emergencies. If you have a dental problem, you can also call NHS 111 for addresses of emergency dentists. Dental treatment through the NHS is not entirely free, so consider private treatment (again, hotels should be able to recommend a dentist) and claim on your insurance policy.

Medical Express) on a paying basis. In case of emergency, anyone – EU or non-EU – will be treated free of charge.

If you have an accident or other problem needing medical

Pharmacies (also known as chemists) are plentiful around London, and pharmacists are trained to dispense medications and advise on ailments. Some medicines are only available with a prescription. It is worth noting that prescription drugs are not free even if you are entitled to NHS treatment; if you are not, you will be charged the full price, and so will need to make an insurance claim. **Boots** is the largest chain of pharmacies in the UK. Most pharmacies are closed on Sundays, but those listed in the Directory, below, have extended hours.

Travel and Health Insurance

All visitors to London should have a comprehensive travel insurance policy providing adequate cover for all eventualities including potential legal expenses, theft, lost luggage or other property, accidents, cancellations, travel delays and medical cover. Even if you are entitled to use the NHS for medical needs, it can be a good idea to have private medical insurance included too, since this may allow you to get quicker treatment with fewer formalities. Your insurance company should provide you with a 24-hour emergency number in case of need.

DIRECTORY

In an Emergency

Police, Fire and Ambulance services
Tel 999 or 112.
Calls are free.

Police

City of London Police
Tel 101 (non-emergencies).
w cityoflondon.
police.uk

Metropolitan Police
Tel 0300 123 1212.
w met.police.uk

West End Central Police Station
27 Savile Row W1.
Map 12 F2.
Tel 020 7437 1212.

Lost Property

Transport for London Lost Property Office
200 Baker St NW1.
Map 3 C5.
Tel 0343 222 1234.
Open 9am–5pm daily.
w tfl.gov.uk

Health Services

Medical Express (Private)
117A Harley St, W1.
Tel 0800 9800 700.
w medicalexpress
clinic.com

NHS
w nhs.uk
To locate a hospital, look under "Find and choose services".

NHS 111

Tel 111
(24-hr health information and nurse-led advice).

University College Hospital
Accident and Emergency,
235 Euston Rd NW1.
Map 5 A4.
Tel 0845 155 5000.

Dentists

24-Hour Emergency Dental Clinic
8F Gilbert Place WC1.
Map 13 B1.
Tel 020 3199 0178.
w 24hour-london-
emergencydentist.co.uk

Late-Opening Pharmacies

Bliss Chemist
5–6 Marble Arch W1.
Map 11 C2.
Tel 020 7723 6116. Open 9am–midnight daily.

Boots the Chemist
302 Regent St W1.
Map 13 A3.
Tel 020 7637 9418.
Open 7:45am–8pm
Mon–Fri, 9am–7pm Sat,
noon–6pm Sun.
w boots.com

Superdrug
508–520 Oxford St W1.
Map 11 C2. Tel 020 7629 1649. Open 7am–11pm
Mon–Fri, 8am–10pm Sat,
12:30–6:30pm Sun.
w superdrug.com

Banking and Local Currency

Visitors to London will find that there are plenty of national and foreign banks lining the city's high streets, and they usually offer the best rates of exchange. Privately owned bureaux de change have variable exchange rates and commissions – some charge more for changing smaller amounts of money – but they do stay open long after the banks have closed.

A typical high street bank ATM, familiarly known as a cashpoint or "hole-in-the-wall"

Banks and Bureaux de Change

Banking hours vary. The minimum opening hours for all banks are 9:30am–3:30pm Mon–Fri, but many branches now stay open till 5 or 5:30pm, especially in central London; some also open on Saturdays from about 10am to 4pm. All banks are closed on Sundays and public holidays (see p63). The commission charged on currency exchange will vary from bank to bank.

When banks are closed, there are plenty of other facilities for changing cash across the city. You will find bureaux de change at airports, main rail stations, in large stores, and at many other locations. **Chequepoint**, **Thomas Cook** and **Travelex** are some of the larger companies. The central London (Piccadilly) branch of **Money Corporation** is open 24 hours daily.

Credit Cards and Travel Money

Major credit cards such as Visa and MasterCard, and debit cards such as Delta, Maestro and Cirrus, are widely accepted all over London. Fewer businesses accept American Express cards.

British credit and debit cards operate on a chip-and-PIN security system; you must enter your PIN into a card reader to validate the purchase. If you have a North American or other card that does not use chip-and-PIN technology, your card will have to be swiped and you'll need to sign a slip.

Contactless technology is fast being adopted across the capital, notably in its public transport system, enabling small payments (no more than £30) to be made quickly using a contactless-enabled card or mobile device.

Another useful way to carry money is with a prepaid money card. Like a debit card, you can use it in shops and restaurants, and withdraw money from cash machines. It is easy to top up the cards online or with an app. Money cards can be obtained at the post office or ordered online; one example is the Travelex MasterCard Cash Passport.

ATMs

There are ATM cash machines (also known as cashpoints), from which you can obtain cash with any of the major credit or debit cards, at all bank branches, many post offices and many other locations, such as stations. The cards accepted by each ATM are indicated on the machine, which usually gives instructions in several languages. Avoid using the

---

DIRECTORY

Bureaux de Change

All have branches across London.

Chequepoint
Tel 1 800 528 4800.
w americanexpress.com

Money Corporation
18 Piccadilly, W1.
Map 13 A3.
Tel 08456 210 210.
Open 24-hrs daily.
w moneycorp.com

Thomas Cook
Tel 0845 246 4353.
w thomascook.com/money

Travelex
Tel 0845 872 7627.
w travelex.co.uk

Lost Credit Cards

American Express
Tel 01273 696 933.

MasterCard
Tel 0800 964 767.

Visa
Tel 0800 891 725.

Main High Street Banks

The businesses whose logos are shown below are some of the UK's major high-street banks, with branches all over London. Many have currency-exchange facilities, but proof of identity may be required.

National Westminster logo

Santander logo

Barclays Bank logo

HSBC logo

independent ATMs found in some small shops, as they often carry expensive extra charges. Avoid using ATMs in dark streets at night, and don't use an ATM if any part of it looks damaged or as if it has been tampered with, especially the card slot. Be aware of anyone standing close to you when using an ATM, and shield the keypad with your hand as you enter your PIN.

Currency

Britain's currency is the pound sterling (£), which is divided into 100 pence (p). Since there are no exchange controls in Britain, there is no limit to how much cash you may import or export. Some large stores in London accept payments in US dollars and Euros, but often at a poor exchange rate.

English banknotes of all denominations feature the Queen's head on one side

Banknotes

English notes used in the UK are £5, £10, £20 and £50. Scotland has its own notes which, despite being legal tender throughout the UK, are often accepted with reluctance.

£50 note

£20 note

£10 note

£5 note

Coins

Coins in circulation are £2, £1, 50p, 20p, 10p, 5p, 2p and 1p (they are shown here slightly smaller than actual size). They all have the Queen's head on the other side.

2 pounds (£2)

1 pound (£1)

50 pence (50p)

20 pence (20p)

10 pence (10p)

5 pence (5p)

2 pence (2p)

1 penny (1p)

Communication and Media

London is a hub of news organizations, book and magazine publishers, and television networks (though these last are steadily moving to other parts of the country). Visitors benefit from an efficient and inexpensive telecommunications system. Though public telephones can still be found around the city – including the famous, now largely defunct, red telephone box – the mobile phone is king and there is a plethora of mobile networks and phone shops to meet demand. Visitors can stay connected via the free Wi-Fi readily available all over the capital.

International and Local Telephone Calls

All London landline telephone numbers have 11 digits and begin with the code 020. Phone numbers in central London continue with 7 and in outer London with 8, although some business numbers continue with 3. If you are calling from another London landline, you do not need to dial the 020, but only the remaining eight digits. Every other part of Britain has its own area code, beginning with 01 or 02.

Whenever possible, avoid making calls from hotels – above all, long-distance – as most add hefty surcharges, and some even charge for freephone lines. There are several special-rate numbers within the UK. Phone numbers beginning 03 are low-cost numbers used mostly by public bodies, such as the police. All 0800 or 0808 numbers are free to call from UK landlines (but not from mobile phones). 0844, 0845, 0870 and 0871 numbers are reduced-rate lines that are used by many companies and organizations for information services. Numbers beginning 09 are premium-rate and so particularly expensive.

To call Britain from abroad, dial 00 44, but then omit the initial zero from the UK area code. So to call the London number 020 7123 4567 from abroad, you would dial 00 44 20 7123 4567. To call abroad from London, dial 00 and then the usual country code (for example, Australia: 61, USA and Canada: 1).

British Telecom logo

Mobile Phones

All UK mobile phone numbers begin with 07. Calling a mobile from a landline is considerably more expensive than calling another landline.

There is a very high level of mobile ownership in London and signal coverage is good all over the city. UK mobiles use the European-standard 900 and 1900 MHz frequencies, so mobiles from other European countries work so long as they have their roaming facility enabled. North American and Asian cell phones will not operate unless they have a tri- or quad-band facility (which is increasingly standard on current phones). New laws mean that data roaming charges throughout Europe have been drastically reduced, and will be abolished by June 2017, so it is now cheaper than ever for Europeans to use their own phones while in London.

If you are visiting from outside the EU and anticipate using the phone a great deal, it may well be more economical to buy a cheap "pay-as-you-go" British mobile (a basic phone can cost as little as £10) from one of the main local providers such as **O2**, **EE** or **Vodafone**, all of which have shops all over the city.

Public Telephones

Though few and far between, BT public phoneboxes can still be found on the city's streets and in every railway station.

Some are the old-style red ones, others are much more modern in appearance; whichever type, they generally have the same technology inside. You can pay with coins, or by credit or debit card.

The minimum call cost is 60p for the first 30 minutes to a UK landline; and 10p for each 10 minutes after that. For a short call, use 10p or 20p pieces, as payphones only return unused coins. For credit-card calls, the minimum charge can be anything from £1.20 to £6.50.

Old BT phonebox   Modern BT phonebox

Useful Dialling Codes

- The area code for London is 020.
- Phone numbers in central London start with 7 or 3, and in outer areas with 8. The 020 prefix must be used if dialling from outside these two areas.
- British Telecom directory enquiries is 118 500.
- If you have any problems contacting a number, call the operator on 100.
- To make an international call, dial 00 followed by the country code (USA and Canada: 1; Australia: 61; New Zealand: 64), the area code and the number. (To the UK from abroad, the country code is 44.) The international operator number is 155 (freephone).
- In an emergency, dial 999 or 112. All emergency calls are free.

Internet and Email

Internet access is very easy to find in London. Public libraries, tourist information centres and some other public buildings have free terminals. Most hotels and a growing number of B&Bs and hostels offer Wi-Fi access. Charges are increasingly rare. There are also many free Wi-Fi hotspots across London, in arts centres, cafés, restaurants and pubs, so using your personal devices is easy. The Cloud is a free Wi-Fi service provider used in many of these destinations. The service only requires you to log in for access and does not have a data allowance (fair usage policy applies). Leading internet providers in London also provide reliable hotspots.

Postal Services

Standard post in the UK is handled by the **Royal Mail**. There are main post offices providing all postal services in every London district, as well as many smaller sub-post offices attached to newsagents and other small shops – these can handle all normal mail. Main post offices are usually open from 9am to 5:30pm Monday to Friday, and to 12:30pm on Saturday. Post offices also exchange money and handle international money transfers.

Post within the UK can be sent by first- or second-class mail. First-class costs a little more and is quicker. Stamps can be bought from post offices or any shop with a "Stamps sold here" sign. Newsagents usually sell them, but may only have UK first- and second-class stamps, so for international mail you may need to find a post office. Hotels nearly always sell stamps, and larger ones may have mail boxes. Public post boxes come in different shapes and sizes – some are sunk into

Old-style pillar box

Newsagent stocking a range of international newspapers

walls – but are always red, and can be found throughout the city. There are several collections a day (Mon–Sat); collection times are indicated on the box.

International letters and cards sent from London take about three days to reach European destinations, and four to six days to North America, Japan or Australasia. A competitively priced Airsure service is available for express deliveries (2–4 days worldwide), as well as a much slower but cheaper surface mail option.

Newspapers and Magazines

London's main local paper is the *Evening Standard*, distributed free in the centre of town from noon on weekdays. *Time Out London* magazine, published each Tuesday, is London's most comprehensive listings guide.

A range of international newspapers and magazines, including *USA Today*, *International Herald Tribune* and major European papers, is on sale at many newsstands and newsagents around central London. For more specialist foreign press, one of the best places to go is Old Compton Street in Soho.

TV and Radio

The UK's analogue signal has been turned off; all radio and TV is digital. The publicly owned BBC operates several television stations, including BBC One,

BBC Two and BBC News. Other free-to-air channels are the independent ITV, Channel 4 and Five. Extra channels available include BBC4 (arts-oriented) and various movie, shopping and music channels. In addition, many hotels also have satellite systems. If you want to be able to view a wide range of US and other international channels (such as ESPN), ask whether a hotel has Sky Plus or an enhanced Freeview package.

The BBC also has a large number of radio stations, of which Radios 1 (97–99 FM) and 2 (88–91 FM) focus on pop music of different kinds, Radio 3 (90.2 FM) on classical and jazz, Radio 4 (92–96 FM) on speech and drama, and Radio 5 (909/693 AM) on news and sport. BBC London (94.9 FM) is good for keeping up with local issues and interests.

GETTING TO LONDON

London is one of Europe's central hubs for international air and rail travel. By air, travellers face a bewildering choice of carriers from Europe, North America, Australasia, the Far East and every other part of the globe. Stiff competition on some routes, especially from major European countries and North America, means that low-fare deals can often be found, so it's always worth shopping around. Since 1994, the Channel Tunnel has provided an efficient high-speed train link –

Eurostar – between France, Belgium and the UK, as well as a fast, weatherproof Channel crossing for drivers. Eurostar trains depart from St Pancras International Station. Many European cruises sail from or finish at ports not far from London, such as Southampton, Dover or Tilbury, and there are efficient passenger and car ferry services from Europe, using large ferries and faster jetfoils and catamarans, across the North Sea and the English Channel.

Station concourse at St Pancras International

Arriving by Rail

Eurostar runs frequent daily trains to London from Paris, Brussels and Lille, where the Paris and Brussels lines meet. Nonstop trains from Paris (Gare du Nord) take 2 hours 25 minutes; from Brussels, 2 hours. Some trains also stop at Calais before entering the Channel Tunnel on the French side, and at Ashford and Ebbsfleet on the English. If you travel by train from any other part of Europe and want to connect with Eurostar, it's best to do so at Lille, as you change trains in the same station – quicker and far easier than doing so in Paris. Check-in on Eurostar is only 30 minutes before departure, so it's generally far quicker than flying.

Eurostar trains arrive in London at St Pancras International, on the northern edge of central London, next to King's Cross Underground station. The station is on six Underground lines, so is well connected with every part of the city. Eurostar fares vary a good deal according to flexibility

and the time of day you travel (early morning trains are often the cheapest), so check current rates on the website when booking. Information and bookings for connecting trains from other parts of Europe can be found on the Voyages–sncf website.

London has eight mainline rail stations at which trains from different parts of Britain terminate: Paddington serves the West Country, Wales and the South Midlands; Liverpool Street serves East Anglia and Essex; King's Cross, St Pancras and Euston cover northern Britain; and Charing Cross, Victoria and Waterloo cover southern England, and also the main Channel ferry ports.

The current UK railway system is complicated and can be confusing. Lines are run by several different companies, but they are coordinated by **National Rail**, which operates a joint information service. Fare structures are especially complex: tickets can be very

expensive or surprisingly cheap, depending on when you book and when you want to travel. Going to a station the same day you want to travel and buying a ticket over the counter is always the most expensive way to travel. Whenever possible, book trains in advance and check alternative fares, bearing in mind that the best fares may only be available online. The National Rail website has a useful cheapest fare finder feature, which then links you to the relevant company site to make the booking. Also helpful is **Trainline**, an independent booking agency which often has discounted tickets. Tickets booked online can be collected at the station and a handy app stores journeys and booking references. Fares on suburban rail services around London are less complex, so there is no need to book ahead. Rail lines within London accept payment by Oyster card *(see p374)* and contactless credit/debit cards.

An information point at a London railway station

Cross-Channel ferry heading to Calais

Arriving by Coach

International and national coach services from every part of Europe and the UK arrive in London at Victoria Coach Station on Buckingham Palace Road, about five minutes' walk from Victoria rail and Underground stations, and with several local bus stops outside. If you're planning to travel to any UK destinations outside of the London area, it's slower but nearly always cheaper to do it by coach than by train, with fares as low as £1 on some London–Oxford services (although train companies may lower fares on the same routes).

National Express operates the most extensive UK coach network, with around 1,000 destinations covered, and is also associated with Eurolines international coach services. **Megabus** has especially low fares to many UK destinations, and also discount train offers. **Green Line** runs buses between London and the surrounding counties, and has a service to Luton Airport *(see p373)*.

Arriving by Sea and Tunnel

The **Eurotunnel** shuttle – the other train service using the Channel Tunnel – is a drive-on, drive-off service for cars between Calais and Folkestone, where the Tunnel connects with the M20 motorway to London. There are usually four shuttles per hour, with a journey time of about 35 minutes.

If you prefer to brave the elements, there are still plenty of ferry services between southeast England and Continental ports. Harwich in Essex has ferries from Hook of Holland in the Netherlands with **Stena Line**. Dover is the busiest port, with frequent services from France: from Dunkerque and Boulogne with **DFDS Seaways** and from Calais with **P&O Ferries** and DFDS. Newhaven–Dieppe ferries are also operated by DFDS.

There are also several routes across other parts of the Channel, which take longer, but may leave you better located for the west of England: to Portsmouth from Caen, Cherbourg, Le Havre and St Malo with **Brittany Ferries**, or from Le Havre with DFDS; to Poole from Cherbourg with Brittany Ferries; or to Poole or Weymouth from St Malo and the Channel Islands with **Condor Ferries**.

Crossing times to Dover are around 1 hour 15 minutes; in other parts of the Channel, it takes more like 5-6 hours, although in summer, fast jetfoils and catamarans cut this to 2–3 hours.

There are also ferry services from Spain: from Santander to Plymouth or Portsmouth with Brittany Ferries; and from Bilbao to Portsmouth with P&O. Crossings take around 24 hours, on comfortable mini cruise ships.

Driving time from Dover or the Channel Tunnel to central London is usually around 2 hours; from Portsmouth, 2–2½ hours. If you bring a car to London, always try to arrange a place to stay with free parking, otherwise this can become extremely expensive.

DIRECTORY

Rail Services

Eurostar
London St Pancras International.
Tel 0344 8224 777.
w eurostar.com

National Rail
Tel 0845 748 4950.
w nationalrail.co.uk

Rail Europe
Tel 1 800 622 8600 (USA),
0844 848 5848 (UK).
w uk.voyages-sncf.com

Trainline
Tel 0871 244 1545.
w thetrainline.com

Coach Services

Green Line
Tel 0844 801 7261.
w greenline.co.uk

Megabus
Tel 0900 160 0900.
w megabus.com/uk

National Express
Tel 08717 818 181.
w nationalexpress.com

Channel Tunnel and Ferries

Brittany Ferries
Tel 0871 244 0744.
w brittany-ferries.com

Condor Ferries
Tel 01202 207 216.
w condorferries.co.uk

DFDS Seaways
w dfdsseaways.co.uk

Eurotunnel
Tel 08443 353 535.
w eurotunnel.com

P&O Ferries
Tel 0871 664 2121.
w poferries.com

Stena Line
Tel 0844 770 7070.
w stenaline.co.uk

Arriving by Air

London's two main airports, Heathrow and Gatwick, are augmented by smaller facilities at Luton, Stansted and London City (see pp372–3). Check which airport you will land at, and plan your journey from there. All the airports have train or coach links; Heathrow is also connected to central London by Underground. Because the airports are so far apart from each other, travelling between them is best avoided.

Access to the Underground from a terminal at Heathrow

British Airways passenger jet at Heathrow airport

Airlines and Fares

Heathrow and Gatwick have long-haul connections with every part of the world, on scores of airlines. The main US airlines offering scheduled flights to London include **Delta**, **United**, **American Airlines** and **US Airways**, while from Canada, there are frequent services with **Air Canada**. **British Airways** and **Virgin Atlantic** also fly from many North American cities. The flight time from New York is about 7½ hours; from Los Angeles, about 10 hours.

The choice of carriers from Australasia and Asia is enormous too: **Qantas**, **Air New Zealand** and British Airways may be the obvious first choices, but operators such as **Singapore Airlines** and **Emirates** offer alternatives.

All the main European scheduled airlines, such as British Airways, Air France, **Iberia** and **Lufthansa**, offer frequent connections, mostly to Heathrow or Gatwick, but they now carry less traffic than the low-cost airlines. **Ryanair** has budget flights from across Europe, Ireland and the UK, mostly into Stansted, while **easyJet** runs almost as extensive a European and British network from Stansted, Luton and Gatwick.

Very few airlines now offer reduced prices for children. Low-cost flights can normally be booked only through each airline's own website. Note that low-cost airlines regularly add extra charges on top of the fare – such as one for checking in luggage. Ryanair, for example, charges £15 if you cannot download and print your own boarding card, and need one to be issued by ground staff at the airport.

Security

Security is tighter than ever at London airports. Allow at least 2 hours to check in and get through security before your departing flight, especially – because of its size – at Heathrow. Allow the same time to catch low-cost flights if you are checking in a bag, since in the interests of keeping costs down, there are not many check-in staff, so lines move slowly.

Heathrow (LHR)

Heathrow in west London is one of the world's busiest airports. It has five terminals, so it's important to know which one your flight will arrive at or depart from. Terminals 1, 2 and 3, the oldest, share an Underground station and Heathrow Central rail station; Terminal 4 has its own Underground station; Terminal 5, which opened in 2008, has Underground and rail stations. A free shuttle bus runs between the Terminals. Most British Airways flights use Terminal 5; most other long-haul airlines use Terminals 3 or 4. There are shops and other facilities in every terminal.

There are several ways into London from Heathrow. The fastest rail service is the **Heathrow Express**, with trains every 15 minutes from around 5am to 11:30pm daily to Paddington station on the west side of central London. Journey time is about 15 minutes to Terminals 2 and 3 (from which you can take the free transfer service to Terminal 4) and a further 6 minutes to Terminal 5. Fares are quite high, at around £25 single, £39 return (slightly less if you buy online). **Heathrow Connect** trains run on the same lines but

Heathrow Terminal 5, used exclusively by British Airways

with several stops, and take 25–30 minutes to reach Paddington. Fares are around £9.50 single.

The Underground offers a much cheaper way of getting into London, but is also much slower. Trains run frequently, calling at all Heathrow terminals from around 5am to midnight Monday to Saturday; 5:50am–11:30pm Sunday. Unlike the Heathrow Express, the Tube runs right into the city centre; allow about 45 minutes to get to Leicester Square. As on all London public transport, it's cheaper with an Oyster card *(see p374)*; the adult fare from Heathrow into the city centre is £5.50.

National Express and other companies run a number of bus routes from Heathrow to Oxford, central London London, London airports and other destinations. The main bus station is at Terminals 1, 2 and 3, but buses

also stop at 4 and 5. A taxi to central London costs about £50. Driving time is between 30 minutes and 1 hour. It's worth noting that local minicab companies offer much cheaper rates *(see p381)*.

London City Airport, within sight of the city's Docklands area

London City Airport (LCY)

London City Airport is the closest airport to central London, located in the Docklands business area just east of London's financial district (the City). Unlike some other airports, it was created primarily for business travellers, so flights are quite expensive. It offers flights to a number of

European destinations, and a luxury service to New York.

London City has its own station on the Docklands Light Railway (DLR), which connects with the Underground network at Tower Hill and Bank. Buses also operate to and from the airport. A taxi to the City costs about £28 and takes 30 minutes; to the West End £40, taking around 45 minutes.

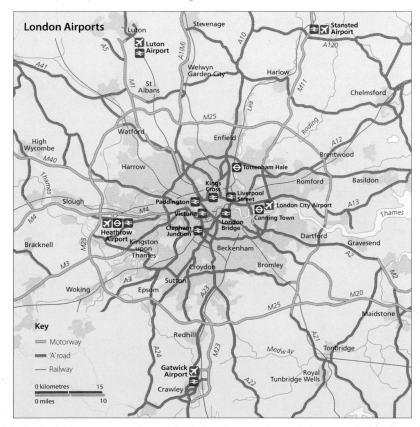

London Airports

Luton
Luton Airport
Stevenage
Stansted Airport
A10
A120
A5
A1(M)
A41
Welwyn Garden City
Harlow
M11
Chelmsford
St Albans
M1
Lea
Roding
A12
M25
High Wycombe
Watford
Enfield
Brentwood
M40
Thames
Harrow
A41
Tottenham Hale
Romford
Basildon
Slough
Kings Cross
Liverpool Street
Paddington
London City Airport
A13
Thames
Victoria
Canning Town
M4
M4
Heathrow Airport
London Bridge
Clapham Junction
Bracknell
M25
Kingston upon Thames
Beckenham
Dartford
Gravesend
A2
M3
Croydon
Bromley
M2
Woking
A3
Sutton
Epsom
A23
M20
Maidstone
M25

Key
━━ Motorway
━━ 'A' road
─── Railway

0 kilometres 15
0 miles 10

Redhill
A24
M23
Medway
A21
Tonbridge
Gatwick Airport
A22
Royal Tunbridge Wells
Crawley

Gatwick (LGW)

Gatwick airport lies due south of central London, and handles long-haul, European and low-cost flights. There are two terminals – North and South – so as at Heathrow, you need to be clear on which you need. The train station and main bus stops are at the South Terminal, from where there is a free shuttle train to the North. Allow around 20 minutes to transfer between terminals. There are banks, shops, cafés and other facilities at both.

There is a choice of three rail services from Gatwick into London, all from the same station. The **Gatwick Express** is the fastest, with trains every 15 minutes to Victoria Station. It runs from 4:35am to midnight daily and takes about 30 minutes (a little longer on Sundays), but it isn't cheap; the fare is just under £20 single, £35 return. Cheaper tickets can be bought online. **First Capital Connect** runs around four trains per hour over the same period to St Pancras International via several stops including East Croydon and London Bridge. Journey time is about an hour, and a single fare around £10. **Southern Railway** has several trains each hour to London Victoria, with a journey time of 30–50 minutes and a single fare of around £11.

Entrance to Stansted's spacious modern passenger terminal

National Express and other companies run buses from the South Terminal to Heathrow and central London (and many towns in southern England), and **easyBus** runs frequently from the North and South terminals to Earl's Court/West Brompton in London. Buses are not limited to easyJet passengers, and fares begin at £2. A taxi into central London will set you back around £90, and can take 1–2 hours. As at Heathrow, minicab companies at Gatwick offer better rates.

Stansted (STN)

Around 40 miles northeast of London, Stansted is the airport in southeast England most popular with low-cost airlines, and so has a huge number of flights from destinations all over Europe.

The rail link into London is the **Stansted Express** train, which runs every 15 minutes from around 6am to 12:30am. Trains run to Liverpool Street, on the east side of central London, with a stop at Tottenham Hale (where you can transfer to the Victoria Underground line). Trains from Liverpool Street to Stansted run from approximately 4:40am to 11:30pm daily. The full journey takes 45 minutes. Adult fares to Liverpool Street are £23.40 single, £33.20 return (cheaper online). **Abellio Greater Anglia** trains also run roughly once an hour to London Stratford station near to East London's Olympic Park, with several stops, taking one hour for a fare of £23.50.

Several bus services run from Stansted to London. National Express runs to Victoria Coach Station (prices start at £5, book ahead) and many other destinations around the region, but easyBus is again the cheapest, with tickets to Baker Street Underground station

Gatwick's free monorail service linking the two terminals

Airport	To city centre	Average journey time	Average taxi fare
London City	10 km (6 miles)	Tube and DLR: 40 minutes	£28
Heathrow	23 km (14 miles)	Rail: 15 minutes Tube: 45 minutes	£50
Gatwick	45 km (28 miles)	Rail: 30 minutes Bus: 70 minutes	£90
Luton	51 km (32 miles)	Rail: 35 minutes Bus: 70 minutes	£60
Stansted	55 km (34 miles)	Rail: 45 minutes Bus: 75 minutes	£90

from £2. A taxi to central London can take 1 hour 30 minutes and cost £90 to £100.

Luton (LTN)

Luton airport lies northwest of London near the M1 motorway, and is used almost exclusively by charter flights and low-cost airlines, especially easyJet. A shuttle bus connects the terminal with Luton Airport Parkway train station (about a 5-minute drive), from around 5am to midnight daily. First Capital Connect has about four trains each hour to London St Pancras – a journey of around 25–40 minutes for an adult single fare of £14. **East Midlands Trains** operate on the same route, and are a little cheaper, at £12. Green Line buses (route 757) run every 15 minutes almost 24 hours

daily between the airport and London Victoria Coach station, with adult fares around £10 (see p369); easyBus has frequent services to Victoria via Baker Street, with tickets from £2. National Express runs from Luton to Heathrow, Gatwick, Stansted and other destinations. A taxi into London will cost around £60, and take about 45 minutes.

Airport Hotels

Given the long check-in times at the main airports, it can be a good idea – even necessary – to stay nearby the night before departure, especially if you have an early-morning flight. There is a large number of hotels in the vicinity of Heathrow and Gatwick; many of these frequently have discount offers. All of them provide shuttle

Relaxing bar of the popular Sheraton Skyline hotel

buses to the airport terminals – in budget hotels this may be charged extra. The **Premier Inn**, **Travelodge**, **Sofitel** and **Holiday Inn** chains have cheap, functional rooms close to the airports. A selection of airport hotels is listed below, but there are many more to choose from.

DIRECTORY

Major Airlines

Air Canada
W aircanada.com

Air New Zealand
W airnewzealand.com

American Airlines
W aa.com

British Airways
W britishairways.com

Delta Airlines
W delta.com

easyJet
W easyjet.com

Emirates
W emirates.com

Iberia
W iberia.com

Lufthansa
W lufthansa.com

Qantas
W qantas.com.au

Ryanair
W ryanair.com

Singapore Airlines
W singaporeair.com

United Airlines
W united.com

US Airways
W usairways.com

Virgin Atlantic
W virgin-atlantic.com

Travel Websites

W bestfares.com
W cheapflights.com
W ebookers.com
W expedia.com
W flights.com
W orbitz.com
W priceline.com
W travelnow.com
W travelocity.com

Airport Information

Gatwick
Tel 0844 892 0322.
W gatwickairport.com

Heathrow
Tel 0844 335 1801.
W heathrowairport.com

London City Airport
Tel 020 7646 0088.
W londoncityairport.com

Luton
Tel 01582 405 100, 0906 211 500 00 (flight information).
W london-luton.co.uk

Stansted
Tel 0844 335 1803.
W stanstedairport.com

Airport Transport

Abellio Greater Anglia
Tel 0345 600 7245.
W abelliogreateranglia.co.uk

easyBus
W easybus.co.uk

East Midlands Trains
Tel 08457 125 678.
W eastmidlandstrains.co.uk

First Capital Connect
Tel 0845 026 4700.
W firstcapitalconnect.co.uk

Gatwick Express
Tel 0845 850 1530.
W gatwickexpress.com

Heathrow Connect
Tel 0845 678 6975.
W heathrowconnect.com

Heathrow Express
Tel 0845 600 1515.
W heathrowexpress.com

Southern Railway
Tel 0845 127 2920.
W southernrailway.com

Stansted Express
Tel 0845 600 7245.
W stanstedexpress.com

Hotels

Holiday Inn London Heathrow Ariel
Tel 0871 423 4901.
W ihg.com

Premier Inn Heathrow (Bath Road)
Tel 0871 527 8508.
W premierinn.com

Sofitel London Gatwick
Tel 01293 567 070.
W sofitel.com

Travelodge Gatwick Airport
Tel 0871 984 6031.
W travelodge.co.uk

GETTING AROUND LONDON

London has one of the busiest, most extensive public transport systems in Europe; it also has all the problems of overcrowding to match. Initiatives are underway to make walking and cycling around the city safer and more appealing. Within central and outer London, most of the public transport systems – city and river buses, the Underground, overground rail lines – are coordinated by Transport for London (TfL), which operates a common ticketing system centred on the pay-as-you-go Oyster card, which passengers use to "touch in" each time they use public transport.

The Transport System

The Underground railway – or "Tube", is generally the fastest, most convenient way to get around the city. The Docklands area, some other parts of east London and Greenwich are served by the Docklands Light Railway (DLR), which connects with the Tube network principally at Bank, Tower Hill, Canary Wharf and Stratford. Tube and DLR lines do not run to every part of the city, however; in particular, large parts of south London are reliant on overground rail connections. Bus routes cover every part of London. There are also riverbus boat services (see pp64–5).

Avoid travelling on public transport during morning and evening "rush hour" – 8–10am and 5–7pm Monday to Friday – if at all possible. For detailed information on every aspect of transport in London, check the TfL website. The site has an invaluable "Journey Planner" feature, to help you get around. TfL also has several Travel Information Centres. Those at Heathrow and Piccadilly Circus Underground stations and Euston, King's Cross, Liverpool Street and Victoria mainline stations are especially helpful, and provide free maps and other information. Mobile apps such as Citymapper are also very useful for those navigating the city.

Oyster Cards and Travelcards

London's public transport is relatively expensive compared to that of many European cities,

Heritage bus

but if you use one of the multi-journey cards available to visitors you will cut costs considerably. For Tube, DLR and local train fares, London is divided into six main fare zones radiating out from Zone 1 in the centre (on buses, there is a flat fare for each trip, no matter how far you travel). If you aim to pack all your sightseeing into one or two days and expect to take multiple trips around the city, the best ticket to get will be a one-day off-peak Travelcard, which gives unlimited travel on all systems after 9:30am on weekdays (or any time on Saturday and Sunday) within zones 1–4 or 1–6 for a flat fee. If you expect to travel more freely, it is better to get a pay-as-you-go Oyster card, which you can preload and top up with as much credit as you wish (note that a £5 deposit is required when purchasing an Oyster card and you will need one card per person). It is also possible to use a contactless credit/debit card to pay for journeys in much the same way as the Oyster card. Whenever you use public transport, you "touch in" with your card on a yellow Oyster Card reader, and the corresponding amount is deducted. On Underground, DLR and overground trains, you must also remember to "touch out" where you finish your journey, or you will be charged a maximum fare. Buses do not accept cash so a ticket, Oyster card or contactless payment is required.

Travelcards and Oyster cards can be bought at Tube and local rail stations, Travel Information Centres and hundreds of small shops that have the TfL Ticket Stop" sticker in the window. You can also obtain them before arriving in London, on Eurostar, Gatwick Express or Stansted Express trains, or online, with advance delivery to 63 countries, through the Visit London and TfL websites.

Travel is free on all buses for under-16s; the Underground and DLR are free for under-11s, and have reduced fares for 11–15-year-olds. A one-day Travelcard for 11–15s costs £6 for main fare zones 1–6.

BAKER STREET

A London Underground sign at a station

Walking

Once you get used to traffic driving on the left, London can be enjoyably explored on foot. There are two types of pedestrian crossing in London: striped "zebra" crossings, marked by beacons; and push-button crossings at traffic lights. Traffic should stop if you wait at a zebra crossing, but at push-button crossings, cars will not stop until they have a red light. Look out for instructions painted on the road, which tell you from which direction you can expect traffic to appear.

Pre-paid Oyster card being placed on a card reader

A pedestrian zebra crossing

Cycling

The TfL website's cycling page is invaluable for those cycling around the city, including useful information about the Cycle Superhighway – safe, designated cycle routes throughout London. Cycle routes are signposted around the city. **Santander Cycle Hire**, London's bike hire scheme, has 6,000 bikes available at docking terminals across the city. The **London Bicycle Tour Company** delivers and collects bikes to and from your location. With your rented bike, you should be given a helmet, lock and other accessories.

Green Travel

Travelling around by foot, Tube, bus, train or riverbus is more energy-efficient than driving or taking a taxi. London's Congestion Charge helps discourage driving in the city centre. The distance between some Tube stations can be covered on foot in less time than it takes to go underground. London continues to invest in improved conditions for cyclists, and this can be the fastest way to get around the city. Several "green" minicab companies, such as **Gogreencar** and **Climatecars**, use hybrid or alternative-fuel vehicles.

Driving in London

Driving is usually the worst way of getting around town. Traffic moves at an average of 11 mph (18 kmh) for much of the day, parking is scarce and expensive, and in central London, there is the added cost of the Congestion Charge – a £11.50-a-day fee paid in advance for private

vehicles entering the charging zone (roughly: the City, the West End, and Mayfair in the west; and south as far as Elephant & Castle) between 7am and 6pm Monday to Friday. If you are determined to drive, remember to drive on the left.

All the well-known car-rental firms, such as **Europcar**, **Auto Europe** and **Hertz**, operate in London. Renting in advance or as an add-on with your flight will get the best rates. To drive out of central London takes about an hour in any direction; if you want to tour the countryside, it can be easier to take a train to a city outside London and rent there.

Parking

Parking is prohibited at all times wherever the street is marked with red or double yellow lines by the kerb. If there is a single yellow line, parking is normally allowed from 6:30pm to 8am Monday to Saturday and all day Sunday, but exact hours vary, so always check the signs along each street. Where there is no line at all, parking is free at all times, but this is rare in central London. Rental car drivers are still liable for parking fines.

DIRECTORY

Transport for London
Tel 0343 222 1234 (info), 0845 900 1234 (Congestion Charge). Congestion Charge payable in advance online, by text message, by phone or by post. A Penalty Charge Notice (PCN) will be issued should you not pay in time.
w tfl.gov.uk

Cycling

London Bicycle Tour Company
Tel 020 7928 6838.
w londonbicycle.com

London Cycling Campaign
Tel 020 7234 9310.
w lcc.org.uk

Santander Cycle Hire
Tel 0343 222 6666.
w tfl.gov.uk

Green Travel

Climatecars
Tel 020 7350 5960.
w climatecars.com

Gogreencar
Tel 020 7502 3670.
w gogreencar.co.uk

Driving

Auto Europe
Tel 1 888 223 5555 (USA), 0800 358 1229 (UK).
w autoeurope.com

Europcar
Tel 0871 384 9900 (UK).
w europcar.com

Hertz Rent a Car
Tel 1 800 654 3001 (USA), 0870 841 5161 (UK).
w hertz.com

A cycle path in one of London's parks

Travelling by Underground

The underground railway system, known as the Tube, has some 270 stations, each identified by the Underground logo. Trains run every day except Christmas Day, from about 5:30am till midnight Monday to Thursday; 5:30am till 1am on Friday and Saturday; and 6:30am to 11:30pm on Sunday. A programme to run 24-hour services at weekends on some lines is under discussion; its progress can be checked on the Transport for London website: www.tfl.gov.uk. The Docklands Light Railway (DLR) in east and southeast London connects with the Tube and also runs to London City Airport. For schedules and information, call 0343 222 1234 or check the TfL website.

London Underground train

Planning Your Journey

There are 12 Tube lines, all named and colour-coded (red for Central, blue for Victoria, and so on), which intersect at various stations. Some lines, like the Jubilee, have a single branch; others, like the Northern, have more than one, so it's important to check the digital boards on the platform and the destination on the front of the train. The Circle Line is a continuous loop around central London with an extension to Hammersmith. Maps of the entire Tube system

(see inside back cover) are posted at each station. Note that the Tube map is topological, not geographical; it isn't to scale, nor can it be relied upon for directions. From it, you can work out where to change lines to travel to any station on the system. All eight of London's mainline rail stations *(see p368)* have associated Tube stations. Due to the ongoing Tube improvement programme, services are sometimes suspended, usually at weekends. When this happens, replacement buses are provided. Check for line closures before travelling.

Buying a Ticket

All Tube and DLR stations fall within one of six main fare zones *(see p374)*. The zones you travel through determine the cost of your journey. Unless you plan on making very few journeys by Tube, it will usually be best to travel with a multi-journey Travelcard or an Oyster card *(see p374)*. However, you can also buy single or return tickets from ticket offices and ticket machines, or pay using a contactless credit or debit card. All Underground and DLR stations have touch-screen machines giving step-by-step instructions in a variety of languages. They accept coins, notes and credit and debit cards; you can also use them to top up your credit on an Oyster card. To check current fares, select the ticket type you need, choose the station you wish to travel to, and the fare will be displayed on screen.

How to read the Journey Planner Maps
(see inside back cover)

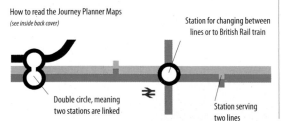

Double circle, meaning two stations are linked

Station for changing between lines or to British Rail train

Station serving two lines

Tube Architecture

The Underground's reputation for exciting architecture was established in the 1930s. In 1999, the Jubilee Line Extension opened to great acclaim, with six imposing and elegant stations designed by a group of top architects including Will Alsop (North Greenwich), Norman Foster (Canary Wharf) and Matthew Hopkins (Westminster). A similarly light, spacious style has been adopted in the impressive Tube, DLR, bus and mainline rail hub at Stratford, gateway to the Queen Elizabeth Olympic Park.

Inside Canary Wharf Underground station

Making a Journey by Underground

1 When you first enter the station, check which line, or lines, you need to take. The times of first and last trains are also posted at every station.

Feed your ticket into the slot at the front of the machine; retrieve it from the slot at the top.

2 Buy your ticket or Travelcard from a ticket office or ticket machine at the station. Keep your ticket; you will need it to exit at your destination. Pre-bought Oyster cards can be topped up at machines or online for later trips. You can also use contactless credit/debit cards to make a journey.

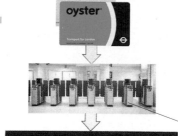

Touch an Oyster card or contactless credit/debit card on the yellow card reader.

3 The platforms are on the other side of the ticket barriers.

Central line →

The ticket office is near the ticket barriers in most stations.

4 Follow the directions to the line on which you need to travel. In some cases this can be a complicated route, but it will be well signposted.

5 You will eventually find yourself with a choice of platforms for the line you want. Look at the list of stations if you are not sure which direction to take.

6 All platforms have electronic indicators displaying the final destination of the next two or three trains and how long you will have to wait before they arrive. On lines with branches, they also indicate the route of each train.

7 Once you have begun your journey, you can check on your progress using the line chart displayed in every carriage. The name of the next station is announced before you arrive, and as you pull into each station, you will see its name posted along the walls.

On all DLR and some Tube trains, push a button to open the carriage doors.

8 After leaving the train, look for signs giving directions to exits or to platforms for any connecting lines.

Travelling by Bus and Boat

The red double-decker bus is one of London's most recognizable symbols, but the design of London buses has changed a great deal over the years. The old, classic open-backed Routemaster buses have been withdrawn (with the exception of two "heritage" routes), and in their place there are modern, square-sided double-deckers, single-deckers for less busy routes, and a modernized Routemaster bus with access at the back and front of the bus. Travelling by bus is an enjoyable, easy way to see London, especially in the middle of the day, and much cheaper than going by Tube or DLR if you have an Oyster card. On the minus side, bus journeys can be slow, especially during rush hour (8–10am and 5–7pm Monday to Friday).

Finding the Right Bus

Bus maps showing all the main routes are available free from Travel Information Centres, or can be downloaded from the Visit London and Transport for London websites. All London bus stops have bus route signs displaying the routes that run from that stop, with lists of their main destinations. On streets that are used by several bus routes – for example Oxford Street in the West End – routes are bunched together at different stops near each other, so make sure you find the right one. Stops also have local area maps showing which of the adjacent bus stops, identified by a letter, you need for buses to a particular area. If in doubt, ask the bus driver when boarding.

Using London Buses

Buses halt at stops marked with the London bus logo. Many have electronic display boards indicating when the next bus is due (this information can also be accessed via an app). Some stops are "request" stops, where drivers will not stop unless they are waved down by a passenger. If they do not stop despite being hailed, it means that the bus is full and no passenger has asked to get off. Destinations are displayed clearly on the front of the bus, and on many buses, the next upcoming stop is indicated on electronic information boards, or announced by an automatic voice system. However, if you are unsure which stop you need, ask the driver to alert you, and stay on the lower deck.

Board buses at the front, so that you can touch in your Oyster Card on the yellow Oyster reader by the driver's cab, or show your Travelcard. Fares are the same for each bus trip no matter how far you travel; the £1.50 is payable by ticket, Oyster or contactless card only. Inspectors – sometimes in plain clothes – often check whether passengers have valid tickets or passes.

Bus Stops

Buses halt at all major stops, such as train stations and popular shopping and visitor destinations, on their routes. At some stops, called request stops, the driver will not halt unless alerted. If you want to board, raise your arm as the bus approaches the stop; when you want to get off, ring the bell once before your stop.

Useful Bus Routes

Several of London's bus routes are particularly convenient for the capital's main sights and shops. If you arm yourself with an Oyster card or Travelcard and are in no particular hurry, sightseeing or shopping by bus can be great fun. The cost of a journey by public transport is far less than any of the charges levied by tour operators, although you won't have the commentary that tour companies give you as you pass sights (*see p358–9*). There are also some sights or areas in London that are either hard to get to by Underground, or can be reached much more directly by bus. Buses run regularly from the city centre to, for instance, the Royal Albert Hall (*see p209*) and Chelsea (*see pp196–201*).

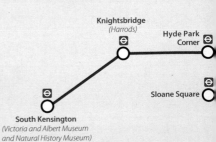

Marble Arch

Knightsbridge
(Harrods)

Hyde Park Corner

Sloane Square

South Kensington
(Victoria and Albert Museum and Natural History Museum)

Thames Clipper boat heading towards Waterloo Bridge

Night Buses

Some main bus routes run 24 hours daily. Night bus services (indicated by the letter "N" added before the route number) also run on many popular routes from 11pm until 6am, generally 3–4 times per hour up to 2–3am, but often only once an hour after that. Many night bus routes originate in or pass through Trafalgar Square, then run out into the suburbs. In the centre they are often very crowded, especially at weekends, but empty out quickly as they move further out. Plan your journey carefully; London is so big that even if you board a bus going in the right direction, you can still be a long walk from your accommodation. As always, be aware of personal security when travelling at night.

Riverboats

Some of London's most spectacular views can only be seen from the River Thames. River trips have also been integrated into London's transport system. **Thames Clippers** has a riverbus service with catamarans running every 20 minutes from 6am to 1am daily in both directions, on a route between Waterloo and Woolwich, via the London Eye, Tower Bridge, Greenwich and other stops at the various river piers. They also operate the **Tate Boat**, a direct boat between the Tate Britain and Tate Modern museums (every 40 minutes in each direction, 10am to 5pm), as well as special services for events at the O2 Arena. Oyster cards can be used on board, and Travelcard holders get discounted tickets. For more information, check with Thames Clippers or www.tfl.gov.uk.

DIRECTORY

Riverboat Services

Tate Boat
Tel 020 7887 8888.
w tate.org.uk/tatetotate

Thames Clippers
Tel 020 7001 2222.
w thamesclippers.com

For information on river cruises see "Cruise Highlights" on p65.

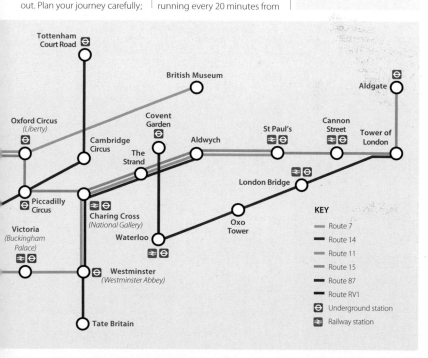

KEY

— Route 7
— Route 14
— Route 11
— Route 15
— Route 87
— Route RV1
⊖ Underground station
⇌ Railway station

SSSSSSS

Travelling by Rail

London's local and suburban train lines (also known as the "overground") are used by hundreds of thousands of commuters every day. For visitors, rail services are most useful for trips to the outskirts of London and areas of the city without nearby Underground connections (especially in south London). If you are planning to travel outside of the capital, always try to book rail tickets in advance, and check to see what alternative fares are available; for more on rail tickets *see p368.*

Useful Routes

Two of the most popular rail lines for visitors to London are those from Charing Cross (via London Bridge) and, on weekdays, Cannon Street to Greenwich *(see pp240–47)*; and from Waterloo to Hampton Court *(see pp260–63)*. A First Capital Connect line runs right through London, north to south, from Luton via St Pancras International to Gatwick. The North London line makes a loop around north London all the way from the East End to Kew *(see pp266–7)* and Richmond.

Using Trains

London has eight main railway termini serving different parts of Britain. Each terminus is also the starting-point for local and suburban lines that cover the whole of southeast England. There are over one hundred smaller London stations. Rail services travel overground and vary between trains that stop at every station, faster suburban trains, and express trains that run nonstop to major destinations. Some train doors will open automatically, others at the touch of a button.

Rail Tickets

Travelcards and Oyster cards are valid on nearly all overground rail services that fall entirely within the London area (defined as Transport for London fare zones 1–6, plus three more suburban zones), so using one or the other will generally be much more economical, and a lot quicker, than buying individual tickets. Be aware, though, that on most overground trains, peak travel times include the evening rush hour (4–7pm Monday–Friday) as well as the morning one (before 9:30am), so with an Oyster you will be charged more during these times. Many small stations do not have staffed ticket counters, just machines.

Return tickets for rail travel

Day Trips

Southern England has a lot to offer visitors besides London. By rail or by bus *(see p369)*, getting out of the city is fast and easy. For details of sights, contact Visit Britain (www.visitbritain.com; 020 7578 1000). National Rail (0845 748 4950) has details of all rail services.

Boating on the River Thames at Windsor Castle

Audley End
Village with a stunning Jacobean mansion nearby.
🚆 from Liverpool Street.
64 km (40 miles); 1 hr.

Bath
Beautiful Georgian city, with Roman baths.
🚆 from Paddington.
172 km (107 miles); 1 hr 25 mins.

Brighton
Lively and attractive seaside resort home to the Royal Pavilion.
🚆 from Victoria or London Bridge.
85 km (53 miles); 1 hr.

Cambridge
University city with fine art gallery and ancient colleges.
🚆 from Liverpool Street or King's Cross.
86 km (54 miles); 1 hr.

Canterbury
Its cathedral is one of England's oldest and greatest sights.
🚆 from Victoria.
100 km (62 miles); 1 hr 25 mins.

Hatfield House
Elizabethan palace with remarkable contents.
🚆 from King's Cross or Moorgate to Hatfield station.
33 km (21 miles); 20 mins.

Oxford
Like Cambridge, famous for its ancient university.
🚆 from Paddington.
90 km (56 miles); 1 hr.

St Albans
Cathedral and Roman theatre.
🚆 from King's Cross or Moorgate.
40 km (25 miles); 30 mins.

Salisbury
Famous for its cathedral, and close to Stonehenge.
🚆 from Waterloo.
135 km (84 miles); 1 hr 40 mins.

Windsor
Riverside town with Britain's grandest royal castle.
🚆 from Paddington, change Slough.
32 km (20 miles); 30 mins.

Travelling by Taxi

London's black cabs are as much of an institution as its red buses. Black cabs (some of which, it should be pointed out, are not actually black – you will often see blue, green, red or even white cabs) are the only cabs licensed to pick up passengers who hail a cab on the street, and their drivers have to take a stringent test on their knowledge of London and its traffic routes before they are awarded a licence. Minicabs, which by law must be booked in advance, not hailed, are a cheaper alternative for specific journeys.

Always approach the first taxi in the line at a taxi rank

Finding a Cab

Licensed London taxis, or black cabs, are large, distinctive vehicles – of which there are now several models – whose yellow "Taxi" sign is lit up whenever the taxi is free. You can hail them on the street, phone for them, or find them at taxi ranks, especially at airports, main rail stations and major hotels. If a cab stops for you, it must take you anywhere within a radius of 9.6 km (6 miles), as long as it is in the Metropolitan Police district, which includes most of the Greater London area and Heathrow Airport.

Taxi Fares

All black cabs have meters that start ticking at around £2.20 as soon as the driver accepts your custom. The fare then increases by the minute, or for each 311 m (340 yds) travelled. There are three tariff time bands: the cheapest is 6am–8pm Monday–Friday; the next most expensive, 8–10pm Monday–Friday and 6–10pm Saturday and Sunday; the most expensive is 10pm–6am. The meter must be clearly visible in the vehicle. It is usual to tip taxi and minicab drivers. If you lose anything in a licensed taxi, contact Transport for London's lost property office *(see p363)*. You will need the driver's cab licence number, displayed in the back of the taxi.

Minicabs

Licensed minicabs are badged with a blue-and-white TfL sticker, usually on the back window. Do not use unlicensed cabs cruising for business. TfL's Cabwise service is a good way of finding a safe cab: text "CAB" to 60835 and you will be sent phone numbers for one black cab office and two reliable minicab companies in the area. If using a non-UK mobile, text your location (street name and postal district) to 00 44 7797 800 000 to access the same service.

Mobile phone apps such as Uber allow you to book a taxi using your phone location and pay safely and conveniently through the app with a credit or debit card.

DIRECTORY

Complaints (Transport for London)
Tel 0343 222 1234.
W tfl.gov.uk

Computer Cabs
Tel 020 7908 0271.
W computercab.co.uk

Dial-a-Minicab
Tel 0800 019 6768.
W dialaminicab.com

Gett Taxis
W gett.com/uk/

Lady Minicabs (women-only drivers)
Tel 020 7272 3300.

Radio Taxis
Tel 020 7272 0272.
W radiotaxis.co.uk

Uber
W get.uber.com/go

The light, when lit, shows the cab is available.

The meter displays your fare as it increases, and surcharges for extra passengers, luggage or unsocial hours. Fares are the same in all licensed black cabs.

Fare   Surcharges

Licensed Taxi Cabs

London's cabs are a safe way of travelling around the city. They can carry a maximum of five passengers, are all accessible for wheelchair users and have ample luggage space.

STREET FINDER

The map references given with all sights, hotels, restaurants, shops and entertainment venues described in this book refer to the maps in this section only (*see How Map References Work opposite*). A complete index of street names and all the places of interest marked on the maps can be found on the following pages.

The key map below shows the area of London covered by the Street Finder, with the postal codes of the various districts. The maps include the sightseeing areas (which are colour-coded), as well as the whole of central London, with all the districts important for hotels, restaurants, pubs and entertainment venues.

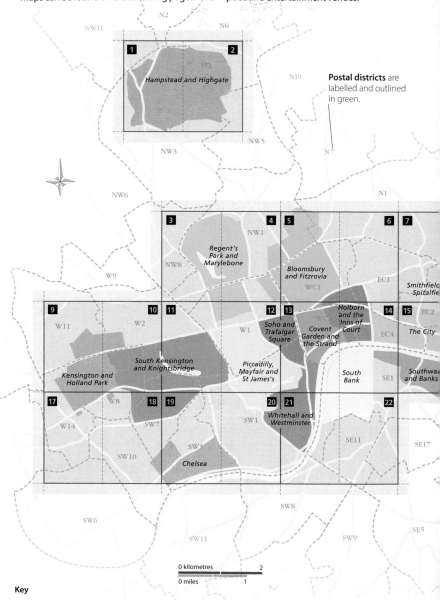

Postal districts are labelled and outlined in green.

Key

– – Postal district boundary

How the Map References Work

The first figure tells you which *Street Finder* map to turn to.

⓬ Wesley's Chapel–Leysian Mission

49 City Rd EC1. **Map** 7. B4. **Tel** 020 7253 2262. 🚇 Old St, Moorgate. **Open** 10am–4pm Mon–Sat. **Closed** between Christmas & New Year, public & bank hols (except Good Friday). ♿ 🕇 9:45am (not 1st Sun of month), 11am Sun, 12:45pm Wed. 📷 groups book ahead. 🎧 Free lunchtime recitals: Thu. **W** **wesleyschapel.org.uk**

The letter and number give the grid reference. Letters go across the map's top and bottom; figures along its sides.

The map continues on map 15 of the *Street Finder.*

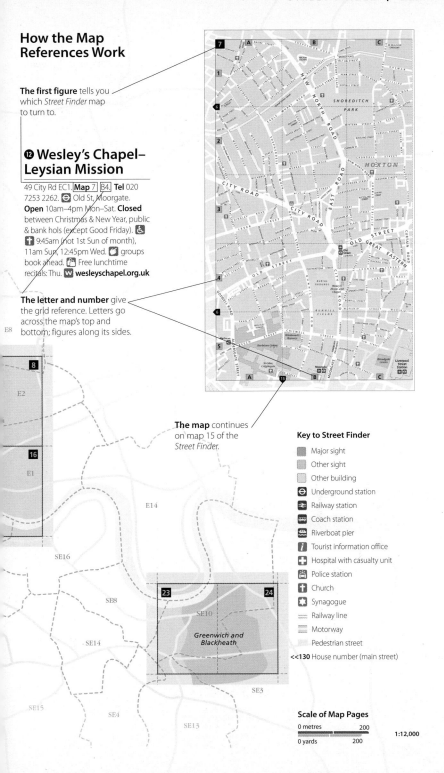

Key to Street Finder

- 🟫 Major sight
- 🟦 Other sight
- ⬜ Other building
- 🚇 Underground station
- 🚉 Railway station
- 🚌 Coach station
- ⛴ Riverboat pier
- *i* Tourist information office
- ➕ Hospital with casualty unit
- 🚔 Police station
- 🕇 Church
- ✡ Synagogue
- ╍ Railway line
- ▭ Motorway
- Pedestrian street
- <<**130** House number (main street)

Scale of Map Pages

0 metres   200
0 yards   200

1:12,000

Street Finder Index

Place	Ref	Place	Ref
Bishops Ave, The NW2	1 B1	Bream's Bldgs EC4	14 E1
Bishop's Bridge Rd W2	10 E1	Brechin Pl SW7	18 F2
Bishop's Rd SW11	19 B5	Brecon Rd W6	17 A4
Bishopsgate EC2	8 D5	Bremner Rd SW7	10 F5
	15 C1	Brendon St W1	11 B1
Bishopsgate Church		Bressenden Pl SW1	20 F1
Yard EC2	15 C1	Brewer St W1	13 A2
Bishopswood Rd N6	2 D1	Brick La E1, E2	8 E5
Black Prince La SE11	21 C2		8 E3
Black Prince Rd SE1	21 C2	Brick St W1	12 E4
Black Prince Rd SE11	22 D2	Bridge Pl SW1	20 F2
Blackall St EC2	7 C4	Bridge St SW1	13 C5
Blackfriars Bridge EC4	14 F2	Bridgefoot SE1	21 C3
Blackfriars La EC4	14 F2	Bridgeman St NW8	3 A2
Blackfriars Rd SE1	14 F3	Bridgeway St NW1	5 A2
Blackfriars Underpass EC4	14 F2	Bridport Pl N1	7 B1
Blackheath SE3	24 D5	Bridstow Pl W2	9 C1
Blackheath Ave SE10	24 D3	Brill Pl NW1	5 B2
Blackheath Hill SE10	23 B4	Britannia Row N1	7 A1
Blackheath Rise SE13	23 B5	Britannia St WC1	5 C3
Blackheath Rd SE10	23 A4	Britannia Wlk N1	7 B3
Blackheath Vale SE3	24 A5	British Library WC1	5 B3
Blackwall La SE10	24 E1	British Museum WC1	5 B5
Blagrove Rd W10	9 A1	British Telecom	
Blandford Sq NW1	3 B5	Tower W1	4 F5
Blandford St W1	12 D1	Brittania Rd SW6	18 D5
Blantyre St SW10	18 F5	Britten St SW3	19 A3
Blenheim Cres W11	9 A2	Britton St EC1	6 F5
Bletchley St N1	7 B2	Brixton Rd SW9	22 E5
Blewcoat School SW1	13 A5	Broad Sanctuary SW1	13 B5
Bliss Cres SE13	23 A5	Broad Wlk NW1	4 D2
Blisset St SE10	23 A4	Broad Wlk, The W8	10 E4
Blomfield St EC2	15 C1	Broadbridge Clo SE3	24 F3
Bloomfield Terr SW1	20 D3	Broadcasting House W1	12 E1
Bloomsbury Pl WC1	5 C5	Broadgate Centre EC2	7 C5
Bloomsbury Sq WC1	5 C5	Broadley St NW8	3 A5
Bloomsbury St WC1	13 B1	Broadley Terr NW1	3 B4
Bloomsbury Way WC1	13 C1	Broadwall SE1	14 E3
Blue Anchor Yrd E1	16 E2	Broadway SW1	13 A5
Blythe Rd W14	17 A1	Broadway Mkt E8	8 F1
Boadicea St N1	5 C1	Broadwick St W1	12 F2
Boating Lake NW1	3 C3		13 A2
Boating Lake SW11	20 D5	Broken Wharf EC4	15 A2
Bolney St SW8	21 C5	Brompton Cemetery	
Bolsover St W1	4 F5	SW10	18 D4
Bolton Gdns SW5	18 D3	Brompton Oratory SW7	19 A1
Bolton St W1	12 E3	Brompton Pk Cres SW6	18 D4
Boltons, The SW10	18 E3	Brompton Pl SW3	19 B1
Bond Way SW8	21 C4	Brompton Rd SW3	11 B5
Bonhill St EC2	7 C4		19 B1
Bonnington Sq SW8	21 C4	Brompton Sq SW3	19 B1
Boot St N1	7 C3	Bromwich Ave N6	2 F3
Borough High St SE1	15 B4	Bronsart Rd SW6	17 A5
Borough Mkt SE1	15 B4	Brook Dri SE11	22 E1
Borough Rd SE1	14 F5	Brook Gate W1	11 C3
Borough Rd SE1	15 A5	Brook Ms North W2	10 F2
Boscobel St NW8	3 A5	Brook St W1	12 E2
Boston Pl NW1	3 B4	Brook St W2	11 A2
Boswell St WC1	5 C5	Brooke St EC1	6 E5
Boundary St E2	8 D4	Brookmill Rd SE8	23 A5
Bourdon St W1	12 E2	Brook's Ms W1	12 E2
Bourne St SW1	20 D2	Brookville Rd SW6	17 B5
Bouverie Pl W2	11 A1	Brougham Rd E8	8 F1
Bouverie St EC4	14 E2	Brown St W1	11 B1
Bow La EC4	15 A2	Brownlow Ms WC1	6 D4
Bow St WC2	13 C2	Brownlow St WC1	6 D5
Bower Ave SE10	24 D3	Brunswick Ct SE1	16 D5
Bowling Grn La EC1	6 E4	Brunswick Gdns W8	10 D4
Bowling Grn St SE11	22 E4	Brunswick Pl N1	7 B3
Boyfield St SE1	14 F5	Brunswick Sq WC1	5 C4
Brackley St EC1	7 A5	Brushfield St E1	8 D5
Brad St SE1	14 E4	Bruton La W1	12 E3
Braganza St SE17	22 F3	Bruton Pl W1	12 E3
Braham St E1	16 E1	Bruton St W1	12 E3
Braidwood St SE1	15 C4	Bryanston Ms East W1	11 C1
Bramber Rd W14	17 B4	Bryanston Pl W1	11 B1
Bramerton St SW3	19 A4	Bryanston Sq W1	11 C1
Bramham Gdns SW5	18 D2	Bryanston St W1	11 C2
Branch Hill NW3	1 A4	Buck Hill Wlk W2	11 A3
Branch Pl N1	7 B1	Buckingham Gate SW1	12 F5
Brand St SE10	23 B3		13 A5
Bray Pl SW3	19 C2	Buckingham Palace SW1	12 F5
Bread St EC4	15 A2		

Place	Ref	Place	Ref
Buckingham Palace		Canterbury Pl SE17	22 F2
Gardens SW1	12 E5	Capland St NW8	3 A4
Buckingham Palace		Caradoc Clo W2	9 C1
Rd SW1	20 E2	Caradoc St SE10	24 D1
Buckingham St WC2	13 C3	Cardigan St SE11	22 D3
Buckland St N1	7 C2	Cardinal's Wharf SE1	15 A3
Bull Wharf La EC4	15 A2	Cardington St NW1	5 A3
Bulls Gdns SW3	19 B2	Carey St WC2	14 D1
Bulmer Pl W11	9 C3	Carlingford Rd NW3	1 B5
Bunhill Fields EC1	7 B4	Carlisle La SE1	14 D5
Bunhill Row EC1	7 B4		22 D1
Burdett Ms W2	10 D1	Carlisle Pl SW1	20 F1
Burgh House NW3	1 B4	Carlos Pl W1	12 E3
Burgh St N1	6 F2	Carlow St NW1	4 F1
Burial Grounds EC1	7 B4	Carlton House Terr SW1	13 A4
Burlington Arcade W1	12 F3	Carlyle Sq SW3	19 A3
Burlington Gdns W1	12 F3	Carlyle's House SW3	19 B4
Burnaby St SW10	18 F5	Carmelite St EC4	14 E2
Burney St SE10	23 B3	Carnaby St W1	12 F2
Burnsall St SW3	19 B3	Carnegie St N1	6 D1
Burnthwaite Rd SW6	17 C5	Carol St NW1	4 F1
Burrell St SE1	14 F3	Caroline Gdns E2	8 D3
Burslem St E1	16 F2	Caroline Pl W2	10 D2
Burton St WC1	5 B4	Caroline Terr SW1	20 D2
Burton's Ct SW3	19 C3	Carriage Dri East SW11	20 D5
Bury Pl WC1	13 C1	Carriage Dri North SW11	19 C5
Bury St EC3	16 D1		20 D4
Bury St SW1	12 F3	Carriage Dri West SW11	19 C5
Bush House WC2	14 D2	Carroun Rd SW8	22 D5
Buttesland St N1	7 C3	Carter La EC4	14 F2
Buxton St E1	8 E4	Cartwright Gdns WC1	5 B3
Byward St EC3	16 D2	Cartwright St E1	16 E2
		Casson St E1	8 E5
C		Castle Baynard St EC4	14 F2
			15 A2
Cable St E1	16 F2	Castle La SW1	12 F5
Cade Rd SE10	23 C4	Castletown Rd W14	17 A3
Cadogan Gate SW1	19 C2	Cathcart Rd SW10	18 E4
Cadogan Gdns SW3	19 C2	Cathedral St SE1	15 B3
Cadogan La SW1	20 D1	Catherine Gro SE10	23 A4
Cadogan Pier SW3	19 B4	Catherine St WC2	13 C2
Cadogan Pl SW1	19 C1	Catton St WC1	13 C1
Cadogan Sq SW1	19 C1	Causton St SW1	21 B2
Cadogan St SW3	19 C2	Cavendish Ave NW8	3 A2
Cale St SW3	19 A3	Cavendish Pl W1	12 E1
Caledonian Rd N1	5 C2	Cavendish Sq W1	12 E1
	6 D1	Cavendish St N1	7 B2
Callender Rd SW7	10 F5	Caversham St SW3	19 C4
Callow St SW3	18 F4	Caxton St SW1	13 A5
Calshot St N1	6 D2	Cedarne Rd SW6	18 D5
Calthorpe St WC1	6 D4	Cenotaph SW1	13 B4
Calvert Ave E2	8 D3	Central Criminal	
Calvert Rd SE10	24 E1	Court EC4	14 F1
Calvin St E1	8 D5	Central Mkt WC2	13 C2
Camberwell New Rd SE5	22 E5	Central St EC1	7 A3
Cambridge Circus WC2	13 B2	Chadwell St EC1	6 E3
Cambridge Gdns W10	9 A1	Chadwick St SW1	21 A1
Cambridge Pl W8	10 E5	Chagford St NW1	3 C4
Cambridge Sq W2	11 A1	Chaldon Rd SW6	17 A5
Cambridge St SW1	20 F3	Challoner St W14	17 B3
Camden High St NW1	4 F1	Chalton St NW1	5 A2
Camden St NW1	4 F1	Chamber St E1	16 E2
	5 A1	Chambers St SE16	16 F5
Camden Wlk N1	6 F1	Chambord St E2	8 E3
Camera Pl SW10	18 F4	Chance St E1, E2	8 D4
Camlet St E2	8 D4	Chancel St SE1	14 F4
Camley St NW1	5 A1	Chancery La WC2	14 D1
Campden Gro W8	9 C4	Chandos Pl WC2	13 B3
Campden Hill W8	9 C4	Chandos St W1	12 E1
Campden Hill Rd W11	9 C4	Chapel Mkt N1	6 E2
Campden Hill Sq W8	9 B4	Chapel Side W2	10 D2
Campden St W8	9 C4	Chapel St NW1	3 B5
Canadian Embassy SW1	13 B3	Chapel St SW1	12 D5
Canal Wlk N1	7 B1	Chapter Rd SE17	22 F3
Canning Pl W8	10 E5	Chapter St SW1	21 A2
Cannon La NW3	1 B4	Charing Cross Pier WC2	13 C3
Cannon Pl NW3	1 B4	Charing Cross Rd WC2	13 B1
Cannon Row SW1	13 B5	Charlbert St NW8	3 A2
Cannon St EC4	15 A2	Charles Dickens	
Cannon St Rd E1	16 F1	Museum WC1	6 D4
Canon St N1	7 A1	Charles La NW8	3 A2
Canrobert St E2	8 F2	Charles Sq N1	7 C3

Each place name is followed by its postal district number and then by its Street Finder reference

Dean Ryle St SW1	21 B1	Duke Humphrey Rd SE3	24 D5	Edith Terr SW10	18 E5	**F**
Dean St W1	13 A1	Duke of Wellington		Edith Vlls W14	17 B2	
Dean's Yd SW1	13 B5	Pl SW1	12 D5	Edwardes Sq W8	17 C1	Fabian Rd SW6	17 B5
Decima St SE1	15 C5	Duke of York St SW1	13 A3	Effie Rd SW6	17 C5	Fair St SE1	16 D4
Delaford St SW6	17 A5	Duke St SW1	12 F3	Egerton Cres SW3	19 B1	Fairclough St E1	16 F1
Delancey St NW1	4 E1	Duke St W1	12 D2	Egerton Dri SE10	23 A4	Fairholme Rd W14	17 A3
Delverton Rd SE17	22 F3	Duke St Hill SE1	15 B3	Egerton Gdns SW3	19 B1	Fakruddin St E1	8 F4
Denbigh Pl SW1	20 F3	Duke's La W8	10 D4	Egerton Pl SW3	19 B1	Falconwood Ct SE3	24 E5
Denbigh Rd W11	9 B2	Duke's Rd WC1	5 B3	Egerton Terr SW3	19 B1	Falkirk St N1	8 D2
Denbigh St SW1	20 F2	Duke's Pl EC3	16 D1	Elaine Gro NW5	2 E5	Fan Museum SE10	23 B3
Denbigh Terr W11	9 B2	Dunbridge St E2	8 F4	Elcho St SW11	19 B5	Fane St W14	17 B4
Denham St SE10	24 F1	Duncan Rd E8	8 F1	Elder St E1	8 D5	Fann St EC1	7 A5
Denman St W1	13 A2	Duncan St N1	6 F2	Eldon Gro NW3	1 B5	Fanshaw St N1	7 C3
Denning Rd NW3	1 B5	Duncan Terr N1	6 F2	Eldon Rd W8	18 E1	Faraday Museum W1	12 F3
Dennis Severs' House E1	8 D5	Dunloe St E2	8 E2	Eldon St EC2	7 C5	Farm La SW6	17 C5
Denny St SE11	22 E2	Dunraven St W1	11 C2	Elgin Cres W11	9 A2	Farm St W1	12 E3
Denyer St SW3	19 B2	Dunston Rd E8	8 D1	Elia St N1	6 F2	Farmer's Rd SE5	22 F5
Derbyshire St E2	8 F3	Dunston St E8	8 D1	Eliot Hill SE13	23 B5	Farncombe St SE16	16 F5
Dereham Pl EC2	8 D4	Durant St E2	8 F2	Eliot Pl SE3	24 D5	Farnham Royal SE11	22 D3
Dericote St E8	8 F1	Durham St SE11	22 D3	Eliot Vale SE3	23 C5	Farringdon La EC1	6 E4
Derry St W8	10 D5	Durham Terr W2	10 D1	Elizabeth Bridge SW1	20 E2	Farringdon Rd EC1	6 E4
Design Museum W8	9 C5	Durward St E1	8 F5	Elizabeth St SW1	20 E2	Farringdon St EC4	14 F1
Devonshire Clo W1	4 E5	Dutton St SE10	23 B4	Ellen St E1	16 F2	Fashion and Textile	
Devonshire Dri SE10	23 A4	Dyott St WC1	13 B1	Ellerdale Clo NW3	1 A5	Museum SE1	15 C4
Devonshire Pl W1	4 D5			Ellerdale Rd NW3	1 A5	Fashion St E1	8 E5
Devonshire Sq EC2	16 D1	**E**		Elliott's Row SE11	22 F1	Faunce St SE17	22 F3
Devonshire St W1	4 E5			Elm Pk Gdns SW10	18 F3	Fawcett St SW10	18 E4
Devonshire Terr W2	10 F2	Eagle Ct EC1	6 F5		19 A3	Feathers Pl SE10	23 C2
Dewey Rd N1	6 E1	Eagle St WC1	13 C1	Elm Pk Rd SW3	18 F4	Featherstone St EC1	7 B4
Diamond Terr SE10	23 B4	Eagle Wharf Rd N1	7 A2		19 A3	Felton St N1	7 B1
Diana, Princess of		Eamont St NW8	3 B2	Elm Pl SW7	18 F3	Fenchurch Ave EC3	15 C2
Wales Memorial		Earl St EC2	7 C5	Elm St WC1	6 D4	Fenchurch Bldgs EC3	16 D2
Playground W2	10 D3	Earlham St WC2	13 B2	Elsham Rd W14	9 A5	Fenchurch St EC3	15 C2
Dilke St SW3	19 C4	Earl's Court Exhibition		Elvaston Pl SW7	18 E1		16 D2
Dingley Rd EC1	7 A3	Centre SW5	17 C3	Elverson Rd SE8	23 A5	Fentiman Rd SW8	21 C4
Dinsdale Rd SE3	24 E2	Earl's Court Gdns SW5	18 D2	Elverton St SW1	21 A1		22 D5
Disbrowe Rd W6	17 A4	Earl's Court Rd SW5,		Elwin St E2	8 E3	Fenton House NW3	1 A4
Disney Pl SE1	15 A4	W8	18 D2	Elystan Pl SW3	19 B2	Fernshaw Rd SW10	18 E4
Diss St E2	8 E2	Earl's Court Sq SW5	18 D3	Elystan St SW3	19 B2	Ferry St E14	23 B1
Ditch Alley SE10	23 A4	Earl's Terr W8	17 B1	Emba St SE16	16 F5	Festival/South Bank	
Dock St E1	16 E2	Earl's Wlk W8	17 C1	Embankment Gdns SW3	19 C4	Pier SE1	14 D3
Dockhead SE1	16 E5	Earlswood St SE10	24 D1	Emerald St WC1	6 D5	Fetter La EC4	14 E1
Dr Johnson's House EC4	14 E1	Earsby St W14	17 A2	Emerson St SE1	15 A3	Field Rd W6	17 A4
Doddington Gro SE17	22 F3	East Ferry Rd E14	23 A1	Emma St E2	8 F2	Fieldgate St E1	16 F1
Doddington Pl SE17	22 F4	East Heath NW3	1 B3	Emperor's Gate SW7	18 E1	Filmer Rd SW6	17 B5
Dodson St SE1	14 E5	East Heath Rd NW3	1 B4	Endell St WC2	13 B1	Finborough Rd SW10	18 E4
Dolben St SE1	14 F4	East Pier E1	16 F4	Enderby St SE10	24 D1	Fingal St SE10	24 F1
Dolphin Sq SW1	21 A3	East Rd N1	7 B3	Endsleigh Gdns WC1	5 A4	Finsbury Circus EC2	7 B5
Dombey St WC1	5 C5	East Smithfield E1	16 E3	Endsleigh St WC1	5 A4		15 B1
Donegal St N1	6 D2	East Tenter St E1	16 E2	Enford St W1	3 B5	Finsbury Mkt EC2	7 C5
Donne Pl SW3	19 B2	Eastbourne Ms W2	10 F1	English Grounds SE1	15 C4	Finsbury Pavement EC2	7 B5
Doon St SE1	14 E3	Eastbourne Terr W2	10 F1	Enid St SE16	16 E5	Finsbury Sq EC2	7 B5
Doric Way NW1	5 A3	Eastcastle St W1	12 F1	Ennismore Gdns SW7	11 A5	Finsbury St EC2	7 B5
Dorset Rd SW8	21 C5		13 A1	Ennismore Gdns Ms SW7	11 A5	First St SW3	19 B1
	22 D5	Eastcheap EC3	15 C2	Ensign St E1	16 F2	Fisherton St NW8	3 A4
Dorset St NW1, W1	3 C5	Eastney St SE10	23 C1	Epirus Rd SW6	17 C5	Fishmongers' Hall EC3	15 B2
Doughty Ms WC1	6 D4	Eaton Gate SW1	20 D2	Epworth St EC2	7 C4	Fitzalan St SE11	22 D2
Doughty St WC1	6 D4	Eaton La SW1	20 E1	Erasmus St SW1	21 B2	Fitzgeorge Ave W14	17 A2
Douglas St SW1	21 A2	Eaton Ms SW1	20 D1	Errol St EC1	7 B4	Fitzjames Ave W14	17 A2
Douro Pl W8	10 E5		20 E1	Essex Rd N1	6 F1	Fitzjohn's Ave NW3	1 B5
Dove House St SW3	19 A3	Eaton Ms North SW1	20 D1	Essex St WC2	14 D2	Fitzroy Pk N6	2 E1
Dove Row E2	8 F1	Eaton Ms West SW1	20 D2	Essex Vlls W8	9 C5	Fitzroy Sq W1	4 F4
Dover St W1	12 F3	Eaton Pl SW1	20 D1	Estcourt Rd SW6	17 B5	Fitzroy St W1	4 F5
Down St W1	12 E4	Eaton Sq SW1	20 D1	Estelle Rd NW3	2 E5	Flask Wlk NW3	1 B5
Downing St SW1	13 B4	Eaton Terr SW1	20 D2	Esterbrooke St SW1	21 A2	Flaxman Terr WC1	5 B3
Downshire Hill NW3	1 C5	Ebbisham Dri SW8	22 D4	Eustace Rd SW6	17 C5	Fleet Rd NW3	2 D5
Draycott Ave SW3	19 B2	Ebor St E1	8 D4	Euston Rd NW1	4 F4	Fleet St EC4	14 E1
Draycott Pl SW3	19 C2	Ebury Bridge SW1	20 E3		5 A4	Fleming Rd SE17	22 F4
Draycott Terr SW3	19 C2	Ebury Bridge Rd SW1	20 E3	Euston Sq NW1	5 A3	Fleur de Lis St E1	8 D5
Drayton Gdns SW10	18 F3	Ebury Ms SW1	20 E1	Euston St NW1	5 A4	Flitcroft St WC2	13 B1
Druid St SE1	16 D4	Ebury Sq SW1	20 E2	Evelyn Gdns SW7	18 F3	Flood St SW3	19 B3
Drummond Cres NW1	5 A3	Ebury St SW1	20 E2	Evelyn Wlk N1	7 B2	Flood Wlk SW3	19 B3
Drummond Gate SW1	21 B3	Eccleston Bridge SW1	20 E2	Eversholt St NW1	4 F2	Floral St WC2	13 C2
Drummond St NW1	4 F4	Eccleston Ms SW1	20 D1		5 A3	Florence Nightingale	
	5 A3	Eccleston Pl SW1	20 E2	Ewer St SE1	15 A4	Museum SE1	14 D5
Drury La WC2	13 C1	Eccleston Sq SW1	20 F2	Exeter St WC2	13 C2	Florida St E2	8 F3
Drysdale St N1	8 D3	Eccleston St SW1	20 E1	Exhibition Rd SW7	11 A5	Flower Wlk, The SW7	10 F5
Duchess of Bedford's		Edge St W8	9 C4		19 A1	Foley St W1	4 F5
Wlk W8	9 C5	Edgware Rd W2	3 A5	Exmouth Market EC1	6 E4	Folgate St E1	8 D5
Duchess St W1	4 E5		11 B1	Exton St SE1	14 E4	Forbes St E1	16 F2
Duchy St SE1	14 E3	Edith Gro SW10	18 E4	Eyre St Hill EC1	6 E4	Fordham St E1	16 F1
Dufferin St EC1	7 B4	Edith Rd W14	17 A2	Ezra St E2	8 E3	Fore St EC2	7 B5

Each place name is followed by its postal district number and then by its Street Finder reference

Each place name is followed by its postal district number and then by its Street Finder reference

Each place name is followed by its postal district number and then by its Street Finder reference

Each place name is followed by its postal district number and then by its Street Finder reference

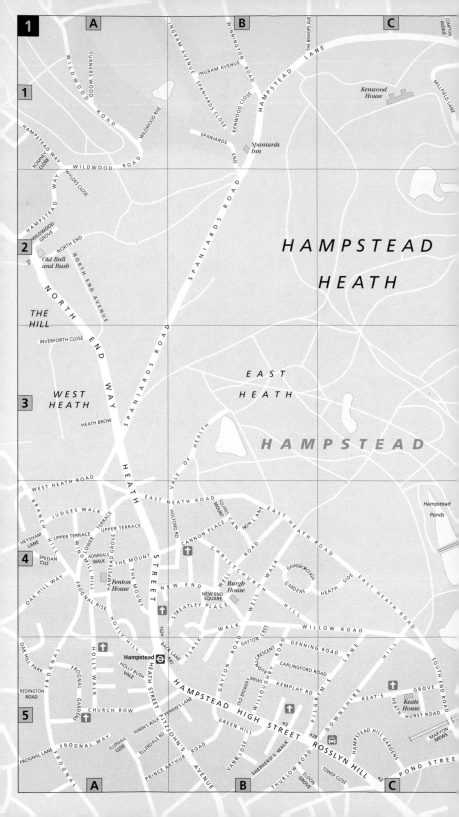

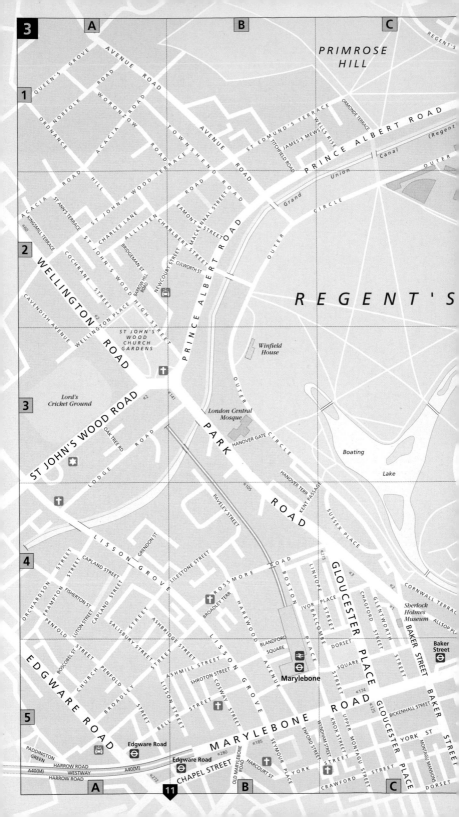

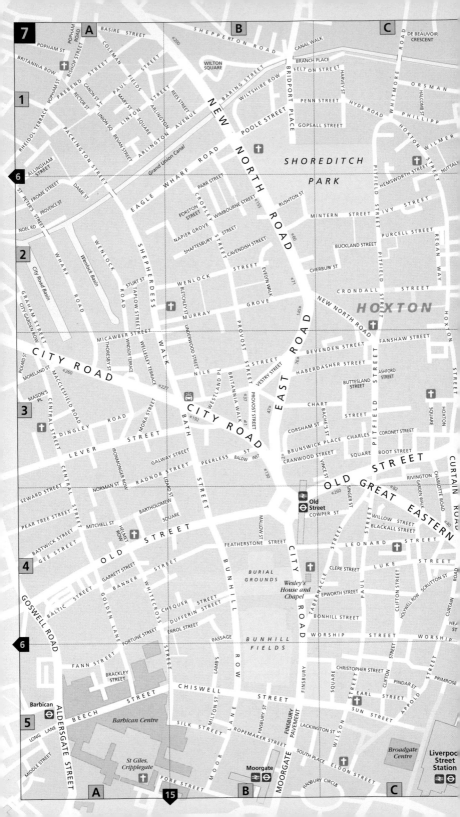

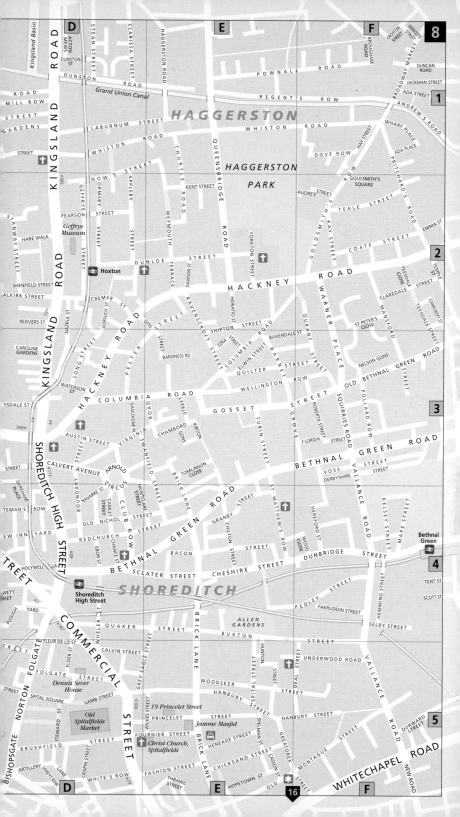

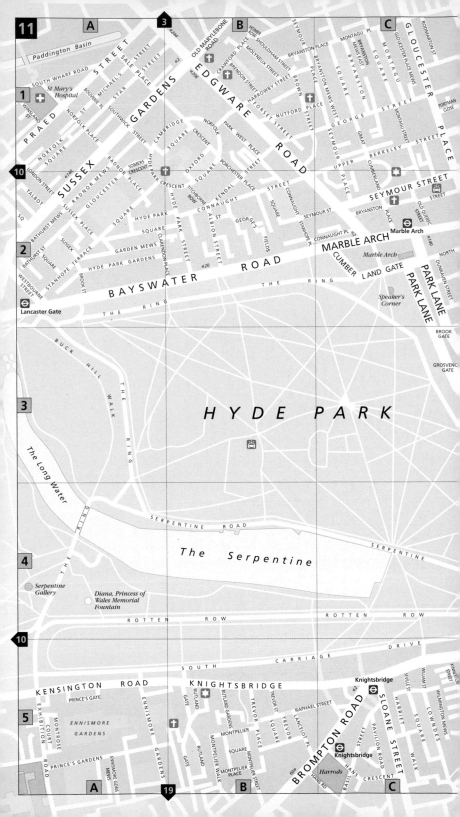

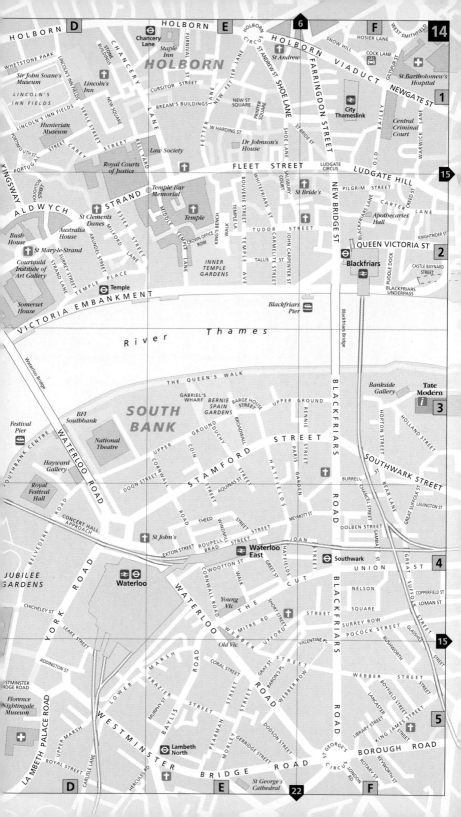

D **E** **F**

NEW STREET

DEVONSHIRE SQUARE

MIDDLESEX STREET

BELL LANE

LEYDEN ST

TOYNBEE ST

WENTWORTH

PETTICOAT LANE

GRAVEL LANE

OLD CASTLE STREET

COMMERCIAL STREET

STREET

GUNTHORPE ST

OSBORN STREET

WHITECHAPEL ROAD

FIELDGATE ST #34

MULBERRY ST

PLUMBER'S ROW

GREENFIELD ROAD

SETTLES STREET

MYRDLE STREET

FORDHAM STREET

NEW ROAD

HOUNDSDITCH

BEVIS MARKS

BURY STREET

DUKE'S PLACE

CREECHURCH LANE

MITRE ST

STONEY LANE

Whitechapel Art Gallery

Aldgate East ⊖

WHITECHAPEL HIGH STREET

#105

WHITE CHURCH LANE

ADLER STREET

COMMERCIAL ROAD

BACK CHURCH LANE

HENRIQUES STREET

BATTY STREET

CHRISTIAN STREET

CANNON STREET RD

1

St Botolph

Aldgate ⊖

ALDGATE HIGH STREET #133

MANSELL STREET

LEMAN STREET

STREET

GOWER'S WALK

FAIRCLOUGH STREET

ELLEN STREET

FORBES STREET

STUFFIELD ST

WICKER ST

PONLER ST

BURSLEM STREET

St Katharine Cree

St Botolph

ALDGATE

MINORIES

JEWRY ST

VINE STREET

FRIARS

ALIE STREET

NORTH TENTER ST

E TENTER ST

W TENTER ST

ST MARK STREET

SCARBOROUGH STREET

SOUTH TENTER STREET

HOOPER STREET

PINCHIN STREET

2

STREET

FENCHURCH BUILDINGS

LLOYD'S AVE

LLOYD'S AVENUE

CROSSWALL

HAYDON STREET

PORTSOKEN STREET

GOODMANS YARD

PRESCOT ST #1

CHAMBER STREET

CABLE STREET

HINDMARSH

CLOSE

Fenchurch Street ⊖

HART ST

CRUTCHED FRIARS

SEETHING LANE

PEPYS STREET

COOPER'S ROW

Tower Gateway DLR ⊖

ROYAL MINT STREET

CARTWRIGHT STREET

JOHN FISHER STREET

DOCK STREET

ENSIGN STREET #15

TRINITY SQUARE

Tower Hill ⊖

BYWARD ST

TOWER HILL

TOWER HILL

BLUE ANCHOR YARD

EAST SMITHFIELD

THE HIGHWAY

PENNINGTON STREET

3

All Hallows by the Tower

THAMES STREET

TOWER BRIDGE APPROACH

Tower of London

ST KATHARINE'S WAY

St Katharine Docks

THOMAS MORE STREET

NESHAM STREET

VAUGHAN WAY

ASHER WAY

KENNET STREET

Tower Pier

HMS Belfast

Tower Bridge

ST KATHARINE'S WAY

St Katharine's Pier

MEWS STREET

ST KATHARINE'S WAY

VAUGHAN WAY

WAPPING HIGH STREET

SAMPSON ST

KNIGHTEN ST

W PIER

NW PIER

NE PIER

4

The Scoop

Greater London Authority Headquarters

POTTERS FIELDS

WEAVERS LANE

BRIDGE ROAD

THE QUEEN'S WALK

SHAD THAMES

River Thames

STREET

BARNHAM ST

DRUID ST

FAIR

GAINSFORDS STREET

QUEEN ELIZABETH STREET

LAFONE STREET

CURLEW STREET

SHAD THAMES

BERMONDSEY WALL WEST

TOOLEY STREET

1838

STREET

MILL STREET

JACOB STREET

WOLSELEY STREET

GEORGE ROW

CHAMBERS STREET

BERMONDSEY WALL EAST

WILSON GROVE

MARIGOLD ST

5

TOWER

DRUID STREET

BRUNSWICK CT

INNER STREET

WHITE'S GROUNDS

TANNER STREET

POPE STREET

RILEY STREET

PURBROOK ST

MALTBY STREET

NECKINGER STREET

STREET

ABBEY STREET

ENID ST

DOCKHEAD

JAMAICA ROAD

BEVINGTON STREET

FARNCOMBE STREET

SCOTT LIDGETT CRESCENT

EMBA ST

JANEWAY ST

MARINE STREET

OLD JAMAICA ROAD

ST JAMES'S RD

JAMAICA ROAD

Bermondsey ⊖

KELTON'S ROAD

D **E** **F**

IVERNA GARDENS
CHENSTON GARDENS
STANFORD RD
COTTESMORE GDNS
VICTORIA GROVE
QUEEN'S GATE TERRACE
IMPERIAL COLLEGE ROAD

VILLAS
KELSO PLACE
ELDON ROAD
LAUNCESTON PLACE
KYNANCE PL
PETERSHAM PLACE
Petersham Place
ELVASTON PLACE
Elvaston Place
QUEEN'S GATE
QUEEN'S

ALLEN STREET VILLAS
MARLOES ROAD
KENSINGTON
Natural History Museum

STRATFORD ROAD
ROAD
CORNWALL GARDENS
QUEEN'S GATE PLACE
QUEEN'S GATE MEWS

1

LEXHAM GARDENS
CORNWALL
EMPEROR'S GATE
GRENVILLE PLACE
MCLEOD'S MEWS
SOUTHWELL GDNS
GLOUCESTER ROAD
QUEEN'S GATE GARDENS
QUEEN'S GATE PLACE MEWS
ATHERSTONE MEWS

PENNANT MEWS
249
ROAD

ROAD
CROMWELL
ROAD
Gloucester Road
CROMWELL
ROAD
QUEENSBERRY PLACE

19

REDFIELD LANE
KNARESBOROUGH
COLLINGHAM PLACE
ASHBURN GARDENS
COURTFIELD RD
ASHBURN PLACE
STANHOPE MEWS WEST
STANHOPE GARDENS
STANHOPE MEWS EAST
STANHOPE
QUEEN'S GATE
HARRINGTON ROAD

EARLS
KENWAY ROAD
HOGARTH ROAD
COLLINGHAM GARDENS
COLLINGHAM PLACE
COLLINGHAM ROAD
COLBECK MEWS
GLOUCESTER ROAD
CLAREVILLE STREET
MANSON PLACE

2

COURT
EARLS COURT GARDENS
BARKSTON
COURTFIELD
HARRINGTON GARDENS
WETHERBY PL
CLAREVILLE GROVE
CLAREVILLE GROVE
ONSLOW GARDENS
CRANLEY PLACE

Earls Court
PENYWERN ROAD
HESPER MEWS
BRAMHAM GARDENS
COLLINGHAM GARDENS
WETHERBY GARDENS
ROSARY GARDENS
BINA GARDENS
BRECHIN PLACE
OLD BROMPTON ROAD
ONSLOW GARDENS
SELWOOD TERRACE

Earls Court
ROAD
BOLTON GARDENS
BOLTON GARDENS
GLEDHOW GARDENS
ROAD
ELM PLACE

3

ROAD
EARLS COURT SQUARE
RICK LANE
237
BROMPTON
ROAD
COLEHERNE COURT
THE LITTLE BOLTONS
CRESSWELL GARDENS
CRESSWELL PLACE
DRAYTON GARDENS
THISTLE GROVE
ROLAND WAY
ROLAND GARDENS
CRANLEY MEWS
CRANLEY GARDENS
EVELYN GARDENS
EVELYN GARDENS

KEMPSFORD GARDENS
279
243
1
OLD
REDCLIFFE
THE BOLTONS
THE BOLTONS
PRIORY WALK
HARLEY GARDENS
GILSTON ROAD
MILBORNE GROVE
ELM PARK GARDENS

West Brompton
COLEHERNE ROAD
REDCLIFFE
WESTGATE TERRACE
SQUARE
HARCOURT TERRACE
REDCLIFFE MEWS
TREGUNTER ROAD
REDCLIFFE ROAD
BEAUFORT ST
279

4

FINBOROUGH
GARDENS
CATHCART ROAD
SEYMOUR WALK
FULHAM ROAD
CALLOW ST
ELM PARK ROAD
PARK WALK
CHELSEA PARK GDNS

BROMPTON
IFIELD ROAD
HOLLYWOOD ROAD
FAWCETT STREET
NETHERTON GROVE
LIMERSTON STREET
CAMERA PL

CEMETERY
ROAD
FAWCETT STREET
REDCLIFFE PL
413

BROMPTON PARK CRESCENT
SEAGRAVE ROAD
BROMPTON PARK CRES
GERTRUDE STREET
SHALCOMB STREET
HOBURY STREET
LANGTON STREET
LAMONT ROAD

BILLING ROAD
FERNSHAW ROAD
EDITH GROVE
SLAIDBURN STREET
510

19

Fulham Broadway
HILARY CLOSE
WANDON RD
GUNTER GROVE
HORTENSIA ROAD
EDITH TERRACE
WORLD'S END PASSAGE
ANN LANE
465

WANDSWORTH
BRITANNIA RD
MAXWELL ROAD
HOLMEAD ROAD
RUMBOLD ROAD
KING'S
LOTS ROAD
CREMORNE
TADEMA ROAD
ROAD
BLANTYRE STREET

5

HARWOOD ROAD
CEDARNE RD
WATERFORD RD
MOORE PARK RD
FULHAM
WANDON RD
ROAD
UPCERNE ROAD
TETCOTT ROAD
BURNABY STREET
ASHBURNHAM ROAD
19

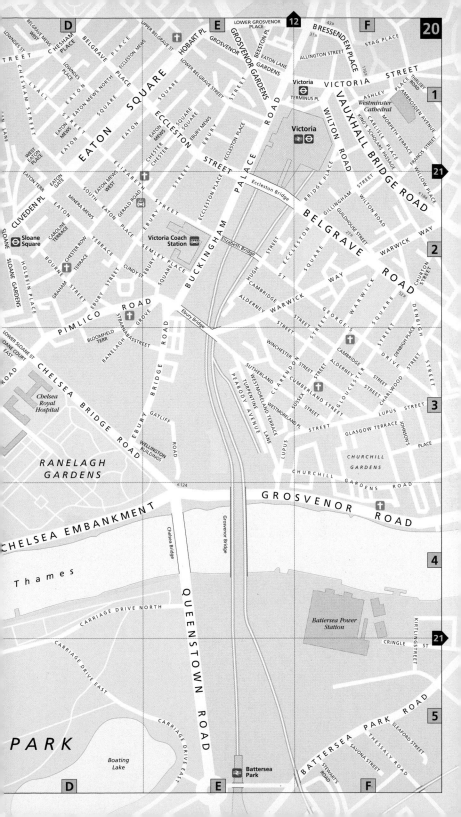

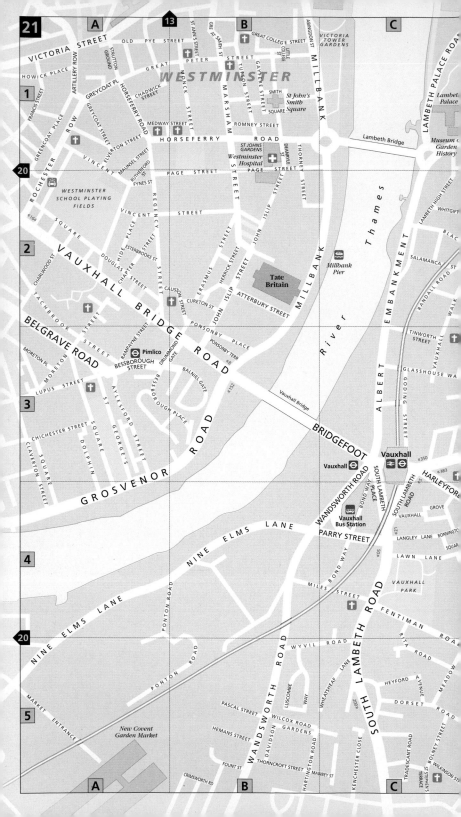

General Index

Roman Bath **122**
Roman London 19, **20–21**
Guildhall 163
Roman Road Market **337**
Rome: The Pantheon (Canaletto) 98
Romney, George 230, 238
Ronnie Scott's 113
Roosevelt, Franklin D
statue of 101, 276
Roper, Margaret 200
Roper, William 200
Roper's Garden **200**, 273
Street-by-Street map 198
Rosa, Salvator 111
The Rose Playhouse **186**
Rossetti, Dante Gabriel
Cheyne Walk 197, 198
Downshire Hill 237
Liberty 113
Venus Venticordia 42
Rothko, Mark 184
Rothschild, Baron Ferdinand 130
Rotten Row 277
Roubiliac, Louis François 230
Nightingale Monument 83
Rousseau, Henri 111
Royal Academy of Arts 10, 28, **94**
London's Best: Museums and Galleries 44, 47
Street-by-Street map 92
Summer Exhibition 61
Royal Academy of Music
Street-by-Street map 226
Royal Albert Hall 202, **209**, **345**
Street-by-Street map 204
Royal Avenue 273
Royal Botanic Gardens *see* Kew Gardens
Royal ceremonies **58**
Royal College of Art **209**
Street-by-Street map 204
Royal College of Music **208**
Street-by-Street map 204
Royal College of Organists 204
Royal Courts of Justice 136, **142**
Street-by-Street map 139
Royal Exchange **151**
Street-by-Street map 149
Royal family **38–9**
Crown Jewels 158, 159, **160**
Royal Festival Hall 34, **192**, 278
Great days in London 11, 12
Street-by-Street map 190
Royal Geographical Society 205
Royal Hospital **201**
Chelsea and Battersea walk 272
Royal Institute of British Architects 229
Street-by-Street map 227
Royal Mews **100**
Royal Observatory Greenwich 47, **246–7**
Royal Opera Arcade **96**
Royal Opera House 13, **119**, **344**
Street-by-Street map 117
Royal Salutes 58, 59, 60, 61, 63
Rubens, Peter Paul
Apsley House 101

Rubens, Peter Paul (cont.)
Banqueting House 27, 75, 84
Courtauld Gallery 121
National Gallery 108, 111
Rugby Union 63, **350**
Rules (restaurant) 117
Ruskin, John 113
Russell Square 54, **132**
Street-by-Street map 127
Rysbrack, John
statue of George II 243

S

Saarinen, Eero 101
Saatchi Gallery 47, **201**
Sadleir, Ralph 252
Safety **362–3**
St Albans, day trips to 380
St Alfege Church 51, **244–5**
Street-by-Street map 242
St Andrew, Holborn **144**
St Anne's, Limehouse 51, **253**
St Anne's Church Tower 113
St Bartholomew-the-Great 50, **169**
Street-by-Street map 167
St Bartholomew-the-Less
Street-by-Street map 166
St Bartholomew's Hospital
Street-by-Street map 166
St Botolph, Aldersgate **169**
St Bride's **143**
London's Best: Churches 50, 51
St Clement Danes 51, **142**
Street-by-Street map 139
St Etheldreda's Chapel **145**
St George's, Bloomsbury **132**
London's Best: Churches 50, 51
Street-by-Street map 127
St Giles, Cripplegate **169**
St Helen's Bishopsgate **162**
St James's *see* Piccadilly, Mayfair and St James's
St James's Church 51, **94**
Street-by-Street map 93
St James's, Garlickhythe 51
Street-by-Street map 148
St James's Palace 92, **95**
London's Best: Ceremonies 56
Street-by-Street map 93
St James's Park **96**
Great days in London 10, 12, 13
London's Best: Parks and Gardens 53, 54, 55
outdoor concerts 55
St James's Park Station **85**
St James's Square **95**
Street-by-Street map 93
St James's Street 10
St Jerome in his Study (Antonello da Messina) 110
St John's Gate **168**
St John's Smith Square **85**, **345**
St Katharine Cree **162**
St Katharine Docks 69, **162**
Great days in London 11, 12, 13
St Leonard's Church **175**
St Luke's Church 273
St Magnus the Martyr 51, **156**

St Margaret's Church **78**
Street-by-Street map 74
St Martin-in-the-Fields **106**
concerts **345**
London's Best: Churches 48, 50, 51
Street-by-Street map 105
St Martin's Theatre
Street-by-Street map 116
St Mary Abchurch
Street-by-Street map 149
St Mary Aldermary
Street-by-Street map 148
30 St Mary Axe ("the Gherkin") 36, 163
St Mary-le-Bow **151**
London's Best: Churches 50, 51
Street-by-Street map 148
St Mary-le-Strand **122**
London's Best: Churches 49, 51
St Mary, Rotherhithe **252**
St Mary Woolnoth
London's Best: Churches 49, 51
Street-by-Street map 149
St Marylebone Parish Church **228–9**
Street-by-Street map 226
St Mary's, Battersea **257**
St Nicholas Cole Abbey
Street-by-Street map 148
St Olave's House 68
St Pancras International **133**
St Pancras Old Church and Graveyard **134**
St Pancras Parish Church 51, **134**
St Paul's Cathedral 146, **152–5**
floorplan 152–3
Great days in London 12, 13
Great Fire 26
A guided tour of St Paul's 154–5
London's Best: Churches 49, 51
A River View of London 67
Street-by-Street map 148
Visitors' checklist 153
St Paul's Church **118**
London's Best: Churches 48, 50
Street-by-Street map 117
St Saviour's Dock 69
St Stephen Walbrook **150**
London's Best: Churches 49, 51
Street-by-Street map 149
Sales 317
Salisbury, day trips to 380
The Saltonstall Family (Des Granges) 87
Sam Wanamaker Playhouse 181
Sambourne, Linley 222
Samson and Delilah (van Dyck) 47
The Sanctuary
Street-by-Street map 74
Sargent, John Singer 42–3, 88, 195
Saunders, Nicholas 119
Savoy Chapel **120**
Savoy Hotel 66, **120**
The Scale of Love (Watteau) 111
Scarves, shopping **329**, 330
Schaufelburg, Ernest 120

Acknowledgments

Dorling Kindersley would like to thank the following people whose help and assistance contributed to the preparation of this book.

Main Contributor

Michael Leapman was born in London in 1938 and has been a journalist since he was 20. He has worked for most British national newspapers and writes about travel and other subjects for several publications, among them *The Independent, Independent on Sunday, The Economist* and *Country Life*. He has written ten books, including *London's River* (1991) and the award-winning *Companion Guide to New York* (1983, revised 1991). In 1989 he edited the acclaimed *Book of London*.

Contributors

James Aufenast, Yvonne Deutch, Guy Dimond, George Foster, Iain Gale, Fiona Holman, Phil Harriss, Lindsay Hunt, Christopher Middleton, Yvette Murrell, Steven Parissien, Alice Park, Christopher Pick, Bazyli Solowij, Matthew Tanner, Mark Wareham, Jude Welton, Ian Wisniewski. Dorling Kindersley wishes to thank the following editors and researchers at Webster's International Publishers: Sandy Carr, Matthew Barrell, Siobhan Bremner, Serena Cross, Annie Galpin, Miriam Lloyd, Ava-Lee Tanner.

Additional Photography

Max Alexander, Peter Anderson, Stephen Bere, June Buck, Peter Chadwick, Michael Dent, Philip Dowell, Mike Dunning, Philip Enticknap, Andreas Einsiedel, Rhiannon Furbear, Steve Gorton, Christi Graham, Alison Harris, Peter Hayman, Stephen Hayward, Will Heap, John Heseltine, Roger Hilton, Sean Hunter, Ed Ironside, Colin Keates, Dave King, Bob Langrish, Neil Lukas, Neil Mersh, Nick Nichols, Sofía Nieto, Robert O'Dea, Ian O'Leary, Vincent Oliver, John Parker, Tim Ridley, Ellen Root, Rough Guides/Viktor Borg, Rough Guides/Roger Norum, Rough Guides/Suzanne Porter, Rough Guides/Natascha Sturny, Rough Guides/ Mark Thomas, Kim Sayer, Chris Stevens, James Stevenson, James Strachan, Doug Traverso, David Ward, Mathew Ward, Stuart West, Steven Wooster, Nick Wright.

Additional Illustrations

Ann Child, Gary Cross, Tim Hayward, Arghya Jyoti Hore, Fiona M Macpherson, Janos Marffy, David More, Chris D Orr, Richard Phipps, Rockit Design, Michelle Ross, John Woodcock.

Cartography

Andrew Heritage, James Mills-Hicks, Chez Picthall, John Plumer (DK Cartography). Advanced Illustration (Cheshire), Contour Publishing (Derby), Euromap Ltd (Berkshire). Street Finder maps: ERA Maptec Ltd (Dublin) adapted with permission from original survey and mapping from Shobunsha (Japan).

Cartographic Research

James Anderson, Roger Bullen, Tony Chambers, Ruth Duxbury, Jason Gough, Ailsa Heritage, Jayne Parsons, Donna Rispoli, Jill Tinsley, Andrew Thompson, Lorwerth Watkins.

Design and Editorial

Managing Editor Douglas Amrine
Managing Art Editor Geoff Manders
Senior Editor Georgina Matthews
Series Design Consultant David Lamb
Art Director Anne-Marie Bulat
Production Controller Hilary Stephens
Picture Research Ellen Root, Rhiannon Furbear, Susie Peachey
DTP Editor Siri Lowe
Revisions Team Louise Abbott, Keith Addison, Namrata Adhwaryu, Ashwin Adimari, Emma Anacootee, Elizabeth Atherton, Sam Atkinson, Lydia Baillie, Chris Barstow, Oliver Bennett, Kate Berens, Hilary Bird, Julie Bowles, Chloe Carleton, Michelle Clark, Carey Combe, Vanessa Courtier, Lorna Damms, Hannah Dolan, Jessica Doyle, Caroline Elliker, Nicola Erdpresser, Jane Ewart, Simon Farbrother, Gadi Farfour, Fay Franklin, Leonie Glass, Simon Hall, Marcus Hardy, Mohammad Hassan, Kaberi Hazarika, Sasha Heseltine, Paul Hines, Phil Hunt, Stephanie Jackson, Gail Jones, Laura Jones, Nancy Jones, Bharti Karakoti, Sumita Khatwani, Stephen Knowlden, Priya Kukadia, Esther Labi, Maite Lantaron, Michelle de Larrabeiti, Chris Lascelles, Jude Ledger, Jeanette Leung, Darren Longley Carly Madden, Tanya Mahendru, Hayley Maher, Ferdie McDonald, Alison McGill, Caroline Mead, Jane Middleton, Rebecca Milner, Sonal Modha, Fiona Morgan, Casper Morris, Hassan Muhammad, Claire Naylor, George Nimmo, Catherine Palmi, Louise Parsons, Marianne Petrou, Andrea Powell, Leigh Priest, Rada Radojicic, Mani Ramaswamy, Marisa Renzullo, Erin Richards, Nick Rider, Ellen Root, Liz Rowe, Simon Ryder, Ankita Sharma, Tracy Smith, Sadie Smith, Susannah Steel, Kathryn Steve, Anna Streiffert, Rachel Symons, Andrew Szudek, Hollie Teague, Priyanka Thakur, Hugh Thompson, Ajay Verma, Richa Verma, Karen Villabona, Diana Vowles, Matthew Walder, Andy Wilkinson, Sophie Wright.

Special Assistance

Christine Brandt at Kew Gardens, Sheila Brown at The Bank of England, John Cattermole at London Buses Northern, the DK picture department, especially Jenny Rayner, Pippa Grimes at the V&A, Emma Healy at the V&A Museum of Childhood, Alan Hills at the British Museum, Emma Hutton and Cooling Brown Partnership, Gavin Morgan at the Museum of London, Clare Murphy at Historic Royal Palaces, Ali Naqei at the Science Museum, Patrizio Semproni, Caroline Shaw at the Natural History Museum, Gary Smith at National Rail, Monica Thurnauer at Tate, Simon Wilson at Tate, Alastair Wardle.

Photographic Reference

The London Aerial Photo Library, and P and P F James.

Photography Permissions

Dorling Kindersley would like to thank all the museums, galleries, churches and other sights that allowed us to photograph at their establishments.

Picture Credits

a = above; b = below/bottom; c = centre; f = far; l = left; r = right; t = top.

Works of art have been reproduced with the permission of the following copyright holders:
Three Studies for Figures at the Base of the Crucifixion, (1944, detail), Francis Bacon © Estate of Francis Bacon/DACS, London 2011 86cl; *Untitled* (1964) © Larry Bell Larry Bell Studio Annex / TAOS 233 Ranchitos Road Taos, New Mexico United States 185tc; Fish 1926, Constantin Brancusi © ADAGP, Paris and DACS, London 2008 183bl; *From the Freud Museum* (1991–6) © Susan Hiller 184cr; Bust of *Lawrence of Arabia* © The Family of Eric H. Kennington, RA 155bl; *Self-Portait with Knickers* Sarah Lucas 2000 Copyright the artist, courtesy Sadie Coles HQ, London 89tl; *Quattro Stagioni* 1993–4, © Cy Twombly 183crb.

The Publishers are grateful to the following individuals, companies and picture libraries for permission to reproduce their photographs:

123RF.com: William Perugini 269cr; **41 Hotel:** 285tr. **Alamy Images:** Brian Anthony 134tl; Simon Balson 255tl; Mike Booth 158cla; Paul Brown 60bc; Paul Carstairs 62br; Construction Photography 224; Cliff Hide Travel 245tc, , Stephen Finn 135br; David Gee 264c; Martyn Goddard 363tl; Jim Hodson 36clb; Scott Hortop Travel 227crb; Richard Green 127br; Lynn Hilton 164; Eric Nathan 140tl; Picturebank 172br; Percy Ryall 187tl; Maurice Savage 261br; Doug Taylor 223tc; Tribaleye Images/J Marshall 182cla; SuperStock 110c; Steve Vidler 74tr; View Pictures Ltd 353cl, Tony Watson 100tl; **The Albemarle Connection:** 95tr; L'Anima Restaurant: 303tr; **Arcaid:** Richard Bryant, Architect Foster and Partners 128t; Richard Bryant 253cr; **Arcblue:** Peter Durant 193clb; **The Art Archive:** 23bl, 30cla, 30bc, 31bl, 32br, 32clb, 33cra, 39crb; British Library, London 22crb; Imperial War Museum, London 34bc; Museum of London 19b, 31br, 32bl; Science Museum, London 31crb; Stoke Museum Staffordshire Polytechnic 27bl, 29crb, 39bc; Victoria and Albert Museum, London 24clb, 25bc, 29tr; **AWL Images:** Rex Butcher 188; **Axiom:** James Morris 168tl.
Governor and Company of the Bank of England: 149tc; Bibendum Restaurant Ltd: 293br; **Bridgeman Art Library, London:** 25t; British Library, London 18, 23ca, (detail) 25br, 28cb, (detail) 38c, 38bl; © Coram in the care of the Foundling Museum 133tc; Courtesy of the Institute of Directors, London 33ca; Guildhall Library, Corporation of London 28br, 80cl; ML Holmes Jamestown – Yorktown Educational Trust, VA (detail) 21bc; Master and Fellows, Magdalene College, Cambridge (detail) 27clb; William Morris Gallery, Walthamstow 23tl, 253bc; Museum of London 26–7; O'Shea Gallery, London (detail) 26crb; Royal Holloway & Bedford New College 161bc; Russell Cotes Art Gallery and Museum, Bournemouth 42tr; Thyssen-Bornemisza Collection, Lugano Casta 263bl; Westminster Abbey, London (detail) 38bc; White House, Bond Street, London 32c. **British Airways:** Adrian Meredith Photography: 370cla; © **The British Museum:** 20ca, 21ca, 44tr, 128–9 all pics except 128t, 130–31 all pics; **Brittany Ferries:** 369tl; **BT Group plc:** 366c. Buen Ayre Restaurant: 305br.
Camera Press: London: Cecil Beaton 83tl; **Charlotte Street Hotel:** 284bl, 288bc; **Chez Bruce:** 306bc; **The Clerkenwell Kitchen:** 302tc; **Clos Maggiore:** 296bl; **Collections:** Oliver Benn 64br; Philip Craven 266cla; Julie Hamilton 234tr; John Miller 167bl; Liz Stares 267bl; **Colorific!:** Steve Benbow 59tl; **Conran Restaurants:** 318bc; **Corbis:** 90, Bettmann 6–7;

Demotix / Kriss Lee 255cc; Sarah J Duncan 132clb; 99tc; EPA / WILL OLIVER 62cr; Jason Hawkes 70–71; Angelo Hornak 65c, 187br; Hulton-Deutsch Collection 33tl; INFphoto.com / infuklo-108 35crb; JAI/Alan Copson 40, 173bl; Gideon Mendel 36c; London Aerial Photo Library 193bl, 193cla; Kim Sayer 10bl; Splash News 43c; Sportsfile / Brendan Moran 254bl; View / Paul Riddle 255crb; Patrick Ward 65tl; **Courtesy of the Corporation of London:** 59c, 150tr; **Courtauld Institute, London:** 45br, 121bl; **Cutty Sark Trust:** 242cla. **Copyright Dean and Chapter of Westminster:** 82bl, 83br; **Dewynters Ltd.:** David Crosswaite 117cra; **Dr Johnson's House: Dorling Kindersley:** courtesy of Guildhall / Max Alexander 163bl; courtesy of Imperial War Museum / Max Alexander 194br; Courtesy of London Zoo / Max Alexander 352bl; Courtesy of The Clink Prison Museum / Max Alexander 179tc; courtesy of The Hunterian Museum at the Royal College of Surgeons / Max Alexander 141tr; Jamie Marshall 78tl; The Science Museum, London 204bc; courtesy of Theatre Royal, Drury Lane / Max Alexander 338cl; Laurie Noble Collection 191tc; **Dreamstime.com:** Anizza 60cr; Anthony Baggett 338cb; Beataaldridge 156cra; Basphoto 265tr; Beaucroft 195tr; Rafael Ben-ari 66br, 192tl; Mike Clegg 37br, 63br; Piero Cruciatti 36br; Danielal 99bl; Chris Dorney 66clb; Thomas Dutour 285bl; Nicola Ferrari 37tl; Eric Flamant 57tr; Michael Foley 97b; Vlad Ghiea 100clb; Hackneykate 254clb; Hpphoto 36cr; Savo Ilic 271br; Dragos Daniel Iliescu 250tr; Inigocia 376br; Irstone 107br, 352c; Kmiragaya 355tr; Slawek Kozakiewicz 37cr, 251bl; Ld1976d 295br; Amanda Lewis 195cl, 237tl; Lowerkase 66cla; Mariagroth 221tc; Meunierd 37tr; Krisztian Miklosy 280cl; Minacarson 126bc; Ml12nan 69tr; Paweł Opaska 138clb; Stuwilson65 355br; Tea 364cl; Hai Huy Ton That 271cr; Ugo Toldi 360tl; Ttatty 292br; Marco Valdifiori 237br; Hilda Weges 353br; **Courtesy of the Governors and the Directors Dulwich Picture Gallery:** 47tr, 256bl. **E&O, Ricker Restaurants:** 300tr; **Francis Edwards:** 319bl; **English Heritage:** 258cr, 264b; Jonathon Bailey 245bl; **English Life Publications Ltd:** 259br; **Mary Evans Picture Library:** 20bl, 20bc, 21bl, 21br, 24bl, 26bl, 29bc, 29br, 31tl, 31ca, 31bc, 34bl, 38br, 39tl, 39clb, 39bl, 39br, 76bc, 76clb, 116bl, 118bl, 139tl, 143tl, 181cl, 209br, 220tr, 230br. **Courtesy of Fan Museum:** Helene Alexander Collection 247b; **Fotolia:** Balliolman 114. **The Goring Hotel, London:** 286tl; **Geffrye Museum, London:** 252tl; **Getty Images:** Gregory Bajor 248; Walter Bibikow 124; Miguel Carminati 72; Alan Copson 356–7; Flickr/Richard Newstead 2–3; Heritage Images 109tl, Peter Macdiarmid 185br; Eric Nathan 146; SuperStock 111br; **Gaucho:** 307tr; **Green Tourism Business Scheme:** 361tr; greenwichmarket.net: 242clb.
Hakkasan Mayfair: 299bc; **Handel House Museum:** James Mortimer 101t; **Robert Harding Picture Library:** 35cra, 46cra, 56cla, 246tr, 339tr, 363cl, 380bl; Philip Craven 212t; Nigel Francis 372tr; Sylvain Gradadam 295tl; Brian Hawkes 25cb; Michael Jenner 25cra, 231tr; Nick Wood 67bl; **Harrods:** (printed by kind permission of Mohamed al Fayed) 316bl; **Hayes-Davidson** (computer generated images): 178clb; **Hayward Gallery:** Richard Haughton 279tl; **Reproduced with permission of Her Majesty's Stationery Office (Crown Copyright):** 160 all pics; John Heseltine: 55tr; **Historic Royal Palaces (Crown Copyright):** 5ca, 5tr, 7t, 41c, 158tr, 159clb, 260–61 all except 260br and 261br, 262–3 all except 263bl; **The Hulton Getty:** 28bl, 132tr.

The Image Bank, London: Gio Barto 59b; Derek Berwin 35tc; Romilly Lockyer 17tl, 17br, 76cla; Terry Williams 143c; Inamo Restaurant: 297tr; iStockphoto.com: Alan Crawford 370br; DMP1 36bl; EdStock 37bl, 39cr; oversnap 61br; peterspiro 375br.
Peter Jackson Collection: 28–9; Jewish Museum, London: 251tr.
The Laughing Gravy: 305tl; Leon Restaurants: 292cla; Leighton House: 220bl; Little Angel Marionette Theatre: 355cl; London Ambulance Service: Tim Saunders 363cla; London Aquarium: 11tr, 192cr; London Bridge Hotel: 285tl; London City Airport: 371tr; London Transport Museum: 32cla.
Madame Tussauds: 226cla, 228cra, 228t; Mansell Collection: 23br, 24cl, 24br, 25bl, 26cl, 26clb, 27br, 31cla; Rob Moore: 119tr; Museum of London: 17crb, 20clb, 21tc, 21crb, 22tl, 25crb, 45tc, 167crb, 170–71.
Reproduced by courtesy of the Trustees, The National Gallery, London: (detail) 41tc, 108–9 all except 108t, 110tr, 110b, 111ca, 111bl; National Portrait Gallery, London: 4t, 45tl, 105cra, 106br; National Postal Museum, London: 30bl; By permission of the Keeper of the National Railway Museum, York: 32–3; National Trust Photographic Library: Wendy Aldiss 27cra; John Bethell 258tl, 259tr; Michael Boys 42br; Natural History Museum, London: 206tr, 207crb; John Downs 16clb, 207tc, Derek Adams 206b, 206cl.
Ottolenghi: 281tc, 306tl; OXO Tower Restaurant/Harvey Nichols: 304tr.
Palace Theatre Archive:112tc; Parliamentary Copyright House of Lords 2012: Photography by Chris Moyse 77crb; Pictor International, London: 64cl, 178br; Pictures Colour Library: 58br; Popperfoto: 33crb, 34tl, 34tr, 34cl, 39tc, 43br; Post House Heathrow: Tim Young 373tr; La Poule au Pot: 301bl; Press Association Ltd: 33bl, 33br; Public Record Office (Crown Copyright): 22b.
RBS Group: 364bl, 364cb; Andrew Laenen 58crb; Jonathon Player 294cla; The Ritz, London: 95bl; The River Cafe: 307bl; Royal Academy of Arts, London: 94tr; The Board of Trustees of The Royal Armouries: 45tr, 161t, 161br; Trustees of the Royal Botanic Gardens, Kew: Andrew McRob 52cl, 266–7 all pics except 266cla, 267bl; The Royal Collection © 2013 Her Majesty Queen Elizabeth II: 1c, 8–9, 57bl, 97c, 98tr, 98cla, 98ca, 99br, 260br; Derry Moore 99cra; Royal College of Music, London: 208c.
Image Courtesy of the Saatchi Gallery, London: Matthew Booth 293tl; St Paul's Cathedral: Sampson Lloyd 152cb, 154cla, 155tr; Salt Yard: 302br; The Savoy Group: 120cr; Science Museum, London: 210–11 all pics; Society of London Theatre/tkts: 339br; Somerset House: Peter Durant/arcblue.com 121tr; Spencer House Ltd: 92bl;

Southbank Press Office: 190clb; Stephen Cummiskey 190cla; Graeme Duddridge 278cla; STA Travel Group: 360bc; The Stafford London: 290tc; Superstock: Loop Images/ Tom Hanslien 202, /Alex Hare 176, /Ricky Leaver 232, 240; Londonstills.com 268; Nomad 196; Prisma 218; Travelshots 282–3; Syndication International: 41tr, 56clb, 57crb, 62bl, 63c; Library of Congress; 29bl.
Tate London 2001: 86–7 all pics, 88 all pics, 89br, 182–3, 184–5, 279br. Transport for London: 359br, 374br, 376tr, 376–7 all maps and tickets, 378bl, 379tl; Travel Pictures: Stuart Black 102.
Courtesy of the Board of Trustees of The Victoria and Albert Museum: 41br, 44br; 214–5 all pics; purchased with the assistance of the NACF and the Goldsmith's Company 215cra; 216–7 all pics.
W Hotel London: 286br, 289tl; By kind permission of the trustees of The Wallace Collection, London: 44cla, 230cl; Philip Way Photography: 68clb, 154bl, 181br; Courtesy of the Trustees of the Wedgwood Museum, Barlaston, Stoke-on-Trent, Staffs, England: 30br; Vivienne Westwood: Patrick Fetherstonhaugh 35br; The Wimbledon Lawn Tennis Museum: Micky White 257tr; The Wolseley: 298tl; Photo © Woodmansterne: Jeremy Marks 41tl, 153cra.
Zefa: 56br; Bob Croxford 61c.

Front Endpaper: Alamy: Construction Photography Ltr; lynn hilton Rcra; AWL Images: Rex Butcher Rbr; Corbis: Rbl; Fotolia: Ballrolman Rtr; Getty Images: Walter Bibikow Rtl; Miguel Carminati Rfbl; Eric Nathan Rcrb; Superstock: age fotostock/Charles Bowman Ltc; Loop Images/Tom Hanslien Lbl, /Alex Hare Rfbr, /Ricky Leaver Ltl; Nomad Lbc; Prisma Lclb; Travel Pictures: Stuart Black Rftl.

Cover: Front main and spine top –
4Corners: SIME / Maurizio Rellini.
Map cover – 4Corners: SIME / Maurizio Rellini.
All other images © Dorling Kindersley
For further information see www.DKimages.com

The London Underground

Legend:

- Bakerloo
- Central
- Circle
- District
- Hammersmith & City
- Jubilee
- Metropolitan
- Northern
- Piccadilly
- Victoria
- Waterloo & City
- DLR
- Emirates Air Line
- London Overground
- TfL Rail
- District open weekends and on some public holidays

- O Interchange stations
- Step-free access from street to train
- Step-free access from street to platform
- National Rail
- Riverboat services
- Trams ✈ Airport
- Victoria Coach Station
- Emirates Air Line

 tfl.gov.uk

 24 hour travel information
0343 222 1234*
*Service and network charges may apply. See tfl.gov.uk/terms for details.

Improvement works may affec